About the Author

A major leader in the international critical thinking movement, Richard Paul is a passionate reformer who sees educational problems at the heart of our social and economic ones. He sees ineffectual educational systems mirroring obsolete economic and social institutions and structures, economic and social malaise exacerbating educational bankruptcy. He sees that, although the 12st Century is upon us, we are still trapped in 19th Century thinking and 20th Century arrogance and narrow-mindedness.

We are not educating our children, Paul argues, and we are not planning, as rational people would, for the economic and social well-being of our country. These two needs are deeply interconnected. In a world of shallow values, instant gratification, and quick fixes, critical thinking is a tool necessary for survival. We need its sharp cutting edge to slice through propaganda generated daily not only by self-serving educational bureaucrats but also by a rainbow of vested interest groups all too ready to sacrifice the well-being of the country to their short-term gain.

Through Paul's efforts, and those of thousands of like-minded persons, critical thinking is finally becoming a national educational goal (so say the National Goals Panel, the U.S. Departments of Commerce and Labor, and the U.S. Department of Education). Yet just as the concept of critical thinking is finally gaining currency — and a window of opportunity is opening up — individuals and groups are ripping it from its substantial intellectual foundations and reducing it to easy-to-learn tricks, gimmicks, and quick fixes. Paul is leading the counter-attack on the pseudo critical thinking that is springing up everywhere in the educational marketplace — from textbooks to state assessment instruments designed to bolster the falling images of state departments of education.

Director of the Center for Critical Thinking, and Chair of the National Council for Excellence in Critical Thinking, author of over 50 articles and five books on critical thinking at every grade level (K–3, 4–6, 6–9, high school, and university), a committed teacher, Paul has given hundreds of workshops at the K–12 level and made a series of eight critical thinking video programs for PBS.

His views on critical thinking have been canvassed in *The New York Times, Education Week, The Chronicle of Higher Education, American Teacher, Educational Leadership, Newsweek, U.S. News and World Report,* and *Reader's Digest.*

Besides publishing extensively in the field, he has organized two national and eleven international conferences on critical thinking. He has given invited lectures at many universities and colleges, including Harvard, University of Chicago, University of Illinois, University of Amsterdam, and the Universities of Puerto Rico and Costa Rica, as well as workshops and lectures on critical thinking in every region of the United States. Paul worked with the late Edward M. Glaser on revising the Watson-Glaser Critical Thinking Appraisal. Working with Gerald Nosich, he has developed a model for the national assessment of critical thinking at the post-secondary level for the U.S. Department of Education. He is actively sought as a keynote speaker and staff development leader.

About the Center for Critical Thinking and Moral Critique

The Center conducts advanced research and disseminates information on critical thinking and moral critique. It works closely with the Foundation for Critical Thinking, the National Council for Excellence in Critical Thinking, the College Board, numerous school districts, the Association for Supervision and Curriculum Development, the National Education Association, and the U. S. Department of Education to facilitate implementation of high standards of critical thinking instruction from kindergarten through the university.

Its major work includes:

- International Conferences on Critical Thinking
  Each summer, in early August, the Center hosts the oldest and largest critical thinking conference with registrants from virtually every state of the union and numerous foreign countries. Over 300 distinguished experts in the field present 350 sessions on critical thinking and critical thinking instruction over four days. These sessions are designed to meet the needs of the widest variety of educational levels and concerns from kindergarten through graduate school. A variety of subject matters and subject fields are used as examples of critical thinking infusion. The two days preceding the conference are used for intensive sessions that lay a foundation for the conference and for critical thinking instruction.

- Staff Development Services
  The Center provides staff development services at every level of education from kindergarten through graduate school. Staff development programs emphasize an exploration of the rich, underlying concepts of critical thinking and how to excite students to the power and potential of developing a mind that reasons well. There is a focus on the critique and redesign of instruction to infuse critical thinking principles into subject matter instruction. Seminars and workshops in critical thinking for business management are also available through the Center.

About the Foundation for Critical Thinking

The Foundation for Critical Thinking is an independent, non-profit, institution not associated with Sonoma State University. It publishes a variety of critical thinking resources.

Resources for Instruction
- PBS Videotapes
- Ground-Breaking Books
- Four Grade-Level Critical Thinking Handbooks
- The Leaders of the Critical Thinking Movement on Audio and Videotape
- Audio and Videotapes for Critical Thinking Staff Development

About the National Council for Excellence in Critical Thinking

Information regarding the National Council for Excellence in Critical Thinking may be secured by calling the National Office. *(707) 546-0629.*

The Center for Critical Thinking
& Moral Critique
Sonoma State University
Rohnert Park, CA 94928
(707) 664–2940

The Foundation for Critical Thinking
4655 Sonoma Mountain Road
Santa Rosa, CA 95404
(800) 833-3645

Richard W. Paul

CRITICAL
THINKING

What Every Person Needs to Survive
In a Rapidly Changing World

Edited by
Jane Willsen and A.J.A. Binker
Foundation for Critical Thinking
1993

Acknowledgments

"The Critical Thinking Movement in Historical Perspective", originally appeared as, "The Critical Thinking Movement: A Historical Perspective", in *National Forum*, Winter 1985.

"Critical Thinking in North America", originally appeared as, "Critical Thinking in North America: A New Theory of Knowledge, Learning, and Literacy", in *Argumentation* 3, 1989.

"Critical Thinking: Fundamental to Education for a Free Society", and "Ethics without Indoctrination", originally appeared in *Educational Leadership*, September 1984, May 1988.

"Critical Thinking and the Critical Person", originally appeared in *Thinking: The Second International Conference*, Lawrence Erlbaum, 1987.

"Dialogical Thinking: Critical Thought Essential to the Acquisition of Rational Knowledge and Passions", appeared in *Teaching Thinking Skills: Theory and Practice*, W. H. Freeman, Co., 1987.

"McPeck's Mistakes: Why Critical Thinking Applies Across Disciplines and Domains", originally appeared as, "McPeck's Mistakes", in *Informal Logic*, Winter, 1985.

"Bloom's Taxonomy and Critical Thinking Instruction: Recall is Not Knowledge", originally appeared as, "Bloom's Taxonomy and Critical Thinking Instruction", in *Educational Leadership,* May, 1985.

"Critical Thinking and General Semantics: On the Primacy of Natural Languages", was originally a talk entitled, "Critical Thinking and the Way We Construct the Meaning of Things", presented at the 36th Annual Alfred Korzybski Memorial Lecture, October 30, 1987.

"Philosophy and Cognitive Psychology: Contrasting Assumptions" and "The Contributions of Philosophy to Thinking", are forthcoming as one paper, "Critical and Reflective Thinking: A Philosophical Perspective", in *Dimensions of Thinking and Cognitive Instruction: Implications for Educational Reform,* Lawrence Erlbaum, 1990.

"Critical Thinking, Human Development, and Rational Productivity", originally appeared as, "Human Factors in Learning", in the *Proceeding of the 6th Annual Rupert N. Evans Symposium April 25–26, 1985,* 1985.

ISBN number: 0–944583–08–3

Library of Congress number: 93–72690

To the memory of the late Edward Glaser, friend and scholar,
whose foundational book,
An Experiment in the Development of Critical Thinking (1941),
laid the cornerstone for the critical thinking movement.

Table of Contents

IV Contrasting Viewpoints

Appendices

Acknowledgments

I wish to acknowledge the enthusiastic and tireless support and good will I received from my many colleagues at the Center for Critical Thinking and Moral Critique and the Foundation for Critical Thinking, including that of J. J. Jones, David Grady, Jessie Foster, Annalise O'Brien, Wes Hiler, Kelly Ann Grogan, Stuart Grose, Mike Lanham, Lincy Castro, Emiko Lewis, Jeanette Martinez, Rena Ferrick, Joyce Miller-Carpini, and Charles Evans. Their team-spirit and practical problem-solving are a continual source of strength and joy to me. Special thanks go to Jill Binker for her editing abilities and long-standing dedication to the cause of critical thinking.

I owe a special debt of gratitude to John Pruess, Renee Denise, and Trish Taylor for their exemplary trouble-shooting abilities and patience in many hours of overload. They demonstrate daily how critical thinking can be brought into the heart and soul of an organization and continually breathe new life and energy into it.

And finally, I want to express my appreciation for the dedicated support, deep insight, and committed vision of my newest friend and colleague, Jane Willsen. Her incisive questions and practical sensitivity, her unflinching sense of "Can do!" and of how always to find new and better ways, have contributed mightily to my work, its fruitfulness, and its personal satisfaction.

Foreword

Although the papers included in this volume have been written at different times and for a variety of occasions, they have a unity that explains their collection into a single book. All have been written with the express purpose of persuading educators and others concerned with education of the need to place critical thinking at the heart of educational reform. They represent a point of view too often at the periphery of the discussion of what is wrong with education. Their scope reflects something of the breadth with which critical thinking ought to be conceived.

No one in education today has accepted the responsibility to conceptualize education as a whole, or to assess, at any given time, whether it is succeeding or rather, degenerating into mere training, socialization, or indoctrination. No one is keeping education focused on essential questions and concerns and, consequently, attention is typically diffused to any of an endless number of "immediate," day-to-day, and specific lower-order "imperatives." Basic facts and questions — like whether or not students are learning to reason well — are lost in the shuffle. No one is held accountable for the integrity of the core issues.

Indeed, as a result, global failures such as the failure of schooling to improve students' ability to reason are not even recognized as such, except episodically, and then almost always by a scattered few. To the extent that the study of critical thinking develops into a recognized and respected field within education, it can serve as a voice responsible for conceptualizing the whole. It can keep attention focused on the central educational pillars such as, "What is an *educated* person?" For can we not say that if students learn to think critically as a result of their schooling, then, *ipso facto*, they have become educated persons? And if, on the other hand, they merely commit to memory any number of specific facts about this or that domain of study, if they pass any number of courses or gain any number of academic credits or degrees but remain undisciplined in their thinking, then, whatever else can be said of them, they have not yet become educated persons. Whether they recognize it or not — and almost inevitably, by virtue of the defective nature of their thinking they do not — they are still walking in circles in the vestibule of education; they have not yet entered its hallowed chambers.

What is worthwhile in education and in life is never easy: no one ever legitimately claimed that critical thinking would be. Critical thinking is complex because it involves overcoming not only intellectual barriers to progress, but psychological barriers as well. We are comfortable, as a rule, with our ideas, our belief structures, our view of the world. Certainly, if we thought our ideas were flawed, irrational, shallow, or biased in an unfair way, we would have *already* changed them. When questioned about the validity of our ideas or beliefs, particularly the foundational ones, we typically interpret the question to be a challenge to our integrity, often even to our identity.

That we hold tenaciously to our beliefs, however ill-founded, is testimony to the struggle that a commitment to critical thinking will trigger. Yet a commitment to critical thinking is as exhilarating as it is exhausting. Imagine the satisfaction of looking through the inventory of one's beliefs and finding that many of them were consciously, deliberately, and painstakingly chosen for their accuracy, their depth, their clarity, their consistency — in other words, their legitimate merit!

Intellectually, critical thinking is challenging because we must prepare the way for new ideas by rooting out old ones, by breaking down remnants from popular, if incoherent, illogical and insupportable ideologies and prejudices of the day. Until we have thought deeply and critically we are apt to be persuaded by deeply flawed ideas, such as

• the view that every person's opinion, regardless of how poorly it is supported, deserves equal respect;

• the view that all language users hold bona fide, unique definitions for every word they use;

• the view that language itself is vague, rather than our use of it;

• the view that there are no general intellectual standards; and

• the view that appropriate intellectual standards are a reflection of gender, race, culture, or period in history.

However tempting these views can be at any point in time or from any given point of view, or how intuitive they might seem, each is readily refuted under closer scrutiny.

Awash as our culture is with these and many other ideologies and prejudices, we cannot help but have unconsciously absorbed some of them. And, unfortunately because we did not think our way into what we have unconsciously absorbed, we must now laboriously and painfully think our way out. These are bothersome presuppositions, not explicit constructions and conclusions. We want only products of our rational and deliberate thought, for that is the goal of critical thinking.

How will we reach our goal? Where is the path? The fact is there are many paths and they crisscross and double back. Given the complexity of the challenge, our inherent tendencies toward self-deception, and our tenacious grip on unconsciously absorbed beliefs, an effective introduction to critical thinking requires that we come at it from many different angles and prepare ourselves for a lifetime of diligent and rigorous intellectual work. We must hear the story many times, and appreciate many different versions and variations. We must retell the story to ourselves and to others to hear how it sounds, to tighten up our understanding, sharpen our insights, and uncover new and important implications.

If there is one phrase that encapsulates this challenge, it is intellectual discipline. Yet, we live in an age in which intellectual discipline is rare and in which schooling and the media are as rich in trivial information as they are devoid, or virtually devoid, of reasoned discourse. We are the targets of an unprecedented campaign of misinformation about what is important, and why. We are simultaneously put upon by a multiplicity of cultural voices — not to mention an army of academic and professional specialists — besieged with information yet left in ignorance, devoid of the tools that could make sense of the chaos that surrounds us.

We are given no glimpse into the inner sanctum. We *fail to see the sense in which critical thinking provides a common denominator for all fields of knowledge.* We are given no common standards upon the basis of which we might form our judgment and build our design. We are perplexed and unsure as to how to construct a comprehensive view that would enable us to gain perspective on diversity in culture, language, and knowledge. Often, we blindly accept hollow models we have picked up from the platitudes, truisms, and arrogance of everyday chatter as substitutes for a well-reasoned, disciplined, comprehensive view.

One major obstacle to the successful construction of such a comprehensive view is a lack of understanding of the basis for intellectual criteria and standards. We don't know where the target is, so how can we aim for it? Where do we get appropriate criteria and the standards? What intellectual criteria should we use and how can we justify them?

In this volume, these issues are treated in a way that will certainly not satisfy everyone, for there is no attempt made to couch the analysis in the jargon of a particular discipline nor in the light of some traditional or specialized mode of argumentation. I am, almost always, more concerned to address those who think across multiple disciplinary lines than I am to address those who bury themselves within the boundaries, the jargon, and the presuppositions of any given one. Critical thinking in its legitimate, comprehensive sense applies to every academic discipline as readily as it applies to life beyond the ivory tower.

Of course, this book in no way contains the last word on critical thinking. Indeed, it is merely one of many opening salvos in a field just now beginning to emerge. In the future the field will draw, as it is just now beginning to do, illuminating contributions from sociologists, anthropologists, historians, economists, scientists, and mathematicians. At present the field is still dominated by philosophers and cognitive psychologists.

Critical thinking will come to be the first field in intellectual history, I believe, that crosses fields at the same time that it draws its contributing scholars from the very fields it crosses. As such it will, I hope, provide for the intellectual perspective and synthesis so typically and significantly absent today from both education and educational research.

Before I close I should provide some explanation of the origin of this new volume. The first two editions of *Critical Thinking: What Every Person Needs To Survive in a Rapidly Changing World*, the parent of this volume, were massive in nature (673 pages of fine print). At the recommendation of many, I have divided the original edition into two overlapping books: one which maintains the original title, and is intended for a general audience, and this one which is targetted principally to educators, *Critical Thinking: How to Prepare Students for a Rapidly Changing World*. Both volumes contain some of the same articles, those which seemed fundamental to both, since the volumes will not be marketed as a set. Each book becomes a more manageable read. I hope that this decision aids in bringing the basic concept of critical thinking to a yet wider audience. The intellectual quality of the original, for better or worse, was nowhere compromised.

One final point. Perceptive readers may discern in these papers many influences including but not limited to Plato, Aristotle, Aquinas, Bacon, Descartes, Tom Paine, Jefferson, John Stuart Mill, John Henry Newman, Freud, Marx, Thoreau, Max Weber, William Graham Sumner, Piaget, John Dewey, C. Wright Mills, Erving Goffman, Bertrand Russell, Ludwig Wittgenstein, John Wisdom, Gilbert Ryle, and J. L. Austin. Certainly there is no idea in it that does not have many historical predecessors. Nevertheless, it seems to me that a rich appreciation of what it would take to cultivate fairminded critical persons in fairminded critical societies is just now beginning to form. I hope this book contributes to this raw beginning.

Introduction

The goal of this book is to persuade the reader on two points. The first is that in a world of accelerating change and complexity, a new form of thinking and learning is required, a form of thinking and learning that involves much more intellectual discipline and skills of self-evaluation than we have yet learned to accept. The second is that the economic progress of the future will be increasingly tied to social, educational, and even "moral" progress. In the future, it will become harder and harder for societies to achieve economic success while they exploit, and maintain in a subservient role, the large mass of people. The economic well-being of the future will require the intellectual empowerment and freedom of ordinary, not just extraordinary people.

The Logic of Adapting to Accelerating Change and Complexity

Critical thinking is the essential foundation for adaptation to the everyday personal, social, and professional demands of the 21st Century and thereafter. The most inescapable imperative of the future is continuous change, change that involves complex adjustments to the increasingly complex systems that dominate our lives. Therefore, the distinguishing characteristics of those who will not only survive but flourish in the future, will be traits and abilities, both intellectual and emotional, that entail excellence in evaluating and responding to complex changing conditions.

Yet the mind is not by nature adaptable to changes of the breadth and depth that we are facing. Rather the mind is instinctively designed for habit, associating "peace of mind" with routine. The mind's natural inclination is to reduce the new to the old, the complex to the simple, and everything as much as possible, to familiar, well-grooved patterns and habits. It is not natural for the human mind to continuously re-think its systems, its routines, its habits — in fact, it is downright threatening.

If we juxtapose the nature of the future with the nature of the human mind, confusion is the inevitable result. We cannot arrest the accelerating changes of our future, nor can we simplify the challenges to come. Therefore, we must adapt our minds. We must ready them for complexity and change. What will the particulars of this adaptation be?

We need to construct, through socialization, education, and new social practices, a new "second nature" for the mind. We must work within the human propensity toward habit by learning how to shape our minds to a qualitatively different kind of habit: the habit of not only continually changing but of continually expecting to change. We must cultivate the habit of continually raising our systems of routine to a conscious level with the express purpose of reshaping them in an unending series of acts of intellectual self-improvement. No domains of our lives — as teachers, parents, citizens, workers — will be spared if legitimate "peace of mind" is to be restored.

It will never again do to think exclusively within one fixed belief system. The cruel illusion of security in permanence will continue to tantalize us, but we must prepare ourselves to live within flux rather than constancy, to be comfortable with the unexpected and problematic, to expect the unexpected, even, in fact, to create the unexpected and problematic as a "natural" part of day-to-day living and thinking. Ceaseless, incessant, perpetual adjustments to novel, unfamiliar intricacy now becomes the only permanent rule. Skill in turning systems inside out, frequently restructuring and recasting them, will be the basis for high-paid labor and the challenge of sound leadership.

For our adaptations to succeed, we must enhance our abilities to evaluate ideas, changing conditions, and events. We will prevail to the extent that we cultivate minds that habitually probe the logic of the systems of the status quo as well as the logic of the possible variations and alternative systems, approaching each with questions that enable us to assess both strengths and weaknesses.

EDUCATION IN A NEW KEY: THINKING, KNOWING, & LEARNING

Our political, social, educational, and economic institutions, unfortunately, are totally unprepared for this kind of revolutionary change. Let's look into one institutional domain as a point of reference. When one lays 21st Century global imperatives against the routines of modern education, for example, the misfit is obvious. Not only are school administrators and teachers insulated from these imperatives, but even if they recognized them, they are not by preparation, practice, or inclination ready to respond. If for no other reason, their own education was severely lacking in stress on intellectual abilities, intellectual traits, and intellectual standards. They have not learned the art of disciplined reasoning. They are often poor problem solvers; they tend to approach all problems from the point of view of expediency and the protection of their images. In any case, they show no sign of recognizing the profound difference between students memorizing the conclusions of others and students reasoning to those conclusions on the basis of their own disciplined thought. They are locked in the past. They do not know that they are. They are not striving to free themselves.

What is at the root of this distorted vision, this rigidity? What new understandings and insights do we need? First and foremost, we need to understand the kind of labor or work a mind needs to do to deeply transform itself. We need to deeply understand the relationship between thinking, knowing, and learning. For we don't simply need to learn *faster*. We need to learn *better*. High quality thinking and learning is essential to our future. But why can't we understand this and what it entails?

Why do we continue to believe that it is possible to "give" people the knowledge they need, quickly and painlessly? What is the simple truth we keep missing? The answer is basic and profound. It is found in understanding how a mind can construct the truth, and so "discover" it, through the art of disciplined, collaborative reasoning.

Because we do not come to our experience with blank slates for minds, because our thinking is already, at any given moment, moving in some direction, because we can form new ideas, beliefs, and patterns of thought only through the scaffolding of our previously formed thought, it is essential that we learn to think critically in environments in which a variety of competing ideas are taken seriously. Critical thinking requires counter-thinking, opposition and challenge, as well as support. We need reasons that are meaningful to us, some persuasive logic, to move our minds from one set of ideas or beliefs to another. In other words, we must "argue" ourselves out of our present thinking and into thinking that is more or less novel to us if we are to gain genuine knowledge. This is the way that the mind engages in labor.

There is no way around the need for minds to think their way to knowledge. Thought is the key to knowledge. Knowledge is discovered by thinking, analyzed by thinking, organized by thinking, transformed by thinking, assessed by thinking, and, most importantly, *acquired* by thinking. There is no way to take the thinking out of knowledge, or the struggle out of thinking, just as there no way to create a neat and tidy, step-by-step path to knowledge that anyone can mindlessly follow. If we want to learn science we must start to think scientifically; if we want to learn math we must start to think mathematically. It is scientific thinking that gains, mathematical thinking that gains, historical thinking that gains, scientific, mathematical, and historical knowledge.

New Forms of Intellectual Engagement & Collaboration

We need others, therefore, to help us in this "labor," to probe and question our thinking, to present their thinking as a contrast that enlivens and stimulates ours. When we talk as if knowledge could be divorced from thinking, and thinking divorced from struggle, something gathered up by one person and given to another in the form of a collection of sentences to remember, we distort the nature of knowledge and the conditions under which it is acquired. Knowledge is not to be confused with belief nor with those things, like printed texts or spoken lectures, which represent knowledge. Humans are quite capable of believing things that are false (or things that are true) without actually knowing them to be so. A book contains knowledge only in a derivative sense, only because minds can analytically and thoughtfully read it and through that active critical process, and only thus, gain knowledge. Opinion alone is available to the uncritical reader.

To this day we have refused to face these facts about knowledge, thought, and learning. To this day we commonly teach as if mere recall were equivalent to knowledge, or we foolishly assume critical thinking to be present when, typically, it is not. For example, we routinely assume critical thinking is available to anyone who, at any given moment, wills to use it. Hence parents, teachers, and other authorities regularly order those under their charge to "Think!" The truth is that they do not know how to think effectively, and nothing in their environment helps them recognize that *the art* of thinking can be learned. This is precisely the purpose of formal education, yet, what goes on in schools is unrelated. In fact, reading, writing, listening, and speaking can all be done critically or uncritically and it is only when done critically that any of these modes of communication become bona fide instruments of knowledge or truth.

TRANSFORMING "THE SELF-DECEIVING ANIMAL"

The nature of thinking and the manner and conditions under which it can be disciplined to acquire knowledge is just one of many things about which we regularly deceive ourselves. In fact, we humans are best defined not as "the rational" but as "the self-deceiving animal." We consistently deceive ourselves about the state of, the degree of, and the nature of our knowledge, our freedom, and our character. We are the only creatures whose speech and activity obscures and distorts who and what we are. Our fervent beliefs we confuse with knowledge or proof, our emotionally-held opinions with convictions, our stubbornness with determination, our judgmentalism with judgment, our point of view with reality. We confound fact and opinion, data and interpretation, evidence and conclusion, information and knowledge. And we do all this with ease, with skill if you will, both individually and collectively. Social life effortlessly and skillfully fosters collective illusions while personal life fosters individual ones.

Yet this is not how we perceive ourselves. Verbal, even behavioral, commitments to the ideal of reasonability are pervasive in daily life. Virtually every human action is implied to be "reasonable" in context. When people act we expect them to be receptive to requests for reasons and we expect their responses themselves to be reasonable, to make logical sense of what they have done. At the same time most people assume that whatever is commonly believed is true. So when schools teach what is commonly believed, they are taken to be teaching the truth. If they were to teach what flies in the face of common belief, and they virtually never do, they would be taken to be biased or narrow. The result is that subjects like social studies become an undisciplined amalgam of what is so and what we have chosen to believe is so (but is not).

The concept of having knowledge is reduced to believing what those around us believe. Being free is reduced to acting as we would *like* to act, which turns out suspiciously similar to acting as those around us act, which turns out amazingly like acting as we have been conditioned to act. The "real" options become the commonly believed options. The "right" choice, the commonly believed choice. Thinking is reduced to responding, reasoning to psychological association. Self-deception reigns supreme.

Hence, it should not be surprising that all societies view themselves as committed to objectivity, reason, and rational learning, while only a feeble minority in each culture recognize the rarity of these values and the presence of dominant forms of irrationality and collective self-delusion. For most, dissent fills them with amazement or disgust; what would appear irrational to a rational person appears to them rational. The result in all cultures is self-perpetuating cycles of irrationality. Growth in authentic knowledge and freedom, growth in social justice and discipline of mind, are consistently impeded thereby.

SCHOOLING AS COLLECTIVE SELF-DECEPTION

Schooling is a classic example. No culture sees itself as indoctrinating its young or discouraging intellectual development. Each sees itself as concerned with education worthy of the name. The rhetoric of reason and objective learning is everywhere. Yet classroom instruction around the world, at all levels, is typically didactic, one-dimensional, and indifferent, when not antithetical, to reason. Blank faces are taught barren conclusions in dreary drills. There is nothing sharp, nothing poignant, no exciting twist or turn of mind and thought, nothing fearless, nothing modest, no struggle, no conflict, no rational give-and-take, no intellectual excitement or discipline, no pulsation in the heart or mind. Students are not expected to ask for reasons to justify what they are told to believe. They do not question what they see, hear, or read, nor are they encouraged to do so. They do not demand that subject matter "make sense" to them. They do not challenge the thinking of other students nor expect their thinking to be challenged by others. Indeed, they do not expect to have to think at all. They mechanically repeat back what they were told, or what they think they were told, with little sense of the logicalness or illogicalness of what they are saying. Schooling for most is drab, empty, passive, and sluggish, a mass of permissions, rules, sanctions, and authorizations.

And, if truth be told, teachers are not typically disturbed by these facts. Indeed, they are disturbingly comfortable with them. Equally disturbing is the fact that what teachers teach very often does not even make logical sense to the teachers themselves. Typically they cannot explain the logic of their own subject matter except at a superficial level. Very often they did not, when they were students, question what was presented to them for belief. Very often their own academic learning was heavily dependent, as it is now for their students, on rote memorization and superficial recall. Though not yet common, some teachers are making this discovery:

After I started teaching, I realized that I had learned physics by rote and that I really did not understand all I thought I knew about it. My thinking students asked me questions for which I always had the standard textbook answers, but for the first time it made me start thinking for myself, and I realized that these canned answers were not justified by my own thinking and only confused my students who were showing some ability to think for themselves. To achieve my academic goals I had to memorize the thoughts of others, but I had never learned or been encouraged to learn to think for myself.

It is not for nothing that the meaning of the word "docile" has gone from its original meaning of "teachable" to its present, ironic, meaning of "passive, lacking initiative, easily managed." Teaching has historically cultivated, and continues to cultivate, intellectual deficiencies in the name of knowledge and skill. As early as the 17th Century, insightful commentators began to think along the lines of, though not necessarily as vehemently as, Commenius, who summed up the schools of his day as "the slaughter house of the mind." Genuine knowledge is not gained, and the capacity for freedom is stunted, in the wearisome, the tedious, the humdrum environment that exists in most schools today.

INDIFFERENCE TO SOCIAL & PERSONAL PREJUDICE

Social and personal prejudice is another classic example of mass self-deception. At the level of public discourse everyone is opposed to prejudice. Publically we scorn and ridicule it. As a practical matter, however, we show little interest in understanding or eradicating it, and more often than not we react to anyone who disagrees with us as if they, simply because they do not share our view, are prejudiced. At the same time we routinely assume our own views to be true and unprejudiced. No social group in any culture has yet made a real commitment to eradicate its own prejudices precisely because no social group thinks of itself as acting on prejudices. The common general admission to being prejudiced is merely a matter of lip service, of saying what one is expected to say, a misleading facade, a mere mask of social humility. Hence, when the newspapers of every country of the world selectively record and interpret events to square with the world view and prejudices of their own culture, the readers, whose world views and prejudices are presupposed as self-evident facts, do not object. People apparently are opposed only to the prejudices of others against them, not to their own prejudices against others.

To put the point in other words, issues and events, which to be approached fairly must be approached from many points of view, are one-sidedly analyzed and answered within one, or at most two, socially dominant point(s) of view. Prejudiced conclusions are taken to be knowledge based on insight, and a mode of pseudo-freedom results as people define only those options as reasonable which square with preconceived beliefs. "Free" choice, manipulated choice, and prejudiced choice, become one and the same phenomenon.

MORAL, EDUCATIONAL, & ECONOMIC REFORM:
INCREASINGLY INTERTWINED

Educational, social, and economic reform focused on explicit consciousness of the comprehensive need for fairminded critical thinking offers hope for the gradual elevation of human life and practice from the irrational to the rational. Only if we raise children to think critically, as a matter of course — about their use of language, the information they take in, the nature of the propaganda which surrounds them, the prejudices they assume to be self-evident truths — only if we educate children to probe the logical structure of thought, to test proposed knowledge against experience, to scrutinize experience from alternative perspectives; only if we reward those who think for themselves, who display intellectual courage, humility, and faith in reason; only then do we have a fighting chance that children will eventually become free and morally responsible adults and hence eventually able to create genuinely free and moral societies.

Knowledge, freedom, true moral sensitivity, and the ability to adapt to accelerating change and complexity are not gifts that can be casually passed on from generation to generation. They must each be achieved, created, won, person by person, society by society. Even to this day robust freedom and genuine morality are still largely unachieved human ideals. Their future realization depends on a deeper, more realistic commitment to what has not yet been significantly cultivated: societies that genuinely value fairminded thought and just action.

Finally, rationality and fairminded critical thought are essential to global social and economic development and prosperity. Irrational productivity is a major problem in the global village. Rational productivity is not a matter of manufacturing more and more stuff to accumulate or consume. It is a matter, ultimately, of serving human good and preserving a precarious environment. The standards for assessing the utility of production are changing at an accelerating rate and increasingly require critical re-examination. We can no longer afford the kind of schooling that at best transforms students into narrow specialists and at worst leaves them without job skills, functional literacy, or self-confidence.

The conditions for and the nature of productivity are not things-in-themselves, but products of multitudes of human decisions embodied in human life and behavior. But again, the human world we have created has been created so far with a minimum of self-directed critical thought, a minimum of public or "cultural" rationality. We are always to some extent acting in ways that negate human good, that undermine our own long-range best interest. The global tensions between government as a would-be servant of the public good, and unbridled capitalism, have not yet been faced. In many parts of the world, the tensions between democratization, capitalism, nationalism, and ethnicity, not to mention new versions of socialism, are just now beginning to be faced. Both the developed and the underdeveloped world desperately need a more genuinely educated, more well-informed, more cosmopolitan, more rational citizenry. Economic life cannot be separated, in the last analysis, from political, social, and personal life. Each and every dimension of life has implications for the quality of life of every other dimension. And every dimension increasingly requires and presupposes the capacity to adapt to accelerating change and complexity.

Harnessing social and economic forces to serve the public good and the good of the biosphere, while encouraging and rewarding individual initiative, requires mass publics around the world skilled in cooperative, fairminded, critical discourse. Such publics do not yet exist, except in embryo. Their cultivation has not yet been taken seriously by any culture.

A NEW WAY OF THINKING & RESPONDING & LIVING

For all of these reasons it is essential that we foster a new conception of self-identity, both individually and collectively, and a new practical sense of the value of self-disciplined, openminded thought. As long as we continue to feel threatened by those who think differently from us, we will listen seriously only to those who start from our premises, who validate our prejudices, and end up with our conclusions. We will continue to stereotype, to distort — in order to reject — what the "others," the "outsiders," say. We must learn, in other words, something quite new to us: to identify not with the content of our beliefs but with the integrity of the process by which we arrived at them. We must come to define ourselves, and actually respond in everyday contexts, as people who reason their way into, and can be reasoned out of, beliefs. Only then will we feel unthreatened when others question our beliefs, only then will we welcome their questions as a reminder of the need to be ready to test and retest our beliefs daily at the bar of reason, only then will we learn to think within multiple points of view, with a sense of global perspective.

The problem of knowledge, freedom, and productivity requires that we, for the first time in our history, take true intellectual discipline and the "fitness" of our minds seriously, since both are necessary conditions for the ability to adapt to accelerating change and complexity. We must create new conditions in school and society under which intellectual virtues long ignored — intellectual courage, intellectual humility, intellectual perseverance, intellectual integrity, faith in reason, and fairmindedness — can develop. We must learn to be comfortable with, indeed to value, rational self-criticism. We must begin to devote as much time to intellectual habits as we now do to physical ones, and admit, finally, that rationality and openness of mind are not automatic or "natural" states that can be left to themselves to emerge and flourish. To begin to do this, we must reconceptualize the nature of teaching and learning in every context of life. We must make disciplined practical reasoning and problem solving into a normal occurrence in everyday situations, not extraordinary performances of an elite few.

In short, knowledge, freedom, and social progress are deeply inter-twined. Education — in the broad sense of any skilled act of disciplined, self-evaluated learning — has a crucial role to play in fostering these crit-ical values. Yet, though there is growing insight into the nature of this role and the importance of the task it represents, and though the pressure for change in this direction is growing progressively, we should harbor no illusions about the nature of the task ahead. In the successful societies of the future, it is clear everyone will regularly "teach" and "learn," and that the "teaching-learning acts" of daily life will be embedded in collabora-tive problem solving and brokering. But such success will not occur quickly or easily. Only through slow, painful change, with much frustra-tion and circling about, only with multiple misunderstandings and con-fusion, will we work our way, eventually, into rational lives in rational societies, into societies in which accelerating change and intensifying complexity are not threats but "givens" in a world of new ways of think-ing, and responding and living.

Richard W. Paul
Center for Critical Thinking and Moral Critique
Rohnert Park, CA
June 10, 1993

Section I

Overview: *What Critical Thinking Is and Why It Is Essential*

Chapter 1

Accelerating Change, the Complexity of Problems, and the Quality of Our Thinking

with Jane Willsen

Abstract

The goal of this chapter is to trace the general implications of what are identified as the two central characteristics of the future: accelerating change and intensifying complexity. If change continues to move faster and faster, and if the changes that do occur become more and more complex, how are we to deal with the world? More specifically, how are we to understand how this change and complexity will play itself out? How are we to prepare for it? Paul and Willsen focus on the economic and educational dimensions of these questions. They lead us into and through the vision of four of our most penetrating thinkers: Robert Reich, Lester Thurow, W. Edward Deming, and Robert Heilbroner. The general thesis is that the visions of these thinkers are complementary and that collectively they provide us with a rich and pointed picture of what we must do, not because they are "visionaries," but because they have done the profound analytic work which enables them to shed a clear light on very general patterns, all of which add up to accelerating change, intensifying complexity, and critical thinking. The chapter ends with an analysis of the implications for parenting, work, and education of the foundational fact that "the work of the future is the work of the mind, intellectual work, work that involves reasoning and intellectual self-discipline."

✦✦ The Nature of the Post-Industrial World Order

*T*he world is swiftly changing and with each day the pace quickens. The pressure to respond intensifies. New global realities are rapidly working their way into the deepest structures of our lives: economic, social, environmental realities — realities with profound implications for teaching and learning, for business and politics, for human rights and human conflicts. These realities are becoming increasingly complex; and they all turn on the powerful dynamic of accelerating change. This chapter explores the general character of these changes and the quality of thinking necessary for effectively adapting to them.

1

Can we deal with incessant and accelerating change and complexity without revolutionizing our thinking? Traditionally our thinking has been designed for routine, for habit, for automation and fixed procedure. We learned how to do something once, and then we did it over and over. Learning meant becoming habituated. But what is it to learn to continually re-learn? To be comfortable with perpetual re-learning? This is a new world for us to explore, one in which the power of critical thinking to turn back on itself in continual cycles and re-cycles of self-critique is crucial.

Consider, for a moment, even a simple feature of daily life: drinking water from the tap. With the increase of pollution, the poisoning of ground water, the indirect and long-term negative consequences of even small amounts of a growing number of chemicals, how are we to judge whether or not public drinking water is safe? Increasingly governments are making decisions about how many lives to risk against the so many dollars of cost to save them. How are we to know whether the risk the government is willing to take with our lives is equivalent to our willingness to risk? This is just one of hundreds of decisions that require extraordinary thinking.

Consider also the quiet revolution that is taking place in communications. From fax machines to E-Mail, from bulletin board systems to computer delivery systems to home shopping, we are providing opportunities for people to not only be more efficient with their time, but to build invisible networks where goods, services, and ideas are exchanged with individuals the world over. But how is one to interface with this revolution? How much is one to learn and how fast? How much money should one spend on this or that new system? When is the new system cost effective? When should one wait for a newer development?

These communication innovations have re-introduced a way of life lost in the industrial revolution of the late 1800s. Farmers used to work at home, doctors' offices were routinely downstairs from where they lived. All that is coming back, not for farmers or doctors, but for millions of service and technical professionals for whom, "I work at home," is now a common refrain. But how are we to take these realities into account in planning our lives and careers?

Yes, technological growth brings new opportunities, new safety devices, more convenience, new lifestyles. But we must also juggle and judge work and child care, efficiency and clogged transportation systems, expensive cars and inconvenient office space, increased specialization and increasing obsolescence. We are caught up in an increasing swirl of challenges and decisions.

These changes ask and offer much at the same time, if only we can make sense of them and put them into perspective. For example, what are we to make of altered forms of community, for community in a world of automatic tellers, home shopping, self-service, delivery services, malls, video rentals, and television? How shall we evaluate these social changes and their implications for our lives?

Or consider another facet of the accelerating change: that young people today can expect to make from four to seven career changes in their lifetimes. The question, "What do you want to be when you grow up?" is a poignant reminder of a vision from the past. Our children and students can no longer anticipate the knowledge or data that they will need on the job, because they can no longer predict the kinds of jobs that will be available or what they will entail.

What is more, even if the young could predict the general fields in which they will work, about half of the information which is current in each field will be obsolete in six years. Will people recognize which half? Will they know how to access and use it?

Accelerating change is intermeshed with another powerful force, the increasing complexity of the problems we face. Consider, for a moment, solid waste management. This problem involves every level of government, every department: from energy to water quality, to planning, to revenues, to public health. Without a cooperative venture, without bridging the territorial domains, without overcoming the implicit adversarial process within which we currently operate, the responsible parties at each tier of government cannot even *begin* to solve these problems. When they do communicate, they often do not speak honestly about the issues given the human propensity to mask the limitations of one's position and promote one's narrow but deeply vested interests.

Consider the issues of depletion of the ozone layer, world hunger, overpopulation, and AIDS. Without a grasp of the elements, and internal relationships of the elements, in each of dozens of interrelating systems from specific product emissions to social incentives, from effective utilization of the media to human learning, we are adrift in a stormy sea of information. Without a grasp of the of political realities, economic pressures, scientific data on the physical environment and its changes — all of which are simultaneously changing the as well — we stand no chance of making any significant positive impact on the deterioration of the quality of life for all who share the planet.

These two characteristics, then, accelerating change and increasing complexity — with their incessant demand for a new capacity to adapt, for the now rare ability to think effectively through new problems and situations in new ways — sound the death knell for traditional methods of learning how to survive in the world in which we live. How can we adapt to reality when reality won't give us time to master it before it changes itself, again and again, in ways we cannot anticipate? As we struggle to gain insight, let's look more closely at the operating forces.

Robert Heilbroner, the distinguished American economist, in *Twenty-First Century Capitalism*, identifies capitalism as a global force that brings us "kaleidoscopic changefulness," a "torrent of market-driven change." As he illustrates in example after example, "If capitalism is anything, it is a social order in constant change — and beyond that, change that seems to have a direction, an underlying principle of motion, a logic." The logic, however, is the logic of "creative destruction, the unpredictable displacement of one process or product by another at the hands of giant enterprise" (p. 20).

Furthermore, along with kaleidoscopic change, along with the continual social transformations that follow from those changes, come "both wealth and misery," development and damage, a "two-edged sword" that makes instability permanent in unpredicted and unpredictable forms. Basic change continually destabilizes the system at the micro-level, making for multiple imbalances and upheavals. The complexity and speed of change means that we shall always have to make unpredictable adjustments to both the upsides and downsides that result from this upheaval, for we cannot hope to predict the myriad of micro-level system changes that are continually emerging and putting pressure on the system at the macro level.

We can no longer rely on the past to be the guide for the future. Technology will continually race ahead, creating links that make the world smaller and smaller. New opportunities will continually emerge but within them are embedded new problems, hence the need for acute readiness and disciplined ingenuity. At every step along the way, however, polished, satiny voices will tempt us astray with slick, simplistic messages that appear to guide us back to the "tried and true." Often, these voices in fact coax us into policies and practices that continually sacrifice our long-term interests to someone's short-term gain. In business, education, and politics, the same sirens echo.

Many American business and labor leaders have yet to come to terms with these realities. They yearn for a world of stability in which they can play a predictable game in a predictable way. As Laura Tyson, Chairwoman of the President's Council of Economic Advisors has put it,

> ... the vast majority of American companies ... [continue] to opt for traditional hierarchical work organizations that ... [make] few demands on the skills of their workers. In fact, most American companies interviewed by the Commission on the Skills of the American Workforce continue to prefer this approach, which dooms most American workers to a low-wage future. If American workers are to look forward to anything more than low-wage employment, changes in work organization are required to upgrade their skills and productivity so that American companies can afford to pay higher wages and still compete in world markets. ("Failing Our Youth: America's K–12 Education," p. 52)

What our businesses are failing to change is what European and Japanese companies are changing: namely, "making their high-wage labor more productive not simply by investing in more equipment but by organizing their workers in ways that ... [upgrade] their skills." World-class, internationally-competitive companies recognize the need to play a new game and have re-organized themselves accordingly. As Tyson explains,

High productivity work-place organizations depend on workers who can do more than read, write, and do simple arithmetic, and who bring more to their jobs than reliability and a good attitude. In such organizations, workers are asked *to use judgment and make decisions* rather than to merely follow directions. Management layers disappear as workers take over many of the tasks that others used to do — from quality control to production scheduling. Tasks formerly performed by dozens of unskilled individuals are turned over to a much smaller number of skilled individuals. Often, teams of workers are required to monitor complicated computer-controlled production equipment, to interpret computer output, to perform statistical quality control techniques, and to repair complex and sensitive equipment. (p. 53) [our emphasis]

These new kinds of workers, of course, are not asked merely to "use judgment and make decisions," rather they are asked to use *good* judgment and make *well-thought-out* decisions. How will workers acquire these fundamental abilities to think deeply and well? Are educators able to "make meaning" out of these exhortations of our leaders?

Bold changes in business organization and practices require parallel changes in education. Yet the U.S. public school systems, like most U.S. businesses, remain mired in the past, focused on lower order skills, and unresponsive to the need for higher order abilities. Again, as Laura Tyson puts it, "[Higher-order tasks] ... require higher-order language, math, scientific, and reasoning skills that America's K–12 education system is not providing."

Our students deserve at least a fighting chance to compete, to rise to the challenges of the day. Reconstructing and adapting our business and educational systems to teach our managers as well as our teachers and administrators how to create these higher order workplaces and classrooms, and then to expect them to do so in the ordinary course of their professional obligations, is our first major challenge. Today, at every level, we are failing this test, failing our students and workers, jeopardizing our future. What is missing is a genuine sense of what accelerating change entails and a shared public vision of the need for fundamental changes. Many of our leading economic analysts are struggling to create just such a new frame of reference within which we can come to terms with the new imperatives.

✦ The Vision of Robert Reich: The Thinking of Workers as the New Capital

Robert Reich, Secretary of Labor, in his seminal book, *The Work of Nations*, offers a shocking perspective. No longer will economies be tied to the fate of national corporations. No longer will we be sheltered by the power of our enormous industrial complex, our major corporations. No longer can we say, "What is good for General Motors is good for the United States!" The new form of "wealth" will no longer principally reside in the number of dollars in American pockets. Rather it will reside in the quality of the minds of our workers. As Reich puts it,

> We are living through a transformation that will rearrange the politics and economics of the coming century. There will be no national products or technologies, no national corporations, no national industries. There will no longer be national economies, or at least not as we have come to understand that concept. All that will remain rooted within national borders are the people who comprise a nation. Each nation's primary assets will be its citizens' skills and insights. (p. 3)

The changes triggered and fueled by new opportunities will bring an economy

> ... replete with unidentified problems, unknown solutions, and unknown means of putting them together — mastery of old domains of knowledge isn't nearly enough to guarantee a good income. Nor, importantly, is it even necessary.... What is more valuable is the capacity to effectively and creatively use the knowledge. (p. 182)

Routinely, jobs and production, the income that those jobs generate, and its multiplying effects in commerce, are leaping national boundaries, seeking optimum conditions for competition. We are facing competition for the production work that Americans have habitually taken as their birthright. The competitors are everywhere, as growing pressures of overpopulation and environmental problems make more people willing to work for lower wages and more governments willing to offer incentives to incoming business.

Certainly, many industries are still located here in the United States; however, there is a hemorrhage of routine production work that is moving to Mexico, to Asia, to Central and South America where workers are able to produce the same product for international markets at a significant savings to the organization. U.S. workers are bewildered and afraid, watching their standard of living decline with every year.

> In the emerging global economy, even the most impressive of positions in the most prestigious of organizations is vulnerable to worldwide competition if it entails easily replicated routines. The only true competitive advantage lies in skill in solving, identifying, and brokering new problems. (p. 184)

Reich claims that the distinguishing characteristic of workers who will retain their jobs will be the ability to "add value" to the production process. This translates into being able to identify and solve problems at every level relative to the job function. It means taking initiative and responsibility for the continuous improvement of production and efficiency, from the shop floor to the executive suite. To the extent that our labor force can shift into a cooperative venture with management, sharing responsibility for enhanced performance and production, jobs are more likely to be retained within our national boundaries.

The possession of capital will not in itself be a sure source of national wealth because American capital, as all other "national" capital, will be drawn to and invested in the nations where the work forces produce the highest level of return. Profit will stem from successful problem solving and brokering. Reich identifies a spiral wherein increasing opportunities for problem solving will provide the fodder for increasing our workers' capacity to solve more and more complex problems. Mastery of each new task requires new learning, thus enhancing each worker's capacity to contribute to the next new task.

Enhancing our capacity to solve problems will also produce more job opportunities, and up the spiral we will march as our workers continue to become better at solving the problems we face and continue to expand our inventories of skills and experience. The effectiveness and quality of our workers' thinking will drive us up the spiral, and will provide the basis for the wealth of the nation.

But do our workers and managers see this spiral? Do we see that it is the effectiveness and quality of our thinking which enables us to climb it? What is patently clear is that the spiral flows both up and down. What is unclear is whether we have the vision and determination to reverse our current course. Assuming we do have the will, we still need to know how to proceed.

Reich identifies four components of the kind of critical thinking that the highly-paid workers of today and the future will increasingly need to master: *1)* abstraction, *2)* system thinking, *3)* experimentation and testing, and *4)* collaboration. He calls the critical thinkers in possession of these basic abilities "symbolic analysts." Let us look briefly at how Reich characterizes each of these four *generic* abilities.

COMMAND OF ABSTRACTIONS

> The capacity for abstraction — for discovering patterns and meanings — is, of course, the very essence of symbolic analysis, in which reality must be simplified so that it can be understood and manipulated in new ways.... Every innovative scientist, lawyer, engineer, designer, management consultant, screenwriter, or advertiser is continuously searching for new ways to represent reality which will be more compelling or revealing than the old.... [But] for most children in the United States and around the world, formal education entails just the opposite kind of learning. Rather than construct meanings for themselves, meanings are imposed upon them. (pp. 229–230)

THINKING WITHIN SYSTEMS

The education of the symbolic analyst emphasizes system thinking. Rather than teach students how to solve a problem that is presented to them, they are taught to examine why the problem arises
and how it is connected to other problems. Learning how to travel
from one place to another by following a prescribed route is one
thing; learning the entire terrain so that you can find shortcuts to
wherever you may want to go is quite another. (p. 231)

TESTING IDEAS

Instead of emphasizing the transmission of information, the
focus is on judgment and interpretation. The student is taught to
get *behind* the data — to ask why certain facts have been selected,
why they are assumed to be important, how they were deduced,
and how they might be contradicted. The student learns to examine reality from many angles, in different lights, and thus to visual-
ize new possibilities and choices. The symbolic-analytic mind is
trained to be skeptical, curious, and creative. (p. 230)

LEARNING TO COLLABORATE AND COMMUNICATE

... in America's best classrooms ... the emphasis has shifted.
Instead of individual achievement and competition, the focus is on
group learning. Students learn to articulate, clarify, and then restate
for one another how they identify and find answers. They learn
how to seek and accept criticism from peers, solicit help, and give
credit to others. They also learn to negotiate — to explain their
own needs, to discern what others need and view things from others' perspectives. (p. 233)

How many critical thinkers (symbolic analysts) will we have the foresight
to develop? For each student we fail to reach, we create an economic dependent; for each student we help to possess the requisite abilities and traits,
we create a producer who can carry not only himself or herself, but those
dependents inevitable in any society. How urgent do we perceive the problem to be? How clearly do we understand the problem and its dimensions?

✦ The Vision of Lester Thurow: Two Forms of Capitalism at War in a World of Economic Revolutions

The world that Lester Thurow looks out upon is a world of multiple
revolutions: a green revolution, a materials-science revolution, a telecom-
munications-computer-transportation-logistics revolution. These revolu-

tions require fundamental changes in all economies around the world. We live in a multi-polar world: the global economy is no longer pivoting solely around the United States as it did in the fifties and sixties.

As Thurow sees it, "Nowhere are the necessary changes going to be harder to make than in the United States, for in the past century it has been the most successful economy in the world." (*Head to Head,* p. 16) Our tendency, Thurow believes, will be to continue the strategies that brought us success in the past, even though those strategies no longer fit a "multi-polar" world.

For example, military power is now a distinct disadvantage rather than an advantage, a drain on the national treasury and a limitation on investments necessary for competition. Here are the new questions that in Thurow's view can be used to measure world economic strength.

> Who can make the best products? What expands their standards of living most rapidly? Who has the best-educated and best-skilled work force in the world? Who is the world's leader in investment — plant and equipment, research and development, infrastructure? Who organizes best? Whose institutions — government, education, business — are world leaders in efficiency? (pp. 23–24)

Much of Thurow's argument is based on a distinction between the two forms of capitalism currently in competition for world leadership: communitarian and individualistic capitalism. In every way, Thurow argues, it is clear that communitarian capitalism (such as in Germany and Japan) wins out over individualistic capitalism (such as in U.S. and Great Britain). This is reflected in many statistics including those of the World Economic Forum relating to American, German, and Japanese management (p. 162).

RANKING OF QUALITY OF MANAGEMENT IN 23 INDUSTRIAL NATIONS
World Economic Forum, Swiss-run publisher of *World Competitiveness Report*

	GERMANY	JAPAN	USA
PRODUCT QUALITY	3	1	12
ON-TIME DELIVERY	2	1	10
AFTER-SALES SERVICE	2	1	10
QUANTITY AND QUALITY OF ON-THE-JOB TRAINING	2	1	11
FUTURE ORIENTATION	3	1	22

Thurow sums up the problem as follows:

> Japan and Germany, the countries that are outperforming Amer-
> ica in international trade, do not have less government or more
> motivated individuals. They are countries noted for their careful
> organization of teams — teams that involve workers and managers,
> teams that involve suppliers and customers, teams that involve
> government and business.... But American mythology extols only
> the individual — the Lone Ranger or Rambo.... History is littered
> with the wrecks of countries whose mythologies were more impor-
> tant than reality. (p. 298)

In essence, Thurow's analysis calls for a transformed American global
view in which we recognize the obsolescence of some of our most fundamental traditional assumptions and the need to shift our world view — to
make no less than a fundamental intellectual paradigm shift.

But isn't this asking a lot of a nation that has never put a premium on
the ability to think critically? Isn't this asking a lot of a nation that historically has been able to solve its problems with sheer hard work and physical courage? Isn't this asking a lot of a nation that believes deeply in the
tried and true, that has been conditioned to think of itself as leading not
following and as being the most progressive, as being always *number one?*

Thurow nowhere discusses how this shift is to occur, how the electorate is to be persuaded into such a radical re-orientation. We tend to
seek security in the familiar, in the established, in the traditional: if we
don't find it immediately, we look harder, but in the same places! Since
most Americans have not been prepared by their education to do the requisite critical thinking that would support a paradigm shift such as
Thurow suggests, how are they to do it?

If Thurow is right in his analysis of world economic conditions, then it
will not be sufficient for a small minority of highly paid workers to learn to
think critically as "symbolic analysts." It will not be enough for a few to be
comfortable with abstractions, to be able to think in terms of alternative
systems, to test ideas for their strengths, and to recognize the value of collaboration. But here, again, is the most pressing problem of the day: How
are we to persuade educators, how are we to persuade citizens, how are we
to persuade parents, that a new economic era is dawning? How are we to
persuade the general public, which itself has not learned to think critically,
that it is now in our collective national interest to set as our first priority the
development of critical thinking abilities and traits in all of our children?

✦ The Vision of W. Edwards Deming:
Everyone a Critical Thinker
Contributing to Continuous Improvement

W. Edwards Deming, the American marvel who, after WWII, designed
the highly successful Japanese style of management and production,

built his whole approach on the assumption that the most important asset of any company is the capacity of the individuals in it to use their ability to think critically to improve their collective performance. Success can be found, in his view, in the ability to devise structures that systematically encourage and reward the critique and improvement of process. He therefore established a system of interrelated networks of "workers and managers" (quality control circles, so called) who use "critical reflection in a formal but unthreatening setting so as to establish what it is good to do." (Holt, p. 383)

When procedures are designed to bring the maximum degree of constructive critical thinking to bear on the problems of production, virtually everyone has a potential contribution to make. The quality of the contribution will not be a function of the worker's position in the hierarchy, but the quality of the critical thinking he or she brings to bear on the problem. This, again, requires the paradigm shift that American businesses seem reluctant to make.

Unfortunately, though Deming is now popular and much has been written about the Deming way and "total quality management," most writings emphasize the "techniques" and "procedures" of Deming while leaving out the critical thinking they require to succeed. They have tried to "formalize" Deming, to reduce Deming to a series of procedures and charts. The inevitable result is a caricature of Deming: Total Quality Control without the "quality." Only excellence in thinking can produce genuine, continuous improvement in quality, and excellence in thinking cannot be produced with simplistic procedures and slogans.

But we are still captive of a traditional American assumption that might be expressed as follows: "Every idea of importance can be expressed simply and learned easily. The true challenges of life are to be found in everyday hard work and extraordinary courage and neither of those require deep or 'intellectual' thinking."

The necessary paradigm shifts, however, do entail the cultivation of critical thinking across the work force, up and down the lines of labor and management, across industries, across educational levels, and into the everyday discussions of national and international issues. This shift is painfully against the American grain, contrary to our traditional folk wisdom, and incompatible with much current thinking of both business and labor leaders.

✦ The Vision of Robert Heilbroner: The Challenge of Large-Scale Disorder

Robert Heilbroner argues, as do Reich and Thurow, that though capitalism will be dominant in the 21st Century, there will be serious conflicts between opposing forms of capitalism. As a result of these conflicts, a new and perplexing dimension to the picture will emerge: the

challenge of "macro-disorder," of economy-wide and world-wide problems arising from the market mechanism following its own logic without making critical adjustments. This problem calls for solutions we
have yet to think through. He calls this problem that of negative "exter-
nalities," of market failures that have large-scale, and to date uncontrolled, negative consequences.

Addressing these large-scale problems requires a new brand of both
leadership and followership. We need leaders who become comfortable
talking about and thinking through complexities. We need "followers"
with the thoughtful ability and patience to grasp the very complexities
being explained. Here are some of the large-scale problems that Heilbroner has in mind:

> The overcutting of forests, the overfishing of the seas, the over-
> consumption of gasoline, ... the indeterminacy of the outlook for
> investment and for technology; the unequal distribution of
> incomes; the volatility of credit; the tendency towards monopoly;
> over-regulation; the technological displacement of labor and the
> technological impetus towards cartelization; the inflationary ten-
> dencies of a successful economy and the depressive tendencies of
> an unsuccessful one; the vacillation between optimism and pes-
> simism, ... the approach of ecological barriers, ... the international-
> izing tendency of capital that continues to outpace the defensive
> powers of individual governments. (p. 104)

He summarizes our situation as follows:

> ... the problems of capitalist disorder — too many to recite, too
> complex in their origins to take up one at a time ... arise from the
> workings of the system.... The problems must be addressed by the
> assertion of political will ... the undesired dynamics of the eco-
> nomic sphere must be contained, redressed, or redirected by the
> only agency capable of asserting a counter-force to that of the eco-
> nomic sphere. It is the government. (pp. 108–109)

The unanswered questions are, "Who or what is going to direct governments to make rational decisions in the long-term public interest? Where
are we to turn to find this new kind of leader? How are we to cultivate the
new kind of electorate?"

If the electorates in the various countries do not learn to think critically
about large and vexing questions in the environment, in the economy, in
health care and overpopulation, it is likely that government policies will
be directed by small groups whose short-range interests *easily* triumph
over long-range public good. We are facing basic problems in our capacity
to govern ourselves. But all government is finally government made up of
people, and people can rise only to the height of their own ability. The
crucial issue is, "Will we develop the thinking abilities and intellectual
traits of our citizens to a level that will be sufficient for survival?"

✦ The Challenge of the Future

The world of the 21ˢᵗ Century — virtually all commentators agree — will see intensifying economic competition between forms of capitalism. Governmental, economic, social, and environmental problems will become increasingly complex and interdependent. Basic causes will be both global and national. The forces to be understood and controlled will be corporate, national, trans-national, cultural, religious, economic, and environmental, all intricately intertwined. Critical thinking will become a survival need, an external imperative for every nation and for every individual who must survive on his or her own talents, abilities, and traits.

A battle for economic vitality is being fought. Yet consider how unprepared we have been, and continue to be, for that battle. Consider the size of our national debt, the decay of our infrastructure. Consider the intensification of social divisions and divisiveness, the obsolescence of our systems of public education. Consider our traditional but increasingly dangerous assumption that the solutions to our problems lie in a dependence on traditional wisdom. Consider our traditional anti-intellectualism, our traditional parochialism. Can we free ourselves from our own narrow modes of thinking?

Can we accept the fact of accelerating change and complexity? Can we develop intellectual humility and flexibility? Can we develop faith in reason as a tool of discovery? Can we learn to think within points of view other than our own? Can we accept that we are no longer the dominant economic force in the world? Can we learn to think in the long-term and not simply in terms of short-term advantages? Can we begin to make decisions that are in the long-range interest of our children and their well-being? Can we become habitual thinkers rather than reactors and learn to continually inform our action with deep thought? These are the challenges we face. How we respond to them will determine our national fate.

✦✦ *Implications*

What, then, do we need to do?

As a society, our challenge is to recognize that the work of the future is the work of the mind, intellectual work, work that involves reasoning and intellectual self-discipline. Our challenge is to demonstrate intellectual courage in facing our traditional indifference to the development of our minds, our traditional arrogance in assuming that our common sense will always provide the answers, and that our example will always lead the world. We are unaccustomed to this kind of challenge. We are uncomfortable with things *intellectual*. The very word smacks of subversive, egghead, ivory tower, out of touch, impractical, unrealistic. Our collective mindset is now working against us and we must own that fact. We need to "discover,"

and then genuinely explore in depth this whole notion of substantive critical thinking, of thinking based on intellectual discipline and standards. We
need to transform our schools, our businesses, and our lives accordingly.
Are we willing to evaluate our own thinking? Are we willing to set ideology
aside? Are we willing to re-think our most basic thinking?

To date, we are still under the sway of the misconception that thinking
more or less "takes care of itself," that simply by studying "hard" subjects
or "concentrating" we can think well. In general, we still treat knowledge
as something that can be given to us and inserted into our minds by
memory alone. We must begin now to set ourselves a course that will take
many, many years to reach.

1) *We must parent differently.* We must respond differently to our children's
"Why?" questions. We must not give them short didactic answers, but
must encourage them to conjecture as to the answers. We must call
more attention to the extent of our own ignorance and not try to convince our children that adults have good answers for most of their
questions.

We must dialogue more with our children about complexities in their
lives and in ours. We must help them to discover their own capacity to
figure things out, to reason through situations. We must hold them
responsible to think and not simply to rotely respond. We must step
more into their points of view and help them to step more into the
points of view of others. We must help them to identify their own
assumptions, clarify their emerging concepts, question their habitual
inferences. We must raise our children so that critical thinking
becomes an integral part of their everyday lives. They must learn to
accept its responsibility and come to discover its power and challenge.

2) *We must work differently.* We must bring the reality of cooperative critical
thinking into the workplace in a thorough way. This means that we
must abandon quick-fix strategies and recognize the counterfeits of substantial change. We must become aware of the difference, for example,
between the jargon of "Total Quality Management" (which we now
have in abundance) and the reality (which we almost entirely lack).

Both managers and workers need to learn how to begin to think in a
new way: we must learn how to discipline our thinking to a new level
of clarity, precision, relevance, depth, and coherence. CEO's need to
learn how to think within alternative models of how to organize and
run businesses. Leaders in industry need to learn to broaden their perspectives and think about the long-range interests of the economy and
not simply about short-range, vested interests of their businesses. Labor
leaders need to concentrate more on support for programs that cultivate broad-based job skills and abilities, that emphasize the basic thinking skills of workers, and less on immediate bread and butter issues.

We must each take it upon ourselves to become lifelong learners, searching for ways to continuously upgrade our reasoning skills, our critical reading skills, our ability and propensity to enter into the points of view of others. Complex problems have many facets, and intellectual humility requires that we become used to exploring multiple perspectives before we make a decision. No more "Ready!... Fire!... Aim!"

3) We must educate differently. We can no longer afford the high cost of educators who have few or no critical thinking skills, and little or no motivation to develop them. Teachers and administrators who do not themselves think critically, cannot design changes in curriculum and instruction that foster critical thinking. We must come to terms with the most fundamental problem in education today and that is "the blind leading the blind." Many educators do not realize that they are functionally blind to the demands of our post-industrial world.

As CEO and Chairman of Apple Computer, John Sculley, has put it,

> In the new economy, strategic resources no longer just come out of the ground. The strategic resources are ideas and information that come out of our minds.
>
> The result: as a nation, we have gone from being resource-rich in the old economy to resource-poor in the new economy almost overnight! Our public education has not successfully made the shift from teaching the memorization of facts to achieving the learning of critical thinking skills. We are still trapped in a K–12 public education system which is preparing our youth for jobs that no longer exist.

✦ Is There Room for Any Optimism?

Yet there is room for optimism, but only under certain conditions. We have the theoretical foundation and expertise to bring critical thinking to our children, but do we have the vision and the will? If we do, we have an ace in the hole. What Deming did not anticipate was the opportunity of systematically enhancing the critical thinking of the workers as well as the students in our schools, and the competitive advantage that this would provide.

Those countries with the foresight to systematically cultivate the critical thinking of their citizens of all ages, through the educational systems in schools and the workplace, will enjoy a significant competitive advantage over countries that do not make this effort. This is particularly true when this foresight extends to emphasizing high-quality, Deming-style production models. At present, no country in the world systematically fosters critical thinking. Opportunities await those nations who can see the potential to invest intensely in this specific effort.

What we can be sure of is that the persuasiveness of the argument for critical thinking will only grow year by year, day by day — for the logic of the argument is simply the only prudent response to the accelerating change, to the increasing complexity of our world. No gimmick, no crafty substitute, can be found for the cultivation of quality thinking. The quality of our lives can only become more and more obviously the product of the quality of the thinking we use to create them.

Critical thinking is ancient, but until now its practice was for the elite minority, for the few. But the few, in possession of superior power of disciplined thought, used it as one might only expect, to advance the interests of the few. We can never expect the few to become the long-term benevolent caretakers of the many.

The many must become privy to the superior intellectual abilities, discipline, and traits of the traditional privileged few. Progressively, the power and accessibility of critical thinking will become more and more apparent to more and more people, particularly to those who have had limited access to the educational opportunities available to the fortunate few.

The only question is how long and how painful the process will be and what we shall sacrifice of the public good in the meanwhile. How many of our citizens will live lives unemployed and unemployable in the post-industrial age?

We must sooner or later abandon the traditional attempt to teach our fellow citizens *what* to think. Such efforts cannot prepare us for the real world we must, in fact, face. We must concentrate instead on teaching ourselves *how* to think, thus freeing us to think for ourselves, critically, fairmindedly, and deeply. We have no choice, not in the long haul, not in the face of the irrepressible logic of accelerating change and increasing complexity.

✦ References

Holt, R. "The Educational Consequences of W. Edwards Deming." *Phi Delta Kappan.* Jan. 1993.

Heilbroner, Robert. *Twenty-First Century Capitalism.* House of Anansi Press, Limited, Concord, Ontario. 1992.

Reich, Robert. *The Work of Nations.* Vintage Books, New York, NY. 1992.

Sculley, John. Remarks to then President-Elect Clinton, December, 1992.

Thurow, Lester. *Head to Head.* William Morrow and Company, Inc., New York, NY. 1992.

Tyson, Laura D'Andrea. "Failing Our Youth: America's K–12 Education." *New Perspectives Quarterly.* edited by Nathan Gordels. Winter, 1993.

Chapter 2

Critical Thinking:
Identifying the Targets

with Jane Willsen

Abstract

The goal of this chapter is to set out clearly what critical thinking is in general and how it plays itself out in a variety of domains: in reading, in writing, in studying academic subjects, and on the job. Richard Paul and Jane Willsen provide down-to-earth examples that enable the reader to appreciate both the most general characteristics of critical thinking and their specific manifestations on the concrete level. It is essential, of course, that the reader become clear about the concept, including its translation into cases, for otherwise she is apt to mis-translate the concept or fail to see its relevance in a wide variety of circumstances. The danger of misunderstanding and mis-application is touched upon in this chapter at the end, but is developed at great length in another chapter, "Pseudo Critical Thinking in the Educational Establishment" (p. 47).

✔ Is this a good idea or a bad idea?

✔ Is this belief defensible or indefensible?

✔ Is my position on this issue reasonable and rational or not?

✔ Am I willing to deal with complexity or do I retreat into simple stereotypes to avoid it?

✔ If I can't tell if my idea or belief is reasonable or defensible, how can I have confidence in my thinking, or in myself?

✔ Is it appropriate and wise to assume that my ideas and beliefs are accurate, clear, and reasonable, when I haven't really tested them?

✔ Do I think deeply or only on the surface of things?

✔ Do I ever enter sympathetically into points of view that are very different from my own, or do I just assume that I am right?

✔ Do I know how to question my own ideas and to test them?

✔ Do I know what I am aiming for? Should I?

Effectively evaluating our own thinking and the thinking of others is a habit few of us practice. We evaluate which washing machine to buy after reading *Consumer Reports*, we evaluate which movie to go see after studying the reviews, we evaluate new job opportunities after talking with friends and colleagues, but rarely do we explicitly evaluate the quality of our thinking (or the thinking of our students).

But, you may ask, how can we know if our thinking is sound? Are we relegated to "trial and error" to discover the consequences of our thinking? Do the consequences always accurately tell the tale? Isn't thinking all a matter of opinion anyway? Isn't my opinion as good as anyone else's? If what I believe is true for me, isn't that all that matters?

In our education and upbringing, have we developed the ability to evaluate, objectively and fairly, the quality of our beliefs? What did we learn about thinking during our schooling?

How did we come to believe what we do believe, and why one belief and not another? How many of our beliefs have we come to through rigorous, independent thinking, and how many have been down-loaded from the media, parents, our culture, our spouses or friends? As we focus on it, do we value the continuing improvement of our thinking abilities? Do we value the continuing improvement of our students' thinking abilities? Important research findings indicate that we need to look closely at this issue. Mary Kennedy reports the findings on the opposite page in the *Phi Delta Kappan*, May, 1991, in an article entitled, "Policy Issues in Teaching Education."

How can we improve our thinking without effective evaluation practices? Can we learn how to evaluate our thinking and reasoning objectively? Let's look at one concrete example for clues into the elements of effective evaluation in a familiar field. In platform diving, there are criteria to be met to receive a score of "10" and standards that judges and competitors alike use to evaluate the dive. These standards guide the divers in each practice session, in each effort off the board. Without these criteria and standards, how would the diver and the judges know what was excellent and what was marginal? Awareness of the criteria and standards are alive in the divers' and coaches' minds. Do we have parallel criteria and standards as we strive to improve our abilities, our performances in thinking?

There is nothing more common than evaluation in the everyday world but for sound evaluation to take place, one must establish relevant standards, gather appropriate evidence, and judge the evidence in keeping with the standards.

There are appropriate standards for the assessment of thinking and there are specific ways to cultivate the learning of them. The research into critical thinking establishes tools that can help us evaluate our own thinking and the thinking of others, if we see their potential benefit and are willing to discipline our minds in ways that may seem awkward at first. This chapter briefly lays out those tools in general terms and acts as a map, so to speak, of their dimensions. We present examples of student

Important Research Findings

First Finding: ...national assessments in virtually every subject indicate that, although our students can perform basic skills pretty well, they are not doing well on thinking and reasoning. American students can compute, but they cannot reason.... They can write complete and correct sentences, but they cannot prepare arguments.... Moreover, in international comparisons, American students are falling behind...particularly in those areas that require higher-order thinking.... Our students are not doing well at thinking, reasoning, analyzing, predicting, estimating, or problem solving.

Second Finding: ...textbooks in this country typically pay scant attention to big ideas, offer no analysis, and pose no challenging questions. Instead, they provide a tremendous array of information or 'factlets', while they ask questions requiring only that students be able to recite back the same empty list.

Third Finding: Teachers teach most content only for exposure, not for understanding.

Fourth Finding: Teachers tend to avoid thought-provoking work and activities and stick to predictable routines.
Conclusion: "If we were to describe our current K–12 education system on the basis of these four findings, we would have to say that it provides very little intellectually stimulating work for students, and that it tends to produce students who are not capable of intellectual work.

Fifth Finding: ... our fifth finding from research compounds all the others and makes it harder to change practice: teachers are highly likely to teach in the way they themselves were taught. If your elementary teacher presented mathematics to you as a set of procedural rules with no substantive rationale, then you are likely to think that this is what mathematics is and that this is how mathematics should be studied. And you are likely to teach it in this way. If you studied writing as a set of grammatical rules rather than as a way to organize your thoughts and to communicate ideas to others, then this is what you will think writing is, and you will probably teach it so.... By the time we complete our undergraduate education, we have observed teachers for up to 3,060 days.

Implication: "We are caught in a vicious circle of mediocre practice modeled after mediocre practice, of trivialized knowledge begetting more trivialized knowledge. Unless we find a way out of this circle, we will continue re-creating generations of teachers who re-create generations of students who are not prepared for the technological society we are becoming."

(FIGURE 1 CONDENSED FROM "POLICY ISSUES IN TEACHING EDUCATION" BY MARY KENNEDY IN THE *PHI DELTA KAPPAN*, MAY, 91, PP 661–66.)

thinking that demonstrate critical and uncritical thinking as we define those terms. In other chapters, we identify approaches to teaching critical thinking that are flawed, and explain why they undermine the success of those who attempt to use them.

✦ Critical Thinking: A Picture of the Genuine Article

Critical Thinking is a systematic way to form and shape one's thinking. It functions purposefully and exactingly. It is thought that is disciplined, comprehensive, based on intellectual standards, and, as a result, well-reasoned.

Critical Thinking is distinguishable from other thinking because the thinker is thinking with the awareness of the systematic nature of high quality thought, and is continuously checking up on himself or herself, striving to improve the quality of thinking. As with any system, critical thinking is not just a random series of characteristics or components. All of its components - its elements, principles, standards and values - form an integrated, working network that can be applied effectively not only to academic learning, but to learning in every dimension of living.

Critical thinking's most fundamental concern is excellence of thought. Critical thinking is based on two assumptions: first, that the quality of our thinking affects the quality of our lives, and second, that everyone can learn how to continually improve the quality of his or her thinking.

Critical Thinking implies a fundamental, overriding goal for education in school and in the workplace: always to teach so as to help students improve their own thinking. As students learn to take command of their thinking and continually to improve its quality, they learn to take command of their lives, continually improving the quality of their lives.

COMPREHENSIVE CRITICAL THINKING HAS THE FOLLOWING CHARACTERISTICS

• It is thinking which is responsive to and guided by INTELLECTUAL STANDARDS, such as relevance, accuracy, precision, clarity, depth, and breadth. Without intellectual standards to guide it, thinking cannot achieve excellence. [Note: most so-called "thinking skill" educational programs and approaches have no intellectual standards.]

The chart on the right gives an overview of the concept of critical thinking supported by thirteen years of research from the Center of Critical Thinking and Moral Critique, Sonoma State University, California.

What is Critical Thinking?

A Unique Kind of Purposeful Thinking
— IN ANY SUBJECT AREA OR TOPIC, WHETHER ACADEMIC OR PRACTICAL, REQUIRING **INTELLECTUAL FITNESS TRAINING FOR THE MIND** AKIN TO PHYSICAL FITNESS TRAINING FOR THE BODY

In Which the Thinker Systematically and Habitually
— **ACTIVELY DEVELOPS TRAITS** SUCH AS INTELLECTUAL INTEGRITY, INTELLECTUAL HUMILITY, FAIRMINDEDNESS, INTELLECTUAL EMPATHY, AND INTELLECTUAL COURAGE

Imposes Criteria and Intellectual Standards Upon the Thinking
— **IDENTIFIES THE CRITERIA OF SOLID REASONING,** SUCH AS PRECISION, RELEVANCE, DEPTH, ACCURACY, SUFFICIENCY, AND **ESTABLISHES A CLEAR STANDARD** BY WHICH THE EFFECTIVENESS OF THE THINKING WILL BE FINALLY ASSESSED

Taking Charge of the Construction of Thinking
— **AWARENESS OF THE ELEMENTS OF THOUGHT** SUCH AS ASSUMPTIONS AND POINT OF VIEW, THAT ARE PRESENT IN ALL WELL-REASONED THINKING; **A CONSCIOUS, ACTIVE AND DISCIPLINED EFFORT** TO ADDRESS EACH ELEMENT IS DISPLAYED

Guiding the Construction of the Thinking According to the Standards
— **CONTINUALLY ASSESSING** THE COUSE OF CONSTRUCTION DURING THE PROCESS, **ADJUSTING, ADAPTING, IMPROVING,** USING THE CANDLES OF CRITERIA AND STANDARDS TO LIGHT THE WAY

Assessing the Effectiveness of the Thinking According to the Purpose, the Criteria, and the Standards.
— **DELIBERATELY ASSESSING THE THINKING TO DETERMINE ITS STRENGTHS AND LIMITATIONS,** ACCORDING TO THE DEFINING PURPOSE, CRITERIA AND STANDARDS, **STUDYING THE IMPLICATIONS** FOR FURTHER THINKING AND IMPROVEMENT

• It is thinking that deliberately supports the development of INTELL-ECTUAL TRAITS in the thinker, such as intellectual humility, intellectual integrity, intellectual perseverance, intellectual empathy, and intellectual self-discipline, among others. [Note: most "thinking skill" programs ignore fundamental intellectual traits.]

• It is thinking in which the thinker can identify the ELEMENTS OF THOUGHT that are present in all thinking about any problem, such that the thinker makes the logical connection between the elements and the problem at hand. For example, the critical thinker will routinely ask himself or herself questions such as these about the subject of the thinking task at hand:

What is the *purpose* of my thinking?

What precise *question* am I trying to answer?

Within what *point of view* am I thinking?

What *information* am I using?

How am I *interpreting* that information?

What *concepts* or ideas are central to my thinking?

What *conclusions* am I coming to?

What am I taking for granted, what *assumptions* am I making?

If I accept the conclusions, what are the *implications*?

What would the *consequences* be, if I put my thought into action?

For each element, the thinker must be able to reflect on the standards that will shed light on the effectiveness of her thinking. [Note: Most "thinking skill" programs ignore most or all of the basic elements of thought and the need to apply standards to their evaluation.]

• It is thinking that is ROUTINELY SELF-ASSESSING, SELF-EXAMIN-ING, and SELF-IMPROVING. The thinker takes steps to assess the various dimensions of her thinking, using appropriate intellectual standards. [Note: Most "thinking skill" programs do not emphasize student self-assessment.] *But what is essential to recognize is that if students are not assessing their own thinking, they are not thinking critically.*

• It is thinking in which THERE IS AN INTEGRITY TO THE WHOLE SYSTEM. The thinker is able not only to critically examine her thought as a whole, but also to take it apart, to consider its various parts, as well. Furthermore, the thinker is committed to thinking within a system of inter-related traits of mind; for example, to be intellectually humble, to be intellectually perseverant, to be intellectually courageous, to be intellectually fair and just. Ideally, the critical thinker is aware of the full variety of ways in which thinking can become distorted, misleading, prejudiced, superficial, unfair, or otherwise defective. The thinker strives for wholeness and integrity as fundamental values. [Note: Most "thinking skills" programs are not well integrated and lack a broad vision of the range of thinking abilities, standards, and traits that the successful critical thinking student will develop. Many tend to instruct students with a technique such as mapping of ideas in diagrams or comparing two ideas, yet these ask little of the student and can readily mislead student and teacher to believe that such techniques will be sufficient.]

• It is thinking that YIELDS A PREDICTABLE, WELL-REASONED ANSWER because of the comprehensive and demanding process that the thinker pursues. If we know quite explicitly how to check our thinking as we go, and we are committed to doing so, and we get extensive practice, then we can depend on the results of our thinking being productive. Good thinking produces good results. [Note: Because most "thinking skills" programs lack intellectual standards and do not require a comprehensive process of thinking, the quality of student response is unpredictable, both for the students and for the teacher.]

• It is thinking that is responsive to the social and moral imperative to not only enthusiastically argue from alternate and opposing points of view, but also to SEEK AND IDENTIFY WEAKNESSES AND LIMITATIONS IN ONE'S OWN POSITION. When one becomes aware that there are many legitimate points of view, each of which—when deeply thought through—yields some level of insight, then one becomes keenly aware that one's own thinking, however rich and insightful it may be, however carefully constructed, will not capture everything worth knowing and seeing. [Because most "thinking skills" programs lack intellectual standards, the students are unable to identify weaknesses in their own reasoning nor are they taught to see this as a value to be pursued.]

WHAT DOES COMPREHENSIVE CRITICAL THINKING LOOK LIKE?

The following section highlights examples of legitimate, substantial, comprehensive critical thinking in a variety of contexts. These examples will provide the reader with concrete samples of the criteria, the standards and characteristics integral to genuine critical thinking.

✦ Identifying the Target: Critical Thinking at School

Critical thinking has an appropriate role in virtually every dimension of school learning, very little that we learn that is of value can be learned by automatic, unreflective processes. Textbooks, subject matter, classroom discussion, even relationships with classmates are things to be "figured out" and "assessed." Let's look at two students who are each "reading" a passage from a story and see if we can identify the consequences of critical and uncritical reading habits and abilities.

ARE WE HITTING THE TARGET?
ASSESSING STUDENT THINKING IN READING

Consider the following example of two students engaging in reading the same story. This example is being taken from an important article by Stephen Norris and Linda Phillips, "Explanations of Reading Comprehension: Schema Theory and Critical Thinking Theory," in *Teachers College Record*, Volume 89, Number 2, Winter 1987. We are privy to conversations between each of the two students, Colleen and Stephen and an experimenter. We are thus invited to reconstruct, from the students' responses, our own appraisal of the quality of their thinking. The utility of intellectual standards such as clarity, relevance, accuracy, consistency, and depth of thinking come into sharp focus once one begins to assess specific thinking for "quality."

In what follows we will present episode-by-episode Stephen and Colleen's thinking aloud as they work through the passage. The experimenter's questions are given in brackets. We have chosen to make our example detailed, because we see this as the best route for providing specificity to otherwise vague generalizations about the relationship between reading and thinking. To simulate the task for you we present the passage without a title and one episode at a time as was done with the children.

Episode 1

The stillness of the morning air was broken. The men headed down the bay.

Stephen

The men were heading down the bay, I'm not sure why yet. It was a very peaceful morning. [Any questions?] No, not really. [Where do you think they're going?] I think they might be going sailing, water skiing, or something like that.

Colleen

The men are going shopping. [Why do you think that?] They're going to buy clothes at The Bay. [What is The Bay?] It's a shopping center. [Any questions?] No. [Where do you think they're going?] They're going shopping because it seems like they broke something.

Commentary

Stephen recognizes that there is insufficient information for explaining what the men are doing. On questioning, he tentatively suggests a couple of alternatives consistent with the information given, but indicates there are other possibilities. Colleen presents one explanation of the story, and seems fairly definitive that the men are going to buy clothes at The Bay, a chain of department stores in Canada. On being queried she maintains her idea that the men are going shopping but offers an explanation inconsistent with her first one that they are going to buy clothes. To do this she assumes that something concrete was broken, which could be replaced at The Bay.

Episode 2

The net was hard to pull. The heavy sea and strong tide made it even difficult for the girdie. The meshed catch encouraged us to try harder.

Stephen

It was not a very good day as there were waves which made it difficult for the girdie. That must be some kind of machine for doing something. The net could be for pulling something out of the water like an old wreck. No, wait! It said "meshed catch." I don't know why but that makes me think of fish and, sure, if you caught fish you'd really want to get them. [Any questions?] No questions, just that I think maybe the girdie is a machine for helping the men pull in the fish or whatever it was. Maybe a type of pulley.

Colleen

I guess The Bay must have a big water fountain. [Why was the net hard to pull?] There a lot of force on the water. [Why was it important for them to pull the net?] It was something they had to do. [What do you mean?] They had to pull the net and it was hard to do. [Any questions?] No. [Where do you think they're going?] Shopping.

Commentary

For both children the interpretations of Episode 2 built on those of Episode 1. Stephen continues to question what the men were doing. He raises a number of alternative interpretation dealing with the context of the sea. He refines his interpretations through testing hypothetical interpretations against specific details, and hypotheses of specific word meanings against his emerging interpretation of the story. At the outset he makes an inference that a girdie is a machine, but leaves details about its nature and function unspecified. He tentatively offers one specific use for the net, but immediately questions this use when he realizes that it will not account for the meshed catch, and substitutes an alternative function. He then confirms this interpretation with the fact from the story that the men were encouraged to try harder and his belief that if you catch fish you would really want to bring them aboard. Finally, he sees that he is in a position to offer a more definitive but tentative interpretation of the word girdie.

Colleen maintains her interpretation of going shopping at The Bay. When questioned about her interpretation, Colleen responds in vague or tautological terms. She seems not to integrate information relating to the terms net, catch, and sea, and it seemed satisfied to remain uniformed about the nature of the girdie and the reason for pulling the net. In the end, she concludes definitively that the men are going shopping.

Episode 3

With four quintels aboard, we were now ready to leave. The skipper saw mares' tails in the north.

Stephen

I wonder what quintels are? I think maybe it's a sea term, a word that means perhaps the weight aboard. Yes maybe it's how much fish they had aboard. [So you think it was fish?] I think fish or maybe something they had found in the water but I think fish more because of the word "catch." [Why were they worried about the mares' tails?] I'm not sure. Mares' tails, let me see, mares are horses but horses are not going to be in the water. The mares' tails are in the north. Here farmers watch the north for bad weather, so maybe the fishermen do the same thing. Yeah, I think that's it, it's a cloud

Colleen

They were finished their shopping and were ready to go home. [What did they have aboard?] Quintels. [What are quintels?] I don't know. [Why were they worried about the mares' tails?] There were a group of horses on the street and they were afraid they would attack the car. [Any questions?] No.

formation which could mean
strong winds and hail or something which I think could be dangerous if you were in a boat and a
lot of weight aboard. [Any questions?] No.

Commentary

Stephen is successful in his efforts to incorporate the new information
into an evolving interpretation. From the outset Stephen acknowledges
that he does not know the meaning of quintel and seeks a resolution of
this unknown. He derives a meaning consistent with his evolving interpretations and with the textual evidence. In his attempt to understand
the expression mares' tails he first acknowledges that he does not know
the meaning of the expression. Thence, he establishes what he does know
from the background knowledge (mares are horses, horses are not going
to be in the water, there is nothing around except sky and water, farmers
watch the north for bad weather) and textual information (the men are
on the bay, they have things aboard, the mares' tails are in the north) and
inferences he has previously made (the men are in a boat, they are fishing). He integrates this knowledge into a comparison between the concerns of Alberta farmers with which he is familiar, and what he takes to be
analogous concerns of fishermen. On seeing the pertinence of this analogy he draws the conclusion that the mares' tails must be a cloud formation foreboding inclement weather. He claims support for his conclusion
in the fact that it would explain the skipper's concern for the mares' tails,
indicating that he did not lose sight of the overall task of understanding
the story.

Colleen maintains her original interpretation but does not incorporate
all the new textual information into it. She works with the information
on the men's leaving and the mares' tails, but appears to ignore or remain
vague about other information. For example, she says the cargo was comprised of quintels but indicates no effort to determine what these things
are. She cites the fact that the men were ready to leave and suggests that
they have finished their shopping, but does not attempt to explain the
use of such words as skipper, cargo, and aboard in the context for shopping for clothes. She interprets mares' tails as a group of horses the possibly would attack the men, but gives no account of what the horses might
be doing on the street. Basically, she appears to grow tolerant of ambiguity and incompleteness in her interpretation.

Interestingly, each student believes that he or she has read the passage. The question becomes, what does it mean "to read" something?
Comprehensive, legitimate critical thinking enables us to explore the

meaning of the concept "to read" and to come to understand that there is a spectrum of quality of readings, some superficial and mechanical, some deep and thorough.

Specifically, Colleen has scrambled to piece together meanings that have little relationship to the writer's ideas. Colleen has "read" the passage but we can quickly see that the quality of her thinking lacks characteristics that we equate with sound reasoning, with critical thinking. She has been ineffective in thinking within the system of meanings inherent in what was said in the passage she tried to read. That her responses were inconsistent did not seem to disturb her, almost as if she had no sense of how to figure out what she was reading. The consequences for Colleen in this episode of thinking are minimal. However, consider how vulnerable she will be outside school, when much more than grades or teacher approval is riding on her ability to think effectively in other systems, such as health care, parenting, upgrading job skills or becoming a proficient consumer.

On the other hand, Stephen has "read" the passage by means of critical reasoning, effectively decoding not only the words but the writer's thoughts. He has taken the initiative to reconstruct in his mind as much as he can of the logic of the images and concepts that the writer conveyed through the system of language. Stephen also explored the implications of his ideas and was clear about what he understood and failed to understand. He demonstrated intellectual perseverance in striving to make sense when struggling with difficult passages. He expected to make sense of the passage, to grasp the author's ideas, and finally he did. These habits, traits and abilities are among those we find in individuals for whom critical thinking is a comprehensive, substantial system of thought embedded, ideally, in every aspect of their lives.

Although Colleen and Stephen have each "read" the passage, a useful distinction can be drawn between "critical reading" and "uncritical reading."

Most reading is performed at the lower end of the spectrum in school today. Very little instruction is given in the thinking skills that critical readers use. Colleen will only be able to improve with professional assistance, that is, with instruction that helps her assess her thinking using intellectual standards and a sense of the elements of thought. She needs help in learning how to think through the elements of a problem. Of course, instruction alone is insufficient. She will also need to apply her will and acquire self-discipline. She will need extensive practice and expectations placed on her effort.

As we stretch ourselves to develop our bodies we naturally feel some physical stress. So, too, do we feel intellectual stress as we stretch our minds to develop our thinking. Students must learn intellectual perseverance, intellectual responsibility, intellectual integrity to develop true intellectual "fitness." This is a lifetime process that merely begins in school.

Most students are not well informed about the consequences of their uncritical thinking habits. It is likely that no one has presented these ideas to them so that they realistically grasp the possibility of intellectual development. Let's now look at two student written responses and examine the quality of the thinking displayed, keeping in mind the implications for the students' future effectiveness.

ARE WE HITTING THE TARGET?
ASSESSING STUDENT THINKING IN WRITING

The Assignment: The students in Ms. Tamari's 8th grade class were asked to write a paragraph in which they were to explain what the most important characteristics of a "friend" are and why they are most important. Here are the written responses of two students, Susan and Carl.

Susan

A friend is someone who cares a lot about you, who likes to be with you, and who helps you out when you get in trouble. The most important characteristics of a friend are loyalty, helpfulness, and honesty. First, it's important for a friend to be loyal because you want to depend on your friend. If someone is not loyal that person may turn against you, especially if she meets someone he or she likes better than you. Second, it's important for a friend to be helpful, because often a person needs help and if you have no friends it can be real hard to feel so alone. And finally, it's important for a friend to be honest because very few people will tell you something about yourself that you don't want to hear. An honest friend will try to help you improve, even though she knows it may hurt your feelings. It's okay to hear some things from a friend because you know that she isn't trying to hurt you.

Observations

Susan is basically doing a good job critically analyzing which characteristics are desirable in a friend. First of all, it is clear that she understands the issue. First she clarifies the concept of a friend. Then she asserts three characteristics of a good friend. Then she takes each one in order and gives good reasons in support of each of them. Her writing is clear, relevant to the issue, systematic, well-reasoned, and reflects deep thinking for her age.

Now let's look at the writing of Carl.

Carl

The most important thing is to have a lot of friends who like to do the things you like to do. Then you can go places and have fun. I mostly like other boys for my friends because they like sports like me. Girls sometimes play sports too but not as good as boys. I like to play baseball, football, and basketball. Sometimes I like to play Hockey. There are no good places to play in my neighborhood and sometimes my mother makes me come in too early. She sometimes makes me very mad because she screws up my life. All she ever wants me to do is work around the house. I don't think she knows anything about having friends. Maybe if she had played sports when she was little she'd let me play more and not just think about work, work, and more work.

Observations

Almost all of Carl's writing is irrelevant to the issue of what are the most desirable characteristics of a friend. He seems simply to be writing thoughts down as they occur to him in a stream of consciousness, in an associational way. Carl begins by confusing the question "What are the most important characteristics in a friend?" with "Is it important to know a lot of people who share pleasures with you?" He then moves to the question "Who do I like?" Then he moves to the question"What do I like to do?" and then on to "What's wrong with my neighborhood?" The final question, "Why doesn't my mother let me do what I want to do?" indicates that he has ended up far off course, yet it is unlikely that he realizes it. Until Carl learns to discipline his mind to stick to the question at hand, he will have trouble doing any quality thinking.

Learning to write out our thinking is one of the best ways to improve it. It goes without saying that excellence in writing requires excellence in thinking. Writing requires that one systematize one's thinking, arranging thought in a progression that makes the system of one's thought accessible to others. When the writer's thinking lacks a clear purpose, lacks focus, lacks documentation and logic, and standards by which to judge the merit of the ideas, these flaws are revealed in the written work.

Writing, then, which is excellent is excellently thought through, is produced by someone with definite standards for both thinking and writing. (See the chapters: "Why Students and Teachers Don't Reason Well" and "Pseudo Critical Thinking in the Educational Establishment.") It is obvious as we read the responses of Carl and Susan that each has a very different understanding of what is well-thought-out thinking and writing, critical and uncritical thinking and writing. The consequences for Carl's uncritical thinking are minimal in 8th grade, but how will he be affected when he demonstrates the same confusions on the job?

School instruction is focused on "subject matter." We usually, but wrongfully, think of school subjects as little more than masses of facts and definitions to be memorized. We don't often recognize that what is really important about school subjects is that they—when properly learned—provide us raw materials upon which to practice thinking in a more proficient and insightful manner. They introduce us to new "systems" in which to think. As you read the next section, see if you can think of school subjects in this more illuminating and penetrating way.

ARE WE HITTING THE TARGET?
ASSESSING STUDENT THINKING IN ACADEMIC SUBJECTS.

Subject Matter, Especially in High School and College Courses
Though we often do not think of it this way, all subject matter — history, literature, geography, biology, chemistry, physics, mathematics — is part of a system of logically ordered parts. A historian studies a period and creates a "story" that puts events into meaningful patterns. In literature we study periods with their distinctive visions, their distinctive values, their distinctive modes of expression. One period is "romantic," one is "classic," one is "realist," and so forth. Or we study the outlook of an author, the way he or she sees the world: Dickens, Austen, Hemingway, Faulkner. In geography we develop systems for dividing up the surface of the earth: into continents, countries, climates. We develop organized, logical ways to look at the surface, especially the physical surface, of the earth. In geology, we use a system to arrange time into geological time periods, and correlate principal physical and biological features with those periods. In biology, we develop systems for making sense of multiple forms of living and pre-living things. In math, we develop systems—arithmetic, geometry, algebra, calculus—for dealing with the quantitative dimensions of the world.

Everywhere there are systems inherent in subject matter, networks of logically ordered parts functioning in relation to each other for a definite human purpose. Critical thinking, with its *system-unlocking orientation*, is the perfect set of tools to take command of the systems inherent in subject matter. It is perfect, that is, only if we understand what it is and how to use it. Most students, unfortunately, have never been introduced to critical thinking, so cannot systematically use it to guide and empower their learning. Most students try to learn what is in fact systematized, by randomly memorizing fragments of the system as if they had no relation to each other. Compare the two following students talking about studying history.

Anna: "I don't really like history too much. There is too much to try to remember. And it's all about olden times, with a lot of dates and different wars and people doing things we don't do anymore. You learn about presidents and kings and what they did and about when things happened. History is all about the past. It's boring and I never use it. How could you? Things are really different now. "

Carra: "We do it differently in Mrs Brown's class. Do you know that we're all part of history? For example, in my mind I remember all of my past as a kind of story I tell myself. That's how I remember things and that's also how I figure things out. Think about it. Whenever you talk about yourself, you're like a historian trying to help people figure things out about you. Everyone is really interested in their own history and in the history of the people they know. That's what gossip is all about. Also the news. It's like the history of yesterday. In her class we talk about how the history writer puts together the story he writes. We also look at how the story might be told differently, I mean 'cause what we read is only a tiny part of what the writer knows, and what the writer knows is only a tiny part of what actually happened. You have to look at it from different points of view or else you don't have a chance of figuring out what most likely really happened. We are learning how to tell the difference between "facts" and how different people filter and interpret the facts depending on their own interests. We also try to notice what is left out of the history stories we read. Mrs Brown says we are learning to think like history writers do and face the problems that they face. I think its fun to try to figure out history . . . how to tell a story in the most honest way, and how to see when people twist a story to make themselves look good."

Observations

Anna and Carra, in their reactions to history, model the distinction between the way subjects have traditionally been taught (as a lot of stuff to remember for a test) and the way they should be taught (as a way to figure things out). The traditional student never gets the real point of the subject and hence does not transfer what she learns to the "real" world. By teaching history in a critical manner students can readily transfer what they learn to "life-centered" situations. They can improve their own everyday historical thinking.

Critical thinking is valuable, of course, not only in school but in the world beyond school as well. If we are teaching properly, our students not only learn how to apply critical thinking effectively to their reading, writing, and subject-matter learning, they also begin to apply it to their everyday lives. The wonderful result is they not only reason historically about what is in their history textbook, for example, they also begin to reason much better about the "historical" issues in their daily life, as Carra is doing above. They not only reason scientifically about what is in their science textbook, they also begin to reason scientifically about the 'scientific" questions in their daily life. They not only hear about ethical principles when talking about characters in stories in their literature class, they also begin to use ethical reasoning when dealing with the ethical issues embedded in their lives.

Indeed, if we do our job correctly, students begin to discover that all the kinds of reasoning that they learn to do at school have application in the "real" world. They not only start to talk about and value reasoning in school, they also begin to discover how actually to do it, how to realistically and effectively to apply intellectual standards to their own thought in virtually every context of their lives. The result is that students, for the first time in their lives, begin to evaluate their own thinking and do so in a way which is increasingly disciplined and objective. Let's look at three examples of college students beginning to discover the value of applying intellectual standards to their own work and thinking.

Mandy: "I am often inconsistent. The most difficult aspect of my weakness is my attempt at achieving consistency between that of word and deed. That is, I use a double standard. I often say one thing and do another."

Kristin: "This semester I have learned how to organize my thinking through critical thinking. In organizing my thinking logically I have learned to break down my thought processes down into specific parts. By breaking my thought process down into specific parts I can see some of my strengths and weaknesses. When I do not organize my thought logically, my writing often becomes trivial, irrelevant and vague."

Laurie: "It is important to recognize key concepts when one thinks. If I need to figure out a problem and do not understand the key concepts, I will not be able to come to a logical conclusion. I am more and more aware of the need to pay attention to key concepts. One particular example occurred this winter when I went snowboarding for the first time. The relevant concepts of snowboarding are: one needs to torque the body, the back leg is your anchor, and the edges of the board are used to slow down and in turn control the speed of the board. My friend explained to me that it usually takes a whole day to learn to snowboard, but because I paid close attention to the concepts and kept them carefully in mind, I was able to learn quickly. Most students do not realize that concepts are important in learning. In fact, I think that most students don't know what concepts are. I certainly didn't."

These examples demonstrate that some students are prepared to take advantage of critical thinking instruction, though others are less ready. The teacher's challenge, however, is to meet the students needs and respond effectively with appropriate instruction.

✦ Identifying the Target: Critical Thinking in the Workplace

With accelerating change and the increasing complexity of problems facing us at the dawn of the 21st Century, we are striving to compete within the new global economic realities. John Sculley, CEO of Apple Computer, Inc. reported to President-elect Clinton in December of 1992:

Most Americans see our largest corporations going through massive restructurings, layoffs, and downsizing. People know something has changed and they are scared because they don't fully understand it and they see people they know losing their jobs.

They also see their neighbors buying high-quality, lower-priced products from abroad, and they ask why can't we build these same products or better ones here at home?

The answer is, we can. But only if we have a public education system which will turn out a world-class product. We need an education system which will educate all our students, not just the top 15–20 percent.

A highly-skilled work force must begin with a world class public education system. Eventually, the New Economy will touch every industry in our nation. There will be no place to hide!

In the New Economy, low-skilled manual work will be paid less. The United States cannot afford to have the high-skilled work being done somewhere else in the world and end up with the low-wage work.

This is not an issue about protectionism. It is an issue about an educational system aligned with the New Economy and a broad educational opportunity for everyone. maximum flexibility.

In the old economy, America had a real advantage because we were rich with natural resources and our large domestic market formed the basis for economies of scale.

In the New Economy, strategic resources no longer just come out of the ground (such as oil, coal, iron, and wheat). The strategic resources are ideas and information that come out of our minds.

The result is, as a nation, we have gone from being resource-rich in the old economy to resource-poor in the New Economy almost overnight! Our public education system has not successfully made the shift from teaching the memorization of facts to achieving the learning of critical thinking skills. We are still trapped in a K–12 public education system which is preparing our youth for jobs that no longer exist.

Critical thinking is valuable not only in school but in the world beyond school as well. Increasingly, our ever-changing economy demands abilities and traits characteristic of comprehensive critical thinking. They enable us not only to survive but to thrive. They are essential to the new management structures to which successful businesses will routinely and increasingly turn. Consider the news item opposite, from a small town in Wisconsin. It illustrates well a trend which is going to grow enormously, and that is toward high productivity work-place organizations that "depend on workers who can do more than read, write, and do simple arithmetic, and who bring more to their jobs than reliability and a good attitude. In such organizations, workers are asked to use judgment and make decisions rather than to merely follow directions. Management layers disappear as workers take over many of the tasks that others used to do...." [Laura D'Andrea Tyson, Chairwoman of the President's Council of Economic Advisors]. Ladysmith, Wisconsin gives us an opportunity to see this trend displayed.

Mill Interviews 83 for Jobs

Between June 10 and 17, City Forest Corporation completed assessments of 83 candidates for jobs at the soon-to-be-opened paper mill in Ladysmith. The mill, formerly operated by Pope & Talbot, has been idle since last Aug 14.

Candidates for positions at the mill went through a half day "assessment center" to determine their potential for the new work concept to be implemented at the mill. The assessment center included several group problem-solving sessions as well as an oral presentation, written presentation and traditional interview.

When the mill reopens, it will operate under a "self-directed team" method. With that approach there are no first line supervisors. Instead, workers are organized into teams which are responsible for much of the decision making and problem solving previously handled by the supervisor.

Each of the four production shifts will have a team leader. The production teams will be supported by a maintenance team...and a staff team made up of management and other staff support. The beauty of this new system is that it place more of the control of the day-to-day operation in the hands of the individuals who are doing the hands-on work.

—*Ladysmith News*, Ladysmith, Wisconsin Thursday, June 24, 1993.

How important, then, is our role as teachers? Can we rely on parents to understand and to provide these essential abilities and traits for their children? Will the children master them on the streets or with their friends? It seems unlikely. How important, then, is it that we, ourselves, devote our professional energies to examining and assessing our own thinking? Can we do a proficient job of helping our students if we are not equally committed to improving our own abilities, traits and habits as well?

Our professional responsibility extends to recognizing that we may very well find that we need to assert our will, our initiative, our discipline and curiosity to secure the best materials and resources available to meet this obligation. How much care, then, should we use in selecting materials that will take us where we want to go, to a deep and comprehensive understanding and working knowledge of legitimate critical thinking?

✦ Off the Target
Pseudo-Critical Thinking Approaches and Materials

Critical thinking cannot be seen, touched, tasted or heard directly, and thus it is readily subject to counterfeit, readily confused with thinking that sounds like, but is not critical thinking, with thinking that will not lead students to success in school and beyond. Critical thinking is readily falsified in the commercial world by those who seek to capitalize on its growing legitimacy. We increasingly need a regular *Consumer Report* that enables the reader to effectively recognize the counterfeits of good thinking which are multiplying daily, to help us recognize the latest gimmick *du jour*. The characteristics of comprehensive critical thinking outlined in this chapter make available just a beginning set of criteria by which professionals and parents can evaluate educational resources in this field.

Educators, business and governmental leaders must begin to distinguish the genuine from the counterfeit, the legitimate from the specious, the incomplete from the comprehensive. Smooth, slick, and shallow thinking are everywhere around us, filled with promises of simple, quick, instant solutions, or misdirecting us into schemes that misspend our own or public monies. Other chapters of this book will provide many examples, principally from the field of education. The reader will doubtless be able to add other examples from his or her own experience.

That we need sound critical thinking to protect ourselves and the public good is intuitively obvious, once we are clear about what critical thinking is and what it can do. Identifying the target precisely, however, is the first step in facing the challenges ahead.

Chapter 3

The Critical Thinking Movement in Historical Perspective

Abstract

In this paper, originally published in National Forum *(1985) and revised for this edition, Richard Paul discusses the history of critical thinking and intellectual discipline in education. He argues that, from the earliest days, education in the U.S. has emphasized passive learning, lower-order training, and indoctrination. He begins with a cameo of the critical thinking movement today, briefly reflects back to Socrates, then explores the history of intellectualism and anti-intellectualism in U.S. schooling and the teaching profession. He concludes with a discussion of the series of reform efforts and their predictable failure.*

✦ Critical Thinking Emerges as a Movement

*T*he critical thinking movement is beginning to have a palpable effect on the day-to-day life of some American schooling, though it is becoming increasingly obvious that it will be many years before we routinely graduate students who can think critically about the problems they face and the tasks they must do. The transition from theory to practice is as vexing as one might have realistically expected. At present, though the public awareness of the importance of critical thinking grows with every increase in public awareness of the accelerating pace of change and complexity, there is still no one area of the country that has emerged as leading the way. It appeared in the mid-1980's that California would be the needed bellwether. In 1981, the massive 19-campus California State University system instituted a graduation requirement in critical thinking intended to achieve:

> ... an understanding of the relationship of language to logic, leading to the ability to analyze, criticize, and advocate ideas, to reason inductively and deductively, and to reach factual or judgmental conclusions based on sound inferences drawn from unambiguous statements of knowledge or belief.

Within two years, the even larger community college system established a parallel requirement. The California Department of Education launched into what was billed as an assessment program heavily emphasizing critical thinking skills. Guiding policy statements from the Department — from the *California State Frameworks*, to *It's Elementary, Caught in the Middle,* and *Second to None* — all claim that critical thinking is at the core of mandatory reforms. However, things are not as quickly achieved as conceived. In California, for example, the serious efforts that many expected to help prepare teachers to teach for critical thinking have not been made. This raises at least three issues: Do California's educational leaders, and those in other states, mean what they say? Do those people charged with the duty to redesign classroom instruction understand what critical thinking requires? And finally, is the educational establishment so insulated that meaningful change requires, at best, a twenty-year plan?

While public education continues to thrash about, still seeking to establish the educational miracle of foundational change through various combinations of painless quick-fixes, the critical thinking movement continues to grow. In every academic discipline and at every level of education there is increased interest in infusing critical thinking into instruction. There is a growing consensus in the assessment community that critical thinking, problem-solving, and higher order communication must be given a new primacy in educational evaluation. In the 1992 Goals Report of the National Education Goals Panel, reasoning and critical thinking are given special prominence in two key objectives:

> • The percentage of students who demonstrate the ability to reason, solve problems, apply knowledge, and write and communicate effectively will increase substantially.

> • The proportion of college graduates who demonstrate an advanced ability to think critically, communicate effectively, and solve problems will increase substantially.

Special prominence has also been given to the importance of critical thinking in a long series of reports on medical education, nursing, and allied health. More and more articles and books are being written about critical thinking, many of them focused on particular subject domains. The number of conferences and workshops on critical thinking continues to grow. The number of centers for critical thinking has also increased dramatically. A National Council for Excellence in Critical Thinking has emerged. More and more prominent leaders are calling attention to the importance of critical thinking for the economic future of the nation. All this is progress that will continue to increase the pressure for fundamental change. This powerful emergence of critical thinking did not occur overnight.

Until the mid-1980's, the movement was no more than a small, scattered group of educators calling for a shift from a didactic paradigm of knowledge and learning to a Socratic, critically reflective one. The early stirrings of the modern critical thinking movement can be traced back to Edward Glaser's *An Experiment in the Development of Critical Thinking* (1941) and his development with Watson of the Watson-Glaser Critical Thinking Appraisal (1940). But let's briefly survey the history of the core ideas and the thinkers who generated them.

The deepest intellectual roots are ancient, traceable to the teaching practice and vision of Socrates 2,400 ago who discovered by a method of probing questioning that people could not rationally justify their confident claims to knowledge. Confused meanings, inadequate evidence, or self-contradictory beliefs often lurked beneath smooth but largely empty rhetoric. Since his time, Socrates' insight has been variously articulated by a scattering of intellectuals, certainly by the 18th, and increasingly in the 19th and 20th centuries: Voltaire, John Henry Newman, John Stuart Mill, and William Graham Sumner are a few that come readily to mind. Consider Mill:

> ... since the general or prevailing opinion on any object is rarely or never the whole truth, it is only by the collision of adverse opinions that the remainder of the truth has any chance of being supplied. (*On Liberty,* 1859)

Or Newman:

> ... knowledge is not a mere extrinsic or accidental advantage, ... which may be got up from a book, and easily forgotten again, ... which we can borrow for the occasion, and carry about in our hand ... [it is] something intellectual ... which reasons upon what it sees ... the action of a formative power ... making the objects of our knowledge subjectively our own. (*Idea of A University,* 1852)

Or Sumner:

> The critical habit of thought, if usual in a society, will pervade all its mores, because it is a way of taking up the problems of life. People educated in it cannot be stampeded by stump orators and are never deceived by dithyrambic oratory. They are slow to believe. They can hold things as possible or probable in all degrees, without certainty and without pain. They can wait for evidence and weigh evidence, uninfluenced by the emphasis and confidence with which assertions are made on one side or the other. They can resist appeals to their dearest prejudices and all kinds of cajolery. Education in the critical faculty is the only education of which it can be truly said that it makes good citizens. (*Folkways,* 1906)

This view of knowledge and learning holds that beliefs, without reason and the judgment of the learner behind them, are for that learner mere prejudices; that critical reflection on the part of each learner is an essential precondition of knowledge and of rational action. Until now this view has made little headway against a deeply if unconsciously held contrary mind-set. The everyday world — especially in the U.S. where the agenda has been filled with one pragmatic imperative after another, a nation with a "mission" to perform and a "destiny" to fulfill — provides little time for self-formed, self-reasoned beliefs called for by Socrates and his successors.

✦ Historical Roots of Anti-Intellectualism In United States' Schools

Let us not forget that schools in the U.S. were established precisely to transmit by inculcation self-evident, true beliefs conducive to right conduct and successful "industry". The best seller of 17ᵗʰ Century North America was Michael Wigglesworth's *Day of Doom*, a detailed description of the terrifying fate of condemned sinners. To question this fate was heresy. In 1671, governor Sir William Berkeley of Virginia could say with pride:

> ... there are no free schools, nor printing in Virginia, for learning has brought disobedience, and heresy ... into the world, and printing has divulged them.... God keep us from both!

"Free schools" were set up, as in Massachusetts (1647), "to teach all children to read and write ... [to combat] that old deluder Satan," or, to ensure that "children and servants" are "catechized" (1675). In Plymouth Colony (1671) "Education of Children" was mandated because "Children and Servants [were]... in danger [of] growing Barbarous, Rude, or Stubborn" and hence were becoming "pests". This was hardly the climate in which analytic thinking and critical questioning could thrive. All questioning began and ended with a *"Nil desperandum, Christo duce."* (Don't despair, Christ leads us.) This sense of having a mission or mandate from God has discouraged self-reflective questioning. At times it has generated arrogant self-delusion.

As late as 1840, U.S. schools taught ordinary students nothing but the three R's, some basic catechism, and a smattering of patriotic history. The school term was short and attendance irregular. In 1800, for example, average Americans attended school only 82 days out of their entire lives. By 1840 it had increased to only 208 days.

When the time in school increased, it was not because of a demand for critical thinking, but for better reading and writing, skills increasingly necessary in the commercial and industrial activities of the day. To get a sense of the quality of reading instruction, one need only hear the assessment of Horace Mann:

> I have devoted especial pains to learn, with some degree of numerical accuracy, how far the reading, in our schools, is an exercise of the mind in thinking and feeling and how far it is a barren action of the organs of speech upon the atmosphere. My informa-

tion is derived principally from the written statements of the school committees of the respective towns — gentlemen who are certainly exempt from all temptation to disparage the schools they superintend. The result is that more than $^{11}/_{12}$ths of all the children in the reading classes do not understand the meanings of the words they read; and that the ideas and feelings intended by the author to be conveyed to, and excited in, the reader's mind, still rest in the author's intention, never having yet reached the place of their destination. *(Second Report to the Massachusetts Board of Education,* 1838)

There was an expansion in schooling, triggered not by a change in the basic U.S. mind-set, but by the increasing use of machinery, the rapid expansion of transportation, and the new waves of non-Anglo-Saxon immigrants. For a long time the *McGuffy Readers*, with their parables about the terrible fate of those who gave in to sloth, drunkenness, or wastefulness were as close as the average student got to reflective thinking. Americans were learning to be "doers," not "thinkers". The basic truths necessary for successful living seemed eminently available, for all who cared to sit up and take notice:

Remember, that time is money, ... that credit is money, ... that money is of the prolific, generating nature, that six pounds a year is but a groat a day ... that the good paymaster is lord of another man's purse. (Ben Franklin, 1770)

In 1860 the average American spent little more than a year in school, and by 1900 spent little more than two years. In 1880, 17% of the population still could not read or write. With their homespun views and simplistic picture of the world in hand, the American public was confident it could judge quite well, not only the matters immediately before it, but also what was best for the well being of other peoples far away. Increasingly in this time, the question of empire was before the public, and the electorate was expected to decide, for example, whether or not it was justifiable to "rule a people without their consent." Those, like Senator Beveridge, who favored imperialism, as did the majority of voters, easily formulated a logic whose fallaciousness was not penetrated by the voting majority:

The opposition tells us that we ought not to govern a people without their consent. I answer: The rule of liberty, that all just government derives its authority from the consent of the governed, applies only to those who are capable of self-government. I answer: We govern the Indians without their consent, we govern our territories without their consent, we govern our children without their consent.... Shall we save them ... to give them a self-rule of tragedy? It would be like giving a razor to a babe and telling it to shave itself. It would be like giving a typewriter to an Eskimo and telling him to publish one of the great dailies of the world. (U.S. Senator Albert Beveridge, 1899)

Senator Beveridge could link, without fear of significant dissent from an electorate of thinking people, the voice of liberty, our guns, Christ's gospel, and our profit:

> Ah! as our commerce spreads, the flag of liberty will circle the globe, and the highways of the ocean — carrying trade to all mankind — will be guarded by the guns of the republic. And, as their thunders salute the flag, benighted peoples will know that the voice of liberty is speaking, at last, for them; that civilization is dawning, at last, for them — liberty and civilization, those children of Christ's gospel, who follow and never precede the preparing march of commerce. It is the tide of God's great purposes made manifest in the instincts of our race, whose present phase is our personal profit, but whose far-off end is the redemption of the world and the Christianization of mankind.

It should be no surprise therefore that William Graham Sumner, one of the founding fathers of anthropology, was appalled by the manner in which history was taught and the level of uncritical thinking that followed it:

> The examination papers show the pet ideas of the examiners.... An orthodoxy is produced in regard to all the great doctrines of life. It consists in the most worn and commonplace opinions.... It is intensely provincial and philistine ... [containing] broad fallacies, half-truths, and glib generalizations. [We are given] ... orthodox history ... [so] ... that children shall be taught just that one thing which is "right" in the view and interest of those in control and nothing else.... "Patriotic" history ... never can train children to criticism. (*Folkways*, 1906)

Higher education was little better. It began in the 17th and 18th centuries in primarily upper class "seminaries," providing a classical education though not, of course, in the Socratic sense. Students were drilled in Latin and Greek and theology. Inculcation, memorization, repetition, and forensic display were the order of the day. Not until the latter half of the 19th Century was higher education possible for someone not in the upper class, and then only at the new Land Grant Colleges (150 new colleges opened between 1880 and 1900). These colleges were established to promote "education of the industrial classes in the several pursuits and professions in life." Their emphasis was "agriculture and the mechanic arts." Students graduated with an agricultural, commercial, technical, industrial, scientific, professional, or theological focus. Higher education turned out graduates fit to enter farms, businesses, professions, or the clergy. Their "civic" education was not fundamentally liberal but nationalistic, not fundamentally emancipatory but provincial.

THE TEACHING PROFESSION FALLS IN LINE

The history of teaching fits into this picture like a perfectly carved puzzle piece. In the early days, teachers were selected from those who had no other job and could read, write, and cipher. From the start, teaching was a low prestige, low paying job. Normal schools did not begin springing up until after 1830, and then their curriculum mainly consisted of a review of the subjects taught in elementary school, such as reading, writing, arithmetic, and spelling. Eventually, and in the spirit of industrialism, science, and technology, education — still conceived fully within the traditional U.S. world view — came to be considered, and is still largely considered, a "science" of methods of "delivery."

At no point along the way, even to this day, have prospective teachers been expected to demonstrate their ability to lead a discussion Socratically, so that students explore the evidence that can be advanced for or against their beliefs, note the assumptions upon which their beliefs are based, their implications for, or consistency with, other espoused beliefs. Nor have they been expected to demonstrate ability to think analytically or critically about the issues of the day. The state of affairs (*circa.* 1920–35) is satirically suggested by journalist and social critic H. L. Mencken:

> The art of pedagogics becomes a sort of puerile magic, a thing of preposterous secrets, a grotesque compound of false premises and illogical conclusions. Every year sees a craze for some new solution of the teaching enigma, an endless series of flamboyant arcana.... Mathematical formulae are marked out for every emergency; there is no sure-cure so idiotic that some superintendent of schools will not swallow it. The aim seems to be to reduce the whole teaching process to a sort of automatic reaction, to discover some master formula that will not only take the place of competence and resourcefulness in the teacher but that will also create an artificial receptivity in the child. Teaching becomes a thing in itself, separable from and superior to the thing taught. Its mastery is a special business, a sort of transcendental high jumping. A teacher well grounded in it can teach anything to any child, just as a sound dentist can pull any tooth out of any jaw. *(Baltimore Sun,* 1923)

✦ 1930's to Today: An Endless Series of Pseudo-Reforms

From 1930 to now, education has undergone a series, indeed an endless series, of reform movements, all of which have come aground for one fundamental reason: none provided a means for transforming the thinking of teachers. Critical thinking was not brought into the classroom in a large-scale way. Teachers still taught as they had been taught, that is, *didactically.* Educators still tacitly maintained the view that knowledge was something one memorizes. Students still got the grades they wanted by simply feeding back to teachers what had been fed to them. No intellectual standards were introduced into the classroom. Indeed, to this day, most teachers and educators still have no real conception of the nature of intellectual standards and what it is to hold students to them. Most grading of student performances is still largely a mixture of reward for lower order recall and verbal agreement with the views of the teacher.

In place of substantial reform, professional educators learned to become masters of lip service, adroit at the art of taking on the language of reform without its substance. This 63-year process of pseudo-reform following pseudo-reform began with the bastardization of the views of John Dewey, the movement of so-called "progressive" education. A deep and well-thought-out conception of education was transformed into a series of slogans and catch-phrases. Progressive classrooms became caricatures of what Dewey advocated.

Today, the educational marketplace is deluged with reformist ideas, each being swiftly transformed, one after another, into caricatures of their more insightful originators. And so it will continue unless we recognize that the quality of any reform can be no better than the quality of the thinking of those who put that reform into action. So it will continue unless we recognize that there is no mindless or robotic way to reform education, that every reform, to be substantial, must be implemented by those whose thinking is substantial, that *critical thinking* must be an intrinsic part of every dimension of every reform.

What good is "outcome-based" education, for example, if the "outcomes" are not well-thought-out, if they are no more than jargon or platitude, or lower-order learning masked under higher order terms? What good is education for "self-esteem" if it is based on the false assumption that we can "give" students self-esteem by continually giving them positive feedback — while we ignore the skills and abilities the possession of which gives them a real sense of empowerment? What good is an emphasis on "cooperative learning" that ignores the intellectual standards whose possession prevents the process from descending into "cooperative mis-learning?" What good is an emphasis on "writing across the curriculum" when students are not learning how to intellectually assess their writing, resulting in smooth, articulate fluff being routinely mistaken for deep, substantial thought? What good is an emphasis on "diversity", when teachers are unable to critically assess which forms of "diversity" and "unity" are appropriate and which forms are not? What good is "restructuring" when those engaged in it do not know how to critically assess alternative suggestions or how to distinguish vague platitude from substantial principle or how to assess whether students are learning at a lower or higher order? What good is "total quality management" when the quality of thinking that goes into the "management" of "quality" is intellectually undisciplined?

The system in place in education has displayed a remarkable ability to take on the appearance of any number of reforms without changing in any substantial way. We have not yet learned the fundamental lesson: No substantial change can occur in education without a substantial change in the thinking of educators.

To formulate substantial "outcomes" in such a way that we can truly assess whether they are being achieved requires critical thinking in the design and application of the teaching and assessment process. To achieve genuine self-esteem, students need to develop the skills and abilities which give them a sense of real empowerment. To engage in successful cooperative learning, students need to bring to the process the intellectual standards by which they can assess and improve the quality of their learning. To effectively emphasize "writing across the curriculum", students need intellectual standards to assess their writing and that of their peers. An appropriate emphasis on "diversity" requires students to critically assess which forms of "diversity" and "unity" are justified and which are not. Productive "restructuring" requires that those engaged in it know how to critically assess proposals effectively. "Total Quality Management" that deserves the name must be based on *thinking of quality*, thinking that is tested again and again by appropriate intellectual standards.

Consider this sobering thought: When, between 1917 and 1934, inductees into the armed forces were systematically tested using the *Army Alpha Test* (an I.Q. test based on the Stanford Benet) it was estimated that the average U.S. citizen was probably somewhere around 13 or 14 years old intellectually — about the intellectual level to which, I understand, most present day T.V. programming today is geared. Can we conclude then that most Americans are intellectually incapable of rising above childish reasoning, or should we rather hypothesize that as a nation both socially and scholastically we have not yet challenged most people to think for themselves beyond the most primitive levels? Are we, and if so will we remain, what William J. Lederer characterized us as in his best selling book of the 1960's, *A Nation of Sheep?*

If Boyer, Sizer, Adler, Bloom and others are right, if the Rockefeller Commission on the Humanities, the International Educational Achievement Studies, the College Board, the Education Commission of the States, the National Assessment of Educational Progress, and the Association of American Medical Colleges are right, then our overemphasis on "rote memorization and recall of facts" does not serve us well. We must exchange our traditional picture of knowledge and learning for one that generates and rewards "active, independent, self-directed learning" so that students can "gather and assess data rigorously and critically." We need to abandon "methods that make students passive recipients of information" and adopt those that transform them into "active participants in their own intellectual growth."

It is time to bite the bullet. It is time to focus on the prime condition for all reform: quality thinking. Educators who have not learned to think critically cannot transform education for the better; as a nation, we can no longer afford to subsidize their efforts, however well-intentioned. Finally, we need to resolutely, we need to adamantly press for a long-term, thorough emphasis on critical thinking for both teachers and administrators.

To achieve this we need a new kind of educational leadership, not one which mirrors the status quo, not one which mouths platitudes and high-sounding words. Rather we need leaders with the intellectual courage to admit forthrightly that education is filled with shallow thinking and the shallow practices that inevitably follow from it. We need leaders willing to look seriously at the prospect of long-term evolution that puts quality of thinking first, at every level of reform.

Such leadership can only come from that minority of administrators, teachers, and parents who are willing to put the well-being of students above the propaganda, the defensiveness, the self-flattery of the status quo. That leadership is only now beginning to emerge. The reality of everyday schooling is still to be transformed. Those committed to fundamental change must be patient, persistent, firm, steadfast, insistent, and tenacious. They must continually use their own capacity for critical thinking to out-think those who would defend the status quo, who invent specious reasons why basic change is impossible, or who present superficial change as though it were basic. It will be many years before the back of the present paradigm is truly broken, and the paradigm of critical thinking for all students everywhere finally replaces it in the trenches of everyday schooling.

Chapter 4

Pseudo Critical Thinking
in the Educational Establishment

Abstract

Unfortunately, there is not simply good and bad thinking in the world, both easily recognized as such. There is also bad thinking that appears to be good and therefore wrongfully, sometimes disastrously, is used as the basis of very important decisions. Very often this "bad thinking" is defended and "rationalized" in a highly sophisticated fashion. However flawed, it successfully counterfeits good thinking and otherwise intelligent people are taken in. Such thinking is found in every dimension of human life and in every dimension it does harm; in every dimension it works against human well-being. Very often it is generated in a structural way, as a likely or probable by-product of how we have arranged and ordered things. This is illustrated in the American educational establishment. The manner in which it is structured and operates makes likely the continuous generation of more bad, albeit highly sophisticated, thinking: pseudo-critical thinking, in short. However, because the educational bureaucracy is a powerful shaping force in education, bad thinking at the bureaucratic level leads directly to bad teaching at the classroom level. In this chapter, Paul illustrates this destructive pattern using the California Department of Education (as his model of educational bureaucracy at work) and the new California State Reading and Writing Assessment instrument (as the resultant bad practice). He argues that this poorly designed assessment tool leads directly to bad teaching practices and the exacerbation of a profound problem in instruction: the failure to teach students to reason well in every subject they study. If the educational bureaucracy doesn't understand what reasoning is and how to assess it in reading and writing, argues Paul, is it likely that higher order reading and writing will be taught? No, he claims. And thus the educational bureaucracy creates a deep and serious problem in education.

A Guide to the Reader

✦ Introduction

Sometimes when people think poorly, they do so out of simple ignorance. They are making mistakes, they don't know they are making mistakes, but they would willingly correct their mistakes if they were pointed out to them. Often mistakes in thinking are quite humble. No one is apt to take them for models of how to think.

Such thinking may be quite uncritical, but is not pseudo critical thinking. Pseudo critical thinking is a form of intellectual arrogance masked in self-delusion or deception, in which thinking which is deeply flawed is not only presented as a model of excellence of thought, but is also, at the same time, sophisticated enough to take many people in. No one takes a rock to be a counterfeit diamond. It is simply other than diamond. But a zircon mimics a diamond and is easily taken for one and hence can be said to be a pseudo diamond.

There is much "sophisticated" but deeply flawed thinking which is presented as a model for thought. This is nothing new in the history of thought and knowledge. Medieval philosophy and theology, for example, was used as a sophisticated tool to resist, quite unknowingly of course, the advance of science. When deeply flawed thinking is embedded in teaching, then the development of thought and knowledge in the student is retarded or arrested. Teachers at every level of education, for example, tell students how to think. They point out thinking which they in effect encourage students to emulate. When what they point out as a model is deeply flawed, and yet sophisticated enough to take many in, it is a form of destructive pseudo critical thinking.

> *When deeply flawed thinking is embedded in teaching, then the development of thought and knowledge in the student is retarded or arrested.*

Pseudo critical thinking is everywhere in the world, for everywhere there are people who take themselves to be models of good thinking and who are engaged in influencing others by their model. Sometimes they foster an approach to thinking quite explicitly — by, for example, designing a program that purports to foster critical thinking. But more often they simply implicitly propagandize for a form of flawed thinking, not aware of the thinking that they are modeling. In any case, it is a rare person, one who really does think critically, who recognizes fundamental flaws in his or her own thinking. Most people are victims of their bad thinking. They do not know how to analyze and assess thinking. Consequently, most believe that their thinking is instinctively and naturally of good quality. Most believe, in other words, that his or her own thinking is that of a fairminded person who judges persons and events in an impartial and accurate way. Often people, then, inadvertently buy into one or more kinds of pseudo critical thinking: in business, in politics, and, of course, in personal, emotional, and family life. The pseudo critical thinking that I propose to concentrate on in this chapter is pseudo critical thinking in the educational establishment.

I will use as my major illustration, the California State Department of Education's new assessment tool for reading and writing. Its development and nature provide an illuminating example of how deeply-flawed thinking is generated and worked into the system, from the statewide to the classroom level. Of course, we must remember that there is local and statewide bureaucracy and that they exist in symbiosis, each feeding the other. And teachers themselves have learned to think the way they do in bureaucratic settings, so very often they are in effect asking for, from the system, what the system by its nature is ready to give them. It is therefore somewhat misleading to say that the flawed thinking at the statewide bureaucratic level is *the* cause — it is rather *a* cause — of flawed thinking in the classroom.

Before we proceed to our "exemplar," I would like to set the stage for what we shall do by providing the reader in advance with one — hopefully intuitive — example of why it might be that flawed thinking is regularly generated in the educational establishment. It is important that the reader comes to see why the blunders and mistakes of the California reading and writing assessment, which I shall presently document, are not exceptions in a generally good record, but rather representative examples of a typically bad product in a system that, like many others, typically generates bad products.

Consider one way in which the educational environment invites flawed thinking. It is an environment in which many whose education may in fact have been quite narrow and flawed, (see "Research Findings," p. 19) take themselves to be experts in one form of knowledge or another,

> . . . *most people recognize that there is something incoherent about saying that one is well educated but thinks poorly.*

and of course, not only in a form of knowledge *per se* but in the kind of thinking that has created or discovered the knowledge. These experts — called teachers and administrators — are presumed to be qualified to tell the young not only what to think but how to think about mathematical, scientific, social, and literary questions, for example. It would be odd for someone to say, "I'm a qualified teacher but my thinking is deeply flawed." That is to say, most people recognize that there is something incoherent about saying that one is well educated but thinks poorly. Imagine someone saying, "Jack is very well educated, but with just one minor exception; his thinking is unclear, imprecise, inaccurate, irrelevant, narrow, insignificant, and shallow. Other than that, he is well educated." Clearly this would be absurd. Hence to believe oneself an educator is pretty much tantamount to believing oneself a critical thinker, at least in *some* academic domain. Chemistry teachers take themselves to be experts in sound chemical thinking. Math teachers take themselves to be experts in sound mathematical thinking, and so on.

Yet many educators have been miseducated. Many are poor reasoners. Many confuse issues and questions, are easily diverted from the relevant to the irrelevant. Many lack a comprehensive educational philosophy. Many do virtually no serious reading. Many cannot speak knowledgeably

---

... many educators have been miseducated. Many are poor reasoners. Many confuse issues and questions, are easily diverted from the relevant to the irrelevant.

---

outside a narrow field. And many are not even up-to-date in their own field. Furthermore, the educational environment dominant in the schools is not traditionally conducive to critical thinking or to the development of further learning on the part of teachers and administrators. Much of the inservice is episodic, intellectually unchallenging, and fragmented. At most schools there is very little discussion on or about serious educational issues, and when there is such discussion it is often simplistic. And that is not all. The kind of instruction that is prevalent at all levels is didactic instruction. The kind of testing that is prevalent is multiple-choice focused on recall. Most students pass their courses by relying on rote memorization. Most teachers, even college professors, passed most of their courses in the same way. (see "Research Findings," p. 19) It is the thesis of this chapter that the models for thinking and the assessment of thinking presented in the schools are generally deeply flawed, and that the reason why this is so is systemic. I will also make recommendations at the end of this chapter as to the kind of action that is called for.

✦ The Bureaucracy
Ignores Reasoning & Intellectual Standards

Much of the pseudo critical thinking derives from the lack of a coherent understanding of the role of reasoning and intellectual standards in disciplined thought. What do I mean by this? Consider that as soon as we set our minds to the task of figuring anything out — a poem, a book, our bank account, a problem in our personal relationships, whatever — we are engaged in the task of reasoning, and reasoning can be done well or poorly. It can be assessed. And to assess it, we need intellectual standards. The California Department of Education English Language Arts Assessment (ELAA) committees are not clear about the role of reasoning in reading and writing, and therefore they are not clear about the role of intellectual standards in the assessment of reasoning in reading and writing. Unfortunately, when one is confused on a basic point such as this, the confusion inevitably spreads to other matters as well. And so we should not be surprised to find a variety of confusions in their work.

I will enumerate for your convenience some of the major ones just below. In the next section, I list flaws characteristic of the educational establishment in general. Each item in this second list I analyze in detail, to provide a background set of understanding in preparation for an in-

> *The general point, running through-out, is that the ill-constructed California reading and writing assessment is not an anomaly.*

depth analysis of the California reading and writing assessment. The reason for this is simple. If one understands the general pattern of misunderstanding, then specific instances of the pattern are much easier to see. A third list of flaws follows the analysis of the test. This final list makes clear the significance and instructional implications of the flawed character of the test. The general point, running throughout, is that the ill-constructed California reading and writing assessment is not an anomaly. The mistakes it makes are painfully predictable, mistakes being made all over the country in any number of ill-designed tests, in any number of ill-conceived curricula, in any number of ill-thought-through assignments.

You shall read, then, three lists of flaws. Remember that each has a somewhat different, but related, purpose. Now, the first list.

The California Department of Education English Language Arts Assessment materials, as we shall show below, contain all of the following flaws:

- Its treatment of intellectual standards is confused and erroneous.
- It confuses recall with knowledge.
- It confuses subjective preference with reasoned judgment.
- It confuses irrational with rational persuasion.
- Its key terms are often vague.
- Some key terms are dangerously ambiguous.
- It inadvertently encourages "subjectivism."
- Its scoring is arbitrary.
- It is both invalid and unreliable.

But before we look at the detail of these manifestations of pseudo critical thinking in the California Department of Education's assessment materials, let's make clearer what some of the common confusions of pseudo critical thinking amount to in the domain of educational assessment and why they occur. With these understandings in hand, it will be easier to explain what precisely is wrong with California's reading and writing assessment.

✦ What Does Pseudo Critical Thinking Look Like in Educational Assessment?

The advance of knowledge has been achieved not because the mind is capable of memorizing what teachers say but because it can be disciplined to ask probing questions and pursue them in a reasoned, self-critical way. Scholars pursuing knowledge submit their thinking to rigorous discipline, just as the discipline within which they think must itself submit to the broader discipline of more encompassing intellectual standards. Each academic discipline, in other words, develops special standards in virtue of its specialized concepts, procedures, and assumptions, but each also must submit to general standards which enable it to share its knowledge with

> *Pseudo critical thinking is revealed in educational assessment when the assessment theory or practice — or the approaches to teaching, thinking, or knowledge that follow from it — fails to take into account fundamental conditions for the pursuit or justification of knowledge.*

all disciplines and enable all genuine knowledge to be integrated comprehensively and tested for coherence. All research must be put, therefore, into a form of reasoning taken seriously in a field and the reasoning must then submit to the reasoned critique of others, both within and ultimately without the field, who share not only its standards but the standards of good thinking generally. Every field must be intellectually accountable to every other field by demonstrating its commitment to clarity, precision, accuracy, relevance, consistency, depth, and coherence.

Pseudo critical thinking is revealed in educational assessment when the assessment theory or practice — or the approaches to teaching, thinking, or knowledge that follow from it — fails to take into account fundamental conditions for the pursuit or justification of knowledge. The result is the unwitting or unknowing encouragement of flawed thinking. What are some of the common ways, then, that the assessment of thinking or, indeed, any approach to the teaching of thinking might be flawed? Here are three. These are not by any means the only ones, but they are very common, very basic, and very important.

FIRST BASIC FLAW —
THE LACK OR MISUSE OF INTELLECTUAL STANDARDS

This is one of the most common flaws. It derives from the fact that though all of us think, and think continually, we have not been educated to analyze our thinking and assess it. We don't have explicit standards already in mind to assess our thinking. We may then fall back on "mental process words" to talk about good thinking, words such as analyzing,

---

. . . though all of us think, and think continually, we have not been educated to analyze our thinking and assess it.

---

identifying, classifying, and evaluating. These are words that name *some* of what thinking does. We use our thinking to identify things, to classify them, to analyze them, to apply them, and to evaluate them. It is tempting, then, to think of critical thinking as *merely* thinking engaged in identification, classification, analysis, application, evaluation, and the like. But it is important to remember that responsible critical thinking requires intellectual standards. Hence, it is not enough to classify, one must do it well, that is, in accord with the appropriate standards and criteria. *Misclassification*, though a form of classification, is not an ability. The same goes for analysis, application, and evaluation.

It might be helpful to remember that all critical thinking abilities have three parts: a process, an object, and a standard. Here are various critical thinking abilities which can serve as examples. As you read them see if you can identify the intellectual standard in each.

- the ability to evaluate information for its relevance
- the ability to accurately identify assumptions
- the ability to construct plausible inferences
- the ability to identify relevant points of view
- the ability to distinguish significant from insignificant information

The standards used in these examples are "relevance," "accuracy," "plausibility," and "significance." Each of these standards would, needless to say, have to be contextualized. Nevertheless — and this is the key point — there can be no critical thinking without the use of intellectual standards.

Hence, if an approach to teaching or thinking focuses on the use of mental processes without a critical application of standards to that use,

---

There can be no critical thinking without the use of intellectual standards.

---

and persuades many to do the same, then, it is an example of pseudo critical thinking. There are in fact many such approaches in use in education today.

SECOND BASIC FLAW — MISCONCEPTIONS BUILT INTO THE SYSTEM

Flaws occur when thinking or an approach to thinking embodies a misconception about the nature of thinking or about what makes for excellence in it. I will explain just two of the most common misconceptions. The first involves confusing *reasoned judgment* (which is one of the most important modes of thinking leading to the possibility of knowledge) with *subjective preference* (which is not a basis for attaining knowledge). The second misconception involves confusing *recall* (which is a lower order use of the mind) with *knowledge* (which requires higher order thinking). Here are the explanations in brief. See if you can follow the examples and relate them to your experience.

Reasoned Judgment Confused with Subjective Preference

Many pseudo critical thinking approaches present all judgments as falling into two exclusive and exhaustive categories: fact and opinion. Actually, the kind of judgment most important to educated people and the kind we most want to foster falls into a third, very important, and now almost totally ignored category, that of reasoned judgment. A judge in a court of law is expected to engage in reasoned judgment; that is, the judge is expected not only to render a judgment, but also to base that judgment on sound, relevant evidence and valid legal reasoning. A judge is not expected to base his judgments on his subjective preferences, on his personal opinions, as such. You might put it this way, judgment based on sound reasoning goes beyond, and is never to be equated with, fact alone or mere opinion alone. Facts are typically used in reasoning, but good reasoning does more than state facts. Furthermore, a position that is well-reasoned is not to be described as simply "opinion." Of course, we sometimes call the judge's verdict an "opinion," but we not only expect, we demand that it be based on relevant and sound reasoning.

Here's a somewhat different way to put this same point. It is essential when thinking critically to clearly distinguish three different kinds of questions: *1)* those with one right answer (factual questions fall into this category), *2)* those with better or worse answers (well-reasoned or poorly reasoned answers), and *3)* those with as many answers as there are differ-

---

When questions that require better or worse answers are treated as matters of opinion, pseudo-critical thinking occurs.

---

ent human preferences (a category in which mere opinion does rule). Here are examples of the three types: *1)* What is the boiling point of lead? *2)* How can we best address the most basic and significant economic problems of the nation today? and *3)* Which would you prefer, a vacation in the mountains or one at the seashore? Only the third kind of question is a matter of sheer opinion. The second kind is a matter of reasoned judgment — we can rationally evaluate answers to the question (using universal intellectual standards such as clarity, depth, consistency and so forth).

When questions that require better or worse answers are treated as matters of opinion, pseudo critical thinking occurs. Students come, then, to uncritically assume that everyone's "opinion" is of equal value. Their capacity to appreciate the importance of intellectual standards diminishes, and we can expect to hear questions such as these: What if I don't like these standards? Why shouldn't I use my own standards? Don't I have a right to my own opinion? What if I'm just an emotional person? What if I like to follow my intuition? What if I don't believe in being "rational?" They then fail to see the difference between offering legitimate reasons and evidence in support of a view and simply asserting the view as true. The failure to teach students to recognize, value, and respect good reasoning is one of the most significant failings of education today.

Recall Confused With Knowledge

A second common confusion which leads directly to pseudo critical thinking is recall confused with knowledge. As I suggested above this confusion is deeply embedded in the minds of many "educators." It results from the fact that most instruction involves didactic lectures and most testing relies fundamentally on recall. Educators confuse students recalling what was said in the lecture with knowing the *how* and the *why* behind what was said. For example, a teacher might give you information, some of which is true and some of which is not, and you may not know which is which. Another way to see this point is to figure out why we don't think of parrots as gaining any knowledge when they learn to repeat words. Tape recorders get no credit for knowledge either. Do you see the point?

We tend to assume, to carry the point a bit further, that all information in a textbook is correct. Some, of course, is not. We attain genuine knowledge only when the information we possess is not only correct but, additionally, we know that it is and why it is. So, strictly speaking, I don't know that something is true or correct if I have merely found it asserted to be so in a book. I need to have a greater understanding — for example, I need to know what supports it, what makes it true — to properly be said to know it.

So if someone tells me Jack has flown to Paris for the weekend, I don't know if he actually did. I might believe that he had (because I trust the person who told me) and my belief might even be correct (through happen stance), but still I don't yet know for sure that he did. I am operating

---

We attain genuine knowledge only when the information we possess is not only correct but, additionally, we know that it is and why it is.

---

on the basis of "hearsay." The failure to appreciate the significance of this distinction causes a lot of problems in schooling because many who teach do not really know their own subjects well enough to explain clearly why this or that *is* so, and why this or that *is not* so. They know what the textbook says, certainly, but not why the textbook says what it says, or whether what it says is so or not. Having knowledge (for such confused persons) is nothing other than remembering what the textbook said.

THIRD BASIC FLAW — THE MISUSE OF INTELLECT

"Skilled" thinking can easily be used to obfuscate rather than to clarify, to maintain a prejudice rather than to break it down, to aid in the defense of a narrow interest rather than to take into account the public good. If we teach students to think narrowly, without an adequate emphasis on the essential intellectual traits of mind (intellectual humility, intellectual honesty, fairmindedness, etc.) the result can then be the inadvertent cultivation of the manipulator, the propagandist, and the con artist. We unknowingly end up, then, undermining the basic values of education and public service, properly conceived.

It is extremely important to see that intelligence and intellect can be used for ends other than those of gaining "truth" or "insight" or "knowledge." One can learn to be cunning rather than clever, smooth rather than clear, convincing rather than rationally persuasive, articulate rather than accurate. One can become judgmental rather than gain in judgment. One can confuse confidence with knowledge at the same time that one mistakes arrogance for self-confidence. In each of these cases a counterfeit of a highly desirable trait is developed in place of that trait. There

> *One can learn to be cunning rather than clever, smooth rather than clear, convincing rather than rationally persuasive, articulate rather than accurate.*

are many people who have learned to be skilled in merely appearing to be rational and knowledgeable when, in fact, they are not. Some of these have learned to be smooth, articulate, confident, cunning, and arrogant. They lack rational judgment, but this does not dissuade them from issuing dogmatic judgments and directives. They impress and learn to control others, quite selfishly. Unless we carefully design schooling to serve the "higher" ends of education, it can easily, as it now often does, degenerate into merely serving "lower" ends. When this happens, schooling often does more harm than good. It spreads the influence and resultant harm of pseudo critical thinking.

With the above understandings in mind, we are prepared to examine the new California Assessment Program and its evaluation of reading and writing.

✦ The California Assessment Program: English Language Arts Assessment

California
Assessment
Program

INTRODUCTION

California has developed the reputation of being a leader in educational reform. It was the first state to mandate critical thinking instruction at all educational levels. However, it is now becoming apparent that at the K–12 level at least, the mandate is not on solid ground, for pseudo critical thinking approaches, and the misunderstandings that underlie them, are becoming rampant in the state. The jargon of reform is everywhere, but substance is virtually nowhere. Unfortunately, the California Department of Education is oblivious of the danger, in fact, is very much part of the problem. Not only is it failing to provide sound leadership in integrating critical thinking into instruction, it is developing an assessment program which is shot-through with pseudo critical thinking confusions.

It is now deeply involved in developing what it calls "authentic" assessment that focuses on student "performances" found in the student "construction of meaning" in language arts and social studies. Now all of these terms — "authentic" and "performance" and "construction of meaning"

— are part of the buzz words of the day in educational circles. Of course, the theoretical insights that led to emphasis on these words are important, so let's briefly review them.

Testing and assessment in this country has come under increasing fire, and for good reason. Much of what has traditionally been tested in the popular, machine scorable, multiple choice tests has contributed to little more than trivial pursuit, more and more emphasis in instruction on the lowest order of thinking: rote memorization. Growing numbers of critics have pointed out that the items on which we have been testing students do not involve reasoning and have little relationship to the kinds of tasks that students will later be called upon to "perform." The tests fail, in other words, to "authentically" test higher order "performances." The reform of assessment has increasingly looked to an increased emphasis on "authentic" items that involve "performances" of a "higher order."

Furthermore, research by cognitive psychologists and others have clearly established the fact that when humans deeply learn something — in contrast to, say, storing it temporarily in short-term memory — that learning involves the "construction of meaning." Here's how you might

---

The reform of assessment has increasingly looked to an increased emphasis on "authentic" items that involve "performances" of a "higher order."

---

look at it. In order to get about successfully in the world in which we live we have to continually "make sense" of things, to give a meaning to what is surrounding us. As we do this we develop networks, systems of meanings that enable us quickly to size up what's in front of us. The result is we don't see "meaningless" colors and shapes and sounds. We see trees, and people, and dogs, and speeding cars, and smog. We immediately construct "meaning" out of our experience. Our experience is made by our minds to "fit into" meanings we have already constructed, or, if we cannot do this, we set about constructing a new meaning out of the old ones.

Now, what puzzled educational researchers was what has come to be called the problem of "transfer." Why don't students take what they are studying at school and use it in their daily acts of "constructing meanings?" Why don't they use scientific concepts when they make everyday predictions or form everyday theories about people and events? Why don't they use concepts from their social studies textbooks when they go about interpreting social situations and trying to figure out solutions to their social problems? Their conclusion was that the students don't use what they study in school in their everyday life because they are not engaged in the construction of meaning in class. In class, they are merely, or at least mainly, memorizing, not constructing meaning, not integrating school learning with everyday life.

Now we are ready to bring the three theoretical concepts together — "authentic," "performance," and the "construction of meaning." In authentic performances students construct meaning. They do not simply memorize. So why not focus school instruction on just such matters? Why not give them tasks that are "authentic?" Why not help them, in "performing" those tasks, to actually "construct meaning," in other words, to integrate what they are learning into the network of meanings they are already using to make sense of the world. This is the basic theoretical idea behind the ELAA materials, and, as far as it goes, there can be no objection. But as one wise person once said, "The important truths are in the details." And the details of the ELAA materials are horrendous.

A close examination of the details of the California Language Arts Assessment reveal that it is flawed in all of the following ways:

• The overall conception is not theoretically coherent. It is filled with vagueness and confusion. This is probably the result of the committee adopting the key buzz words without clearly understanding the theory underlying them. The buzz words are then used vaguely and the details are filled out with terms from the agendas of the various stake-holders.

• It does not provide a realistic model of reasoning, of critical reading and writing. Indeed, it is clear that the developers of the assessment do not realize that both reading and writing intrinsically involve the use of reasoning and that reasoning can be done well or poorly.

• The overall conception does not call attention to definite and clear intellectual standards. The criteria given are typically vague and applied inconsistently. Important intellectual standards are missing.

The test, in fact, leads the teachers in the direction of malpractice, that is, into the systematic misassessment of reading and writing, leading the students in turn to become inaccurate, imprecise, and undisciplined readers and writers.

• There is no way that a teacher might grasp an organized and systematic approach to the role of reasoning in reading and writing by studying the materials being disseminated. The test, in fact, leads the teachers in the direction of malpractice, that is, into the systematic misassessment of reading and writing, leading the students in turn to become inaccurate, imprecise, and undisciplined readers and writers.

A TANGLE OF CONFUSIONS

Let's now look at the details and shed light on some of the theoretical confusions that undermine the approach.

First of all, the ELAA commentators open by confusing knowledge with recall and "constructing meaning" with "reasonably constructing meaning." Since these confusions are basic and lead to indiscriminate scoring, let's look at how this occurs.

California's *New English-Language Arts Assessment: An Integrated Look*, begins by announcing a paradigm shift. As the English Language Arts Assessment (ELAA) document explains, "At the heart of the framework is a paradigm shift in which 'constructing meaning' replaced 'gaining knowledge' as the primary goal." Or, as it says later, "Since the construction of meaning is the essence of both reading and writing, the new assessment allows students to shape the outcome rather than to identify correct meanings that test makers have posited."

It is clear that the writers of the assessment are either not clear about the difference between recall and knowledge, or they are wrongly assuming that the attainment of knowledge is not intrinsically connected to the construction of meaning, or both. Briefly, let's make these relationships clear.

RATIONAL AND IRRATIONAL CONSTRUCTIONS

"Constructing meaning" is a process that is common to all learning which becomes deep-seated in the mind of the learner. It applies, however, just as much to the formation of flawed, irrational meanings as it does to the formulation of defensible, rational meanings. Deep-seated irrational fears, for example, result as much from the personal construction of meaning as do insights and understandings. Knowledge, on the other hand, though also the result of the construction of meaning, requires a clear-cut exercise of the rational faculties of the mind. For example, to appropriately judge a person accused of murder to be guilty or innocent, one's thinking must be guided by a careful and rational use of evidence, legal criteria (the criteria for "murder"), and the canons of sound reasoning. When a jury appropriately attains the knowledge of guilt or innocence, that knowledge, expressed in their verdict, is a product of a rational, a reasoned, construction of meaning. Of course, a jury may not function as it ought. It may be irrational and prejudiced, and the judge may overturn its verdict precisely because it did not properly discharge its responsibility to be "rational."

There is nothing wrong, therefore, with focusing attention on the need of students to "construct meaning" but it must be underscored that the *mere* construction of meaning, as such, is not a significant achievement, since it is done as much by Archie Bunker as by Einstein.

But the authors of The California Student Assessment System are confused on this point, for they talk as if the construction of meaning is an end in itself. They forget that "prejudice," "stereotypes," "misconceptions," "illusions," "delusion," "self-deceptions," "false beliefs," and all manner of other intellectually flawed creations of the mind, are just as much "constructions" and as "meaningful" constructions as ones more insightful and discerning.

We should rather be interested in fostering in children adherence to those intellectual standards that maximize their construction of genuine

---

> *. . . it must be underscored that the* mere *construction of meaning, as such, is not a significant achievement, since it is done as much by Archie Bunker as by Einstein.*

"knowledge," for otherwise they are likely to engage in a great deal of "irrational" construction and they will not know they are doing so. Education must discriminate between the quality of students' constructions of meaning, both in their reading and in their writing. But this can only defensibly be done by judging them by means of those intellectual standards common to educated thought. A construct that is unclear is not to be confused with one that is clear. One that is inaccurate is not to be confused with one that is accurate. One that is relevant to an assigned task is not to be confused with one that is irrelevant. One that is superficial is not to be confused with one that is deep.

Hence we do not need to decide between emphasizing the construction of meaning and the goal of attaining knowledge. If we properly understand the "dual" character of "meaning construction," we will immediately recognize the need to focus on the "reasoned" and "reasonable" construction of meaning, and not indiscriminately credit *any* construction of meaning.

To underscore the point, the human mind naturally and inevitably constructs meaning. The mere fact that students construct meanings tells us nothing about the quality of those constructs. For example, in the extended example on reading as a form of thinking which we cited (pp. 24–27), both readers, Stephen and Colleen, constructed meanings. But you will remember that the meanings constructed by Colleen were absurd. Both students reasoned about the text's meaning, but there was a stark contrast in the quality of reasoning in the two cases.

The point should now be clear. We want to work with our students' capacity to construct meaning from a text, but we want to do this while teaching them to discipline their reading, to learn how to fit their interpretations to the logic of the words of the text. We want them to develop definite intellectual standards for their reading and not feel free to treat a text as if it were "silly putty," to be shaped into any "meaning" they choose.

In passing, in the workplace, there is no economic value in constructing irrational, fanciful, lively, and entertaining meaning if it is irrational and reflects a flawed understanding of the text. Employers are not looking for a flashy, individualized response to a piece of writing, but rather a solid grasp of the meaning intended by the author. This is a fundamental premise of written communication! We should therefore continually

---

Employers are not looking for a flashy, individualized response to a piece of writing, but rather a solid grasp of the meaning intended by the author. This is a fundamental premise of written communication!

---

underscore the pivotal role of intellectual standards, not only in assessment but in any form of intellectual work whatsoever, including of course, reading and writing.

Intellectual Standards *That Apply to Thinking in Every Subject*	
Thinking that is:	*Thinking that is:*
Clear .... vs	Unclear
Precise .... vs	Imprecise
Specific .... vs	Vague
Accurate .... vs	Inaccurate
Relevant .... vs	Irrelevant
Plausible .... vs	Implausible
Consistent .... vs	Inconsistent
Logical .... vs	Illogical
Deep .... vs	Superficial
Broad .... vs	Narrow
Complete .... vs	Incomplete
Significant .... vs	Trivial
Adequate *(for purpose)* ....vs	Inadequate
Fair .... vs	Biased or One-Sided

A PSEUDO COMMITMENT TO INTELLECTUAL STANDARDS

Intellectual standards are essential to the appropriate assessment of reading and writing. At some level, the assessment authors are aware of this necessity. Their description of their own criteria imply both impartiality and commitment to intellectual standards. For example, the authors of the English-Language Arts Assessment often speak of their commitment to "encourage students to read widely and in depth." (Depth implies criteria for distinguishing "deep" from "shallow" readings.) Secondly, they imply impartial assessment when they state the three-fold purpose of the new English-Language Arts Assessment (p. I-2):

1) To establish standards for evaluating students' performance when they read diverse kinds of materials for different purposes.

2) To measure how well students are able to construct meaning.

3) To improve the instructional program by providing an assessment that reflects the Framework.

They use language that implies a concern with rational judgment: for example, the ELAA report says when speaking of "meaning-making," that,

We want students to think critically as they explore interests, clarify values, solve problems, resolve conflicts, generate new ideas, synthesize/apply learnings, set goals, and make decisions in response to the literature they read. (p. I - 2)

Now, the processes of thinking critically, clarifying values, solving problems, setting goals, and making decisions all presuppose the importance of rationality, of engaging in sound reasoning. To clarify values, for

---

It becomes clear, from here on, that the California testing experts' glossy, global statements about critical thinking and meaning-making and standards are losing their luster.

---

example, requires that we rationally analyze them. Solving problems is not the product of an arbitrary construction of meaning, but requires, amongst other things, an objective and accurate analysis of the nature of the problems, of the information relevant to the problems, and such like. Effective goal setting requires that we accurately identify possible competing goals and reasonably assess which make most sense. And certainly, decisions can reasonably or unreasonably be arrived at. It becomes clear, from here on, that the California testing experts' glossy, global statements about critical thinking and meaning-making and standards are losing their luster. Empty platitudes and vacuous ideals are a specialty of virtually all bureaucracies. So common are they now that they are hardly noticed anymore.

THE PROBLEM OF SCORING

As you might expect, all of the confusions above come home to roost in the design for scoring student "performances" in reading and writing. For example, in explaining the design with respect to assessing elementary reading, the authors introduce us to a 15-point list under the head of the reading performances of effective readers.

Effective readers *connect* with, *reflect* on, and *challenge* the text. Readers do not need to show evidence of all the performances listed here. The discerning and insightful reader may display a broad spectrum of reading behaviors or may investigate a few selected behaviors in great depth. The exemplary reader may show variety, complexity, breadth, and/or depth. Through their writing and graphics, these readers show convincing evidence of their ability to construct meaning. They may:

1. Experiment with ideas; think divergently; take risks; express opinions (e.g., speculate, hypothesize, explore alternative scenarios; raise questions; make predictions; think metaphorically).

2. Explore multiple possibilities of meaning; see cultural and/or psychological nuances and complexities in the text.

3. Fill in gaps; use clues and evidence in the passage to draw conclusions; make plausible interpretations of ideas, facts, concepts, and/or arguments.

4. Recognize and deal with ambiguities in the text.

5. Revise, reshape and/or deepen early interpretations.

6. Evaluate; examine the degree of fit between the author's ideas or information and the reader's prior knowledge or experience.

7. Challenge the text(s) by agreeing or disagreeing, arguing, endorsing, questioning, and or wondering.

8. Demonstrate understanding of the work as a whole.

9. Show sensitivity to the structure of the text(s): how the parts work together; how characters and/or other elements of the work(s) change.

10. Show aesthetic appreciation of the text(s); see linguistic and structural complexities.

11. Allude to and/or retell specific passages(s) to validate and/or expand ideas.

12. Make connections between the text(s) and their own ideas, experiences, and knowledge.

13. Demonstrate emotional engagement with the text(s).

14. Retell, summarize, and/or paraphrase with purpose.

15. Reflect on the meaning(s) of the text(s), including larger or more universal significance; express a major understanding about or insight into a subject, an aspect of self, or of life in general.

The Escape Hatch

First off, it is clear that since each scorer can pick and chose from such a wide variety of criteria (a number of which as we shall see are extremely vague), the impartiality of application of the criteria is suspect. Also note that any and all of these activities can be done either defensibly or indefensibly. Hence, if these are to be assessed in order to be credited or discredited, criteria must be provided for each of the individual "performances" cited (over 50 are buried in the list). We need some explanation of how they expect someone assessing student reading to apply them. Consider each of the following. The assessor is left to her own intuitions in determining whether or not a student's reading:

• is insightful; discerning; perceptive;

• is sensitive to linguistic, structural, cultural and psychological nuances and complexities;

• entertains challenging ideas; grounds meaning in acute perceptions of textual and cultural complexities.

Do the assessors really know how to *impartially* assess whether or not a student reader is being "sensitive to a psychological nuance" or to a "structural nuance" or a "cultural nuance?" Or can they impartially determine whether or not the student reader is entertaining a "challenging" idea? Or whether a student perception is "acute" or not? Isn't it highly probable that different assessors are going to have somewhat different conceptions of each of these matters, for example, one thinking a given idea is "quite challenging" and another thinking it is not? Surely this much is clear! No criteria, however, are provided, and this invalidates any attempt to use the results to assess one student's performances year after year, as well as to assess all California students collectively, year after year. Instead, having given us an array of vague descriptors, the authors now largely set them aside and focus instead on a six-point "Scoring Guide" that is to be used in distinguishing student reading into the following categories:

• *Exemplary* Reading Performance ....(Six Points)

• *Discerning* Reading Performance ....(Five Points)

•*Thoughtful* Reading Performance ....(Four Points)

• *Literal* Reading Performance ....(Three Points)

• *Limited* Reading Performance ....(Two Points)

• *Minimal* Reading Performance ....(One Point)

These general descriptors are of very little use. For example, consider the words "discerning" and "thoughtful." It is not obvious that one is better off being "discerning" than being "thoughtful." It is also not obvious why "literal" is above "limited." It is certainly not clear why the lowest score is "minimal" reading. What ever happened to just plain "poor" reading? Has it disappeared or is it one of many forms of "minimal" reading. (See Colleen's reading on pp. 24–27.) Is it "minimal" or just plain "poor?")

But that is not all. Each of the terms listed in each of the six point scoring guide create further problems for the conscientious scorer. Consider the terms in the first category alone, that of "exemplary reading performance." A person who takes seriously the characterizations of this first category should be prepared to notice and assess whether or not the student is:

filling in gaps	drawing on evidence
drawing meaning	objecting to text features
entertaining ideas	considering the authority of the author
raising questions	considering the quality of the author's sources
taking exception	suggesting ways of rewriting the text
agreeing; disagreeing	embracing the ideological position of a text
exploring possibilities	resisting the ideological position of a text
developing connections	revising their understanding as they read
making connections	carrying on an internal dialogue

The State Department Criteria for an Exemplary Reading Performance

1) An exemplary reading performance is insightful, discerning and perceptive as the reader constructs and reflects on meaning in a text. Readers at this level are sensitive to linguistic, structural, cultural, and psychological nuances and complexities. They fill in gaps in a text, making plausible assumptions about unstated causes or motivations, or drawing meaning from subtle cues. They differentiate between literal and figurative meanings. They recognize real or seeming contradictions, exploring possibilities for their resolution or tolerating ambiguities. They demonstrate their understanding of the whole work as well as an awareness of how the parts work together to create the whole.

Readers achieving score point six develop connections with and among texts. They connect their understanding of the text not only to their own ideas, experience, and knowledge, but to their history as participants in a culture or larger community, often making connections to other texts or other works of art. Exceptional readers draw on evidence from the text to generate, validate, expand, and reflect on their own ideas.

These readers take risks. They entertain challenging ideas and explore multiple possibilities of meaning as they read, grounding these meanings in their acute perceptions of textual and cultural complexities. They often revise their understanding of a text as they re-read and as additional information or insight becomes available to them. They sometimes articulate a newly developed level of understanding.

Readers demonstrating a score point six performance challenge the text. They carry on an internal dialogue with the writer, raising questions, taking exception, agreeing, disagreeing, appreciating or objecting to text features. They may test the validity of the author's ideas, information, and/or logic by considering the authority of the author and the nature and quality of the author's source(s). They frequently suggest ways of rewriting the text, speculating about the ideology or cultural or historical biases that seem to inform a text, sometimes recognizing and embracing and sometimes resisting the ideological position that a text seems to construct for its reader.

MUST THE STUDENT JUST DO IT OR DO IT WELL?

Even more problematic than the likely disagreement among assessors as to the application of the vague standards provided is, as I suggested above, the problem of the assessors being given many criteria that name processes that can, in principle, be done well or poorly. The directions do not explain whether, to be credited, the student is obliged to use the cited processes well or simply use them in any way whatsoever. That is, there is

> *Unfortunately, once we examine the actual student writing examples along with the commentary provided, it becomes painfully clear that the assessors were simply looking to see if the student in any sense used the process and did not have, or did not use, criteria to assess how* well *the students used the processes credited.*

no indication as to whether the assessor is to evaluate the "quality" of the way the student is doing these things or simply certify the fact of doing these things — however poorly. Remember, a student who is drawing an *absurd* meaning is still drawing a meaning. A student who is making a *trivial* connection is still making a connection. A student who is drawing on *irrelevant* evidence is still drawing on evidence. A student who is raising a *silly* or *superficial* question is still raising a question. And so forth, and so on.

Unfortunately, once we examine the actual student writing examples along with the commentary provided, it becomes *painfully clear* that the assessors were simply looking to see if the student in any sense used the process and did not have, or did not use, criteria to assess how *well* the students used the processes credited. The California State Department of Education falls directly into the trap of failing to discriminate between these crucial differences. The assessors are left to their own devices. They can draw these distinctions or fail to draw them. It is clear that most failed to draw them. This is a fatal flaw in the assessment. It renders the results of the assessment virtually useless.

THE MISASSESSMENT OF ELEMENTARY READING

The only elementary reading passage which is given with scored examples is from a story by John Gardiner called *Stone Fox*. It is an emotionally explosive story, one chosen perhaps to ensure an emotional response. The children are simply asked to give some of their "thoughts, feelings, and questions" about what they are reading. No other kind of writing is given as an example.

Insufficient Directions Are Given

Now the first remarkable feature of the *Stone Fox* reading prompt is that the student readers are given no indication whatsoever of the purpose for which they are reading the story. This is ironic in the light of the fact that the CAP materials emphasize the fact that one can read and write "for different purposes" (p. I-3). And yet, here, the students are asked to read for no particular purpose. Are they to read in a casual fashion, simply for amusement? Or are they to do a "close reading" for detail? Are they to be analytical and reflective, or not? The students are given no indication of how they will be assessed. Hence, they are asked to engage, at best, in an ill-defined "performance." Nothing is given in the way of directions to the students except "Read to see what happens" and a place to the right in which the student *may* write notes under a column head titled, "My thoughts, feelings, and questions about what I am reading." The students were apparently not even told that they should try to write out as much of their thoughts, feelings, and questions as they could. Some readers might presumably have thoughts, feelings, and questions they would not bother to express.

Consider that you are a student reading the story. You see a column at the right which says, "My thoughts, feelings, and questions about what I am reading." How should you understand it? Wouldn't you wonder which thoughts ... which feelings ... based on what? What am I to think about? Why am I to think about it?

In any case, since the student reader is not told that she is going to be evaluated on what she writes and is told none of the criteria, why should she be motivated to fully express her thoughts and feelings? Consider, on the other hand, what the directions might have said.

Possible Directions

When we read a story we have to try to understand and follow its meaning. We try to figure out what it is saying and we try to connect it with our own life in some way. We want you to read this story and see what it means to you. Why do you think it was written? Do you think that it was written well? Do you think it is true to life? Does it illustrate anything that you believe is important? Please write in as many of your thoughts on these questions as possible as you read. Help us to understand what is going on in your mind as you are reading and trying to relate this story to your life.

Can One Evaluate Purely Subjective Responses to Stories?

When the student reads that she is directed to express her "feelings," with no explanation given why she is so directed, then how can we legitimately go on to judge those feelings and "score" them one through six?

Suppose the student quite sincerely said, "In my view this is a sentimental story that insults my intelligence. I feel disgusted when I read it and bored silly." How should the assessor evaluate that "feeling" response? Is there any way to discredit it according to the directions? Certainly not. It is as good a response to a request for "feelings" as any other. To put the point succinctly, *either we help students understand the difference between a request for a purely subjective response,* (How do you feel when you read this?) *and a request for a more reasoned response* (What feeling do you judge the author wants you to feel and why? In your judgment is the author successful? Tell us the reasons why you think so.) *or we must not indulge in any assessment of the students "feelings."* We have no legitimate grounds for doing so. The student can legitimately take the request to be one that asks for a subjective response and a purely subjective response cannot be impartially assessed or scored.

THE MISASSESSMENT OF WRITING AT THE ELEMENTARY LEVEL

Different kinds of writing will be assessed at different levels: Elementary: persuasive writing ... Middle School: *problem solution, evaluation* and *speculation about cause and effect* ... High School: *evaluation, speculation about cause and effect, interpretation* and *controversial issues* plus a *reflective essay.* (p. I–4)

The grade four writing assessment is designed to reflect a variety of purposes for which children write:

1) **Expressive** writing
   ("This is what I see, think, and feel ...")

2) **Persuasive** writing
   ("This is what I believe and why I think you should believe it ...");

3) **Narrative** writing
   ("This is what happened ..."); and

4) **Informational** writing
   ("This is what I know and how I know it ...").

Criteria For Persuasive Writing

Persuasive writing is explained in the following terms (p. III–12):

> Persuasive writing requires students to choose positions, to make judgments, to offer proposals, and to argue convincingly for their beliefs and ideas. However, some students may choose to explore both sides of an issue and then offer a compromise, ... Effective writers use evidence such as examples or anecdotes to support their arguments. Convincing arguments may appeal to logic, emotions, and/or philosophical beliefs.

Persuasive writers establish themselves as informed, knowledgeable individuals. They orient readers... More than any other kind of writing, argument requires writers to consider their audience.... The best persuasive writers systematically develop arguments with a strong sense of coherence and movement throughout the piece.

California's Standards for Exceptional Writing (Six Points)

An exceptional score (6 points) must meet the following standards:

Focus/coherence

Position. Writers of six-point papers usually assert and maintain a clear position throughout the piece; they present evidence and explanations in a purposeful way. Occasionally these writers will effectively evaluate both sides of an issue and offer a reasonable compromise; or they may conclude that neither position is preferable, or they may suggest a third position.

Organization. Writers arrange reasons, examples, information and/or personal anecdotes in a discernible and effective pattern resulting in an overall persuasive effect.

Coherence. Writers provide overall links or transitions; they present arguments, evidence, and reasons logically so that the overall effect is one of coherence.

Elaboration

Depth/Density of Arguments. Writers thoroughly develop and elaborate their reasons, examples, information and/or anecdotes. Some writers may develop only one reason or example, but they do so in depth; others may choose to develop several appropriate reasons, examples, and so forth.

Relevance of Arguments. Writers choose and present appropriate reasons, examples, information, and so forth to support their argument(s). They show their arguments are valid based on prior knowledge, personal experience and reflection.

Audience Awareness. Writers choose and present arguments with a clear awareness of reader needs. They often show credibility and a sense of authority by revealing source(s) of information. They may anticipate possible reader response by including some counter-arguments.

Style

Word Choice. These writers use lively, interesting concrete language that carries precise meanings and emotions. Word choice is appropriate to the writer's purpose.

Sentence Variety. Writers vary sentence length and type, making the writing interesting and readable.

Voice. Writers evidence confidence, conviction, belief and sometimes enthusiasm.

Problems With the Criteria In Assessing Writing

Once again there are a host of problems with the criteria, the most serious being that, just as in the criteria for reading, there is no indication of whether the students are expected to do any of the above well, or simply do them in any form whatsoever. For example, consider the claim that "convincing arguments may appeal to logic, emotions, and/or philosophical beliefs." Suppose a student uses "convincing" but "fallacious" logic — is the student to be credited? Or suppose the student appeals to the emotions of the reader by engaging in *name-calling* ("This stupid communist idea...!") — is the student to be credited? The formulators of the criteria are seemingly oblivious of the problem.

A GRADE FOUR ESSAY JUDGED TO ILLUSTRATE HIGH-RANGE ACHIEVEMENT

"Good-evning ladies and gentelmen. I come to you tonight with a few simple facts. The pack you are ready to face down is this very munit filled with children. It is the favorit place to play of many children, as well as myself. Do you anistly think that children at the age of two und three are going to enjoy a mall more than a park?! I would also like to bring to your atichun that we already have over five stores in one plazua. You can get there very esley. I admit that it's about a half hour away, but

wouldn it be 'hole lot of trouble to spend a little more cash & as long as you know that children are happy and safe. You, and only

you can make that chois to make that difreace!! How would you feel if you were a child playing in your favorit place to play, beutiful shady trees, and fresh green grass. A perfict place to play, take your dog for a walk, play with another pet, or even just sit around and look at the beutiful sky. And then after knoing it had been there for over 100 years, and their going to tare it down! Oh! The feeling

thoes poor children must haved Please! Please! Just stop and think about this matter! This is very sereous. I didnt come here to wach thoes C.A.T.s tare up that park! Pleas consiter my slotion. I bid yoy good night."

The CAP Commentary

From the opening ... this writer exudes confidence, focuses on an audience and takes a firm stand on the issue. These attributes of persuasive writing are maintained throughout the piece.

Support for the writer's credible arguments in favor of a park versus a mall are drawn from personal experiences. She uses examples: "We already have over five stores in our plaza," and notes that the park is a "perfect place to play, take your dog for a walk." She includes reflection,

"Do you honestly think that children at the age of two or three are going to enjoy a mall ...?" Her arguments are appropriate and appeal to reason (safety) and emotions ("I didn't come here to watch those C.A.T.s tare up that park!")

This writer is consistently aware of and appeals to her audience with appropriate tone and lively language.

The Problem of Subjectivity, Once Again

The problem of subjectivity that was so apparent in the elementary reading assessment reappears again in the writing assessment. It is clear in this, and in other examples, that the commentators are using the criteria for good persuasive writing literally and not making any real judgments of reasonability. Hence, if the student says anything which can be construed as falling under one of the criteria then that is credited. For example, if she uses an emotional appeal then credit the emotion criterion (however irrelevant or inappropriate it might be); if she says something which can be described as "reflection," then credit the reflection criterion (however irrelevant or inappropriate the "reflection" might be). Any kind of a move that would work with an audience, in the view of the commentator, is credited as good (regardless of how irrational it might be). But the

---

To suggest that this is good persuasive writing is to teach children exactly the wrong lesson. It fails to show them the vital distinction between reason and its counterfeit.

---

significant question for anyone concerned with the traditional values of education is whether a *reasonable* audience should be persuaded or "moved." The important distinction for students to grasp is that between what might be called "low level rhetorical appeals" and those appeals which would convince or "move" a reasonable audience. No such distinction is recognized by ELAA. The criteria are used crudely, without any important intellectual distinctions in evidence.

The implication of this is that if a student wrote a very rational appeal, which recognized the weaknesses in her position and the need to qualify her claims, she would be downgraded because she would not be "exuding confidence," "taking a firm stand on the issue," etc. Indeed, though her presentation might appeal to a "jury of reasonable persons," the graders of the ELAA would not be impressed.

In this particular essay, for example, though it is good for children to display confidence, etc., the issue of park versus mall should be decided on rational grounds. Yes, it is important that the park is a favorite place for children and that they are safe there, but this is really a decision about options, and alternatives, and relative costs and benefits. This issue should be decided by looking at these factors and weighing them as rationally as possible, not on the basis of emotional appeals, like that of the child. To suggest that this is good persuasive writing is to teach children exactly the wrong lesson. It fails to show them the vital distinction between reason and its counterfeit.

Suppose the child has to present a case before an audience she knows to be racist; if one reads and applies the criteria presented for good persuasive writing in ELAA, the student who plays on those racist sentiments

---

What apparently matters in the mind of the ELAA assessors is that one successfully persuades, not that one argues reasonably. But it is harder to imagine a distinction which it is more vital for the educated person to grasp.

---

will score higher than one who opposes them. What apparently matters in the mind of the ELAA assessors is that one successfully persuades, not that one argues reasonably. But it is harder to imagine a distinction which it is more vital for the educated person to grasp. Indeed, one might almost regard it as a criterion of being educated that one sees the difference between fairminded, reasonable argument, and self-seeking, low-level, persuasive rhetoric. The demagogues may often win the day, but do we want to use public monies to generate armies of demagogues, all having mastered the art of demagogery at the public expense?

In another example, which contains some very good reasoning about why another child should feel good about himself, the commentators say, "She arranges her reasons and evidence in a sophisticated pattern." There is no mention of whether the reasons and evidence are relevant or

---

It is not that the reasons are arranged in a sophisticated pattern, but that they are good reasons!

---

irrelevant, true or false, good or bad. Yet, again, isn't this what really matters? It is not that the reasons are arranged in a sophisticated pattern, but that they are *good* reasons!

In another, mid-range, example, about how to solve problems between children and parents, the commentators say (among other things), "Audience awareness is evident throughout, although appeals lack the vigor and exactness of higher score point papers. The use of bullets to summarize the writer's arguments is an effective tool and adds to her sense of conviction." Why is the writer criticized for a lack of vigor and praised for conveying a sense of conviction? Neither is a virtue in itself. What matters is that one exhibits the *appropriate* degree of vigor and conviction, depending on the strength of one's case. Vigorously arguing a weak case and displaying conviction despite poor supporting reasons ought to be marked down, not praised.

The Young Hitler Scores High on the CAP Test

We can now make our point dramatically by considering how the following piece of persuasive, but highly irrational, writing should be graded according to the ELAA criteria.

... the greatest revolution Germany has undergone was that of the purification of the Volk [people] and thus of the races, which was launched systematically in this country for the first time ever. *[From the opening the writer exudes confidence, focuses on an audience and takes a firm stand on the issue.]*

The consequences of this German racial policy will be more significant for the future of our Volk than the effects of all the other laws put together. For they are what is creating the new man. They will preserve our Volk from doing as so many historically tragic past prototypes of other races have done: lose their earthly existence forever because of their ignorance as regards a single question. *[The writer arranges reasons, examples and information in a discernible and effective pattern resulting in overall persuasive effect.]*

For what is the sense of all our work and all our efforts if they do not serve the purpose of preserving the German being? And what good is any effort on behalf of this being if we omit the most important thing to preserve it pure and unadulterated in its blood? *[The writer asserts and maintains a clear position throughout. He also chooses and presents arguments with a clear awareness of reader needs.]*

Any other mistake can be rectified, any other error can be corrected, but what one fails to do in this area can often never be amended. Whether our work in this area of purifying our race and thus our Volk has been fruitful is something you can best judge for yourselves here during these few days. For what you are encountering in this city is the German being. Come and see for yourselves whether he has become worse under National Socialist leadership or whether he has not indeed become better. Do not gauge only the increasing number of children being born — gauge above all the appearance of our youth. *[The writer presents evidence and explanations in a purposeful way.]*

How lovely are our girls and our boys, how bright is their gaze, how healthy and fresh their posture, how splendid are the bodies of the hundreds of thousands and millions who have been trained and cared for by our organizations! *[The writer shows his arguments are valid based on personal knowledge and reflection.]*

Where are better men to be found today than those who can be seen here? It is truly the rebirth of a nation, brought about by the deliberate breeding of a new being *[The overall effect is one of coherence.]*

—*(Hitler Speech 1937)*

This piece asserts and maintains a clear position throughout and presents evidence and explanations in a purposeful way; the writer arranges reasons, examples, information and/or personal anecdotes in a discernible and effective pattern resulting in overall persuasive effect; the overall effect is one of coherence; the writer shows his arguments are valid based on prior knowledge, personal experience and reflection; the writer chooses and presents arguments with a clear awareness of reader needs; the writer evidences confidence, conviction, belief, and sometimes enthusiasm.

Clearly, for all these reasons we have to give this piece of Hitler's writing a Point 6 score! It meets the CLAS criteria, as does much of his writing. Hitler's writing was widely recognized to meet the needs of his audience, to exude confidence, etc. Is that really what we want to praise? Is that the model of persuasive writing that we want to hold up to our children? If so, shame on the California Learning Assessment System!

THE MISASSESSMENT OF WRITING AT THE HIGH SCHOOL LEVEL

Introduction — Same Problem: Next Level

At the high school level the Writing Assessment assesses four types of writing, Autobiographical Incident, Interpretation, Reflective Essay, and Speculation About Causes and Effects, some of which are successors to the elementary level Persuasive writing.

The same general faults that were mentioned earlier in connection with the elementary level are to be found at this level too. For example, the scoring guide for *interpretation* makes it clear that only subjective reactions to and subjective interpretation of fiction are really being considered. But *interpretation* is important in many other contexts, e.g. history, and in history it is crucial to distinguish between subjective response and objective interpretation, between reasons that persuade irrational audiences and reasons which persuade rational and fairminded persons, between something which is rhetorically convincing and something which is true. None of these distinctions is recognized in the CLAS.

To be specific in our criticisms, consider the scoring guide for **Speculation About Causes and Effects**; once again writing of this kind is judged almost entirely by *subjective* standards, by standards appropriate to one's response to fiction.

Here is what is said about writing of this kind which should score Point 6, for Exceptional Achievement:

A six point essay **engages the reader immediately**. It seems **purposeful**. The writer **seems aware of reader's questions and needs throughout** the essay. The essay seems to be not just written but **written to particular readers**. The writer **convinces the readers of the plausibility** of the speculation.

A six-point essay demonstrates qualities all readers admire: conviction, enthusiasm, freshness. These essays may use an unconventional rhetorical approach. A six-point essay may **take chances and succeed.**

Presenting the Situation. The six-point essay writer clearly defines, identifies, or describes the situation to be speculated about. Though it does not dominate the essay at the expense of speculation, the situation is nevertheless presented fully and precisely. The writer limits the occasion appropriately, focusing reader attention on just those aspects of the situation that the writer will speculate about.

Writers of six-point essays may describe or detail the situation that is established in the prompt, or they might create the situation by using narrative or anecdotal techniques. In either case, they will **use concrete language, rich in sensory detail**.

The writer of the six-point essay acknowledges readers' concerns. For real world situations, the writer of the six-point essay acknowledges the reader's experience or familiarity with a situation and, using narrative or descriptive strategies, builds on this awareness to focus reader attention on a comparable situation. ...

Whether the essay arises from a factual assessment of a real situation or from a fanciful guess about a fanciful situation, the writer **consistently demonstrates broad knowledge and clear understanding of the situation. In this way the writer establishes authority.**

Logic and Relevance of Causes and Effects. In the six-point essay, the proposed causes and effects are clearly related to the particular situation that the writer has defined. Writers use imaginative, inventive argument to convince the reader of the logic of their speculation. The best writers are clearly considering possibilities and are seeing multiple perspectives.... Because speculation is essentially a persuasive type of writing, the best writers will be continually aware of readers' needs. They might refer to the readers directly, trying to enlist their support ...

Elaboration of Argument. The six-point essay **provides substantial elaboration**, convincing the reader that the writer's conjectures are valid for the situation. These writers elaborate their speculated causes and effects **with carefully chosen evidence that is logically and fully developed. Such evidence is chosen because it is relevant and convincing.** It is developed fully with precise, explicit detail to convince the reader both of the logic and the authenticity of the proposed cause and effect.

Some strategies writers may use to develop their arguments are the following:

* Cite facts, opinions, projections, and personal experiences or observations (anecdotes) to explain or validate a cause or an effect.

* Elaborate on possibilities arising from proposed causes and effects, showing possible "domino effects" that might determine the direction of the developing situation.

* Give specific examples of comparable causes and effects that have arisen in analogous situations. (p. III–64)

How may we best make the point that these criteria again fail to recognize the crucial distinctions of which we have been speaking — between subjective responses and good reasons, etc? Perhaps the simplest way is to look at another example of persuasive writing, this time **Speculating About Causes and Effects,** and consider how we should grade it according to the CLAS criteria.

Just as every people, as a basic tendency of all its earthly actions possesses a mania for self-preservation as its driving force, likewise is it exactly so with Jewry too. Only here, in accord with their basically different dispositions, the struggle for existence of Aryan peoples and Jewry is also different in its forms. The foundation of the Aryan struggle for existence is the soil, which he cultivates and which provides the general basis for an economy satisfying primarily its own needs within its own orbit through the productive forces of its own people.

Because of the lack of productive capacities of its own the Jewish people cannot carry out the construction of a state, viewed in a territorial sense, but as a support of its own existence it needs the work and creative activities of other nations. Thus the existence of the Jew himself becomes a parasitical one within the lives of other people. Hence the ultimate goal of the Jewish struggle for existence is the enslavement of productively active peoples. In order to achieve this goal, which in reality has represented Jewry's struggle for existence at all times, the Jew makes use of all weapons that are in keeping with the whole complex of his character.

Therefore in domestic politics within the individual nations he fights first for equal rights and later for super-rights. The characteristics of cunning, intelligence, astuteness, knavery, dissimulation, etc, rooted in the character of his folkdom, serve him as weapons thereto.

They are as much stratagems in his war of survival as those of other peoples in combat.

In foreign policy he tries to bring nations into a state of unrest, to divert them from their true interests, and to plunge them into reciprocal wars and in this way gradually rise to mastery over them with the help of the power of money and propaganda.

His ultimate goal is the denationalization, the promiscuous bastardization of other peoples, the lowering of the racial level of the highest peoples as well as the domination of this racial mish-mash through the extirpation of the folkish intelligentsia and its replacement by the members of his own people.

The end of the Jewish world struggle therefore will always be a bloody Bolshevization. In truth this means the destruction of all the intellectual upper classes linked to their peoples so that he can rise to become the master of a mankind become leaderless. *Hitler's Secret Book*, pp. 212-213.

Hitler's Assessment Based on CAP Criteria

- This piece of writing certainly engages the reader immediately;
- it seems purposeful;
- the writer seems aware of reader's questions and needs throughout;
- the piece seems not just to be written but written to particular readers;

• the writer convinced those readers of the plausibility of the speculation;

• the writing shows conviction and enthusiasm;

• the writer clearly defines the situation to be speculated about, acknowledges the reader's experience or familiarity with the situation, and consistently demonstrates broad knowledge and clear understanding of the situation;

• the writer uses imaginative, inventive argument to convince the reader of the logic of his speculation;

• the writer elaborates on possibilities arising from the proposed causes and effects, showing possible "domino effects" that might determine the direction of the developing situation; etc., etc.

Can there be any doubt that Hitler's writing in the category merits a Point 6 grade?! If that is so then once again, shame on the California Learning Assessment System, which has again failed to see the difference between a *proper* and *improper* use of rhetoric and reason.

Summary Judgment
on the California Assessment of Reading & Writing

An assessment of reading and writing should not only underscore the role of reasoning in both, but also firmly establish defensible intellectual standards, appropriately and specifically explained and consistently and

---

No assessment of intellectual work, nor foundation for teaching, should be based on an approach in which intellectual standards are confused and erroneous, confusing recall with knowledge, subjective preference with reasoned judgment, irrational with rational persuasion.

---

appropriately applied. No assessment of intellectual work, nor foundation for teaching, should be based on an approach in which intellectual standards are confused and erroneous, confusing recall with knowledge, subjective preference with reasoned judgment, irrational with rational persuasion. No assessment of intellectual work should use its key terms vaguely or oscillate between two significant uses of a term or score in an arbitrary manner. And, most important of all, no intellectual assessment should encourage irrational subjectivism.

For example, it is striking that in the context of reading and listening, there is little discussion of the need to create an accurate interpretation: there are many contexts in which it is not appropriate for the readers to "create their own meaning" and where accuracy is what is required. This may be equally true if the author is addressing a particular question or problem, or using particular basic concepts; very often the good response to what is said or written is good precisely because it is based on an accurate construal of the text. Nothing in this assessment mentions the virtue of accuracy.

Most importantly however, this approach is flawed again and again because what gets credited is anything that could be construed as fulfilling one of the criteria and the criteria are the wrong ones for the purpose. If the writer is using any emotion (however discreditable) then it is marked positively; if she is giving anything that could be called evidence,

---

Underneath all of this is a question of values. We are obliged to educate our students, not simply to shape them.

---

even if it is bad evidence, it is credited; any kind of a move that would work with an audience, in the view of the reader is credited as good (regardless of how irrational it might be). The end result is that if a student wrote a very rational appeal, one that would persuade a rational audience, it is going to be graded down because it wouldn't appeal to an irrational judge (because it won't be maintaining a strong line, it won't necessarily be persuasive; it will be putting in qualifications; it will be speaking in terms of greys and greys don't persuade; it will not be engaging in hyperbole and hyperbole is effective; it won't be trying to negate everything about the other side, it will be recognizing reasonable objections; it will express the degree of confidence that is appropriate but no more). Given a list of what a rational person would do, you will be able to see that the criteria for success under CLAS are negating these rational qualities and therefore encouraging irrational beliefs about how you communicate to people, indeed encouraging people to become manipulators!

Underneath all of this is a question of values. We are obliged *to educate* our students, *not simply to shape them.*

The educated person is reasonable; the educated person isn't simply concerned with winning. The educated person wants to win when winning is the appropriate thing. However, when the other side is more reasonable, then the educated person, who is more interested in getting at the truth than in winning, will want to make concessions.

If the goal of education is simply to enable people to get what they want, then we should teach them tools of manipulation, ways to win battles, ways to undermine positions whether those positions are rational or not, ways to just get what they want, irrespective of fairness, and of the evidence. Inadvertently and unknowingly, this is what CLAS is supporting. CLAS does not have in mind a clear difference between the educated, fairminded, and rational person, on the one hand, and the person who is simply good at manipulating, winning, and defeating others, on the other.

In effect what CLAS has said is that the name of the game is to persuade the audience by whatever methods work and we'll credit anything that works. Shouldn't they instead have said, "Since we are obliged and committed to educating children, and since this requires they learn to reason well as readers, writers, and thinkers, we will not credit flawed reasoning. We will only credit well-reasoned responses."

To Summarize Some of Our Criticisms of the CLAS Approach:

1) The overall conception fails to capture the practices of critical readers, writers, and thinkers the world over.

2) The overall conception does not call attention to definite and clear intellectual standards, and without them, it becomes impossible for both teacher and student to engage in "objective" assessment.

3) The overall conception does not provide an organized and systematic approach to posing, analyzing, and reasoning through problems embedded in everyday personal and professional reading and writing.

4) The teacher who takes this approach seriously will misteach reading and writing.

5) The student who learns through this approach will mislearn the art of reading and writing.

Given these failings, it is clear that the California Learning Assessment System falls into the category of pseudo critical thinking, and will not help students and teachers to develop their critical thinking abilities, but will hinder this process. Indeed, when classroom teachers receive copies, as they surely will, of test items, sample answers, commentary, and scores, they will use them as a guide for instruction. Thousands of school children will lose an opportunity to begin to become critical readers and writers. Thousands of school children will themselves learn to confuse recall with knowledge, subjective preference with reasoned judgment, irrational with rational persuasion. They will learn to use language vaguely and to think that their subjective pronouncements are not to be criticized. Their reasoning skills will remain abysmally low.

✦ Is The California Assessment Fiasco a Fluke?
The Educational Bureaucracy and Self-Deception

One of the most significant facts about the California language arts test fiasco is that *it is not a fluke*. But of course, *neither is it a plot* to undermine education. *The situation is worse than either.* As a fluke it could be corrected. As a plot the perpetrators could be severely dealt with when exposed. No, the pathetic side of the case is that there are systemic reasons why educational bureaucracies, framed as they are, will continue to generate just such fiascos regularly and predictably. And predictably, many will be taken in. Furthermore, because classroom teachers have emerged from a long-term training that reflects a similar background to that of the test designers, they also will fall easily into line with the flawed thinking passed down to them.

To deal with the problem at its roots, we must own the fact that there are significant problems in education due to its wide-spread and large-

---

One of the most significant facts about the California language arts test fiasco is that it is not a fluke. But of course, neither is it a plot to undermine education. The situation is worse than either.

---

scale bureaucratization. Large-scale bureaucratization entails, or at least makes highly probable, a high degree of narrow specialization — and specialization tends to bring fragmentation, narrowness of vision, politicization, and self-deception in its wake. The fragmentation and narrowness of vision makes it difficult to effect fundamental changes because the parts do not work together in a rational way and no one sees clearly that this is so, since each element in the structure becomes an end in itself, to itself.

It is almost impossible for the most pressing problems of education to become "issues" in educational bureaucracies because the focus is inevitably on the political, the narrow, the fragmented part or parts. With each part serving itself as an ultimate end — including those on the top — the whole is left to take care of itself. No one is left responsible for it. The executive wing is also focused on itself and typically is satisfied with or driven to manufacture an illusion of serving the announced or official goals and ends. Meanwhile, the politicization and self-deception helps hide those realities most unpleasant to think about, and to have to face, and consequently those realities most in need of change.

This includes, of course, the most significant one today: the fact that modern American bureaucratic schooling is a system that preserves at its heart a mode of instruction that is a hold-over from the 19th Century and whose consistent effect is a superficial one. Most students in most classes most of the time are not actively engaged in learning what is worth learning. Most students are, on their side, not taking their education seriously. On the teaching side, they are not given challenging instruction. They are not engaged in genuine intellectual work. They are not developing intellectual standards or discipline. And, most assuredly, they are not learning to reason scientifically, mathematically, geographically, economically, sociologically, or morally. (See "Research Findings," p. 19.)

On the shoddy foundation of didactic instruction and passive, lower order learning, the rhetoric of high goals and ideals, the propaganda of the schools, is overlaid. Modern educational bureaucracy has developed

---

On the shoddy foundation of didactic instruction and passive, lower order learning, the rhetoric of high goals and ideals, the propaganda of the schools, is overlaid.

---

multiple ways to appear to be, and to appear to be doing, what it is not. In the K–12 domain especially, the history of education in the 20th Century is a triumph of propaganda and self-deception. This is documented in story after story of wave after wave of pseudo reform following pseudo reform, of new buzz words and new jargon replacing old buzz words and old jargon — each set of new words serving as a new mask to obscure the one-and-the-same consistent lower order face. (Cf "Critical Thinking in Historical Perspective chapter.) Unfortunately, virtually everyone in the game has a stake in making their playing of it look more honorable, more lofty, more noble and effective than it really is.

You may remember that it is only some three years now since every state in the union, through the massaging and manipulation of statistics by its own state department of education, proudly announced that its students had scored above the national average!!! This is the kind of self-serving propaganda and trickery that is the daily fare of educational reality.

State departments of education, as I have suggested, are a particularly interesting manifestation of the workings of the educational establishment. Each consists of huge bureaucracies, interlaced with committees that are in turn tied into networks of teachers and administrators spread across their states. The microcosm we analyzed in this chapter (the California State Department of Education's new English-Language Arts Assessment materials) is still officially in draft stage, but already is being highly touted as a refined, future-oriented, testing instrument. We've seen what the ELAA has done. Let's see what CLAS and the Department of Education says it has done. The test is being represented to the public and to teachers within the state and the nation as having,

> The goal ... to evaluate students' capacities for insightful, pro-
> ductive thinking with tests that support the finest curriculum and
> instructional programs in the language arts ... [*California's Learning
> Assessment System*, CDE Publication]

> The most important single component of the new assessment
> system will be the **statewide performance standards**, and the
> most important outcome of the assessment process will be the
> internalization of those standards in the thinking and work of
> teachers, students, and parents. The **performance standards will
> undergird all aspects of the educational enterprise; serving as
> the center of the seamless web of teaching, learning and assess-
> ment.** [*Some Principles and Beliefs about the Role of Assessment in California's
> School Reform Plan*, February 15, 1993, CDE]

Let's see what the legislature mandated, Senate Bill 662 (Hart):

> Develop a system for producing **valid, reliable** individual scores
> and to develop and implement common statewide performance
> standards of student achievement as a basis for reporting all test
> results and setting targets for improvement.

It sounded simple enough but it provided us with a classic model of
pseudo critical thinking in the educational establishment. The manner in
which it is structured provides a textbook case. By mirrors, illusion, and

---

*The result is that the most fundamental problem in
education today — that students are not learning to
reason well — is not only ignored, it is intensified.*

---

standard self-deception, it creates the appearance of substantial change
and reform. In fact, nothing is really being changed. The result is that the
most fundamental problem in education today — that students are not
learning to reason well — is not only ignored, it is intensified.

FRAGMENTATION AND VESTED INTERESTS

There are a number of reasons why it is unlikely that fundamental
reforms will be effected by state departments of education or that this critique, by itself, will bring about fundamental change. In the first place,
most of the positions within the state departments of education are for
specialists, for example, positions for those specializing in nutrition, for
those specializing in transportation, for those specializing in the laws
regarding education, for those specializing in learning disorders, for those
specializing in a and b and c and d and e and f and g. Virtually no one,
however, has a responsibility directly connected to the fundamental goals

of education (except possibly the director of instruction). Each specialist has his or her own special interest to focus on and a special group of stake-holders to represent.

When there is a need to develop an assessment instrument, like the one we examined of the California Department of Education, a large group of teachers and administrators from around the state are appointed. For example, there are 33 members of the CAP English-Language Arts committee. In addition to the main committee there is a supporting committee ("Reserve Team") consisting of 46 additional members. According to the California State Department: "These development team teachers have been responsible for shaping the test format, developing prompts for the assessment, and constructing scoring rubrics." (p. I-2)

Many political considerations go into the selection of the members of the development teams; most of the members, for example, are not scholars with publications that could be used as the basis of selection. There is an effort made to balance the committee by region, gender, race, and ethnicity. In addition, many members will have personal agendas to advance. There are usually three "Consultants/Advisors" selected from

---

The test becomes, then, both invalid and unreliable. In fact, it becomes a hot-bed of pseudo critical thinking, with a variety of misconceptions and flaws emerging. But while its intellectual value is low, its political value is high.

---

universities to bring in the over-arching theoretical framework. These consultants are usually the pipeline to the latest buzz words and to the theory behind them. The consultants concede to each other the right to get their favored terms into the language of the test materials.

The result of this process, as we have seen, is that the official "standards" embodied in the test become extraordinarily numerous. Many of them remain vague and ill-defined. Others take on a dangerous ambiguity. The diverse criteria and the open-ended nature of the directions combined with the ill-defined nature of the terms, opens the way to arbitrary and inconsistent grading of student responses. The test becomes, then, both invalid and unreliable. In fact, it becomes a hot-bed of pseudo critical thinking, with a variety of misconceptions and flaws emerging. But while its intellectual value is low, its political value is high. The various political interests around the state are served. The media has a simplistic event to cover. Parents can delight in the fact that the scores will go up. (How can they go down when anything can count as a good answer?) The politicians will gain because they can speak of their state as in the vanguard. And so it goes. A new pseudo reform is put in place and the educational bureaucracy grinds on until the next wave of public criticism requires it to generate a new and fresh illusion of change, a new catalogue of counterfeit, bogus, and superficial "reforms."

✦ So What Can We Do? Recommendations

There is a pressing need to develop networks of educators, parents, politicians, and business people who see the need for truly fundamental reform. That reform must be advanced simultaneously on many levels, for it is not going to result from action on one level alone. Because it must go to the roots of things, because it must be substantial, because it involves deep understandings, it must be incremental, evolutionary, and long-term. Everyone with the insight to see the problem comprehensively should act within the sphere of his or her greatest influence. There is a role for everyone concerned to exercise influence for the better: for parents, for public citizens, for business people, for civic leaders, for superintendents, for teachers, for college professors, and ... yes, even for those in state educational bureaucracies. Let us consider each briefly in turn.

WHAT CAN PARENTS DO?

Insightful parents can make the case for an emphasis on intellectual discipline and reasoning in the school curriculum. They can ask whether there is any long-term inservice in critical thinking and reasoning. They can ask what intellectual standards the students are being taught and how they are being taught them. They can make the case to other parents. They can write letters to the local papers. They can organize groups of parents who petition the school board. And most important they can develop a home environment in which the reasonability and intellectual discipline of their children is fostered, in which both they and their children routinely ask and give good reasons in support of their decisions and reason together about issues of importance not only to the family but to the broader society as well.

WHAT CAN CITIZENS DO?

Insightful public citizens can make the case for an emphasis on intellectual discipline and reasoning in the school curriculum in virtue of the need to develop voters who will help the country maintain a democratic form of government. They, too, can go to the local school board and ask whether there is any long-term inservice in critical thinking and reasoning. They, too, can make the case to parents and other citizens. They can contact civic groups. They can write letters to the local papers. They can organize groups of interested citizens to petition the school board.

WHAT CAN BUSINESS PEOPLE DO?

Insightful business people can use the respect that their success commands to exercise influence, alone or in concert with others, over educational decisions about what to teach and how to teach it. Since their success will be increasingly dependent upon their bringing critical thinking into the inner workings of their own businesses, on workers learning how to continually relearn and improve in their performances and in the systems they use, they will have ready access to models and paradigms that can be used to illuminate what should be happening in the classroom. Increasingly, cutting-edge businesses are moving away from an emphasis on hierarchy to an emphasis on group problem solving. Since critical thinking is essential to effective group problem solving, progressive business people will be able to talk intelligibly with educators and other citizens about how problem solving structures function in business and how parallel classroom problem solving groups might be set up. And, certainly, there are any number of civic groups that business people with insight might address on the problem of educational reform, putting emphasis, of course, on the missing foundation: the failure of teachers to learn how to think critically themselves and to teach for that thinking in their instruction, the failure to focus education, in other words, on "carefully-reasoned" problem solving. Finally, insightful business people can form alliances with insightful educators, to create symbiotic, reflective, mutually useful dialogues on what each group can learn from the other and how each can profit by working together.

WHAT CAN CIVIC LEADERS DO?

Insightful civic leaders can draw public attention to the need for intellectual discipline and reasoning in instruction. They can articulate publicly the key links to developing responsible citizens, moral persons, and workers on the cutting edge of development. They can use their access to a more public forum by focusing the discussion of educational reform on the historical problem of the educational bureaucracy and its tendency to generate pseudo reform. They can create a public awareness of the importance of reasoning, critical thinking, and problem solving. They can help organize civic groups. They can use their superior access to other persons of leadership and influence to facilitate significant pressure on the educational bureaucracies. They can make contact with insightful and responsible politicians who are in a position to facilitate appropriate legislation.

WHAT CAN SUPERINTENDENTS DO?

Insightful superintendents can make the case for an emphasis on intellectual discipline and reasoning in the school curriculum to the school board, administration members, teachers, and parents. They can ensure that there is long-term inservice in critical thinking and reasoning. They can ensure that students are being taught intellectual standards in depth. They can create incentives to teachers motivated to move in this direction. They can make the case to civic groups. Most importantly they can model reasonability and help create an atmosphere conducive to making the school a network of communities of inquiry.

WHAT CAN TEACHERS DO?

Insightful teachers can make the case for an emphasis on intellectual discipline and reasoning in the school curriculum. They can request and help design long-term inservice in critical thinking and reasoning. They can bring intellectual standards into the classroom. They can make the case to parents. They can work with other teachers to foster a school environment in which reasonability and intellectual discipline are accepted school norms. Most importantly, they can routinely ask for and give good reasons in the classroom. They can foster student reasoning in history, science, math, and so forth. They can ensure that students must regularly assess their own work using intellectual standards.

WHAT CAN COLLEGE PROFESSORS DO?

Insightful college professors can make the case for an emphasis on intellectual discipline and reasoning in the college curriculum. They can request and help design long-term faculty development in critical thinking and reasoning. They can bring intellectual standards into the classroom. They can do research on the significance of critical thinking and reasoning in their discipline. They can work with schools and departments of education to ensure that those studying to become teachers take classes that require reasoning and disciplined thought. They can articulate the need for prospective teachers to learn how to design assignments that require reasoning and critical thinking. Most importantly, they can routinely foster reasoning in their own classrooms and ensure that their students must regularly assess their own work using intellectual standards.

WHAT CAN THOSE IN STATE-WIDE BUREAUCRACIES DO?

Insightful members of state-wide bureaucracies (who recognize the systemic ways that educational bureaucracies have fostered pseudo reforms and constructed ill-designed assessments) can play a number of significant roles. They can inform themselves and others they work with of the fundamental changes that are being made in businesses adopting structures contrary to those of traditional bureaucratic organization. They can foster movement toward problem-solving teams. They can raise broader and deeper issues. They can recommend hiring people with broader vision and more developed reasoning abilities. They can help to work against narrow specialization. At the same time, they can argue for more appropriate use of experts, so that those who lack expertise in a subject will not become, for example, principal designers in tests or assessment instruments in that subject. They can argue for the construction of assessment instruments that assess reasoning in every subject area and so help to integrate emphases across subject areas.

CAVEAT

Doubtless you noticed my emphasis on "insightful" in characterizing those who can make important contributions to reform. It is important to underscore the problem of pseudo reform, which emerges when well-meaning persons use their intelligence inadvertently to re-duplicate an old problem in new form, creating the illusion of change. Many persons today are unwilling to think through the implications of accelerating change and intensifying complexity. Many are subconsciously wedded to rigid ideas and a static way of thinking. Many are taken in by their own platitudes and high-sounding words. These facts guarantee that a long struggle will be required to work through the superficial and work into the substantial.

✦ Final Conclusion

Pseudo critical thinking is more or less inevitable in the educational bureaucracies, given the way we have traditionally arranged and ordered things. This is illustrated, as we have seen, in the way the American educational establishment goes about designing assessment. Unfortunately, faulty assessment leads to faulty teaching, which leads to more faulty thinking in society, in business, in politics, and in everyday social life. The California Department of Education is a model case of American educational bureaucracy at work and the new California reading and writing assessment instrument is the typical resultant bad practice. Good thinking is now a fundamental human need. And though it will take generations to fully evolve from a society in which pseudo critical thinking is dominant to one in which sound, fairminded, ethically-informed reasoning is dominant, every step in that direction will reduce the amount of suffering and injustice that exists and increase, by degrees, human well being and quality of life. It is our intellectual and moral responsibility to make some contribution to this evolution. Though we are only at the beginnings of this evolution, the irresistible dynamic of accelerating change and intensifying complexity will eventually force it upon us. I hope we learn our lessons sooner rather than later, that the price of waste and unnecessary human misery may be as little as possible.

✦ References

All of the references in this chapter (unless otherwise noted) are from the *Samplers for English Language Arts Assessment,* for Elementary and High School, disseminated statewide in the Spring, 1993, by the California Department of Education.

Chapter 5

Critical Thinking:
Basic Questions and Answers

Abstract

In this interview for Think *magazine (April '92), Richard Paul provides a quick overview of critical thinking and the issues surrounding it: defining it, common mistakes in assessing it, its relation to communication skills, self-esteem, collaborative learning, motivation, curiosity, job skills for the future, national standards, and assessment strategies.*

Question: Critical thinking is essential to effective learning and productive living. Would you share your definition of critical thinking?

Paul: First, since critical thinking can be defined in a number of different ways consistent with each other, we should not put a lot of weight on any one definition. Definitions are at best scaffolding for the mind. With this qualification in mind, here is a bit of scaffolding: critical thinking is thinking about your thinking while you're thinking in order to make your thinking better. Two things are crucial: *1)* critical thinking is not just thinking, but thinking which entails self-improvement and *2)* this improvement comes from skill in using standards by which one appropriately assesses thinking. To put it briefly, it is self-improvement (in thinking) through standards (that assess thinking).

To think well is to impose discipline and restraint on our thinking — by means of intellectual standards — in order to raise our thinking to a level of "perfection" or quality that is not natural or likely in undisciplined, spontaneous thought. The dimension of critical thinking least understood is that of intellectual standards. Most teachers were not taught how to assess thinking through standards; indeed, often the thinking of teachers themselves is very "undisciplined" and reflects a lack of internalized intellectual standards.

Question: Could you give me an example?

Paul: Certainly, one of the most important distinctions that teachers need to routinely make, and which takes disciplined thinking to make, is that between reasoning and subjective reaction. If we are try-ing to foster quality thinking, we don't want students simply to assert things; we want them to try to reason things out on the basis of evi-dence and good reasons. Often, teachers are unclear about this basic difference. Many teachers are apt to take student writing or speech which is fluent and witty or glib and amusing as good thinking. They are often unclear about the constituents of good reasoning. Hence, even though a student may just be asserting things, not reasoning things out at all, if she is doing so with vivacity and flamboyance, teachers are apt to take this to be equivalent to good reasoning. This was made clear in a recent California state-wide writing assessment in which teachers and testers applauded a student essay, which they said illustrated "exceptional achievement" in reasoned evaluation, an essay that contained no reasoning at all, that was nothing more than one subjective reaction after another.

The assessing teachers and testers did not notice that the student failed to respond to the directions, did not support his judgment with rea-sons and evidence, did not consider possible criteria on which to base his judgment, did not analyze the subject in the light of the criteria, and did not select evidence that clearly supported his judgment. Instead the student *1)* described an emotional exchange, *2)* asserted — without evidence — some questionable claims, and *3)* expressed a vari-ety of subjective preferences. The assessing teachers were apparently not clear enough about the nature of evaluative reasoning or the basic notions of criteria, evidence, reasons, and well-supported judgment to notice the discrepancy. The result was, by the way, that a flagrantly mis-graded student essay was showcased nationally (in ASCD's *Devel-oping Minds*), systematically misleading the 150,000 or so teachers who read the publication.

Question: Could this possibly be a rare mistake, not representative of teacher knowledge?

Paul: I don't think so. Let me suggest a way in which you could begin to test my contention. If you are familiar with any thinking skills programs, ask someone knowledgeable about it the "Where's the beef?" question, namely, "What intellectual standards does the program artic-ulate and teach?" I think you will first find that the person is puzzled about what you mean. And then when you explain what you mean, I think you will find that the person is not able to articulate any such standards. Thinking skills programs without intellectual standards are tailor-made for mis-instruction. For example, one of the major pro-grams asks teachers to encourage students to make inferences and use analogies, but is silent about how to teach students to assess the infer-ences they make and the strengths and weaknesses of the analogies they use. This misses the point. The idea is not to help students to make *more* inferences but to make *sound* ones, not to help students to come up with *more* analogies but with more *useful* and *insightful* ones.

Question: What is the solution to this problem? How, as a practical matter, can we solve it?

Paul: Well, not with more gimmicks or quick-fixes. Not with more fluff for teachers. Only with quality long-term staff development that helps the teachers, over an extended period of time, over years not months, to work on their own thinking and come to terms with what intellectual standards are, why they are essential, and how to teach for them. The city of Greensboro, North Carolina has just such a long-term, quality, critical thinking program. So that's one model your readers might look at. In addition, there is a new national organization, the National Council for Excellence in Critical Thinking Instruction, that is focused precisely on the articulation of standards for thinking, not just in general, but for every academic subject area. It is now setting up research-based committees and regional offices to disseminate its recommendations. I am hopeful that eventually, through efforts such as these, we can move from the superficial to the substantial in fostering quality student thinking. The present level of instruction for thinking is very low indeed.

Question: But there are many areas of concern in instruction, not just one, not just critical thinking, but communication skills, problem solving, creative thinking, collaborative learning, self-esteem, and so forth. How are districts to deal with the full array of needs? How are they to do all of these rather than simply one, no matter how important that one may be?

Paul: This is the key. Everything essential to education supports everything else essential to education. It is only when good things in education are viewed superficially and wrongly that they seem disconnected, a bunch of separate goals, a conglomeration of separate problems, like so many bee-bees in a bag. In fact, any well-conceived program in critical thinking requires the integration of all of the skills and abilities you mentioned above. Hence, critical thinking is not a set of skills separable from excellence in communication, problem solving, creative thinking, or collaborative learning, nor is it indifferent to one's sense of self-worth.

Question: Could you explain briefly why this is so?

Paul: Consider critical thinking first. We think critically when we have at least one problem to solve. One is not doing good critical thinking, therefore, if one is not solving any problems. If there is no problem there is no point in thinking critically. The "opposite" is also true. Uncritical problem solving is unintelligible. There is no way to effectively solve problems unless one thinks critically about the nature of the problems and of how to go about solving them. Thinking our way through a problem to a solution, then, is critical thinking, not something else. Furthermore, critical thinking, because it involves our working out afresh our own thinking on a subject, and because our own thinking is always a unique product of our self-structured experience, ideas, and reasoning, is intrinsically a new "creation", a new "making", a new set of cognitive and affective structures of some kind. All thinking, in short, is a creation of the mind's work, and when it is disciplined so as to be well-integrated into our experience, it is a new creation precisely because of the inevitable novelty of that integration. And when it helps us to solve problems that we could not solve before, it is surely properly called "creative".

The "making" and the "testing of that making" are intimately interconnected. In critical thinking we make and shape ideas and experiences so that they may be used to structure and solve problems, frame decisions, and, as the case may be, effectively communicate with others. The making, shaping, testing, structuring, solving, and communicating are not different activities of a fragmented mind but the same seamless whole viewed from different perspectives.

Question: How do communication skills fit in?

Paul: Some communication is surface communication, trivial communication — surface and trivial communication don't really require education. All of us can engage in small talk, can share gossip. And we don't require any intricate skills to do that fairly well. Where communication becomes part of our educational goal is in reading, writing, speaking and listening. These are the four modalities of communication which are essential to education and each of them is a mode of reasoning. Each of them involves problems. Each of them is shot through with critical thinking needs. Take the apparently simple matter of reading a book worth reading. The author has developed her thinking in the book, has taken some ideas and in some way represented those ideas in extended form. Our job as a reader is to translate the meaning of the author into meanings that we can understand. This is a complicated process requiring critical thinking every step along the way. What is the purpose for the book? What is the author trying to accomplish? What issues or problems are raised? What data, what experiences, what evidence are given? What concepts are used to organize this data, these experiences? How is the author thinking about the world? Is her thinking justified as far as we can see from our perspective? And how does she justify it from her perspective? How can we enter her perspective to appreciate what she has to say? All of these are the kinds of questions that a critical reader raises. And a critical reader in this sense is simply someone trying to come to terms with the text.

So if one is an uncritical reader, writer, speaker, or listener, one is not a good reader, writer, speaker, or listener at all. To do any of these well is to think critically while doing so and, at one and the same time, to solve specific problems of communication, hence to effectively communicate. Communication, in short, is always a transaction between at least two logics. In reading, as I have said, there is the logic of the thinking of the author and the logic of the thinking of the reader. The critical reader reconstructs (and so translates) the logic of the writer into the logic of the reader's thinking and experience. This entails disciplined intellectual work. The end result is a new creation; the writer's thinking for the first time now exists within the reader's mind. No mean feat!

Question: And self esteem? How does it fit in?

Paul: Healthy self-esteem emerges from a justified sense of self-worth, just as self-worth emerges from competence, ability, and genuine success. If one simply feels good about oneself for no good reason, then one is either arrogant (which is surely not desirable), or, alternatively, has a dangerous sense of misplaced confidence. Teenagers, for example, sometimes think so well of themselves that they operate under the illusion that they can safely drive while drunk or safely take drugs. They often feel much too highly of their own competence and powers and are much too unaware of their limitations. To accurately sort out genuine self-worth from a false sense of self-esteem requires, yes you guessed it, critical thinking.

Question: And finally, what about collaborative learning? How does it fit in?

Paul: Collaborative learning is desirable only if grounded in disciplined critical thinking. Without critical thinking, collaborative learning is likely to become collaborative mis-learning. It is collective bad thinking in which the bad thinking being shared becomes validated. Remember, gossip is a form of collaborative learning; peer group indoctrination is a form of collaborative learning; mass hysteria is a form of speed collaborative learning (mass learning of a most undesirable kind). We learn prejudices collaboratively, social hates and fears collaboratively, stereotypes and narrowness of mind, collaboratively. If we don't put disciplined critical thinking into the heart and soul of the collaboration, we get the mode of collaboration which is antithetical to education, knowledge, and insight.

So there are a lot of important educational goals deeply tied into critical thinking just as critical thinking is deeply tied into them. Basically the problem in the schools is that we separate things, treat them in isolation and mistreat them as a result. We end up with a superficial representation, then, of each of the individual things that is essential to education, rather than seeing how each important good thing helps inform all the others.

Question: One important aim of schooling should be to create a climate that evokes children's sense of wonder and inspires their imagination to soar. What can teachers do to "kindle" this spark and keep it alive in education?

Paul: First of all, we kill the child's curiosity, her desire to question deeply, by superficial didactic instruction. Young children continually ask why. Why this and why that? And why this other thing? But we soon shut that curiosity down with glib answers, answers to fend off rather than respond to the logic of the question. In every field of knowledge, every answer generates more questions, so that the more we know the more we recognize we don't know. It is only people who have little knowledge who take their knowledge to be complete and entire. If we thought deeply about almost any of the answers which we glibly give to children, we would recognize that we don't really have a satisfactory answer to most of their questions. Many of our answers are no more than a repetition of what we as children heard from adults. We pass on the misconceptions of our parents and those of their parents. We say what we heard, not what we know. We rarely join the quest with our children. We rarely admit our ignorance, even to ourselves. Why does rain fall from the sky? Why is snow cold? What is electricity and how does it go through the wire? Why are people bad? Why does evil exist? Why is there war? Why did my dog have to die? Why do flowers bloom? Do we really have good answers to these questions?

Question: How does curiosity fit in with critical thinking?

Paul: To flourish, curiosity must evolve into disciplined inquiry and reflection. Left to itself it will soar like a kite without a tail, that is, right into the ground! Intellectual curiosity is an important trait of mind, but it requires a family of other traits to fulfill it. It requires intellectual humility, intellectual courage, intellectual integrity, intellectual perseverance, and faith in reason. After all, intellectual curiosity is not a thing in itself — valuable in itself and for itself. It is valuable because it can lead to knowledge, understanding, and insight, because it can help broaden, deepen, sharpen our minds, making us better, more humane, more richly endowed persons. To reach these ends, the mind must be more than curious, it must be willing to work, willing to suffer through confusion and frustration, willing to face limitations and overcome obstacles, open to the views of others, and willing to entertain ideas that many people find threatening. That is, there is no point in our trying to model and encourage curiosity, if we are not willing to foster an environment in which the minds of our students can learn the value and pain of hard intellectual work. We do our students a disservice if we imply that all we need is unbridled curiosity, that with it alone knowledge comes to us with blissful ease in an atmosphere of fun, fun, fun. What good is curiosity if we don't know what to do next, how to satisfy it? We can create the environment necessary to the discipline, power, joy, and work of critical thinking only by modeling it before and with our students. They must see our minds at work. Our minds must stimulate theirs' with questions and yet further question, questions that probe information and experience, questions that call for reasons and evidence, questions that lead students to examine interpretations and conclusions, pursuing their basis in fact and experience, questions that help students to discover their assumptions, questions that stimulate students to follow out the implications of their thought, to test their ideas, to take their ideas apart, to challenge their ideas, to take their ideas seriously. It is in the totality of this intellectually rigorous atmosphere that natural curiosity thrives.

Question: It is important for our students to be productive members of the work-force. How can schools better prepare students to meet these challenges?

Paul: The fundamental characteristic of the world students now enter is ever-accelerating change, a world in which information is multiplying even as it is swiftly becoming obsolete and out of date, a world in which ideas are continually restructured, retested, and rethought, where one cannot survive with simply one way of thinking, where one must continually adapt one's thinking to the thinking of others, where one must respect the need for accuracy and precision and meticulousness, a world in which job skills must continually be upgraded and perfected — even transformed. We have never had to face such a world before. Education has never before had to prepare students for such dynamic flux, unpredictability, and complexity, for such ferment, tumult, and disarray. We as educators are now on the firing line. Are we willing to fundamentally rethink our methods of teaching? Are we ready for the 21st Century? Are we willing to learn new concepts and ideas? Are we willing to learn a new sense of discipline as we teach it to our students? Are we willing to bring new rigor to our own thinking in order to help our students bring that same rigor to theirs? Are we willing, in short, to become critical thinkers so that we might be an example of what our students must internalize and become?

These are profound challenges to the profession. They call upon us to do what no previous generation of teachers was ever called upon to do. Those of us willing to pay the price will yet have to teach side by side with teachers unwilling to pay the price. This will make our job even more difficult, but not less exciting, not less important, not less rewarding. Critical thinking is the heart of well-conceived educational reform and restructuring because it is at the heart of the changes of the 21st Century. Let us hope that enough of us will have the fortitude and vision to grasp this reality and transform our lives and our schools accordingly.

Question: National Standards will result in national accountability. What is your vision for the future?

Paul: Most of the national assessment we have done thus far is based on lower-order learning and thinking. It has focused on what might be called surface knowledge. It has rewarded the kind of thinking that lends itself to multiple choice machine-graded assessment. We now recognize that the assessment of the future must focus on higher – not lower – order thinking, that it must assess more reasoning than recall, that it must assess authentic performances, students engaged in bona fide intellectual work.

Our problem is in designing and implementing such assessment. In November of this last year, Gerald Nosich and I developed and presented, at the request of the U.S. Department of Education, a model for the national assessment of higher order thinking. At a follow-up meeting of critical thinking, problem-solving, communication, and testing scholars and practitioners, it was almost unanimously agreed that it is possible to assess higher-order thinking on a national scale. It was clear from the commitments of the Departments of Education, Labor, and Commerce that such an assessment is in the cards. [See figure 1, "Today's and Tomorrow's Schools".]

Today's and Tomorrow's Schools

Schools of Today	Schools of Tomorrow
• Focus on development of basic skills	• Focus on development of thinking skills
• Testing separate from teaching	• Assessment integral to teaching
• Students work as individuals	• Cooperative problem solving
• Hierarchically sequenced — basics before higher order	• Skills learned in context of real problems
• Supervision by administration	• Learner-centered, teacher-directed
• Elite students learn to think	• All students learn to think

figure 1   From "What Work Requires of Schools" *A Scans Report for America 2000,* The Secretary's Commission on Achieving Necessary Skills, U.S. Department of Labor, June 1991

The fact is we must have standards and assessment strategies for higher-order thinking for a number of reasons. First, assessment and accountability are here to stay. The public will not accept less. Second, what is not assessed is not, on the whole, taught. Third, what is mis-assessed is mis-taught. Fourth, higher-order thinking, critical thinking abilities, are increasingly crucial to success in every domain of personal and professional life. Fifth, critical thinking research is making the cultivation and assessment of higher-order thinking do-able.

The road will not be easy, but if we take the knowledge, understanding, and insights we have gained about critical thinking over the last twelve years, there is much that we could do in assessment that we haven't yet done — at the level of the individual classroom teacher, at the level of the school system, at the level of the state, and at the national level. Of course we want to do this in such a way as not to commit the "Harvard Fallacy", the mistaken notion that because graduates from Harvard are very successful, that the teaching at Harvard necessarily had something to do with it. It may be that the best prepared and well-connected students coming out of high school are going to end up as the best who graduate from college, no matter what college they attend. We need to focus our assessment, in other words, on how much value has been added by an institution. We need to know where students stood at the beginning, to assess the instruction they received on their way from the beginning to the end. We need pre- and post-testing and assessment in order to see which schools, which institutions, which districts are really adding value, and *significant* value, to the quality of thinking and learning of their students.

Finally, we have to realize that we already have instruments available for assessing what might be called the fine-textured micro-skills of critical thinking. We already know how to design prompts that test students' ability to: identify a plausible statement of a writer's purpose; distinguish clearly between purposes, inferences, assumptions, and consequences; discuss reasonably the merits of different versions of a problem or question; decide the most reasonable statement of an author's point of view; recognize bias, narrowness, and contradictions in the point of view of an excerpt; distinguish evidence from conclusions based on that evidence; give evidence to back up their positions in an essay; recognize conclusions that go beyond the evidence; distinguish central from peripheral concepts; identify crucial implications of a passage; evaluate an author's inferences; draw reasonable inferences from positions stated; and so on.

With respect to intellectual standards, we are quite able to design prompts that require students to: recognize clarity in contrast to unclarity; distinguish accurate from inaccurate accounts; decide when a statement is relevant or irrelevant to a given point; identify inconsistent positions as well as consistent ones; discriminate deep, complete, and significant accounts from those that are superficial, fragmentary, and trivial; evaluate responses with respect to their fairness; distinguish well-evidenced accounts from those unsupported by reasons and evidence; tell good reasons from bad.

With respect to large scale essay assessment we know enough now about random sampling to be able to require extended reasoning and writing without having to pay for the individual assessment of millions of essays.

What remains is to put what we know into action: at the school and district level to facilitate long-term teacher development around higher-order thinking, at the state and national level to provide for long-term assessment of district, state, and national performance. The project will take generations and perhaps in some sense will never end. After all, when will we have developed our thinking far enough, when will we have enough intellectual integrity, enough intellectual courage, enough intellectual perseverance, enough intellectual skill and ability, enough fairmindedness, enough reasonability? One thing is painfully clear. We already have more than enough rote memorization and uninspired didactic teaching, more than enough passivity and indifference, cynicism and defeatism, complacency and ineptness. The ball is in our court. Let's take up the challenge together and make, with our students, a new and better world.

Chapter 6

The Logic of
Creative and Critical Thinking

Abstract

In this paper Richard Paul develops an extended explication of the relation-ship between creative and critical thinking. He does so by first setting out the relationship in general, arguing that both are perfections of thought which are, in fact, inseparable in everyday reasoning. "Creativity", according to Paul, masters a process of "making" or "producing", "criticality" a process of "assessing" or "judging". He then argues that insofar as the mind — in thinking — is thinking well, it must, virtually simultaneously, both produce and assess, make and judge that making.

Having set out this relationship in general, Paul works out the details with respect to a series of theoretically basic structures and processes: 1) thinking through the logic of things, 2) taking command of reasoning and logic, 3) making fundamental assumptions about learning and knowing, 4) understanding the logic of concepts, 5) understanding the logic of academic disciplines, 6) the logic of language, 7) the logic of questions, 8) the logic of student thinking, 9) the logic of teaching, 10) the logic of reading, writing, speaking, and listening, and 11) the logic of logic. Throughout, the underlying theme of the paper is sustained: that intellectual discipline and rigor are not only quite at home with originality and productivity but that both so-called "poles" of thinking are really inseparable aspects of excellence of thought.

Beyond exploring the relation of creativity and criticality, this paper is one of the best in the collection for giving the reader a unified sense of the importance to critical thinking of the concept, "the logic of..." On Paul's analysis, this concept is indispensable and, if one reads with a sensitivity to it, one will find that it plays a role in virtually everything he writes.

✦ Introduction

C reative and critical thinking often seem to the untutored to be polar opposite forms of thought, the first based on irrational or unconscious forces, the second on rational and conscious processes, the first undirectable and unteachable, the second directable and teachable. There is some, but very little, truth in this view. The truth in it is that there is no way to generate creative geniuses, nor to get students to gen-

101

erate highly novel ground-breaking ideas, by some known process of systematic instruction. The dimension of "creativity", in other words, contains unknowns, even mysteries. So does "criticality" of course. Yet there are ways to teach simultaneously for both creative and critical thinking in a down-to-earth sense of those terms. To do so, however, requires that we focus on these terms in practical everyday contexts, that we keep their central meanings in mind, and that we seek insight into the respect in which they overlap and feed into each other, the respect in which they are inseparable, integrated, and unitary. This paper will develop these insights.

OVERVIEW

Good thinking is thinking that does the job we set for it. It is thinking that accomplishes the purposes of thinking. If thinking lacks a purpose, that is, is aimless, it may chance upon something of value to the thinker, but more often it will simply wander into an endless stream of unanalyzed associations from one's unanalyzed past: "hotdogs remind me of ball games, ball games remind me of Chicago, Chicago of my old neighborhood, my old neighborhood of my grandmother, of her pies, of having to eat what I didn't like, which reminds me ... which reminds me ... which reminds me...." Few people need training in aimless thinking such as this, or in daydreaming or fantasizing. For the most part we are "naturals" at aimless thinking.

Where we have trouble is in purposeful thinking, especially purposeful thinking that involves figuring things out, thinking, in other words, that poses problems to be solved and intricacies to reason through. "Criticality" and "creativity" have an intimate relationship to the ability to figure things out. There is a natural marriage between them. Indeed, all thinking that is properly called "excellent" combines these two dimensions in an intimate way. Whenever our thinking excels, it excels because we succeed in designing or engendering, fashioning or originating, creating or producing results and outcomes appropriate to our ends in thinking. It has, in a word, a *creative* dimension.

But to achieve any challenging end, we must also have *criteria*: gauges, measures, models, principles, standards, or tests to use in judging whether we are approaching that end. What is more, we must apply our criteria (models, gauges, measures, models, principles) in a way that is discerning, discriminating, exact, fastidious, judicious, and acute. We must continually monitor and assess how our thinking is going, whether it is plausibly on the right track, whether it is sufficiently clear, accurate, precise, consistent, relevant, deep, or broad for our purposes.

We don't achieve excellence in thinking with no end in view. We don't design for no reason, fashion and create without knowing what we are trying to fashion and create. We don't originate and produce with no sense of why we are doing so. Thinking that is random, thinking that roams aimlessly through half-formed images, that meanders without an organizing goal is not a candidate for either "creativity" or "criticality". It is not a candidate for excellence.

Why? When the mind thinks aimlessly, its energy and drive are typically low, its tendency is commonly toward inertness, its results usually barren. What is aimless is also normally pointless and moves in familiar alliance with indolence and dormancy. But when thinking takes on a challenging task, the mind must then come alive, ready itself for intellectual labor, engage the intellect in some form of work upon some intellectual object — until such time as it succeeds in originating, formulating, designing, engendering, creating, or producing what is necessary for the achievement of its goal. Intellectual work is essential to *create* intellectual products, and that work, that production, involves intellectual standards *judiciously* applied, ... in other words, creativity and criticality interwoven into one seamless fabric.

Like the body, the mind has its own form of fitness or excellence. Like the body, that fitness is caused by and reflected in activities done in accordance with standards (criticality). A fit mind can successfully engage in the designing, fashioning, formulating, originating, or producing of intellectual products worthy of its challenging ends. To achieve this fitness, the mind must learn to take charge of itself, to energize itself, press forward when difficulties emerge, proceed slowly and methodically when meticulousness is necessary, immerse itself in a task, become attentive, reflective, and engrossed, circle back on a train of thought, recheck to ensure that it has been thorough, accurate, exact, and deep enough.

Its generativeness and its judiciousness can only be artificially separated. In the process of actual thought they are one. Such thought is systematic when being systematic serves its end. It can also cast system aside and ransack its intuitions for a lead — when no clear maneuver, plan, strategy, or tactic comes to mind. Nor is the generative, the productive, the creative mind without standards for what it generates and produces. It is not a mind lacking judiciousness, discernment, and judgment. It is not a mind incapable of acuteness and exactness. It is not a mind whose standards are unclarity, imprecision, inaccuracy, irrelevance, triviality, inconsistency, superficiality, and narrowness. The fit mind generates and produces precisely because it has high standards for itself, because it cares about how and what it creates.

Serious thinking originates in a commitment to grasp some truth, to get to the bottom of something, to make accurate sense of that about which it is thinking. This "figuring out" cannot simply be a matter of arbitrary creation or production. There must be specific restraints and requirements to be met, something outside the will to which the will must be bent, some unyielding objectivity we must painstakingly take into account and neither ignore nor thrust aside. It is exactly the severe, inflexible, stern fact of reality that forces intellectual criticality and productivity into one seamless whole. If there were no "objectivity" outside our process of "figuring out", then we would have literally nothing to figure out. If what we figure out can be anything we want it to be, anything we fantasize it as being, then there is no logic to the expression "figure out".

In a sense, of course, all minds create and produce in a manner reflective of their fitness or lack thereof. Minds indifferent to standards and disciplined judgment tend to judge inexactly, inaccurately, inappropriately, prejudicially. Prejudices, hate, irrational jealousies and fears, stereotypes and misconceptions — these too are "created", "produced", "originated" by minds. Without minds to produce them, they would not exist. Yet they are not the products of "creative" minds. They reflect an undisciplined, an uncritical mode of thinking and therefore are not properly thought of as products of "creativity". In short, except in rare circumstances, creativity presupposes criticality and criticality creativity. This is the essential insight behind this paper.

In what follows, therefore, we shall explore the intimate connection between a well-grounded sense of creativity in thinking, the sense of thinking as a *making*, as a process of *creating* thought, as a process that *brings thoughts into being* to organize, shape, interpret, and make sense of our world — thinking that, once developed, enables us to achieve goals, accomplish purposes, solve problems, and settle important issues we face as humans in a world in which rapid change is becoming the only constant. This sense of *thought as a creative making* is the most important sense of creativity, pedagogically speaking, and cannot be understood, as I have briefly argued, separate from understanding the development of "critical judgment" and a critical mind. When a mind does not systematically and effectively embody intellectual criteria and standards, is not disciplined in reasoning things through, in figuring out the logic of things, in reflectively devising a rational approach to the solution of problems or in the accomplishment of intellectual or practical tasks, that mind is not "creative". In this sense, there is a reciprocal logic to both intellectual creation and critical judgment, to the intellectual "making" of things and to the on-going "critique" of that making. Let us examine that reciprocal logic more closely.

✦ Thinking That Grasps the Logic of Things

All intellectual products, in order to be intellectually assessed and validated, require some logic, some order or coherence, some intellectual structure that makes sense and is rationally defensible. This is true whether one is talking of poems or essays, paintings or choreographed dances, histories or anthropological reports, experiments or scientific theories, philosophies or psychologies, accounts of particular events or those of general phenomena or laws. A product of intellectual work that makes no sense, that cannot be rationally analyzed and assessed, that cannot be incorporated into other intellectual work, or used — and hence that cannot play a role in any academic tradition or discipline — is unintelligible. Whether we are designing a new screw driver, figuring out how to deal with our children's misbehavior, or working out a perspective on religion, we must order our meanings into a system of meanings that make sense to us, and so, in that respect, have a logic.

This is to say that there is an important role for reason and reasoning, for constructing and working within a logic, for creative producing and critical assessing of what is produced, in every intellectual enterprise. Let us now explore that role in brief.

WHAT IS REASONING? WHAT IS LOGIC?

The words 'reasoning' and 'logic' each have both a narrow and a broad use. In the narrow sense, 'reasoning' is drawing conclusions on the basis of reasons, and, in the narrow sense, 'logic' refers simply to the principles that apply to the assessment of that process. But in the broad sense, 'reason' and 'reasoning' refer to the total process of figuring things out, and hence to every intellectual standard relevant to doing that. And parallel to this sense is a broad sense of 'logic' which refers to the basic structure that one is, in fact, figuring out (when engaged in reasoning something through).

One can draw conclusions about poems, microbes, numbers, historical events, languages, social settings, psychological fears, everyday situations, character traits — indeed, about anything whatsoever. And this drawing of conclusions is part of a broader process of reasoning things through. The particular inferences made have a specific logic that can be assessed and the total process of reasoning things through has a general logic that also can be assessed. In this broad sense of 'logic', one focuses on the logic of the poem or the logic of a microbe or the logic of numbers or the logic of a historical event or the logic of a language, and so forth. In the narrow sense, one focuses on the logic of this or that inference within a given poem or about a given microbe or within some train of mathematical thought. Hence, Sherlock Holmes tries to figure out the logic of the murder by making a number of specific inferences from the available evidence. The broader logic contains the narrower logic.

IN THE BROAD SENSE, WHAT MAKES GOOD REASONING GOOD REASONING?

Becoming adept at drawing justifiable conclusions on the basis of good reasons is more complex than it appears. This is because drawing a conclusion is always the tip of an intellectual iceberg. It is not just a matter of avoiding a fallacy in logic (in the narrow sense). There is much more that is implicit in reasoning than is explicit, there are more components, more "logical structures" that we do not express than those we do. To become skilled in reasoning things through we must become practiced in making what is implicit explicit so that we can "check out" what is going on "beneath the surface" of our thought.

Thus, when we draw a conclusion, we do so in some circumstances, making inferences (that have implications and consequences) based on some reasons or information (and assumptions), using some concepts, in trying to settle some question (or solve some problem) for some purpose within some point of view.

Good reasoners can consider and plausibly assess any of these elements as they function in their thought in any act of reasoning something out. Good reasoners therefore use good logic in both the narrow and the broad sense. Furthermore, in most circumstances in which we are *using* logic we are *creating* it simultaneously. This needs explanation.

✦ Whenever We Are Reasoning Something Through We Are Ipso Facto Engaged in Creative Thinking

In the broad sense, all reasoned thinking is thinking within a logic, and when we have not yet learned a given logic — e.g., not yet learned the logic of the internal combustion engine, the logic of right triangles, or the logic of dolphin behavior — our minds must bring that logic into being, create it in the fabric, within the structure, of our established ways of thinking. Hence, when we are thinking something through for the first time, to some extent, we create the logic we are using. We bring into being new articulations of our purposes and of our reasons. We make new assumptions. We form new concepts. We ask new questions. We make new inferences. Our point of view is worked out in a new direction, one in which it has never been worked out before.

Indeed, there is a sense in which all reasoned thinking, all genuine acts of figuring out anything whatsoever, even something previously figured out, is a new "making", a new series of creative acts, for we rarely recall our previous thought whole cloth. Instead we generally remember only some part of what we figured out and figure out the rest anew, based on the logic of that part and other logical structures more immediately available to us. We continually create new understandings and re-create old understandings by a similar process of figuring.

In what follows, I will articulate a frame of reference that highlights the intimate interplay between creative and critical thinking, between the thinking that creates a set of logically interrelated meanings and the thinking that assesses the logic being created. I will begin with a basic assumption that underlies the model being developed. The theme that shall run throughout is as follows:

In all contexts that demand the reasoned figuring out of something, there are, as it were, *three logics* involved: *1)* the logic to be figured out (the logic it is our aim to create), *2)* the logic we use to do the figuring (chosen by us from the logics we have already learned), and *3)* the logic that results, in the end, from our reasoning (and which needs to be assessed for its "fit", for the degree to which it has captured the logic to be figured out). For example, I may use my understanding of the logic of one D.H. Lawrence novel (say, *Sons and Lovers*) as an initial framework for understanding the logic of another (say, *Lady Chatterley's Lover*). The understanding I end up with may or may not fully make sense of the actual story. The logic I make of it may be inadequate. Or again, in studying history, I may use my understanding of the logic of one economic crisis (say that of the thirties in the USA) to understand another one (say that of the nineties in the USA). The reconstruction I come up with may or may not make sense of the logic of what was actually going on economically in the nineties. In all our learning we must seek out provisional models (mini logical systems) for figuring out what we are trying to learn (the system we are trying to grasp). We then end up with a product of thought, a system we create. That system may or may not be adequate to the task.

A Basic Assumption

In all of our behavior we assume there is order, regularity, and potential intelligibility in everything; that every portion of "reality" can sooner or later be figured out, explained, and related to other portions; that our innate capacity to form conceptions of, and make inferences about, ourselves and the things around us is adequate for our purposes. This basic assumption implies that in some sense there is a discoverable logic to each dimension of reality. Of course, in making this assumption, we need not also assume that what we discover about the logic of things, from our various concepts and inferences, is some form of "Absolute Truth", nor that our knowledge of things exhausts, completely spells out, or totally captures the ultimate nature of things, or even that things have an "ultimate" nature. For one thing, our knowledge is always limited by the perspectives that are inherent in our various ways of forming concepts and making inferences. We are limited, not infinite, creatures; humans, not gods.

✦ The Logic of ...

To say that something has a logic, then, is to say that it can be understood by use of our reason, that we can form concepts that accurately — though not necessarily thoroughly — characterize the nature of that thing. Only when we have conceptualized a thing in some way, and only then, can we reason through it. Since nature does not tell us how to conceptualize it, we must create that conceptualization, individually or socially. Once conceptualized, a thing is integrated by us into a network of ideas (since no concept ever stands alone) and, as such, becomes the subject of many possible inferences.

Furthermore, once we begin to make inferences about something, we can do so either well or poorly, justifiably or unjustifiably, in keeping with the meaning of the concept and the nature of what we know of the thing conceptualized, or not so in keeping. If we are not careful, for example, we may (and very often do) infer more than is implied. If I hear a sound at the door and conceptualize it as "scratching at the door", I may then infer that it is my dog wanting to come in. I have used my reason (my capacity to conceptualize and infer) to interpret the noise as a "scratch" and I have assumed, in the process, that the only creature in the vicinity who could be making that scratch at my door is my dog... my reasoning may be off. I may have mis-conceptualized the noise as a "scratch" (I may even have misheard where the noise is coming from) or I may have wrongly assumed that there are no other creatures around who might make it. Notice that in these acts, I create the conceptualizations that are at the root of my thinking.

We approach virtually everything in our experience as something that can be thus "decoded" by the power of our minds to create a conceptualization and to make inferences on the basis of it (hence to create further conceptualizations). We do this so routinely and automatically that we don't typically recognize ourselves as engaged in processes of reasoned creation. In our everyday life we don't first experience the world in "concept-less" form and then deliberately place what we experience into categories in order to make sense of things.

Rather, it is as if things are given to us with their "names" inherent in them. So we see "trees", "clouds", "grass", "roads", "people", "men", "women", and so on. We apply these concepts intuitively, as if no rational, creative act were involved. Yet, if we think about it, we will realize that there was a time when we had to learn names for things and hence, before we knew those names, we couldn't possibly have seen these phenomena through the mediation of these concepts. In learning these concepts we had to create them in our own minds out of the concepts we already had learned.

I want to highlight the importance of this power of creative conceptualization and inference in human life, for it is precisely this power of mind that we must take charge of in forming disciplined habits of thought, thought which we summarize with the expression 'thinking critically'. In thinking critically we take command of our conceptual creations, assessing them more explicitly than is normally done. Concepts, like all human creations, can be well or poorly designed. Critical judgment is always relevant to the process of design and construction, whether that construction be conceptual or material.

For example, we study living organisms to construct "bio-logic", that is, to establish ways to conceptualize and make valid inferences about life forms. We study social arrangements to construct "socio-logic", that is, to establish ways to conceptualize and make valid inferences about life in society. We study the historical past to construct "the logic of history", ways to conceptualize and make valid inferences about the past. Since no one is born with these logical structures at his or her command, everyone must "create" them.

THE LOGIC OF CONCEPTS

In this paper, we are using the word 'concept' to mean simply "a generalized idea of a class of things". We understand "conceptualization" to be a process by which the mind infers a thing to be of a certain kind, to belong properly to some given class of things. Hence, if I call something, or interpret something to be, an apple, I have placed it into a generalized class of things (the class of all apples). Our minds understand any particular aspect of things in relation to generalized ideas that highlight perceived similarities and differences in our experience. For example, the word 'dog' represents one concept, the word 'cat' another, the word 'cloud' a third, the word 'laughter' a fourth. We reason about, and so interpret the world, by putting the objects of our experience into "categories" or "concepts" each one of which highlights some set of similarities or differences for us, links the thing up with other concepts, and validates a certain set of inferences. For example, if I see a creature before me and take it to be a dog — that is, if I place it mentally into the category of 'dog' — I can reasonably infer that it will bark rather than meow or purr. Of course, I cannot reasonably infer that it will not bite me if I attempt to chase it away. Furthermore, by placing something into the concept of 'dog' I locate the thing in relation to other concepts, such as 'animal', 'furry', 'muzzle', 'paw', 'tail', and so forth.

In learning to speak our native language, we learn thousands of concepts which, when properly used, enable us to make countless legitimate inferences about the objects of our experience. Unfortunately, there is nothing in the way we ordinarily learn to speak a language that forces us to use concepts carefully or that prevents us from making unjustifiable inferences while engaged in their use. Indeed, a fundamental need for critical thinking is given by the fact that as long as the mind remains undisciplined in its use of concepts, it is susceptible to any number of illegitimate inferences.

The process of learning the concepts implicit in a natural language like English, is a process of creating facsimiles of the concepts implicit in the language usage, to which we are exposed. However, we cannot give anyone the meaning of a word or phrase; that meaning must be individually created by every person who learns it. When we mis-learn the meaning of a word, we create in our own minds a meaning that it doesn't have.

THE LOGIC OF ACADEMIC DISCIPLINES

We can now understand each academic discipline to represent a domain in which humans are creating specialized concepts (and inferences that follow from those concepts) that enable them to approach that domain through an ordered set of logical relationships structured by human reason. Critical judgment is essential to all of the acts of construction; all acts of construction are open to critical assessment. We not only assess *what* we create; we assess as we create.

Each student who would learn the logic of a discipline has to create that logic in his or her own mind. Each moment of that creation requires the presence of critical thought and judgment. There is no way to create the logic for the student or simply to "give", transfer, or inject the logic in pre-fabricated form. By the same token, the logic of a text within a discipline enters the student's thinking only through the mediation of the logic of the student's thinking. But the logic of the student's thinking must be continually re-shaped and modified. The logic the student fashions in learning represents, if done well, an analytically modified logic, the result of a process of measured accommodation, not simply one of uncritical assimilation.

Hence, if a student reads a text within a discipline well, that is, critically, the logic he or she creates through reading matches the logic of the text well. Reading proficiently is both a creative task (a making, a creating) and a critical task (an assessing, a judging). The making and the assessing, the creating and the judging are integral to one seamless process of good reasoning. We create the logic of the text in our minds as we critically dialogue with it. We raise and answer probing questions as we read, generating and fashioning ideas and meanings in and through our responses.

This picture is complicated by those domains in which competing logics develop, each rationally defended by different, apparently equally expert, apparently equally rational, proponents. To some extent, of course, questions which call for the adjudication of competing logics emerge in all disciplines. On the other hand, some disciplines, namely those which attempt to conceptualize and make sense of human realities, seem to be inescapably "multi-logical": history, psychology, sociology, philosophy, anthropology, economics, literature, fine arts, and so forth. In these domains, seminal thinkers continue to emerge with alternative and conflicting ideas for reasoning about basic questions in the field. In this case, students have to create and reason within conflicting logics. Problems of confusion abound in this circumstance.

The creativity in reasoning one's way into disciplines which are multi-logical demands exacting and discriminating restraint and self-regulation. In reading, for example, the writings of Freud, Adler, and Jung, I must create in my mind three overlapping systems of thought, systems which complexely agree and disagree. If I come to understand what I have read, I have come to develop the ability to think within three different systems of thought. Only I, through a process of disciplined intellectual work, can generate, fabricate, engender in my mind Freudian, Adlerian, and Jungian thoughts. Only I can create the inner understandings which enable me to draw fine distinctions among their views, fine distinctions which honor the multiple logics they collectively developed. Instruction should provide incentives for students to actively create the logics of these conflicting perspectives and to critically assess that creation at one and the same time.

THE LOGIC OF LOGIC

Critical thinking can now be understood as a deep interest in *the logic of logic,* the art of taking charge of the large variety of ways in which we create concepts and make inferences by means of them, the various ways, in other words, in which we use human reason well or poorly in attempting to make sense of things and our created interpretations of them. Critical thinkers, on this view, attempt to heighten their awareness of the conditions under which their self-created conceptualizations — and inferences from them — are rationally justified. They not only use their innate capacity to reason, they also study how to improve the use of their reason, to discipline and "perfect" it (to make it more clear, precise, accurate, relevant, logical, consistent, respectful of evidence, responsive to good reasons, open to new ideas, and so forth). They habitually, therefore, reason about their reasoning. They routinely scrutinize their thinking as an act of on-going creation which must be continually monitored and checked for its "match".

In this way, critical thinkers maintain an acute and abiding interest in their own intellectual self-improvement. They carefully attend to their personal concept-creating and concept-using practices. They exercise special discipline in taking charge of their thinking by taking charge of the ideas that direct that thinking, by close examination of the ideas which they are generating and using to create an ordered set of meanings.

THE LOGIC OF LANGUAGE

Many of our ideas or concepts come from the languages we have learned to speak (and in which as a matter of course we do our thinking). Embedded in the educated use of words are criteria or standards that we must respect in order to think clearly and precisely by means of those words. We are free, of course, to use a particular word in a special way in special circumstances, but only if we have good reason for modifying its meaning. Such special stipulations should proceed from a clear understanding of established educated use. We are not free, for example, to use the word 'education' as if it were synonymous with the word 'indoctrination' or 'socialization'. We are not free to equate pride with cunning, truth with belief, knowledge with information, arrogance with self-confidence, desire with love, and so on. Each word has its own established logic, a logic that cannot, without confusion or error, be ignored.

Though each word has an established logic, we still have to recreate that logic in our thinking, and we must base that creation on meanings we have previously created. Learning the meaning of a word is therefore not a simple task because in each case we must create a new concept in our minds out of modified old understandings. This requires that our creation be ordered, restrained, regulated, and controlled. The undisciplined creation of meaning in the context of learning the logic of language is nothing more nor less than the mis-learning of that logic.

THE LOGIC OF STUDENT THINKING

Unfortunately many students do not understand the significant relationship between care and precision in language usage and care and precision in thought. Students often say, when talking about the nature of language, that people have their own meanings for all the words they use, not noticing that, were this true, we would not be able to understand each other. Students often speak and write in vague sentences because they have no criteria for choosing words other than that one word rather than another occurred to them. They do not seek to put their sentences into clear logical relationships to one another because they do not recognize any responsibility to do so nor any clear idea of what that would entail. They do not read, write, speak, or listen well because they have never had to think clearly about the logic of reading, writing, speaking, or listening.

All of the rational processes of mind are assumed by them to take care of themselves, automatically and effortlessly. Or better, they are unaware that there are any rational processes of mind to be tended to, in the first place. It goes without saying that students do not generally have any grasp of the creative dimension of all learning. They do not see themselves designing, fashioning, or shaping meanings. They think of themselves as simply absorbing meanings, as simply receiving what is being given to them by the teacher, the textbook, or experience itself.

The result of this common mind-set is that students find it very difficult, if not impossible, to master any well-developed or refined set of conceptual relationships. The logic of their own thinking is vague, fragmented, often contradictory, highly egocentric, typically sociocentric, pervasively undisciplined, and lacking in foundational insights. Since one begins to develop critical thinking significantly only insofar as one begins to discipline one's own thinking with respect to at least one framework of concepts, and since one learns a new set of concepts only by means of a set of previously learned concepts, the development of student thinking must take place over an extended period of time and must be heavily dialogical. Only by moving back and forth between their own undisciplined thought and some set of disciplined concepts, can they work their minds into disciplined thought.

Furthermore, there is the very real danger that, once developed, their emerging discipline in one domain will remain isolated and segregated from the rest of their thinking. Even expert thinkers in one domain are often atrocious in another. The human mind does not necessarily develop as an integrated whole. This is one of the reasons why it is important to emphasize critical thinking as critical thinking, in its most generalizable form. Hence, when learning to think with discipline in one domain of concepts, it is highly useful to be exposed to logically illuminating parallel examples from other domains.

Finally, lacking the discipline of critical thinking and judgment, the creative dimension of student thinking is commonly quite undistinguished. What they "create" is typically poorly designed and constructed. For example, since their own thinking is vague and fragmented, they routinely generate vague and fragmented meanings in the process of learning; their minds bring into being disjointed meanings which often have no single, definite logic whatsoever. It is important to recognize that in a literal sense there is no necessary virtue in "creating" meaning. Prejudices, self-delusions, distortions, misconceptions, and caricatures are all products of the mind as maker and creator.

THE LOGIC OF QUESTIONS

Every question, when well put, imposes specific demands upon us, demands implicit in the logic of the words of the question and in the contexts in which those words are intelligibly used by educated speakers of the language. If I ask, "What is the sum of 434 and 987?", the question requires an answer consonant with the established logic of the word 'addition'. If I ask, "Is Jack your friend or merely an acquaintance?", the question requires an answer in keeping with the logic of the established distinction between the words 'friend' and 'acquaintance'. If I ask you "To what extent are your students learning to think critically?", the question requires that you 1) understand precisely what is implied by the expression 'thinks critically' and 2) assess your students' thinking by some means appropriate to determining the relative standing of your students either with respect to a fixed ideal of critical thinking or some standardized norm to which your students' performances (of thinking) can appropriately be compared. An appropriate answer is one that is constructed in accordance with the logical demands of the question.

Very often, people are cavalier in their putting and answering of questions. They rarely put their own questions precisely, and, when answering the questions of others, they often respond impressionistically or otherwise inappropriately, without care, discipline, or sensitivity to what is implied by the established logic of the question (or by the context in which the question is asked). When called upon to sharpen their questions or to respond more carefully and precisely, many respond with irritation or annoyance, exasperated that they are expected to be clear or precise or accurate or relevant or consistent in their question-asking or -answering behaviors.

This general insensitivity to the logic of questions is part of the broader phenomenon of insensitivity to the logic of language, which is itself part of the even broader phenomenon of insensitivity to the need for care and discipline in our use of reason — our use of concept and inference — in figuring out the logic of the world within and around us. All of these, in turn, are part of the general insensitivity to the need to discipline our mind's creative productions, to shape them in accord with restraining conditions. Sometimes these restraining conditions are given by the logic of language, sometimes by the logic of the material world.

✦ *The Elements of Thought*

As soon as we move from thought which is purely associational and undisciplined, to thought which is conceptual and inferential, which attempts in some intelligible way to figure something out, to use the power of creative reason, then it is possible, and helpful, to think about what might be called "the elements of thought", the basic building-blocks of thinking, the essential dimensions of all reasoning whenever and wherever it creates meaning. There is, in other words, a general logic to the use of reason. We can deduce these elements, these essential dimensions of reasoning, by paying close attention to what is implicit in the attempt on the part of the mind to figure anything out whatsoever. Once we make these elements of thought clear, it will be obvious that each of them can serve as an important touchstone or point of assessment in our critical analysis and assessment of the constructed process and products of our thinking. As meaning makers we must be exacting, discriminating, and fastidious. Without a guiding logic, thinking is aimless and random. Productive thinking needs some structure, some basic logic to follow.

We have already noticed that the attempt to render something intelligible requires the construction of concepts, the creation of interpretations and understandings based on them, and inferences drawn from them. We can now set out the basic set of conditions implicit in these creative, critical acts of the mind, whenever they occur. They are as follows:

1) *Purpose, Goal, or End in View:* Whenever we reason, we reason to some end, to achieve some purpose, to satisfy some desire or fulfill some need. One source of problems in reasoning is traceable to "defects" at the level of goal, purpose, or end. If our goal itself is unrealistic, contra-

dictory to other goals we have, confused or muddled in some way, then the reasoning we use to achieve it is problematic. The goal, purpose, or end of our thinking is something our mind must actively create.

2) *Question at Issue (or Problem to Be Solved):* Whenever we attempt to reason something out, there is at least one question at issue, at least one problem to be solved. One area of concern for the reasoner should therefore be the very formulation of the question to be answered or problem to be solved. If we are not clear about the question we are asking, or how the question relates to our basic purpose or goal, then it is unlikely that we will be able to find a reasonable answer to it, or one that will serve our purpose. The question at issue in our thinking is something our mind must actively create.

3) *Point of View or Frame of Reference:* Whenever we reason, we must reason within some point of view or frame of reference. Any defect in our point of view or frame of reference is a possible source of problems in our reasoning. Our point of view may be too narrow or too parochial, may be based on false or misleading analogies or metaphors, may not be precise enough, may contain contradictions, and so forth. The point of view which shapes and organizes our thinking is something our mind must actively create.

4) *The Empirical Dimension of Our Reasoning:* Whenever we reason, there is some "stuff", some phenomena about which we are reasoning. Any defect, then, in the experiences, data, evidence, or raw material upon which our reasoning is based is a possible source of problems. We must actively decide which of a myriad of possible experiences, data, evidence, etc. we will use.

5) *The Conceptual Dimension of Our Reasoning:* All reasoning uses some ideas or concepts and not others. Any defect in the concepts or ideas (including the theories, principles, axioms, or rules) with which we reason, is a possible source of problems. The concepts and ideas which shape and organize our thinking must be actively created by us.

6) *Assumptions* — The Starting Points of Reasoning: All reasoning must begin somewhere, must take some things for granted. Any defect in the starting points of our reasoning, any problem in what we are taking for granted, is a possible source of problems. Only we can create the assumptions on the basis of which we will reason.

7) *Inferences:* Reasoning proceeds by steps called inferences. To make an inference is to think as follows: "Because this is so, that also is so (or probably so)". Any defect in the inferences we make while we reason is a possible problem in our reasoning. Information, data, and situations do not determine what we shall deduce from them; we create inferences through the concepts and assumptions which we bring to situations.

8) Implications and Consequences — Where Our Reasoning Takes Us: All reasoning begins somewhere and proceeds somewhere else. No reasoning is static. Reasoning is a sequence of inferences that begin somewhere and take us somewhere else. Thus all reasoning comes to an end, yet could have been taken further. All reasoning has implications or consequences beyond those the reasoner has considered. Any problem with these (implications that are false, undesirable consequences), implies a problem in the reasoning. The implications of our reasoning are an implicit creation of our reasoning.

If we taught each school subject in such a way that students had to reason their way into the subject, and if we routinely questioned students so they came to habitually look into each basic dimension of their thinking — purpose, question at issue, point of view, data, concepts, assumptions, inferences, implications and consequences — they would progressively become more disciplined in their reasoning, more self-critical and self-directed in the process and products of their thinking.

THE LOGIC OF READING, WRITING, SPEAKING, AND LISTENING

Reading, writing, speaking, and listening are all "dialogical" in nature. That is, in each case there are at least two logics involved, and there is an attempt being made by someone to translate one logic into the terms of another. Consider reading and listening. In both of these cases we are attempting to make sense of the logic or reasoning of another person. Whatever is written must, if it is reasoned, contain all of the elements of thought, and as a critical reader one can question the text as one goes seeking to determine: What is the central purpose of the writer of the text, what problems or issues does she raise? Within what point of view is she reasoning? What is she assuming or taking for granted? What evidence, information, or data is presented to us? How is that evidence interpreted or conceptualized? What are the key concepts or ideas in the text? What lines of reasoning are formulated? What key inferences are made? Where is the reasoning taking us? What is implied by it? If this reasoning were taken seriously and made the basis for action or policy, what consequences would follow? Furthermore, each of these dimensions of reasoning could be looked at from the point of view of the "perfections" of thought, those intellectual standards which individually or collectively apply to all reasoning. (Is it clear, precise, accurate, relevant, consistent, logical, broad enough, based on sound evidence, utilizing appropriate reasons, adequate to our purposes, and fair, given other possible ways of conceiving things?)

To read well, to read critically, one needs to actively construct an interpretation, imagine alternative meanings, imagine possible objections — one must think creatively. But "creative reading" (as the phrase is often understood) is not good reading — accurate, clear, plausible — unless it is also critical, disciplined reading. Consider the following example of two students engaged in reading a text. (This example is taken from an article by Stephen Norris and Linda Phillips "Explanations of Reading Comprehension: Schema Theory and Critical Thinking Theory" in *Teachers' College Record*, Volume 89, Number 2, Winter 1987). We can see in these two readers a striking difference between good and bad reasoning embedded in the act of reading (the questions and commentaries within the text below are those of Norris and Phillips).

In what follows we will present, episode-by-episode, Steven's and Colleen's thinking aloud as they work through the passage. The experimenter's questions are given in brackets. We have chosen to make our example detailed, because we see this as the best route for providing specificity to otherwise vague generalizations about the relationship between reading and thinking. To simulate the task for you we present the passage without a title and one episode at a time, as was done with the children.

Episode 1

The stillness of the morning air was broken. The men headed down the bay.

Steven

The men were heading down the bay, I'm not sure why yet. It was a very peaceful morning. [Any questions?] No, not really. [Where do you think they're going?] I think they might be going sailing, water skiing, or something like that.

Colleen

The men are going shopping. [Why do you say that?] They're going to buy clothes at The Bay. [What is The Bay?] It's a shopping center. [Any questions?] No. [Where do you think they're going?] They're going shopping because it seems like they broke something.

Steven recognizes that there is insufficient information for explaining what the men are doing. On questioning, he tentatively suggests a couple of alternatives consistent with the information given, but indicates there are other possibilities. Colleen presents one explanation of the story, and seems fairly definite that the men are going to buy clothes at The Bay, a chain of department stores in Canada. On being queried she maintains her idea that the men are going shopping, but offers an explanation inconsistent with her first one that they are going to buy clothes. To do this she assumes that something concrete was broken, which could be replaced at The Bay.

Episode 2

The net was hard to pull. The heavy sea and strong tide made it even difficult for the girdie. The meshed catch encouraged us to try harder.

Steven

It was not a very good day as there were waves which made it diffi-cult for the girdie. That must be some kind of machine for doing some-thing. The net could be for pulling something out of the water like an old wreck. No, wait! It said "meshed catch." I don't know why but that makes me think of fish and, sure, if you caught fish you'd really want to get them. [Any questions?] No questions, just that I think maybe the girdie is a machine for helping the men pull in the fish or whatever it was. Maybe a type of pulley.

Colleen

I guess The Bay must have a big water fountain. [Why was the net hard to pull?] There's a lot of force on the water. [Why was it important for them to pull the net?] It was something they had to do. [What do you mean?] They had to pull the net and it was hard to do. [Any ques-tions?] No. [Where do you think they're going?] Shopping.

For both children the interpretations of Episode 2 built on those of Episode 1. Steven continues to question what the men were doing. He raises a number of alternative interpretations dealing with the context of the sea. He refines his interpretations through testing hypothetical interpretations against specific details, and hypotheses of specific word meanings against his emerging inter-pretation of the story. At the outset he makes an inference that a girdie is a machine, but leaves details about its nature and function unspecified. He tentatively offers one specific use for the net, but immediately questions this use when he realizes that it will not account for the meshed catch, and substitutes an alternative func-tion. He then confirms this interpretation with the fact from the story that the men were encouraged to try harder and his belief that if you catch fish you would really want to bring them aboard. Finally, he sees that he is in a position to offer a more definitive but tentative interpretation of the word girdie.

Colleen maintains her interpretation of going shopping at The Bay. When questioned about her interpretation, Colleen responds in vague or tautological terms. She seems not to integrate informa-tion relating to the terms net, catch, and sea, and she seemed satis-fied to remain uninformed about the nature of the girdie and the reason for pulling the net. In the end, she concludes definitively that the men are going shopping.

Episode 3

With four quintels aboard, we were now ready to leave. The skipper saw mares' tails in the north.

Steven

I wonder what quintels are? I think maybe it's a sea term, a word that means perhaps the weight aboard. Yes maybe it's how much fish they had aboard. [So you think it was fish?] I think fish or maybe some-thing they had found in the water but I think fish more because of the word "catch." *[Why were they worried about the mares' tails?]* I'm not sure. Mares' tails, let me see, mares are horses but horses are not going to be in the water. The mares' tails are in the north. Here farmers watch the north for bad weather, so maybe the fishermen do the same thing. Yeah, I think that's it, it's a cloud formation which could mean strong winds and hail or something which I think could be dangerous if you were in a boat and had a lot of weight aboard. *[Any questions?]* No.

Colleen

They were finished with their shopping and were ready to go home. *[What did they have aboard?]* Quintels. *[What are quintels?]* I don't know. *[Why were they worried about the mares' tails?]* There were a group of horses on the street and they were afraid they would attack the car. *[Any questions?]* No.

Steven is successful in his efforts to incorporate the new information into an evolving interpretation. From the outset Steven acknowledges that he does not know the meaning of quintel and seeks a resolution of this unknown. He derives a meaning consistent with his evolving interpretation and with the textual evidence. In his attempt to understand the expression *mares' tails* he first acknowledges that he does not know the meaning of the expression. Thence, he establishes what he does know from the background knowledge (mares are horses, horses are not going to be in the water, there is nothing around except sky and water, farmers watch the north for bad weather) and textual information (the men are on the bay, they have things aboard, the mares' tails are in the north) and inferences he has previously made (the men are in a boat, they are fishing). He integrates this knowledge into a comparison between the concerns of Alberta farmers with which he is familiar, and what he takes to be analogous concerns of fishermen. On seeing the pertinence of this analogy he draws the conclusion that the mares' tails must be a cloud formation foreboding inclement weather. He claims support for his conclusion in the fact that it would explain the skipper's concern for the mares' tails, indicating that he did not lose sight of the overall task of understanding the story.

Colleen maintains her original interpretation but does not incorporate all the new textual information into it. She works with the information on the men's leaving and the mares' tails, but appears to ignore or remain vague about other information. For example, she says the cargo was comprised of quintels but indicates no effort to determine what these things are. She cites the fact that the men were ready to leave and suggests that they have finished their shopping, but does not attempt to explain the use of such words as skipper, cargo, and aboard in the context of shopping for clothes. She interprets mares' tails as a group of horses that possibly would attack the men, but gives no account of what the horses might be doing on the street. Basically, she appears to grow tolerant of ambiguity and incompleteness in her interpretation.

Notice how both readers illustrate the relationship between creative and critical thinking. Steve is creating an interpretation, actively constructing — building it, if you will — and in so doing, he makes creative and constructive use of previous knowledge and of his imagination, critically assessing his interpretation as he goes. Colleen, on the other hand, is certainly "creative" in one sense: wildly building a bizarre interpretation, un-restrained by mere reality or plausibility. (Later, after reading that the men cut up the fish they have caught, she, believing the fish to be guppies, says that after the men cut them up, they probably put them in an aquarium.) This "creativity run amok" is not the kind of creative thinking we want to foster in our students, does not enable them to make sense of, and sensibly evaluate, what they read. Only a disciplined process of critical analysis enables one to create in one's mind the logic of the text, to construct a system of meanings that mirror, to the best of one's ability, the system of meanings inherent in the text.

✦ Intellectual Standards

All intellectual standards are derived from some humanly created logic or are implied in the very nature of things themselves, including *universal criteria* implicit in intellectual history and educated discourse within that history, *the logic of concepts and words* implicit in educated usage, *the logic of questions* implicit in academic practice and educated usage, and *the logic of subject matter* implicit in the nature of things themselves. For example, it would be unintelligible to say, "I want to reason well but I am indifferent as to whether or not my reasoning is clear, precise, accurate, relevant, logical, consistent, based on appropriate evidence and reasons, ..." By the same token, it would be unintelligible — unless very special circumstances prevailed — to say "I am trying to determine whether or not I am a 'selfish' person, but I am not concerned with what the word 'selfish' implies." The logic of the question, "Is Jack a selfish person?" is basically revealed by understanding the established uses of the word 'selfish' in educated discourse.

✦ The Logic of Teaching

(Assuming that the most basic goal of education is to foster the general, reasoned, intellectual development of students.) To teach a student critically is to devise activities and an environment conducive to the general, reasoned, intellectual development of students. By the model we present, the goal will be seen to entail cultivating students' ability to reason "creatively and critically" (viewed as inseparable dimensions of good thinking) with respect to the logic of any subject matter they study, in such a way as to maximize the development, over an extended period of time, of general intellectual standards and disciplined minds, minds strongly motivated to reason rigorously and analytically with respect to any problem, issue, or intellectual task to which they afterward set themselves. The ability to read, write, speak, and listen as forms of disciplined reasoning, as forms of disciplined questioning, become central goals on the model because each is a basic modality of reason through which we learn much of what we learn. As teachers committed to the intellectual development of our students, we introduce our students not only to the logic of what they are studying but also to the very logic of logic, i.e., critical thinking, so that they begin as soon as possible to discipline their minds in a general and not simply in a subject-specific way. Through that discipline, the created products of their thinking become useful products, products fashioned, to the degree that they develop critical judgment, with acute discrimination and fastidious discernment. That minds will create meanings is not in doubt; that they will create meanings that are sound, insightful, or profound is.

✦ Conclusion

Creativity, as a term of praise, involves more than a mere haphazard or uncritical making, more than the raw process of bringing something into being. It requires that what is brought into being meet criteria intrinsic to what it is we are trying to make. Novelty alone will not do, for it is easy to produce worthless novelty. Intellectual standards and discipline do not stand in the way of creativity. Rather, they provide a way to begin to generate it, as it must be generated: slowly and painfully, one student at a time, one problem at a time, one insight at a time. If we can engage each of our students passionately in genuine intellectual work on genuine intellectual problems worthy of reasoned thought and analysis, and continually help each student to become a more judicious critic of the nature and quality of his or her thought, we have done all we can do to make likely both the critical and the creative development of each student. It is stimulating intellectual work that develops the intellect simultaneously as both a creator and evaluator: as a creator that evaluates and as an evaluator that creates. Fitness of mind, intellectual excellence, is the result.

Chapter 7

Critical Thinking in North America

Abstract

In this paper, Richard Paul sets out his conception of the emerging critical theory of education, in contrast to the standard didactic theory of education. "The root concept of the educated literate person as critical thinker is not theoretically new .... What is new is its progressive development across a variety of academic domains and its unifying foundation as a basis for addressing a variety of emerging educational, social, and economic concerns."

Students are not learning "to work by, or think for, themselves." "Neither are they learning how to gather, analyze, synthesize, and assess information, how to analyze questions and problems, how to enter sympathetically into the thinking of others, how to deal rationally with conflicting points of view. They do not use their native languages clearly, precisely, or persuasively." Most importantly, Paul argues, students gain little knowledge since, for the most part, they could not explain the basis for what they believe. They do not, therefore, become "literate," in Paul's conception of the word.

Paul names the source of these problems as a didactic conception of education — simplistic, fragmented, and inaccurate — which has shaped instructional theory and practice, and which primarily arose from schools' historical role of indoctrinating people to fit into narrow, isolated societies, a situation changing in the modern world of global communication and interdependence. Research and theoretical work on numerous fronts are developing and reflecting a contrasting theory of education which Paul explicates and links to critical thinking. The broadness and complexity of the emerging concept of critical thinking can be seen in the variety of definitions of it. After setting out numerous definitions, Paul sets out one of his own in some detail and explores its key features: perfections of thought, elements of thought, and domains of thought. Paul closes by citing research that supports his view of critical teaching.

✦ Introduction

*T*here is a critical thinking movement gaining momentum at all levels of education today. Its epicenter is in North America but its influence is being felt in Europe and beyond. It is manifested in a burgeoning variety of research projects and papers, in educational manifestoes and mandates, in new curriculum articulations, in far-reaching philosophical critique, and in a spate of efforts to "restructure" schools.

The root concept of the educated literate person as critical thinker is not theoretically new but can be traced to the ancient Socratic model of the learner as a systematic, probing questioner and dialectical reasoner striving to live a reflective and rational life. (Paul, 1987) (Siegel, 1980, 1988) What is new is its progressive development across a variety of academic domains and its unifying foundation as a basis for addressing a variety of emerging educational, social, and economic concerns.

On the economic front, developed nations must increasingly generate workers who can think critically for a living. Evidence of this growing perception is illustrated in an open letter, drafted by the president of Stanford University, Donald Kennedy, co-signed by 36 other college leaders from across the U.S., and sent to 3,000 college and university presidents (Sept. 18, 1987). It warned of "a national emergency ... rooted ... in the revolution of expectations about what our schools must accomplish:"

> It simply will not do for our schools to produce a small elite to power our scientific establishment and a larger cadre of workers with basic skills to do routine work.... Millions of people around the world now have these same basic skills and are willing to work twice as long for as little as one-tenth our basic wages.... To maintain and enhance our quality of life, we must develop a leading-edge economy based on workers who can think for a living.... If skills are equal, in the long run wages will be too. This means we have to educate a vast mass of people capable of thinking critically, creatively, and imaginatively.

On the social and political fronts, both developed and underdeveloped nations face complex problems that cannot be solved except with significant conceptual shifts on the part of large masses of people. Such large-scale shifts presuppose increased reflective and critical thought about deep-seated problems of environmental damage, human relations, overpopulation, rising expectations, diminishing resources, global competition, personal goals, and ideological conflict. Simultaneously, as war and preparation for war waste more and more resources, the battle for world political hegemony, which fuels this waste, becomes increasingly unacceptable. One result is an increasing drive to challenge the world-wide academic *status quo*, a *status quo* whose outdated and simplistic theoretical underpinnings invite serious attack, and to build in its place modes of education better suited to the demands of emerging world problems. A multi-dimensional, interdependent world cannot be fathomed by people schooled in fragmented, monological specialties or steeped in nationalist myopia. Most problems are multi-dimensional, logically messy, require interdisciplinary analysis and synthesis, deeply involve values and priorities, and demand sympathetic consideration of conflicting points of view or frames of reference.

Monological analysis will not solve multilogical problems. Specialists whose main *forte* is reductive thinking within a discipline offer little toward solving such problems. The lay person, bombarded with diverse contradictory explanations and prescriptions, retreats to simplistic pictures of the world. The growing mass media feed this demand for simple-minded answers. A new concept of knowledge, learning, and literacy more in tune with the modern world is emerging, however; one designed to engender people comfortable with dialogical and dialectical thinking, at home with complexity and ambiguity, who can adjust their thinking to accelerating changes, who do not fixate on their present beliefs, people not easily manipulated or taken in by propaganda. (Scriven 1985) The theoretical foundation for this need and its fulfillment is now accumulating a solid research base. Its academic implementation is merely beginning; its full development around the world is years in the future.

✦ Two Conflicting Theories of Knowledge, Learning, and Literacy: The Didactic and the Critical

Most instructional practice in most academic institutions around the world presupposes a didactic theory of knowledge, learning, and literacy, ill-suited to the development of critical minds and literate persons. After a superficial exposure to reading, writing, and arithmetic, schooling is typically fragmented into more or less technical domains each with a large vocabulary and an extensive content or propositional base. Students "take in" and reiterate domain-specific details. Teachers lecture and drill. Students rarely integrate their daily non-academic experiences. Teachers spend little time stimulating student questions. Students are rarely encouraged to doubt what they hear in the classroom or read in their texts. Students' personal points of view or philosophies of life are considered largely irrelevant to education. In most classrooms teachers talk and students listen. Dense and typically speedy coverage of content is usually followed by content-specific testing. Students are drilled in applying formulas, skills, and concepts, then tested on nearly identical items. Instructional practices fail to require students to *use* what they learn when appropriate. Practice is stripped of meaning and purpose.

Interdisciplinary synthesis is ordinarily viewed as the personal responsibility of the student and is not routinely tested. Technical specialization is considered the natural goal of schooling and is correlated with getting a job. Few multi-logical issues or problems are discussed or assigned and even fewer teachers know how to conduct such discussions or assess student participation in them. Students rarely engage in dialogical or dialectical reasoning and few teachers can analyze such reasoning. Knowledge is viewed as verified intra-disciplinary propositions and well-supported intra-disciplinary theories. There is little or no discussion of the nature of prejudice or bias, little or no discussion of metacognition, little or no discussion of what a disciplined, self-directed mind or self-directed thought require. We expect students to develop into literate, educated persons from years of content memorization and ritual performance.

Theory of Knowledge, Learning, and Literacy	
Didactic Theory	*Critical Theory*
1. The fundamental needs of students	
That the fundamental need of students is to be taught more or less *what* to think, not *how* to think (that is, that students will learn how to think if they can only get into their heads what to think).	That the fundamental need of students is to be taught *how* not *what* to think; that it is important to focus on significant content, but this should be accomplished by raising live issues that stimulate students to gather, analyze, and assess that content.
2. The nature of knowledge	
That knowledge is independent of the thinking that generates, organizes, and applies it.	That all knowledge of "content" is generated, organized, applied, analyzed, synthesized, and assessed by thinking; that gaining knowledge is unintelligible without engagement in such thinking. (It is *not* assumed that one can think without some content to think about, nor that all content is equally significant and useful.)
3. Model of the educated person	
That educated, literate people are fundamentally repositories of content analogous to an encyclopedia or a data bank, directly comparing situations in the world with facts that they carry about fully formed as a result of an absorptive process. That an educated, literate person is fundamentally a true believer, that is, a possessor of truth, and therefore claims much knowledge.	That an educated, literate person is fundamentally a repository of strategies, principles, concepts, and insights embedded in processes of thought rather than in atomic facts. Experiences analyzed and organized by critical thought, rather than facts picked up one-by-one, characterize the educated person. Much of what is known is constructed by the thinker *as needed* from context to context, not *prefabricated* in sets of true statements about the world.

Theory of Knowledge, Learning, and Literacy

Didactic Theory	Critical Theory
	That an educated, literate person is fundamentally a seeker and questioner rather than a true believer, therefore cautious in claiming knowledge.

4. The nature of learning

Didactic Theory	Critical Theory
That knowledge, truth, and understanding can be transmitted from one person to another by verbal statements in the form of lectures or didactic teaching.	That knowledge and truth can rarely, and insight never, be transmitted from one person to another by the transmitter's verbal statements alone; that one cannot directly give another what one has learned — one can only facilitate the conditions under which people learn for themselves by figuring out or thinking things through.

5. The nature of listening

Didactic Theory	Critical Theory
That students do not need to be taught skills of listening to learn to pay attention and this is fundamentally a matter of self-discipline achieved through will power. Students should therefore be able to listen on command by the teacher.	That students need to be taught how to listen critically — an active and skilled process that can be learned by degrees with various levels of proficiency. Learning what others mean by what they say requires questioning, trying on, testing, and, hence, engaging in public or private dialogue with them, and this involves critical thinking.

6. The relationship of basic skills to thinking skills

Didactic Theory	Critical Theory
That the basic skills of reading and writing can be taught without emphasis on higher order critical thinking.	That the basic skills of reading and writing are inferential skills that require critical thinking; that students who do not learn to read and write critically are ineffective readers and writers, and that critical reading and writing involve dialogical processes in which probing critical questions are raised

Theory of Knowledge, Learning, and Literacy

Didactic Theory	Critical Theory
	and answered. (For example, What is the fundamental issue? What reasons, what evidence, is relevant to this issue? Is this source or authority credible? Are these reasons adequate? Is this evidence accurate and sufficient? Does this contradict that? Does this conclusion follow? Is another point of view relevant to consider?)

7. The status of questioning

Didactic Theory	Critical Theory
That students who have no questions typically are learning well, while students with a lot of questions are experiencing difficulty in learning; that doubt and questioning weaken belief.	That students who have no questions typically are not learning, while having pointed and specific questions, on the other hand, is a significant sign of learning. Doubt and questioning, by deepening understanding, strengthen belief by putting it on more solid ground.

8. The desirable classroom environment

Didactic Theory	Critical Theory
That quiet classes with little student talk are typically reflective of students learning while classes with a lot of student talk are typically disadvantaged in learning.	That quiet classes with little student talk are typically classes with little learning while classes with much student talk focused on live issues is a sign of learning (provided students learn dialogical and dialectical skills).

9. The view of knowledge (atomistic vs. holistic)

Didactic Theory	Critical Theory
That knowledge and truth can typically be learned best by being broken down into elements, and the elements into sub-elements, each taught sequentially and atomically. Knowledge is additive.	That knowledge and truth is heavily systemic and holistic and can be learned only by many on-going acts of synthesis, many cycles from wholes to parts, tentative graspings of a whole guiding us in understanding its parts, periodic focusing on the parts (in relation to each other) shedding light upon the whole,

Theory of Knowledge, Learning, and Literacy

Didactic Theory	*Critical Theory*
	and that the wholes that we learn have important relations to other wholes as well as their own parts and hence need to be frequently canvassed in learning any given whole. (This assumption has the implication that we cannot achieve in-depth learning in any given domain of knowledge unless the process of grasping that domain involves active consideration of its relation to other domains of knowledge.) That each learner creates knowledge.

10. The place of values

That people can gain significant knowledge without seeking or valuing it, and hence that education can take place without significant transformation of values for the learner.	That people gain only the knowledge they seek and value. All other learning is superficial and transitory. All genuine education transforms the basic values of the person educated, resulting in persons becoming life-long learners and rational persons.

11. The importance of being aware of one's own learning process

That understanding the mind and how it functions, its epistemological health and pathology, are not important or necessary parts of learning. To learn the basic subject matter of the schools one need not focus on such matters, except perhaps with certain disadvantaged learners.	That understanding the mind and how it functions, its health and pathology, are important and necessary parts of learning. To learn subject matter in-depth, we must gain some insight into how we as thinkers and learners process that subject matter.

12. The place of misconceptions

That ignorance is a vacuum or simple lack, and that student prejudices, biases, misconceptions, and ignorance are automatically replaced by their being given knowledge.	That prejudices, biases, and misconceptions are built up through actively constructed inferences embedded in experience and must be broken down through a similar process; hence, that students must reason their way dialogically and dialectically out of their prejudices, biases, and misconceptions.

Theory of Knowledge, Learning, and Literacy

Didactic Theory	Critical Theory

13. The level of understanding desired

That students need not understand the rational ground or deeper logic of what they learn to absorb knowledge. Extensive but superficial learning can later be deepened.	That rational assent is an essential facet of all genuine learning and that an in-depth understanding of basic concepts and principles is an essential foundation for rational concepts and facts. That in-depth understanding of root concepts and principles should be used as organizers for learning within and across subject matter domains.

14. Depth versus breadth

That it is more important to cover a great deal of knowledge or information superficially than a small amount in depth. That only after the facts are understood, can students discuss their meaning; that higher order thinking can and should only be practiced by students who have mastered the material. That thought-provoking discussions are for the gifted and advanced, only.	That it is more important to cover a small amount of knowledge or information in depth (deeply probing its foundation) than to cover a great deal of knowledge superficially. That all students can and must probe the significance of and justification for what they learn.

15. Role definition for teacher and student

That the roles of teacher and learner are distinct and should not be blurred.	That we learn best by teaching or explaining to others what we know.

16. The correction of ignorance

That the teacher should correct the learners' ignorance by telling them what they do not know.	That students need to learn to distinguish for themselves what they know from what they do not know. Students should recognize that they do not genuinely know or comprehend what they have merely memorized. Self-directed recognition of ignorance is necessary to learning.

Theory of Knowledge, Learning, and Literacy

Didactic Theory	*Critical Theory*
17. The responsibility for learning	
That the teacher has the fundamental responsibility for student learning. Teachers and texts provide information, questions, and drill.	That progressively the student should be given increasing responsibility for his or her own learning. Students need to come to see that only they can learn for themselves and that they will not do so unless they actively and willingly engage themselves in the process.
18. The transfer of learning to everyday situations	
That students will automatically transfer the knowledge that they learn in didactically taught courses to relevant real-life situations.	That most knowledge that students memorize in didactically taught courses is either forgotten or rendered "inert" by their mode of learning it, and that the most significant transfer is achieved by in-depth learning which focuses on experiences meaningful to the student and aims directly at transfer.
19. Status of personal experiences	
That the personal experience of the student has no essential role to play in education.	That the personal experience of the student is essential to all schooling at all levels and in all subjects; that it is a crucial part of the content to be processed (applied, analyzed, synthesized, and assessed) by the student.
20. The assessment of knowledge acquisition	
That a student who can correctly answer questions, provide definitions, and apply formulae while taking tests has proven his or her knowledge or understanding of those details. Since the didactic approach tends to assume, for example, that knowing a word is knowing its definition (and an example),	That students can often provide correct answers, repeat definitions, and apply formulae while yet not understanding those questions, definitions, or formulae. That proof of knowledge or understanding is found in the students' ability to explain in their own words, with examples, the meaning and significance of the

Theory of Knowledge, Learning, and Literacy	
Didactic Theory	*Critical Theory*
didactic instruction tends to overemphasize definitions. Students practice skills by doing exercises, specifically designed as drill. Successfully finishing the exercise is taken to be equivalent to having learned the skill.	knowledge, why it is so, and to *spontaneously* recall and use it when relevant.

21. The authority validating knowledge

That learning is essentially a private, monological process in which learners can proceed more or less directly to established truth, under the guidance of an expert in such truth. The authoritative answers that the teacher has are the fundamental standards for assessing students' learning.	That learning is essentially a public, communal, dialogical, and dialectical process in which learners can only proceed indirectly to truth, with much "zigging and zagging" along the way, much back-tracking, misconception, self-contradiction, and frustration in the process. In this process, authoritative answers are replaced by authoritative standards for engagement in the communal, dialogical process of enquiry.

The above dominant pattern of academic instruction and learning assumes an uncritical theory of knowledge, learning, and literacy coming under increasing critique by those concerned with instruction fitted to new interpretations of the emerging economic and social conditions and changing conditions for human survival. (Passmore, 1967) (Scheffler 1973, 1965) Those whose teaching reflects the didactic theory rarely formulate it explicitly. Some would deny that they hold it, though their practice implies it. In any case, it is with the theory implicit in practice that we are concerned.

Now let's examine the two opposing theories systematically in terms of specific contrasting assumptions.

✦ A Glimpse at the Historical and Social Background of Didactic Instruction and Uncritical Learning

The didactic theory of knowledge, learning, and literacy, though unsuited to in-depth learning or critical thinking, has been functional to some extent for the maintenance of routine life in what have been to date largely uncritical societies. Schooling has been first and last a social process, reflecting ascendant social forces and thinking largely subservient to them. Much of what happens in schools results from social and economic decisions made predominantly by non-academics. Epistemo-logic is traditionally subordinate to socio-logic.

We must remember that knowledge, however extensive, is a highly limited social construction out of an infinitude of possible such constructions. Although all humans live in a veritable sea of potentially expressible truths, they express only a few of them, only a few become knowledge. The constraints that we must live within inevitably limit the social production of knowledge. We are therefore highly selective and directional in that production. We don't randomly express truths. We systematically seek the knowledge which serves our interests, meets our needs, and solves our problems. The human mind and social life being what it is, we generate a good deal of pseudo-knowledge intermixed with the genuine. We also avoid producing and disseminating knowledge that might undermine our social engagements and vested interests. Not all learning is ipso facto rational, and irrational practices are often deeply embedded in day-to-day social life. We do this spontaneously and naturally, without guile or conscious malice. We are not *truth* seekers by nature but *functional knowledge* seekers. And widely accepted pseudo-knowledge is often quite functional. Hence, to take an obvious example, in a racist society it is functional to be racist. Rationally unjustified beliefs often enable us to get ahead and stay out of trouble. Ordinary social life, whether we like it or not, is filled with innumerable functional falsehoods.

As long as societies functioned primarily as self-contained systems independent of each other and the repercussions of economic, social, and political conflicts were manageable, functional falsehoods and suppressed knowledge (the avoidance of unpleasant truth) was tolerable. We should remember that the systematic search for particular dimensions of knowledge as an organized and specialized endeavor is itself quite recent in human history. It is at most 2,000 years old while the species is somewhere between 1,000,000 and 3,000,000 years old. Most disciplines have emerged as significant endeavors only within the last 300 or so years. Wholesale mass schooling is only about 100 years old. Schools and socialization historically have armed the mass of people with minimum levels of superficial knowledge, functional falsehoods, and socially approved biases. Only a few were encouraged to approach the ideal of critical thought, and even these only in a limited way. As scientific disciplines emerged it became necessary for some to understand particular disciplines deeply. What Kant called *scientific ignorance* — knowing clearly what we do not yet know — became necessary for advancing intra-disciplinary progress. But most people were not expected to contribute to the advances in specialized disciplines, only to use in a limited way some tools that a technological application of those advances made possible.

Furthermore, the overwhelming majority of people were each expected to find a particular niche within the complex structures of social life, not to engage in social critique, not to detect social contradictions, not to expose pseudo-knowledge or to articulate suppressed knowledge. That learning was all of a piece for the typical (uncritical) learner — truth, half-truth, bias, and falsehood blended together — created no insoluble economic or social problems for society. Problems aplenty there were, but on the whole people in the same societies shared the same basic beliefs, true or false, rational or irrational. Anarchy did not result from the fact that "Truth" meant no more in the last analysis to ordinary people than "We believe it" or "It agrees with our beliefs" or "It was said by someone with authority and prestige."

But the relative homogeneity and isolation of societies began to break down with the advent of science and the emergence of a technological world. More and more individuals became, are increasingly becoming, aware of differences in belief, not just of people outside but of people inside their societies as well. And interdependence has dramatically and increasingly emerged. What were previously local decisions with nothing more than local consequences are becoming international matters. Knowledge production and dissemination can no longer be premised on an intra-societal world and humanity cannot survive indefinitely with masses of people whose ultimate *de facto* test of knowledge is personal desire or social conformity.

✦ *What, Then, Is Critical Thinking?*

It is certainly of the nature of the human mind to think — spontaneously, continuously, and pervasively — but it is not of the nature of the human mind to think critically about the standards and principles guiding its spontaneous thought. It has no built-in drive to question its innate tendency to believe what it wants to believe, what makes it comfortable, what is simple rather than complex, and what is commonly believed and socially rewarded. The human mind is ordinarily at peace with itself as it internalizes and creates biases, prejudices, falsehoods, half-truths, and distortions. Compartmentalized contradictions do not, by their very nature, disturb those who take them in and selectively use them. The human mind spontaneously experiences itself as in tune with reality, as directly observing and faithfully recording it. It takes a special intervening process to produce the kind of self-criticalness that enables the mind to effectively and constructively question its own creations. The mind spontaneously but uncritically invests itself with epistemological authority with the same ease with which it accepts authority figures in the world into which it is socialized.

Learning to think critically is therefore an extraordinary process that cultivates capacities merely potential in human thought and develops them at the expense of capacities spontaneously activated from within and reinforced by normal socialization. It is not normal and inevitable or even common for a mind to discipline itself within a rational perspective and direct itself toward rational rather than egocentric beliefs, practices, and values. Yet it is possible to describe the precise conditions under which critical minds can be cultivated. The differences between critical and uncritical thought are increasingly apparent.

Nonetheless, because of the complexity of critical thinking — its relationship to an unlimited number of behaviors in an unlimited number of situations, its conceptual interdependence with other concepts such as the critical person, the critical society, a critical theory of knowledge, learning, and literacy, and rationality, not to speak of the opposites of these concepts — one should not put too much weight on any particular definition of critical thinking. Distinguished theoreticians have formulated many useful definitions which highlight important features of critical thought. Harvey Siegel has defined critical thinking as "thinking appropriately moved by reasons". This definition highlights the contrast between the mind's tendency to be shaped by phenomena other than reasons: desires, fears, social rewards and punishments, etc. It points up the connection between critical thinking and the classic philosophical ideal of rationality. Yet clearly the ideal of rationality is itself open to multiple explications. Similar points can be made about Robert Ennis' and Matthew Lipman's definitions.

Robert Ennis defines critical thinking as "rational reflective thinking concerned with what to do or believe". This definition usefully calls attention to the wide role that critical thinking plays in everyday life, for, since all behavior depends on what we believe, all human action depends upon what we in some sense *decide* to do. However, like Siegel's definition it assumes that the reader has a clear concept of rationality and of the conditions under which a decision can be said to be "reflective". There is also a possible ambiguity in Ennis' use of 'reflective'. As a person internalizes critical standards the application of these standards to action becomes more automatic, less a matter of conscious effort, hence less a matter of overt "reflection", assuming that Ennis means to imply by 'reflection' a special consciousness or deliberateness.

Matthew Lipman defines critical thinking as "skillful, responsible, thinking that is conducive to judgment because it relies on criteria, is self-correcting, and is sensitive to context". This definition is useful insofar as one clearly understands the difference between responsible and irresponsible thinking, as well as what the appropriate self-correction of thought, the appropriate use of criteria, and appropriate sensitivity to context mean. Of course, it would be easy to find instances of thinking that were self-correcting, used criteria, and responded to context *in one sense* and nevertheless were *uncritical* in some other sense. One's criteria might be uncritically chosen, for example, or the manner of responding to context might be critically deficient in numerous ways.

I make these points not to deny the usefulness of these definitions, but to point out limitations in the process of definition itself when addressing a complex concept such as critical thinking. Rather than to work solely with one definition of critical thinking, it is better to retain a host of definitions, for two reasons: *1)* to maintain insight into the various dimensions of critical thinking that alternative definitions highlight, and *2)* to help oneself escape the limitations of each. In this spirit I will present a number of my definitions of the cluster of concepts whose relationship to each other is fundamental to critical thinking. These concepts are: critical thinking, uncritical thinking, sophistic critical thinking, and fair-minded critical thinking. After so doing, I will analyze one definition at length.

CRITICAL THINKING

    a) the art of thinking about your thinking while you're thinking so as to make your thinking more clear, precise, accurate, relevant, consistent, and fair

    b) the art of constructive skepticism

    c) the art of identifying and removing bias, prejudice, and one-sidedness of thought

    d) the art of self-directed, in-depth, rational learning

    e) thinking that rationally certifies what we know and makes clear wherein we are ignorant

UNCRITICAL THINKING

    a) thought captive of one's ego, desires, social conditioning, prejudices, or irrational impressions

    b) thinking that is egocentric, careless, heedless of assumptions, relevant evidence, implications, or consistency

    c) thinking that habitually ignores epistemological demands in favor of its egocentric commitments

SOPHISTIC CRITICAL THINKING

a) thinking which meets epistemological demands insofar as they square with the vested interests of the thinker

b) skilled thinking that is heedless of assumptions, relevance, reasons, evidence, implications and consistency only insofar as it is in the vested interest of the thinker to do so

c) skilled thinking that is motivated by vested interest, egocentrism, or ethnocentrism rather than by truth or objective reasonability

FAIRMINDED CRITICAL THINKING

a) skilled thinking which meets epistemological demands regardless of the vested interests or ideological commitments of the thinker

b) skilled thinking characterized by empathy into diverse opposing points of view and devotion to truth as against self-interest

c) skilled thinking that is consistent in the application of intellectual standards, holding one's self to the same rigorous standards of evidence and proof to which one hold's one's antagonists

d) skilled thinking that demonstrates the commitment to entertain all viewpoints sympathetically and to assess them with the same intellectual standards, without reference to one's own feelings or vested interests, or the feelings or vested interests of one's friends, community or nation

It is important not only to emphasize the dimension of skills in critical thinking, but also to explicitly mark out the very real possibility of a one-sided use of them. Indeed, the historical tendency for skills of thought to be systematically used in defense of the vested interests of dominant social groups and the parallel tendency of all social groups to develop one-sided thinking in support of their own interests, mandates marking this tendency explicitly. We should clearly recognize that one-sided critical thinking is much more common than fairminded critical thought.

With these cautionary remarks in mind I will provide a definition of critical thinking which lends itself to an analysis of three crucial dimensions of critical thought:

1) the perfections of thought
2) the elements of thought
3) the domains of thought

THE DEFINITION:

Critical thinking is disciplined, self-directed thinking which exemplifies the perfections of thinking appropriate to a particular mode or domain of thinking. It comes in two forms. If the thinking is disciplined to serve the interests of a particular individual or group, to the exclusion of other relevant persons and groups, I call it *sophistic* or *weak sense* critical thinking. If the thinking is disciplined to take into account the interests of diverse persons or groups, I call it *fairminded* or *strong sense* critical thinking.

To this definition should be added the following gloss:

In thinking critically we use our command of *the elements of thinking* to adjust our thinking successfully to the logical demands of a type or *mode of thinking*. As we come to habitually think critically in the strong sense we develop special *traits of mind*: intellectual humility, intellectual courage, intellectual perseverance, intellectual integrity, and confidence in reason. A sophistic or weak sense critical thinker develops these traits only in a restricted way, consistent with egocentric and sociocentric commitments.

I shall now list examples of what I mean by the perfections and imperfections of thought, the elements of thought, and the domains of thought. In each case I will comment briefly on the significance of these dimensions.

The Perfections and Imperfections of Thought

clarity	vs	unclarity
precision	vs	imprecision
specificity	vs	vagueness
accuracy	vs	inaccuracy
relevance	vs	irrelevance
consistency	vs	inconsistency
logicalness	vs	illogicalness
depth	vs	superficiality
completeness	vs	incompleteness
significance	vs	triviality
fairness	vs	bias or one-sidedness
adequacy (for purpose)	vs	inadequacy

Each of the above are general canons for thought. To develop one's mind and to discipline one's thinking to come up to these standards requires extensive practice and long-term cultivation. Of course coming up to these standards is relative and often has to be adjusted to a particular domain of thought. Being *precise* while doing mathematics is not the same thing as being precise while writing a poem or describing an experience.

Furthermore, one perfection of thought may come to be periodically incompatible with the others: *adequacy to the purpose*. Because the social world is often irrational and unjust, because people are often manipulated to act against their interests, because skilled thought is often used to serve vested interest, thought adequate to these purposes may require skilled violation of the common standards for good thinking. Skilled propaganda, skilled political debate, skilled defense of a group's interests, skilled deception of one's enemy may require the violation or selective application of any of the above standards. The perfecting of one's thought as an instrument for success in a world based on power and advantage is a different matter from the perfecting of one's thought for the apprehension and defense of fairminded truth. To develop one's critical thinking skills merely to the level of adequacy for success is to develop those skills in a lower or *weaker* sense. It is important to underscore the commonality of this weaker sense of critical thinking, for it is dominant in the everyday world. Virtually all social groups disapprove of members who make the case for their competitors or enemies however justified that case may be. Skillful thinking is commonly a tool in the struggle for power and advantage, not an angelic force that transcends this struggle. It is only as the struggle becomes mutually destructive and it comes to be the advantage of all to go beyond the onesidedness of each that a social ground is laid for fairmindedness of thought. There is no society yet in existence that in a general way cultivates fairness of thought in its citizens.

THE ELEMENTS OF THOUGHT

Both sophistic and fairminded critical thinkers are skilled compared to uncritical thinkers. The uncritical thinker is often unclear, imprecise, vague, illogical, unreflective, superficial, inconsistent, inaccurate, or trivial. To avoid these imperfections in thought requires some command of the elements of thought. These include an understanding of and an ability to formulate, analyze and assess these elements:

1) The problem or question at issue
2) The purpose or goal of the thinking
3) The frame of reference or points of view involved
4) Assumptions made
5) Central concepts and ideas involved
6) Principles or theories used
7) Evidence, data, or reasons advanced
8) Interpretations and claims made
9) Inferences, reasoning, and lines of formulated thought
10) Implications and consequences involved

The principles of thought that underlie command of these elements may be formulated and grouped in a variety of ways. I favor a formulation that highlights the intimate relation between the component skills of critical thinking with the *traits* of a critical thinker. These abilities to command the elements of thought must be reflected in the critical thinkers' insights into the diverse demands of differing question types and domains of thought.

THE DOMAINS OF THOUGHT

The ability to command the elements of thought to achieve the perfections of thought depends on a thinker's ability to adjust his or her thinking to differing question types and domains of thought. Of course there is no *one* way to classify questions into types or thinking into domains. In fact, critical thinkers must be comfortable adjusting their thinking not only to different question types, but also to conceptualizing each question from various analytic points of view. Often one should understand a question from a "subject-matter" point of view: to grasp, for example, that it is biological, or psychological, or mathematical, or economic. But this is rarely enough, for the same subject area may contain questions of different types, may have more than one conceptual framework within it, and many of the most important questions we face are multi-disciplinary or interdisciplinary in nature. Or one question may be analyzed from different perspectives within the logic of questions. For example, virtually all questions can be analyzed from the perspective of the distinction between empirical, conceptual, and evaluative components. Some questions are more empirical than conceptual or more evaluative than empirical. Sometimes we need to adjust our thinking about a question to take these parameters into account. Few students, for example, can address fundamentally conceptual questions; for example, questions like these:

Is a whale a fish?

Is a human fetus a person?

Is Communism compatible with democracy?

Is Capitalism compatible with democracy?

Can one ever be certain about what is right?

Are humans essentially rational or irrational?

What is the difference between freedom fighters and terrorists?

Are there such things as male and female qualities or are all such qualities a matter of social conditioning?

Can computers think?

Do animals have language?

And this is by no means all, for sometimes one must know whether a question is being raised against the background of a given social system, a given socio-logic. I have alluded to this variable before in terms of the use within social systems of "functional falsehoods". What is justified as an answer to a question, given one social system as the defining context, may very well be different within the logic of another social system. We need to know, therefore, whether we must reason within the logic of a given social system or more broadly. A question may be answerable within one system and not within another, or not in the same sense, or in the same sense but with a different answer.

Going still further, one may have to recognize, in asking a question, whether we are framing it within the logic of a technical or natural language. The question, "What is fear?" asked with the technical language of physiology and biology in mind, may well be a different question from that same interrogative sentence asked in ordinary English, a *natural* language.

Finally we often need to know, when reasoning about a question, whether it is most appropriately treated within an established logic (monological issues), or whether it is plausible to approach it from diverse points of view (multilogical issues). If one dominant theory or established procedure or algorithm exists for settling a question, it is rational to use it. Many of the routine problems of everyday life as well as many of the standard problems in highly technical or scientific disciplines are of this sort. However, students must learn how to identify those higher order problems to which multiple theories, frames of reference, or competing ideologies apply, and hence which cannot legitimately be approached monologically. Instruction rarely addresses these multilogical issues, even though most of the pressing problems of everyday social, political, and personal life are of this kind. Moreover, there is good reason to use a multilogical approach even to monological issues, when students initially approach them. I shall return to this important point presently.

Schooling, as structured today, lacks *organized* emphasis on any of these dimensions of thought: its perfections, its elements, or its typology. Educators assume good thinking follows from the systematic coverage of content and problem-solving algorithms and the memorization that traditional didactic instruction inevitably fosters. The result is students who do not think about the general perfections, the elements, or the typology of thought, students who think about knowledge and learning solely within the traditional didactic model and, as a result, can function comfortably only with lower-order, monological problems. As Lauren Resnick has put it:

> Mass education was, from its inception, concerned with inculcating routine abilities: simple computation, reading predictable texts, reciting religious or civic codes. It did not take as goals for its students the ability to interpret unfamiliar texts, create material others would want and need to read, construct convincing arguments, develop original solutions to technical or social problems. The political conditions under which mass education developed encouraged instead the routinization of basic skills as well as the standardization of teaching and education institutions. (p. 5)

Resnick characterizes the kind of (higher order) thinking typically neglected in the schools as follows:

- Higher order thinking is *nonalgorithmic*. That is, the path of action is not fully specified in advance.

- Higher order thinking tends to be *complex*. The total path is not "visible" (mentally speaking) from any single vantage point.
- Higher order thinking often yields *multiple solutions,* each with costs and benefits, rather than unique solutions.
- Higher order thinking involves *nuanced judgment* and interpretation.
- Higher order thinking involves the application of *multiple criteria,* which sometimes conflict with one another.
- Higher order thinking often involves *uncertainty*. Not everything that bears on the task at hand is known.
- Higher order thinking involves *self-regulation* of the thinking process. We do not recognize higher order thinking in an individual when someone else calls the plays at every step.
- Higher order thinking involves *imposing meaning*, finding structure in apparent disorder.
- Higher order thinking is *effortful*. There is considerable mental work involved in the kinds of elaborations and judgments required. (p. 3)

Important consequences follow from this tendency of schools to emphasize lower order thinking: *1)* students do not learn how to think in an interdisciplinary way, *2)* they are uncomfortable thinking within multiple points of view, *3)* they tend to look for recipes and algorithmic procedures for settling questions, *4)* they tend to do poorly when faced with unfamiliar issues, and *5)* they tend to gravitate toward an uncritical dogmatism or an equally uncritical relativism. Not only do most students fail to achieve any sense of how to adjust their thinking to the nature of the issue or domain about which they are thinking, but their spontaneous "lower order" thinking prevents them from developing into autonomous thinkers and independent learners.

✦ *The Logic of Learning Versus the Logic of Proof*

Higher order (multilogical) thinking applies to two basic conditions: *1)* when the question at issue is multilogical and *2)* when one is unfamiliar with the logic of the question at issue and hence must think one's way into its background logic. Standard instruction is ill-suited to both of these conditions. Multilogical issues are usually ignored and monological domains are presented as finished products. Students seldom have an opportunity to think their way into a new domain of knowledge, but are instead expected to learn to think within finished procedures, algorithms, or concepts. Most mathematics instruction illustrates this point. Rather than being introduced to problems that bridge the gap between familiar and novel problem types, students are introduced to finished algorithms and procedures. Consequently most students have large gaps in their thinking, since the algorithms they learn are only superficially understood. They are rarely expected to *think* their way to these algorithms. They learn to identify the need for one by recognizing the form in which problems are (artificially) framed in their texts.

History instruction illustrates a parallel point. Students read the finished products of professional historians rather than problems and data which enable them to think historically. Students have little sense of how to engage in historical thinking and so do not recognize the historical dimension of the problems they face in everyday life. What they learn in history class seems totally unrelated to their concerns or values.

We need a shift to higher-order thinking in every domain of learning: in monological domains like mathematics, so that students *think* their way non-algorithmically into mathematical systems, and in multilogical domains like history and sociology so that they come to appreciate the true (multilogical) nature of these domains.

The main point is this, higher-order thinking is required for all deep-seated original learning, even within domains that, once mastered, can routinely be canvassed in a lower order, monological way. To genuinely grasp a new logical domain, one must thoughtfully transfer logical structures that one does understand to the new domain and use the familiar logic analogically to mentally construct the unfamiliar one. This requires higher order thinking on the part of all learners in all original learning. It requires argumentation pro and con as students explore alternative analogies and strategies. Standard schooling has yet to assimilate this insight.

A couple of examples from research into math and science instruction will illustrate this point. Math and science provide paradigms of monological disciplines. Algorithms and quantifiable laws abound. Most textbooks contain no theoretical disputes. Students are mainly expected to learn established procedures, technical definitions, and practices. Yet even here we are discovering the importance of having students *think* their way, on their own terms, with much theoretical disputation, to comprehension and insight. The work of Easley at Illinois (1983a, 1983b, 1984a, 1984b) Schoenfeld at Berkeley, (1979, 1985, 1986, 1987, in press), and many others [Collins, Brown, and Newman (in press), Crosswhite (1987), Kilpatrick (1987), Driver (1978, 1986, 1987), Smith (1987b, 1987a, 1983), and Roth (1984, 1986, 1987)] demonstrate this need.

Schoenfeld puts the claim bluntly: "I believe that most instruction in mathematics is, in a very real sense, deceptive and possibly fraudulent." He supports this claim by citing cases in which it can be demonstrated that even advanced students of mathematics have fundamental misconceptions about the mathematical symbols and algorithms they manipulate:

> I taught a problem-solving course for junior and senior mathematics majors at Berkeley in 1976. These students had already seen some remarkably sophisticated mathematics. Linear algebra

and differential equations were old hat. Topology, Fourier transforms, and measure theory were familiar to some. I gave them a
straightforward theorem from plane geometry (required when I
was in the tenth grade). Only two of eight students made any
progress on it, some of them by using arc length integrals to
measure the circumference of a circle. (Schoenfeld, 1979) Out of
the context of normal course work these students could not do
elementary mathematics. (pp. 28–29)

In sum, all too often we focus on a narrow collection of well-
defined tasks and train students to execute those tasks in a routine, if not algorithmic fashion. Then we test the students on
tasks that are very close to the ones they have been taught. If
they succeed on those problems we and they congratulate each
other on the fact that they have learned some powerful mathematical techniques. In fact, they may be able to use such techniques mechanically while lacking some rudimentary thinking
skills. To allow them and ourselves, to believe that they "understand" the mathematics is deceptive and fraudulent. (p. 29)

Schoenfeld compares stereotypical standard practice with multilogical
mathematics instruction that focuses on class discussion, debate, argumentation, and interdisciplinary application. He cites Harold Fawcett's
geometry classes at the Ohio state University laboratory school, described
in the 1938 NCTM Yearbook, *The Nature of Proof*:

Simply put, Fawcett believed that mathematics can help you
think — in particular, that a course in geometric proof can help
students to learn to reason clearly about a wide range of situations. Following Dewey, Fawcett hoped to help his students
develop "reflective thinking" — "active, persistent and careful
consideration of any belief or supposed form of knowledge in
the light of the grounds that support it and the further conclusions to which it tends". Following Christofferson, Fawcett
sought to develop in his students "an attitude of mind which
tends always to analyze situations, to understand their interrelationships, to question hasty conclusions, to express clearly,
precisely, and accurately non-geometric as well as geometric
ideas". Among his goals for students were that in situations sufficiently important to them, his students would: ask that
important terms be defined; require evidence in support of
conclusions they are pressed to accept; analyze the evidence
and distinguish fact from assumption; recognize stated and
unstated assumptions; evaluate them; and finally, evaluate the
arguments, accepting or rejecting the conclusion. Moreover,
they would do so reflectively, constantly re-examining the
assumptions behind their beliefs and that guide their actions.
(pp. 37–38 Schoenfeld)

Katherine Roth (in press) comments on the problem of science instruction in a similar way:

> Students memorize facts and formulae, they plug in these facts and formulae to pass tests, and they use these to solve "textbook" problems. However, they do not use these facts and formulae to explain real-world phenomena that they observe and experience. To students, the facts and formulae are school knowledge, perhaps a third vine to add to the Pines and West (1983) metaphor. Students use this vine of knowledge to "get by" in school. However, this vine is unconnected with really making sense of their disciplinary vine, and it is totally irrelevant to students' everyday ways of thinking — their intuitive knowledge vine. Thus, students end instruction still finding their intuitive theories, or misconceptions, as most useful in explaining their world. Connections between their own understandings and the disciplinary concepts are rarely made. (p. 23)

She and others doing similar research continually call for an approach that requires much classroom "debate" and hence multilogical thinking:

> Most of the teachers using conceptual conflict as an instruction strategy frequently encouraged students to debate among themselves. They did not easily cave in to students' desires to be told the "right" answer. Instead, the teachers asked questions to help students clarify their explanations and to develop better support for their thinking. (ibid)

We should not assume, of course, that the change required is simply in a manner of teaching on the part of the teacher. It also requires a fundamental change in the teachers' thinking about their own learning. Consider this letter from a teacher with a Master's degree in physics and mathematics, with 20 years of high school teaching experience in physics:

> After I started teaching, I realized that I had learned physics by rote and that I really did not understand all I knew about physics. My thinking students asked me questions for which I always had the standard textbook answers, but for the first time it made me start thinking for myself, and I realized that these canned answers were not justified by my own thinking and only confused my students who were showing some ability to think for themselves. To achieve my academic goals I had to memorize the thoughts of others, but I had never learned or been encouraged to learn to think for myself.

✦ Conclusion

The pace of change in the world is accelerating, yet educational institutions have not kept up. Indeed, schools have historically been the most static of social institutions, uncritically passing down from generation to generation out-moded didactic, lecture-and-drill-based, models of instruction. Predictable results follow. Students, on the whole, do not learn how to work by, or think for, themselves. They do not learn how to gather, analyze, synthesize, and assess information. They do not learn how to analyze the diverse logics of the questions and problems they face and hence how to adjust their thinking to them. They do not learn how to enter sympathetically into the thinking of others, nor how to deal rationally with conflicting points of view. They do not learn to become critical readers, writers, speakers, or listeners. They do not learn how to use their native languages clearly, precisely, or persuasively. They do not, therefore, become "literate", in the proper sense of the word. Neither do they gain much genuine knowledge since, for the most part, they could not explain the basis for their beliefs. They would be hard pressed to explain, for example, which of their beliefs were based on rational assent and which on simple conformity to what they have heard. They do not see how they might critically analyze their own experience or identify national or group bias in their own thought. They are much more apt to learn on the basis of irrational than rational modes of thought. They lack the traits of mind of a genuinely educated person: intellectual humility, courage, integrity, perseverance, and faith in reason.

Fortunately, there is a movement in education today striving to address these problems in a global way, with strategies and materials for the modification of instruction at all levels of education. It arises from an emerging new theory of knowledge, learning, and literacy which recognizes the centrality of independent critical thought to all substantial learning, which recognizes the importance of higher order multilogical thinking for childhood as well as adult learning, to foundational learning in monological as well as multilogical disciplines. This educational reform movement does not propose an educational miracle cure, for its leading proponents recognize that many social and historical forces must come together before the ideals of the critical thinking movement will be achieved. Schools do not exist in a social vacuum. To the extent that the broader society is uncritical, so, on the whole, will society's schools. Nevertheless the social conditions necessary for fundamental changes in schooling are increasingly apparent. The pressure for fundamental change is growing. Whether and to what extent these needed basic changes will be delayed or side-tracked, and so require new periodic resurgences of this movement, with new, more elaborate articulations of its ideals, goals, and methods — only time will tell.

✦ References

Collins, A., Brown, J. S., & Newman, S. (in press). "The New Apprenticeship: Teaching Students the Craft of Reading, Writing, and Mathematics." In L. B. Resnick (Ed.), *Cognition and Instruction: Issues and Agendas.* Hillsdale, J. N.: Erlbaum.

Crosswhite, F. J. (1987). "Cognitive Science and Mathematics Education: A Mathematics Educator's Perspective." In A. Schoenfeld (Ed.), *Cognitive Science and Mathematics Education,* pp. 256–277. Hillsdale, NJ: Erlbaum.

Driver, R. (1986). *Restructuring the Physics Curriculum: Some Implications of Studies on Learning for Curriculum Development.* Invited paper presented at the International Conference on Trends in Physics Education, Tokyo, Japan.

Driver, R. (1987). "Promoting Conceptual Change in Classroom Settings: The Experience of the Children's Learning in Science Project". in J. D. Novak (Ed.), *Proceeding of the Second International Seminar on Misconceptions and Educational Strategies in Science and Mathematics.* Ithaca, NY: Cornell University.

Driver, R., & Easley, J. (1978). "Pupils and Paradigms: A Review of Literature Related to Concept Development in Adolescent Science Students. *Studies in Science Education, 5,* 61–84.

Easley, J. (1983a). "A Japanese Approach to Arithmetic." *For the Learning of Mathematics,* 3 (3).

Easley, J. (1983b). "What's There to Talk about in Arithmetic?" *Problem Solving* (Newsletter, The Franklin Institute Press) 5.

Easley, J. (1984a). "Is There Educative Power in Students' Alternative Frameworks?" *Problem Solving* (Newsletter, The Franklin Institute Press), 6.

Easley, J. (1984b). "A Teacher Educator's Perspective on Students' and Teachers' Schemes: Or Teaching by Listening." Unpublished paper, presented at the *Conference on Thinking, Harvard Graduate School of Education.*

Ennis, Robert H. "Goals For A Critical-Thinking/Reasoning Curriculum" Illinois Critical Thinking Project. University of Illinois, Champaign. 1985.

Kilpatrick, J. (1987) "Problem Formulating: Where do Good Problems Come From?" In A. Schoenfeld (Ed.), *Cognitive Science and Mathematics Education,* pp. 123–148. Hillsdale, J. N.: Erlbaum.

Lipman, Matthew. (March, 1988) "Critical Thinking and the Use of Criteria" *Inquiry,* Newsletter of the Institute for Critical Thinking, Montclair State College, Upper Montclair.

Passmore, John. "On Teaching to be Critical." *The Concept of Education,* Routledge & Kegan Paul, London: 1967. pp. 192–211.

Paul, Richard W. *Critical Thinking Handbook: K–3, A Guide for Remodelling Lesson Plans in Language Arts, Social Studies and Science,* Co-authors: A. J. A. Binker, Marla Charbonneau. Center for Critical Thinking and Moral Critique, Sonoma State University, Rohnert Park. 1987.

Paul, Richard W. *Critical Thinking Handbook: 4–6, A Guide for Remodelling Lesson Plans in Language Arts, Social Studies and Science,* Co-authors: A. J. A. Binker, Karen Jensen, Heidi Kreklau. Center for Critical Thinking and Moral Critique, Sonoma State University, Rohnert Park. 1987.

Paul, Richard W. "Teaching Critical Thinking in the Strong Sense: A Focus on Self-Deception, World Views, and a Dialectical Mode of Analysis," *Informal Logic,* May 1982, J. Anthony Blair and Ralph Johnson, editors.

Paul, Richard W. "The Critical Thinking Movement: A Historical Perspective," *National Forum,* Winter 1985, Stephen White, editor.

Paul, Richard W. "Critical Thinking and the Critical Person," *Thinking: Progress in Research and Teaching,* Lawrence Erlbaum Associates, Inc. 1987 Hillsdale, J. N., Perkins, Bishop, and Lochhead, editors.

Paul, Richard W. "Dialogical Thinking: Critical Thought Essential to the Acquisition of Rational Knowledge and Passions," *Teaching Thinking Skills: Theory and Practice,* W. H. Freeman Company, Publishers, NY, NY, 1987, Joan Baron and Robert Steinberg, editors.

Paul, Richard W. "Critical Thinking: Fundamental to Education for a Free Society," *Educational Leadership,* September 1984, Ronald Brandt, editor.

Paul, Richard W. "Ethics Without Indoctrination," *Educational Leadership,* May 1988, Ronald Brandt, editor.

Resnick, Lauren, *Education & Learning to Think,* National Academy Press, Washington DC, 1987.

Roth, K. J. (1984). "Using Classroom Observations to Improve Science Teaching and Curriculum Materials." In C.W. Anderson (Ed.), *Observing Science Classrooms: Perspectives from Research and Practice.* (1984 Yearbook of the Association for the Education of Teachers in Science.) Columbus, OH: ERIC Center for Science, Mathematics, and Environmental Education.

Roth, K. J. (1985). *Food for Plants: Teacher's Guide.* (Research Series No. 153). East Lansing, MI: Michigan State University, Institute for Research on Teaching.

Roth, K. J. (1986). "Conceptual-Change Learning and Student Processing of Science Texts." (Research Series 167). East Lansing, MI: Institute for Research on Teaching, Michigan State University.

Roth, K. J. (1987). *Helping Science Teachers Change: The Critical Role of Teachers' Knowledge about Science and Science Learning.* Paper presented at the annual meeting of the American Educational Research Association, Washington, DC.

Schoenfeld, A. H. (1985). *Mathematical Problem Solving.* New York: Academic Press.

Schoenfeld, A. H. (1986). "On Having and Using Geometric Knowledge." in J. Hiebert (Ed.), *Conceptual and Procedural Knowledge: The Case of Mathematics,* pp. 225–264. Hillsdale, NJ: Erlbaum.

Schoenfeld, A. H. (1987). "What's All the Fuss About Metacognition?" in A. Schoenfeld (Ed.), *Cognitive Science and Mathematics Education,* pp. 189–215. Hillsdale, NJ: Erlbaum.

Schoenfeld, A. H. (In press). "When Good Teaching Leads to Bad Results: The Disasters of 'Well Taught' Mathematics Classes." *Educational Psychologist.*

Scriven, Michael "Critical For Survival" *National Forum* Winter 1985. pp. 9–12.

Scheffler, Israel *Reason and Teaching.* Bobbs-Merrill, New York: 1973.

Scheffler, Israel *Conditions of Knowledge,* Scott Foresman, Chicago. 1965.

Siegel, Harvey *Educating Reason: Rationality, Critical Thinking, and Education,* Routledge. 1988.

Siegel, Harvey "Critical Thinking As an Educational Ideal," *The Educational Forum,* November 1980, pp. 7–23.

Smith, E. L., (1983). "Teaching for Conceptual Change: Some Ways of Going Wrong." In H. Helm and J. Novak (Eds.), *Proceeding of the International Seminar on Misconceptions in Science and Mathematics.* Ithaca, NY: Cornell University.

Smith, E. L., and Anderson, C. W. (1987a). *The Effects of Training and Use of Specially Designed Curriculum Materials on Conceptual Change Teaching and Learning.* Paper presented at the annual meeting of the National Association for Research in Science Teaching, Washington, DC.

Smith, E. L., (1987b). "What Besides Conceptions Needs to Change in Conceptual Change Learning?" In J. D. Novak (Ed.), *Proceedings of the Second International Seminar on Misconceptions and Educational Strategies in Science and Mathematics.* Ithaca, J. N.: Cornell University.

Chapter 8

Why Students — and Teachers — Don't Reason Well

Abstract

Paul begins this essay by developing the notion that all human action presupposes the use of humanly created logical systems that model, abridge, and summarize the features of the world about us, and that abstract inferential systems, and the reasoning they make possible, are as natural to us as a species as swimming is to a dolphin or flying is to a bird. As Paul puts it, we are continually "making inferences within a system we have created — about what is going on in our lives." Unfortunately, according to Paul, to reason well we must do more than simply engage in it. We must become aware of that engagement and use our knowledge of the nature of that engagement to improve it. Paul compares the good reasoner to the good ballet dancer, the good chess and tennis players. All three must explicitly study the principles and practice the moves involved (with explicit standards of performance in mind).

Having suggested what good reasoning requires, Paul presents evidence to show that most students are not good at it. What is more, he presents evidence to suggest that most teachers are not good at it either — at least not at assessing it when students are called upon to use it in their work. One of the major reasons, combining with ignorance of what reasoning requires, is a systematic confusion between intelligent subjectivity (wit, articulateness, cleverness without substance), and reasoned objectivity (careful, disciplined, reasoning about an issue), between subjective opinion (however "bright"), and reasoned judgment (however mundane).

Paul documents this problem with an analysis of a major mistake in a California Department of Education statewide assessment of reasoned evaluation in writing. He follows up this documentation of a mistake on the part of testing experts with the same mistake made by teachers. He then briefly explicates a model for the analysis and assessment of reasoning (based on the logic of the question at issue) complete with a series of samples of student reasoning, all duly analyzed for the reader.

Paul concludes the paper with a brief argument to the effect that "the logical structures implicit in an educated person's mind are highly systematized." In contrast he argues:

"When the logical structures by which a mind figures out the world are confused, a jumble, a hodgepodge, a mere conglomeration, then that figuring out is radically defective.... Then the mind begins it knows not where, takes things for granted without analysis or questioning, leaps to conclusions without sufficient evidence..., meanders without a consciousness of its point of view.... Then the

mind wanders into its own prejudices and biases, its own egocentricity and socio-centricity. Then the mind is not able to discipline itself by a close analysis of the question at issue and ignores the demands that the logic of that question puts on it and us as rational, logic-creating, logic-using animals."

✦ The Ability to Reason: A Defining Feature of Humans

*O*ur capacity to reason is at the heart of all disciplined thinking. It explains how we alone of all the creatures of the earth have been able to develop full-fledged academic disciplines: biology, physics, botany, zoology, chemistry, geography, history, psychology, sociology, etc. We can go beyond immediate, instinctive reactions to reflective, reasoned responses precisely because we are able to develop small-scale and large-scale systems in which to intellectually operate and act. These systems enable us to mentally manipulate our possible responses to situations — to formulate them explicitly, to hold them at intellectual arm's length, to analyze and critique them, and to decide what their implications are for us. Let me explain.

We understand the various particulars of everyday life by constructing abstract models or systems that abridge and summarize their features. In simplest form, we call these models or systems *ideas*. For example, our abstract concept of a bird is a model or system for thinking about actual birds in order to make sense of their behavior — in contrast to the behavior, say, of cats, dogs, turtles, beetles, and people. As we construct these abstract systems or models, we are enabled to use the reasoning power of our minds to go beyond a bare unconceptualized noticing of things to the making of inward interpretations of them, and hence derivations from them. In short, our concepts provide our minds with systems in which to experience and think; our minds operate (reason) within them to invest the world we experience with meanings rich in implications and consequences. Much of this is done, of course, quite automatically and subconsciously.

I can reason to any number of conclusions as the result of my having one simple model for a thing. For example, if I recognize a creature to be a dog, I can quickly infer it will:

1) bark rather than meow or chirp
2) wag its tail when pleased
3) growl when irritated
4) be unable to fly
5) have no feathers
6) be unable to live under water
7) be carnivorous

8) need oxygen
9) have teeth
10) have paws rather than feet, etc.

This word ('dog') is part of a much larger logical map upon which our minds can move in virtue of our capacity to reason. As we act bodily in the world, we act intellectually in our minds. These intellectual moves guide our actions in the world. Without these maps and the capacity to locate particulars on them, we would either thrash about aimlessly or be paralyzed by the bewildering mystery of things and events before us. In every situation in our lives we "construct" a response that results from how we are modeling the situation in our minds.

Hence, put us in any situation and we start to give it meaning, to figure it out with the logical structures we have at our disposal. So quickly and automatically do we make inferences — as the result of the way we are modeling the situation in our minds — that we do not typically notice those inferences.

For example, we see dark clouds and infer rain. We hear the door slam and infer someone has arrived. We see a frowning face and infer the person is angry. Our friend is late and we infer she is being inconsiderate. We meet a tall boy and infer he is good at basketball, an Asian and infer he will be good at math. We read a book, and infer what the various sentences and paragraphs, indeed what the whole book, is saying. We listen to what people say, and make a continual series of inferences as to what they mean. As we write we make inferences as to what others will make of what we are writing. We make inferences as to the clarity of what we are saying, as to what needs further explanation, as to what needs exemplification or illustration. We could not do this without "logical structures" by means of which to draw our inferences.

Many of our inferences are justified and reasonable. But, of course, many are not. One of the most important critical thinking skills is the skill of noticing and reconstructing the inferences we make, so that the various ways in which we inferentially shape our experiences become more and more apparent to us. This skill, this sensitivity or ability, enables us to separate our experiences into analyzed parts. We learn to distinguish the raw data of our experience from our interpretations of those data (in other words, from the inferences we are making about them). Eventually we realize that the inferences we make are heavily influenced by our point of view and the assumptions we have made. This puts us in the position of being able to broaden the scope of our outlook, to see situations from more than one point of view, to become more openminded. This requires that we recognize our point of view as a "logical system" that guides our inferences, a system that we can exchange for another (an alternative point of view), depending on our assumptions.

Often, then, different people make different inferences because they bring to situations a different point of view. They see the data differently. Or, to put it another way, they have different assumptions about what they see. For example, if two people see a man lying in a gutter, one might infer, "There's a drunken bum." The other might infer, "There's a man in need of help." These inferences are based on different assumptions about the conditions under which people end up in gutters and these assumptions are connected to the point of view about people that each has formed. The first person assumes: "Only drunks are to be found in gutters." The second person assumes: "People lying in the gutter are in need of help." The first person may have developed the point of view that people are fundamentally responsible for what happens to them and ought to be able to take care of themselves. The second may have developed the point of view that the problems people have are often caused by forces and events beyond their control. The two are modeling the situation differently. They are using a different system for experiencing it.

In any case, if we want our students to become good reasoners, we must become concerned to help them begin to notice the inferences they are making, the assumptions they are basing those inferences on, and the point of view about the world they are taking — hence the systems in which they are thinking. To help our students do this, we need to give them clear examples of simple cases, and lots and lots of practice analyzing and reconstructing them. For example, we could display the above inferences in the following way:

Person One:
Situation: "A man is lying in the gutter."
Assumption: "Only bums lie in gutters."
Inference: "That man's a bum."

Person Two:
Situation: "A man is lying in the gutter."
Assumption: "Anyone lying in the gutter is in need of help."
Inference: "That man is in need of help."

Our goal of sensitizing students to the inferences they make and to the assumptions that underlie their thinking enables them to begin to gain command over their thinking (the way they are using logical structures to model the world). Of course, it may seem odd to put any effort into making explicit such obvious examples. In the harder instances, however, the value of the explication becomes more evident. In any case, because all human thinking is inferential in nature, and all inferences are embedded in a system, we cannot gain command of our thinking unless we can recognize, one way or another, the inferences embedded in it and the assumptions that underlie it.

Consider the way in which we plan and think our way through everyday events. We think of ourselves as washing up, eating our breakfast, getting ready for work, arriving on time, sitting down at our desks, making plans for lunch, paying bills, engaging in small talk, etc. Another way to put this is to say that we are continually interpreting our actions, giving them meanings — making inferences within a system we have created — about what is going on in our lives.

And this is to say that we must choose among a variety of possible systems for thinking about things. Again, consider some simple cases. As I am sitting in my easy chair, am I "relaxing" or "wasting time"? Am I being "determined" or "stubborn", or worse, "pig-headed"? Did I "join" the conversation or "butt in"? Is Jack "laughing with me" or "laughing at me"? Am I "helping him" or "being taken advantage of"? Every time I interpret my actions within one of these systems that each word in the language represents, every time I give them a meaning, I make one or more inferences on the basis of one or more assumptions within some point of view.

As humans we continually make assumptions about ourselves, our jobs, our mates, our children, about the world in general. We take some things for granted, simply because we can't always be questioning everything. Sometimes we take the wrong things for granted. For example, I run off to the store (assuming that I have enough money with me) and arrive to find that I have left my money at home. I assume that I have enough gas in the car only to find that I have run out. I assume that an item marked down in price is a good buy only to find that it was "marked up" before it was "marked down". I assume that it will not, or that it will, rain. I assume that my car will start when I turn the key and press the starter. I assume that I mean well in my dealings with others. We make hundreds of assumptions, use hundreds of concepts, make hundreds of inferences, without noticing that we are doing so. Most of them are quite sound and justifiable. Some however are not.

The question then becomes: "How can we teach our students to begin to recognize the inferences they are making, the assumptions they are basing those inferences on, and the point of view, the perspective on the world that they are beginning to form?" That is, "How can we help students to recognize how they are reasoning about the world?"

✦ Our Students Are Not Learning to Reason Well

Though we are "logic-creating" and "logic-using" animals, we typically operate with little awareness of this fact. We create and apply logical systems without knowing that we are doing so. Our intellectual modeling of the world is done *sub rosa*, without mindfulness. It is small wonder, then, that we often reason poorly.

Imagine a ballet dancer improving her ballet without knowing that she is a dancer or how and when she is dancing. Imagine a chess player who does not know she is playing chess. Or a tennis player who does not know she is playing tennis. We can hardly imagine people developing these physical and intellectual abilities without high consciousness of how and what they are doing in the doing of it. Yet we expect students to develop the ability to reason well without any mindfulness of the nature of reasoning, the elements of reasoning, or the criteria for assessing reasoning. We expect students to become good reasoners, in other words, without any knowledge of the logic of reasoning. Not surprisingly our approach doesn't work. Most students are very poor reasoners.

WHAT DOES RESEARCH ON LEARNING AND TEACHING TELL US?

By any measure whatsoever, most students are not learning to reason well. A recent summary of research by Mary Kennedy regarding student learning and instruction at the K–12 level documents serious reasoning deficiencies on the part of students. (See figure next page.)

✦ California State-Wide Test Fiasco: Teachers and Testers Who Don't Understand Reasoning

Before teachers will be able to help students to reason well, it is essential that they learn what reasoning is and how to assess it. A recent statewide test in California demonstrated that many teachers, and even some educational testing experts, have serious misunderstandings about the nature of reasoning and how to assess it.

The student essay below (figure 2) should have been graded at the lower rather than the higher end of the continuum of eight levels: "minimal evidence of achievement" or, at best, "limited evidence of achievement" rather than the highest grade of "exceptional achievement". For though the essay may have "flair and sparkle" (as one teacher expressed it), it is a poor example of evaluative reasoning, since it systematically confuses the objective goal of reasoned evaluation with the very different goal of explaining subjective preference, an important distinction in critical thinking which the teacher-evaluators apparently missed entirely.

First of all, the instructions themselves are confused. They begin with a clear requirement of "objective" evaluation:

"Students were asked to write an evaluative essay, make judgments about the worth of a book, television program, or type of music and then support their judgments with reasons and evidence. Students must consider possible criteria on which to base an evaluation, analyze their subject in the light of the criteria, and select evidence that clearly supports their judgments."

Important Research Findings

First Finding: "...national assessments in virtually every subject indicate that, although our students can perform basic skills pretty well, they are not doing well on thinking and reasoning. American students can compute, but they cannot reason.... They can write complete and correct sentences, but they cannot prepare arguments.... Moreover, in international comparisons, American students are falling behind...particularly in those areas that require higher-order thinking.... Our students are not doing well at thinking, reasoning, analyzing, predicting, estimating, or problem solving."

Second Finding: "...textbooks in this country typically pay scant attention to big ideas, offer no analysis, and pose no challenging questions. Instead, they provide a tremendous array of information or 'factlets', while they ask questions requiring only that students be able to recite back the same empty list."

Third Finding: "Teachers teach most content only for exposure, not for understanding."

Fourth Finding: "Teachers tend to avoid thought-provoking work and activities and stick to predictable routines."

Conclusion: "If we were to describe our current K–12 education system on the basis of these four findings, we would have to say that it provides very little intellectually stimulating work for students, and that it tends to produce students who are not capable of intellectual work."

Fifth Finding: "... our fifth finding from research compounds all the others and makes it harder to change practice: teachers are highly likely to teach in the way they themselves were taught. If your elementary teacher presented mathematics to you as a set of procedural rules with no substantive rationale, then you are likely to think that this is what mathematics is and that this is how mathematics should be studied. And you are likely to teach it in this way. If you studied writing as a set of grammatical rules rather than as a way to organize your thoughts and to communicate ideas to others, then this is what you will think writing is, and you will probably teach it so.... By the time we complete our undergraduate education, we have observed teachers for up to 3,060 days."

Implication: "We are caught in a vicious circle of mediocre practice modeled after mediocre practice, of trivialized knowledge begetting more trivialized knowledge. Unless we find a way out of this circle, we will continue re-creating generations of teachers who re-create generations of students who are not prepared for the technological society we are becoming."

(Figure 1 condensed from "Policy Issues in Teaching Education" by Mary Kennedy in the *Phi Delta Kappan*, May, 91, pp 661–66.)

Evaluative Essay Sample

EVALUATION. Students were asked to write an evaluative essay, make judgments about the worth of a book, television program, or type of music and then support their judgments with reasons and evidence. Students must consider possible criteria on which to base an evaluation, analyze their subject in light of the criteria, and select evidence that clearly supports their judgments. Each student was assigned one of the following evaluative tasks:

- To write a letter to a favorite author telling why they especially liked one of the author's books.
- To explain why they enjoyed one television program more than any others.
- To justify their preference for a particular type of music.

The tasks made clear that students must argue convincingly for their preferences and not just offer unsupported opinions.

This is a sample essay from a student who demonstrated exceptional achievement.

Rock Around the Clock

"Well, you're getting to the age when you have to learn to be responsible!" my mother yelled out.

"Yes, but I can't be available all the time to do my appointed chores! I'm only thirteen! I want to be with my friends, to have fun! I don't think that it is fair for me to baby-sit while you go run your little errands!" I snapped back. I sprinted upstairs to my room before my mother could start another sentence. I turned on my radio and "Shout" was playing. I noted how true the song was and I threw some punches at my pillow. The song ended and "Control" by Janet Jackson came on. I stopped beating my pillow. I suddenly felt at peace with myself. The song had slowed me down. I pondered briefly over all the songs that had helped me to control my feelings. The list was endless. So is my devotion to rock music and pop rock. These songs help me to express my feelings, they make me wind down, and above all they make me feel good. Without this music, I might have turned out to be a violent and grumpy person.

Some of my favorite songs are by Howard Jones, Pet Shop Boys, and Madonna. I especially like songs that have a message in them, such as "Stand by Me", by Ben E. King. This song tells me to stand by the people I love and to not question them in times of need. Basically this song is telling me to believe in my friends, because they are my friends.

My favorite type of music is rock and pop rock. Without them, there is no way that I could survive mentally. They are with me in times of trouble, and best of all, they are only a step away.

California classroom teachers wrote comments like these after reading and scoring students' evaluative essays:

- "Evidence of clear thinking was heavily rewarded in our scoring."
- "I am struck by how much some students can accomplish in 45 minutes; how well they can sometimes marshal the ideas; and with how much flair and sparkle they can express themselves."
- "More emphasis should be placed on critical thinking skills, supporting judgments, and tying thoughts and ideas together. Far too many papers digress, summarize, underdevelop, or state totally irrelevant facts."
- "Students generally need to develop skills in giving evidence to support their judgments. I plan to spend more time on these thinking skills next year."

Figure 2, Source: California State Department of Education, 1988. Reprinted in, "California: The State of Assessment", Anderson, Robert L. *Developing Minds*, edited by Art Costa, pp. 314–25.

Unfortunately, this request for reasoned evaluation is blended in the second half of the instruction with what might possibly be taken, with a little stretching and selective reading, as a request for the expression of a "subjective" preference:

> Each student was assigned one of the following evaluative tasks: to write a letter to a favorite author telling why they especially liked one of the author's books, to explain why they enjoyed one television program more than any others, or to justify their preference for a particular type of music. The tasks made clear that students must argue convincingly for their preferences and not just offer unsupported opinions.

Let's look closely at this confusion. In the first place, there is still an emphasis on objective evaluation ("The tasks made clear that students must argue convincingly for their preferences and not just offer unsupported opinions") while the task itself is defined as the justification of a "preference".

Now most people prefer books, television programs, and types of music for fundamentally subjective, not objective, reasons. They like a particular book, television program, or song for no reason other than that they like it, that is, because they enjoy it or find pleasure in it or are interested or absorbed or excited or amused by it. Their reasons for liking what they like are not the result of an objective evaluation. They have no relation to the objective quality of what is judged. They are about the personal responses of the experiencer, not about the objective qualities of that which is experienced.

Most people, to take the point a step further, do not have "evidence" — other than the stuff of their subjective reactions — to justify their preferences. They prefer because of the way they feel not because of the way they reason. To choose because of these subjective states of feeling is precisely to lack criteria of evaluation or evidence that bears upon objective assessment. When challenged to support subjective preferences, people usually can do little more than repeat their subjective reactions ("I find it boring, amusing, exciting, dull, interesting, etc.") or rationalize them ("I find it exciting because it has a lot of action in it.")

A *reasoned evaluation* of a book, a program, or a type of music requires more than this; it requires some knowledge of the qualities of what we are evaluating and of the criteria appropriate to the evaluation of those qualities. One needs to be well-informed about books, about programs, about music if one is to claim to be in a position to objectively evaluate them. If one is not well-informed, one is unable to render a justified evaluative judgment, though one can always subjectively react and freely express one's subjective reactions as (mere) personal preferences. This is what the student (graded as having written an objective evaluation of "exceptional achievement") actually does. But his evaluators, not having this distinction clear in their own minds, completely miss the difference.

The sample student essay can, for analytic purposes, be divided into three parts. We shall comment briefly on each in turn. The first segment of the essay is an account of a highly emotional exchange between the student and his mother:

> "Well, you're getting to the age when you have to learn to be responsible!" my mother yelled out. "Yes, but I can't be available all the time to do my appointed chores! I'm only thirteen! I want to be with my friends, to have fun! I don't think that it is fair for me to baby-sit while you run your little errands!" I snapped back. I sprinted upstairs to my room before my mother could start another sentence.

It is clear that in this segment there is no analysis, no setting out of alternative criteria, no clarification of the question at issue, no hint at reasoning or reasoned evaluation.

In the second part, the student makes a sweeping claim about a purported causal relationship between listening to rock music and his asserted, but unsupported, ability to control his emotions. He does not consider "possible criteria on which to base an evaluation". He does not present any evidence, though he does cite two examples, one where a song prompts him to punch his pillow and one where another song prompts him to stop. This gives little credence to the notion that rock music leads to his "controlling" his emotions. If anything, his examples seem to imply that, rather than learning control from, he is learning to be controlled by, the music he listens to. His major claim that "Without this music, I might have turned out to be a violent and grumpy person" is without reasoned or evidentiary support. He merely brashly asserts that it is true:

> I turned on my radio and "Shout" was playing. I noted how true the song was and I threw some punches at my pillow. The song ended and "Control", by Janet Jackson came on. I stopped beating my pillow. I suddenly felt at peace with myself. The song had slowed me down. I pondered briefly over all the songs that had helped me to control my feelings. The list was endless. So is my devotion to rock music and pop rock. These songs help me to express my feelings, they make me wind down, and above all they make me feel good. Without this music, I might have turned out to be a violent and grumpy person.

In the third, and final, section of the essay the student closes his remarks with a series of subjective, unsupported, even irrelevant statements:

> Some of my favorite songs are by Howard Jones, Pet Shop Boys, and Madonna. I especially like songs that have a message in them, such as "Stand by Me", by Ben E. King. This song tells me to stand by the people I love and to not question them in time of need. Basically this song is telling me to believe in my friends, because they are my friends.

My favorite type of music is rock and pop rock. Without them, there is no way that I could survive mentally. They are with me in times of trouble, and best of all, they are only a step away.

If this is reasoning, it is very bad reasoning: "Believe in your friends because they are your friends", "If you feel you cannot survive without rock music, then it follows that you can't." Of course, a more appropriate interpretation of what is going on is that the student is not reasoning at all but merely asserting his subjective opinions. Consider, the student doesn't examine alternative criteria on which to base an evaluation of music. He doesn't analyze rock music in the light of evaluative criteria. He doesn't provide evidence that clearly supports his judgment. His writing is vague where it needs to be precise, logically rambling where it needs to be critically reasoned. We don't really know what he means by songs "controlling" his feelings. We are not provided with any evidence on the basis of which we could assess whether there is any truth in his sweeping claims about himself, for example, that he could not survive mentally without rock music. Indeed, common sense experience strongly suggests, we believe, that the student is simply deluding himself on this point, or, alternatively, engaging in unbridled hyperbole.

When a blatantly weak essay such as this is disseminated nationally as an example of "exceptional achievement" in the writing of a *reasoned* evaluative essay, then it is clear that there are large numbers of educators who are not clear about the assessment of reasoning. Remember, the California Assessment Program of the California State Department of Education is the second largest assessment unit in the country. (I should add that Dale Carlson, the head of CAP, is now putting a major effort into rectifying this problem.)

THE MANY WAYS TEACHERS MIS-ASSESS REASONING

If many teachers take bad reasoning to be good, do they also take good reasoning to be bad? Unfortunately the answer appears to be, "Yes." This became apparent in a Center for Critical Thinking research project in which teachers were provided with a well-reasoned response to the California prompt, in addition to the poorly reasoned one. The participants were teachers enrolled in critical thinking workshops. They were given the two essays to assess after receiving a morning's instruction on critical thinking. What is significant is the myriad of confusions and misunderstandings about the assessment of reasoning that emerged and the inconsistencies in both grading and in justifying grades.

Here is the "well-reasoned response" they were asked to assess alongside the poorly-reasoned "Rock Around the Clock".

This second essay (next page) was written by one of the research staff members of the Center who made sure that it was responsive to the directions and displayed all of the critical thinking abilities called for:

1) it distinguished mere subjective preference from well-reasoned assessment,

2) it was responsive to the logic of the question at issue,

3) it formulated and discussed alternative relevant criteria,

4) it distinguished having evidence relevant to a question from lacking such evidence,

5) it displayed intellectual humility,

6) it displayed intellectual integrity,

7) it drew only those conclusions the evidence warranted.

The results highlighted the problem. On one occasion 81 teachers and administrators assessed the two essays. The poorly-reasoned essay was given an average score of 5.4 (out of 8) while the well-reasoned essay was given an average score of 3.9. Forty-nine of the teachers gave the poorly-reasoned essay a 6, 7, or 8, while only 18 teachers gave the well-reasoned essay a 6, 7, or 8.

Can I Prove Rock Music is Better?

It's certainly hard to objectively judge music based on justifiable criteria because most people don't have any real standards for the music they listen to other than they like it. My friends and I are probably no different from other people. We listen to music we like because we like it. But this assignment asks me to give good reasons why we like what we like. I'm not sure I can, but I'll try.

I first wonder what would be a really good reason for liking any kind of music (other than it sounds good to you). Well, I suppose that one possible good reason for preferring one kind of music to another is that it expresses better the problems we face and what we can do to solve those problems.

Does this give me a good reason for preferring rock music to other kinds? Perhaps so. Certainly, rock music is often about problems that we have: problems of love and sex, school and parents, drugs and drink. I'm not sure, however, whether the "answers" in the songs actually are really good answers or just answers that appeal to us. They might even increase our prejudices about parents, teachers, school, and love. I'm not sure.

Another possible good reason for preferring one kind of music to another is that it is written better or more skillfully performed. Can I truthfully say that rock music is more skillfully written or performed than other kinds of music? In all honesty I cannot.

So what is my conclusion? It is this. I am unable to give any objective reason for liking rock music. My friends and I are like most people. We like the music we listen to just because we like it. For better or for worse, that's all the reason we have. What do you think? Can 15 million teenagers be wrong?

Even more illuminating than the raw scores were the reasons given by the teachers and administrators. Multiple confusions surfaced, as I suggested above, about the nature of reasoning and the appropriate way to assess it. Let's look at some of the responses. Try to imagine students actually receiving these grades along with the often mistaken, confused, or unintelligible commentary.

I have divided teacher assessments for convenience into two groups. The first consists of those teachers who grade the poorly reasoned essay higher than the well-reasoned essay. The second consists of those teachers who grade the poorly reasoned essay lower than the well-reasoned essay. Reading the teachers' justifications for their grades reveals a great deal of misunderstanding of the nature of reasoning. [First Essay: "Rock Around the Clock" (the poorly reasoned essay) Second Essay: "Can I Prove Rock Music is Better?" (the well-reasoned essay)]

First Group of Teachers

The following teachers give a high grade to the poorly reasoned essay and a low grade to the well-reasoned essay. In virtually every case, the teachers reveal no awareness of the importance of intellectual humility, wherein one does not claim to justify a conclusion when one lacks the evidence to do so, instead, one gives good reasons for suspending judgment.

1) *A Physical Education Teacher: [#1]* "The first essay better fulfills the criteria for the assignment because the writer justifies (his or her) preference for a particular type of music. I think I would give it a 7 though because it was kind of confusing how the writer got on the subject.

   [#2] "The second essay did not justify a preference for any particular type of music. So the writer did not meet the criteria for the assignment. Strangely enough it was easier to read but possibly because the way the writer feels is how I feel about music in general. I think the essay deserves a '0'."

2) *An English Teacher: [#1]* "I would give this essay a 7 because he/she gave experience from his/her life to support their opinion — gave reasons and evidence by example.

   [#2] "I would give this essay a grade of 2 because he/she did not prove a point — merely rambled from one thing to another searching for a reason."

3) *A Math Teacher: [#1]* "I would give the first essay a 5 because it did not support the judgment well but did make many references.

   [#2] "I would give the second essay a 3 because it is not very evaluative! It did analyze the subject but provided no real support of any judgment."

4) *A Math Teacher: [#1]* "I would give this paper a grade of 7 because criteria were evident, analysis was good and it had lots of supporting evidence.

[#2] "I would give this paper a 3 because criteria are given but nothing was analyzed and no supporting evidence."

5) *Freshman Studies Teacher: [#1]* "I would give 'Rock Around the Clock' a grade of 6 because: *a)* a more flowing style of writing than a series of loosely related points, *b)* a personal approach, *c)* specific information as to records and effects of the songs, *d)* valid and accurate comparisons, *e)* personalization, *f)* availability, *g)* a well-supported point of view, and *h)* R&R as an avoidance tool.

[#2] "I would give 'Can I Prove Rock Music is Better?' a 3 because *a)* statement of problem OK, *b)* no exploration about 'Why we like it', *c)* discusses what it is about, not why we listen. Do we listen to the words or music?, *d)* the idea of 'better performances' not followed through on, and *e)* How do they know they are like 'most people'?"

6) *A Math Teacher: [#1]* "The first essay: grade 6. The writer has set up some criteria for his choice, the music gives him a calming influence.... Since the writer is given the opportunity to set his own criteria, this will suffice. He gives examples to justify his conclusions.

[#2] "The second essay: grade 3. An attempt is made to give reasons for supporting the music but no conclusions are made. The writer cannot make an argument for his case in any area. It is difficult, as the writer has said, to justify choice or preference, but since one can choose one's own criteria it would seem any position well-argued and justified would fulfill the assignment. The author did not succeed in doing that."

7) *Subject Taught Not Identified: [#1]* "'Rock Around the Clock' Score: 6. This student does not give any clear criteria to start off as to possible criteria to base their evaluation on. This student based their evaluation on how it made them feel or respond. It was based on reactions — not facts to choose music by, but at least this student used something to justify their preference.

[#2] "'Can I Prove Rock Music Is Better?' Score: 2 Too vague — never really makes a decision about their preference of music. This student talks about possible criteria but never really says anything about it. Shows no support to justify the preference."

8) *Former English Teacher: [#1]* "I would give this essay a grade of 8 because: *a)* essay cites specific examples, *b)* catchy opening, *c)* the criteria used was based on student's personal experience, *d)* student was asked to justify their preference. I think she did.

[#2] "I would give this essay a grade of 2 because: *a)* very generalized, *b)* few, if any, concrete examples, *c)* essay is not personalized to any extent, *d)* no specific conclusions drawn."

9) *Special Ed. Teacher: [#1]* "Point total: 7. This essay listed three criteria on which to base a judgment. It gave examples of each — maybe better examples could be found. The writer attempted to analyze a basically subjective issue in concrete terms — what the songs do for them: not objective, but a fairly concrete assessment of music's subjectivity.

[#2] "Point total: 0. This essay did not seriously attempt to answer the issue at hand. Instead it concluded, quite lamely, that no objective statement of worth could be made. While this may be accurate in the broadest sense, no effort was made to justify that position."

10) *English Teacher: [#1]* "I would give this essay a 7 because the author is not afraid to take a stand. Although the 'proof' is emotionally based, that was the direction of his/her argument.

[#2] "I would give this essay a 3 because the writer was not able to take a position. He/she beats around the bush and asks the reader to make the decision when that was the assignment to the writer. The insecurity and negative attitude runs through the entire paper."

SECOND GROUP OF TEACHERS

The following teachers give a low grade to the poorly reasoned essay and a high or higher grade to the well-reasoned essay. In some cases the teachers revealed some awareness of the importance of intellectual humility. Some are, however, confused or mistaken in part about reasoning and its assessment. For most, thankfully, this confusion is conjoined with some insight into reasoning. For some few others, the fact that they graded the poorly-reasoned essay lower is not based on insight but chance. This is apparent from some of the reasons they give.

1) *A Library-Media Teacher: [#1]* "Grade: 3 or 4. Reasons: My first thought that it wasn't a typical essay but rather starts out with a rather clever, attention-getting device. In that sense, the student did catch my attention — and also confused me somewhat. That is, it doesn't start out as a typical essay. The student is a good writer in that their word choices make sense and there are supporting reasons for why they chose rock music and pop music.... Now that I read this again, I can see that really the writer has only supplied one reason for their selection: the control/expression of feelings. Well, it's the same old problem in grading a paper, i.e., the student writes well but hasn't followed the criteria strictly.

[#2] "Grade: 7. Reasons: Just a first critical response before I re-read it. It strikes me as thoughtful and honest (which always impresses me). Now I'll see how it fits the criteria. The writer states he needs good reasons for his judgment. I don't think that 'good' is the word he wants.... Why do we like what we like? That's a provocative question!... A quickie, yes, I think they've fulfilled most of the criteria, just not in the usual fashion. Also, it's an essay (as I define one)."

2) *A Special Ed. Teacher: [#1]* "The student in this essay never really makes a statement that involves an evaluation of a judgment made concerning a type of music, except to say 'My favorite type of music is rock and pop rock. Without them there is no way I could survive mentally.' He does try to show what he means by this statement when he offers examples of music that affect his mood. He lacks a clear evaluation or supportive evidence toward the topic. I think his statement about surviving mentally is a bit much. I give it a 4.

[#2] "This student doesn't know what he thinks and he lets you know it continually. His closing paragraph summarizes what he is trying to put down in the essay and it is the most straightforward part of the essay. His title doesn't quite jibe with the rest of the essay. He was supposed to prove rock music is better, but what he really talked about was whether there was any justification for why people like rock music. I give it a 5."

3) *A Social Studies Teacher: [#1]* "I would give essay one a grade of 6. Essay number one lists reasons for liking rock music, but it is very superficial in analyzing them in the light of the criteria. It really does not approach the subject in a way that logically lists possible criteria as a basis for analysis and then applies the criteria to the music. The essay is generally Bull Shit with only a general connection to the instructions.

[#2] "I would give essay #2 an 8 because the possible criteria for analyzing the issue are covered...."

4) *An English Teacher: [#1]* "Score: 3. The writer in essay one has discussed how he/she feels about rock and pop music, but generalities are given and his/her statements aren't supported with evidence. The assignment is to 'justify' preference, not discuss that it makes him/her 'feel good' period. No criteria have been established, so the essay just rambles on about 'feelings' and not much else. Reasons and evidence are lacking.

[#2] "Score: 5. This essay does a little bit better in attempting an argument. The essay establishes two 'criteria' on which to base his/her essay.... Examples of 'answers' in paragraph 3 are needed as

evidence.... Paragraph 4 isn't developed. Needs reasons and evidence/ examples. Weak Conclusion."

5) *A Physical Education Teacher: [#1]* "I would grade the essay 0. The essay does not show their judgment about worth with reason and evidence as asked in the directions. There are no criteria for evaluation, analysis with criteria or evidence that clearly supports the judgments.

[#2] "I would grade the essay 5. The essay attempts to set up criteria for evaluation, yet not as completely as it could have been done. There was an attempt to analyze the subject with the criteria, but not complete. There was no evidence to clearly support the judgment."

6) *A Second Grade Teacher: [#1]* "The first essay should have a 3 because the stated criterion is subjective. The conclusion comes down to, 'I like it because I like it.'

[#2] "The second essay would have a 6 because there was a search for good criteria and no evidence was found to support the good criteria."

7) *A Counselor: [#1]* "I would give this essay a 1 because the student did select a topic to evaluate which fit the directions. However, she reported her subjective taste (how some songs have affected her, which songs she likes) rather than evaluating 'rock music'.

[#2] "I would give this essay a 7 because: a) she selects an appropriate topic, 2) she considered what criteria would be appropriate to evaluate rock music, c) she made judgments based on the criteria she listed, 4) her conclusion was based on her criteria/judgment. However, she might have considered/used other criteria."

8) *A Sixth Grade Language Arts Teacher: [#1]* "A grade of 1. There was no evaluation, went strictly by senses.

[#2] "A grade of 8. The writer did a good job on a subject that is a matter of preference no matter how you look at it! He tried to objectively judge rock music, but in the end... 'We like it just because we like it.'"

9) *A First Grade Teacher: [#1]* "I would give 'Rock Around the Clock' a 4 because the writer did give some facts for liking rock music but wrote mostly from emotion without questioning if her facts were sound. For example, 'believe in my friends because they are my friends'.

[#2] "I would give 'Can I Prove Rock Music is Better?' a 7. The writer stated the purpose, criteria, facts, and gave a conclusion. The writer considered more than just feeling. More facts for liking rock music are needed."

✦ Introduction to the Analysis and Evaluation of Reasoning

There are two obstacles that stand in the way of fostering sound reasoning K–12: *1)* teachers must learn how to devise assignments that require reasoning, and *2)* teachers must learn how to analyze and evaluate reasoning objectively. This process will not happen overnight, but the sooner it begins, the sooner it can be achieved.

We will shortly take a look at three assignments that call for reasoning as well as at three examples of student work for each of those assignments: student work with no reasoning in it, student work with poor reasoning in it, and student work with good reasoning in it. In each case, we will provide a brief commentary to help make clear what one should look for in the reasoning. But first we will provide a brief overview of what is involved, in general, in the analysis and evaluation of reasoning.

WHAT IS INVOLVED IN ANALYZING AND EVALUATING REASONING?

The fundamental criteria to use in analyzing and evaluating reasoning comes from an analysis of the purpose of the reasoner and the logic of the question or questions raised. For example, if a person raises the question, say, as to whether democracy is failing in the USA (in the light of the dwindling number of people who vote and the growing power of vested interest groups with significant money to expend on campaign contributions), we can establish general criteria for assessing the reasoning by spelling out what in general one would have to do to settle the question. Those criteria would include such matters as the following:

1) An Analysis of the Concept of the Ends of Democracy. What would it be for democracy to succeed? What would it be for it to fail? What do we take the fundamental objective of democracy to be? For democracy to succeed is it enough that it simply ensure the right of the people at large to vote or must it also serve the well being of the people as well?

2) Collection of the Facts About the Numbers of People Not Voting. What is the actual number of people not voting? Is it growing? By what percentage?

3) An Interpretation of the Significance of the Facts Collected in #2. What are the reasons why growing numbers of people are not voting? What are the implications of those facts?

4) Collection of Facts About the Number of Vested Interest Groups Influencing Elections. How many vested interested groups are influencing elections today in comparison to the past? What is the nature and extent of their influence in money spent?

5) An Interpretation of the Significance of the Facts Collected in #4. What is the significance of the growing influence of vested interest groups on election outcomes? What is gained and lost by means of that influence?

6) Synthesis of Numbers 1 through 5. What is the overall significance of what we have found out in 1 through 5? What does it all add up to? What exactly are we gaining and losing as a result of the growing influence of vested interest groups and diminished numbers of voters? In attempting to put everything together we would want to see reflection on this issue from more than one point of view. We would want to assess how the reasoner responds to reasonable objections from other points of view.

These are some of the considerations relevant to reasoning well about the issue. A rational analysis of someone's response to this issue would involve, then, checking to see if the above considerations were reasonably addressed, to see if the reasoner had done a plausible job in analyzing the functions of democracy, collecting relevant facts and information, interpreting those facts, and putting everything together, with a sensitivity to more than one point of view, into one coherent line of reasoning.

Many of the teachers assessing the reasoning of the essays on rock music above failed to analyze or review the logic of the question at issue. Instead they read the essays impressionistically, allowing the grade they gave to be determined more by whether their impressions were positive or negative than by any close analysis of the degree to which the student responded adequately to the demands inherent in the precise question at issue.

It is the logic of the question at issue which is the "system for thinking" that should guide our reasoning. If we do not develop skill in explicating that logic, our reasoning is apt to become impressionistic, guided by our prejudices and biases, by our egocentrism and ethnocentrism, rather than disciplined by rational considerations.

✦ *Three Examples of Student Reasoning*

What follows below are three assignments designed to call for reasoning on the part of the students, along with three examples of student "reasoning" in response to those assignments. Two of the assignments are in history and the other in literature. The three issues the students are asked to develop their reasoning on involve: reasoning about the character of the American people, reasoning about the meaning of a poem, and reasoning about the comparative importance of inventions. It would be useful if you thought a little about your own assessment of the students' reasoning before you looked at ours'. You could then compare the two.

AMERICAN HISTORY: REASONING ABOUT THE AMERICAN CHARACTER

Question at Issue: "Are the Americans you know capable of the kind of mass hysteria which occurred in 1919 and is described in a textbook as the 'Red Scare'?"

Directions: One of the most important reasons to write our history is to discover who we are and who we are not, how we can develop ourselves, what faults we have to watch out for, and what strengths we can build upon. Read the passage in your textbook on the "Red Scare". Then write a couple of paragraphs in which you try to figure out whether the Americans you know are "capable" or "not capable" of reacting as many Americans did in 1919. (See textbook, p. 731.) Be sure you show us your reasoning. Support and explain why you think as you do.

Reading Excerpt: The "Red Scare"
(from *America: Past and Present*, by Divine, Breen, Fredrickson, and Williams; Scott, Foreman and Company, 1984, p. 731.)

The first and most intense outbreak of national alarm came in 1919. The heightened nationalism of World War I, aimed at achieving unity at the expense of ethnic diversity, found a new target in bolshevism. The Russian Revolution and the triumph of Marxism frightened many Americans. A growing turn into communism among American radicals (especially the foreign-born) accelerated the fears, although the numbers involved were tiny — at most there were sixty thousand Communists in the United States in 1919. But they were located in the cities, and their influence appeared to be magnified with the outbreak of widespread labor unrest.

A general strike in Seattle, a police strike in Boston, and a violent strike in the iron and steel industry thoroughly alarmed the American people in the spring and summer of 1919. A series of bombings led to panic. First the mayor of strike-bound Seattle received a small brown package containing a homemade bomb; then an alert New York postal employee detected sixteen bombs addressed to a variety of famous citizens (including John D. Rockefeller); and finally, on June 2, a bomb shattered the front of Attorney General A. Mitchell Palmer's home. Although the man who delivered it was blown to pieces, authorities quickly identified him as an Italian anarchist from Philadelphia.

In the ensuing public outcry, Attorney General Palmer led the attack on the alien threat. A Quaker and progressive, Palmer abandoned his earlier liberalism to launch a massive roundup of foreign-born radicals. In a series of raids that began on November 7, federal agents seized suspected anarchists and Communists and held them for deportation with no regard for due process of law. In December, 249 aliens — including such well-known radical leaders as Emma Goldman and Alexander Berkman — were sent to Russia aboard the *Buford,* dubbed the "Soviet Ark" by the press. Nearly all were innocent of the charges against them. A month later, Palmer rounded up nearly four thousand suspected Communists in a single evening. Federal agents broke into homes, meeting halls, and union offices without search warrants. Many native-born Americans were caught in the dragnet and spent several days in jail before being released; aliens rounded up were deported without hearings or trials.

For a time, it seemed that this Red Scare reflected the prevailing views of the American people. Instead of condemning their government's actions, citizens voiced their approval and even urged more drastic steps. One patriot said his solution to the alien problem was simple: "S.O.S. — ship or shoot." General Leonard Wood, the army chief of staff, favored placing Bolsheviks on "ships of stone with sails of lead," while evangelist Billy Sunday preferred to take "these ornery, wild-eyed Socialists" and "stand them up before a firing squad and save space on our ships." Inflamed by public statements like these, a group of legionnaires in Centralia, Washington, dragged a radical from the town jail, castrated him, and hanged him from a railway bridge. The coroner's report blandly stated that the victim "jumped off with a rope around his neck and then shot himself full of holes."

The very extremism of the Red Scare led to its rapid demise. Courageous government officials in the Department of Labor insisted on due process and full hearing before anyone else was deported. Prominent public leaders began to speak out against the acts of terror. Charles Evans Hughes, the defeated GOP candidate in 1916, offered to defend six Socialists expelled from the New York legislature; Ohio Senator Warren G. Harding, the embodiment of middle-class values, expressed his opinion that "too much has been said about bolshevism in America." Finally, Palmer himself, with evident presidential ambition, went too far. In April 1920, he warned of a vast revolution to occur on May 1; the entire New York City police force, some eleven thousand strong, was placed on duty. When no bombings or violence took place on May Day, the public began to react against Palmer's hysteria. Despite a violent explosion on Wall Street in September that killed thirty-three people, the Red Scare died out by the end of 1920. Palmer passed into obscurity, the tiny Communist party became torn with factionalism, and the American people tried hard to forget their momentary loss of balance.

Student #1

The people I know are not like the people who lived in 1919. They obey the law and, though they might make some mistakes or do some things they ought not to, they would never hurt someone who was innocent. Most of the people I know go to church and believe in God. They are good Christians. They read the Bible. They try to raise their children to be good and avoid evil. They are kind people. So I don't believe that what happened in 1919 could ever happen again. It won't happen in my neighborhood.

Commentary on the Student's Reasoning

There is very little reasoning in this student's work and, on the whole, what there is seems uncritical and self-serving: in essence, "My friends are good. Therefore they wouldn't do anything bad." There are obvious objections to this reasoning. Presumably, most of the people in 1919 also went to church and believed in God. Presumably, they too would have thought themselves to be good Christians. Presumably, their friends thought of them as kind and as trying to raise their children to be good and to avoid evil. As a result, the student has not really responded to the logic of the question which implicitly requires that we think about mass hysteria, how it occurs, and how it influences otherwise morally sensitive people to behave in a morally insensitive way.

Student #2

Certainly there are always people who go overboard. That is human nature. And it is unreasonable to think that we will ever abandon human nature. The American people rightly recognized the threat that communism posed to our way of life and fought against it. After all, if we had defeated it then we would not have to have fought the Cold War and spent so much money and resources to defeat the communists after WW II. So what is the lesson. Watch out for human nature. Don't go overboard. But on the other hand, don't forget who your enemies are and don't give up the fight against them just because some people punish them too severely or go to an extreme.

Commentary on the Student's Reasoning

There is more reasoning in this student's work, but still not very good reasoning: in essence, "It is human nature for some people to lose control. So (by implication) some of us might do so, but whether or not some of us might act as some people in 1919 did, the people in 1919 were right to fight against communists". This reasoning is weak because it largely ignores the issue raised. The question at issue is not whether it was right for the people in 1919 to oppose communism, such as it was, in the USA at the time. The question is rather how it came to pass that, as we expressed above, otherwise morally sensitive people came to behave in a morally insensitive way. The student didn't take this question seriously.

Student #3

It is hard to answer the question as to what anyone is capable of. Perhaps what we are capable of is largely a result of the circumstances we are under. If we assume that all humans share human nature and that because of human nature we are capable of acting out of intense fear or insecurity or hate, then a lot depends upon whether something or someone is able to stir those things up in us. Perhaps, of course, there is a way to raise people so that they have so much good character that even when someone tries to stir up the "worst" in them, they do not give in, they resist the temptation to let their worst side take control of them. The question could then be asked whether I and my friends and neighbors are in the first or the second group. Since we have never been "tested" in a crisis situation, since we have never felt deeply threatened, I don't think I can honesty say we would pass the test. I don't know whether we would act like a "Charles Evans Hughes" or a "Billy Sunday". It's a scary thought.

Commentary on the Student's Reasoning

This is better reasoning than in either of the two passages above: in essence, "Everyone has a worse and a better side. Everyone's worse side can be appealed to. Whether you have the "character" to withstand an appeal to your worse cannot be known until you are "tested". My friends and I have not been tested. Therefore, we cannot know whether we have the character to withstand such an appeal. Therefore, we don't know whether we would or would not act as many did in 1919."

ENGLISH: INTERPRETING POEMS

Question At Issue: What is John Donne saying in his poem "Death Be Not Proud"?

Directions: Carefully read the poem below, trying to figure out what the poet is saying. Be careful to explain what your interpretation is and what exactly it is based on. Show us your reasoning. Make sure your interpretation is consistent with (all of) what the poem says.

Death Be Not Proud
(John Donne 1572–1631)

Death be not proud, though some have called thee
Mighty and dreadful, for, thou art not soe,
For, those, whom thou think'st, thou dost overthrow,
Die not, poore death, nor yet canst thou kill mee.
Much pleasure, then from thee, much more must flow,
And soonest our best men with thee doe goe,
Rest of their bones, and soules deliverie.
Thou art slave to Fate, Chance, kings, and desperate men,
And dost with poyson, warre, and sicknesse dwell,
And poppie, or charmes can make us sleepe as well,
And better then thy stroake; why swell'st thou then?
One short sleepe past, wee wake eternally,
And death shall be no more; death, thou shalt die.

Student #1

I don't like this poem. It is boring and confusing. The guy does not spell correctly. He talks a lot about death but he does not say anything. I don't see why he thinks death is mighty or why he thinks it can't kill him. He says a lot of confusing things. At one time he says it gives pleasure and then talks about bones resting, which makes no sense. Then he talks about flowers and sleeping.

Finally he says that death shall be no more and that it shall die. I don't get it. Why doesn't he just say what he wants to say? This is a terrible poem. Why do we have to read such stupid stuff?

Commentary on the Student's Reasoning

This student provides us with virtually no reasoning at all. Rather than attempt to figure out what the poet is saying by closely reading what is said, the student rejects the poem, dismisses it emotionally. The result is that the student flagrantly mis-reads the poem and blames his mis-reading on the poem itself and the poet. The student needs to be introduced to the concept of critical reading in which the reader uses the text as evidence to use in interpreting the meaning.

Student #2

Mr. Donne says that death should not be proud. It is not mighty or dreadful. He says this because death is like sleep and when you go to sleep you rest. Therefore, because it is restful even the best people sleep, even slaves. And sleeping is better than being poisoned or being sick. Finally, he says that we only sleep a while and then we awake. And then death is gone. In fact, it is dead. He thinks this is good.

Commentary on the Student's Reasoning

There is more reasoning in this student's work but most of it ignores the evidence of what the poem says. The poem does not say or imply, for example, that "because it [death] is restful even the best people sleep, even slaves". The poem does not say or imply that "sleeping is better than being poisoned or being sick". Finally, it is clear that the student is not getting the major point of the poem, namely, that because of the promised resurrection, last judgment, and eternal life in heaven or hell, there is a sense in which "death" is not real and lasting, but only something that will "die". Like the first student, this student also needs to be introduced to the concept of critical reading in which the reader uses the text as evidence in interpreting meaning.

Student #3

It is clear that Donne believes in God or at least in an afterlife. This is implied in the first four lines which I interpret as saying something like this: "Don't think you're so powerful because no one really dies but only appears to die" (People who "die" are really just awaiting their resurrection). This interpretation is supported in the next line which implies that what we call death is really a kind of "sleepe" and is not, therefore, very bad. In fact, as he says sleep often gives us "pleasure". The next lines make a different kind of point but still are a criticism of the view that death is "mighty" and "dreadful". Death, he says, is not able to control "Fate, Chance, kings, and desperate men". Furthermore, not only is it not able to control these other forces, it can't even get away from such unpleasant associates as "poyson, warre, and sicknesse". Finally, he reasons, narcotics makes us sleep as well as death does and when everyone is resurrected for final judgment (which I infer is what he means) then death itself will be gone forever, and therefore "shalt die".

Commentary on the Student's Reasoning

Finally, we have a student who illustrates the process of critical reading, carefully reasoning her way through the poem, using the words of the poem to carefully back up her interpretation.

HISTORY: REASONING ABOUT THE SIGNIFICANCE OF INVENTIONS

Question at Issue: "Of two inventions discussed in your textbook, which was the most important and why?"

Directions: The textbook for the course describes a number of important inventions, including those of Gutenberg, Edison, and George Washington Carver. Take two inventions, either from those mentioned in the book or some other inventions you know of, and compare their importance. Defend your answer by giving reasons in favor of your judgment.

Student #1

An invention that is very important is the printing press. It was invented by Johann Gutenberg, who was a man that lived in Germany. He invented the printing press in the Fifteenth Century. The first book ever printed by Gutenberg was the Bible. But he soon printed many other books as well. The first printing press worked by using movable type.

Another important invention mentioned in the textbook was the dehydration of foods. This was invented by George Washington Carver. When you dehydrate foods you take the water out of them. George Washington Carver wanted many people to use his inventions, so he did not take out any patents on them. He made many other inventions besides dehydration. He even thought of more than 300 uses for the peanut, including facial cream, shoe polish, and ice cream.

Both inventions are very important. Many people read books that are printed on a printing press. Many people eat food that has been dehydrated. But to me the printing press was more important than dehydration.

Commentary on the Student's Reasoning

The student does not provide any reasoning to support his conclusion. He discusses no criteria for assessing inventions for their importance, nor any evidence to support one or the other with respect to those criteria. Most of the factual detail is irrelevant to the issue.

Student #2

R-r-r-r-ring.

The first sound I hear in the morning is my alarm clock going off. It's an invention I truly hate.

R-r-r-r-ring.

It is not a pretty sound, and as soon as I hear it I feel myself getting angry. If only I didn't have to get up so early! All my muscles cry out that I want to sleep! Most mornings when I hear that sound, I even cover my ears with my pillow in the hope that I won't hear it going off.

It is an old-fashioned wind-up alarm clock that loses ten minutes a day. It is not a digital alarm clock because all the digital alarm clocks I've ever tried have alarms that are too soft to awaken a really sound sleeper. And believe me I am a *very* sound sleeper.

R-r-r-r-ring. But no matter what I do, or how I feel, I end up wide awake and out of bed and getting dressed for school.

Once I am awake I look at my other clock, the one that is hanging on the wall over my dresser. It is a great invention too. It's a digital clock that keeps perfect time. It has a red LED display and it glows in the dark. It has an emergency battery backup, so that even if the electricity cuts out in the night, my wall clock never loses a second.

Which of the two inventions is more important? That's the question I ask myself as I head off for school. And then the answer comes to me. No matter how perfectly the digital wall clock keeps time, without the alarm clock I wouldn't be awake to see it. So without doubt the alarm clock wins the prize as most important.

Commentary on the Student's Reasoning

The student provides some reasoning but when considered closely it is apparent that the reasoning is absurd. The notion that without the alarm clock people would never wake up is ridiculous. What does this student think happened before the alarm clock was invented? Furthermore, does she really think that loud alarms cannot be built into digital clocks? Once again, the student has not learned to think about the logic of the question at issue. Therefore, the student gives no time to reflecting on the general criteria by means of which we might assess the social worth of inventions by relating that worth to the most basic human values, like the preservation of life, the minimization of pain and suffering, the development of a more just society, and so forth. It is only in terms of the concepts of basic human values that criteria can be generated that give a solid logic to the question and hence a means to assess the reasoning which purports to settle the question.

Student #3

Two inventions mentioned in the book are television and the dehydration of food. Each is important in different ways. The television set, for example, affects many people's lives. I watch television almost every night and so do all of my friends. But it's not just me and my friends. The same is true for people all across the country, and in most foreign countries as well. Television allows more people to be entertained than was ever possible before. We witness world news, nature programs, comedies and many other programs. Television lets us see much of what is going on in the world.

Dehydration of foods is important in a very different way. The main effects of dehydration are that it allows food to be kept for a long time without spoiling, and to be shipped for a lower cost. I don't know how many people in the world today use dehydrated foods, but I'm pretty sure that it's far smaller than the number of people who enjoy TV. So that seems to show that TV is more important.

And yet I don't feel right saying that one invention is more important than another simply because it has affected more people. If dehydration is used more than it is now, it could help cut down on the number of people who are starving in the world. Saving just a few people from dying of starvation is more important than taking a lot of people and entertaining them.

Commentary on the Student's Reasoning

The student provides some reasoning which might at first appear absurd, but on reflection makes good sense. This student is thinking about the logic of the question at issue and hence is reflecting on the general criteria by means of which we might assess the social worth of inventions by relating that worth to the most basic human values: like the quality or preservation of life, the minimization of pain and suffering, the development of a more just society, and so forth. To say that this student's reasoning is better than the first two students — because she does respond to the logic of the question at issue — does not mean that her reasoning is perfect, for perhaps there are yet further considerations that might be mentioned about the effects of television which might persuade us that television itself is making so large a contribution to the quality or preservation of human life that it is indeed more important than food dehydration. We may know the basic logic of a question without knowing whether we yet have the best answer to that question, the answer that best fulfills its logic.

✦ Conclusion

The whole of this book is concerned with the process of developing students who reason through what they are learning so as to grasp the logic of it, students who know clearly the difference between coming to terms with the logic of something and merely rotely memorizing it. But reasoning is not a matter to be learned once and for all. It is a matter of life-long learning, a matter of bringing insightful mindfulness into the fabric of our thinking and our action. For the teacher, it is a matter of learning how to design instruction so that students take command of the logic of their own thinking while they are thinking and through that insightful grasp, improve it.

We figure things out better if we can monitor what we are doing, intellectually, in trying to figure them out, so that we go beyond simply using logical structures, so that we go beyond simply making logical moves, so that we start to intentionally, deliberately, and willfully examine and take apart the logical structures we are using, so that we designedly, purposively, and alertly assess our use of the structures in everyday situations, and, of course, so that we do these things well: clearly, accurately, precisely, etc.

To understand logical structures is to integrate them, to establish logical connections between them, to make it possible for the mind to make an extended series of nuanced inferences, deductions, and derivations. "This is so, therefore that also is so, and that, and that." The logical structures implicit in an educated person's mind are highly systematized. The well-educated person is able to reason quite directly and deliberately, to begin somewhere, know where one is beginning, and then reason with awareness from that point to other points, all with a given question in mind, with specific evidence in mind, with specific reasons to advance, with specific conclusions to support, with consciousness of one's point of view and of contrasting points of view. The good reasoner is always reasoning within a system that disciplines and restrains that reasoning.

When the logical structures by which a mind figures out the world are confused, a jumble, a hodgepodge, a mere conglomeration, then that figuring out is radically defective, typically in any of a variety of ways: incomplete, inaccurate, distorted, muddled, inexact, superficial, rigid, inconsistent, and unproductive. Then the mind begins it knows not where, takes things for granted without analysis or questioning, leaps to conclusions without sufficient evidence to back them up, meanders without a consciousness of its point of view or of alternative points of view. Then the mind wanders into its own prejudices and biases, its own egocentricity and sociocentricity. Then the mind is not able to discipline itself by a close analysis of the question at issue and ignores the demands that the logic of that question puts on it and us as rational, logic-creating, logic-using animals.

Section II

Critical Thinking in the Strong Sense

Chapter 9

Critical Thinking:
Fundamental to Education for a Free Society

Abstract

In this paper, written for Educational Leadership *(1984), Paul argues that educational reform will not produce meaningful change unless educators explicitly grasp five inter-related truths: that students, as all people, tend to reason egocentrically; that multi-dimensional problems, traditionally ignored, ought to be central in schooling; that indoctrination into prevailing views has inappropriately been the major academic response to real world problems; that children from the earliest years need to be encouraged to think for themselves through dialogue, discussion, and constructive debate; and, finally, that "teaching strategies need to be revamped across the board" to stress the development of dialogical and dialectical thought. Paul summarizes his thesis at the close: "An open society requires open minds. Collectively reinforced egocentric and sociocentric thought, conjoined with massive technical knowledge and power, are not the foundations for a genuine democracy."*

✦ The Emerging Critical Thinking Movement

*T*he "critical thinking movement" is now, after a long and halting start, building up a head of steam. Predictably, numerous quick-fix, miracle cures have sprung up, and turning to them is tempting, especially given the increasing variety of imperatives and mandates under which schools operate. I argue in this paper for a different understanding of how to proceed. I advocate both a short-term and a long-term strategy, based on an analysis of where we now stand and what we should strive for ultimately.

I argue that our strategy should reflect a realistic appraisal of the following factors: *1)* the basic cognitive and affective tendencies of the human mind in its normal, uncritical state, *2)* the categorically different problem types and the reasoning appropriate to them, *3)* the social and personal conditions under which cognitive and affective processes develop, *4)* the present critical thinking skills of teachers and students, and *5)* the fundamental intellectual, affective, and social obstacles to the further development of such skills.

I emphasize the need to recognize and highlight a fundamental difference between two distinct conceptions of critical thinking: a "weak" sense, understood as a set of discrete micro-logical skills extrinsic to the character of the person, skills that can be tacked onto other learning; and a "strong" sense, understood as a set of integrated macro-logical skills and abilities intrinsic ultimately to the character of the person and to insight into one's own cognitive and affective processes. If we chose the latter we concern ourselves not only with the development of *technical reason* — skills which do not transform one's grasp of one's basic cognitive and affective processes — but also with the development of *emancipatory reason* — skills and abilities which generate not only fundamental insight into, but also some command of one's own cognitive and affective processes. In the strong sense, we emphasize comprehensive critical thinking skills and abilities essential to the free, rational, and autonomous mind. In the weak sense, we are content to develop what typically comes down to "vocational" thinking skills which by themselves have little influence on a person's intellectual, emotional or moral autonomy. If we aspire to strong sense critical thinking skills and abilities for our long-term goals, and we take stock of where we now stand, careful consideration of the available evidence will, sooner or later, persuade us of something like the following points:

1) that we have deep seated tendencies to use reason to maximize getting, and justify getting, what we, often unconsciously, want, and that this means we use cognitive and affective processes to maintain self-serving or pleasant illusions, to rule out or unfairly undermine ideas in opposition to our own, to link our identity with ideas that are "ours" (and so experience disagreement as ego-threatening), and otherwise to distort or misinterpret our experience to serve our own advantage;

2) that we must distinguish two kinds of problems: problems in technical domains wherein one self-consistent, close-textured system of ideas and procedures determines the settlement of issues, and, in contrast, problems in the logically messy "real world" of everyday life, wherein opposing points of view and contradictory lines of reasoning are relevant and realities of power and self-delusion make rational settlement of issues much harder;

3) that until now, the schools, to the extent they have addressed problem-solving, have focused on technical problems and technical reason and procedures, and have either illicitly reduced real world problems to them or have tacitly inculcated into students the pre-fabricated "self-evident answers" of the dominant social majority or some favored minority;

4) that our capacity to control our cognitive and affective processes often depends on the character of our early lives both at home and school and that very special preparation is necessary for children to develop

into adults comfortable with and skilled in weighing, reconciling, and assessing contradictory arguments and points of view through dialogue, discussion, and debate; and,

5) that teaching strategies need to be revamped across the board — especially in social studies and basic academic competencies — to stress the development of dialectical knowledge and skills, and thus self-formed, self-reasoned conviction.

✦ Short Term Strategy: Develop Micro-Logical, Analytic Critical Thinking Skills

The best short term strategy is to facilitate the understanding and teaching of micro-logical analytic critical thinking skills within established subject areas. This requires teaching the use of the elementary critical, analytic vocabulary of the English language, a working knowledge of such mundane terms as *premise, reason, conclusion, inference, assumption, relevant, irrelevant, consistent, contradictory, credible, doubtful, evidence, fact, interpretation, question-at-issue, problem,* etc. Teachers should be encouraged to take at least one university level course in critical thinking wherein they practice the basic micro-logical skills associated with these terms, and so learn to isolate and distinguish issues, premises, assumptions, conclusions, inferences, and master the rudiments of argument assessment.

The nationally normed tests, such as the Watson-Glaser and the Cornell Critical Thinking Tests should be available and teachers should learn how to formulate test questions modeled on them.

A full range of critical thinking books and materials, both university level and K–12, should be made available to teachers and regular brainstorming sessions established. Teachers need to begin to think critically about thinking skills, to get a handle on what makes sense to them and what they can immediately begin to do. An important caveat should be entered here, however. Unlike the domain of technical skills, teachers, and people generally, are naturally disinclined to recognize the degree to which they do not think critically. People tend to retreat to simplistic approaches that do not lay an appropriate foundation for higher level (strong sense) critical thought or to dismiss the need for any new learning at all. ("All good teachers naturally teach critical thinking.") Most people, including the most uncritical, take offense at the suggestion that they lack skill in this area. This ego-identification with critical thinking (*others* need it) is a continual obstacle to reform. To the extent that people lack critical thinking skills, they conceptualize those who have them as "prejudiced", "closedminded", "overly academic", "negative", or "nit-picky".

We must therefore emphasize from the start that the ability to think critically is a matter of degree. No one is without any critical skills whatsoever and no one has them so fully that there are *no* areas in which uncritical thinking is dominant. Openmindedness may be the proper, but it is not the "natural", disposition of the human mind. More on this presently.

Additional short term goals should include the following:

1) Getting master teachers trained in critical thinking;

2) Encouraging teachers and curriculum specialists to attend the growing numbers of critical thinking conferences;

3) Developing a school-wide attitude in which reasoning within unorthodox and conflicting points of view and respectful, reasoned disagreement is considered essential and healthy (a very difficult goal to achieve of course);

4) Looking for what Bloom has called "latent" curricula and "unspoken" values that may undermine the critical spirit (again, very difficult); and,

5) Establishing a working relationship with at least one university critical thinking instructor.

The ideal, as I see it, is to take those first steps that initiate the teaching of relatively "self-contained" critical thinking skills — testing for inferences that do or do not follow, recognizing assumptions and clear-cut contradictions, giving initial formulations of reasons to support conclusions, considering evidence rather than relying on authority, and so forth — and that develop an environment conducive to strong sense critical thinking. In the process, wherever possible, students should have opportunities to advance ideas of their own and give reasons to support them, as well as opportunities to hear the objections of other students. If this is done carefully in an atmosphere of co-operation and while learning critical analytic terms, the students will begin to use critical distinctions to defend their ideas. When this vocabulary integration begins, a very healthy process has been set in motion which, properly nurtured, can lead to primitive emancipatory thinking skills.

✦ Long Term Strategy: Develop Macro-Logical, Integrative Thinking Skills

An effective long range strategy should have two parts: 1) an on-going explication of the obstacles to the development of strong-sense critical thought, and 2) an increasing recognition of the distinctive nature and importance of dialectical issues and how they can be brought into the curriculum. It is not enough to recognize that all human thought is embedded in human activity and all human activity embedded in human thought. We also need to recognize that much of our thinking is subconscious, automated, and irrational. The capacity to explicate the roots of the thinking "hidden" from us and to purge it when irrational are crucial. Long-term strategy must have an explicative/purgative as well as a constructive/developmental dimension. Because of the limitations of space, however, we can do no more here than set out each side of this global orientation in rough outline.

OBSTACLE ONE: THE DENIAL OF THE NEED

Without ignoring the many ways in which they intersect, consider the degree to which we live in two very different worlds: a world of technical and technological order and clarity, and a world of personal and social disorder and confusion. We are increasingly adept at solving problems in the one domain and increasingly endangered by our inability to solve problems in the other.

Various explanations have been given for this unhappy state of affairs. One of the most popular identifies the root causes to be two-fold: 1) a lack of willingness on the part of those who are right, and know they are, to "stand tall" and refuse to be pushed around by those who are wrong (and are being irrational, stubborn, or malevolent), and 2) the difficulty of getting the "others", our opposition, to see the rationality and fairmindedness of our views and the irrationality and closedmindedness (or malevolence) of their own. President Reagan, to take a recent striking example, put it succinctly when he claimed that one country, the USSR, is the "focus of all evil in the world", an "evil empire" which understands nothing but force and power and steel-eyed determination. That a one-dimensional explanation of this sort can still, not only catch the public's fancy, but seem intelligible to many national leaders, not to mention some "intellectuals", testifies, in my view, to the primitive state of much of our thinking about non-technical, non-technological human problems.

President Reagan's nationalistic expostulations remind me of a tendency to ethnocentrism deep in our own, and perhaps in all cultures. Consider this passage from a 19th century speech:

> Fellow Americans, we are God's chosen people. Yonder at Bunker Hill and Yorktown His providence was above us. At New Orleans and on ensanguined seas His hand sustained us. Abraham Lincoln was His minister, and His was the altar of Freedom the boys in blue set on a hundred battle-fields. His power directed Dewey in the East and delivered the Spanish fleet into our hands on the eve of Liberty's natal day, as He delivered the elder armada into the hands of our English sires two centuries ago. His great purposes are revealed in the progress of the flag, which surpasses the intentions of congresses and cabinets, and leads us like a holier pillar of cloud by day and pillar of fire by night into situations unforeseen by finite wisdom, and duties unexpected by the unprophetic heart of selfish-

ness. The American people cannot use a dishonest medium of exchange; it is ours to set the world its example of right and honor. We cannot fly from our world duties; it is ours to execute the purpose of a fate that has driven us to be greater than our small intention. We cannot retreat from any soil where Providence has unfurled our banner; it is ours to save that soil for liberty and civilization. For liberty and civilization and God's promise fulfilled, the flag must henceforth be a symbol and the sign of all mankind — the flag!

Such passages bring to mind the views articulated by the children interviewed by Piaget in his study for UNESCO on the causes of war.

Michael M. (9 years, 6 months old): Have you heard of such people as foreigners? *Yes, the French, the Americans, the Russians, the English ....* Quite right. Are there differences between all these people? *Oh yes, they don't speak the same language.* And what else? *I don't know.* What do you think of the French, for instance? Do you like them or not? Try and tell me as much as possible. *The French are very serious, they don't worry about anything, an' it's dirty there.* And what do you think of the Russians? *They're bad, they're always wanting to make war.* And what's your opinion of the English? *I don't know ... they're nice ....* Now look, how did you come to know all you've told me? *I don't know ... I've heard it ... that's what people say.*

Maurice D. (8 years, 3 months old): If you didn't have any nationality and you were given a free choice of nationality, which would you choose? *Swiss nationality.* Why? *Because I was born in Switzerland.* Now look, do you think the French and the Swiss are equally nice, or the one nicer or less nice than the other? *The Swiss are nicer.* Why? *The French are always nasty.* Who is more intelligent, the Swiss or the French, or do you think they're just the same? *The Swiss are more intelligent.* Why? *Because they learn French quickly.* If I asked a French boy to choose any nationality he liked, what country do you think he'd choose? *He'd choose France.* Why? *Because he was born in France.* And what would he say about who's the nicer? Would he think the Swiss and the French equally nice or one better than the other? *He'd say the French are nicer.* Why? *Because he was born in France.* And who would he think more intelligent? *The French.* Why? *He'd say that the French want to learn quicker than the Swiss.* Now you and the French boy don't really give the same answer. Who do you think answered best? *I did.* Why? *Because Switzerland is always better.*

Marina T. (7 years, 9 months old): If you were born without any nationality and you were given a free choice, what nationality would you choose? *Italian.* Why? *Because it's my country. I like it better than Argentina where my father works, because Argentina isn't my country.* Are Italians just the same, or more, or less intelligent than the Argentinians? What do you think? *The Italians are more intelligent.* Why? *I can see the people I live with, they're Italians.* If I were to give a child from Argentina a free choice of nationality, what do you think he would choose? *He'd want to stay an Argentinian.* Why? *Because that's his country.* And if I were to ask him who is more intelligent, the Argentinians, or the Italians, what do you think he would answer? *He'd say Argentinians.* Why? *Because there wasn't any war.* Now who was really right in the choice he made and what he said, the Argentinian child, you, or both? *I was right.* Why? *Because I chose Italy.*

For both the President of the United States and these children the world is nationalistically simple: the forces of good (embodied in ourselves) stand opposed by the forces of evil (those who oppose us). The need for emancipatory reason is a need of "the other", the stranger, the foreigner, the opposition.

From this perspective, the schools' job is to pass on our thought to children, exposing them to all of the reasons why our's is right and superior and unquestionable and, at the same time, developing technical abilities and technological power to defend (enforce) our views. The school's task, in short, is to inculcate cultural patriotism and facilitate vocational training.

The distinguished conservative U.S. anthropologist, William Graham Sumner, sharply challenged this view, though he had no illusions about the difficulty of transforming the schools into vehicles for human and social emancipation (1906):

Schools Make Persons All on One Pattern: Orthodoxy

School education, unless it is regulated by the best knowledge and good sense, will produce men and women who are all of one pattern, as if turned in a lathe .... The examination papers show the pet ideas of the examiners .... An orthodoxy is produced in regard to all the great doctrines of life. It consists of the most worn and commonplace opinions which are current in the masses. It may be found in newspapers and popular literature. It is intensely provincial and philistine .... The popular opinions always contain broad fallacies, half-truths, and glib generalizations of fifty years before .... The boards of trustees are almost always made up of "practical men", and if their faiths, ideas, and prejudices are to make the norm of education, the schools will turn out boys and girls compressed to that pattern .... (There is a desire) that children shall be taught just that one thing which is "right" in the view and interest of those in control, and nothing else.

Sumner saw the essential link between education and critical thinking:

Criticism is the examination and test of propositions of any kind which are offered for acceptance, in order to find out whether they correspond to reality or not. The critical faculty is a product of education and training. It is a mental habit and power. It is a prime condition of human welfare that men and women should be trained in it. It is our only guarantee against delusion, deception, superstition, and misapprehension of ourselves and our earthly circumstances. It is a faculty which will protect us against all harmful suggestion .... Our education is good just so far as it produces a well-developed critical faculty ....

He even has a conception of what a society would be like were critical thinking — in what I call the strong sense — a fundamental social value:

> The critical habit of thought, if usual in a society, will pervade all its mores, because it is a way of taking up the problems of life. Men educated in it cannot be stampeded by stump orators and are never deceived by dithyrambic oratory. They are slow to believe. They can hold things as possible or probable in all degrees, without certainty and without pain. They can wait for evidence and weigh evidence, uninfluenced by the emphasis and confidence with which assertions are made on one side or the other. They can resist appeals to their dearest prejudices and all kinds of cajolery. Education in the critical faculty is the only education of which it can be truly said that it makes good citizens.

Sumner's concept of a "developed critical faculty" clearly goes much beyond that envisioned by those who link it to a shopping list of atomic skills. He understands it as a pervasive organizing core of mental habits, and a shaping force in the character of a person. It is fairmindedness brought into the heart of everyday life, into all of its dimensions. As a social commitment, it transforms the very nature of how life is lived and human transactions mediated. Sumner does not tell us however how to nurture or develop this faculty and this commitment. He does not explain how it relates to strategies successful in technical domains. Finally, he does not tell us how to initiate this development, though he clearly believes it can begin very early.

OBSTACLE TWO: THE FAILURE OF COGNITIVE PSYCHOLOGY AND PROBLEM-SOLVING THEORISTS TO CALL ATTENTION TO THE LOGIC OF DIALECTICAL ISSUES

A major weakness in cognitive psychology and problem solving theory today is the failure to highlight the striking difference between the logic of technical problems and that of dialectical problems. Until one recognizes this difference one tends to reduce all problems to technical ones and so render all knowledge and all problems procedural, if not algorithmic. Both the power and the limitations of technical disciplines lie in their susceptibility to operationalism and routine procedure. Technical domains progress by severely narrowing what qualifies as appropriate subject matter and as appropriate treatment of it. All concepts are specifically designed to serve restricted disciplinary purposes. Additionally, scope is typically further limited to the quantifiable. For these reasons many of the concepts and attendant skills of application are relatively subject specific.

Consider the wide variety of disciplines that can be brought to bear on the study of humans: physics, chemistry, neurology, physiology, biology, medicine, psychology, economics, sociology, anthropology, history, and philosophy. To put this point another way, humans are physical, chemical, neurological, biological, psychological, economic, sociological, historical, and philosophical beings, all at once. Each person is one, not many. To the extent that a human problem is rendered technical, it is reduced to a relatively narrow system of exclusionary ideas; technical precision and manageability is achieved by excluding a variety of other technical and non-technical features. Specialized disciplines develop by generating ever more specialized sub-disciplines, abstracting further and further from the "wholeness" of things.

This becomes clearer when we consider those disciplines — history, psychology, sociology, anthropology, economics, and philosophy — whose study of humankind does not appear to admit, beyond a range of foundational premises, to discipline-wide unanimity. In each of these fields a variety of alternative systems or viewpoints compete. Generate a question within them and you typically generate a field of conflicting lines of reasoning and answers. Raise questions about their application to everyday life problems and debate intensifies. The issues are properly understood as dialectical, as calling for dialogical reasoning, for thinking critically and reciprocally within opposing points of view. This ability to move up and back between contradictory lines of reasoning, using each to critically cross-examine the other, is not characteristic of the technical mind.

Technical knowledge is typically developed by restriction to one frame of reference, one standpoint. Knowledge arrived at dialectically, in contrast, is like the verdict of a jury, with supporting reasoning. There is no fail-safe, technical path to it. At least two points of view must be entertained. It is not, as problem-solving theorists tend to characterize problems, a movement from an initial state through a series of transformations (or operations) to a final (answering) state.

Most of our everyday interest in people is unquestionably in the area of dialectical issues. By and large we don't know them, value them, or relate to them in terms of their technically determinable sub-features. We struggle to know them as multi-dimensional totalities, in short, as real people. We struggle to grasp the world in this same macro-integrative way. Unfortunately, we fail to see the dialectical nature of this task, the need to entertain more than one interpretation of human acts and of the human world. Indeed we rarely see that our perceptions of people and the world are inferences, based on typically unconscious assumptions, concepts, and beliefs. More on this later.

Despite this need for non-technical, dialectical, integrative thinking, most of the work in cognitive psychology and problem-solving theory assumes that all problem solving can be understood on the model of solving technical problems. Since each technical domain generates a dominant logical system and thus criteria and procedures for cognitive moves within it, theorists tend to reduce problem-solving to a technical or "scientific" model. This was true of problem-solving theory from the start

For example, Dewey thought that one could approach all problems through the following ordered scientific steps: *1)* identify the problem, *2)* establish facts, *3)* formulate hypotheses, *4)* test hypotheses, and *5)* evaluate results. Polya formulated a similar general procedure: *1)* Understand the problem. What is the unknown? What data are given? What are the conditions? *2)* Devise a plan. Find the connection between the data and the unknown. You may be obliged to consider auxiliary problems if an immediate connection cannot be found. *3)* Carry out the plan. Check each step. Can you see clearly that the step is correct? Can you prove that it is correct? *4)* Look back. Check the result. Check the argument. Can you derive the result differently? Can you see it at a glance? We find this procedural emphasis even in a relatively recent work on problem-solving. John R. Hayes' characterization, in *The Complete Problem Solver* (1981) is typical:

> *What is a Problem?* If you are on one side of a river and you want to get to the other side but you don't know how, you have a problem. If you are assembling a mail-order purchase and the instructions leave you completely baffled about how to "put tab A in slot B" you have a problem. If you are writing a letter and you can't find the polite way to say, "No, we don't want you to come and stay a month," you have a problem. Whenever there is a gap between where you are now and where you want to be, and you don't know how to find a way to cross that gap, you have a problem.
>
> Solving a problem means finding an appropriate way to cross a gap. The process of finding a solution has two major parts: (1) representing the gap — that is, understanding the nature of the problem, and (2) searching for a means to cross it.

Though these writers have set out and described each step as checklists, the steps still require independent thought and judgment, which cannot be set out and mindlessly followed. Furthermore, the steps are not mutually exclusive. In real life there is no *one* order in which to take each step. I may begin with a vague sense of the problem which I do not thoroughly clarify until the end — *after* gathering facts, considering solutions, and so on. Defining the problem does not necessarily come first.

Most "textbook" and the "real-life" problems problem-solving theorists address are one-system problems (definable and soluble entirely within one discipline or perspective) or self-contained (soluble atomistically rather than as mutually interdependent problems). They implicitly place critical thought squarely in the center of an atomistic, information-processing model of knowledge: the finding, organizing, manipulating, and inferential transforming of technical information.

Just last month, in a *Phi Delta Kappan* article "Improving Thinking Skills — Defining the Problem", Barry Beyer identified insufficient proceduralization as a major problem in instruction in thinking skills. He expressed as self-evident the need for teachers to provide "... step-by-step instructions on how to use specific thinking skills," indeed to spell out "... exactly how to execute a skill". (Every thought that goes through your head?) He demanded that "the crucial part of teaching a skill" is "discussing its operation procedures". (For every conceivable context?) He fails to recognize that the largest and most important form of human thinking, dialectical thinking, cannot, by its very nature, be reduced to an "operational procedure". When we think dialectically we are guided by *principles* not *procedures*, and the application of the principles is often subject to discussion or debate.

The most vexing and significant "real life" problems are logically messy. They span multiple categories and academic disciplines. They are rarely "in" any one of them. The general attitude of mind, for example, that enables one with apparent peace and tranquility to confuse egocentric dogmatism with genuine conviction, to accept vague avowals as true beliefs, to take sentimental credulity for moral insight, to harmonize technical truths with pleasant delusions and superstitions, to wander in and out of a panoply of self-serving reifications, to use confusion to one's advantage, to perform social roles that one does not know one is performing — is not a problem whose solution lies in a discipline, or in a procedure, or in "finding the connection between the data and the unknown", or in "considering an auxiliary problem" or in using special "operators" or in performing a cost-benefit analysis, or in learning mnemonic techniques, or memory codes or study systems or protocol analysis. It is a problem implicit in an uncritical mode of living and so in the very structure of an uncritical mind. Furthermore, if "it works" (enables you to get what you want, perhaps even enables you to become President) is it for you a problem at all? We do not always recognize our problems *as* problems. Once in the ebb and flow of mundane life, its messy criss-crossing of categories, values, and points of view, its inevitable blending of the intellectual, the affective, and the moral, its embodying of irrationality in social practices and beliefs, there is little room for the neat and "abstract" procedures of technical reason.

We need dialogic, point-counter-point, argument for and argument against, scrutiny of individual event against the background of this or that global "totalizing" of it into one's life. We need emancipatory reason, the ability to reason "across", "between", and "beyond" the neatly marshalled data and narrowed, clear-cut concepts of any given technical domain. Because it cannot presuppose or restrict itself to any one "system" or "technical language" or "procedure", it must be dialectical. That is, it must move back and forth between opposing points of view. It must consider how this or that situation might be handled if looked at it this way, or how if looked at that way, what follows from this construal and what from that, what objection can be raised to this and what objection to that. It is the logic that is mocked in the typically closedminded exchanges of mundane human arguments about the personal and social affairs of life. It is the logic that is concept-generating as well as concept-using (since our point of view is shaped as we use it, in a way parallel to "case" law).

Precisely because it is not procedural, not susceptible to a decision-procedure or a set of technical maneuvers, there is the temptation to retreat, as I have noted, either to apodictic self-righteousness (let us pass on to our children our heritage, our wisdom — so they like us can recognize the folly of those who oppose us) or to vacuous or self-contradictory relativism (we cannot teach dialectical thinking skills for they are in the realm of opinion or faith). Both choices ignore the proper role of dialectical reason, which, used as a means of penetrating and assessing the logic of our mundane lives, alone enables us to become intellectually, emotionally, and morally autonomous.

OBSTACLE THREE: CHILDHOOD EGO-IDENTIFICATION WITH ADULT BELIEFS: A FOUNDATION FOR CLOSEDMINDEDNESS

If we do not control the fundamental logical structures — the assumptions, values, and beliefs — that shape our own thought, our own feeling responses, and our own moral judgments, then in a significant sense we are not free. Close scrutiny of how most children come to imbibe those structures and of the evidence that shows that most adults do not recognize them, mandates the admission that we have not yet learned how to make fundamental intellectual, emotional, and moral emancipation the likely result of parenting or schooling. The ultimate court of appeal of a free and open mind is, and must be, the principles of comprehensive reason and evidence — not external authority, ego-identification, or technical expertise — the willingness to listen to and empathize with all contending perspectives on an issue without presupposing any connection between the truth and any pre-selected line of reasoning.

The foundation for this capacity, if it is to flourish, must be laid in the early years of a child's life. It depends on which of the child's behavior is rewarded and which penalized. It depends on how the child's identity comes to be shaped. It depends on the extent that children come to be persuaded, wittingly or unwittingly, that their goodness depends on believing what those who are in authority over them believe. When love and affection are contingent on specific beliefs, then those beliefs become an integral part of the child's identity. They become egocentric extensions of children. Children are thus denied an opportunity to separate their own being from belief structures that adults impose. They literally become dependent on them — intellectually and emotionally — and cannot later, without trauma, subject them to serious critical scrutiny. They are "condemned" to closedmindedness.

Our present process of raising children and of teaching them has, in my judgment, precisely this unhappy effect. Children come to adulthood today as intellectual, emotional, and moral cripples. They are not whole or free persons, in the sense delineated in this paper, and they fail to see that they are not. Like all whose belief-states are ego-identifications they conceive those who disagree with them, however rationally, as *biased*. They may have learned how to effect an adult veneer, how to put on socially accepted masks; at root, however, infantile, egocentric identifications and commitments rule them. They do not know how to conduct a serious discussion of their own most fundamental beliefs. Indeed most do not know what those beliefs are. They cannot empathize with the reasoning of those who seriously disagree with them. If adept at conceptual moves at all, their adeptness is in dodges, such as caricaturing the reasoning of those who seriously disagree with them. They know, like politicians, how to retreat into vagueness to protect their challenged beliefs. They have learned how to avoid "understanding". They refuse to be rationally persuaded *out of* an irrational belief. They have no patience for close and exacting distinctions. They become, at best, anxious, at worst, hostile and belligerent, when their own basic assumptions or beliefs or reasonings are, even quietly and respectfully, called into question.

This fundamental failure to achieve command of one's own faculties, to grasp the root of one's own thought and emotion, has been demonstrated in many graphic studies. I shall illustrate it with one of the most stunning, the experiments of Stanley Milgram on unquestioning obedience to malevolent authority. The results he obtained go to the heart of the question of intellectual, emotional, and moral autonomy.

Most people think of themselves as free agents. They believe that their beliefs have been self-selected as a result of reasonable judgements based on experience and reflective thought. They believe that their behavior is informed by a freely chosen moral perspective and that generally they act in accordance with that perspective. Hence, they believe that though there are evil people in the world, at least people who do evil things, they do not include themselves among them. They believe that they, for example, would never, like so many Germans, have participated in the Nazi extermination of Jews. If a serious conflict arose between the demands of an authority and their own conscience, they are confident that they would follow their conscience. Let us hear the experiment summarized in Milgram's own words:

> A person comes to a psychological laboratory and is told to carry out a series of acts that come increasingly into conflict with conscience. The main question is how far the participant will comply with the experimenter's instructions before refusing to carry out the actions required of him .... Two people come to a psychology laboratory to take part in a study of memory and learning. One of

them is designated as a "teacher" and the other a "learner". The experimenter explains that the study is concerned with the effects of punishment on learning. The learner is conducted into a room, seated in a chair, his arms strapped to prevent excessive movement, and an electrode attached to his wrist. He is told that he is to learn a list of word pairs; whenever he makes an error, he will receive electric shocks of increasing intensity.

The real focus of the experiment is the teacher. After watching the learner being strapped into place, he is taken into the main experimental room and seated before an impressive shock generator. Its main feature is a horizontal line of thirty switches, ranging from 15 volts to 450 volts, in 15-volt increments. There are also verbal designations which range from Slight Shock to Danger — Severe Shock. The teacher is told that he is to administer the learning test to the man in the other room. When the learner responds correctly, the teacher moves to the next item; when the other man gives an incorrect answer, the teacher is to give him an electric shock. He is to start at the lowest shock level (15 volts) and to increase the level each time that man makes an error, going through 30 volts, 45 volts, and so on.

The "teacher" is a genuinely naive subject who has come to the laboratory to participate in an experiment. The learner, or victim, is an actor who actually receives no shock at all. The point of the experiment is to see how far a person will proceed in a concrete and measurable situation in which he is ordered to inflict increasing pain on a protesting victim. At what point will the subject refuse to obey the experimenter?

Conflict arises when the man receiving the shock begins to indicate that he is experiencing discomfort. At 75 volts, the "learner" grunts. At 120 volts he complains verbally; at 150 he demands to be released from the experiment. His protests continue as the shocks escalate, growing increasingly vehement and emotional. At 285 volts his response can only be described as an agonized scream ....

Many subjects will obey the experimenter no matter how vehement the pleading of the person being shocked, no matter how painful the shocks seem to be, and no matter how much the victim pleads to be let out. This was seen time and again in our studies and has been observed in several universities where the experiment was repeated. It is the extreme willingness of adults to go to almost any lengths on the command of an authority that constitutes the chief finding of the study and the fact most urgently demanding explanation.

A commonly offered explanation is that those who shocked the victim at the most severe level were monsters, the sadistic fringe of society. But if one considers that almost two-thirds of the participants fall into the category of "obedient" subjects, and that they represented ordinary people drawn from working, managerial, and professional classes, the argument becomes very shaky.

Not only does this experiment reveal how little most people understand the roots of their own behavior, it also reveals how much human behavior today is typically determined by external authority. Whatever schooling Milgram's participants had, and some had a great deal, that schooling had little effect on their intellectual, emotional, or moral autonomy. Furthermore, it appears that Milgram's participants were heavily influenced by their desire to maintain the approach of the experimenter giving them orders. Having been children who came to do and think what they were told to do and think, Milgram's adult participants maintain their rapport with the experimenter rather than refuse orders which apparently endangered the life of an innocent victim:

> The subjects were so concerned about the show they were putting on for the experimenter that influences from other parts of the social field did not receive much weight. This powerful orientation to the experimenter would account for the relative insensitivity of the subject to the victim ....

This need not be so. The extent to which children ego-identify with this or that belief of authorities around them can be minimized. Children can be raised to value the authority of their own reasoning. They can be encouraged to value making up their own minds thoughtfully and reflectively. They can learn comprehensive principles of rational thought. They can learn to consider it "natural" that people differ in their beliefs and points of view. And they can learn to grasp this not as a quaint peculiarity of people but as a tool for learning. They can learn how to learn from others, even from their "objections", their contrary perceptions, their different ways of thinking.

They can and should learn all this, but they will do so only if parents and teachers recognize the problem created by belief inculcation and its consequent ego-identifications, and learn to nurture and respect the dialogical process. But how can this be done? How can these obstacles be overcome? How can we teach dialectical reasoning and pave the way for human emancipation?

✦ Teaching Basic Academic Competencies as Incipient Higher Order Thinking Skills

Unless one achieves an understanding of the relationship of language to logic one will not develop the ability to analyze, criticize and advocate ideas. We must recognize differences between the structure and purposes of technical languages, the nature and use of concepts within them, and those of natural languages such as English, German, or Swahili. The differences parallel the differences between technical and dialectical issues, and the divergent modes of reasoning they require. Teachers should realize when, on the one hand, they are teaching a technical language, and so presupposing one standpoint and a specialized, technically defined hierarchy of problems and when, on the other, they are in a domain where multiple standpoints apply, and so where concepts are used in a non-technical way, and where opposing lines of thought need to be considered.

Whenever we think, we conceptualize and make inferences from our conceptualization, based on assumptions. In technical domains like math, physics, and chemistry, however, the concepts and assumptions are *given*. They are not generally to be challenged by an alternative point of view. The logic, on the one hand, and the technical language, on the other, are opposite sides of the same coin. But the affairs of everyday life, including the inner life of the mind, are fundamentally conducted within the logic of a natural language, and the key concepts are inevitably used non-technically and (when properly handled) dialectically.

How we read, write, speak, listen, and reason varies, or should vary, in accordance with these fundamental distinctions. Do I read, write, speak, listen, and reason so as to throw myself totally into one well-defined point of view and make its rules, regulations, and operations the controlling variables in my thinking? Or do I read, write, speak, listen, and reason so as to entertain comparisons and contrasts between ideas from competing perspectives? Do I reason monologically or dialogically?

Few students have any experience in this second and crucially important mode of reading, writing, speaking, listening, and reasoning, even though many of their everyday experiences presuppose such abilities. They often talk and listen to people who look at events and situations in a variety of ways. Their parents and peers often see situations differently. They are often frustrated by their inability to come to terms with these conflicts and dilemmas.

If we understand speaking and writing as constructing a point of view, developing ideas in some logical relation to each other, and listening and reading, as entering into someone else's point of view, into *their* organization of ideas, then we can see how the basic academic competencies ought to be understood as incipient higher order thinking.

Furthermore, we will recognize that when we are listening to or reading ideas which conflict with our ego-identified belief states, we have a different problem to combat than when the difficulty is not a matter of resistance but of technical complexity. Learning how to listen to and read (without distortion) lines of reasoning whose possible truth we egocentrically wish to rule out, is an essential experience, indeed the mother's milk of educational development. As in all areas of intellectual and emotional competency, these reading and listening capacities must be built up progressively and over a long time. They are acquired by degrees. They can always be further developed.

Assignments designed to facilitate basic academic competencies may set the stage for intellectual or emotional development, indeed contribute to that development, or they may simply issue in the superficial learning of these skills. They may be learned, in other words, as lower order, or as incipient higher order thinking skills.

✦ Teaching Social Studies

Few recognized that the area we call "social studies" or "social science" is, when rightly conceived, a combination of technical and dialectical issues. The major justification for including them as a universal requirement however is *not* for the technical training they might provide, but for the assumed knowledge, insight, and skills that can be gleaned from their study and applied in everyday personal and social life.

However, clearly one tacit function of instruction in this area is at base "indoctrinative". By this I mean that we teach much of the subject area in a way that assumes, states, or implies (as self-evidently true) claims of a self-serving, sometimes ethnocentric, nature. Of course, the formulations of "goals" are often vague enough so that it is unclear whether a "fact" or an "ideal" is being expressed (for example, "with liberty and justice for all"). Because instruction confuses the technical, the dialectical, and the ethnocentric, and students have no tools for distinguishing them, or little sense of how to proceed to rational judgments if they did, the result is largely non-educational.

Of course, we could understand our "heritage", in another sense, as a commitment to developing the maximum degree of personal and social freedom, as a commitment to intellectual, emotional, and moral autonomy. If that is our fundamental commitment, then, we must approach education dialectically, especially in historical and social studies.

All history is history from a point of view. Alternative perspectives and interpretations of our historical past compete for our assent. Students should be exposed to some of the differing perspectives and reason dialectically between them.

The American Revolution, for example, need not be studied simply from our point of view. The same events could be seen from a British point of view, or from the point of view of a colonial loyalist, or from the point of view of a Native American, whose homeland was being systematically taken by a "foreign" race. Our attitude toward "revolution" as a justifiable political act could be compared between 1776 and now. Students should consider whether the U.S. government's present disapproval of Third World revolutions contradicts its approval of its own.

Or further, students could study the history of the Cold War itself dialectically. More and more of the national budget goes for policies premised on one unexamined interpretation of the origin and nature of the Cold

War. But how often, if ever, do students reason dialectically on this issue? This means, of course, that students learn that the issue is dialectical, that interpretations differ among distinguished historians and that they developed opposing lines of reasoning to justify them, that we can empathize with the Soviet perspective, argue their case, formulate their critique of our behavior and their defense of their own, and bring the Soviet case into dialogical contest with the strongest case of the U.S. side.

Or again, students might consider some opposing analyses of the nature of our society, clarifying some of the differences between conceptualizing events from a "Right" or a "Left" perspective. Some contemporary U.S. trends could be considered from both the the Right and the Left. Instead of seeing these perspectives as empty terms charged with positive or negative stereotypes, students could begin to translate them into analytic tools of dialogical reasoning, and therefore develop an increasingly macro-logical integrative perspective.

Of course, dialectical skills must be developed gradually. One useful teaching tool is the daily newspaper. The news, like history, is perspectival (dialectical). The news is always news from a point of view. Students now have virtually no critical reading or listening or viewing skills for the news media. This process can begin very early. Sesame Street-like skits could be developed which show young children how we take events and "re-present" them and how that "re-presentation" can serve different purposes or ends, can be constructed to convey different implications and impressions.

We are worlds away from taking this task seriously. The sooner we begin the better.

✦ Teaching Science

As elsewhere we must clearly understand the extent to which we want technical competencies and the extent to which we want global (dialectical) competencies. If we merely want to produce as many scientists and engineers as we can, then we should proceed with the strategy that best serves that end. If we doubt that most students will become scientists, engineers, or even technicians, but must live in a technological world in which science and its uses are crucial to the quality of human life, then we will use a somewhat different strategy.

Both approaches need some common foundation, but even here the emphasis may differ. Students do not inevitably understand scientific concepts better, that is, achieve global perspective with respect to them, simply because they can solve increasingly complex textbook problems. Furthermore, going in the other direction, students can gain a great deal of understanding of science, from a global perspective, without being able to solve highly complex textbook problems.

As Ronald Giere, in *Understanding Scientific Reasoning,* points out:

> Learning physics — that is, to produce solutions to problems in physics — is indeed very difficult. But if it is presented correctly, it is possible for anyone to gain some understanding of what physics, especially classical Newtonian physics, is all about. Moreover, discovering that this is so can be a very liberating experience. If you can understand Newtonian physics you can probably understand most any scientific theory presented in a reasonable manner. So learning a little about physics may give you confidence that you can understand scientific theories and even evaluate arguments for or against theoretical hypotheses. An important component in developing the skill to reason intelligently about scientific issues is simply gaining the confidence that you can do it, even if you are not an expert.

With a fuller global grasp of the uses of scientific concepts, the student is better able to think critically about the application of scientific concepts in everyday life, including such mundane issues as these:

1) media reports of scientific discoveries,

2) advertisements that make scientific claims,

3) decisions about food, nutrition, and health,

4) assessment of doctors and of the credibility of their diagnoses, etc.

Finally, only with this global grasp can students begin to aspire to Einstein's call for critical thinking about scientific concepts themselves:

> The eyes of the scientist are directed upon those phenomena which are accessible to observation, upon their apperception and conceptual formulation. In the attempt to achieve a conceptual formulation of the confusingly immense body of observational data, the scientist makes use of a whole arsenal of concepts which he imbibed practically with his mother's milk; and seldom if ever is he aware of the eternally problematic character of his concepts. He uses this conceptual material, or speaking more exactly, these conceptual tools of thought, as something obviously, immutably given; something having an objective value of truth which is hardly ever, and in any case not seriously, to be doubted. How could he do otherwise? How would the ascent of a mountain be possible, if the use of hands, legs, and tools had to be sanctioned step-by-step on the basis of the science of mechanics? And yet in the interest of science it is necessary over and over again to engage in the critique of these fundamental concepts, in order that we may not unconsciously be ruled by them. This becomes evident especially in those situations involving development of ideas in which the consistent use of the traditional fundamental concepts leads us to paradoxes difficult to resolve.

"logical structures" that we do not express than those we do. To become skilled in reasoning things through we must become practiced in making what is implicit explicit so that we can "check out" what is going on "beneath the surface" of our thought.

Thus, when we draw a conclusion, we do so in some circumstances, making inferences (that have implications and consequences) based on some reasons or information (and assumptions), using some concepts, in trying to settle some question (or solve some problem) for some purpose within some point of view.

Good reasoners can consider and plausibly assess any of these elements as they function in their thought in any act of reasoning something out. Good reasoners therefore use good logic in both the narrow and the broad sense. Furthermore, in most circumstances in which we are *using* logic we are *creating* it simultaneously. This needs explanation.

✦ Whenever We Are Reasoning Something Through We Are Ipso Facto Engaged in Creative Thinking

In the broad sense, all reasoned thinking is thinking within a logic, and when we have not yet learned a given logic — e.g., not yet learned the logic of the internal combustion engine, the logic of right triangles, or the logic of dolphin behavior — our minds must bring that logic into being, create it in the fabric, within the structure, of our established ways of thinking. Hence, when we are thinking something through for the first time, to some extent, we create the logic we are using. We bring into being new articulations of our purposes and of our reasons. We make new assumptions. We form new concepts. We ask new questions. We make new inferences. Our point of view is worked out in a new direction, one in which it has never been worked out before.

Indeed, there is a sense in which all reasoned thinking, all genuine acts of figuring out anything whatsoever, even something previously figured out, is a new "making", a new series of creative acts, for we rarely recall our previous thought whole cloth. Instead we generally remember only some part of what we figured out and figure out the rest anew, based on the logic of that part and other logical structures more immediately available to us. We continually create new understandings and re-create old understandings by a similar process of figuring.

In what follows, I will articulate a frame of reference that highlights the intimate interplay between creative and critical thinking, between the thinking that creates a set of logically interrelated meanings and the thinking that assesses the logic being created. I will begin with a basic assumption that underlies the model being developed. The theme that shall run throughout is as follows:

that can be made for alternative political systems, one concludes that one is superior to the others; when, as a result of hearing various sides of a family argument, one becomes persuaded that one way of putting things is more justified and accurate; when, as a result of reading many reports on the need for educational reform, one is prepared to argue for one of them; when, as a result of entertaining various representations of national security and the building of more nuclear weapons, one reasons to a position on the issue; when, after reading and thinking about various approaches to raising children, one opts for one; when, after knowing a person for a number of years and exploring various interpretations of his or her character, one decides that he or she would make a good spouse — *one is reasoning dialectically.* Dialectical thought is the master-principle of all rational experience and human emancipation. It cultivates the mind and orients the person as technical training cannot. It meets our need to bring harmony and order into our lives, to work out an amalgamation of ideas from various dimensions of experience, to achieve, in short, intellectual, emotional, and moral integrity. The proper doing of it is our only defense against closedmindedness.

An open society requires open minds. Collectively reinforced egocentric and sociocentric thought, conjoined with massive technical knowledge and power, are not the foundations for a genuine democracy. The basic insight formulated over a hundred years ago by John Stuart Mill is as true, and as ignored, today as it was when he first wrote it:

> In the case of any person whose judgment is really deserving of confidence, how has it become so? Because he has kept his mind open to criticism of his opinions and conduct. Because it has been his practice to listen to all that could be said against him; to profit by as much of it as was just, and expound to himself, and upon occasion to others, the fallacy of what was fallacious. Because he has felt that the only way in which a human being can make some approach to knowing the whole of a subject, is by hearing what can be said about it by persons of every variety of opinion, and studying all modes in which it can be looked at by every character of mind. No wise man ever acquired his wisdom in any mode but this; nor is it in the nature of human intellect to become wise in any other manner.

If the schools do not rise to meet this social need, what social institution will? If this is not the fundamental task and ultimate justification for public education, what is?

✦ References

Beveridge, Albert J., U.S. Senator. "The March of the Flag," 1898.

Beyer, Barry. "Improving Thinking Skills — Defining the Problem." *Phi Delta Kappan,* March 1984.

Bloom, Benjamin. *All Our Children Learning.* New York: McGraw-Hill. 1981, pp. 22–24.

Campbell, Sarah, ed. *Piaget Sampler: An Introduction to Jean Piaget Through His Own Words.* New York: John Wiley & Sons, 1976.

Dewey, John. cf. *How We Think.* Boston: D. C. Heath & Co., 1933.

Dewey, John. *Logic: The Theory of Inquiry.* New York: Holt, Rinehart, & Winston, 1938, Chapters VI and XXIV.

Giere, Ronald. *Understanding Scientific Reasoning.* New York: Holt, Rinehart & Winston, 1978.

Hayes, John R. *The Complete Problem Solver.* Philadelphia: The Franklin Institute Press, 1981.

Jammer, M. *Concepts of Space: The History of Theories of Space in Physics.* Cambridge: Harvard University Press, 1957. p. xi.

Milgram, Stanley. *Obedience to Authority.* New York: Harper & Row, 1969.

Mill, John Stuart. *On Liberty.* Edited by Alburey Castell. Illinois: AHM Publishing Co., 1947. p. 20.

Polya, Gyorgy. *How to Solve It.* New York: Doubleday Anchor, 1957.

Sumner, William G. *Folkways and Mores.* Edited by Edward Sagarin. New York: Schoken Books, 1959.

Chapter 10

Critical Thinking and the Critical Person

Abstract

Written for Thinking: The Second International Conference *(1987), this paper explores a series of themes familiar to Richard Paul's readers: that most school learning is irrational rather than rational, that there are two different modes of critical thinking and hence two different kinds of critical persons, that strong sense critical thinking is embedded in the ancient Socratic ideal of living an examined life, and that social studies instruction today is, in the main, sociocentric. Paul illustrates this last point with items from a state department of education critical thinking test and illustrations from a popular university-level introductory political science text. Paul closes with an argument in favor of a new emphasis on developing the critical thinking abilities of teachers: "If, in our haste to bring critical thinking into the schools, we ignore the need to develop long-term strategies for nurturing the development of teachers' own critical powers and passions, we shall surely make the new emphasis on critical thinking into nothing more than a passing fad, or worse, into a new, more sophisticated form of social indoctrination and scholastic closedmindedness."*

✦ Introduction

*T*he clarion call for critical thinking instruction from kindergarten to graduate school grows louder. Overburdened educators, responsible for classroom instruction, naturally look for simple answers to the question, "What is critical thinking?". Their ideal would be routine and simple strategies that they could effectively use immediately upon their return to the classroom. Few educators see that their standard instructional procedure and its underlying theory need a complete overhaul before they can help their students become critical thinkers in their daily personal, professional, and civic lives.

This chapter clarifies and develops some of the theoretical and practical implications of the concept of critical thinking. I consider the work of some of the leading critical thinking theorists. I contrast my views with the general approach of cognitive psychologists. I use social studies throughout to illustrate the problem. I, along with most critical thinking theorists, believe that global insights into the multifaceted obstacles to critical reflection, inquiry, and discussion on the part of students, teachers, and people in general are crucial to sound design of critical thinking instruction. Such insights are severely limited unless one clearly and coherently grasps the "big picture". For example, few pay attention to John Passmore's claims that "being critical can be taught only by persons who can themselves freely participate in critical discussion" and that, "In many systems of public instruction ... it is a principal object of teacher training to turn out teachers who will firmly discourage free critical discussion."[1] Rarely do teachers grasp where and when "free critical discussion" is essential, what it means to conduct it, and what is required to empower students to pursue it with understanding and self-command. What follows, I hope, contributes something to those foundational understandings, to the insights on which successful critical thinking instruction depends.

✦ Rational and Irrational Learning

All rational learning presupposes rational assent. And, though we sometimes forget it, all learning is not automatically or even commonly rational. Much that we learn in everyday life is quite irrational. It is quite possible — and indeed the bulk of human learning is unfortunately of this character — to come to believe any number of things without knowing how or why. It is quite possible, in other words, to believe for irrational reasons: because those around us believe, because we are rewarded for believing, because we are afraid to disbelieve, because our vested interest is served by belief, because we are more comfortable with belief, because we have ego identified ourselves, our image, or our personal being with belief. In all these cases, our beliefs are without rational grounding, without good reason and evidence, without the foundation a rational person demands. We become rational, on the other hand, to the extent that our beliefs and actions are grounded in good reasons and evidence; to the extent that we recognize and critique our own irrationality; to the extent that we are not moved by bad reasons and a multiplicity of irrational motives, fears, desires; to the extent that we have cultivated a passion for clarity, accuracy, and fairmindedness. These global skills, passions, and dispositions integrated into a way of acting and thinking characterize the rational, the educated, and in my sense, the critical person.[2]

No one, in this view, is ever *fully* educated. Hence, we should view rational learning not as something completed by schooling but as something struggling to emerge against deep-seated, irrational, and uncritical tendencies and drives. Schools can be structured to foster belief without regard to rational justification. To make rational belief a probable outcome of schooling requires special design and distinctive commitment.

✦ Thinking Critically in the "Strong" Sense

One cannot develop a coherent concept of critical thinking without developing a coherent concept of rationality, irrationality, education, socialization, the critical person, and the critical society, as they bear on and mutually illuminate one another. This holistic approach distinguishes the mode of theorizing of most philosophers working on the concept of critical thinking from that commonly used by most cognitive psychologists concerned with the nature of thinking. Cognitive psychologists often treat cognitive processes and their "pathology" separate from any consideration of the affective, social, or political life of the thinker. The research findings of clinical and social psychologists rarely integrate self-deception, egocentricity, or ethnocentricity into the problem definitions or conclusions of cognitive psychology.[3] Consequently, cognitive psychologists rarely focus on messy real-life multilogical problems that cross disciplines, instead they restrict their attention to artificial or self-contained monological problems, problems whose solutions can typically be found in a field-specific conceptual framework without reference to major personal or social bias. The more basic and difficult human problems, for whose solutions there are competing frameworks, and in which the problem of bias and vested interest looms large, are routinely ignored.

It is hard to go very far into the core concept of the critical person, however, without recognizing the centrality of multilogical thinking, the ability to think accurately and fairmindedly within opposing points of view and contradictory frames of reference. Multilogical problems, whose fairminded treatment requires us to suspend our egocentric tendency to confuse the framework of our own thinking with "reality" and reason within opposing points of view, are among the most significant human problems and among those most resistant to solution. The problems of human understanding, of war and peace, of economic, political, and social justice, of who our friends and who our enemies are, of what we should accept as the most basic framework of our thinking, of our own nature, our goodness and our evil, our history and that of those we oppose, of how we should interpret our place in the world, and how to best satisfy our needs and critically assess our desires — all such problems are at the heart of the basic frustrations and conflicts that plague human life and all require multi-system thinking. We cannot justifiably assume the correctness of any one point of view as the only perspective within which these basic human problems can be most rationally settled. Schooling should improve the student's ability to distinguish monological from multilogical problems and to address each appropriately.

On this view, we distinguish two important senses of critical thinking, a *weak* sense and a *strong* one. Those who think critically only with respect to monological issues and, as a result, consider multilogical issues with a pronounced monological bias have merely mastered weak sense critical thinking. They would lack the ability, and presumably the disposition also, to critique their own most fundamental categories of thought and analysis. They would, as a result, lack the ability to enter sympathetically into, and reconstruct, the strongest arguments and reasons for points of view fundamentally opposed to their own. When their monological thinking arises from an unconscious commitment to a personal point of view, their thinking is egocentric; when it arises from an unconscious commitment to a social or cultural point of view, their thinking is ethnocentric. In either case they think more or less exclusively within their own frames of reference. They might use the basic vocabulary of critical thinking with rhetorical skill — their arguments and reasons might impress those who already shared their framework of thought — but they would lack the basic drives and abilities of what I call *strong sense* critical thinking: *a)* an ability to question deeply one's own framework of thought, *b)* an ability to reconstruct sympathetically and imaginatively the strongest versions of points of view and frameworks of thought opposed to one's own, and *c)* an ability to reason dialectically (multilogically) to determine when one's own point of view is weakest and when an opposing point of view is strongest.

Strong sense critical thinkers are not routinely blinded by their own points of view. They know that they *have* a point of view and therefore recognize on what framework of assumptions and ideas their own thinking rests. They realize they must put their own assumptions and ideas to the test of the strongest objections that can be leveled against them. Critical proponents of a socialist economic system, for example, can analyze economic events from the perspective of an insightful proponent of capitalism. Critical proponents of a capitalist economic system can analyze economic events from the perspective of an insightful proponent of socialism. This implies, by the way, that economics should not be taught in a way which presupposes capitalism, socialism, or any other economic system as *the* correct one. In other words, the issue as to what economic system is most justified is a multilogical issue.

Similarly, the strong sense critical thinker's thought is disciplined to avoid confusing concepts that belong in different categories. For example, they do not confuse "democracy", a political concept, with "capitalism", an economic concept. They realize that any important connection between democracy and capitalism must be argued for, not assumed, that *free enterprise* should not be routinely injected into U.S. social studies texts as a neutral synonym for *capitalism,* any more than *people's democracy* should be routinely injected into Soviet social studies texts as a neutral synonym for *Soviet communism.* They can recognize when terms are used in this question-begging way. A teacher who values strong sense critical thinking fosters these abilities.

The importance of strong sense critical thinking has been underscored, each in his own terms, by most leading critical thinking theorists: Robert Ennis,[4] Harvey Siegel,[5] Israel Scheffler,[6] Michael

Scriven,[7] Matthew Lipman,[8] R. S. Peters,[9] John Passmore,[10] Edward Glaser,[11] Ralph Johnson,[12] J. Anthony Blair,[13] and others. I exemplify the point briefly with four of them: Ennis, Siegel, Scriven and Peters.

Robert Ennis defines critical thinking as "reasonable reflective thinking that is concerned with what to do or believe". He argues that the various component cognitive skills essential to critical thinking cannot lead to genuine "rational reflective thinking" unless used in conjunction with, as the manifestation of, a complex of dispositions. For example, in and of themselves, the component cognitive skills of critical thinking can be used to serve either closedminded or openminded thought. Those with genuine openmindedness, Ennis claims, will: *a)* Seriously consider points of view other than their own ("dialogical thinking"); *b)* reason from premises with which they disagree — without letting the disagreement interfere with their reasons ("suppositional thinking"); *c)* withhold judgment when the evidence and reasons are insufficient.[14]

Harvey Siegel argues that students cannot become genuine critical thinkers unless they develop "the critical spirit", and that students will not develop the critical spirit unless they are taught in "the critical manner":

> The critical manner is that manner of teaching that reinforces the critical spirit. A teacher who utilizes the critical manner seeks to encourage in his or her students the skills, habits, and dispositions necessary for the development of the critical spirit. This means, first, that the teacher always recognizes the right of the student to question and demand reasons; and consequently recognizes an obligation to provide reasons whenever demanded. The critical manner thus demands of a teacher a willingness to subject all beliefs and practices to scrutiny, and so to allow students the genuine opportunity to understand the role reasons play in justifying thought and action. The critical manner also demands honesty of a teacher: reasons presented by a teacher must be genuine reasons, and a teacher must honestly appraise the power of those reasons. In addition, the teacher must submit his or her reasons to the independent evaluation of the student. Teaching in the critical manner is thus teaching so as to develop in the students skills and attitudes consonant with critical thinking. It is, as Scheffler puts it, an attempt to initiate students into the rational life, a life in which the critical quest for reasons is a dominant and integrating motive.[15]

Siegel's point is that for students to develop the passions of strong sense critical thinkers (the passion for accuracy, clarity, and fairmindedness), teachers must continually model those passions in their manner of teaching. The component micro-skills of critical thinking (the ability to clarify an issue, distinguish evidence from conclusions, recognize assumptions, implications, and contradictions, and so on) do not become the skills of a (strong sense) critical thinker, except insofar as they are integrated into "a life in which the critical quest for reasons is a dominant and integrating motive."

Michael Scriven represents (strong sense) critical thinking skills as not only requiring "a whole shift of values for most of us"[16] but also as essential for survival in a world in which "the wrong decision can mean injury or long-term commitment to a disastrous form of life such as addiction or criminality or resented parenthood."[17] For students to "transfer" their critical thinking skills to such situations, they need to practice fairminded thought on controversial (multilogical) issues:

> The real case, in dealing with controversial issues is the case as put by real people who believe in what they are saying. But the schools — and to a varying but often equal extent the colleges — are not willing to let there be that kind of serious discussion of the argument on both sides of controversial issues. Of course, they don't mind having the bad guys' position represented by someone who doesn't agree with it, in the course of dismissing it. But only the completely naive would suppose that such a presentation is likely to make the best case for the position. The notions of a fair hearing, or of confronting your accuser which are so deeply entrenched in our system of justice obviously transfer immediately to the intellectual sphere. If you want to hear the arguments for a political position other than those of the majority parties, for example the political position that the largest countries on earth espouse, you cannot possibly assume that it will be fully and fairly represented by someone to whom it is anathema.[18]

Unfortunately, many teachers will naturally fear highlighting controversial issues in the classroom. It is fair to say, I believe, few teachers have had much experience working with such issues. Many know only processes for laying out and testing for "right" answers, not assessing contradictory arguments in terms of their relative strength in dialogical or dialectical settings. There are, in other words, both affective and cognitive obstacles to the genuine fostering of fairmindedness. Some of the affective obstacles are in educators themselves.

R. S. Peters has developed the significance of the affective side of reason and critical thought in his defense of the necessity of "rational passions":

> There is, for instance, the hatred of contradictions and inconsistencies, together with the love of clarity and hatred of confusion without which words could not be held to relatively constant meanings and testable rules and generalizations stated. A reasonable man cannot, without some special explanation, slap his sides with delight or express indifference if he is told that what he says is confused, incoherent and perhaps riddled with contradictions.
>
> Reason is the antithesis of arbitrariness. In its operation it is supported by the appropriate passions which are mainly negative in character — the hatred of irrelevance, special pleading and arbitrary fiat. The more developed emotion of indignation is aroused when

some excess of arbitrariness is perpetuated in a situation where people's interests and claims are at stake. The positive side of this is the passion for fairness and impartial consideration of claims.

A man who is prepared to reason must feel strongly that he must follow the arguments and decide things in terms of where they lead. He must have a sense of the giveness of the impersonality of such considerations. In so far as thoughts about persons enter his head they should be tinged with the respect which is due to another who, like himself, may have a point of view which is worth considering, who may have a glimmering of the truth which has so far eluded himself. A person who proceeds in this way, who is influenced by such passions, is what we call a reasonable man.[19]

What implications does this have for students and teachers? It entails that the affective life of the student must be brought into the heart of classroom instruction and dealt with in the context of the problem of thinking fairmindedly. Students must come to terms not only with how they feel about issues both inside and outside the curriculum, but also with the rationality or irrationality of those feelings. The teacher, on the other hand, must model rational passions and set the example of showing no favoritism to particular positions. The students must become convinced that the teacher is a fair and reasonable referee, an expert in nurturing the process by which truth and understanding is sought, not an authoritative judge of what is actually true or false. Questions rather than assertions should characterize the teacher's speech. The classroom environment should be structured so that students feel encouraged to decide for themselves what is and is not so. Teachers should treat no idea or point of view as in itself absurd, stupid, or "dangerous", whatever their personal views or those of the community. They should shield their students from the pressure to conform to peers or the community. Free and open discussion should be the sacred right in all classrooms.

It should be clear that strong sense critical thinking is embedded in a personal, social, and educational ideal. It is not simply a complex of atomistic cognitive skills. To think critically in this sense requires, as Passmore points out, "initiative, independence, courage, (and) imagination".[20] Let us now look briefly at the historical foundation for his concept.

✦ *Critical Thinking and the Socratic Ideal*

The concept of strong sense critical thinking, of critical thought integrated into the personal and social life of the individual, is not new. It was introduced into Western intellectual tradition in the chronicles of the life and death of Socrates (470-399 BC), one of the most important and influential teachers of ancient Greece. As a teacher, he was committed to the importance of ideas and their critique in the conduct of everyday human life. It is to him that the precept "the unexamined life is not worth living" is attributed. It is in him that the ideal of conscientious civil disobedience and critical autonomy of thought is first to be found. He illustrated the possibility and the value of sharpness of mind, clarity of thought, and commitment to practical insight based on autonomous reason. He championed reason, the rational life, and a rationally structured ethic, the intimate fusion of reason and passion. He disclaimed authority on his own part but claimed the right to independently criticize all authoritative beliefs and established institutions. He made it clear that teachers cannot be educators in the fullest sense unless they can criticize the received assumptions of their social groups and are willing to nurture a climate of questioning and doubt among their students. He demonstrated the intimate connection between a passionate love of truth and knowledge, the ability to learn through the art of skilled questioning, and the willingness to face personally and socially embarrassing truths. He spoke often with those who had a sophistic (weak sense) command of critical thinking skills, who could, through their skills of persuasion and knowledge of the vulnerabilities of people, make the false appear true and the true false.

Socrates taught by joining in discussions with others who thought they knew or understood a basic or important truth, for example, what justice is, or knowledge or virtue. When questioned by Socrates — who probed the justification and foundation for the belief, examining its consistency or inconsistency with other beliefs — it became clear that his discussants did not know or understand what they at first thought they did. As a result of Socrates' mode of questioning, his "students" realized that they lacked fundamental knowledge. Of course not all of Socrates' discussants appreciated the discovery. But those who did developed a new drive to seek out knowledge. This included an appreciation of dialectical thinking, a recognition of the need to subject putative knowledge to probing questioning, especially from the vantage point of opposing points of view. Socrates' students became comfortable with and adept in the art of dialectical questioning. All beliefs had first to pass the test of critical scrutiny through dialectical challenges before they were to be accepted.

The social reaction to Socrates' mode of teaching through probing questions illustrated the inevitable antagonism between schooling as socialization into accepted beliefs and practices and schooling as education in the art of autonomous thought. Although he did not foster any doctrines of his own (other than the values of intellectual integrity and critical autonomy), he was executed for "not believing in the gods the state believes in ... and also for corrupting the young" (see Plato's *Apology*).

Socrates' practice laid the cornerstone for the history of critical thought. He provided us with our first historic glimpse into how the organizing concepts by which humans live rarely reflect the organizing concepts through which they express their thoughts publicly. We must keep this example in mind when we conceptualize and elaborate the problem of learning to think critically. If we do, we certainly will not conceive of critical thinking in narrow intradisciplinary terms, nor will we ignore the significance of the affective dimensions of thought. It is intriguing to imagine classrooms in which the example of Socrates is highlighted and encouraged as a model of education.

✦ *The Egocentrically Critical Person*

Piaget's basic model for the egocentric mind, developed by studying the thinking of children, has significant application, with appropriate translation, to much adult thinking and therefore significant application for the design of critical thinking instruction. Few adults have experience in reciprocal critical thought, that is, in reasoning within their antagonists' point of view. Few have experience in making the structure of their own thought conscious. Few, as Socrates discovered, can explain intelligibly how they came to their beliefs, or provide rational justifications for them.

The egocentrism of most adult thought parallels the egocentrism of childish thought, as Piaget characterized it in *Judgment and Reasoning in the Child:*

> Egocentrism of thought necessarily entails a certain degree of unconsciousness with the egocentric thinker 'in a perpetual state of belief', (p. 137)
> [The egocentric thinker:]
> - [is] confident in his own ideas,
> - [is] naturally...(untroubled) about the reasons and motives which have guided his reasoning process,
> - [seeks] to justify himself in the eyes of others ... only under the pressure of argument and opposition...,
> - [is] incapable either by introspection or retrospection of capturing the successive steps...[his] mind has taken (pp. 137–138)
> - [is] not conscious of the meaning assigned to the concepts and words used ... (p. 149)
> - suffers from illusions of perspective, (p. 165)
> - ignorant of his own ego, takes his own point of view to be absolute, and fails to establish...that reciprocity which alone would ensure objectivity (p. 197)
> - [is] intelligent without being particularly logical,
> - [uses] thought ... at the service of desire,
> - simply believes ... without trying to find the truth, (p. 203)
> - assimilates everything he hears to his own point of view. (p. 208)
>
> He does not try to prove whether such and such of his idea does or does not correspond to reality. When the question is put to him, he evades it. It does not interest him, and it is even alien to his whole mental attitude. (p. 247)[21]

We naturally tend to think egocentrically, especially in domains of significant personal or social interests. Egocentrism is, in some sense, as typical of adult as childish thought. It takes a special cultivated discipline to recognize and attempt to correct for it. This becomes apparent when one formulates basic safeguards against egocentric thought and attempts to cultivate an interest in students or people in general in using them. Consider, for example, the platitude "one cannot disagree with a position one does not understand," that in other words "judgment presupposes understanding". Cultivating it as a critical principle means taking steps to ensure one clearly understands what someone else is saying before one "disagrees". In my experience most people, including some with a good deal of schooling, tend to uncritically assume understanding when they have done little or nothing to test it, and as a result, are much too quick to "disagree". Most people are surprised if, after they disagree with something said, the speaker says, "What exactly did you take me to be saying that you are disagreeing with?" Often they will be puzzled and say, "Well, perhaps you should say it again," or words to that effect.

Or consider a more profound safeguard against egocentric thought, an attempt to probe the justification for one's belief by sympathetically formulating the strongest arguments for rejecting that belief from opposing points of view. After confidently stating a belief few can summarize strong arguments and reasons that have persuaded intelligent, rational others to believe in opposing positions.

Each of us, to the extent that we are egocentric, spontaneously think along lines that serve to justify our fears, desires, and vested interests. Few have developed a "Socratic" character. As a result, most everyday critical thought is egocentric. We unconsciously tend to think in the following ways: "Your thinking is well founded and insightful to the extent that it agrees with or supports my own. If it does not, then, as a matter of course, it is 'wrong' and I am obliged to criticize it." Much adult "critical" thought is not fairminded but rather egocentrically motivated and structured, lacking fairmindedness at its very core. Is it not also fair to say that few adults had opportunities in school to grapple with their own tendencies to think irrationally?

✦ The Sociocentrically Critical Person and the Ideal of a Critical Society

In my view, Piaget rightly identifies uncritical thought with a tendency toward egocentrism, and critical thought with a tendency toward reciprocity. He recognizes, but does not explore, how egocentricity develops into and partially merges with sociocentricity:

> The child begins with the assumption that the immediate attitudes arising out of our own special surroundings and activities are

the only ones possible. This state of mind, which we shall term the unconscious egocentricity (both cognitive and affective) of the child is at first a stumbling-block both to the understanding of his own country and to the development of objective relations with other countries. Furthermore, to overcome his egocentric attitude it is necessary to train the faculty for cognitive and affective integration; this is a slow and laborious process consisting mainly in efforts at 'reciprocity', and at each new stage of the process, egocentricity re-emerges in new guises farther and farther removed from the child's initial center of interest. There are the various forms of sociocentricity — a survival of the original egocentricity — and they are the cause of subsequent disturbances or tensions, any understanding of which must be based on an accurate analysis of the initial stages and of the elementary conflicts between egocentricity and understanding of others (Reciprocity).[22]

One manifestation of the irrational mind is to uncritically presuppose the truth of beliefs and doctrines embedded in social life or values. We intellectually and affectively absorb common frames of references from the social settings in which we live. Our interests and purposes find a place within a socially absorbed picture of the world. We use that picture to test the claims of contesting others. We imaginatively rehearse situations within portions of that picture. We rarely, however, describe that picture *as* a picture, as an image constructed by one social group as against that of another. We cannot easily place that picture at arm's length, so to speak, and for a time suspend our acquiescence to it. (For example, I cannot avoid feeling uncomfortable when an acquaintance of another culture stands "too close" to me while we talk, just as that acquaintance cannot avoid feeling somewhat offended that I continually move "too far away" for conversation. To each of us, the proper distance seems obviously and objectively proper.) That our thought is often disturbed and distorted by ethnocentric tendencies is rarely an abiding recognition. At best, it occurs in most people in fleeting glimpses, to judge by how often it is recognized explicitly in everyday thought.

Although many talk about and research ethnocentrism or sociocentrism as a problem in education, there are no reasonable, effective means of combatting it. Institutions and beliefs tend to become "sacred" and "cherished"; the thinking that critiques them seems "dangerous", "subversive", or at least "disturbing" and "unsettling". Habits, customs, and faiths become deeply embedded in how we define ourselves, and intolerance, censorship, and oppression never seem to be such by those who carry them out in the name of "true belief".

Socrates is not the only thinker to imagine a society in which independent critical thought became embodied in the day-to-day lives of individuals; others, including William Graham Sumner, North America's distinguished conservative anthropologist, have formulated the ideal:

The critical habit of thought, if usual in a society, will pervade all its mores, because it is a way of taking up the problems of life. Men educated in it cannot be stampeded by stump orators and are never deceived by dithyrambic oratory. They are slow to believe. They can hold things as possible or probable in all degrees, without certainty and without pain. They can wait for evidence and weigh evidence, uninfluenced by the emphasis or confidence with which assertions are made on one side or the other. They can resist appeals to their dearest prejudices and all kinds of cajolery. Education in the critical faculty is the only education of which it can be truly said that it makes good citizens.[23]

Until critical habits of thought pervade our society, however, schools, as social institutions, will tend to transmit the prevailing world view more or less uncritically, transmit it as reality *itself*, not as a *picture* of reality. Our ability to solve social and international problems becomes constrained by the solutions credible and plausible within our prevailing ideas and assumptions. When solutions are suggested from contrary world views, they appear patently false to us because they appear to be based on false ideas, that is, ideas that don't square with "reality" (with our ideas of reality). Of course, those who live in other societies will themselves interpret our proposed solutions as patently false because they appear to them to be based on false ideas; that is, ideas that don't square with reality (with their ideas of reality). Hence, one society's freedom-fighters are another society's terrorists, and vice verse. Each is outraged at the flagrant propaganda of the other and is forced to conclude that the other must be knowingly distorting the facts, and hence is evil to the core. Citizens in any country who question the prevailing labels commonly have their patriotism questioned, or worse.

Ideas, in other words, do not enter into school life in neutral but in socially biased ways. Helping students think critically entails developing their ability to recognize and so to question this process.

Sociocentrically critical people may use the vocabulary of critical thinking. They may develop facility in its micro-skills. But they inadvertently function as apologists for the prevailing world view, nevertheless. They may conceive of themselves as hard-headed realists, fundamentally beyond "ideology" or naive "idealism", but the lack of reciprocity in their thought demonstrates their closedmindedness.

A critical society emerges only to the extent that it becomes socially unacceptable to routinely presuppose, rather than explicitly identify and argue for, one's fundamental ideas and assumptions. In the schools of a critical society, both teachers and students would recognize multilogical issues as demanding dialogical rather than monological treatment. Reasoning within opposing points of view would be the rule, not the rare exception. Social studies instruction in particular would play a significant role in fostering reciprocal multilogical thinking and so would contribute in a special way to the nurturing in the citizenry of values and skills essential to the conduct of everyday life in a critical manner.

✦ Social Studies and the Fostering of Rational Belief

We can assess any school program for its educative value by determining the extent to which it fosters *rational* as against *irrational* belief formation. To the extent that students merely memorize what the teacher or textbook says, or presuppose the correctness of one point of view, and so develop no sense of what would justify rational belief, to that extent the school fosters irrational learning and irrational belief.

Social studies instruction is an excellent area to canvass in this regard because societies naturally inculcate an uncritical monological nationalistic perspective, despite the multilogical nature of the major issues in the field. The tendency is natural because people within a country or culture naturally ego identify with it and hence assume rather than question the policies of its leaders. Thus, the history of those policies and of the social representation of them continually gravitates in a self-serving direction. Reason inadvertently serves an intellectually dishonorable function: the rationalization of the prevailing structure of power and the idealization of national character. Karl Mannheim identified this as the inevitable development of *ideology*.[24] Louis Wirth suggests the practical problems for thought that it engenders:

> Even today open, frank, and "objective" inquiry into the most sacred and cherished institutions and beliefs is more or less seriously restricted in every country of the world. It is virtually impossible, for instance, even in England and America, to enquire into the actual facts regarding communism, no matter how disinterestedly, without running the risk of being labeled a communist. (p. XIV, preface)[25]

Yet, the field is clearly multilogical; that is to say, the issues in the field can be intellectually defined, analyzed, and "settled" from many perspectives. There are inevitably — to put it another way — *schools* of social thought. Whether one looks at the classic theorists (Durkheim, Weber, Marx, Mannheim, Sumner, etc.), or more recent theorists (Sorokin, Parsons, Mills, Merton, Pressman, Garfinkel, Berger, etc.), clearly there is no one agreed-upon frame of reference in which social behavior can be represented and understood. Those more "conservative" inevitably come to different conclusions about people and world events than those more "liberal". There is no way to abstract all discussion and study from basic disputes arising from conflicting frames of reference. For students to rationally understand social events, they must not only recognize this but also enter the debate actively. They need to hear, and themselves make the case for, a variety of conservative, liberal, and radical interpretations of events. They need to develop the critical tools for assessing differences among these views. These skills develop only with dialectical practice. There is no alternative.

When students cover a conflict between two countries — especially when one is their own — they should hear the case not just for one but both countries' perspectives. Often other perspectives are also relevant.

U.S. textbook writers canvassing the Cold War, for example, do not identify themselves as arguing for one selective representation of it. They do not identify themselves as having a pro-U.S. bias. They do not suggest that they represent only one out of a number of points of view. They imply rather that they give an "objective" account, as though the issues were intrinsically monological and so settleable by considering merely one point of view. They imply that the reader need not consider other points of view on the Cold War. They imply that the facts speak for themselves and that they (the textbooks) contain the facts, all the facts, and nothing but the facts. There is nothing dialogical about their modes of canvassing the material nor in the assignments that accompany the account the student is inevitably led to believe.

That some of the most distinguished historians have concluded that the United States bears a large share of the blame for the Cold War is never, to my knowledge, even casually mentioned. It would seem bizarre to most students in the United States, and their teachers, to hear a distinguished historian like Henry Steele Commager speak of the Cold War as follows:

> How are we to explain our obsession with communism, our paranoid hostility to the Soviet Union, our preoccupations with the Cold War, our reliance on military rather than political or diplomatic solutions, and our new readiness to entertain as a possibility what was long regarded as unthinkable — atomic warfare?[26]

The notion that U.S. citizens might be obsessed or the victims of "paranoid hostility" completely contradicts how textbooks in the U.S. characterize the country, its philosophy, behavior, and values.

Or consider Arnold Toynbee's characterization:

> In examining America's situation in the world today, I can say, with my hand on my heart, that my feelings are sympathetic, not malicious. After all, mere regard for self-interest, apart from any more estimable considerations, would deter America's allies from wishing America ill .... (But) today America is no longer the inspirer and leader of the World Revolution ... by contrast, America is today, the leader of a world-wide, anti-revolutionary movement in defense of vested interests. She now stands for what Rome stood for. Rome consistently supported the rich against the poor in all foreign communities; and since the poor, so far, have always been far more numerous than the rich, Rome's policy made for inequal-

ity, for injustice, and for the least happiness for the greatest numbers. America's decision to adopt Rome's role has been deliberate, if
I have gauged it right.[27]

These views would shock most U.S. citizens. Their schooling has given
them no inkling that the United States' and Britain's most distinguished
historians could have such a low estimation of our policies. They *would*
understand the recent California State Assembly resolution, endorsed on
a vote of 52–0, that the Vietnam war was waged for a noble purpose.

Similar points can be made about every major issue in history and
social studies. They can all be approached from more than one point of
view. All history, to put it another way, is history-written-from-a-point-of-
view, just as all social perception is perception-from-a-point-of-view.
There are, inevitably, different philosophies of history and society based
on different presuppositions about the nature of people and human society. Different schools of historical and social research inevitably use different organizing concepts and root metaphors.

Therefore, a rational approach to historical, sociological, and anthropological issues must reflect this diversity of approach. Just as juries
must hear both the pro and con cases before coming to a judgment,
irrespective of the strength of the case for either, so, too, must we insist,
as rational students of history and human society, on hearing the case
for more than one interpretation of key events and trends so that our
own view may take into account this relevant evidence and reasoning.
Intellectual honesty demands this, education requires it. It is irrational
to assume *a priori* the correctness of one of these perspectives, and intellectually irresponsible to make fundamental frame of reference decisions for our students.

Once students consider conflicting perspectives, they should actually
argue the cases for them, role playing the thought of those who insightfully hold them. This requires students to learn how to collect the "facts"
each side marshals to defend its views and analyze their divergent use of
key terms. For example, what exactly differentiates those we label *freedom fighters* from those we label *terrorists*? How can we define them without presupposing the truth of someone's ideology? These crucial terms
and many others current in social disputes are often used in self-serving
ways by nations and groups, begging most of the crucial social and moral
issues. Students need skills in breaking down ideologically biased uses of
language. This requires them to develop concepts that do not presuppose
specific national ideological slants. This, in turn, requires them to engage
in the argumentation for and against their application in key cases.

Unfortunately, even when critical thinking becomes an explicit
instructional objective and significant attention is given to formulation of
curriculum, unless teachers and curriculum specialists have internalized
the concept of strong sense critical thinking, instruction usually fosters

sociocentric weak sense critical thinking skills rather than strong sense skills. Consider the following critical thinking writing prompts from a series of similarly constructed items for a state-wide testing program:

Critical Thinking Writing Prompt
History-Social Science

The Cold War: Cuban Missile Crisis

Directions: Read the conversation below that might have taken place between two United States citizens during the Cuban missile crisis in 1962.

Speaker 1: These photographs in the newspaper show beyond a doubt that Russians are building missile bases in Cuba. It's time we took some strong action and did something about it. Let's get some bombers down there.

Speaker 2: I agree that there are Russian missiles in Cuba, but I don't agree with the solution you suggest. What would the world think about America dropping bombs on a neighboring small island?

Speaker 1: I think the only way to deal with the threat of force is force. If we do nothing, it's the same as saying it's okay to let them put in missiles that will threaten the whole hemisphere. Let's eliminate those missile bases now with military force.

Speaker 2: The solution you propose would certainly eliminate those bases, but innocent people might be killed, and world opinion might be against us. What if we try talking to the Russians first and then try a blockade of their ships around Cuba, or something like that?

Speaker 1: That kind of weak response won't get us anywhere. Communists only understand force.

Speaker 2: I think we should try other less drastic measures that won't result in loss of life. Then, if they don't work, use military action.

Imagine that you are a concerned citizen in 1962. Based on the information above, write a letter to President Kennedy about the missile crisis. Take a position and explain to President Kennedy what you think should be done about the missiles in Cuba and why.

- State your position clearly.
- Use information from the conversation above and from what you know about the missile crisis to support your position.

Critical Thinking Writing Prompt
History-Social Science

The Cold War: Cuban Missile Crisis

Directions: Read the information below and answer the questions that follow.

In 1962 an international crisis erupted when the Soviet Union installed missile-launching equipment in Cuba. Because Cuba is only 90 miles from Florida, many Americans felt threatened by the missile bases. On October 26, 1962, President Kennedy sent the following letter to the Soviet Union's premier, Nikita Khrushchev:

> You would agree to remove these weapons systems from Cuba under appropriate United Nations' supervision ... the first ingredient is the cessation of work on missile cites in Cuba ....

Nikita Khrushchev responded in a letter shortly thereafter by saying:

> We accept your proposal, and have ordered the Soviet vessels bound for Cuba but not yet within the area of American warships' piratical activities to stay out of the interception area.

1. Based on the information above about the Cuban missile crisis, what do you think the central issue or concern is?

_____

_____

2. List two facts in the information about the missile crisis.

_____

_____

3. Do you see any words in either President Kennedy's or Premier Khrushchev's letters that might be considered biased or "loaded"? Find which one or ones are "loaded" and list why they are "loaded".

_____

_____

4. Based on the information above, which side do you think is the aggressor? Why?

_____

_____

5. Khrushchev had spoken earlier of the need for "peaceful coexistence" between the U.S. and USSR. Is arming Cuba with missiles *consistent* with this statement about peaceful coexistence? Why or why not?

_____

_____

6. If you had an opportunity to interview Khrushchev in 1962, what question would you ask to find out why he placed missiles in Cuba?

_____

_____

7. President Kennedy was convinced that there actually were missile bases in Cuba. If you were President Kennedy in 1962, what information would *you* need to conclude that missile bases actually existed in Cuba?

_____

_____

8. If Cuba had been permitted to install missile bases, what affect would this have had on Cuba's relationships with other countries?

_____

_____

_____

Critical Thinking Writing Prompt
History-Social Science

The Cold War: Cuban Missile Crisis

Directions: Read the information below about missiles in Cuba and answer the questions that follow.

In 1962, an international crisis erupted when the Soviet Union installed missile-launching equipment in Cuba. Some of the facts relating to the incident are:

- Photographs of Cuba taken by United States planes show missile sites under construction in Cuba.
- Long-range missiles are observed near the sites.
- Russian supply ships are bringing missile base equipment and technicians to Cuba.
- Cuba is only 90 miles from the United States.
- The President's military advisers recommend that the missiles be removed.

1. What is the central issue?

_____

2. Write one question you might want to ask the United States military advisers.

_____

3. Write one question you might want to ask Soviet Premier Khrushchev.

_____

4. What does the United States assume that Cuba will do with the missiles?

_____

5. List two actions the United States might have taken in response to this crisis.

_____

_____

6. List two facts that support one of the actions identified in item 5.

_____

_____

7. Imagine you are a concerned citizen who has been following the above events with great interest. You decide to write a letter to the editor of the local newspaper. Write your letter on this sheet of paper. In your letter, take a stand on the situation in Cuba and clearly explain your reasons.

> • State your position clearly.
> • Use information from the list and from what you know about the missile crisis to support your position.

Editor
Daily Bugle
Yourtown, USA

Dear Editor:

_____

_____

_____

_____

In every case, the student has *none* of the facts to which a Soviet might call attention, or any sense of how a Soviet might use them to develop an opposing line of reasoning.

Imagine, in contrast, a test item that provided a list of facts to which United States observers might allude (such as those preceding), followed by a list of facts to which Soviets might allude, including perhaps these: *a)* the United States already had placed many of its own missiles within 90 miles of the Soviet border; *b)* Cuba is a sovereign country; *c)* the United States had rejected Soviet complaints that it had put missiles too close to their borders by saying that the countries where the missiles were placed were sovereign countries.

After giving students the two lists of facts, one could give short arguments in favor of the opposed positions. Then the students might be asked to answer the same kinds of questions as the original prompt. Other contrasting lists of facts could be provided regarding many of the tense situations that have characterized the Cold War, and the students could be given a variety of dialogical writing and role-playing assignments. Through such assignments the students could come to understand how Soviets actually reason about the conflicts and tensions that have characterized the history of the two countries. They would learn not to presuppose that their country is always right. They would develop a much more realistic sense of how governments of all kinds often act in ways they themselves (the various governments) would disapprove of were "the enemy" to do what they do.

One of the major ways in which sociocentric bias is introduced into social studies texts is through the fostered illusion of "scientific" objectivity. Nothing suggests that the authors are taking a position on issues about which reasonable people could disagree, or at least that they are taking such a position only when they explicitly admit to it.

The textbook *American Democracy in World Perspective*,[28] written by four professors at the University of California for use in college political science courses, is an exemplary case in this regard. Virtually everything in its 700-plus pages is oriented toward persuading the reader that the United States has the best form of government, comes closest to "perfect" democracy, and that the fate of freedom in the world depends on the United States: "As democracy fares in the United States, so will it, in the long run, fare throughout the world."

The text divides all governments into two basic types, democratic and non-democratic, the non-democratic ones are divided into authoritarian and totalitarian ones, in accord with the figure 1.[29]

Numerous features stand out in this chart. *Democracy* is a term that we apply to ourselves (a *positive* term with which virtually all people identify). *Authoritarian* and *totalitarian* are *negative* terms with which virtually no one identifies. The United Sates is characterized by a term that expresses an ideal, whereas its enemies, the USSR and its allies, are characterized by terms that in effect condemn them. The chart, presented as purely descriptive, obscures its tendentious character. By the same token, the distinction between authoritarianism and totalitarianism provides, under the guise of pure description, a means whereby support of dictators by the United States can be justified as the "better" of two evils. It does not take too much imagination to reconstruct how an equally tendentious chart might be fabricated for a "neutral" Soviet social studies text (see figure 2).

The authors also imply that most Americans believe in *reason and experience*, whereas Communists believe in *dogmatism*:

> By using reasons and experience, man has scored impressive advances in the mastery of nature .... Democrats believe that reason and experience can be fruitfully used in the understanding and

The World Political Spectrum

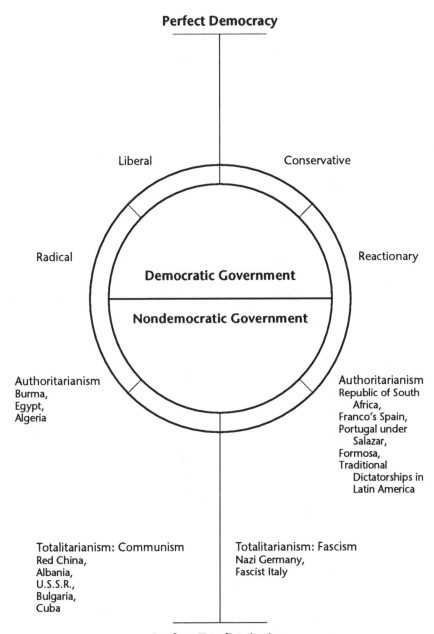

Perfect Democracy

Liberal

Conservative

Radical

Reactionary

Democratic Government

Nondemocratic Government

Authoritarianism
Burma,
Egypt,
Algeria

Authoritarianism
Republic of South
Africa,
Franco's Spain,
Portugal under
Salazar,
Formosa,
Traditional
Dictatorships in
Latin America

Totalitarianism: Communism
Red China,
Albania,
U.S.S.R.,
Bulgaria,
Cuba

Totalitarianism: Fascism
Nazi Germany,
Fascist Italy

Perfect Totalitarianism

The World Political Spectrum

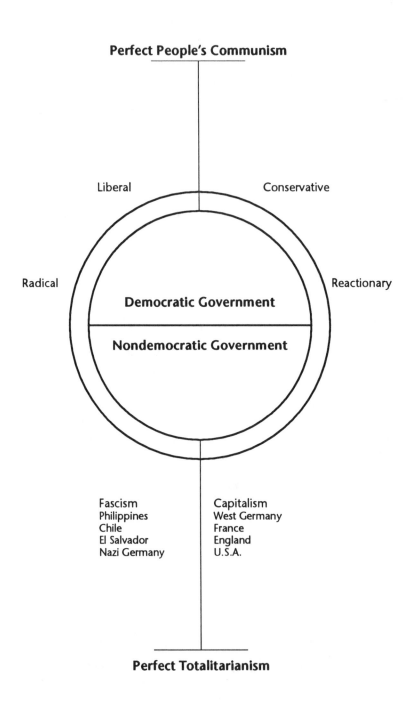

Perfect People's Communism

Liberal   Conservative

Radical   Democratic Government   Reactionary

Nondemocratic Government

Fascism   Capitalism
Philippines   West Germany
Chile   France
El Salvador   England
Nazi Germany   U.S.A.

Perfect Totalitarianism

> harmonious adjustment of human relations .... In contrast, dogma-
> tists (such as Communists or Fascists) reject this belief in reason
> and experience.[30]

At the same time, the text gives lip service to the need for free discussion of issues in social studies.

> In trying to present a fair and balanced picture of American
> democracy, we have not sought to avoid controversial issues. The
> United States owes its existence to controversy and conflict, and
> throughout its history, as today, there has never been a dearth of
> highly controversial questions.[31]

I know of no textbook presently used in a large public school system
that focuses on the multilogical issues of social studies or highlights the
importance of strong sense critical thinking skills. Monological thinking
that presupposes a U.S. world view clearly dominates. At the same time,
students do not recognize that they are learning, not to think, but to
think like "Americans", within one out of many possible points of view.

✦ Concluding Remarks: The Critical Teacher

To be in the best position to encourage critical thinking in their students, teachers must first value it highly in their personal, social, and
civic lives. A teacher of critical thinking must be a critical person, a person comfortable with and experienced in critical discussion, critical
reflection, and critical inquiry; must be willing to make questions rather
than assertions the heart of his or her contribution to student learning;
must explicitly understand his or her own frame of reference and that fostered in the society at large; must be willing to treat no idea as intrinsically good or bad; must have confidence in reason, evidence, and open discussion; must deeply value clarity, accuracy, and fairmindedness; and
must be willing to help students develop the various critical thinking
micro-proficiencies in the context of these values and ideals. To do so,
teachers must be students of human irrationality, egocentricity, and prejudice. Their interest must be both theoretical and practical. They must
experience (and recognize) irrational drives and behavior in themselves as
well as others. A teacher must be patient and capable of the long view, for
people, schools, and society change only in the long run, never quickly,
and always with some frustration, conflict, and misunderstanding.

Few now realize that the critical teacher is rare and that most of the
critical thinking cultivated in students today is, at best, monological and
technical, and, at worst, sociocentric and sophistic. The concept of
strong sense critical thinking — of what it is to live or teach critically —
has as yet had little perceptible influence on schools as a whole. If, in our
haste to bring critical thinking into the schools, we ignore the need to

develop long-term strategies for nurturing the development of teachers' own critical powers and passions, then we shall truly make the new emphasis on critical thinking into nothing more than a passing fad, or worse, into a new, more sophisticated form of social indoctrination and scholastic closedmindedness.

✦ Footnotes

1 John Passmore, "On Teaching to be Critical," included in *The Concept of Education*, Routledge & Kegan Paul, London: 1967, pp. 192–211.

2 For a sense of the dimensions requiring critical thinking, see the Phi Kappa Phi *National Forum* special issue on *Critical Thinking*, which I edited and which includes articles by Neil Postman, Sabini and Silver, Matthew Lipman, Edward Glaser, Robert Ennis, Michael Scriven, Ernest Boyer, and me. Winter 1985.

   See also my "Critical Thinking; Fundamental to Education For a Free Society," *Educational Leadership*, September 1984; "Teaching Critical Thinking in the Strong Sense," *Informal Logic*, 1982, Vol. 4, p. 3; and "Bloom's Taxonomy and Critical Thinking Instruction," *Educational Leadership*, May 1985.

3 "Dialogical Thinking: Critical Thought Essential to the Acquisition of Rational Knowledge and Passions," delivered at the *Connecticut Thinking Skills Conference*, March 11–13, 1985, forthcoming in *Teaching Thinking Skills: Theory and Practice*, W.H. Freeman, New York, edited by Joan Baron and Robert J. Sternberg. 1987.

4 Robert Ennis heads the Illinois Critical Thinking Project, co-authored the Cornell Critical Thinking Tests, and has written many seminal articles on critical thinking, beginning with his "A Concept of Critical Thinking," *Harvard Educational Review*, 1962, Vol. 32(1), 81–111.

5 Harvey Siegel has developed a number of ideas implicit in the writings of Israel Scheffler. Most important for critical thinking theory is Siegel's contribution "Critical Thinking as Educational Ideal," *The Educational Forum*, November 1980, pp. 7–23.

6 See Israel Scheffler's *Reason and Teaching*, Bobbs-Merrill, New York: 1973; and *Conditions of Knowledge*, Scott Foresman, Chicago: 1965.

7 See Scriven's "Critical For Survival" in the *National Forum's* special issue on critical thinking and his textbook, *Reasoning*, McGraw-Hill, New York: 1976.

8 Matthew Lipman has developed a multitude of innovative instructional strategies for bringing critical reflection into classroom discussions, third through twelfth grades, in the process of creating the *Philosophy for Children Program*.

9 See R. S. Peters' *Reason and Compassion*, Routledge & Kegan Paul, London: 1973.

10 Passmore, op. cit.

11 Edward Glaser is one of the founding fathers of the critical thinking movement in the United States. Its early stirrings can be traced back to his *An Experiment in the Development of Critical Thinking* (1941) and his development with Watson of the *Watson-Glaser Critical Thinking Test* (1940).

12, 13 Ralph Johnson and J. Anthony Blair have been the major Canadian leaders in the Informal Logic/Critical Thinking movement. They have organized two major international conferences at the University of Windsor, have written many important papers in the field, edit *Informal Logic* (the major journal for those working on the theory of critical thinking), and have written an excellent text, *Logical Self-Defense,* McGraw-Hill, Toronto: 1977.

14 Ennis, "Critical Thinking," a handout developed in July 1985. *Illinois Critical Thinking Project,* University of Illinois/Champaign.

15 "Critical Thinking as Educational Ideal," op. cit., p. 11.

16 *Reasoning,* op. cit., p. ix.

17 "Critical for Survival," op. cit., p. 9

18 Ibid.

19 *Reason and Compassion,* op. cit., p. 79.

20 op. cit., p. 198

21 Piaget, Jean. *Judgment and Reasoning in the Child,* Littlefield, Adams, Totowa, NJ: 1976. Compare R. S. Peters: "The connection of being unreasonable with egocentricity is obvious enough. There is lacking even the stability in behavior that comes from acting in the light of established beliefs and practices. Beliefs tend to be infected with arbitrariness and particularity. Little attempt is made to fit them into a coherent system. A behavior is governed largely by wants and aversions of an immediate, short-term character. Little account is taken of the viewpoint or claims of others. Indeed, the behavior of others is seen largely in a self-referential way as it impinges on, threatens or thwarts the demands of the greedy, restless ego, ..." op. cit., p. 97.

22 Piaget, from "The Development in Children of the Idea of the Homeland and of Relations with Other Countries," *The International Social Science Bulletin,* Vol. III, no. 3, 1951, pp. 561–578.

23 William Graham Sumner, *Folkways,* originally 1906, reissued by Dover Publications, New York: 1959, p. 633.

24 See Karl Mannheim's magnificent classic *Ideology and Utopia,* a seminal work whose contribution to the theory of critical thinking has yet to be absorbed.

25 Ibid., Louis Wirth in his preface to Mannheim's *Ideology and Utopia.*

26 Commager, Henry Steele *The Atlantic,* March 1982.

27 Toynbee, Arnold *America and the World Revolution,* Oxford University Press, New York and London: 1962, p. 92.

28 Eberstein, Pritchett, Turner, and Mann, *American Democracy in World Perspective,* Harper & Row, New York: 1967, all quotes pp. 3–5.

29 op. cit., chart printed on inside covers.

30 op. cit., p. 5.

31 Ibid.

Chapter 11

Critical Thinking and the Nature of Prejudice

with Kenneth R. Adamson

Abstract

In this paper, originally prepared as a result of an Anti-Defamation League conference on Critical Thinking and Prejudice, *Paul and Adamson argue that there are seven basic flaws in "traditional research into the nature of prejudice". Efforts in prejudice reduction, based on traditional research, tend to merely reshape and redirect prejudice rather than to lessen it. This research problem originated in the failure of theoreticians to take seriously the ground-breaking work of William Graham Sumner in* Folkways *(1906). Sumner developed the view that prejudice is the norm rather than the exception in everyday belief formation. His concept ties in well with Piaget's research into egocentrism and sociocentrism of thought.*

Only a well-conceived critical education, Paul and Adamson argue, "an education that cultivates the rationality of students, ... liberates students from modes of thinking that limit their potential and narrow their perspective" lessens "the natural drive toward prejudice". For Paul and Adamson, "prejudice is a rich, complex, multi-dimensional phenomenon, grounded in ... the primary, instinctual nature of human thinking." Removing it, "requires the development of our secondary, more latent, nature, our capacity to develop as fairminded, rational persons." Such an emphasis "should not focus on the content of particular prejudices ... but on the mechanisms of prejudice and their role in the struggle for power, advantage, and money." The authors conclude: "A credible program of prejudice reduction ought not focus on the prejudices of others, prejudices against us, for we are ideally situated to change our own mode of thinking, not to change the thinking of others."

✦✦ Introduction

*T*raditional research into the nature of prejudice has these seven basic flaws: *1)* Researchers tend to approach prejudice as an aberration, something abnormal or atypical, something outside the normal mechanisms of thought, desire, and action — in palpable contrast to the main source, direction, and nature of human cognitive and affective life. *2)* They tend to emphasize the dysfunctional nature of prejudice, to

229

ignore the many advantages in power, wealth, status, and peace of mind that come from prejudiced states of mind. 3) They tend to focus on negative prejudices, "prejudices-against;" and assume that positive prejudices, "prejudices-for", are independent of negative ones and largely benign. 4) They play down or ignore prejudices against belief systems and ideologies, as though prejudices were only against people as such. 5) They fail to emphasize how prejudice is embedded in the pervasive problem of everyday human irrationality. 6) They tend to focus on the content of prejudices, rather than on the mode of thinking generating them. 7) They fail to recognize that significant prejudice reduction requires long-term strategies for developing fair and openminded persons in fair and openminded societies.

We emphasize, in contrast, the normality and universality of prejudice, its "functionality" in advancing the vested interests of favored groups, the harm in positive prejudices, the significance of prejudice against belief systems and ideologies, the embeddedness of prejudice in egocentric minds and sociocentric societies, the mode of thinking that leads to prejudice formation, and the need to focus efforts of prejudice reduction on long-term strategies for fostering openminded persons in openminded societies. We also emphasize the problem of self-serving interest in prejudice reduction: the revulsion we feel when thinking about "their" prejudices against "us;" the apathy we feel when thinking about "our" prejudices against "them".

Few in favor of prejudice reduction focus on their own prejudices, pro or con. Most grossly underestimate the strength and significance of their own prejudices while expressing anger toward and scorn for the prejudices of "others" against them. We argue that prejudice has root causes inherent not only in the human mind but also in traditional human social and cultural arrangements and practices. By largely ignoring the root causes of prejudice, contemporary approaches to prejudice reduction do little except minimize some forms of it while other forms — typically those that further vested interests — thrive. If we do not strike at the roots of prejudice, we do little to lessen the damage and injury it does, though we may shift who is damaged and to what extent.

Prejudices, on this view, are not isolatable things-in-themselves, not mental or affective atoms. Individual prejudices always spring from roots more basic than themselves. Just as a permanent underground stock of a plant continually produces and sustains the stems and leaves, so a deep-seated substratum of beliefs and drives continually creates and sustains prejudices and other irrationalities. Egocentric minds and sociocentric societies are permanent breeding grounds for prejudice. Opposing particular prejudices is pointless unless we take significant steps against what generates them in the first place. Pruning prejudiced plants does not eliminate the plant itself. To date in human history virtually all groups organized for prejudice reduction are organized to reduce particular prejudices, most notably prejudices against them. Rather than being indifferent to prejudices in favor of themselves, they actively cultivate them. Of course they cultivate them under other names such as loyalty, patriotism, or self-defense. Hence, any energy spent on prejudice reduction *reforms* rather than *reduces* prejudice, redirects rather than eradicates it. For these reasons, we argue, both research into prejudice and our conception of prejudice reduction requires a major reorientation.

✦✦ *The Concept of Prejudice*

The English word "prejudice" derives from the Latin stems *pre* meaning "before" and *judicium* meaning "judgment" or "sentence". Literally speaking, therefore, it means "judging or sentencing before the evidence has been considered". Its early recorded uses link it conceptually to injury, detriment, hurt, loss, or damage caused to persons by a judgment or action in which their rights were disregarded.

From the earliest uses one finds the word and its grammatical cognates used with conceptual connections to the affective and the behavioral as well as to the cognitive. Consider the following entries from the *Oxford English Dictionary:*

1. a judgment formed before due examination or consideration; a premature or hasty judgment ...

2. the action of judging an event beforehand

3. preconceived opinion; bias or leaning favorable or unfavorable

4. a feeling, favorable or unfavorable, toward any person or thing, prior to or not based on actual experience; a prepossession; a bias or leaning toward one side; an unreasoning predilection or objection

5. a preconceived idea as to what will happen

6. to affect injuriously or unfavorably by doing some act, or as a consequence of something done

7. to injure materially; to damage

Words with equivalent historical roots exist in French (préjugé), German (Vorurteil), Portuguese (preconceito), and other European languages. Each essentially refers to the human capacity to form prejudgments and preconceptions without adequate reason or before the relevant evidence is in, then to feel and act accordingly to the detriment of others. This core of meaning implies that people can be prejudiced in any dimension of thought, feeling, or action, not only with respect to ethnic or racial groups. Furthermore, the concept of prejudice formation is clearly linked to other basic concepts, such as 'bias', 'subjectivity', 'irrationality', 'narrowmindedness', 'closedmindedness', 'oversimplification', 'stereotype', 'distortion', 'rationalization', 'self-deception', 'egocentricity', 'sociocentricity', 'ethnocentricity', 'fallaciousness', and so forth. Indeed any sound empirical or theoretical work on why people tend to think, feel, or act in these flawed ways sheds light on the nature or phenomenology of prejudice.

The network of words conceptually intertwined with the word *prejudice* re-enforces the seminal nature of prejudice in human life. Prejudice is not likely to become intelligible or treatable as a thing-in-itself. Rather, we should understand it as integral to our understanding of how and why humans, with the raw capacity to form beliefs and feelings upon the basis of adequate reasons and evidence, so often form them otherwise. To put this another way, the question "Why do people often think, feel, and act in a prejudiced way?" is a paraphrase of the question "Why do people often think, feel, and act in a way that does not make sense given the available evidence?" Furthermore, the tendency of people to be emotionally attached to their prejudices, to hold to them even in the face of overwhelming contrary reasons and evidence, suggests that prejudiced thought and action serve powerful motives or interests. To overturn prejudice we must overturn irrationality, narrowmindedness, self-deception, egocentricity, and sociocentricity. We must understand both the psychological and social functions of prejudiced thought, sentiment, and behavior. And most importantly we must recognize how deep-rooted prejudice is in normal human cognition in every dimension of human life.

✦ *The Status of Research Into Prejudice*

Interestingly, in one of the seminal works in the field of anthropology and sociology, *Folkways* (1906), William Graham Sumner laid a foundation for what could have (but did not) become a global account of the nature of prejudice and a systematic approach to prejudice reduction. His basic thesis was that the overwhelming majority of beliefs and sentiments, both those expressed and those acted upon, are grounded in the folkways and mores of human societies. These foundational bases for belief and sentiment, these sustaining grounds for action and reaction, according to Sumner, are not chosen by people on the basis of reason, evidence, or reflection but rather produced by "frequent repetition of petty acts" which generate "habit in the individual and custom in the group". The principal conditioners of beliefs and sentiments are "pleasure and pain". (Sumner, p. 3)

Sumner implies that prejudgments and preconceptions are inevitable because "the first task of life is to live". "Men begin with acts, not with thoughts." (Sumner, p. 2) For primitive peoples, Sumner notes,

> Custom regulates the whole of a man's action, — his bathing, washing, cutting his hair, eating, drinking, and fasting. From his cradle to his grave he is the slave of ancient usage. (p. 4)

Sumner sees little deviation from this pattern in modern life: "All men act in this way with only a little wider margin of voluntary variation."

People divide people into "ingroups" and "outgroups", forming positive prejudices toward their own group (its beliefs, sentiments, and patterns of behavior) and negative prejudices toward outgroups:

> The relation of comradeship and peace in the we-group and that of hostility and war toward others-groups are correlative to each other. The exigencies of war with outsiders are what make peace inside, lest internal discord should weaken the we-group for war. These exigencies also make government and law in the ingroup, in order to prevent quarrels and enforce discipline. Thus war and peace have reacted to each other and developed each other, one within the group, the other in the intergroup relation. (p. 12)

Sumner labels this pattern in human life "ethnocentrism" and argues that it shapes a cast of mind found in virtually all social groups:

> Ethnocentrism is the technical name for this view of things in which one's own group is the center of everything, and all others are scaled and rated with reference to it. Each group nourishes its own pride and vanity, boasts itself superior, exalts its own divinities, and looks with contempt on outsiders. (p. 13)

Sumner sees patriotism as a common manifestation of ethnocentrism, typically leading to chauvinism:

> The masses are always patriotic. For them the old ethnocentric jealousy, vanity, truculency, and ambition are the strongest elements of patriotism. Such sentiments are easily awakened in a crowd. They are sure to be popular. Wider knowledge always proves that they are not based on facts. That we are good and others are bad is never true. Every group of any kind whatsoever demands that each of its members shall help defend group interests. (p. 15)

Again and again Sumner develops the thesis that basic beliefs and sentiments, folkways and mores, wherever found, are grounded in tradition and are not subjected, except in rare circumstances, to rational reflection and critique:

> The tradition is its own warrant. It is not held subject to verification by experience. The notion of right is in the folkways. It is not outside of them, of independent origin, and brought to them to test them. In the folkways, whatever is, is right. (p. 28)

Conformity of behavior in society reflects conformity of thought and sentiment:

> All are forced to conform, and the folkways dominate social life. Then they seem true and right, and arise into mores as the norm of welfare. Thence are produced faiths, ideas, doctrines, religions, and philosophies, according to the stage of civilization and the fashions of reflection and generalization. (p. 38)

Even the mores of society, its articulated principles of right conduct, rarely reflect or stimulate reasoned belief:

> They do not stimulate thought, but quite the contrary. The thinking is already done and is embodied in the mores. They never contain their own amendment. They are not questions, but answers, to the problem of life. They present themselves as final and unchangeable, because they present answers which are offered as "the truth". (p. 79)

Or again:

> The trained reason and conscience never have heavier tasks laid upon them than where questions of conformity to, or dissent from, the mores are raised. It is by dissent and free judgment of the best reason and conscience that the mores win flexibility and automatic adjustment. Dissent is always unpopular in the group. (p. 95)

Sumner paints a picture of human life in which prejudiced sentiment and belief, highly resistant to reason and evidence, are pervasive:

> The most important fact about the mores is their dominion over the individual. Arising he knows not where or how, they meet his opening mind in earliest childhood, give him his outfit of ideas, faiths, and tastes, and lead him into prescribed mental processes. They bring to him codes of action, standards, and rules of ethics. They have a model of the man-as-he-should-be to which they mold him, in spite of himself and without his knowledge. (pp. 173–4)

Sumner's personal repugnance toward prejudiced thought and sentiment is given in hundreds of examples that fill the nearly 700 pages of his book. Here is one such example:

> The tyranny is greatest in regard to "American" and "Americanism". It follows that if anything is base and bogus it is always labeled "American". If a thing is to be recommended which cannot be justified, it is put under "Americanism". (p. 177)

Sumner, using the concepts of suggestion and pathos, explores the apparatus of social conditioning which universally indoctrinates people and inculcates beliefs and sentiments. He spells out how they are "protected from severe examination", "cherished with such a pre-established preference and faith that it is thought wrong to verify" them, how they work "to preclude verification", and to "create an atmosphere of delusion". (p. 181)

In Sumner's view, and we believe his view is basically sound, belief and sentiment usually are formed precisely as prejudgments and preconceptions. Normally, the basic framework for belief and sentiment is prejudiced. Prejudgment and preconception is the rule, rational assent the exception. As Sumner puts it:

> The notion that "the group thinks" deserves to be put to the side of the great freaks of philosophy which have been put forth from age to age. Only the elite in any society, or any age, think, and the world's thinking is carried on by them by the transplanting of ideas from mind to mind, under the stress and strain of clashing argument and tugging debate. If the group thinks, the thought costs nothing, but in truth thought costs beyond everything else .... (p. 207)

Or again:

> ... the masses always enforce conformity to the mores. Primitive taboos are absolute. There is no right of private judgment. Renegades, apostates, deserters, rebels, traitors, and heretics are but varieties of dissenters who are subject to disapproval, hatred, banishment, and death. In higher stages of civilization this popular temper becomes a societal force which combines with civil arrangements, religious observances, literature, education, and philosophy. Toleration is no sentiment of the masses for anything which they care about. What they believe they believe, and they want it accepted and respected. (p. 232)

In fact, Sumner titles Chapter 15, "The Mores Can Make Anything Right and Prevent Condemnation of Anything". He closes the chapter with the admonition that the mores of a social group form "a moral and civil atmosphere through which everything ... [is] seen and rational judgment ... made impossible". Only in the exceptional case does Sumner allow for the formation of unprejudiced beliefs:

> It is only by high mental discipline that we can be trained to ... form rational judgments on current cases. This mental independence and ethical power are the highest products of education. (p. 532)

Of course, Sumner does not confuse *education* in the sense in which he defends it with mere *schooling:*

> School education, unless it is regulated by the best knowledge and good sense, will produce men and women who are all of one pattern, as if turned in a lathe .... An orthodoxy is produced in regard to all the great doctrines of life. It consists of the most worn and commonplace opinions which are current in the masses. It may be found in newspapers and popular literature. It is intensely provincial and philistine .... The popular opinions always contain broad fallacies, half-truths, and glib generalizations of fifty years ago. (p. 630–31)

Sumner contrasts typical schooling with genuine education based on the cultivation of critical thought:

> Criticism is the examination and test of propositions of any kind which are offered for acceptance, in order to find out whether they correspond to reality or not. The critical faculty is a product of edu-

cation and training. It is a mental habit and power. It is a prime condition of human welfare that men and women should be trained in it. It is our only guarantee against delusion, deception, superstition, and misapprehension of ourselves and our earthly circumstances .... Education teaches us to act by judgment. Our education is good just so far as it produces a well developed critical faculty. (pp. 632–33)

Sumner also expresses the possibility of a critical society in which the cultivation of the critical faculties would predominate over education for conformity:

The critical habit of thought, if usual in a society, will pervade all its mores, because it is a way of taking up the problems of life. Men educated in it cannot be stampeded .... They are slow to believe. They can hold things as possible or probable in all degrees, without certainty and without pain. They can wait for evidence and weigh evidence, uninfluenced by the emphasis or confidence with which assertions are made on one side or the other. They can resist appeals to their prejudices and all kinds of cajolery. Education in the critical faculty is the only education of which it can be truly said that it makes good citizens. (p. 633)

Sumner's work, though seminal, is by no means the final word on the subject. Among other things, his book reflects many of his own prejudices. Nevertheless, *Folkways* is unequalled in the literature on prejudice in its scope as a framework for understanding the pervasive social roots of prejudice. Ironically, each of its major theses is missing from the subsequent main stream literature on prejudice:

1. that prejudgment and preconception are the dominant social roots of belief, sentiment, and behavior,
2. that prejudice-for and prejudice-against are intertwined and interdependent,
3. that only a small minority of persons have learned how to critically question their own beliefs and sentiments and to rationally restructure them,
4. that a special education or training is necessary to develop a person's critical faculties, and
5. that a critical society, though possible, has not yet emerged.

Had these theses been taken seriously, subsequent research would have focused on the nature of schooling and socialization. Instead, though the literature is voluminous, the analysis of prejudice has typically been more superficial than Sumner's profound beginnings. After Sumner, prejudgment and preconception are taken as exceptions, prejudice-for played down as innocent and innocuous, the concept of prejudice narrowed to racial and ethnic prejudices, and the bulk of attention focused on socially unpopular prejudices. Consequently, few now recognize the universality of prejudice, its "functionality" in standard social arrangements, or the profound shift needed in schooling for prejudice reduction to be a significant social commitment.

We can document these general tendencies by canvassing the review articles on prejudice in the *Encyclopedia of the Social Sciences* and the *Encyclopedic Dictionary of Psychology*. Otto Klineberg, writing on the concept of prejudice in the *Encyclopedia of the Social Sciences*, defines prejudice as "an unsubstantiated prejudgment of an individual or group, favorable or unfavorable in character, tending to action in a consonant direction". Very quickly, however, it becomes clear that Klineberg's is not the broad approach of Sumner. Klineberg moves quickly to the limited view we have been criticizing:

> Social science research has joined with popular usage in introducing two limitations to this concept. In the first place, favorable prejudices, although they undoubtedly exist, have attracted relatively little attention, perhaps on the principle that they do good rather than harm. It might, however, legitimately be argued that even favorable prejudices should be discouraged, since they too represent unwarranted generalizations, often of an irrational nature. Second, although prejudice may extend far and wide to apply to objects as disparate as trade-union leaders, women, or exotic foods, in practice it has been considered as dealing primarily, if not exclusively, with populations or ethnic groups distinguished by the possession of specific inherited physical characteristics ("race") or by differences in language, religion, culture, national origin, or any combination of these. (p. 439)

He discounts the universality of prejudice by considering it only as a derivation from psychoanalysis:

> One view of the universality of prejudice seems to derive from an erroneous interpretation of psychoanalytic theory. This theory, particularly in its orthodox form, regards hostility or aggression (Freud's Thanatos) as instinctive and universal; prejudice would then be simply one manifestation of this instinct. Not all psychoanalysts would accept this formulation, but even those who would add that although aggression must manifest itself in some form, there is no one form (for example, prejudice) which must be regarded as inevitable. There is still considerable argument as to whether hostile aggression is universal, but in any case it can be expressed in so many different ways that inference to the universality of prejudice remains exceedingly doubtful. (p. 441)

He then focuses the bulk of his article on problems concerning prejudice against minority groups. He makes a passing reference to the ease with which a "healthy" nationalism "moves into an exaggerated chauvinism which is not only for 'us' but *against* 'them'." He then treats what he calls "economic factors" in which he alludes to the commonly "motivated" nature of prejudice, how it enables

> the dominant group to maintain others in a state of sub-servience, to exploit them, to treat them as slaves or serfs, to reduce their power to compete on equal terms for jobs, and to keep them "in their place". (p. 443)

Quite importantly, he calls attention to the unconscious nature of prejudice and hence to the link of prejudice to self-deception:

> *They,* whom we keep in an inferior position, are happier than they would be otherwise; *they,* whom we persecute because of their beliefs, can be saved only if they accept the true (that is to say, *our*) religion; *they,* whom we destroy, are planning to destroy *us,* and we are simply exercising the right to protect ourselves. It is arguments like these, presented in all sincerity, which so often in the past, and not so rarely in the present, have given to men the conviction that what they are doing is somehow noble and beautiful, in Hooten's telling phrase, they "can rape in righteousness and murder in magnanimity". (p. 443)

But he does not follow this up with any link into standard folkways and mores or into the ways they are inculcated. Rather he implies that prejudice is abnormal rather than normal in society:

> The fact remains that under the same cultural conditions, sur-rounded by the same institutions and tempted by the same desire for gain, some people show prejudice and others do not. (p. 443)

He alludes to Adorno's *The Authoritarian Personality* as a possible explanation for this abnormality in development.

The limitations in the research on the nature of prejudice is mirrored in Klineberg's review of the literature on "The Reduction of Prejudice". Far from suggesting that the fundamental cause of prejudice can be found, as Sumner found it, in the inculcative, indoctrinative socialization processes which bypass and diminish a person's capacity for reflective critical thinking, Klineberg favorably mentions the possible use of propaganda techniques to reduce prejudice. He shows no sensitivity to the distinction between schooling based on inculcation and indoctrination on the one hand, and that centered on the cultivation of critical thought on the other. Indeed he ends his article on what he calls an optimistic note by ejaculating,

> There is hope, too, in the fact that "authoritarians" are con-formist. If prejudice becomes unfashionable, even the hard core of resistance to change may give way to progress.

Henri Tajfel gives a similar account of the literature on prejudice in the *Encyclopedic Dictionary of Psychology*:

1. He says that the term has been narrowed, for these two reasons:

> The first is that it is generally applied to people's views about social groups and their members rather than more generally to 'persons' or 'things'. The second is that, in practice, the term has been mainly restricted in psychological theory and research to hostile or unfavorable views about human groups other than one's own ("outgroups"). It has been used by psychologists in the context of intergroup hostility, conflicts, persecution or discrimination.

2. It focuses on discrimination and hostile attitudes toward minorities, and

3. Although Allport's approach to stereotyping as a general mode of categorizing the social world is briefly discussed, there is no mention of profound implications.

Only by admitting the profound and pervasive nature of prejudiced thought and emotion can we make intelligible the need for profound educational changes to reduce prejudice. A superficial approach to prejudice that views it narrowly, as exceptional rather than routine, cannot be used as the main fulcrum for prejudice reduction.

The best candidate for a follow-up of Sumner's, *Folkways* (1906) is Gordon Allport's *The Nature of Prejudice*. (1954) Like Sumner, Allport approaches prejudice from the broadest of perspectives, attempting to trace prejudice to a variety of roots: "economic exploitation, social structure, the mores, fear, aggression, sex conflict, or any other favored soil". (xvi) However, in attempting to deal with prejudice from a variety of points of view and to point out the limitations of each, the overall effect is diffuse. Furthermore, Allport's work underestimates, as does most of the literature, the significance of positive prejudice: "... we will be concerned chiefly with prejudice *against* ... " (p. 7)

The most significant deficiency of Allport's approach however is his relatively superficial analysis of the nature of the thinking and affect that underlie prejudice. He attempts to account for prejudiced thinking simply as a result of faulty categorization and generalization. Allport sees "irrational categories" as "formed as easily as rational categories". He does not seem to grasp the special difficulties of attempting to cultivate and nurture persons who habitually think rationally. His analysis of rational thinking is too simplistic to help him to realize the need, for example, of profound changes in schooling:

> How to combat this irrational overcategorization is a baffling problem .... All these obstacles are profoundly serious, representing as they do the most firmly entrenched aspects of irrationalism in people and in social groups. (Allport, p. 503)

When Allport talks about the role of critical thinking in the solution of the problem of irrationality — and he does so only by implication — his analysis is simplistic:

> Fairly early children can ... learn that Foreigner 1 is not the same as Foreigner 2. They can be shown how the law of linguistic precedence in learning (p. 305) creates dangers for them, particularly in the form of derogatory epithets such as "nigger" and "wop". Simple lessons in semantics and in elementary psychology are neither dull nor incomprehensible to children. (Allport, p. 512)

Allport's concluding comment on democracy merely points in the direction of the problem. It is a far cry from Sumner's chapter on the task of developing a critical society:

> Democracy, we now realize, places a heavy burden upon the personality, sometimes too great to bear. The maturely democratic person must possess subtle virtues and capacities: an ability to think rationally about causes and effects, an ability to form properly differentiated categories in respect to ethnic groups and their traits, a willingness to award freedom to others, and a capacity to employ it constructively for oneself. All these qualities are difficult to achieve and maintain. It is easier to succumb to oversimplification and dogmatism, to repudiate the ambiguities inherent in a democratic society, to demand definiteness, to "escape from freedom". (Allport, p. 515)

✦ Curriculum Materials Focusing on Prejudice Reduction

Curriculum materials reflect the deficiencies in the research on prejudice. Of the curriculum materials on prejudice we reviewed, one of the best is Book 2 of the series "Challenges of Our Time" entitled *Prejudice and Discrimination*. Its quality notwithstanding, this book reflects the same basic oversimplifications detailed above.

The book contains six chapters, an introduction, and a conclusion. Five of the six chapters address racial or cultural prejudice, the sixth, sexual prejudice. The aim and direction of the book is given in the Forward to the teacher's guide.

> *Prejudice and Discrimination* deals with the problems arising from the social (group-forming) nature of human beings. The prejudices, competition, and conflicts that arise between groups are discussed in terms of ethnic, sexual, racial, and religious discrimination and adjustment. Special emphasis is given to the pluralistic quality of American society: a general discussion of the theme of "a nation of immigrants" is followed by an examination of the specific situations of various ethnic minorities in the United States, including Jews,

indigenous Americans (Indians), Mexican Americans, Puerto Ricans, Chinese Americans, Japanese Americans, and Afro-Americans. One chapter is devoted to anti-Semitism and Nazi persecution of the Jews and another to sexual prejudice in American society. (p. 2)

The book primarily focuses on racial prejudice. It barely touches on other forms of prejudice. It ignores the harm done by national, ideological, professional, personal, and religious prejudice. The chapter entitled "The Jewish People" might have led to a discussion of religious prejudice, but does not. Instead, when addressing the Jewish religion it concerns itself only with prejudice against the Jews culturally. It fails to address ideological prejudice anywhere, except by implication. Thus the authors not only miss the opportunity to analyze prejudice for and against political, economic, philosophical, and social systems, they also fail to address the roots of prejudice: the egocentric/sociocentric mind.

When they do hint at ideological prejudice, they ignore the ideational dimension. The term "Americanization" is introduced in chapter two, "The United States: A Nation of Immigrants", and refers to the pressure felt by immigrants to adopt the values and attitudes held by most Americans. Two questions might be asked: "To what extent was this a prejudice against other ways of seeing and understanding the world?" and, "To what extent was it a demand that all Americans learn to think alike, to share the same assumptions, the same ideas, the same world view?" The book neglects these questions. The lesson ignores how the history of U.S. prejudice involves significant prejudice against foreign *ideas* and *beliefs*, not just against foreign customs and dress, or ethnicity.

The Forward contains a list of 56 objectives for the series "Challenges of Our Time". The volume *Prejudice and Discrimination* includes the following paraphrased objectives: Students will be able to recognize various views of human nature: humans as rational and good, irrational and bad, mixture of both, the anarchist view, the racist view; students will understand the meaning of culture; students will understand the concept of groups and the basic psychological feature of group relations (in-group/out-group, or we-they attitudes.)

The few objectives cited here are quite significant, and, if ambitiously pursued, could lead students to useful and important insights into the nature of prejudiced thought, as well as into the nature of thought in general, for prejudice is grounded in the very *way* beliefs are formed. However, the book takes a less than ambitious approach and leaves untouched the heart of prejudice. For it is not enough to discover that one has this or that prejudice; one must also discover how one generates and multiplies prejudices in an ongoing way. One cannot kill poison oak merely by periodically picking a leaf off the plant. Prejudice producing modes of thinking *must* become the focus of instruction for prejudice reduction. The content of the prejudices is secondary; it does not much matter what particular prejudices particular humans have. It is their profound involvement in "prejudgment" as a habitual mode of thinking and judgment that is the key problem. Only by exposing and examining the roots of prejudice can we effectively begin to eliminate it.

This failure to recognize prejudice formation as a mode of thought is continued in the book's treatment of positive prejudice. In the student text, positive prejudice is defined as: "A preference for certain ideas, values, things, or people". (p. 5) These preferences, the student is told, are not necessarily harmful or unhealthy, and may be required to be loyal to one's group. Quoting again from the student text:

> If one is a member of a group one will usually have a prejudice in favor of it, that is, a preference for it. One will be prejudiced in favor of the group's values. If these values are sound, one's prejudice will probably be sound, too. A prejudice in favor of one's children or one's parents is a good thing in a family. (p. 5)

By approving of positive prejudice, the book potentially undermines all it attempts to accomplish. A positive prejudice is typically accompanied by a negative prejudice, for in being prejudiced in favor of particular groups we more or less automatically oppose those groups in conflict with them. In this sense, positive prejudice is rarely, if ever, harmless. Others are typically affected by our prejudices. This is certainly true of national prejudice. Our prejudice in favor of our nation tends to be accompanied by a prejudice against those nations that differ from or oppose our own. This affects our attitudes toward these nations, and our policies concerning them. We usually develop double standards to protect these prejudices, judging the actions and policies of our country differently than the actions and policies of opposing countries. Our positive prejudice may lead us to think any who say we have wronged them are either liars or fools.

Prejudice, as we have said, is located in a general mode of thinking by which beliefs are formed and maintained. Until we learn to form beliefs on the basis of rational considerations, we form them without such consideration — that is, as prejudices. Approving of positive prejudice encourages this prejudice forming process, as though it could be limited to innocent prejudices. Furthermore, in the confusion, rational preference is obscured.

To rationally prefer some belief implies that we have strong reasons and evidence to support it, and conversely, good reason to oppose conflicting beliefs. It also of course requires us to consider the case against our preferences or against the way we manifest our preference in action. *Blind* loyalty to a group is not, for example, a rational preference. Neither is the practice of giving preferred status in a society to particular ethnic and religious groups. A prejudiced preference, on the other hand, implies a preference based not on good reasons, but on considerations that will not stand up to critical assessment. Unknowingly, it is this prejudiced preference which the lesson encourages. Egocentricity and sociocentricity generate positive and negative prejudices as part of egocentric and socio-centric activities of mind, and it is these fundamental drives that must be overcome to make any significant progress toward prejudice reduction. We cannot work against prejudice if we encourage the very processes that create it.

To sum up, although this book introduces the student to some important concepts and tendencies, it is on the whole superficial, and contains fundamental confusions. Inadvertently, the book reflects the narrow focus of contemporary research on prejudice reduction.

✦✦ *Prejudice and Human Desire*

Human action arises from human motives and human motives arise from human desire and perceived interest. Getting what we want and what advances our prestige, wealth, power, and peace of mind naturally structures and shapes how we conceive of and understand the situations and circumstances of our daily lives. We categorize, make assumptions, interpret, and infer from within a viewpoint we routinely use to advance our personal ends and desires. We are, in a word, naturally prejudiced in our favor. We reflexively and spontaneously gravitate to the slant on things that makes it easiest to gratify our desires and justify doing so, including the desire to be correct. We naturally shrink at the thought of being wrong, and conversely, delight in the thought of being right, and so often resist the attempts of others to "correct" us, especially when this involves beliefs that are fundamental and part of our personal identity.

The thinking, then, most natural or instinctive in humans Freud called "pleasure-principle thinking". This mode of thinking requires the absence of intellectual virtues, for the presence of these virtues would prevent us from thinking one-sidedly in ways that structure or shape situations to our advantage. "How-can-I-think-of-this-situation-in-such-a-way-as-to-get-what-I-want-out-of-it?" is a reflex in the thinking of humans. Consider these two examples.

A small child who wanted to play her audio tape for a guest was told by the guest to first ask her mother if that was all right. The child ran to her mother and said, "She wants to hear my tape!" She instinctively knew not to say, "I want to play my tape. Could I play it for her?"

A toddler who was told by his mother that he could not play outside because it was raining, looked thoughtfully out the window and then ejaculated: "Yes, I can play outside. It isn't raining, its only drizzling!" Already these children are learning to structure their requests and interpret evidence in ways that help them get their way.

The extent to which these perceived interests and the means adopted to realize them are unexamined is the extent to which these ends and means are prejudices. We begin with self-serving assumptions, and from these assumptions proceed to build a system of beliefs. This system may be quite complex and sophisticated, but if the assumptions upon which it rests are a result of prejudgments, the beliefs built on them are prejudices. 'Prejudice', then, refers to the manner in which the belief is formed and held, not to its falsity. A prejudice is not necessarily a false belief, and may, on examination, be rationally defensible. Prior to this examination however it is no less a prejudice.

✦ Prejudice and the Illusion of Morality

To be prejudiced in favor of our perceived interests entails that we become prejudiced against whomever or whatever appears to oppose or stand in the way of furthering them. It is not enough to be taught to be honest, kind, generous, thoughtful, concerned with others, and respectful of human rights. The human mind can easily construe situations in ways that conceive selfish desire as self-defense, cruelty as discipline, domination as love, intolerance as conviction, and in general, evil as good. The mere conscious desire to do good does not remove prejudiced conceptions which shape perceptions to further our interests or keep us from forming such conceptions. To minimize our egocentric drives, we must develop critical thinking in a special direction. We need not only intellectual *skills* but intellectual *character* as well. Indeed, we must develop and refine our intellectual skills as we develop and refine our intellectual character, to embed the skills in our character and shape our character through the skills.

Much of our thinking is directed at deciding to perform some action from among a range of possible actions. Whatever action we decide to take will inevitably influence others in some way, often trivially, sometimes profoundly. There is, then, a distinctly moral dimension to thinking that must not be ignored. People not only *can*, but often *do* create the illusion of morality in a variety of ways. One major way is the systematic confusion of group mores with universal moral standards.

When people act in accordance with the injunctions and taboos of the group to which they belong they naturally feel righteous. They receive much praise in moral terms, and may even be treated as moral leaders, if they speak or act in a way that impresses the group. For this reason, few people distinguish moral or religious conformity or demagoguery from genuine moral integrity. Group norms are typically articulated in the language of morality and a socialized person inwardly experiences some sense of shame or guilt in violating a social taboo, and anger or moral outrage at others who do so. In other words, what commonly seems to be the inner voice of conscience is often nothing more than the internalized voice of social authority, the voice of our parents, our teachers, and other "superiors" speaking within us. Genuine moral integrity requires what might be called "intellectual character" and this requires rational assent, for moral decisions require thoughtful discrimination between what is merely socially permitted and what is genuinely morally justified.

The other major way in which humans systematically create the illusion of morality is egocentrically structured self-deception. This, as we have mentioned, is the shaping and justification of self-serving perceptions and viewpoints. When engaged in such spontaneous thought, we systematically confuse our viewpoint with reality itself. We do not experience ourselves as selecting among a range of possible perceptions; quite the contrary, it seems to us that we simply observe things *as they are*. What is really egocentric intellectual arrogance we experience as righteous moral judgment. This leads us to conceive those who disagree with us as fools, dissemblers, or worse. Since our inner voice tells us that our motives are pure, that we see things as they really are, those who set themselves against us or threaten to impede us often seem the manifestation of evil. If they use violence to advance their ends, we experience their action as aggressive, as blind to human rights and simple justice. But if we use violence, it is not even conceived as violence but as justifiable self-defense, as the restoring of law and order, as the protection of right and justice. We habitually use double standards to assess the beliefs and actions of ourselves and others. The one we apply to ourselves is sympathetic, open-ended, and forgiving, the one we apply to others is unsympathetic, rigid, and unforgiving.

✦ Prejudiced in Favor of Our Interests

Consider the common sense truth that human groups typically have vested interests and spend a significant part of their time and energy advancing them. Developing a point of view, a framework of beliefs that serve these interests, is crucial to "success". The result is that prejudiced thinking is usually functional. Fairminded thinking impedes success by diffusing effort and nurturing self-restraint that limits "profit" and "advantage". This basic truth lies at the root of much worldly prejudice. One finds it in all special interest groups, whether professional, economic, religious, ethnic, or otherwise. This can be illustrated by a recent segment of the history of the American Medical Association.

A professional association like the AMA routinely pursues the perceived vested interests of its members. This pursuit is part and parcel of developing a frame of reference and mode of thinking prejudiced in favor of these interests. For example, because the approach of the AMA to health care is predominantly pharmacological and surgical, we can predict that members will be unsympathetic to such things as home birth, holistic medicine, and chiropractic. Also, since the approach to medical practice is committed to a particular conception of free enterprise and private practice, we can be confident that the AMA will reject socialized medicine. Since the profession is based on perceived interests, on pharmacology and surgery, and on a conception of free enterprise and private practice, members of the AMA generally oppose positions that appear to negate or question views favoring these positions. They also fail to grant that there may be elements of significant truth in these opposing positions.

Consequently, few doctors read books which advocate an opposing position, such as socialized medicine or chiropractic. Thus, few doctors hear or understand the strongest arguments against the dominant thinking within their profession. They think this unnecessary because they are confident in their positions *a priori*, before the evidence. In other words, they are prejudiced in favor of views into which they were socialized by the culture of medical school and medical practice.

Consider, as an illustration, the AMA's position on chiropractic therapy. Prior to the early 1970's, some advocates of chiropractic made exaggerated claims regarding the types of disorders it could effectively treat — citing as treatable, cancer, high blood pressure, diabetes, and infectious disease. This provided a reasonable ground for AMA skepticism regarding chiropractic. However, this legitimate AMA concern for patient care soon escalated into a general caricature of chiropractic. So powerful was this negative prejudice that the AMA conspired against the chiropractic profession. It took a court ordered permanent injunction to restrain the AMA (Chester A. Wilks vs. American Medical Association). On August 27, 1987, the United States District Court decided in this case that, "the AMA and its members participated in a conspiracy against chiropractors in violation of the nation's antitrust laws". (*JAMA*, p. 81) According to the Permanent Injunction Order:

> In the early 1960's, the AMA decided to contain and eliminate chiropractic as a profession. In 1963 the AMA's Committee on Quackery was formed. The committee worked aggressively, both overtly and covertly, to eliminate chiropractic. One of the principle means used by the AMA to achieve its goal was to make it unethical for medical physicians to professionally associate with chiropractors. (*JAMA*, p. 81)

In the early 1970's, chiropractic therapy began to change, and claims of its effectiveness became more reasonable. The AMA, however, did not begin to alter its position toward chiropractic until 1977, after several lawsuits had been brought against the AMA a year earlier. Although policy had now "officially" changed, this new policy was not passed on to the members of the AMA. Quoting again from the Permanent Injunction Order:

The AMA's present position on chiropractic, as stated to this court, is that it is ethical for a medical physician to professionally associate with chiropractors provided the physician believes that such association is in the best interests of his patients. This position has not previously been communicated by the AMA to its members. (*JAMA*, p. 81)

An initially legitimate concern for patient health became a prejudice. Of course, the initial concern may have also included a desire on the part of the AMA to "protect its turf". In the case of Wilks vs. the AMA,

The court concluded that the AMA had a genuine concern for scientific methods in patient care, and that this concern was the dominant factor in motivating the AMA's conduct. However, the AMA failed to establish that throughout the entire period of the boycott, from 1966 to 1980, this concern was objectively reasonable .... Finally, the court ruled that the AMA's concern for scientific method in patient care could have been adequately satisfied in a manner less restrictive of competition and that a nationwide conspiracy to eliminate a licensed profession was not justified by the concern for scientific method. On the basis of these findings, the court concluded that the AMA had failed to establish the patient care defense. (*JAMA*, p. 82)

Even though "AMA witnesses, including the present Chairman of the Board of Trustees of the AMA, testified that some forms of treatment by chiropractors, including manipulation, can be therapeutic in the treatment of conditions such as back pain syndrome" (*JAMA*, p. 82), this prejudice against chiropractic persists among physicians today. Few physicians know about instances in which chiropractic manipulation of the joints and spine are, or can be, therapeutic. Few advise their patients to seek chiropractic care, and many even attempt to dissuade from visiting chiropractors those patients who express a desire to do so.

This is merely one illustration out of a virtually endless series of examples of professional prejudice. In addition to professional prejudice, of course, there are many other forms of prejudice: personal, cultural, religious, ideological, social, scientific, and national. Each, if analyzed, yields parallel insights. Later we will look at national prejudice.

The central problem of prejudice reduction in the world is that *self-announced prejudice almost never exists*. Prejudice nearly always exists in obscured, rationalized, socially validated, functional forms. It enables people to sleep peacefully at night even while flagrantly abusing the rights of others. It enables people to get more of what they want, or get it more easily. It is often sanctioned with pomp and ceremony. It sometimes appears as the very will of God. Unless we admit to these powerful tendencies in ourselves, in our social institutions, in what we sometimes take to be our most lofty actions, we will not face the problem of prejudice realistically. We will fail to attack it at its roots. We will avoid taking those measures which could empower our children to move in the direction of genuine fairmindedness. It is not mere coincidence that most groups concerned with prejudice concern themselves with the prejudices of *others*. Only on the rarest of occasions do groups focus any attention on their own prejudices for or against others.

✦✦ Taking Prejudice Reduction Seriously: The Role of Education

Whether in or out of school, the dominant mode of social learning is didactic, dogmatic, fragmented, and unconducive to independent critical thought. The belief that knowledge can be directly transmitted by simple statement and memorization is so embedded in the public and academic mind that instruction in this mode is a virtual addiction. Part of the reason for this is that schooling became a large scale social commitment at the turn of the century so that people might have the basic skills to fill the nation's need for manufacturing, not that people might become autonomous critical thinkers. (Tucker, 1980) The very design of schools of the day reflected that of factories. (Keating and Oakes, 1988) But the roots of the didactic paradigm of knowledge and learning long pre-dates the turn of the century.

For thousands of years most children in most societies were expected to do what their parents did, and what their parents did was essentially what their parents and their parent's parents had done for many generations. Today, parents, peer groups, mass media, and teachers transmit beliefs with little sensitivity to or explicit awareness of what it would be to give good reasons and evidence to support those beliefs.

Didacticism, the direct transmission of beliefs taken to be true, is accepted as the transmission of knowledge itself, and rote recall accepted as proof of knowledge acquisition. At all levels of schooling the main mode of instruction is didactic lecturing and the main mode of learning is reiterating what is said or written. Students memorize information and facts, but rarely think critically about what they take in, since this is not required to pass the tests. Students do not connect what they learn in school to their experience outside of school. Nor do they make interdisciplinary connections, as, for example, between what they learn in history and what they learn in civics. Since this type of instruction requires little or no critical thinking, uncritical modes of thought are undisturbed, and the modes of thought conducive to prejudice formation flourish, not only undiminished, but accelerated.

In short, the mere reiteration of facts and formulas should not be confused with assimilation of knowledge. When knowledge is separated from thinking and presented as a thing in itself, it ceases to be knowledge. One need not think about or understand what one memorizes in order to memorize it. Knowledge, on the other hand, cannot be separated from thinking minds. Knowledge is produced by thinking, grasped by thinking, transformed by thinking, and assessed by thinking. We gain genuine knowledge through disciplined dialogue, through critically analyzed experience, through controlled experiment, through careful consideration of divergent points of view, through the critical examination of assumptions, implications, and consequences, through a sensitivity to contradiction and inconsistency, and through carefully developed reasoning. To work toward these ends entails a large scale educational commitment, one largely absent from contemporary educational theory and practice.

✦ Two Modes of Thinking and Learning

There are two basic modes of learning: association and logic. The first is unmediated, spontaneous, and automatic; the second mediated, thoughtful, and deliberate. Understanding the fundamental differences between them sheds further light on the nature of education and the generation of prejudices.

ASSOCIATIONAL THINKING AND LEARNING

What we find together in our experience we associate in our minds. If we are frequently punished for not eating our spinach we associate spinach with punishment. If it often rains in the summer, we associate rain with summer. If our parents generally speak of African-Americans disparagingly, we associate negativity with African-American persons. When entertainment media portray scientists as socially dysfunctional, carpenters as ignorant, blondes as flaky, we associate those groups with those characteristics. This is the lowest and simplest kind of learning. It is effortless and automatic. However it is often unjustified. (What is "connected" in our experience might well be unconnected in fact; what was "separate" in our experience might well be connected.)

When we subconsciously and mindlessly accept our associations as the truth (What do you associate with 'blond topless waitress' or 'communist sympathizer'?), we uncritically accept what are typically stereotypes and prejudices. Mere association is in fact a classic basis for prejudgment. We do not then figure out for ourselves what underlies our conclusions, we do not then typically recognize that we are coming to conclusions at all. Our associations seem to us bare facts.

Of course, many of our associations are transitory connections that we quickly forget, precisely because we have not figured them out for ourselves. These flit in and out of our minds. As such they are not a significant problem for the mind. But others are. Others are repeated thousands of times and become deeply rooted in our subconscious thought, laying the foundation for hundreds of prejudices, pro and con. Peer group indoctrination is of this later sort.

The only way to use associative learning as a basis for genuine knowledge is to go beyond it to logic. We use logic when we figure out whether our associations have a basis in reason or fact: Does the association make sense? Do we have evidence or reasons to support it? Does it fit in with other things we know? For example, by studying climate we could come to recognize that there is no necessary relationship between rain and summer. By studying human nature and paying closer attention to the African-American persons we meet, we can break down our prejudiced association of African-Americans with negativity. And by reflecting on spinach and punishment, we can readily see there is no objective relationship between them. We can figure out why the connections we had formed through mere association do or do not make sense, do or do not stand to reason, are or are not based on sound inferences.

CRITICAL THINKING AND THE LOGIC OF THOUGHT

The word 'critical' comes from the root 'skeri': to cut, take apart, or analyze; and from the Greek word 'kriterion': a standard for judging. The word 'logic' comes from the Greek word 'logos': word, speech, account, thought, reckoning. When we think critically we do not thoughtlessly accept things as we find them. We use our power of thought to take things apart, to analyze them; we use our power of language, logos, to account for things. We set up standards for judgment and use them to give things a conscious reckoning. We do this to genuinely understand what we experience, to go beyond mere association.

When we analyze the logic of things, rather than blindly associate them, we raise our learning to a higher order through critical thought. We begin the process of developing our capacity for rational assent. We begin to develop standards for belief. We begin to question what we read, what we hear and what we subconsciously infer. We forge logical rather than simply associative connections. We often say to ourselves: "Let me see, does that make sense?" Then we talk our way through inferences, reminding ourselves of the key things we know as we proceed. Sometimes we devise an experiment or test of some kind or ask others for their thinking, which we then analyze and consider.

Much school learning relies on association rather than logic. In the rush to cover content, we give students conclusions and constructions that someone else developed. Students retreat to association to achieve recall. They rarely use their own logical powers to reflect on what is taught to them to determine whether they can make sense of it. They rarely form standards of judgment or give a personal reckoning to the conclusions they are didactically taught. They seldom take apart what is presented as connected or put together what is presented as separate. They do not therefore typically determine whether these connections make good sense to them, whether their own thought justifies them. The result is that they often mis-learn, they often forget, they often confuse, they rarely effectively use, what they learn.

Most students' work reflects associations formed about school in general or about particular subjects or assignments. These associations usually minimize higher order learning, for they represent mind-sets contrary to independent logical thought. Students do not learn to think in critically reflective and fairminded ways precisely because it is not taught, encouraged, or modeled in their instruction.

In other words, students do not expect to have to think for themselves while in school. They associate school with passivity, with someone else telling them things to remember for tests. In history classes they expect to be given names, dates, events, and their results. Fair game is asking them to repeat them. In math classes they expect to be given formulas to use according to fixed procedures. Fair game is giving them problems that can be solved by routine use of the formulas covered immediately before the test.

English classes have several operative associations. If asked to read a story students expect to be asked to recall randomly selected details or to give their subjective reactions. They do not expect to have to distill the plot, figure out the meaning of a story, or back up their subjective reactions with evidence from it. They expect the teacher ultimately to let them know the "real" meaning of the story and what if anything they should remember for the test. They expect to be given lists of words and sentences to "do" according to directions. ("Underline each noun.") If asked to write they expect either to repeat what the text or the teacher said, to copy the encyclopedia, or to write out their subjective impressions and associations as these occur to them. They have only a foggy notion of what it means to think logically. They have no sense of how to develop an idea logically. They do not realize that their thought depends on assumptions that they might probe or examine. They do not recognize that their interpretations represent inferences. They do not know how to marshal evidence for their conclusions. They do not know how to check their thinking or that of others for contradictions. They do not see that their thinking, like all thinking, takes place within a point of view or frame of reference. One might say that they are critically illiterate. The associational and impressionistic dominate their thought. Rather than form the foundation for modes of learning and thinking which undermine prejudices, the mode of instruction in schools typically fosters prejudgment and stereotypes.

✦ A Critical Education

An education that cultivates the rationality of students is a significant challenge. A critical education provides the tools and skills necessary for independent thinking and learning. It liberates students from modes of thinking that limit their potential and narrow their perspective. It appeals to reason and evidence. It encourages students to discover as well as to process information. It stimulates students to use their own thinking to come to conclusions and solutions, to defend positions on issues, to consider a wide variety of points of view, to analyze concepts, theories, and explanations, to clarify issues and conclusions, to evaluate the credibility of sources, to raise and pursue root questions, to solve non-routine problems, to transfer ideas to new contexts, to make interdisciplinary connections, to evaluate arguments, interpretations, and beliefs, to generate novel ideas, to question and discuss each others' views, to compare perspectives and theories, to compare ideals with actual practice, to examine assumptions, to distinguish relevant from irrelevant facts, to explore implications and consequences, and to come to terms with contradictions and inconsistencies. Only such a pervasive shift in instruction and school climate will get at the roots of student thinking.

A shift in classroom procedure from a didactic mode to a dialogical mode of teaching, where student questions, objections, and opinions can be freely and comfortably expressed, will of course take time, as teachers will need to learn new strategies, a new conception of knowledge and learning, and new habits of classroom response.

GETTING INTO THE LOGIC OF WHAT WE LEARN

Getting into the habit of reflecting upon the logic of what one learns is key to critical thought. Not only does this require figuring things out for oneself, it also requires pursuing the roots of what one learns until one establishes logical foundations for it. This involves tying any given thing learned into a basic logic one already understands. For example, to study history, the critical thinker does not simply memorize names, events, and dates, or thoughtlessly accept statements regarding causes and results. Nor is it enough to reflect upon alternative historical explanations. One must also reflect upon the very logic of historical thought itself: What is it to think historically? To what extent is historical thinking a dimension of all of our thinking about the world? To what extent, in other words, is all human thinking historical? This reflection need not be esoteric and distracting. The key is to recognize that everything we learn is temporally sequenced, that we continually see the present in light of how we have come to see the past, and that each of us has internalized a selective memory of what has happened to us, emphasizing what seemed to us to be significant in our experience.

When we grasp that all humans shape their present by their reading of their past and their anticipation of the future in the light of the past, we are ready to come to terms with the logic of history. We then approach not only all historical texts but all interpretation of experience with the awareness that all recording or interpreting of the past is selective, presupposes value judgments about what is important, and organizes what is recorded within one out of a number of rationally defensible frames of reference or points of view. The best basis for reasoning well within a domain of human learning or experience is to figure out how the basic elements of thought interrelate within that domain.

ETHICAL REASONING AND PREJUDICE

Consider the ethical domain as an example. Prejudiced thought is often unethical, or rationalizes unethical behavior. But how are we to understand the basic logic of moral reasoning? How are we to understand the ingredients or elements of thought at work in everyday moral thought? We can distinguish at least these three elements:

1) General principles of morality, such as "Do not cheat, deceive, exploit, harm, or steal from others," "Respect the rights of others, including their freedom and well-being," "Help those most in need of help, seek the common good, and strive to make the world more just and humane." These tend to be shared by people everywhere, at least as expressed ideals.

2) Conflicting general perspectives of the world, such as conservatism, liberalism, theism, atheism, mainstream U.S., Soviet, Chinese, or Japanese world views. These tend to determine how people conceptualize moral situations.

3) Data, information, or facts relevant to a particular moral issue. Our particular moral judgments are ultimately judgments about particular situations, actions, or persons. We come to our conclusions, at least in part, on the basis of what we take to be "the facts of the case". (Paul, 1988b)

To reason more critically about moral issues, we must reason with full cognizance of these elements, be able to distinguish the general moral principles advanced, the perspective on the world into which those principles are integrated, and the factual allegations presupposed or expressed. Quite commonly, for example, people disagree in their general perspective on the world. One is conservative, the other liberal; one approaches the issue from a mainstream French point of view, the other from a Chinese. Awareness of these elements does not guarantee resolution of a moral issue, but it does enable reasoners to focus more particularly on possible problem areas, and, most importantly, gain insight into how and why their own reasoning may be biased. For example, our personal, professional, or national perspective on the world is often based on conditioned associations which have, over time, become uncritically held prejudgments. As thinkers who aspire to fairmindedness we often have to probe the assumptions that underlie our reasoning; often we find no rational foundation for them.

✦ Traits of Mind and Modes of Learning

The traits of mind and character we develop reflect our use of both logic and association. It makes a profound difference if and how we foster the mind's capacity for rational thought. People easily use their logical powers to justify prejudice, narrowmindedness, and intellectual arrogance. When we are prejudiced, we typically reason logically from prejudiced premises to prejudiced conclusions. Our inferences are logically flawless; these are not the problem. It is the deep seated starting points of our reasoning that are flawed.

We can see this most readily in others. Hence, when the Soviet government sent troops into Afghanistan, they had no trouble justifying their involvement logically. They reasoned as follows:

> When a government that represents the interests of the people is threatened by subversion from outside capitalist forces, it is the moral responsibility of the Soviet Union to stand by their side to protect them until they can successfully defend themselves. The government of Afghanistan represents the interests of the people and is threatened by subversion by the CIA. *Therefore,* it is the moral responsibility of the Soviet Union to protect them.

We easily see the questionableness of the assumption that the government of Afghanistan represents the interests of the people precisely because we do not share it. We are amazed that the Soviets can be so blinded by their prejudices. What we fail to see, of course, is that we are blinded by our own assumptions, which do not seem to us to be prejudices. They seem rather self-evident truths. We, for example, assume that when the CIA intervenes to overturn a government, it does so to serve the interests of its people.

To find the roots of the problem we need only review the contrary social conditioning and accompanying associations of the U.S. and U.S.S.R. U.S. citizens are conditioned to associate the United States with these images and ideas: the stars and stripes, George Washington, Abraham Lincoln, the Bill of Rights, freedom, democracy, land of opportunity, justice for all, human rights, leader of the free world, U.S. military, defense of the free world, etc. Soviets, in turn, are conditioned to associate the USSR with these images and ideas: hammer and sickle, Karl Marx, Lenin, freedom, people's democracy, land of the people, classless society, justice for all, freedom from want and exploitation, defender of the world's poor and workers, great hope for humanity and socialism, etc. The network of conditioned associations operate implicitly to generate a virtually unending series of prejudiced conclusions on both sides. Each side is prejudiced by its own positive associations with itself. Of course this is not all, since both countries also have negative associations about the other.

U.S. citizens associate the Soviet Union with bread-lines, cold and calculating bureaucrats, a monolithic power structure, slavery, totalitarianism, a drive to conquer the world for communism, Siberian labor camps, inefficiency, unhappy people, grey buildings, drab clothes, and long suffering. Soviets, in turn, associate the United States with the wealthy dominating the poor, massive slums, malnourished poor, drug dealers, prostitutes, gangsters, racism, pornography, right-wing leadership, political corruption, greed, and a ruling-class drive to prevent the workers of the world from self-determination.

Neither side questions its own associations and the prejudices these associations spawn. Each side uses all of its logical powers to trick or outmaneuver the other. Each is self-righteous in its thought and action. Neither side is intellectually humble. Neither side is fairminded. All this is done in a spirit of confident sincerity, with neither side believing itself to have committed any breach of intellectual integrity.

As long as individuals or groups refuse to recognize the conditioned associations that operate at the base of their thinking they cannot develop the traits of mind and character necessary for a significant transcendence of prejudice. Their logical skills will mainly be used to *maintain* rather than to *critique* their prejudices. Their thinking will remain primarily associational and impressionistic, easily influenced by desire, egocentricity, and sociocentricity, typically self-serving, resistant to criticism, and characterized by a lack of intellectual and moral character.

The contrasting mode of thinking is, in a sense, unnatural, and requires a sustained effort to develop. It is primarily logical and driven by a commitment to a consistent and fair use of logical principles. The drive for integrity in thought is characterized by the intellectual virtues: intellectual humility, perseverance, courage, fairmindedness, integrity, and confidence in reason. The challenge, then, is this: to encourage a shift from an egocentric, prejudice forming mode of thinking to a critically reflective and fairminded one.

TEACHING FOR INTELLECTUAL VIRTUE

Such a shift in thinking requires that students *learn intellectual skills* as they *develop traits of mind*. These perfections of mind are acquired if students progressively recognize the importance and value of these virtues as they think in ways consonant with them. Modes of thinking and educational practices are, then, inseparable. Students cannot develop intellectual skills incompatible with classroom practice. Nor can students be expected to develop intellectual traits if these traits are not modeled in an environment favorable to their development.

Nevertheless, there are specific ways in which each of the intellectual virtues can be cultivated and encouraged. *Intellectual fairmindedness* can be fostered by encouraging students to consider evidence and reasons for positions they disagree with, as well as those with which they agree. Students can also be encouraged to show reciprocity when disputes arise or when the class is discussing issues, evaluating the reasoning of story characters, or discussing other cultures. *Intellectual humility* can be fostered in any situation in which students are not in a position to know, by encouraging them to explore the basis for their beliefs. Teachers can model intellectual humility by demonstrating a willingness to admit limits in their own knowledge and in human knowledge generally. *Intellectual courage* is fostered through a consistently openminded atmosphere. Students should be encouraged to honestly consider or doubt any belief. Students who disagree with their peers or text should be given support. Probing questions could be asked regarding unpopular ideas which students have hitherto been discouraged from considering. *Intellectual good faith* or *integrity* can be modeled and fostered by teachers' being sensitive to their own inconsistencies in the application of rules or standards, and helping students to explore their own. When evaluating or developing criteria for evaluation, students should assess both themselves and others, noting their tendency to favor themselves. *Intellectual perseverance* can be fostered by going back to previous problems to reconsider or re-analyze them, as opportunity presents itself. By reviewing and discussing the kinds of difficulties that were inherent in previous problems worked on, and exploring why it is necessary to struggle with them over an extended period, students come to see the value in pursuing important ideas at length. *Confidence in reason* can be fostered by giving students multiple opportunities to try to persuade others and by encouraging students who disagree to reason with one another. These are a few of the many ways in which the traits of mind that define intellectual virtues can be fostered.

✦✦ *National Prejudice*

It was stated at the beginning of this paper that there are seven fundamental deficiencies in current research on prejudice. In this and the following section we exemplify how each of these seven areas are more common than is admitted. National prejudice will be used as an illustration.

The natural drive toward prejudice is grounded, as we have argued, in egocentricity and its social extension, sociocentricity. We often make ourselves, our group, and our nation the standard by which others are compared and judged, and we do this typically on the basis of prejudgments. We do not, for example, experience a wide variety of societies and then make a comparative judgment based on independent standards. Rarely do we learn to think within the frame of reference of any group or society other than our own. Rather we begin with a host of prejudgments that we and ours are best, and then interpret and experience the events of our world upon the basis of these prejudgments. Not only our thinking but our very identity becomes shaped by thought and experience grounded in prejudgment. If someone questions or criticizes our family, religion, or nation we usually feel personally attacked and rush to the defense. Once they become part of our personal and social identity, prejudices are hard to admit and even harder to dislodge.

An uncritical national perspective is often acquired in childhood, transmitted by parents, peers, and the media. Piaget noticed this tendency and commented, " ... everything suggests that, on discovering the values accepted in his immediate circle, the child felt bound to accept the circle's opinions of other national groups". These acquired images of other countries are typically not as favorable as that of one's own country, and are sometimes extremely negative. An us/them dichotomy results, one typically carried into adulthood as a network of prejudgments. We do not see beliefs based on these prejudgments as one possible perspective among many, but as the unquestionable truth. Without realizing it, we seek to confirm our prejudgments and tend to ignore what disconfirms them. We pay attention to what is negative about them and positive about us. Several things follow from this.

First, we rarely see in those people and groups we dislike the positive characteristics we take ourselves to have. Second, we rarely see in ourselves and our favored friends the faults we identify in groups we dislike. And third, we ascribe to ourselves and our friends intentions we withhold from those we dislike.

Consider the first of these drives as illustrated in beliefs concerning economic and political arrangements. Western style "free enterprise" and "democracy" are presented to the ordinary citizen as unquestionably and obviously the best choice among economic and political structures. Most North Americans could not persuasively argue for them, but are emotionally attached to these beliefs regardless. In short, most Westerners are deeply prejudiced in favor of their own economic and political arrangements and prejudiced against those that differ from their own. Any study of these systems, say, in school, occurs within this framework and carefully protects the favored prejudices. Students do not learn the merits of other systems, but continually compare them invidiously to their own beliefs, and confirm their judgments as a result. Furthermore, we typically compare other systems' worse points with our systems' best points, negative facts about other systems with positive ideals within ours. This is routinely done with virtually no objection from the academic community, which itself usually reflects social prejudices. These tendencies, unrecognized and unchecked, embed our deeply held prejudgments in thought and action.

Prejudice also protects our viewpoints, interests, actions, and institutions from unsettling criticism. As mentioned previously, these beliefs often constitute the bulwark of our personal and cultural identity, and we often find it psychologically painful to think we might be wrong, especially regarding fundamentals. Prejudice gives us peace of mind, protects us from the possibility of having to admit fundamental error, allows us to pursue vested interests, and when others are harmed in some way by our pursuit of our interests, enables us to continue with a clear conscience. We need only search our own memories to find abundant examples of times we dogmatically defended some favored position or belief, only to change our minds later. Our egocentric and sociocentric thinking prevents us from considering the merits of other positions. Our rigid idealization of ourselves generates a rigid negation of those who question us, oppose us, or simply stand in our way.

In addition, prejudice offers a confident and comforting retreat from the complexities and uncertainties of life, for problems are more easily identified and solutions more readily proposed, since there are few grey areas or complexities in prejudice. But the protection and solace of this retreat also provides for the flourishing of dogmatism, closedmindedness, double standards, oversimplification, injustice, and inequity. No one political or social system has all of the truth, neither does any political or social system contain all falsehood. But a dichotomous world view, acquired and preserved through prejudice, prevents recognition of whatever merit there might be in opposing systems. Honest and open dialogue among an array of different and opposing points of view is rare and its absence rarely noted.

Prejudice, again, is the typical, the normal state of affairs in everyday life, not an aberration; it serves a multitude of functions, from providing peace of mind to the gaining of power, wealth, and status; prejudice "for" a position is as common and potentially destructive as prejudice "against"; it is commonly directed against beliefs and ideologies as well as against ethnic and racial groups. It is one with the problem of human irrationality. National prejudice reflects this complexity. An examination of how the news media reinforces national prejudice suggests the kind of ambitious and thorough approach to prejudice reduction necessary to significantly lessen it.

✦ Prejudice and the Mainstream U.S. World View

One must first become aware of how a prejudice is expressed before one can recognize instances of it. Consider some of the more basic mainstream U.S. national prejudices.

We see ourselves as citizens of the most powerful country in the world. We see our country as moderate, peace-loving, just, democratic, free, honest in international dealings, supportive of human rights and consistently opposed to terrorism. Though subject to mistakes, the U.S. is seen as right on all fundamental issues, even when it stands alone against world opinion. Internally the country is understood to be the freest, with the greatest degree of equality of opportunity to rise to the top.

These are only a few of the many possible attitudes that could have been listed, attitudes that influence the way we view our country and its actions and policies. Since we assume that we are peace-loving, we have difficulty conceiving of our country as an aggressor in any conflict. Any who so conceive us fail to see that we are acting in self-defense, protecting ourselves, our allies, or our legitimate interests. We only "intervene" in the affairs of other countries to help them toward a more democratic government, even if they do not appreciate it at the time. We are criticized only because we are misunderstood, or because leftist propaganda has generated the criticism. Even when virtually every country of the world is against us (for example, in denying Arafat a visa) it is simply because they do not understand (in this case, because they do not grasp the threat of terrorism).

NEWS MEDIA AND NATIONAL PREJUDICE

All human thinking depends on our beliefs, beliefs that form the basis of classification, interpretation, and experience. Many of these beliefs are uncritically formed at an early age and retained and defended as prejudices. We rarely recognize how we acquired them or how they influence our perceptions. We experience but do not monitor *how* we experience events, nor do we identify what beliefs underlie which interpretations. As beliefs differ, expectations and interpretations also differ, but we do not observe this process in operation. For example, when citizens are raised to believe that the motives of their leaders are "pure" while the motives of leaders of "enemy" countries are "evil" or self-serving, events concerning these countries are experienced accordingly. The experiencer does not notice why, or link that experience to social conditioning. This difference in perspective focuses the attention of the viewer on some elements of the event and away from others, and often leads to widely disparate interpretations and experiences. News items about an intervention in *our* newspapers present interpretations of events based upon *our* assumptions and beliefs, while *their* newspapers present interpretations of the events based upon *their* assumptions and beliefs. We (and they) do not recognize that we both shape the news in a self-serving sociocentric way.

National prejudice is by no means peculiar to the United States. Every nation has its prejudiced image of itself as a nation, an image that greatly determines how events are interpreted. Consider this point made by Jerome Frank (1982), which vividly illustrates how national prejudice influences our image of other nations:

> Enemy-images mirror each other — that is, each side attributes the same virtues to itself and the same vices to the enemy. "We" are trustworthy, peace-loving, honorable, and humanitarian, "they"

are treacherous, warlike, and cruel. In surveys of Americans conducted in 1942, the first five adjectives chosen to characterize both
Germans and Japanese (enemies) included warlike, treacherous,
and cruel, none of which appeared among the first five describing
the Russians (allies); in 1966 all three had disappeared from American characterizations of the Germans and Japanese (allies), but
now the Russians (no longer allies, but more rivals than enemies)
were warlike and treacherous. In 1966 the Mainland Chinese predictably, were seen as warlike, treacherous, and sly. After President
Nixon's visit to China, these adjectives disappeared from our characterizations of the Chinese, whom we now see as hardworking,
intelligent, artistic, progressive, and practical.

Several examples illustrate how these tendencies are articulated in the
media. Consider Admiral Trost's article "The Morning of the Empty
Trenches: Soviet Politics of Maneuver and the U.S. Response".

We in the West, whose ethical foundations lie on concepts of
truth and justice, are frequently surprised to find that other civilizations have different ethics. In our relationship with the Soviet
Union, this has had a curious in-side-out effect. We have been lied
to so many times that we now eagerly rush forward at the first sign
that the Soviets are telling the truth. Occasionally, the Soviets may
find it convenient to lie, and we must learn to deal with this.

Admiral Trost claims that the professed ethical foundations of some
civilizations lie on falsehood and injustice. Clearly this is false, for all
nations claim to value truth and justice. However, what a nation considers ethical often differs from what is actually ethical. Motivated by egocentricity and sociocentricity, people idealize their beliefs and actions. We
value truth and justice, but so do they. We see our actions as good and
just, but so do they. We differ, of course, in the things we take as being
true and just.

If we or those we like engage in some activity of a questionable or negative nature, we justify the activity by appealing to motive or intent ("We
meant well."). A clear example from the *San Francisco Chronicle* (1988)
illustrates this:

For the United States the war in Vietnam was humbling, drain-
ing public hubris and setting the precedent for a deficit economy.
Vietnam, with Soviet support, taught America that *purity of motive*
does not always prevail. (Emphasis ours.)

Though most now agree that the war in Vietnam was a tragic mistake,
many still insist that our motives were "pure". Several years ago the California State Assembly passed a resolution by a vote of 52–0, that the Vietnam
war was waged for a "noble purpose". However, if those we dislike engage in
similar actions, we ascribe negative intent to them as easily as we do positive intent to ourselves. The Soviet involvement in Afghanistan is a recent

case in point. We see *ourselves* as intervening to support a struggling democracy (South Vietnam) against an outside aggressor (North Vietnam). We see *them* as invading Afghanistan to prop up a puppet dictatorship. The Soviets see these two instances as reversed: the U.S. is the aggressor, the U.S.S.R. is the liberator. To substantiate this, consider this excerpt from the Soviet press, taken from the front page of *Pravda* dated October 14, 1986. It is written in the form of an open letter to Soviet troops returning from Afghanistan. The headline reads: "To the Soldier Internationalists Returning from the Democratic Republic of Afghanistan".

> Dear Comrades!
> We welcome you warmly, glorious sons of the Homeland. You are returning home having honorably fulfilled your internationalist duty on the soil of friendly Afghanistan.
> At the request of that country's legitimate government, you, soldiers of peace, along with your fighting friends who previously completed their terms of military service in the Democratic Republic of Afghanistan, have helped the Afghan people defend their independence and freedom and the achievements of the national democratic April Revolution, and have helped to ensure the reliable security of the southern borders of our Fatherland.
> Soviet soldiers, along with Afghan soldiers and all of the country's patriots, have courageously opposed and continue to oppose the armed aggression of hostile forces encroaching on the sovereignty of the Afghan state.

The letter continues at some length, and includes such phrases as these: "... we take pride (in) freedom and equality, culture and democracy ... " and, "Lasting peace and reliable security for all people is our ideal." Notice the elements common to the prejudice of many nations: the (stated) love of peace, democracy, equality; disdain for aggression, terrorism, imperialism, and oppression. We defend our interventionist activities in Central America by saying that we must protect this hemisphere from the encroachment of communist influence. The U.S.S.R. defends its interventionist activities in Afghanistan similarly:

> (I)n a situation where imperialism continues to threaten the security of the socialist Fatherland and of our allies and friends and unceremoniously interferes in the affairs of others, we must be on guard.

The next two articles illustrate the use of a double standard to condemn the actions of an "enemy" country while not condemning similar actions of a "friendly" country. Both articles appeared on the front page of the "World News" section of the March 1, 1989, edition of the *San Francisco Chronicle*. The first article is titled "No Attacks on Israel: U.S. Amends Terms For Talks With PLO".

The United States called on the Palestine Liberation Organization yesterday to refrain from attacks on Israeli military and civil-
ian targets inside and outside Israel if it wants to continue its discussions with Washington ....

In December, the United States agreed to open direct talks with
the PLO after Yasser Arafat ... renounced terrorism and said he
accepts Israel's right to exist.

Now the United States is saying that the PLO must abstain from
attacks on Israeli military targets regardless of whether such attacks
fit its definition of terrorism.

In contrasting this article with the one appearing with it, the double
standard becomes immediately apparent. The article is headlined "Israeli
Jets Hit Bases in Lebanon 22 Children Hurt".

Israeli jets bombed Palestinian targets southwest of Beirut yesterday, killing three people and wounding 22 school children, the
police said. The police said a missile fired by one of the jets hit a
school yard in the village of Ainab, wounding the children.

Nothing in this article suggests that Israel be censured for this attack.
Neither is any connection made between the bombing of school yards
and 'terrorism'. To exercise fairmindedness, we should imagine how this
event would have been reported had Palestine attacked Israel and injured
22 Israeli school children. The action would certainly have been labeled
terrorism and condemned. Instead, we condemn Palestine and declare
that "the PLO must abstain from attacks on Israeli military targets," while
Israel is free to "defend" its interests however it likes. Two standards are
applied, a very liberal one for our ally, a strict one for their adversary.

Consider another article from the front page of *Pravda*, April 2, 1988.

Occupied Territories: Despite the draconian repressive measures
of the occupational authorities, Palestinians took to the streets in
the past 24 hours to express protest against the terror unleashed on
them by the aggressors. A UN spokesman stated that on Wednes-
day, Land Day, the Israeli aggressors killed eight people and wound-
ed 250 in carrying out punitive actions against the Palestinians.

We are immediately struck by several words: repressive, terror, aggressors, and punitive actions. These are words U.S. citizens normally associate with the Palestinians and their actions, not the Israelis and their
actions. This article would be written very differently in our press, written to favor our friend and ally, Israel. Sociocentricity inevitably convinces us that our actions and our ally's actions are justified. This attitude is reflected in and perpetuated by the language we use to describe
these events. Our choice of words give important clues in identifying
prejudice: the favorable words reserved for our friends, the negative for
our rivals or enemies.

Of the many forms that prejudice can take, national prejudice has perhaps the greatest potential for destruction. The prejudices of nations have global consequences. The deep-seated problems of environmental change, new complex health problems, worsening human relations, diminishing resources, overpopulation, rising expectations, global competition, and ideological conflict increasingly interact with each other to produce a host of multidimensional, logically messy problems. Our survival as a species demands that the higher potential of human critical thought be significantly tapped. The ability to recognize national prejudice and prejudiced thinking requires cultivation, as do the more general principles of critical thought.

✦✦ *Conclusion*

Prejudice is a rich, complex, multidimensional phenomenon, grounded in what might be called the primary, instinctual nature of human thinking. Removing prejudice requires the development of our secondary, more latent, nature, our capacity to develop as fairminded rational persons. Research into prejudice has truncated the concept while underestimating its roots, thereby delaying deep understanding of the global nature of the problem as well as of the required solution.

To understand the nature of prejudice, we must see it in relation to our basic modes of thinking, in relation to our desires and goals, in relation to our intellectual and moral traits of mind, in relation to our social groups and educational practices. Prejudice formation involves the way we think, the way we form beliefs, and the way we assess beliefs. It is fundamentally uncritical or narrowmindedly critical, governed by egocentricity and sociocentricity, reflecting double standards and inconsistencies. Obviously, humans *can* analyze, synthesize, and assess their thinking in a less than fairminded way. They can easily reshape their thinking to make it self-delusive. They create fantasies that have little relationship to reality and then live in them as though they were reality. They confuse their systems of thought, their viewpoints, ideologies, and cultural perspectives with reality itself. They embody their prejudices in cultural practices, indoctrinate children into narrow and rigid beliefs, and perpetuate closedmindedness, intolerance, and fear. They easily say one thing and do another, compartmentalize their contradictions, believe what their experience denies, ignore evidence, misuse language, value in themselves what they criticize in others, ignore and repeat their mistakes, project their faults onto others, and undermine the conditions of their own survival.

Fairminded critical thinking has always been a part of human thinking, but typically a subordinate part. Intellectuals and other intelligent people often use prejudiced thinking to advance their self-interest. Rather than exposing the narrowness of ideologies, they distinguish themselves as

skilled proponents of them; rather than challenging prejudices and risk-
ing the wrath of the prejudiced, they perpetuate them; rather than taking
on the worthwhile task of helping people become independent thinkers,
they manipulate them, thereby advancing their self-interest. It is certainly
easier to *take advantage of* prejudices and narrowmindedness than to
eradicate them. As a result, human life and societies have often been dominated by the manipulated and the manipulators, by those largely uncritical in their thought and action and those who use their critical abilities
to their narrowly conceived personal advantage. This weak form of critical thinking is the predominant mode of critical thinking developed in
schools and social life.

Because the problem of prejudice formation and preservation reflects
fundamental forms of thought that pervade every dimension of social and
personal life, any successful effort to reduce prejudice must be systematic
and foundational. A sustained and serious effort to reduce prejudice
should extend into three areas of a child's life: the scholastic, the familial,
and the social. Of these three, the scholastic provides the most immediate
opportunity for implementing a comprehensive program of prejudice
reduction. But this cannot be accomplished quickly, nor should we expect
it to be. To effect changes as fundamental and sweeping as these will take
years. This is an argument, not against action, but rather for a realistic
strategy, for steady, deep changes over a long time. As individuals change,
as their mode of thinking shifts from one that encourages prejudiced
thought formation to one antithetical to it, society's folkways and mores
will themselves shift, and so will familial behavior and interaction.

An educational effort to move students from prejudiced to fairminded
thought processes requires critical thinking and the cultivation of intellectual traits of character. (Paul, 1987c, 1988a, 1988b.) It should not focus
on the content of particular prejudices except for illustrative purposes. It
should emphasize the explication of the *mechanisms* of prejudice and
their role in the struggle for power, advantage, and money. It should
begin with the assumption that prejudice recognition and reduction
ought to begin with each of us, with our own prejudices. A credible program of prejudice reduction ought not focus on the prejudices of others,
prejudices against us, for we are ideally situated to change our own mode
of thinking, not to change the thinking of others.

✦ References

Allport, Gordon W. *The Nature of Prejudice.* Addison Wesley Publishing Co.
Cambridge, Mass. 1954.

Frank, Jerome. "Psychological Causes of the Nuclear Arms Race." *CHEMTECH*, Aug.,
1982. p. 467.

JAMA (Journal of the American Medical Association) "Special Communication:
Permanent Injunction Order Against the AMA," Jan. 1, 1988. pp. 81–2.

Keating, P. and Oakes, J. "Access to Knowledge: Breaking Down School Barriers to Learning." *Denver CO: The Education Commission of the States* 1988.

Klineberg, Otto. "Prejudice" *International Encyclopedia of the Social Sciences.* Crowell Collier and MacMillan, Inc. 1968.

Paul, Richard W. (1987a) *Critical Thinking Handbook: K–3, A Guide for Remodeling Lesson Plans in Language Arts, Social Studies, and Science* Co-authors: A. J. A. Binker, Marla Charbonneau. Published by the Center for Critical Thinking and Moral Critique.

Paul, Richard W. (1987b) *Critical Thinking Handbook: 4th–6th Grades, A Guide for Remodeling Lesson Plans in Language Arts, Social Studies, and Science* Co-authors: A. J. A. Binker, Karen Jensen, and Heidi Kreklau. Published by the Center for Critical Thinking and Moral Critique.

Paul, Richard W. (1987c) "Dialogical Thinking: Critical Thought Essential to the Acquisition of Rational Knowledge and Passion," *Teaching Thinking Skills: Theory and Practice,* Joan Baron and Robert Steinberg, editors. W. H. Freeman and Co., 1987.

Paul, Richard W. (1988a) "Critical Thinking and the Critical Person," *Thinking: Progress in Research and Teaching,* by Perkins, et al., editors. Lawrence Erlbaum Associates, Inc., Hillsdale, New Jersey.

Paul, Richard W. (1988b) "Ethics Without Indoctrination," in *Educational Leadership,* Ronald Brandt, ed. May, 1988.

Paul, Richard W. (1989a) *Critical Thinking Handbook: 6th–9th Grades, A Guide for Remodeling Lesson Plans in Language Arts, Social Studies, and Science* Co-authors: A. J. A. Binker, Chris Vetrano, Heidi Kreklau Douglas Martin. Published by the Center for Critical Thinking and Moral Critique.

Paul, Richard W. (1989b) "Critical Thinking in North America: A New Theory of Knowledge, Learning, and Literacy." Forthcoming, *Argumentation,* D. Reidel Publishing Co., Dordrecht, The Netherlands.

Piaget, Jean. "The Transition from Egocentricity to Reciprocity." In Campbell, Sarah F. ed. *Piaget Sampler, An Introduction to Jean Piaget Through His Own Words,* John Wiley and Sons, New York. 1976.

Prejudice and Discrimination Book 2 of *"Challenges of Our Time,"* prepared by the Social Studies Staff of the Education Research Council of America. Allyn and Bacon, Inc., Boston. 1977.

Sumner, William Graham *Folkways* Ginn and Co., Boston. 1940.

Tajfel, Henri. "Prejudice," in *Encyclopedic Dictionary of Psychology,* Rom Harre and Roger Lamb (ed.) MIT Press, Cambridge, Mass. 1983.

Trost, C. A. H., Admiral, U.S. Navy. "The Morning of the Empty Trenches: Soviet Politics of Maneuver and the U.S. Response." *U.S. Naval Institute: Proceedings,* Aug., 1988. p. 15.

Tucker, M. S. "Peter Drucker: Knowledge, Work, and the Structure of Schools." *Educational Leadership,* 1988, 45. pp. 44–46.

Chapter 12

Critical Thinking, Human Development, and Rational Productivity

Abstract

In this paper, originally presented at the Annual Rupert N. Evans Symposium *at the University of Illinois in 1985, Paul argues that productivity, development, and thinking are deeply interrelated. Consequently, societies concerned with their development and productivity must concern themselves with the nature of their educational systems, especially with whether or not the mass of citizens learn to think critically. Paul distinguishes rational from irrational productivity and argues that critical thinking is essential to rational productivity in a democratic world.*

Irrational production, in Paul's view, is productivity which "fails to serve the public good, insofar as it is production wasteful of non-renewable resources, destructive of public health, or at the expense of basic human needs". As both capitalism and democracy develop as world forces, it is important that we recognize the struggle "between the ideal of democracy and protection of the public good, on the one hand, and the predictable drive on the part of vested interests to multiply their wealth and power irrespective of the public need or good, on the other .... To the extent that it is possible for concentrations of wealth to saturate the media with images and messages that manipulate the public against its own interest, the forms of democracy become mere window dressing, mere appearance with no substantial reality."

Paul believes that the human world we have created has been created with a minimum of critical thought, a minimum of public rationality. He is convinced, however, that we can no longer afford mass irrationality. For Paul, the tensions between democracy, unbridled capitalism, and the public good must be increasingly resolved by a genuinely educated, rational, citizenry.

*W*hen we look upon learning in itself or productivity in itself or any other dimension of human life in itself, we look upon it with a partial view, as an abstraction from the real world in which all things exist in relationship. We then fail to see how it derives from relationship its true qualities. We view our object uncritically and narrowly. We fail to achieve the comprehensiveness all genuine and deep understanding presupposes. In this paper, I emphasize the intimate reciprocal relation

267

between learning and productivity, arguing that what we learn about the nature and problems of learning sheds light on the nature and problems of productivity. Hence, just as learning can be rational or irrational, so, too, can productivity. Just as learning can be assessed not only in terms of quantity but quality as well, so, too, can productivity. Finally, I will argue that the nature and quality of life in society is intimately dependent on the nature and quality of human learning which in turn determines the nature and quality of productivity.

A free and rational society requires free and rational learning and thus generates free and rational production. Education, rightly conceived, has as its fundamental end the nurturing of free and rational learning and hence aims to contribute and will contribute to free and rational production. Vocational education should not, then, be seen as independent of the fundamental aims and ends of all education. It should proceed with the same liberating comprehensiveness, the same excellence, and the same command of mind and behavior that we typically think of as the desired hallmarks of a liberal education. My fundamental questions are these:

What is the nature of irrational human learning?

What is the nature of irrational human productivity?

What is the significance for education of irrational learning and irrational productivity as social phenomena?

✦ What Is the Nature of Irrational Human Learning?

All learning has social and psychological as well as epistemological roots. Whatever we learn, we learn in some social setting and in the light of the in-born constitution of the human mind. There is a natural reciprocity between the nature of the human mind as we know it and society as we know it. The human mind — and we must understand it as it is, not as we may judge it ought to be — has a profound and natural tendency toward egocentrism. Human society in turn, has a profound and natural tendency toward ethnocentrism. Both egocentrism and ethnocentrism are powerful impediments to rational learning and rational production. An irrational society tends to spawn irrational learning and inevitably generates irrational productivity. Both socially and individually, irrationality is the normal state of affairs in human life. It represents our primary nature, the side of us that needs no cultivation, that emerges willy-nilly in our earliest behaviors.

No one needs to teach young children to focus on their own interests and desires (to the relative exclusion of the rights, interests, and desires of others), to experience their desires as self-evidently "justified", and to structure experience with their own egos at the center. They do this quite naturally and spontaneously. They and we are spontaneously motivated to learn what gets us what we want. They and we are instinctively motivated to believe whatever justifies our getting what we want. It is not *natural* for us to step outside our egocentric point of view. It is not natural for us to take into account the interests, needs, or points of view of others. We do so only insofar as we are compelled as we experience the force and power of others who require us to respond to their interests and desires and to take into account their point of view. We do so, then, often grudgingly and with limited understanding. We acquire and extinguish beliefs, knowledge, habits, and behaviors insofar as they seem to us to further our, typically unexamined, desires. We begin with visceral learning that is functional in the most immediate and spontaneous way. We learn without knowing we are learning, without making any conscious choice about the conditions of our learning, without recognizing the pitfalls of our learning, without recognizing its selective, its epistemologically naive, its narrow foundations. And, as long as what we learn "works", as long as we can get by with it, we tend not to discover the longer range value of self-critique.

Socialization, which comes close on the heels of egocentric experience, builds upon, rather than significantly modifies, egocentrism. Our egocentrism is partially transformed into ethnocentrism. We spontaneously and subconsciously internalize the world view that is dominant in our society. And just as we don't as individuals recognize the egocentrism of our personal point of view, we don't as members of social groups recognize the ethnocentrism of our collective world view. We take that world view to be as objective, as completely a mirror-image of the world, as we take our personal point of view to be. Indeed, it is a rare individual who can tell where the one ends and the other begins.

The capacity to think critically — to penetrate our egocentrism and ethnocentrism, to give credence to points of view other than our own, to recognize ourselves as *having* a point of view (rather than simply grasping the nature of the world directly and objectively), to seek evidence for our beliefs, to monitor and assess the component elements in our reasoning — is not spontaneous as is our primary egocentrism, but must be laboriously cultivated through education. When we develop abilities to think critically we develop our capacity to function as free agents. As they develop, we come to analyze, assess, and take command of our learning and so of the actions that issue from that learning, including our own productions and productivity. As rational agents, we bring a new dimension to learning and production. We open the way for our own rational production and the collective development of a rational society. We can understand this better by considering the nature of human productivity.

✦ What Is the Nature of Human Productivity?

Production is, quite simply, the creation of some *utility.* The first question to ask, then, in probing the roots of productivity is, *whose utility?* Beyond production for sheer survival, utility must be judged from a human point of view; and all of the diversity and opposition that exists between conflicting points of view is reflected in judgments of the relative utility of diverse forms and modes of production and productivity.

Production and productivity can be looked at both quantitatively and qualitatively. Of greatest significance are the standards we use to assess production qualitatively. I suggest that *the most pressing problem the world faces today* is the problem of irrational production, of that production which wastefully expends human labor and precious resources for ends that would not be valued by rational persons nor be given priority in a rational society.

The modes and nature of production within any given society reflect the nature, development, and values of that society. Insofar as a society is democratic, the modes and nature of production will reflect democratic decision making regarding production. This reflects not only individual decisions that one might make as an autonomous "consumer" and vocational decision-maker but also collective decisions as a citizen who supports some given social and economic philosophy or other. For example, the decision to provide many hundreds of millions of dollars to subsidize the development of nuclear energy rather than solar energy was a "collective" decision, heavily dependent on public funds and resources. So, too, were the development of railroad systems, the airline industries, the public highways, and sewer systems. These general decisions and the precise ways in which they were implemented can be analyzed for their implications for the use of public resources and the meeting of public interest and need. Indeed, there are very few "political" or "social" decisions which do not have economic and moral implications. Every expenditure of public or private resources represents both an economic trade-off (in that other possible uses cannot, then, be furthered) and some implementation of a judgment of value for public or private good. A society is not democratic if its citizens are not disposed to participate in this economic and social decision making in such a way as to knowingly and effectively protect the public good and interest.

✦ What Is Irrational Production?

It is a platitude, but an important platitude to keep in mind, that the productive resources of society should be marshalled to serve public need and public good, as against the vested interests of a relative few at the expense of the public good. *Production is irrational to the extent that it fails* to serve the public good, insofar as it is production wasteful of non-renewable resources, destructive of public health, or at the expense of basic human needs. One valuable rule of thumb is this: any economic practice is of questionable rationality if it can be maintained only by keeping the public in ignorance as to specific nature and modes of operation. The public cannot be understood to sanction that which it does not comprehend.

Production and productivity are to be viewed as collective as well as individual decisions in a functioning democracy. For these decisions to be made in a rational fashion, the public must have been educated to think critically, for when some narrow interest group seeks to maintain some form of irrational production (either as a whole or in part), it is inevitable that public relations and lobbying efforts will be launched which function, at least in part, to obfuscate public recognition of its own interests. For instance, it was in the narrow egocentric interest of asbestos manufacturers to minimize public disclosure of the health hazards of working and building with asbestos. The asbestos industry obscured the public interest to serve its own. As a result of the industry successfully protecting its vested interest, a mode of production was maintained for decades at great expense and loss in public health.

Since it is unrealistic to expect industries with narrow vested interests to abandon those interests for the public good, it becomes necessary that the public be armed with the critical, analytic, fact-finding, and reasoning abilities that critical thinking provides, that they may judge where, when, and to what degree the pursuit of a vested interest is consistent with the public good.

It is easy to find innumerable historical examples in which the public good was flagrantly sacrificed precisely because the public was kept in the dark about the manner in which and the extent to which private interest was secured. Adam Smith himself was well aware of the tendency of private interest to seek its own advancement at the expense of the public good:

> People of the same trade seldom meet together, even for merriment and diversion, but the conversation ends in a conspiracy against the public, or in some contrivance to raise prices. *(Wealth of Nations,* Book 1, Ch 10.)

It is extremely difficult to maintain genuine competition that serves the public good in the face of ever-changing market structures and ever-growing concentrations of economic wealth and power. Multi-national corporations, for example, are increasingly able to function as quasi-monopolies, or, in their capacity to move their productive facilities and great concentrations of wealth from one country to another, as to function as quasi-oligopolies. For example, when a foreign dictator prevents the development of free labor unions and preserves both "political stability" and "low wages" by effective and organized instruments of social and political repression, then the "free" labor force economically competing in "democratic" countries loses effective bargaining power at home. Free labor cannot effectively compete against unorganized repressed labor. A market economy cannot function in the public good when increasing concentrations of wealth produce conditions of radically inequitable bargaining power.

Again and again, questions intrinsic to the nature and mode of production and productivity turn upon decisions and policies that can be argued from divergent points of view and in which the relation of private and public interest are in need of critical explication. The individual citizen's capacity to penetrate the rationalizing smoke screens that can be generated to undermine the public good in service of private gain is a profound on-going problem of public life.

Consider, for example, an argument in the London *Economist* of July 13, 1850, criticizing the "sanitary movement" which was urging that government support the development of a pure water supply and proper sewage disposal. The *Economist* argued that poor housing and high urban death rates,

> sprung from two causes, both of which will be aggravated by these new laws. The first is the poverty of the masses, which if possible, will be increased by the taxation inflicted by the new laws. The second is that the people have never been allowed to take care of themselves. They have always been treated as serfs or children and they have to a great extent become in respect to those objects which the government has undertaken to perform for them, imbeciles .... There is a worse evil than typhus or cholera or impure water, and that is mental imbecility.

Here the public good is defined as allowing poor water treatment and supply to continue. To correct them, say these editors, would *harm* the poor.

As Adam Smith recognized, private vested interests naturally try to increase their wealth regardless of the public good. Hence, ironically, no private interest is in favor of more, but rather in favor of less competition in its own industry (unless an increase in competition would increase its own profits). When it is possible to take advantage of the public, private interests will almost inevitably do so. Thus, during OPEC's oil embargo, U.S. oil companies raised their own prices at home as well as abroad even though internal consumption of Arab oil was no more than 10% of our market. The OPEC action, in other words, provided a convenient excuse to join in a monopolistic practice of a special interest cartel. The result was windfall profits extracted from the U.S. public under artificially created, non-competitive conditions. The public, on the other hand, was continually led to believe that "Arabs" were exclusively to blame, as though U.S. companies hadn't taken advantage of the situation to advance their own interests, irrespective of the public good.

I am arguing that the nature and conditions of production and productivity are never things-in-themselves, forces independent of political and social decisions, but rather intimately bound to such decisions. These decisions may be rational (in the public interest) or irrational (against the public interest). Whether they are the one or the other, can only be determined by full and fair public argument. If a nation is to function as a democracy, then its citizens must be armed with the critical thinking skills which enable them to penetrate the propagandistic arguments which are creatively and adroitly developed by private interests to keep violations of the public good from public recognition. The history of the country is shot through with cases in which the public was deceived into supporting policies in which public interest was sacrificed to private greed. A tremendous price in lives and resources has been paid as a result of the public's inability to think critically to a sufficient degree to protect itself from irrational modes of production. We are, in my opinion, very far from the sort of educational system which nurtures the economic survival skills the public needs to protect itself against highly sophisticated propaganda which routinely advances private greed against public good.

It is crucial that we grasp the inevitable struggle that will continue to be played out between the ideal of democracy and protection of the public good, on the one hand, and the predictable drive on the part of vested interests to multiply their wealth and power irrespective of public need or good, on the other. In a society based not only on the ideal of democracy but also on a market economy that produces large concentrations of capital and vested interest, the power of the voting public is only as great as the information upon which the public can base its votes. To the extent that it is possible for concentrations of wealth to saturate the media with images and messages that manipulate the public against its own interests, the forms of democracy become mere window dressing, mere appearance with no substantial reality. As John Dewey remarked in *Individualism, Old and New*, "financial and industrial power, corporately organized, can deflect economic consequences away from the advantage of the many to serve the privilege of the few". Unfortunately, but predictably, the political parties, heavily dependent for their success upon the raising of large amounts of capital, "have been eager accomplices in maintaining the confusion and unreality". (p. 114) Dewey saw the issue as fundamental to whether the democratic ideal would be achieved, and as being determined by whether *force* or *intelligence* would prevail:

> The question is whether force or intelligence is to be the method upon which we consistently rely and to whose promotion we devote our energies. Insistence that the use of force is inevitable limits the use of available intelligence .... There is an undoubted objective clash of interests between finance-capitalism that controls the means of production and whose profit is served by maintaining relative scarcity, and idle workers and hungry con-

sumers. But what generates violent strife is failure to bring the conflict into the light of intelligence where the conflicting interests can be adjudicated in behalf of the interests of the great majority. (p. 79)

✦ What Is the Significance for Education of Irrational Learning and Irrational Production as Social Phenomena?

Wentworth Eldredge has put part of the background of the problem in a stark light:

The traditional democratic assumption is that rational adults in a rational society have the necessary hereditary intelligence and social training, coupled with a determined interest and sufficient time, to absorb the available facts which will enable them to make in the political process wise decisions among offered choices and upon occasion to invent and make real alternate choices. A majority vote of such reasoning citizens shall constitute the truth and the ship of state will sail a true course .... Most adults have completely inadequate training to understand even remotely the complexity of the contemporary scene. They lack interest and feel hopeless to think and act correctly in other than purely private concerns; and moreover, they have neither the time nor the information — assuming they could cope with the latter if by chance it were made available. They are merely carrying out the trite inculcated orders of their culture which have been drilled into them formally and informally since birth. Most adults are feeble reeds in the wild, whistling storm of a dangerous world they neither made nor could ever understand. To ask for the people's reasoned decision and advice on weighty matters of policy would seem to be a waste of everyone's time and energy, including their own. One might as well inquire of a five-year-old if he wanted polio vaccine injections.

In a rational society three general conditions would prevail:

1) The modes of production would be rational; that is, the bulk of production would be designed to satisfy basic human needs in a manner minimally wasteful of human and natural resources.

2) There would be, as a result, a multiplicity of jobs available to individuals whose performance would have a self-fulfilling quality based on the realization that it contributes to production in the public good.

3) Education would be oriented toward providing citizens with the critical thinking skills to make informed judgments with regard to the social and political decisions that ultimately shape and determine the economic destiny of the nation.

I am arguing that we are far from this democratic ideal of a rational society. If we are committed to it, we must devise means to achieve it. The only satisfactory strategy available to educators lies in making *rational learning* the hallmark of schooling. We can no longer afford the kind of schooling that at best transforms students into narrow specialists or experts who function as *tools* subject to additional *retooling* as dictated by the needs of production narrowly defined and narrowly controlled, and at worst leaves them without either specialized job skills or a general capacity to learn. The ordinary citizen needs the critical thinking skills of a person able to probe the evidential grounds for belief, a person who is swayed not by appeals to fear, prejudice, or ego but rather by the weight of evidence and reason, who is capable of suspending his judgment until such reasonable grounds for beliefs are forthcoming; a person eager to hear reasons and evidence against his or her beliefs if they become available, and to modify his or her views in accordance with them. Today's industrial technology is complex, specialized, and interdependent, but the social uses to which it is put and the human decision-making needed to maintain and direct it must be flexible, analytic, and humane — "ends" as well as "means" oriented.

TWO OBJECTIONS

Before concluding, I should air a couple of obvious objections. One may be put as follows:

> So far you have not dealt with the most obvious problem of productivity, the unproductive worker, the employee who, through lack of knowledge, training, or motivation, fails to perform in an optimal or adequate fashion. What employers want are dedicated, motivated, conscientious, and skilled employees who carry out their tasks as prescribed, not reflective thinkers who ponder the global problems of society.

This objection, you should note, assumes that the fundamental problem of productivity is "the worker". This is, of course, a natural assumption to make if the role one has played is one of traditional management in U.S. industry. From that vantage point, it is natural to key in on employee performance standards and to see those standards as a function of employees in themselves. Studies have demonstrated, however, that in most of the Western world, management and labor both operate with a strong caricature or stereotype of each other. The fact is that each tends to function with a narrow view of its own immediate vested interest. Hence, while it may be in the immediate vested interest of employers to get the most labor from the least investment of capital, it is also in the immediate vested interest of employees to get the highest pay for the least labor. There is minimal incentive in the system to cooperate toward mutual advantage, and maximal incentive to compete as adversaries for available capital.

The Japanese system of management with its guarantees to the worker of life-long employment and its provision for child care, recreation, profit-sharing, and job-retraining (if necessary) suggests the possibility of the accent being focused on cooperation rather than adversarial competition. It seems to me more reasonable to assume that there are no genetic or "moral" differences between Japanese, and say, U.S. workers, but that the differences in productivity are more a function of radically different philosophies of management/employee relations. I don't believe that any significant increase in worker productivity will occur unless, and only to the degree that, the interest of workers is more structurally linked to the interests of employers. This is both a global problem and one that can be addressed at the level of individual companies. One reason for the success of high-tech industries, it seems to me, has been a management/employee model closer to the "Japanese" than to the traditional "American" one. Much worker inefficiency arises from these two interrelated causes: workers don't seem to think; workers don't seem to care.

Present instructional practices and management/employee relations seem perfectly designed to produce the first cause. Students are neither taught nor expected to *think*. Such practices as mindless, purposeless drill, over-proceduralization (first do this, then this, then that — don't worry about understanding it) seem suited to what employers want: workers who keep moving, look busy, *seem* efficient, and don't question. But this very training-for-mindlessness produces workers who don't use their heads. Education and industry encourage "going through the motions."

Regarding the second cause, why *should* workers care about mindless tasks over which they have no control, which they are not encouraged to understand or value, and for which they often get little recognition or reward?

Here is a second objection:

> The dominant trend in business is toward giant corporations. Within them relations are direct, hierarchical, and bureaucratic. Directions flow from the top down. There is minute specialization of tasks. The entire task is accomplished by orchestrating the diverse specialized contributions. Very few specialists are in a position to judge the contributions of other specialists, or to judge the productive process as a whole. What we need are specialists who know their own specialty well, not generalists who judge this process as a whole.

My argument is not an argument against specialization but rather an argument for how to teach specialized skills. It is an argument in favor of specialists with the skills of generalists. There are two different modes of specialization, a narrowing and a broadening one. Most tools nowadays have a narrow specialized function. They are increasingly designed to serve a specific purpose in a specific process. But, as such, they are quickly rendered obsolete. We cannot afford vocational education or training that renders workers obsolete. Precisely because information and technology are quickly being replaced and transformed, we need workers who can adapt to profound changes.

Mindless, routine jobs are quickly being automated. The jobs that remain require increasing ability to adapt, to abandon old and adopt new ways. The same kinds of general critical thinking skills and abilities required for the global decisions of a citizen and consumer are required by specialists to adapt to new information, new technologies, and new procedures. This has been attested to in the call for new emphasis on critical thinking skills in vocational and professional education by the Educational Commission of the States, The National Academy of Sciences, and the Association of American Medical Colleges. As one business leader put it, we do not need "a steady supply of drones moving in a huge beehive". What we do need he suggested with the following example:

> My company took a contract to extract beryllium from a mine in Arizona. I called in several consulting engineers and asked, "Can you furnish a chemical or electrolytic process that can be used at the mine site to refine directly from the ore?" Back came a report saying that I was asking for the impossible — a search of the computer tapes had indicated that no such process existed. I paid the engineers for their report. Then I hired a student from Stanford University who was home for the summer. He was majoring in Latin American history with a minor in philosophy. I gave him an airplane ticket and a credit card and told him, "Go to Denver and research the Bureau of Mines archives and locate a chemical process for the recovery of beryllium." He left on Monday. I forgot to tell him that I was sending him for the impossible. He came back on Friday. He handed me a pack of notes and booklets and said, "Here is the process. It was developed 33 years ago at a government research station at Rolla, Mo." He then continued, "And here also are other processes for the recovery of mica, strontium, columbium and yttrium, which also exist as residual ores that contain beryllium." After one week of research, he was making sounds like a metallurgical expert.

Whereas the specialists' preconceptions, intellectual arrogance, and algorithmic thought prevented them from solving the problem, the student's open mind and general skills enabled him to do so. It is clear that the age of changing specializations needs specialists skilled in the art of changing their specialty, not specialists who, like tools and machines, become obsolete. Those corporations, giant or otherwise, who recognize this will thrive. Those who seek drones with specialities will continually be in trouble and, eventually, I would guess, out of business.

CONCLUSION

We do not live in a disembodied world of objects and physical laws. Neither do we live in a world of nature-created economic laws. We live in a world of people. The fundamental institutional structures, the rules, laws, principles, mores, and folkways are, consciously or unconsciously, created by people. The conditions for and the nature of productivity are not things-in-themselves, but products of multitudes of human decisions embodied in human activity and behavior. The benefits yielded by any mode of production can be viewed narrowly or broadly. They can be treated technically as a function of production curves, of so much raw material and labor costs, of product output and input factors, of production standards expressible in time per unit or units per hour. They can, of course, be viewed from the perspective of management as skill in using labor and equipment or of maximizing profits for investors. In many settings, the narrow view will inevitably prevail as determined by pressing agendas and the imperatives that result from functioning essentially in the service of narrow vested interests. Stockholders do not gather together to hear reports of service to the broader public good but to hear what the balance sheets say, what the present profits are and, given intelligent projections, can be expected to be in the near future.

But educators, whether concerned with "liberal", "professional", or "vocational", programs, should not function as representatives of any vested interest but rather as public servants working to advance the public good. Such a responsibility requires a broad, a comprehensive, and a critical view of society as a whole. Our understanding of the role of our specialization must be determined by our vision of its place in service of a critically sophisticated view of the problems of working to achieve a society that serves the public rather than private interests. Our global vision must shape our understanding of our specialty; our specialty as a thing-in-itself, as a system of narrow loyalties must not be used as a model for generalizing our vision of the world as a whole. The vocational or professional educator who adopts the philosophy, "What's good for General Motors is good for the United States" uncritically confuses vested and public interest.

A market economy is compatible with democracy only insofar as large accumulations of capital cannot be used to harness mass communications to manipulate the public into the service of vested interest and private greed. There is no way to prevent such practices except through the development of sophisticated critical thinking processes on the part of the electorate as a whole. Such processes must be honed in school on complex, controversial issues that force one to deal with opposing points of view and the subtle devices of propaganda and mass manipulation. The result of instruction in critical thinking is independence of thought and flexibility of mind, the very features essential to the metamorphosis of work from routine, mechanical functions (more and more to be automated) to complex problem-solving functions that presuppose the ability to question and redefine the basic problems themselves. Our view should not then be "What's good for General Motors is good for the United States", but "What's good for the United States is good for General Motors", whether it realizes it or not.

Chapter 13

Critical Thinking:
The Background Logic*

Abstract

In this, the most technical of his papers, written for the Second International Symposium on Informal Logic *in Windsor, Canada (1985), Richard Paul develops, at length, the concept of background logic: the notion that the reasoning and thinking which we overtly express can best be understood as surface manifestations of a complex system of thought which is, for the most part, implicit, presupposed, and unexpressed. With this view, Paul implies that comprehending the words and actions of other people and our selves is best understood as the problem of deciphering the use of three logics: the logic of natural languages (such as, English or French), the logic of society (for example, everyday U.S. cultural practices), and personal logic (our personal system of assumptions and meanings). There are three major patterns of life-style that emerge from the ways people orchestrate these logics in pursuing their ends: idealizing, rationalizing, and reasoning. The first option, idealization, is dominant in the lives of uncritical persons. The second, rationalization, is dominant in the lives of selfishly critical persons. The third, fairminded reasoning, is dominant in the lives of fairmindedly critical persons. Most people act, on Paul's view, with minimal awareness of the social and personal meanings that dominate their lives, with little sense of how their minds have been shaped and in turn shape their experience and action. Paul believes that "irrational" language usage is rampant in everyday life. The consequence is far-reaching: "When background logic is left in the background, unformulated, we are dominated rather than freed by the logic of our own thought and social transactions."*

Everywhere and always the quota of generally accepted rules and opinions weighs, however lightly, on the individual spirit, and it is only in theory that the child of 12–14 can submit all rules to a critical examination. Even the most rational of adults does not subject to his 'moral experience' more than an infinitesimal proportion of the rules that hedge him round. Anxious though he was to escape from his 'provisional morality', Descartes retained it to the end of his days.

Jean Piaget, *The Moral*
Judgment of the Child

---

* This essay is somewhat more difficult than most of the others. The reader might defer reading it until most of the others are clearly understood.

✦ Introduction

*E*very human thinks. Thinking is intrinsic to human life. Thought is necessary to and implicit in all human activities. Everything that humans do is "thought-full". So deep-seated and intrinsic to our being is it that we can't stop thinking even if we want to. It is our nature to think. But we do little thinking *about* our thinking. And what we do is rarely fruitful. It is difficult to do, it must be systematically encouraged, and easily degenerates into worry, speculation, or daydreaming. At this point in our evolution as a species we have not learned how to take command of our thinking by mastering the art of thinking about our thinking.

Why is this so? Besides being thinking beings, we are also egocentric ones. When we think, our thought is spontaneously egocentric. This means that our thought is continually oriented toward the goal of getting what we want. We spontaneously form ideas that serve our selfish interests, including a self-serving image of ourselves.

This image is partially conscious and partially unconscious. The conscious part, or much of it, helps obscure that part which is unconscious. Put another way, part of what it means to be egocentric is to project an image of ourselves which conflicts with what we are. This results in strong resistance to seeing ourselves as we are. We naturally and spontaneously resist thinking about how we think, for doing so would disclose self-deceptive and ego-protective acts.

To maintain a positive self-image, we often resist admitting any inconsistency, hypocrisy, or contradiction. When we sense that our actions conflict with our ideals, we tend to respond defensively or hostilely. We often hide our inconsistencies and shortcomings, even from ourselves. To defend our behavior, we often distort not only our motives but their consequences. We routinely defend our distortions. We work hard to maintain the illusion that we are what we are not.

A second reason we generally lack command of our thought is that we are sensual-perceptual beings. We are deeply involved in a world we can see, touch, smell, hear, and taste. And though we freely fabricate mythical entities in our minds, most are entities we can "picture" in sensual terms. But our thought processes cannot be "observed" in sensual-perceptual terms. We cannot look into our minds and simply watch what takes place. Our mind is not a *place* and so we cannot turn to it. Special skills are necessary for thinking about our thinking. These are not observational skills but rather *analytic* ones. We think about our thinking not by looking in a new place, but by using new ways of dissecting what we say and do. We do not need new experiences but insight into what is implicit in our experiences.

Thinking about our thinking is partly a set of linguistic skills. We cannot effectively think about our thinking unless we learn to use words with discipline. This requires that we learn to distinguish educated use from social misuse. Thinking about thinking is partly a set of social skills. We cannot effectively think about our thinking unless we learn to analyze the social settings in which we think, to recognize how our thought is often embedded in our action in a social world.

Thought is logical. That which is logical has logical *components*, logical *relations*, and logical *direction*. For example, one cannot think without beginning one's thought "somewhere", that is, by setting off from *premises* that embody *assumptions*. Secondly, having "begun somewhere", thought proceeds in some *direction* and for some *purpose*, leaving a trail of logical *connections* and relations.

While we are thinking we do not fully know *why* or *how* we think. We do not completely know the functions of our thought, our total set of premises and assumptions, what logical connections we are developing, and the conclusions toward which our thought is tending. Yet the more we learn to think about our thinking the more we come to identify, in the very process of thinking, the logical ingredients of our thought.

✦ Background Logic

Most critical thinking pedagogy and theory focuses on the part of thinking actually spoken or written — what we call "manifest logic". What we say or write, however, is only a small portion of the thinking process — the proverbial tip of the iceberg. Surrounding any line of thought is a large substructure of *background thought, logical connections* not lying on the surface of reasoning, but prior to it, underlying it, or implied by it. In the background of all thinking are foundational concepts, assumptions, values, purposes, experiences, implications, and consequences — all embedded in lines of thought radiating outward in every direction.

These background connections often emerge only after extended dialogical discussion. Two people may begin with a specific question: Was the President right to order the bombing of ...? The discussion predictably moves to other questions, topics, and subjects: Should any country be bound by international law if its interests are served by violating it? What does history tell us about the likely consequences of an action such as this? Does our country have a special historic responsibility to intervene in the affairs of other countries if democracy is threatened? How can we evaluate the motives of public figures in distant countries? Are there universal ethical principles?

Disputants will probably raise points regarding other foreign policy decisions and will discuss further historical background and psychological considerations, domestic policy, news coverage, and so on. Such a broadening movement from sub-issue to sub-issue is often necessary to fully canvass the original issue. While trying to persuade the other, each arguer cites evidence, interpretations, principles, etc., which the other may or may not accept, and so must sometimes be argued. Thus, points that at first blush seem unrelated to the original question become relevant as each reasoner explores the conflicting background thinking surrounding the beliefs of the other.

People engaged in such discussions are often surprised at what the other says. Arguments that to each seem compelling, the other finds weak. The other can provide reasons to defend a seemingly indefensible position, or answer an apparently unanswerable objection. We are all largely unaware of the substructure of belief and thought that underlies what we overtly assert.

One of the reasons we ignore the importance of background logic in our thought is that our schooling did not teach us how to explicate it. In fact for most people background thought doesn't exist. They respond to the surface of what is said or done, oblivious of what is not staring them in the face.

Another reason why background thinking is not taken seriously is our over-fascination with formal procedures and what we take to be scientific objectivity. In an age of science it seems to many that all important problems are questions that should be settled by some objective scientific process that transcends the "subjectivity" of thought. Our obsession with scientific formalism, our scientism, is actually quite old, ultimately traceable perhaps to Aristotle's deductive logic.

Plato's method of intellectual give-and-take, of dialogical exchange between opposing viewpoints, was relegated by many to an inferior role, and formal syllogistic reason officially accepted as the exclusive means of acquiring true knowledge. In place of argumentation between conflicting points of view Aristotle's followers held that definite methods should be developed that lead more or less directly and objectively to the truth. This laid a foundation for a long history of formal approaches to logic: logic largely divorced from context, from the conceptual problems of everyday life and dispute, and from the practical problems faced in an irrational, multi-faceted, deeply disguised world.

Philosophy, in contrast to science, maintained dialectic as its fundamental means of inquiry. Bring opposing philosophers together and it is usually necessary to test each of their views against the objections of the other. This process is at its roots informal, for there are no hard-and-fast rules or formulas for deciding how and when to object to an opposing philosophical position. This point can be generalized to any assessment of reasoning within one point of view by reasoning from another. When one is engaged in multi-dimensional argumentation, one disputes not only the proper answer to a question but often the nature of the question itself. One must often develop new ideas, not simply use established ones. Because the ground rules typically used by a perspective for settling its own questions come under dispute, one cannot use them to adjudicate differences. Informal give-and-take, not formal or procedural skills, become primary and crucial.

Unfortunately, however, the history of "informal" argumentation within philosophy has had no perceptible influence on common practice in everyday life. Philosophy remains an elite subject, largely abstracted from everyday life and practical concerns, at least in the minds of most non-philosophers. Hence the background logic of everyday beliefs and thought is rarely systematically explored, formally or informally. In everyday life it seems anything goes, any move one can get away with is maintained as legitimate thought. The intellectual discipline most philosophers exercise seems irrelevant, pedantic, and unintelligible to most people tackling everyday issues.

Some time after philosophers retreated from the marketplace to their own inner circles, science began its slow but steady development. With it came the emergence of more narrowly defined technical disciplines with increasingly refined procedural approaches, testifying to the power of procedure in settling narrowly defined one-dimensional questions. By the 20th Century even some philosophers began a systematic attempt to make their work "scientific". This meant to many that traditional philosophical argumentation should give way to precise and formalized method. General, comprehensive, philosophical skills seemed to many in need of replacement. Specialized, formal procedures, parallel to those used by the physical sciences, seemed necessary for philosophy itself. Philosophy, it was thought by many, should become specialized and scientific.

This demand that philosophy "professionalize" itself, and thus substitute disciplined *procedure* for freewheeling *dialectic* has diminished in the last 20 years. Likewise, educators increasingly recognize that education based on training in unconnected and isolated disciplines does not prepare one well for most of the issues one faces in everyday life. Furthermore, many concede that an overly narrow or fragmented education — the kind associated with an emphasis on specialization — engenders minds that compartmentalize and cannot easily adapt or generalize specialized understandings. There is also an increasing recognition that narrowly skilled persons may be as irrational in much of their lives as unschooled people tend to be.

Similarly, there is a growing recognition that the comprehensive thinking of a rational person cannot be equated with formal reasoning or the following of narrow rules and procedures. The crucial problems we face in the complexities of everyday life are increasingly recognized to be multi-faceted and resistant to single-discipline approaches.

Unfortunately, the fragmented schooling of today leaves little room for intellectual give-and-take or for interdisciplinary thinking. Too often questions which do not submit to disciplinary procedures are defined away or ignored. People leave school with few of the skills necessary to plumb the background logic of their own beliefs and thought, and so with few convictions, and little sense of the many contradictions that underlie their thoughts, words, and deeds. Most importantly, they lack the ability to strip off surface language and consider alternative ways to talk; little sense of what it would be to question basic labels and categories by which inferences and meanings are multiplied.

Most people unconsciously internalize the basic world view of their peer group and society with little or no conscious awareness of what it would be to rationally decide upon alternative ways to conceptualize everyday situations, persons, and events. Utterances, by themselves and others, are taken at their face value, or twisted by egocentric inclinations and vested interests. Similarly, most people are responsive to and awed by social rituals and the trappings of authority, status, and prestige. They live their lives, as it were, in surface structures. They reduce complex situations to self-serving verbalizations. Thus, not surprisingly, most people do not know how to explicate and clarify an issue, how to enter sympathetically into points of view they have consciously or unconsciously rejected. Deeply insecure, most people are only concerned with injustices inflicted upon themselves personally or upon those they ego-identify with. They easily dehumanize those who thwart, or appear to thwart, their vested interests; they typically resent those whose beliefs conflict with their own. Their reasoning is often infantile at root.

It is tendencies, qualities, and dispositions such as these which give rise to the problem of "uncritical thought". They define the obstacles against which proposed critical thinking pedagogy must be measured. The problem of teaching critical thinking to essentially rational persons in a rational society differs greatly from the problem of teaching it to irrational persons in an unconsciously irrational society. In a society that uncritically defines itself and its social, political, economic, and personal rituals as civilized, rational, and free, there is no impetus to probe beneath the surface of public discourse. When the most fundamental logical structures, the most basic concepts, assumptions, beliefs, inferences, and category-decisions are typically unexpressed, unconscious, and irrational, then the problem of background logic assumes new proportions and the language games implicit in everyday life are in need of a fundamental re-construal. A society incapable of exploring the roots of its own thought and action is not a free society, properly so called. People cannot be said to have freely chosen what they do not recognize to exist. The rest of this paper tries to make a modest contribution to reversing this incapacity, this inability to grasp the foundations and substructure of thought and action.

✦ Some Principles

1) All human behavior is intelligible to us finally only in terms of some background of concepts and distinctions, values and meanings, associations and assumptions, purposes and goals. This background is embedded ultimately, as Wittgenstein put it, in concrete forms of life — in behavior.

Yet there is little awareness of the background logics in use. We absorb these structures uncritically through socialization. We are not encouraged to explicate and assess them.

2) Often background systems of meanings are misused or confused, resulting in a multitude of category mistakes in which persons radically mis-describe their experience. For example, because we commonly characterize ourselves as free, reasonable, just, and caring, we assume that our behavior matches what these words imply. In fact words often substitute for realities named by them. Fundamental contradictions or inconsistencies in our lives typically go unquestioned. Yet to this day no adequate theory of background logic has been developed and the concept remains in need of foundational analysis and clarification.

3) The inferences we make depend upon the concepts we use. Some concepts, being more basic, are implicit in un-monitored inferences that shape our behavior in many domains of life. Three important categories of background logic influence our point of view or perspective as individuals: the natural language we speak (English, French, etc.), the technical languages we study in school (the language of biology, zoology, anthropology, mathematics, etc.), and the social practices that shape the meanings fostered in social situations, the sociocentric logic of our peer group or culture. Presently I will explain how we selectively internalize these networks to define our personal philosophy, our world view, the filter through which we interpret or construct our experience. It is crucial to recognize the differences between these background domains, particularly between the logic of natural languages and that of social behavior. Social behavior often incorporates ordinary language in distorting ways. We learn how to gain advantage by a systematic misuse of everyday language. Before we consider how everyday irrationalities are obfuscated in social practices, however, it is useful to set out four dimensions of background logic implicit in every instance of reasoning.

✦ *Four Dimensions of Background Logic*

Whenever we reason and express our thinking in words, there are four background dimensions of our thought which can be probed. Each of these dimensions expresses a different point of reference and a different order of analytic fact: *1)* the dimension of our thinking *temporally prior to* what we have expressed, *2)* the dimension of our thinking *logically presupposed by* what we have expressed, *3)* the dimension of our thinking *implied by* what we have expressed, and *4)* the dimension of our *thinking developed when our thinking is challenged* by others.

The basic idea behind these distinctions is simple. Before we formulate our reasoning on a subject we must decide on our purpose and how to describe what we think is the central issue or problem we are facing. We

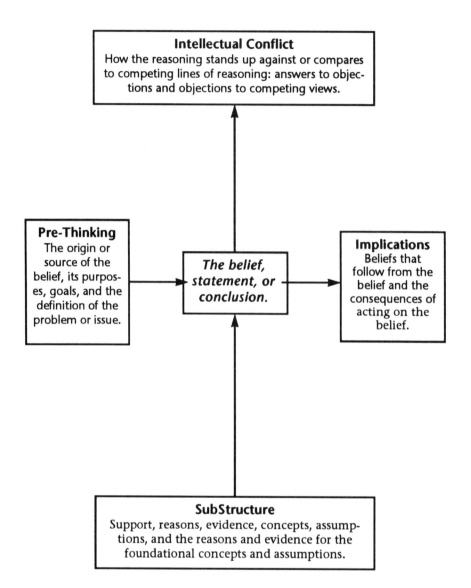

Intellectual Conflict
How the reasoning stands up against or compares to competing lines of reasoning: answers to objections and objections to competing views.

Pre-Thinking
The origin or source of the belief, its purposes, goals, and the definition of the problem or issue.

The belief, statement, or conclusion.

Implications
Beliefs that follow from the belief and the consequences of acting on the belief.

SubStructure
Support, reasons, evidence, concepts, assumptions, and the reasons and evidence for the foundational concepts and assumptions.

Background Logic
There are four directions in which thought can be pursued.

do some *pre-thinking,* in other words. Moreover, once we formulate our thinking there is a *substructure* to it — foundational concepts and assumptions — and a *direction* to it — implications and consequences unexpressed or not fully expressed. Finally, any line of reasoning inevitably *conflicts* with other lines of reasoning. The moves that can be made in exploring any of these conflicts are important "background logic" to understand when attempting to come to terms with any reasoning set out for our assessment. When we look into the background logic of a line of reasoning, therefore, we look into various domains presupposed by it: its pre-thinking, its substructure, its implications, and its possible defense in relation to conflicting lines of thought. We analyze background logic because we recognize that we must delve into these unexpressed domains to come to terms with that part of the thought which is expressed.

This approach can be likened to coming to understand new acquaintances. We learn something of their prior lives, something of their deeper thoughts, something of where they are headed, and something of how they respond to challenges from others. We use what people overtly say and do as guides or indicators of their "background". We understand what people say or do not only by examining directly what they say or do, but also by finding out what lies in the background of what they say and do — how they came to these actions from their past, what is presupposed by these actions at the moment, where these actions take us if we follow them out to their logical consequences, and how these actions stand-up under critique from divergent standpoints.

THE DOMAIN OF PRE-THINKING

Before we reason with respect to an issue or goal, we must frame a goal or formulate an issue or problem. In other words, we must define a problem before we can look for a solution. The problem of deciding on one issue rather than another and of wording an issue one way rather than another goes a long way toward shaping reasoning with respect to it. If, in other words, all reasoning consists in an attempt to settle a question, then all reasoning presupposes an issue to settle, an issue shaped through the thinking of the reasoner. Before we argue with our spouses about some aspect of our marriage, we pre-think the situation or problem. We define it in some way, even if merely to define it as "problematic" rather than "un-problematic". We often fail to notice that the situation did not present itself as a problem, our thinking (our "pre-thinking" in other words) concluded it to be so. Perhaps we began with a feeling of disquiet or frustration then leapt to the conclusion that this particular aspect of the other person or the relationship is problematic. The reasoning behind our interpretation of the original discomfort as arising from this particular thing is often unconscious. We are not aware of having reasoned at all, but seem to have perceived the root of the problem directly.

Or, to take a more scholastic example, consider the history of philosophy. It can fruitfully be viewed as a series of disagreements regarding how best to frame philosophical questions, and hence disagreements about what specifically is at issue. Philosophers, we could say, are intensely concerned with prior questions and prior reasoning. They are invariably concerned with the issues buried in the pre-thinking of actions, judgments, and decisions.

THE DOMAIN OF SUBSTRUCTURE

Just as the domain of pre-thinking spans the initial choices of goals, problems, and issues, the substructural domain spans the concepts and assumptions presupposed in the reasoning. It is not explicit in the manifest logic since few people explicitly discuss their assumptions in their expressed thought. They use but do not focus on them. We need to probe beneath a person's reasoning to make their most fundamental concepts and assumptions explicit.

For example, to understand whether disagreements in manifest thought can be resolved, we must often use skills that probe the "inner" logic of that thought. We must often determine whether assumptions that underlie two lines of thought are reconcilable. We must often explore whether their fundamental ideas are consistent or inconsistent. For example, if an advocate of market capitalism is debating an economic issue — say, "Should the capital gains tax be reduced?" — with an advocate of democratic socialism, the basic concepts and assumptions of capitalism and socialism underlie the reasoning of the debaters. Under what conditions is "competition" more fruitful than "cooperation", or "private interest" the best guide to "public interest"? Exploring issues such as these helps lay bare what I call the substructural dimension of thought. Of course how far we probe into these deeper, underlying issues depends upon our purpose in discussing the issue in the first place. Practical considerations may restrict us to a more superficial analysis, to discussing the manifest logic alone.

Once we begin to explore the concepts and assumptions presupposed in two lines of thought we are often driven to consider background facts and information, the empirical or experiential support for those concepts and assumptions. Hence, advocates of capitalism if pressed to defend the concept of competition will cite a variety of "facts" and "experiences" which they believe justify the concept. If pressed they will cite cases to argue for the concept of competition in *general*. Focus on surface facts — the facts cited in support of positions on the *original* issue — gives way to focus on "infralogical facts", the empirical considerations advanced when probing into foundational concepts and assumptions. We begin talking about a current economic problem; we are then driven to talk about our foundational ideas and what supports them; we then move back to the original issue with a broader sense of perspective, a broader sense of the background logic of both positions.

THE DOMAIN OF IMPLICATIONS

Another domain of background logic we may need to consider, another way we may need to go beyond what is "manifest" in reasoning, is that of implications and consequences. Thinking not only has a pre-history and a substructure, it also has a *direction*. It leads us one way rather than another. It takes us from one set of beliefs to other beliefs that "follow from" the first. Furthermore, beliefs acted upon have consequences, for different things happen when we act on different beliefs. No one can fully explore the implications and consequences of his or her reasoning. We are often circumscribed by pressures to decide and act. Nevertheless implications and consequences are always implicit in what we say and do. Unfortunately few have been taught to recognize anything but the most obvious implications and consequences and many frequently do not even recognize them.

THE DOMAIN OF INTELLECTUAL CONFLICT

A fourth domain of background logic for a line of reasoning is revealed when we set it into conflict with competing lines of thought. Coming to understand the strengths and weaknesses of reasoning in relation to opposing thought adds a further dimension to our grasp of the reasoning. Hence Kant's reasoning adds a dimension to our understanding of the logic of Descartes and Hume, while their reasoning contributes to our understanding of his. By the same token, different stages in the development of a discipline constitute background logic that contributes to the intelligibility and definition of each. We have a much clearer and well-developed sense of the assumptions of Newtonian physics since Einstein and quantum theory. Often then we conclude that we had not fully understood a point of view until it was superseded by another. However confident in a given line of reasoning, however attentive to the basic shaping of issues, however focused on our basic principles, concepts, and assumptions, however conscientious in explicating further implications and collateral consequences, we do not fully understand reasoning until we grasp its force in conflict with other reasoning.

✦ Toward a Richer Understanding of Background Logic

There is no reason, of course, why a portion, even a significant portion, of what is background logic in one context cannot become foreground or manifest logic in another. Indeed an essential characteristic of the critical mind is its passion to penetrate, explicate, and dialectically assess competing background logics. Once background logic is formulated it becomes part of manifest logic. Of course there is no way that one can formulate all the background logic for a line of reasoning, just as there is no way to describe all aspects of a person. We can go as far as we please, but we do not run out of further places to explore in all the directions that follow outward from our thought.

To begin to make effective use of our knowledge of background logic, we must develop a taxonomy of background logical distinctions in addition to the four dimensions above. For example, we must distinguish technical one-dimensional (monological) background logics, specified in fine detail, narrowly defined and procedurally developed, — for example, chemistry or algebra — from the background logic one unconsciously absorbs, for example, in the socialization process. Raised in the United States, we internalize different concepts, beliefs, and assumptions about ourselves and the world than we would have had we been raised in China or Iran, for example.

Furthermore, we must distinguish both technical and cultural background logics from the background logic of natural languages. Natural languages are a resource for virtually unlimited conceptual possibilities. They are much more flexible than technical languages. They are more neutral than the belief systems of cultural groups. As critical thinkers, we should be cognizant, in other words, of the extent to which we are reasoning within the technical concepts of a specialized discipline, within the concepts implicit in our cultural relationships and experience, or within the concepts implicit in the language we speak. Of course, our reasoning might use concepts from all three of these dimensions simultaneously. Critical thinking requires sensitivity to the conceptual problems that may arise from this blending of domains. We will see something more of the importance of these distinctions in the next section of the paper.

✦ *Background Logic and Language Games*

The logic of the English language, and of all other known natural languages, should not be confused with the background logic of the egocentric mind or, for that matter, of the sociocentric mind. All human existence is necessarily multi-dimensional, not only because it involves beings whose nature and behavior can never be reduced to one category alone, but also because it involves some necessary intersection of personal, social, and linguistic background logics. Every interpretation of language usage, in other words, is a complex act in which we respond to cues that reflect three variously-related background logics: that of the egocentric individual, that of the social group, and that of the natural language of the user. Hence sometimes a communication is idiosyncratic, and its meaning can only be understood correctly if one understands something about the specific history or background of the speaker. For example, only if you understand something of the history of the conflict between two people, may you be able to recognize the significance of a given utterance. What may seem a compliment to an outsider may in fact be an insult.

Or, to highlight another background logic, it may be more illuminating to interpret what is said as a social or in-group performance, as a communication that presupposes familiarity with the ideology or rituals of a social group. For example, within a given society, though the leader may ask whether anyone disagrees with his or her view, it may be socially unacceptable to express such disagreement.

Or finally, one might best understand what is being said as expressing straightforwardly what is implied by the words as used by educated speakers of the language, irrespective of the society in which they were raised or of their personal idiosyncrasies. For example, a Japanese person, having learned proficient English in a Japanese school, may express his "Japanese" ideas in English. Language learning in itself does not transform the culture of the person speaking the language. It may be the occasion for such learning but does not necessarily include it.

Psychoanalysts aim at developing facility in decoding highly idiosyncratic utterances, and of disclosing thereby primitive assumptions and concepts which patients unconsciously hold about themselves, about people close to them, or about the nature of their world. All the sophisticated defense mechanisms, so called, can consequently be viewed as various forms of irrational, but highly functional language games by which people fend off unpleasant reality and maintain their unconscious world views. Thus, for an individual, weight-loss may represent a "promised land" of unreal expectations of perfection, and unhealthy eating habits may represent the safety of the familiar, protection from sexual advances, an escape, or an excuse for problems, shortcomings, and unhappiness. Neither food nor weight have these meanings socially or in the natural language: food is sustenance, nutrition, relieves hunger, and can taste good or bad. These idiosyncratic meanings may develop in our minds without our awareness of their development.

The sociocentric or in-group background logic and associated language games are easier to decode than idiosyncratic background logic, since they are more public. If one belongs to the in-group, or if one has studied the world view or perspective presupposed in given social interactions, one can render these meanings explicit, as sociologists do. However, the nature of sociocentric logic, like egocentric logic, is not ordinarily formulated as such, and for good reason. If you paid enough attention to the language which maintains and expresses the inner dynamics of group power to construct a dictionary of basic meanings, you would have a text more like Ambrose Bierce's *Devil's Dictionary*, than like the *Oxford English Dictionary*. You would find at least two layers of meaning at work simultaneously: meanings implied by surface verbalizations and, in contrast, meanings implied by behavior, with frequent contradictions between the two. An outsider or naive person would take the surface meaning to be the sole meaning. The sophisticated in-group member however would respond not simply to the surface meaning but also to latent cues and implied meanings. Goffman's *The Presentation of Self in Everyday Life* presents numerous examples of these contrasting levels of meaning.

A business party, for example, though explicitly defined as a party, and with all of its external forms and trappings — hence a time to relax, have fun, socialize, let your hair down, be yourself without the pressure of having to meet expectations — is not a party in the normal sense. It imposes limitations on behavior, and has innumerable hidden rules and agendas. The poor, naive junior executives who behave appropriately for a more genuinely *social* gathering — friendly teasing, eccentric behavior, careless flirtations — will wonder why they do not get the promotions due them given their job performance. They don't realize that actions at parties *are* part of their job performance.

If there is a split within a society between two opposing behavioral logics, and so between two social groups or classes whose action embodies those logics, then the discrepancy between verbally and behaviorally implied meanings may become a subject for discussion, analysis, and critique. But as long as the "hypocrisy", "deception", or duplicity is more or less universal within a group, it is rarely noticed as such. Things go quite as expected, no disturbances highlight contradictions.

One can distinguish three different modes of living that represent different values and different skills of analysis with respect to decoding language usage within these background systems. Some tend to idealize social interactions, routinely accepting fostered impressions and surface language usage. These people, let us dub them naive idealizers, tend to accept the ideology of their society as descriptive of reality. Their horizons are conceptually and pragmatically limited. They are not adept at manipulating situations to their advantage, since they are minimally aware of the transactions going on beneath overt meanings and behaviors. They tend to be easily manipulated by those sensitized to the deeper levels of transaction.

Clearly, idealizers are not critical thinkers, since they cannot get beyond surface logic. The rationalizers of this world, on the other hand, penetrate the surface level and identify meanings and pay-offs. They function comfortably within meanings not disclosed to the naive. They get used to reading between the lines and to taking advantage of the opportunities for gaining advantage thereby. Those who design political campaigns, with their double messages and manipulative meanings, are an excellent case in point.

Being engaged in manipulations to further their self-interest, rationalizers tend to ignore the discrepancies and inconsistencies in the unspoken social ideology they use to their advantage. Having discovered how to play a game that advances their interests, they see no value in making the game public. Besides, like all humans, rationalizers need to maintain a positive view of themselves. This would be difficult if their manipulative use of other people were made explicit. To put this another way, uncritical idealization invites manipulation, and rationalizers take advantage of openings for power and gain. Idealizers, oblivious of the struggle for power and advantage lurking beneath the surface of social transactions are tailor-made for those seeking advantage. Rationalizers are empowered to get what they want through their deeper understanding of how to use social masks to obtain private ends.

This leaves one final life-style choice with respect to the socio-linguistic activities of everyday life: interesting one's self in making hidden dimensions of discourse explicit, striving to decode as fully as possible the real, deeper, meanings and contradictions in social transactions. I would dub this third choice of life-style that of the reasoner, the genuinely fairminded, critical thinker, the person striving to transform blind conformity into rational conviction. Admittedly a tiny minority, this group is a force for progressive social change and transformation.

Reasoners or fairminded critical thinkers, on this view, learn to see their behavior in terms of the tacit infrastructure of thinking that underlies it. This necessarily requires a willingness to undergo stress, to face personal and social contradictions, to develop rational passions, and, on the whole, to engage in self-transformation. On this view, no one can become fairminded and avoid the "hot" issues that underlie personal and social life, or the necessity of facing, indeed the necessity of *constructing,* some opposition to the social status quo. Most importantly, then, fairminded critical thinking requires a passion for social disclosure not simply for abstract theorizing about social interaction, a passion for synthesis that takes into account the specific relations between, and the problems of overcoming, unformulated but lived, and formulated but unlived logical systems. Insightful critical thinking requires understanding how language is systematically misused to achieve unexpressed, self-serving social and personal ends. Since such activity requires courage and concern for social justice, it is intrinsically a moral activity.

✦ Synthesis

At the same time that our everyday experience presupposes and reflects continual and spontaneous acts of logical synthesis that transcend any particular academic category, our conscious knowledge remains logically fragmented. Our everyday action is socially more sophisticated than our conscious thinking implies. We seem able to take into account at the behavioral level more than we analyze at the intellectual level. Consider this example taken from the research of Hans Toch and Henry Clay Smith:

>Any perception is an awareness that emerges as a result of a most complicated weighing process an individual goes through as his mind takes into account a whole host of factors or cues. It must be emphasized at the very outset how tremendously complex even the simplest perception is — for example, the perception of a star point. For it can be demonstrated that, in perceiving a star point as such, a whole host of indications are weighed and integrated to give us our final experience ... the integration of all these factors is accomplished in a faction of a second and is, more frequently than not, entirely unconscious.

This spontaneous weighing and totalizing process applies in everyday experience to our perception of individuals, groups, ideologies, religions, and any manner of complex or "simple" events. We instantly know how to respond to any number of people playing diverse social roles. Unfortunately, because most of our *de facto* skills of synthesis reflect background logical systems that are egocentric, sociocentric, or both, our skills of *rational* synthesis are not enhanced thereby. The paradox is that while our irrational mind easily uses background logical systems to integrate, synthesize, and structure behavior and events, our rational mind is still highly compartmentalized, reinforced by an academic world whose fundamental interest is narrow and non-synthetic, an interest in keeping disciplinary categories unintegrated and free of dialectical and interdisciplinary thought. The academic world, it would seem, is convinced that there is no significant loss from traditional academic specialization. But we cannot face situations in everyday life in the terms in which we are academically trained. The real world of human action is not compartmentalized into academic categories. The social, the psychological, the philosophical, and the economic are, in the real world, often so entwined that it makes no sense to try to explain any one dimension without explaining the roles of the others.

Consequently, we cannot turn to isolated disciplines for an answer to the problem of uncritical thought in everyday life. The only "neutral" background logic we have at our critical disposal is that of natural languages themselves. Academic or technical languages, in contrast, presuppose the compartmentalizations they themselves have created. We can ask, for example, whether what we in the U.S. call "democratic" is consistent with what the word 'democratic' implies in the English language. We can reflect upon whether modern elections with their well-funded campaigns and reliance on manipulative practices, are consistent with the belief that the people are ruling. The concepts of the English language allow us to abstract from ideologies, academic agendas, and social presuppositions.

We can take any word that expresses an important human value — friendship, love, intimacy, honesty, integrity, equality, justice — analyze what its use implies to educated speakers of the language, and then compare these verbal implications to the world as we find it. We can learn to resist assuming that social situations commonly described by value-laden words really do merit the characterization. To do so requires a disciplined awareness of the difference between what is linguistically implied by given words in the English language and what is commonly described as such within social groups that happen to use English to talk about events in their everyday life. Unfortunately, however, few people can distinguish those uses of language which twist or distort social reality from those which reveal it.

We need to forge critical thinking abilities that focus on a command of background logics. Special intellectual skills are required, both destructive and constructive: on the one hand ability to question the on-going stream of fostered definitions and social conceptualizations, choices of basic concepts and categories that uncritically shape our daily thought and experience, and on the other hand, ability to synthesize across these concepts and categories so that our "totalization", our summing up of people, facts, and events, represents characterizations to which we can give, and do give, conscious assent. We have a responsibility to educate people to have a disposition to see social life as a whole, especially its living contradictions and hypocrisies, to look beyond surface meanings and compartmentalized academic categories, to see not only how everyday life is structured but how it might be structured were we to commit ourselves to live by the moral values we have long verbally espoused.

✦ Some Unresolved Questions

Since all reasoning, all thought, presupposes questions at issue, and since fundamental questions require critical explication of background logic, we need a fuller exploration and specification of what this entails, especially in contrast to discipline-specific training. We need to decide how to frame background logical questions and how to make this deeper mode of questioning socially acceptable. We must not forget that the social world is a real world, one whose background logic transforms the lives and minds of people. When Background logic is left in the background, unformulated, we are dominated rather than freed by the logic of our own thought and social transactions. If we think egocentrically and sociocentrically, we stifle our capacity for insight, intellectual freedom, and self-command.

This brings us to an important question, a question to which our concrete lives provide an answer, even if our words do not: is it rational to be rational in an irrational world? Less paradoxically, is it rational to give up the advantage for personal gain provided by the many who allow themselves to be manipulated? One can gain status, prestige, money, power, easy self-satisfaction, and ego-gratification only if one's actions at least *appear* to validate socially dominant views. Is it worthwhile to make con-

traditions and hypocrisies public to achieve abstract goals such as intellectual and moral integrity? The wisdom of the world, the answer suggested by those most heavily engaged in it, would seem to be,

> No, it is not worth it. To be rational is to be a successful rational-
> izer, accepting and using the ascendant social ideology, to be skilled
> in personal self-deception, able to question fostered appearances
> only when personally advantageous, and if anything else, adept in
> helping your friends and hurting your enemies.

Socrates and Plato might have won the academic debate against
sophistry but history demonstrates they did not win the battle for the
hearts and minds of people. The everyday world of social action is shot
through with sophistry and hypocrisy.

✦ Summary & Conclusion

Academic disciplines with their compartmentalization of thought fail to
provide a plausible approach to everyday uncritical thought. We live as
inferential beings enveloped in unformulated systems. The logical systems
of the schools frequently have little to do with the logic we live. We are
often controlled and confused by, and consequently have never consciously assented to, the inner logic we ourselves create in our behavior. We
don't know how to get perspective, how to critically analyze and synthesize what lies behind our behavior. In contrast, our inner world, the world
of our self-constituted experience is heavily synthesized, but unconsciously, egocentrically, and sociocentrically so. We have not yet developed
insight into the importance of background logic. We have not yet learned
how to probe it and bring it under our intellectual self-command. We have
not yet grasped how unformulated dimensions of thought and action
dominate us. We are so fixated on action, on the agendas of our lives, that
we have not yet interested ourselves in the thought embedded in our
action. To come to a deeper understanding of the unformulated thinking
buried in our lives, we must make background logic accessible to our conscious thought. Instead of impugning the motives of others, we should
learn how to explore the background meanings that make social and personal contradictions and hypocrisies intelligible.

In any case, a fundamental distinction must be drawn between the
logic of natural languages and egocentric or sociocentric uses of them.
Because of his failure to note the latter two, Wittgenstein failed to distinguish irrational from rational language games. He failed to see that many
socially common uses of words are not innocuous. He failed to see how
social groups systematically misuse language for self-serving ends. He
failed to see, for example, how often we "confuse" concepts to obscure
our own hypocrisies, while calling attention to the hypocrisies of our
opponents, the hypocrisies of the "enemy". He failed to recognize the

need to probe the unformulated dimensions of our lives to see patterns that reveal who we really are, how much we live three significantly distinct forms of life: that of the idealizer, that of the rationalizer, and that of the reasoner.

If there are idealizers in the world, given to idiosyncratic speech acts, presumably with thoughts to match, it follows that they live in narrow, self-enclosed worlds, highly vulnerable to manipulation and frustration. If there are rationalizers in the world, given to sociocentric speech acts, presumably again with thoughts to match, it follows that, whatever advantages they gain, they cannot fully assent to the character of their own behavior. If there are fairminded thinkers in the world, with a passion to transcend egocentric or sociocentric life worlds and the irrational language games which define them, it follows that they would strive to engage in discourse which does not presuppose egocentric or sociocentric concepts and values, that they would use words with a rich sense of their implications. If these three life worlds are in some sense logical possibilities for every person, then interpretation of language usage requires an ability to distinguish egocentric, sociocentric, and rational discourse. Because these distinctions cannot be made except in reference to background logical considerations that may not be immediately apparent, and because those background logics may be hidden and denied, the problem of analysis and explication is difficult.

To become a reasoner or fairminded critical thinker requires skills of analysis and synthesis as yet underdeveloped. We get little help from the academic world with its pervasive fragmentation and specialization. We need new skills in the art of totalizing experience, and in the dialectical testing of competing ways to conceptualize experience. We need to see that human social life is still at an uncritical stage of development. Full fledged critical thought is nevertheless possible for the future. It has not yet become socially acceptable except in circumscribed ways under constraining conditions. We cannot yet embrace it. We do not yet know *how* to embrace it. We have not yet learned to live as rational persons.

We need more knowledge of the logic of questions, of background systems of thought, of the power and inner attraction of egocentrism and sociocentrism, and of how to combat the "wisdom of the world", which, till now, meets emerging critical thought with disdain, ignores or suppresses it, and thus answers with a resounding "No!" the question, "Is it rational to be rational in an irrational world?"

Section III

The Affective and Ethical Dimension

Ethics Without Indoctrination

Critical Thinking, Moral Integrity, and Citizenship: Teaching for the Intellectual Virtues

Dialogical Thinking: Critical Thought Essential to the Acquisition of Rational Knowledge and Passions

Power, Vested Interest, and Prejudice: On the Need for Critical Thinking in the Ethics of Social and Economic Development

Chapter 14

Ethics Without Indoctrination

Abstract

In this revised paper, originally published in Educational Leadership *(1988), Richard Paul argues that ethics ought to be taught in school, but only in conjunction with critical thinking. Without critical thinking at the heart of ethical instruction,* indoctrination *rather than ethical* insight *results. Moral principles do not apply themselves, they require a thinking mind to assess facts and interpret situations. Moral agents inevitably bring their perspectives into play in making moral judgments and this, together with the natural tendency of the human mind to self-deception when its interests are involved, is the fundamental impediment to the right use of ethical principles.*

Paul spells out the implications of this view for the teaching of ethics in literature, science, history, and civics. He provides a taxonomy of moral reasoning skills and describes an appropriate long term staff development strategy to foster ethics across the curriculum.

✦ The Problem of Indoctrination

*N*early everyone recognizes that even young children have moral feelings and ideas, make moral inferences and judgments, and develop an outlook on life which has moral significance for good or ill. Nearly everyone also gives at least lip service to a universal common core of general ethical principles — for example, that it is morally wrong to cheat, deceive, exploit, abuse, harm, or steal from others, that everyone has a moral responsibility to respect the rights of others, including their freedom and well-being, to help those most in need of help, to seek the common good and not merely their own self-interest and egocentric pleasures, to strive in some way to make this world more just and humane. Unfortunately, mere verbal agreement on general moral principles alone will not accomplish important moral ends nor change the world for the better. Moral principles mean something only when manifested in behavior. They have force only when embodied in action. Yet to put them into action requires some analysis and insight into the real character of everyday situations.

The world does not present itself to us in morally transparent terms. The moral thing to do is often a matter of disagreement even among people of good will. One and the same act is often morally praised by some, condemned by others. Furthermore, even when we do not face the morally conflicting claims of others, we often have our own inner conflicts as to what, morally speaking, we should do in some particular situation. Considered another way, ethical persons, however strongly motivated to do what is morally right, can do so only if they know what that is. And this they cannot do if they systematically confuse their sense of what is morally right with their self-interest, personal desires, or what is commonly believed in their peer group or community. Because of complexities such as these, ethically motivated persons must learn the art of self-critique, of moral self-examination, to become attuned to the pervasive everyday pitfalls of moral judgment: moral intolerance, self-deception, and uncritical conformity. These human foibles cause pseudo-morality, the systematic misuse of moral terms and principles in the guise of moral action and righteousness.

Unfortunately few have thought much about the complexity of everyday moral issues, can identify their own moral contradictions, or clearly distinguish their self-interest and egocentric desires from what is genuinely moral. Few have thought deeply about their own moral feelings and judgments, have tied these judgments together into a coherent moral perspective, or have mastered the complexities of moral reasoning. As a result, everyday moral judgments are often a subtle mixture of pseudo and genuine morality, moral insight and moral prejudice, moral truth and moral hypocrisy. Herein lies the danger of setting up ill-thought-out public school programs in moral education. Without scrupulous care, we merely pass on to students our own moral blindness, moral distortions, and closedmindedness. Certainly many who trumpet most loudly for ethics and morality in the schools merely want students to adopt *their* ethical beliefs and *their* ethical perspectives, regardless of the fusion of insight and prejudice those beliefs and perspectives doubtless represent. They take themselves to have *the Truth* in their pockets. They take their perspective to be exemplary of all morality rightly conceived. On the other hand, what these same people fear most is someone else's moral perspective taught as the truth: conservatives afraid of liberals being in charge, liberals of conservatives, theists of non-theists, non-theists of theists.

Now, if truth be told, all of these fears are justified. People, except in the most rare and exceptional cases, do have a strong tendency to confuse what they believe with the truth. It is always the others who do evil, who are deceived, self-interested, closedminded — never us. Given this universal blind spot in human nature, the only safe and justified basis for ethical education in the pubic schools is one precisely designed to rule out bias in favor of the substantive beliefs and conclusions of any particular group, whether religious, political, communal, or national. Indeed since one of our most fundamental responsibilities as educators is to *educate* rather than indoctrinate our students — to help them cultivate skills, insights, knowledge, and traits of mind and character that transcend narrow party and religious affiliations and help them to think beyond biased representations of the world — we must put special safeguards into moral education that prevent indoctrination. The world needs not more closed-minded zealots, eager to remake the world in their image, but more morally committed rational persons with respect for and insight into the moral judgments and perspectives of others, those least likely to confuse pseudo with genuine morality.

But how is this to be done? How can we cultivate morality and character in our students without indoctrinating them, without systematically rewarding them merely because they express our moral beliefs and espouse our moral perspective?

The answer is in putting *critical thinking* into the heart of the ethical curriculum, critical thinking for both teachers and students. To bring ethics and morality into the schools in an educationally legitimate way, administrators and teachers must think critically about what to emphasize and what to avoid. Intellectually discriminating minds and morally refined sensibilities must be in charge of both initial curriculum design and its subsequent classroom implementation. This is not an unreasonable demand, for, ethics aside, skill in the art of drawing important intellectual discriminations is crucial to education in any subject or domain, and proficiency in the art of teaching critically — encouraging students to question, think for themselves, develop rational standards of judgment — is the responsibility of all classroom teachers. Any subject, after all, can be taught merely to indoctrinate students and so to inadvertently stultify rather than develop their ability to think within it. Unfortunately, we have all been subjected to a good deal of indoctrination in the name of education and retain to this day some of the intellectual disabilities that such scholastic straight-jacketing produces. To allow ethics to be taught in the public schools this narrowly is unconscionable. It is to betray our ethical responsibility as educators in the name of ethics.

✦ Integrating Critical Thinking and Ethics

If we bring ethics into the curriculum — and we should — we must ensure that we do so morally. This requires us to clearly distinguish between espousing the universal, general principles of morality shared by people of good will everywhere, and the very different matter of defending some particular application of these principles to actual life situations as conceived from a particular moral standpoint (liberal, conservative, radical, theistic, non-theistic, U.S., Soviet, etc.). Any particular moral judgment arises from someone conceptualizing the facts of a situation from some moral perspective or standpoint. Every moral perspective in some way embodies the same general moral principles. The integration of *principles* with purported *facts* within a particular *perspective* produces the judgment that this or that act is morally right or wrong. Precisely because we often differ about the facts or about the proper perspective on the facts, we come to differing moral judgments.

The problem is not at the level of general moral principles. No people in the world, as far as I know, take themselves to oppose human rights or stand for injustice, slavery, exploitation, deception, dishonesty, theft, greed, starvation, ignorance, falsehood, and human suffering. In turn, no nation or group has special ownership over any general moral principle. Students, then, need skill and practice in moral reasoning, not indoctrination into the view that one nation rather than another is special in enunciating these moral principles. Students certainly need opportunities to explicitly learn basic moral principles, but more importantly they need opportunities to apply them to real and imagined cases, and to develop insight into both genuine and pseudo morality. They especially need to come to terms with the pitfalls of human moralizing, to recognize the ease with which we mask self-interest or egocentric desires with high-sounding moral language.

In any case, for any particular instance of moral judgment or reasoning, students should learn the art of distinguishing *principles* (which tell us in a general way what we ought or ought not to do) from *perspectives* (which characterize the world in ways which lead to an organized way of interpreting it) and *facts* (which provide the specific information for a particular moral judgment). In learning to discriminate these dimensions of moral reasoning, we learn how to focus on the appropriate questions at issue. Sometimes the dispute will depend on the facts: (Did John actually take the watch?) But, more often, they will be a matter of perspective (If you look at it this way, Jack did not take advantage of her, but if you look at it that way, he did. Which is more plausible given the facts?) Sometimes they will be a matter of both the facts and how to interpret them. (Do most people on welfare deserve the money they get? Should white collar crime be punished more severely?).

As people, students have an undeniable right to develop their own moral perspective — whether conservative, liberal, theistic, or non-theistic — but they should be able to analyze the perspective they do use, compare it accurately with other perspectives, and scrutinize the facts they conceptualize and judge as carefully as in any other domain of knowledge. They should, in other words, become as adept in using critical thinking principles in the moral domain as we expect them to be in scientific and social domains of learning.

To help students gain these skills, teachers need to see how one adapts the principles of critical thinking to the domain of ethical judgment and reasoning (see figure #1). Teachers also need insight into the intimate interconnection of intellectual and moral virtues. They need to see that being moral is something more than abstract good-heartedness, that our basic ways of knowing are inseparable from our basic ways of being, that how we think and judge in our daily life reflects who we are, morally and intellectually. To cultivate the kind of moral independence implied in being an educated moral person, we must foster in students moral humility, moral courage, moral integrity, moral perseverance, moral empathy, and moral fairmindedness (see figure #2). These moral traits are compatible with all moral perspectives (whether conservative, liberal, theistic, non-theistic, etc.).

Students who learn to think critically about moral issues and so develop moral virtues, can then develop their moral thinking within any tradition they choose. Critical thinking does not compel or coerce students to come to any particular substantive moral conclusions or to adopt any particular substantive moral point of view. Neither does it imply moral relativism, for it emphasizes the need for the same high intellectual standards in moral reasoning and judgment at the foundation of any bona fide domain of knowledge. Since moral judgment and reasoning presupposes and is subject to the same intellectual principles and standards that educated people use in all domains of learning, one can integrate consideration of moral issues into diverse subject areas, certainly into literature, science, history, civics, and society. Let us consider each of these areas very briefly.

✦ Ethics and Literature

Good literature represents and reveals, to the reflective critical reader, the deeper meanings and universal problems of real everyday life. Most of these problems have an important moral dimension or character. They are the kinds of problems all of us must think about and solve for ourselves; no one can simply tell us the "right" answers:

> Who am I? What kind of person am I? What is the world really like? What are my parents, my friends, and other people really like? How have I become the way I am? What should I believe in? Why should I believe in it? What real options do I have? Who are my real friends? Who should I trust? Who are my enemies? Need they be my enemies? How did the world become the way it is? How do people become the way they are? Are there any really bad people in the world? Are there any really good people in the world? What is good and bad? What is right and wrong? How should I decide? How can I decide what is fair and what is unfair? How can I be fair to others? Do I have to be fair to my enemies? How should I live my life? What rights do I have? What responsibilities?

Stimulating students to reflect upon questions like these in relationship to story episodes and their own experience enables them to draw upon their own developing moral feelings and ideas, to reason about them systematically, to tie them together and see where they lead. Careful reflection on episodes in literature — characters making sound or unsound moral judgments, sometimes ignoring basic moral principles or twisting them to serve their vested interests, sometimes displaying moral courage or cowardice, often caught in the throws of a moral dilemma — helps students develop a basic moral outlook on life. Furthermore, since moral issues are deeply embedded in everyday life, they often appear in literature. One need not unnaturally force discussion of literature into a moral framework. Moral issues are inevitably implicit there for the raising. However, it is important to realize that moral issues in literature, like the moral issues of everyday life, are rarely simplistic, and involved students will typically generate opposing viewpoints about how to respond to them. This, too, reflects the nature of the real world with its variety of moral outlooks vying for our allegiance.

As teachers of literature we should not impose authoritative interpretations upon the student; we should help them develop a reasoned, reflective, and coherent approach of their own. Each perspective, of course, should be respected; however, to be considered, each perspective must be *reasoned out*, not simply dogmatically asserted. In discussion, each student must learn the art of appealing to experience and reason, not merely to authority. Each student must therefore learn to reflect upon the grounds of his or her beliefs, to clarify ideas, support them with reasons and evidence, explore their implications, and so forth. Each student must also learn how to sympathetically enter into the moral perspectives of the others, not with the view that all moral perspectives are equally sound, but rather with the sense that we cannot judge another person's perspective until we genuinely understand it. Everyone is due the respect of at least being *understood*. And just as students will feel that they have something worth saying about the moral issues facing characters in stories and want their views to be understood, so they must learn to give that same respect to the others. Students then learn the art of reasoned dialogue, how to use moral reasoning skills to articulate their concerns about rights, justice, and the common good, from whatever moral viewpoint their experience and background predisposes them.

Essay writing is an excellent means of helping students organize their thinking on moral issues in literature. It provides the impetus to formulate moral principles explicitly, to carefully conceptualize and interpret facts, and to give and consider reasons in support of their own and contending moral conclusions. Needless to say we must grade students' moral writing, not on the basis of their substantive perspectives or conclusions, but rather on grounds of clarity, coherence, and sound reasoning. A clearly thought out, well-reasoned, well-illustrated piece of "moral" writing is what we are after. Such writing need not be long and complicated. Indeed it can begin in the early years with one-sentence "essays" such as "I think Jack (in "Jack and the Bean Stalk") was greedy because he didn't need to take all the golden eggs and the golden harp, too."

✦ Ethics and Science

Students should study science to understand, evaluate, and utilize scientific information. Most students will not, of course, become scientists but nevertheless need scientific knowledge to understand and solve problems within everyday personal and vocational life, problems having to do with such diverse areas as medicine, biology, chemistry, engineering, technology, the environment, and business. Science and technology play a greater and greater role in our lives, often generating major moral issues in the process. Scientific information is not simply *used*, it is used, and sometimes misused, for a variety of purposes, to advance the interests of a variety of groups, as those interests are conceived from a variety of perspectives. Its use must always be *assessed*.

In their daily lives students, like the rest of us, are bombarded with scientific information of every kind, typically in relation to some kind of advocacy. And they, like the rest of us, need to make decisions about the implications of that information. What are the real dangers of air pollution? Do people have a right to clean air and water? If so, how clean? What are the consequences of developing nuclear rather than solar power? To what extent should scientists be able to use animals in their experiments? Do animals have moral rights? To what extent should scientists be allowed to experiment with new viruses that might generate new diseases? Under what conditions should people be artificially kept alive? What life and death decisions should be left to doctors? What special moral responsibilities, if any, do scientists have to the broader society? These are but a few of the many weighty moral and scientific issues with which all of us as educated people are faced. Whether we develop an informed viewpoint or not, practical decisions are made everyday in each of these areas, and the public good is served or abused as a result of the rationality or irrationality of those decisions. Although many of these issues are ignored in traditional science instruction, there are good reasons not only to include but to emphasize them. First, they are more interesting and useful to most students than the more traditional "pure-science" emphasis. Second, they help students develop a more unified perspective on their values and personal beliefs and on the moral issues that science inevitably generates when applied to the real world.

✦ Ethics and History

There is no more important subject, rightly conceived, than history. Human life in all of its dimensions is deeply historical. Whatever experiences we have, the accounts that we give of things, our memories, our records, our sense of ourselves, the "news" we construct, the plans we form, even the daily gossip we hear — are historical. Furthermore, since we all have a deep-seated drive to think well of ourselves, and virtually unlimited powers to twist reality to justify ourselves, how we construct history has far-reaching ethical consequences. Not only do virtually all ethical issues have a historical component (moral judgment presupposes an account of what actually happened) but also virtually all historical issues have important ethical implications.

Issues arise among historians when they have conflicting accounts of events. Each major moral standpoint tends to *read* history differently and comes to importantly different moral conclusions as a result. The moral and the historical come together again and again in questions such as these: Morally speaking, what does the past *teach* us? What were the long-term effects of this kind of action as opposed to that? What kind of a world are we living in? What moral ideals can we actually live by and in what way? Is pacifism, for example, realistic? Are we justified in engaging in "unethical" practices in our own defense because our enemies use them to attack or harm us? What does it mean for countries to be "friendly" toward each other? How are friendships between countries like and unlike those between individuals? To what extent have we as a nation (and I as an individual) lived in accordance with the moral ideals we have set for ourselves? For example, was the historical treatment accorded Native Americans and other ethnic groups, has our foreign policy in general, been in keeping with our traditional espoused moral values? Morally speaking, how could our founding fathers justify slavery? Should they be morally criticized for accepting this violation of human rights or are there historical reasons why our criticism should be tempered with "understanding"? If our founding fathers, who eloquently formulated universal moral principles, were capable of violating them, are we now different from them, are we morally *better*, or are we also, without recognizing it, violating basic moral values we verbally espouse?

Once we grasp the moral significance of history, as well as the historical significance of morality, and recognize that historical judgment, like ethical judgement, is necessarily selective, that facts are conceptualized from some point of view, then we are well on our way toward constructing an unlimited variety of assignments in which history is no longer an abstraction from present and immediate concerns but rather an exciting, living, thought-provoking subject. Once students truly see themselves constructing history on a daily basis and, in doing so, coming to conclusions that directly affect the well-being of themselves and others, they will have taken a giant step toward becoming historically sensitive, ethical persons. As Carl Becker said in his presidential address to the American Historical Association over 50 years ago, every person, like it or not, "is his own historian". We must make sure that our students grasp the *moral* significance of that fact.

✦ Ethics, Civics, and the Study of Society

Just as all of us, to be ethical, must be our own historian, so too, to ethically fulfill our civic responsibilities, we must be our own sociologists. That is to say, each of us must study the underlying realities of social events, the unwritten rules and values that unreflectively guide our behavior; otherwise how can we justify using ethical principles to judge people and situations in the real world around us? We should be more than uncritical social observers and superficial moral judges. We have to recognize, as every sociologist since William Graham Sumner has pointed out, that most human behavior is a result of unanalyzed habit and routine based on unconsciously held standards and values. These embedded standards and values often differ from, even oppose, the ideals we express, and yet the conformist thinking which socialization tends to produce resists critical analysis. This resistance was recognized even from the early days of sociology as a discipline:

> Every group of any kind demands that each of its members shall help defend group interests ... group force is also employed to enforce the obligations of devotion to group interests. It follows that judgments are precluded and criticism is silenced. (Sumner, 1906)

Even patriotism, Sumner points out, "may degenerate into a vice ... chauvinism":

> It is a name for boastful and truculent group self-assertion. It overrules personal judgment and character, and puts the whole group at the mercy of the clique which is ruling at the moment. It produces the dominance of watchwords and phrases which take the place of reason and conscience in determining conduct. The patriotic bias is a recognized perversion of thought and judgment against which our education should guard us. (Sumner, 1906)

Ironically, true patriots in a democratic society serve their country by using their critical powers to ensure governmental honesty. Intelligent distrust rather than uncritical trust is the foundation necessary to keep officials acting ethically and in the public good. It was Jefferson who said:

> It would be a dangerous delusion were a confidence in the men of our choice to silence our fears for the safety of our rights. Confidence is everywhere the parent of despotism — free government is founded in jealousy, and not in confidence.

And Madison enthusiastically agreed: "The truth is, all men having power ought to be mistrusted."

What students need in civic education, then, is precisely what they need in moral education: not indoctrination into abstracted ideals, with the tacit implication that the ideals are generally practiced, not slogans and empty moralizing, but assignments that challenge their ability to use civic ideals to assess actual political behavior. Such assignments will, of course, produce divergent conclusions by students depending on their present political leanings. But, again, their thinking, speaking, and writing should be graded on the clarity, cogency, and intellectual rigor of their work, not on the substance of their answers. All students should learn the art of political analysis, the art of subjecting political behavior to critical assessment based on civic and moral ideals, on an analysis of important relevant facts, and on consideration of alternative political viewpoints. Virtually no students graduate today with this art in hand.

This means that words like "conservatism" and "liberalism", the "right" and "left", must become more than vague jargon; they must be recognized as names of different ways of thinking about human behavior. Students need experience actually thinking within diverse political perspectives. No perspective, not even one called "moderate", should be presented as *the* correct one. By the same token, we should be careful not to lead the students to believe that all perspectives are equally justified or that important insights are equally found in all points of view. We should continually encourage and stimulate our students to think and never do their thinking for them. We should, above all, be teachers and not preachers.

✦ Implementation Philosophy

Bringing ethics into the curriculum is essential but difficult. Many teachers are deeply committed to didactic lectorial modes of teaching. If ethics is taught in this way, indoctrination results, and we have lost rather than gained ground. Better no ethics than dogmatic moralizing.

To successfully establish a solid framework of ethical reasoning throughout the curriculum, we need excellent supplemental resources and well-designed in-service. Whenever possible, teachers should have access to books and materials that demonstrate how ethical and critical thinking principles can be integrated into subject matter instruction. They also need opportunities to air whatever misgivings they have about the paradigm shift this model represents for many of them. Above all, one should conceive of a move such as this as part of a long-term strategy in which implementation is achieved progressively over an extended time.

Just as educators should respect the autonomy of students, so in-service design should respect the autonomy of teachers. Teachers can and should be helped to integrate a critical approach to ethics into their everyday teaching. But they must actively think their way to this integration. It should not be imposed on them.

The model I suggest is one I have used successfully in in-service for both elementary and secondary teachers on numerous occasions. I call it the "Lesson Plan Remodeling Strategy" and have written three handbooks and an article explaining it in depth.

The basic idea is simple. Every practicing teacher works daily with lesson plans of one kind or another. To remodel lesson plans is to critique one or more lesson plans and formulate one or more new lesson plans based on that critical process. Thus, a group of teachers or staff development leaders with a reasonable number of exemplary remodels with accompanying explanatory principles can design practice sessions that enable teachers to develop new teaching skills as a result of experience in lesson remodeling.

Lesson plan remodeling can become a powerful tool in staff development for several reasons. It is action oriented and puts an immediate emphasis on close examination and critical assessment of what is taught on a day-to-day basis. It makes the problem of infusion more manageable by paring it down to the critique of particular lesson plans and the progressive infusion of particular principles. It is developmental in that, over time, more and more lesson plans are remodeled, and what has been remodeled can be remodeled again.

✦ Inservice Design

The idea behind inservice on this model is to take teachers step-by-step through specific stages of implementation. First of all, teachers must have an opportunity to become familiar with the basic concepts of critical thinking and ethical reasoning. They should first have an opportunity to formulate and discuss various general principles of morality and then to discuss how people with differing moral perspectives sometimes come to different moral conclusions when they apply these principles to actual events. Questions like "Is abortion morally justified?" or "Under what conditions do people have a right to welfare support?" or "Is capital punishment ever morally justified?" etc., can be used as examples to demonstrate this point.

Working together, the teachers should then construct examples of how they might encourage their students to apply one or more of the moral reasoning skills listed in figure #1. One table might focus on devising ways to help students clarify moral issues and claims *(S-8)*. Another table may discuss assignments that would help students develop their moral perspective *(S-7)*. A third might focus on ways to encourage one of the essential moral *virtues*, say, *moral integrity*. Of course teachers should have examples for each of the moral reasoning skills, as well as model classroom activities that foster them. Teachers should not be expected to work with nothing more than a list of abstract labels. The subsequent examples developed by the teachers working together should be written up and shared with all participants. There should be ample opportunity for constructive feedback.

Once teachers get some confidence in devising examples of activities they can use to help students develop various individual moral reasoning skills, they should try their hands at developing a full remodel. For this, each table has an actual lesson plan and they collectively develop a critique and remodel that embodies moral reasoning skills explicitly set out as objectives of the lesson. As before, exemplary remodels should be available for teachers to compare with their remodels. The following components should be spelled out explicitly:

1. *the original lesson plan* (or an abstract of it)

2. *a statement of the objectives of the plan*

3. *a critique of the original* (Why does it need to be revised? What does it fail to do that it might do? Does it indoctrinate students?)

4. *a listing of the moral reasoning skills to be infused*

5. *the remodeled lesson plan* (containing references to where in the remodel the various moral reasoning skills are infused)

Eventually school-wide or district-wide handbooks of lesson remodels can be put together and disseminated. These can be updated yearly. At least one consultant with unquestionable credentials in critical thinking should be hired to provide outside feedback on the process and its products.

For a fuller explanation of this inservice process and a wide selection of examples, I refer the reader to either *Critical Thinking Handbook: 4th-6th Grades*, or *Critical Thinking Handbook: K-3*, both are subtitled *A Guide for Remodeling Lesson Plans in Language Arts, Social Studies & Science*. Both integrate an emphasis on ethical reasoning into critical thinking infusion, though they do not explicitly express the component critical thinking skills with a moral reasoning emphasis (as I have in figure #1). The handbook examples are easily adaptable as illustrations for the upper grade levels. In any case, handbooks or not, what we should aim at is teacher practice in critiquing and revising standard lesson plans, based on a knowledgeable commitment to critical thinking and moral reasoning. We should not expect that teachers will begin with the knowledge base or even the commitment but only that with exposure, practice, and encouragement within a well planned long-term inservice implementation, proficiency and commitment will eventually emerge.

In my own experience in conducting inservices, I have found it easy to *begin* this process working with teachers. Though the early products of the teachers are of mixed quality, all of what is produced is workable as a basis for the development of further insights and teaching skills. The difficulty is not in getting the process started; it is in keeping it going. One

---

Moral Reasoning Skills

A Moral Affective Strategies
S-1 exercising independent moral thought and judgment
S-2 developing insight into moral egocentrism and sociocentrism
S-3 exercising moral reciprocity
S-4 exploring thought underlying moral reactions
S-5 suspending moral judgment

B Cognitive Strategies: Moral Macro-Abilities
S-6 avoiding oversimplification of moral issues
S-7 developing one's moral perspective
S-8 clarifying moral issues and claims
S-9 clarifying moral ideas
S-10 developing criteria for moral evaluation
S-11 evaluating moral authorities
S-12 raising and pursuing root moral questions
S-13 evaluating moral arguments
S-14 generating and assessing solutions to moral problems
S-15 identifying and clarifying moral points of view
S-16 engaging in Socratic discussion on moral issues
S-17 practicing dialogical thinking on moral issues
S-18 practicing dialectical thinking on moral issues

C Cognitive Strategies: Moral Micro-Skills
S-19 distinguishing facts from moral principles, values, and ideals
S-20 using critical vocabulary in discussing moral issues
S-21 distinguishing moral principles or ideas
S-22 examining moral assumptions
S-23 distinguishing morally relevant from morally irrelevant facts
S-24 making plausible moral inferences
S-25 supplying evidence for a moral conclusion
S-26 recognizing moral contradictions
S-27 exploring moral implication and consequences
S-28 refining moral generalizations

---

figure 1

Essential Moral Virtues

Moral Humility: Awareness of the limits of one's moral knowledge, including sensitivity to circumstances in which one's native egocentrism is likely to function self-deceptively; sensitivity to bias and prejudice in, and limitations of, one's viewpoint. Moral humility is based on the recognition that no one should claim to know more than one actually knows. It does not imply spinelessness or submissiveness. It implies the lack of moral pretentiousness, boastfulness, or conceit, combined with insight into the strengths and weaknesses of the logical foundations of one's beliefs.

Moral Courage: The willingness to face and assess fairly moral ideas, beliefs, or viewpoints to which we have not given serious hearing, regardless of our strong negative reaction to them. This courage arises from the recognition that ideas considered dangerous or absurd are sometimes rationally justified (in whole or in part), and that moral conclusions or beliefs espoused by those around us or inculcated in us are sometimes false or misleading.

Moral Empathy: Having a consciousness of the need to imaginatively put oneself in the place of others in order to genuinely understand them. We must recognize our egocentric tendency to identify truth with our immediate perceptions or longstanding beliefs. This trait correlates with the ability to reconstruct accurately the moral viewpoints and reasoning of others and to reason from moral premises, assumptions, and ideas other than our own. This trait also requires that we remember occasions when we were morally wrong, despite an intense conviction that we were right, as well as consider that we might be similarly deceived in a case at hand.

Moral Integrity: Recognition of the need to be true to one's own moral thinking, to be consistent in the moral standards one applies, to hold one's self to the same rigorous standards of evidence and proof to which one holds one's antagonists, to practice what one morally advocates for others, and to honestly admit discrepancies and moral inconsistencies in one's own thought and action.

Moral Perseverance: Willingness and consciousness of the need to pursue moral insights and truths despite difficulties, obstacles, and frustrations; firm adherence to moral principles despite irrational opposition of others; a sense of the need to struggle with confusion and unsettled questions over an extended period of time, to achieve deeper moral understanding or insight.

Moral Fairmindedness: Willingness and consciousness of the need to entertain all moral viewpoints sympathetically and to assess them with the same intellectual standards without reference to one's own feelings or vested interests, or the feelings or vested interests of one's friends, community, or nation; implies adherence to moral standards without reference to one's own advantage or the advantage of one's group.

figure 2

new lesson plan does not by itself change an established style of teaching. Like all creatures of habit, teachers tend to revert on Monday to their established teaching practices. A real on-going effort is essential for lesson plan remodeling to become a way of life and not just an interesting inservice activity.

✦ The Need for Leadership

I cannot overemphasize the need for leadership in this area. Teachers need to know that the administration is solidly behind them in this process, that the time and effort they put in will not only be appreciated but also visibly built upon. The school-wide or district-wide handbooks mentioned above are one kind of visible by-product that teachers should see. An excellent start is to have key administrators actively participate in the inservice along with the teachers. But the support should not end there. Administrators should facilitate on-going structures and activities to support this process: making and sharing video tapes, sending key personnel to conferences, establishing working committees, informal discussion groups, and opportunities for peer review. These are some among the many possibilities. Administrators should also be articulate defenders of an educational rather than a doctrinaire approach to morality. They should be ready, willing, and able to explain why and how critical thinking and ethics are integrated throughout the curriculum. They should make the approach intelligible to the school board and community. They should engender enthusiasm for it. They should fight to preserve it if attacked by those good hearted but closedminded people who see morality personified in their particular moral perspectives and beliefs. Above all, they should make a critical and moral commitment to a moral and critical education for all students and do this in a way that demonstrates to teachers and parents alike moral courage, perseverance, and integrity.

✦ References

Ralph W. Clark, *Introduction to Moral Reasoning,* West Publishing Company, St. Paul: 1986.

Ronald N. Giere, *Understanding Scientific Reasoning,* Holt, Rinehart, and Winston; New York: 1979.

Kuzirian and Madaras, *Taking Sides: Clashing Views on Controversial Issues in American History,* Dushkin Publishing Group; Guilford, Conn.: 1985.

Richard Paul, "Critical Thinking: Fundamental to Education for a Free Society," *Educational Leadership* 42, September, 1984.

Richard Paul, "Critical Thinking and the Critical Person," Forthcoming in *Thinking: Progress in Research and Teaching,* by Lawrence Erlbaum Associates, Inc. Publishers; Perkins, et al. editors.

Richard Paul, "Dialogical Thinking: Critical Thought Essential to the Acquisition of Rational Knowledge and Passions," *Teaching Thinking Skills; Theory and Practice,* by W.H. Freeman & Company, Publishers, Joan Baron and Robert Steinberg, editors, 1987.

Richard Paul, "Critical Thinking Staff Development: Lesson Plan Remodeling as the Strategy," *The Journal of Staff Development,* Fall 1987, Paul Burden, editor.

Paul, Binker, Jensen, and Kreklau, *Critical Thinking Handbook: 4th–6th Grades, A Guide for Remodeling Lesson Plans in Language Arts, Social Studies and Science,* Published by the Center for Critical Thinking and Moral Critique, (Sonoma State University, Rohnert Park, CA 94928) 1987.

Paul, Binker, Charbonneau *Critical Thinking Handbook: K–3, A Guide for Remodeling Lesson Plans in Language Arts, Social Studies and Science,* Published by the Center for Critical Thinking and Moral Critique, 1987.

Harvey Siegel, "Critical Thinking as an Education Ideal," *The Educational Forum,* Nov. 1980.

William Graham Sumner, *Folkways: A Study of the Sociological Importance of Usages, Manners, Customs, Mores, and Morals,* Dover Publications, Inc., New York: 1906.

Chapter 15

Critical Thinking, Moral Integrity, and Citizenship:
Teaching for the Intellectual Virtues

Abstract

Many are tempted to separate affective and moral dimensions of learning from cognitive dimensions. They argue that the cognitive and affective are obviously separate since many intelligent, well-educated people lack moral insight or sensitivity and many less intelligent, poorly-educated, or uneducated people are morally good. By distinguishing "strong" and "weak" senses of the terms 'critical thinking', 'moral integrity', and 'citizenship' Richard Paul suggests a novel answer to this objection.

Critical thinking, understood as skills alone separate from values, is often used to rationalize prejudice and vested interest. Moral integrity and responsible citizenship, understood merely as "good heartedness", are themselves susceptible to manipulation by propaganda. The human mind, whatever its conscious good will, is subject to powerful, self-deceptive, unconscious egocentricity of mind. The full development of each characteristic — critical thought, moral integrity, and responsible citizenship — in its strong sense requires and develops the others, in a parallel strong sense. The three are developed together only in an atmosphere which encourages the intellectual virtues: intellectual courage, intellectual empathy, intellectual good faith or integrity, intellectual perseverance, intellectual fairmindedness, and faith in reason. The intellectual virtues themselves are interdependent.

*E*ducators and theorists tend to approach the affective and moral dimensions of education as they approach all other dimensions of learning, as compartmentalized domains, and as a collection of learnings more or less separate from other learnings. As a result, they view moral development as more or less independent of cognitive development. "And why not!" one might imagine the reply. "Clearly there are highly educated, very intelligent people who habitually do evil and very simple, poorly-educated people who consistently do good. If moral development were so intimately connected to cognitive development, how could this be so?"

In this paper, I provide the outlines of an answer to that objection by suggesting an intimate connection between critical thinking, moral integrity, and citizenship. Specifically, I distinguish a weak and a strong sense of each and hold that the strong sense ought to guide, not only our understanding of the nature of the educated person, but also our redesigning the curriculum.

There is little to recommend schooling that does not foster what I call intellectual virtues. These virtues include intellectual empathy, intellectual perseverance, intellectual confidence in reason, and an intellectual sense of justice (fairmindedness). Without these characteristics, intellectual development is circumscribed and distorted, a caricature of what it could and should be. These same characteristics are essential to moral judgment. The "good-hearted" person who lacks intellectual virtues will act morally only when morally grasping a situation or problem does not presuppose intellectual insight. Many, if not most, moral problems and situations in the modern world are open to multiple interpretations and, hence, do presuppose these intellectual virtues.

We are now coming to see how far we are from curricula and teaching strategies that genuinely foster basic intellectual and moral development. Curricula is so highly compartmentalized and teaching so committed to "speed learning" (covering large chunks of content quickly) that it has little room for fostering what I call the intellectual virtues. Indeed, the present structure of curricula and teaching not only strongly discourages their development but also strongly encourages their opposites. Consequently, even the "best" students enter and leave college as largely miseducated persons, with no real sense of what they do and do not understand, with little sense of the state of their prejudices or insights, with little command of their intellectual faculties — in short, with no intellectual virtues, properly so-called.

Superficially absorbed content, the inevitable by-product of extensive but shallow coverage, inevitably leads to intellectual arrogance. Such learning discourages intellectual perseverance and confidence in reason. It prevents the recognition of intellectual bad faith. It provides no foundation for intellectual empathy, nor for an intellectual sense of fair play. By taking in and giving back masses of detail, students come to believe that they *know* a lot about each subject — whether they understand or not. By practicing applying rules and formulas to familiar tasks, they come to feel that getting the answer should always be easy — if you don't know how to do something, don't try to figure it out, ask. By hearing and reading only one perspective, they come to think that perspective has a monopoly on truth — any other view must be completely wrong. By accepting (without understanding) that their government's past actions were all justified, they assume their government never would or could do wrong — if it doesn't seem right, I must not understand.

The pedagogical implications of my position include these: cutting back on coverage to focus on depth of understanding, on foundational ideas, on intellectual synthesis, and on intellectual experiences that develop and deepen the most basic intellectual skills, abilities, concepts, and virtues. A similar viewpoint was expressed by Whitehead:

> The result of teaching small parts of a large number of subjects is the passive reception of disconnected ideas, not illuminated with any spark of vitality. Let the main ideas which are introduced into a child's education be few and important, and let them be thrown into every combination possible. The child should make them his own, and should understand their application here and now in the circumstances of his actual life. From the very beginning of his education, the child should experience the joy of discovery. The discovery which he has to make is that general ideas give an understanding of that stream of events which pours through his life. (*The Aims of Education*, p. 14)

To accomplish this re-orientation of curriculum and teaching, we need new criteria of what constitutes success and failure in school. We need to begin this re-orientation as early as possible. Integrating teaching for critical thinking, moral integrity, and citizenship is an essential part of this re-orientation.

✦ Teaching for "Strong Sense" Skills

The term "critical thinking" can be used in either a weak or a strong sense, depending upon whether we think of critical thinking narrowly, as a list or collection of discrete intellectual skills, or, more broadly, as a mode of mental integration, as a synthesized complex of dispositions, values, and skills necessary to becoming a fairminded, rational person. Teaching critical thinking in a strong sense is a powerful, and I believe necessary means to moral integrity and responsible citizenship.

Intellectual skills in and of themselves can be used either for good or ill, to enlighten or to propagandize, to gain narrow, self-serving ends, or to further the general and public good. The micro-skills themselves, for example, do not define fairmindedness and could be used as easily by those who are highly prejudiced as those who are not. Those students not exposed to the challenge of strong sense critical thinking assignments (for example, assignments in which they must empathically reconstruct viewpoints that differ strikingly from their own) will not, as a matter of abstract morality or general good-heartedness, be fair to points of view they oppose, nor will they automatically develop a rationally defensible notion of what the public good is on the many issues they must decide as citizens.

Critical thinking, in its most defensible sense, is not simply a matter of cognitive skills. Moral integrity and responsible citizenship are, in turn, not simply a matter of good-heartedness or good intentions. Many good-hearted people cannot see through and critique propaganda and mass manipulation, and most good-hearted people fall prey at times to the powerful tendency to engage in self deception, especially when their own egocentric interests and desires are at stake. One can be good-hearted and intellectually egocentric at the same time.

The problems of education for fairminded independence of thought, for genuine moral integrity, and for responsible citizenship are not three separate issues but one complex task. If we succeed with one dimension of the problem, we succeed with all. If we fail with one, we fail with all. Now we are failing with all because we do not clearly understand the interrelated nature of the problem nor how to address it.

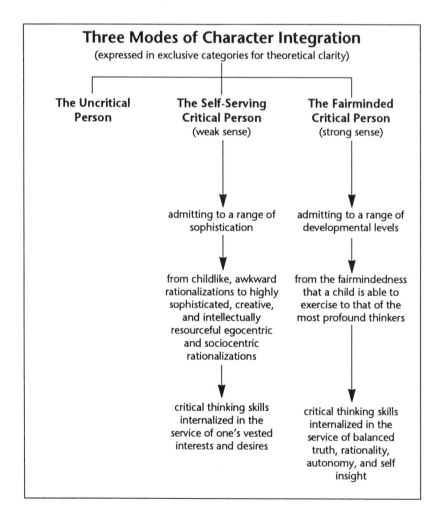

Three Modes of Character Integration
(expressed in exclusive categories for theoretical clarity)

The Uncritical Person	The Self-Serving Critical Person (weak sense)	The Fairminded Critical Person (strong sense)
	admitting to a range of sophistication	admitting to a range of developmental levels
	from childlike, awkward rationalizations to highly sophisticated, creative, and intellectually resourceful egocentric and sociocentric rationalizations	from the fairmindedness that a child is able to exercise to that of the most profound thinkers
	critical thinking skills internalized in the service of one's vested interests and desires	critical thinking skills internalized in the service of balanced truth, rationality, autonomy, and self insight

✦ The Intellectual and Moral Virtues of the Critical Person

Our basic ways of knowing are inseparable from our basic ways of being. How we think reflects who we are. Intellectual and moral virtues or disabilities are intimately interconnected. To cultivate the kind of intellectual independence implied in the concept of strong sense critical thinking, we must recognize the need to foster intellectual (epistemological) humility, courage, integrity, perseverance, empathy, and fairmindedness. A brief gloss on each will suggest how to translate these concepts into concrete examples. Intellectual humility will be my only extended illustration. I will leave to the reader's imagination what sorts of concrete examples could be marshalled in amplifying the other intellectual virtues.

Intellectual Humility: Having a consciousness of the limits of one's knowledge, including a sensitivity to circumstances in which one's native egocentrism is likely to function self-deceptively; sensitivity to bias, prejudice, and limitations of one's viewpoint. Intellectual humility depends on recognizing that one should not claim more than one actually knows. It does not imply spinelessness or submissiveness. It implies the lack of intellectual pretentiousness, boastfulness, or conceit, combined with insight into the logical foundations, or lack of such foundations, of one's beliefs.

To illustrate, consider this letter from a teacher with a Master's degree in Physics and Mathematics, with 20 years of high school teaching experience in physics:

> After I started teaching, I realized that I had learned physics by rote and that I really did not understand all I knew about physics. My thinking students asked me questions for which I always had the standard textbook answers, but for the first time it made me start thinking for myself, and I realized that these canned answers were not justified by my own thinking and only confused my students who were showing some ability to think for themselves. To achieve my academic goals I had to memorize the thoughts of others, but I had never learned or been encouraged to learn to think for myself.

This is a good example of what I call intellectual humility and, like all intellectual humility, it arises from insight into the nature of knowing. It is reminiscent of the ancient Greek insight that Socrates was the wisest of the Greeks because only he knew how little he really understood. Socrates developed this insight as a result of extensive, in-depth questioning of the knowledge claims of others. He had to think his way to this insight.

If this insight and this humility is part of our goal, then most textbooks and curricula require extensive modification, for typically they discourage rather than encourage it. The extent and nature of "coverage" for most grade levels and subjects implies that bits and pieces of knowledge are easily attained, without any significant consideration of the basis for the knowledge claimed in the text or by the teacher. The speed with which content is covered contradicts the notion that students must think in an extended way about content before giving assent to what is claimed. Most teaching and most texts are, in this sense, epistemologically unrealistic and hence foster intellectual arrogance in students, particularly in those with retentive memories who can repeat back what they have heard or read. *Pretending* to know is encouraged. Much standardized testing validates this pretense.

This led Alan Schoenfeld, for example, to conclude that "most instruction in mathematics is, in a very real sense, deceptive and possibly fraudulent". He cites numerous examples including the following. He points out that much instruction on how to solve word problems in elementary math

> ... is based on the "key word" algorithm, where the student makes his choice of the appropriate arithmetic operation by looking for syntactic cues in the problem statement. For example, the word 'left' in the problem "John had eight apples. He gave three to Mary. How many does John have left?" ... serves to tell the students that subtraction is the appropriate operation to perform. (p. 27)

He further reports the following:

> In a widely used elementary text book series, 97 percent of the problems "solved" by the key-word method would yield (serendipitously?) the correct answer.
>
> Students are drilled in the key-word algorithm so well that they will use subtraction, for example, in almost any problem containing the word 'left'. In the study from which this conclusion was drawn, problems were constructed in which appropriate operations were addition, multiplication, and division. Each used the word 'left' conspicuously in its statement and a large percentage of the students subtracted. In fact, the situation was so extreme that many students chose to subtract in a problem that began "Mr. Left ...".

Schoenfeld then provides a couple of other examples, including the following:

> I taught a problem-solving course for junior and senior mathematics majors at Berkeley in 1976. These students had already seen some remarkably sophisticated mathematics. Linear algebra and differential equations were old hat. Topology, Fourier transforms, and measure theory were familiar to some. I gave them a straight-forward theorem from plane geometry (required when I was in the tenth grade). Only two of eight students made any progress on it, some of them by using arc length integrals to measure the circumference of a circle. (Schoenfeld, 1979). Out of the context of normal course work these students could not do elementary mathematics.

He concludes:

> In sum: all too often we focus on a narrow collection of well-defined tasks and train students to execute those tasks in a routine, if not algorithmic fashion. Then we test the students on tasks that are very close to the ones they have been taught. If they succeed on those problems, we and they congratulate each other on the fact that they have learned some powerful mathematical techniques. In fact, they may be able to use such techniques mechanically while lacking some rudimentary thinking skills. To allow them, and ourselves, to believe that they "understand" the mathematics is deceptive and fraudulent.

This approach to learning in math is paralleled in all other subjects. Most teachers got through their college classes mainly by "learning the standard textbook answers" and were neither given an opportunity nor encouraged to determine whether what the text or the professor said was "justified by their own thinking". To move toward intellectual humility, most teachers need to question most of what they learned, as the teacher above did, but such questioning would require intellectual courage, perseverance, and confidence in their own capacity to reason and understand subject matter through their own thought. Most teachers have not done the kind of analytic thinking necessary for gaining such perspective.

I would generalize as follows: just as the development of intellectual humility is an essential goal of critical thinking instruction, so is the development of intellectual courage, integrity, empathy, perseverance, fairmindedness, and confidence in reason. Furthermore, each intellectual (and moral) virtue in turn is richly developed only in conjunction with the others. Before we approach this point directly, however, a brief characterization of what I have in mind by each of these traits is in order:

Intellectual Courage: Having a consciousness of the need to face and fairly address ideas, beliefs, or viewpoints toward which we have strong negative emotions and to which we have not given a serious hearing. This courage is connected with the recognition that ideas considered dangerous or absurd are sometimes rationally justified (in whole or in part) and that conclusions and beliefs inculcated in us are sometimes false or misleading. To determine for ourselves which is which, we must not passively and uncritically "accept" what we have "learned". Intellectual courage comes into play here, because inevitably we will come to see some truth in some ideas considered dangerous and absurd, and distortion or falsity in some ideas strongly held in our social group. We need courage to be true to our own thinking in such circumstances. The penalties for non-conformity can be severe.

Intellectual Empathy: Having a consciousness of the need to imaginatively put oneself in the place of others in order to genuinely understand them, which requires the consciousness of our egocentric tendency to identify truth with our immediate perceptions or long-standing thought or belief. This trait correlates with the ability to reconstruct accurately the viewpoints and reasoning of others and to reason from premises, assumptions, and ideas other than our own. This trait also correlates with the willingness to remember occasions when we were wrong in the past despite an intense conviction that we were right, and with the ability to imagine our being similarly deceived in a case-at-hand.

Intellectual Good Faith (Integrity): Recognition of the need to be true to one's own thinking; to be consistent in the intellectual standards one applies; to hold one's self to the same rigorous standards of evidence and proof to which one holds one's antagonists; to practice what one advocates for others; and to honestly admit discrepancies and inconsistencies in one's own thought and action.

Intellectual Perseverance: Willingness and consciousness of the need to pursue intellectual insights and truths in spite of difficulties, obstacles, and frustrations; firm adherence to rational principles despite the irrational opposition of others; a sense of the need to struggle with confusion and unsettled questions over an extended period of time to achieve deeper understanding or insight.

Faith in Reason: Confidence that, in the long run, one's own higher interests and those of humankind at large will be best served by giving the freest play to reason, by encouraging people to come to their own conclusions by developing their own rational faculties; faith that, with proper encouragement and cultivation, people can learn to think for themselves, to form rational viewpoints, draw reasonable conclusions, think coherently and logically, persuade each other by reason and become reasonable persons, despite the deep-seated obstacles in the native character of the human mind and in society as we know it.

Fairmindedness: Willingness and consciousness of the need to treat all viewpoints alike, without reference to one's own feelings or vested interests, or the feelings or vested interests of one's friends, community, or nation; implies adherence to intellectual standards without reference to one's own advantage or the advantage of one's group.

✦ The Interdependence of the Intellectual Virtues

Let us now consider the interdependence of these virtues, how hard it is to deeply develop any one of them without also developing the others. Consider intellectual humility. To become aware of the limits of our knowledge we need the *courage* to face our own prejudices and ignorance.

To discover our own prejudices in turn we must often *empathize* with and reason within points of view toward which we are hostile. To do this, we must typically *persevere* over a period of time, for learning to empathically enter a point of view against which we are biased takes time and significant effort. That effort will not seem justified unless we have the *faith in reason* to believe we will not be "tainted" or "taken in" by whatever is false or misleading in the opposing viewpoint. Furthermore, merely believing we can survive serious consideration of an "alien" point of view is not enough to motivate most of us to consider them seriously. We must also be motivated by an *intellectual sense of justice*. We must recognize an intellectual *responsibility* to be fair to views we oppose. We must feel *obliged* to hear them in their strongest form to ensure that we do not condemn them out of our own ignorance or bias. At this point, we come full circle back to where we began: the need for *intellectual humility.*

Or let us begin at another point. Consider intellectual good faith or integrity. Intellectual integrity is clearly difficult to develop. We are often motivated — generally without admitting to or being aware of this motivation — to set up inconsistent intellectual standards. Our egocentric or sociocentric side readily believes positive information about those we like and negative information about those we dislike. We tend to believe what justifies our vested interest or validates our strongest desires. Hence, we all have some innate tendencies to use double standards, which is of course paradigmatic of intellectual bad faith. Such thought often helps us get ahead in the world, maximize our power or advantage, and get more of what we want.

Nevertheless, we cannot easily operate *explicitly* or overtly with a double standard. We must, therefore, avoid looking at the evidence too closely. We cannot scrutinize our own inferences and interpretations too carefully. Hence, a certain amount of *intellectual arrogance* is quite useful. I may assume, for example that I know just what you're going to say (before you say it), precisely what you are really after (before the evidence demonstrates it), and what actually is going on (before I have studied the situation carefully). My intellectual arrogance makes it easier for me to avoid noticing the unjustifiable discrepancy in the standards I apply to you and those I apply to myself. Of course, if I don't have to empathize with you, that too makes it easier to avoid seeing my duplicity. I am also better off if I don't feel a keen need to be *fair* to your point of view. A little background *fear* of what I might discover if I seriously considered the consistency of my own judgments also helps. In this case, my lack of intellectual integrity is supported by my lack of intellectual humility, empathy, and fairmindedness.

Going in the other direction, it will be difficult to maintain a double standard between us if I feel a distinct responsibility to be fair to your point of view, understand this responsibility to entail that I must view things from your perspective in an empathic fashion, and conduct this inner inquiry with some humility regarding the possibility of my being wrong and your being right. The more I dislike you personally or feel wronged in the past by you or by others who share your way of thinking, the more pronounced in my character must be the trait of intellectual integrity in order to provide the countervailing impetus to think my way to a fair conclusion.

✦ Defense Mechanisms and the Intellectual Virtues

A major obstacle to developing intellectual virtues is the presence in the human egocentric mind of what Freud has called "defense mechanisms". Each represents a way to falsify, distort, misconceive, twist, or deny reality. Their presence represents, therefore, the relative weakness or absence of the intellectual virtues. Since they operate in everyone to some degree, no one embodies the intellectual virtues purely or perfectly. In other words, we each have a side of us unwilling to face unpleasant truth, willing to distort, falsify, twist, and misrepresent. We also know from a monumental mass of psychological research that this side can be *powerful*, can dominate our minds strikingly. We marvel at, and are often dumfounded by, others whom we consider clear-cut instances of these modes of thinking. What is truly "marvelous", it seems to me, is how little we take ourselves to be victims of these falsifying thoughts, and how little we try to break them down. The vicious circle seems to be this: because we, by and large, lack the intellectual virtues, we do not have insight into them, but because we lack insight into them, we do not see ourselves as lacking them. They weren't explicitly taught to us, so we don't have to explicitly teach them to our children.

✦ Insights, Analyzed Experiences, and Activated Ignorance

Schooling has generally ignored the need for insight or intellectual virtues. This deficiency is intimately connected with another one, the failure of the schools to show students they should not only test what they "learn" in school by their own experience, but also test what they experience by what they "learn" in school. This may seem a hopeless circle, but if we can see the distinction between a critically analyzed experience and an unanalyzed one, we can see the link between the former and *insight*, and the latter and *prejudice*, and will be well on our way to seeing how to fill these needs.

We subject little of our experience to critical analysis. We seldom take our experiences apart to judge their epistemological worth. We rarely sort the "lived" integrated experience into its component parts, *raw data, our interpretation* of the data, or ask ourselves how the interests, goals, and desires we brought to those data shaped and structured that interpretation. Similarly, we rarely seriously consider the possibility that our interpretation (and hence our experience) might be selective, biased, or misleading.

This is not to say that our unanalyzed experiences lack meaning or significance. Quite the contrary, in some sense we assess *all* experience. Our egocentric side never ceases to catalogue experiences in accord with its common and idiosyncratic fears, desires, prejudices, stereotypes, caricatures, hopes, dreams, and assorted irrational drives. We shouldn't assume *a priori* that our rational side dominates the shaping of our experience. Our unanalyzed experiences are some combination of these dual contributors to thought, action, and being. Only through critical analysis can we hope to isolate the irrational dimensions of our experience. The ability to do so grows as we analyze more and more of our experience.

Of course, more important than the sheer *number* of analyzed experiences is their *quality* and *significance*. This quality and significance depends on how much our analyses embody the intellectual virtues. At the same time, the degree of our virtue depends upon the number and quality of experiences we have successfully critically analyzed. What links the virtues, as perfections of the mind, and the experiences, as analyzed products of the mind, is *insight*. Every critically analyzed experience to some extent produces one or more intellectual virtues. To become more rational it is not enough to have experiences nor even for those experiences to have meanings. Many experiences are more or less charged with *irrational* meanings. These important meanings produce stereotypes, prejudices, narrowmindedness, delusions, and illusions of various kinds.

The process of developing intellectual virtues and insights is part and parcel of our developing an interest in taking apart our experiences to separate their rational from their irrational dimensions. These meta-experiences become important benchmarks and guides for future thought. They make possible modes of thinking and maneuvers in thinking closed to the irrational mind.

✦ Some Thoughts on How to Teach for the Intellectual Virtues

To teach for the intellectual virtues, one must recognize the significant differences between the higher order critical thinking of a fairminded critical thinker and that of a self-serving critical thinker. Though both share a certain command of the micro-skills of critical thinking and hence would, for example, score well on tests such as the Watson-Glaser Critical Thinking Appraisal or the Cornell Critical Thinking Tests, they are not equally good at tasks which presuppose the intellectual virtues. The self-serving (weak sense) critical thinker would lack the insights that underlie and support these virtues.

I can reason well in domains in which I am prejudiced — hence, eventually, reason my way out of prejudices — only if I develop mental benchmarks for such reasoning. Of course one insight I need is that when I am prejudiced it will seem to me that I am not, and similarly, that those who are not prejudiced as I am will seem to me to be prejudiced. (To a prejudiced person, an unprejudiced person seems prejudiced.) I will come to this insight only insofar as I have analyzed experiences in which I was intensely convinced I was correct on an issue, judgment, or point of view, only to find, after a series of challenges, reconsiderations, and new reasonings, that my previous conviction was in fact prejudiced. I must take this experience apart in my mind, clearly understand its elements and how they fit together (how I became prejudiced; how I inwardly experienced that prejudice; how intensely that prejudice seemed true and insightful; how I progressively broke that prejudice down through serious consideration of opposing lines of reasoning; how I slowly came to new assumptions, new information, and ultimately new conceptualizations).

Only when one gains analyzed experiences of working and reasoning one's way out of prejudice can one gain the higher order abilities of a fairminded critical thinker. What one gains is somewhat "procedural" or sequential in that there is a *process* one must go through; but one also sees that the process cannot be followed out formulaically or algorithmically, it depends on principles. The somewhat abstract articulation of the intellectual virtues above will take on concrete meaning in the light of these *analyzed experiences*. Their true meaning to us will be given in and by these experiences. We will often return to them to recapture and rekindle the insights upon which the intellectual virtues depend.

Generally, to develop intellectual virtues, we must create a collection of analyzed experiences that represent to us intuitive models, not only of the pitfalls of our own previous thinking and experiencing but also processes for reasoning our way out of or around them. These model experiences must be charged with meaning for us. We cannot be *indifferent* to them. We must sustain them in our minds by our sense of their importance as they sustain and guide us in our thinking.

What does this imply for teaching? It implies a somewhat different content or material focus. Our own minds and experiences must become the subject of our study and learning. Indeed, only to the extent that the content of our own experiences becomes an essential part of study will the usual subject matter truly be learned. By the same token, the experiences of others must become part of what we study. But experiences of any kind should always be critically analyzed, and students must do their own analyses and clearly recognize what they are doing.

This entails that students become explicitly aware of the logic of experience. All experiences have three elements, each of which may require some special scrutiny in the analytic process: *1)* something to be experienced (some actual situation or other); *2)* an experiencing subject (with a point of view, framework of beliefs, attitudes, desires, and values); and *3)* some interpretation or conceptualization of the situation. To take any experience apart, then, students must be sensitive to three distinctive sets of questions:

1) What are the raw facts, what is the most neutral description of the situation? If one describes the experience this way, and another disagrees, on what description *can* they agree?

2) What interests, attitudes, desires, or concerns do I bring to the situation? Am I always aware of them? Why or why not?

3) How am I conceptualizing or interpreting the situation in light of my point of view? How else might it be interpreted?

Students must also explore the interrelationships of these parts: How did my point of view, values, desires, etc., affect what I noticed about the situation? How did they prevent me from noticing other things? How would I have interpreted the situation had I noticed those other things? How did my point of view, desires, etc., affect my interpretation? How *should* I interpret the situation?

If students have many assignments that require them to analyze their experiences and the experiences of others along these lines, with ample opportunity to argue among themselves about which interpretations make the most sense and why, then they will begin to amass a catalogue of critically analyzed experiences. If the experiences illuminate the pitfalls of thought, the analysis and the models of thinking they suggest will be the foundation for their intellectual traits and character. They will develop intellectual virtues because they had thought their way to them and internalized them as concrete understandings and insights, not because they took them up as slogans. Their basic values and their thinking processes will be in a symbiotic relationship to each other. Their intellectual and affective lives will become more integrated. Their standards for thinking will be implicit in their own thinking, rather than in texts, teachers, or the authority of a peer group.

✦ Conclusion

We do not now teach for the intellectual virtues. If we did, not only would we have a basis for integrating the curriculum, we would also have a basis for integrating the cognitive and affective lives of students. Such integration is the basis for strong sense critical thinking, for moral development, and for citizenship. The moral, social, and political issues we face in everyday life are increasingly intellectually complex. Their settlement relies on circumstances and events that are interpreted in a variety of (often conflicting) ways. For example, should our government publish misinformation to mislead another government or group which it considers terrorist? Is it ethical to tolerate a "racist" regime such as South Africa, or are we morally obligated to attempt to overthrow it? Is it ethical to support anti-communist groups that use, or have used, torture, rape, or murder as tools in their struggle? When, if ever, should the CIA attempt to overthrow a government it perceives as undemocratic? How can one distinguish "terrorists" from "freedom fighters"?

Or, consider issues that are more "domestic" or "personal". Should deliberate pollutors be considered "criminals"? How should we balance off "dollar losses" against "safety gains"? That is, how much money should we be willing to spend to save human lives? What is deliberate deception in advertising and business practices? Should one protect incompetent individuals within one's profession from exposure? How should one reconcile or balance one's personal vested interest against the public good? What moral or civic responsibility exists to devote time and energy to the public good as against one's private interests and amusements?

These are just a few of the many complex moral, political, and social issues that virtually all citizens must face. The response of the citizenry to such issues defines the moral character of society. These issues challenge our intellectual honesty, courage, integrity, empathy, and fairmindedness. Given their complexity, they require perseverance and confidence in reason. People easily become cynical, intellectually lazy, or retreat into simplistic models of learning and the world they learned in school and see and hear on TV. On the other hand, it is doubtful that the fundamental conflicts and antagonisms in the world can be solved or resolved by sheer power or abstract good will. Good-heartedness and power are insufficient for creating a just world. Some modest development of the intellectual virtues seems essential for future human survival and well-being. Whether the energy, the resources, and the insights necessary for this development can be significantly mustered remains open. This is certain: we will never succeed in cultivating traits whose roots we do not understand and whose development we do not foster.

Chapter 16

Dialogical Thinking:
Critical Thought Essential to the Acquisition of Rational Knowledge and Passions

Abstract

Passions, Paul argues, can be rational or irrational. To become a rational person we must develop rational passions: "a passionate drive for clarity, accuracy, and fairmindedness, a fervor for getting to the bottom of things, to the deepest root issues, for listening sympathetically to opposition points of view, a compelling drive to seek out evidence, an intense aversion to contradiction, sloppy thinking, inconsistent application of standards, a devotion to truth as against self-interest." These emotional commitments are essential to the development of rationality, and only intensive dialogical and dialectical thinking over years will produce them. Paul develops this thesis at length in one of his most popular papers (Teaching Thinking Skills: Theory and Practice *1987*).*

We all have a natural tendency toward egocentricity — a tendency to assume our perspectives to be the only (or only plausible) one, to resist considering issues from the perspectives of others. This tendency is reinforced rather than combatted by approaches to problem-solving and critical thinking which are technical or monological in nature. Here, as elsewhere, Paul argues for the importance of teaching students the art of dialogical thinking. He notes that most "real-life" problems are multilogical in nature, and thus require consideration from multiple points of view.

The main thrust of the argument in this paper is pedagogical, in that, when students compare and defend multiple points of view on issues, exploring and testing them, they become more truly convinced of what they learn, and thus take that knowledge to heart. Even subjects which are, or can be seen to be, technical should be taught dialogically, since students need to reason back and forth between their own ideas about subjects (e.g., ideas about numbers or about the physical world) and the ideas being presented to them by their teacher, the textbook, or other students. Teaching all subjects through a dialogical approach, Paul emphasizes, encourages students to make their ideas explicit and to critique them, making their own ideas more sophisticated, rather than superimposing "inert school knowledge" upon "activated student ignorance". Students, in other words, need to reason their way to knowledge. Otherwise, their own deep-seated preconceptions will remain alive and ultimately displace what they passively "learned" in the classroom.

*W*hen psychologists concerned with cognitive psychology and problem solving want to test their theories, they choose different kinds of problems than those generally chosen by philosophers concerned with critical thinking and rationality. Cognitive psychologists like to analyze and generalize about problems defined, explored, and settled in a fundamentally self-contained way. They prefer atomic problems, especially those having to do with technology, math, science, and engineering. Mathematical and verbal puzzles are a favorite. They choose problems that can be represented and settled in a definitive way within one frame of reference, for example,

1. A man once offended a fortune-teller by laughing at her predictions and saying that fortune telling was all nonsense. He offended her so much, in fact, that she cast a spell on him which turned him into both a compulsive gambler and, in addition, a consistent loser. That was pretty mean. We would expect the spell would shortly have turned him into a miserable, impoverished wreck. Instead, he soon married a wealthy businesswoman who took him to the casino every day, gave him money, and smiled happily as he lost it at the roulette table. They lived happily ever after. Why was the man's wife so happy to see him lose?

2. You are visiting a strange country in which there are just two kinds of people — truth tellers and liars. Truth tellers *always* tell the truth and liars *always* lie. You hail the first two people you meet and say, "Are you truth tellers or liars?" The first mumbles something you can't hear. The second says, "He says he is a truth teller. He is a truth teller and so am I." Can you trust the directions that these two may give you?

3. Ten full crates of walnuts weigh 410 pounds, whereas an empty crate weighs 10 pounds. How much do the walnuts alone weigh?

4. In how many days of the week does the third letter of the day's name immediately follow the first letter of the day's name in the alphabet?

I call these problems (adapted from Hayes, 1940) and the means by which they are solved *monological*. This implies that they are settled within one frame of reference with a definite set of logical moves. When the right set of moves is made, the problem is settled. The proposed answer or solution can be shown to be the "right" answer or solution by standards implicit in the frame of reference.

Philosophers concerned with critical thinking and rationality are drawn to a very different kind of problem. They tend to choose non-atomic problems, problems that are inextricably joined to other problems and form clusters, with some conceptual messiness about them and often important values lurking in the background. When the problems have an empirical dimension, that dimension tends to have a controversial scope. One must argue how the facts ought to be considered and interpreted and how to determine their significance. When they have a conceptual dimension, there tend to be arguably different ways to pin the concepts down.

Consequently, the problem's precise identification and definition depend upon some arguable choice among alternative frames of reference. I call these questions *multilogical*. More than one kind of incompatible logic can be advanced for their settlement. Indeed, more than one frame of reference can be used to argue their construal.

Since more than one frame of reference is contending for their construal and settlement, we must somehow "test" the frames of reference themselves. To test whole frames of reference without begging the question one must set the frames of reference against each other dialectically, and test the logical strength of one against the logical strength of the rest by appealing to standards not peculiar to any.

If we do not know how to make the case for an answer proposed from a contending frame of reference, we can find a proponent to make the case for it. Then we listen to the case made from a competing frame of reference. Most especially, we try to determine how successfully each constructed logic answers the objections framed from opposing perspectives. A trial by jury with opposing arguments of prosecution and defense illustrates a traditional approach to multilogical issues.

However, if no informed proponents of opposing points of view are available, we have to reconstruct the arguments ourselves. We must enter into the opposing points of view on our own and frame the dialogical exchange ourselves. I contend that this skill of empathy and reciprocity is essential to the development of the rational mind. Only such activity forces us outside our own frame of reference, which, given the primary nature of the human mind, tends to become an inflexible mind set. Unless we counter this tendency early on, it begins a process that becomes progressively harder to reverse.

Even though the lives of children are deeply involved in multilogical questions, and how children respond to these questions has a profound influence on how they later define and address the central issues they will face as adults, children rarely have a real opportunity in school to reflect upon these questions in mutually supportive dialogical settings. I have in mind questions *like* the following (although not necessarily these *precisely*):

Who am I? What am I like? What are the other people around me like? What are people of different backgrounds, religions, and nations like? How much am I like others? How much am I unlike them? What kind of a world do I live in? When should I trust? When should I distrust? What should I accept? What should I question? How should I understand my past, the past of parents, my ethnic group, my religion, my nation? Who are my friends? Who are my enemies? What is a friend? How am I like and unlike my enemy? What is most important to me? How should I live my life? What responsibilities do I have to others? What responsibilities do they have to me? What responsibilities do I have to my friends? Do I have any responsibilities to people I don't like? To people who don't like me? To my enemies? Do my parents love me? Do I love them? What is love? What is hate? What is indifference? Does it matter if others do not approve of me? When does it matter? When should I ignore what others think? What rights do I have? What rights should I give to others? What should I do if others do not respect my rights? Should I get what I want? Should I question what I want? Should I take what I want if I am strong enough or smart enough to get away with it? Who comes out ahead in this world, the strong or the good person? Is it worthwhile to be good? Are authorities good or just strong?

Questions like these underlie most of the satisfactions and frustrations of childhood. The deepest orientation of the person to self and life depends on how the individual responds to them.

✦ Background Principles

Before proceeding with my argument for the need for dialogical thinking to develop rational knowledge and passions, I would like to introduce the following background principles:

1. A reasonable person solves problems or settles questions about what to do or believe by adjusting his or her thinking to the nature of each question. Different questions require different modes of thinking. If a question's settlement presupposes the gathering of some empirical data, a reasonable person uses his or her thinking to facilitate that gathering. If that gathering requires examining sources arguing from more than one point of view, the person looks at multiple sources and listens to the case for more than one point of view. If reasonable doubts can be raised about the accuracy, relevance, completeness, or implications of these data, they raise them. If there are values or purposes implicit in the problem-solving activity that a reasonable person would clarify or question, he or she clarifies or questions them.

2. People have both a primary and a secondary nature. Our primary nature is spontaneous, egocentric, and strongly prone to irrational belief formation. It is the basis for our instinctual thought. People need no training to believe what they want to believe, what serves their immediate interests, what preserves their sense of personal comfort and righteousness, what minimizes their sense of inconsistency, and what presupposes their own correctness. People need no special training to believe what those around them believe, what their parents and friends believe, what they learn from religious and school authorities, what they often hear from or read in the media, and what is commonly believed in the nation in which they are raised. People need no training to think that those who disagree with them are wrong and probably prejudiced. People need no training to assume that their own most

fundamental beliefs are self-evidently true or easily justified by evidence. People naturally and spontaneously identify with their own beliefs and experience most disagreement as personal attack, adopting as a result a defensiveness that minimizes their capacity to empathize with or enter into points of view other than their own.

On the other hand, people need extensive and systematic practice to develop their secondary nature, their implicit capacity to function rationally. They need extensive and systematic practice to recognize their tendencies to form irrational beliefs. They need extensive practice to develop a dislike of inconsistency, a love of clarity, a passion to seek reasons and evidence and to be fair to points of view other than their own. People need extensive practice to recognize that they indeed have a point of view, that they live *inferentially,* that they do not have a direct pipeline to reality, that one can easily have an overwhelming inner sense of the correctness of one's views and still be wrong.

3. Instruction that does not further the development of human rationality, though it may properly be called training, is not *education.* The cultivation of the educated mind and person presupposes the cultivation of rational skills and passions. Insofar as schooling furthers, uses, or reinforces irrational belief formation, it violates its responsibility to *educate.* A society of uneducated persons is incompatible with democracy.

Unfortunately, the rule rather than the exception in schooling today is that students are continually encouraged to believe that there are more or less authoritative answers readily available for most of the important questions and decisions we face, or at least, authoritative frames of reference through which such answers can be pursued. Students are led to believe that they are surrounded by experts whose command of knowledge enables them to definitively settle the important issues they face socially and personally. Students tend to ego-identify with the monological answers of their parents, teachers, or peers. They have no real experience with dialogical thinking.

✦ Most Important Issues of Everyday Life Are Multilogical and Human

We do not live in a disembodied world of objects and physical laws. Instead, we live in a humanly contrived and constructed world. And there is more than one way to contrive and construct the world. Not only our social relations but our inner cognitive and affective lives are inferential in nature. We do not deal with the world-in-itself but the the world-as-we-define-it in relation to our interests, perspective, and point of view. We shape our interests and point of view in the light of our sense of what significant others think, and so live in a world that is exceedingly narrow, static, and closed. To protect ourselves, we assume our view is moral and objective. For the most part, our viewpoints are in fact amoral and subjective. Consider Goffman's (1959) explanation.

> In their capacity as performers, individuals will be concerned with maintaining the impression that they are living up to the many standards by which they and their products are judged. Because these standards are so numerous and so pervasive, the individuals who are performers dwell more than we might think in a moral world. But, *qua* performers, individuals are concerned not with the moral issue of realizing these standards, but with the amoral issue of engineering a convincing impression that these standards are being realized. Our activity, then, is largely concerned with moral matters, but as performers we do not have a moral concern with them. (p. 19)

This is not, as Whitehead (1929) shrewdly points out, how we *describe* ourselves,

> It does not matter what men say in words, so long as their activities are controlled by settled instincts. The words may ultimately destroy the instincts. But until this has occurred, words do not count.

As young children we begin to internalize images and concepts of what we and others are like, of what, for example, Americans are like, of what atheists, Christians, communists, parents, children, business-people, farmers, liberals, conservatives, left-wingers, right-wingers, salespeople, foreigners, patriots, Palestinians, Kiwanis Club members, cheerleaders, politicians, Nazis, ballet dancers, terrorists, union leaders, guerrillas, freedom fighters, doctors, Marines, scientists, mathematicians, contractors, waitresses, are *like*. We then ego-identify with our conceptions, we assume them to be accurate, and spontaneously use them to guide our day-to-day decisions.

Unwittingly, we begin as children — and, unless we get extensive dialogical practice, we continue as adults — to use egocentric and self-serving theories of people and the world. We organize our experience and make judgments from the perspective of assumptions and theories we would not admit to having if questioned. Studies in social perception demonstrate this in detail. Toch and Smith (1968) summarize it as follows:

> The process of reaching a value-judgment, the unconscious weighing that man's brain is able to make of numerous cues during a fraction of a second, is by no means a random and chaotic procedure. The weighing process, resulting in a perception, goes on for a purpose, whether that purpose is seeking food, adjusting one's footsteps to a curbing, picking up a book, reading or underlining certain passages in a book, joining some gang or group, or accepting or rejecting some political ideology. (p. 6)

> We see people as instant wholes. A "theory" is commonly viewed as something used exclusively by scientists. The discussion, however, emphasizes that everyone has, and inevitably uses, theories about people. These theories guide the wholes they perceive and the parts that they fit into the wholes. (p. 10)
>
> We all use theories in dealing with people: We invent concepts, assume relationships between them, and make predictions from our assumptions. Our theories are not, however, useful in the scientific sense, for they are implicit rather than explicit. That is, we are only dimly aware of our theories. As a result, we rarely make any real effort to test them. Yet they rule our impressions and our judgments. (p. 13)

People from different ethnic groups, religions, social classes, and cultural allegiances tend to form different but equally egocentric belief systems and use them equally unmindfully. These different construals of the world represent alternative settlements of the same basic set of issues all people continually face. We must all decide who we are as individuals and members of a community. We must construct a history, a place in time. We must envision an emergent future. We must decide who our friends and enemies are. We must invest our time, energy, and resources in some projects and not others. We must decide what is *ours* and *why* it is ours. We must decide what is just and unjust and what grievances and grudges we have. We must decide to whom to give and from whom to withhold credibility. We must decide what is possible and impossible, what to fear and what to hope for.

All of these decisions determine our fundamental life-style and, ultimately, our destiny. They all presuppose answers to multilogical issues. Yet few of us realize how we internalize and construct a logic, a point of view, an organized way of experiencing, reasoning, and judging. Most of us, unfortunately, think of the world in terms of a monological definition of reality. How we see things simply seems *the correct way* to see them. How others see them simply seems wrong or prejudiced.

This can be illustrated by the flagrant differences between the colonial and British perceptions of the so-called Boston Massacre. The accounts at the time testify to the way in which people automatically presuppose the correctness of their ethnocentric perceptions:

1. A colonial onlooker, standing 20 yards from the colonists, gave sworn testimony to the justices of the peace on April 23, 1775, that the British fired the first shot.

2. A colonial Tory (a sympathizer with the British) wrote on May 4, 1775, to General Gage (the British commander in Boston), that the colonists fired the first shot.

3. A young British lieutenant wrote in his diary on April 19, 1775, that the colonists fired one or two shots, then the British returned the fire without any orders.

4. The commander of the colonial militia, John Parker, in an official deposition on April 25, 1775, said that he ordered the militia to disperse and not to fire, but the British fired on them without any provocation.

5. The *London Gazette* stated on June 10, 1775, to its British readers that the colonists fired on the British troops first.

Most teachers, I suspect, simply assume the account that favors their nation and then teach it as fact. Thus, students are taught to think mono-logically about historical events.

Consequently, most students (and their teachers) fail to grasp the essentially multilogical character of history. Since they don't see that all history is history-from-a-point-of-view, students fail to recognize appropriate logical parallels, for example, that all news is news-from-a-point-of-view. The result is that students do not learn how to read history or the news critically.

✦ *Inert Knowledge and Activated Ignorance*

Whitehead described the problem of inert knowledge — knowledge that we in some sense *have* but do not use when logically relevant, knowledge that just sits there in our minds, as it were, without activating force. Typically, this inability to put knowledge to work is viewed as an inability to *transfer*. In light of the above, I suggest instead that the problem is mainly due to our already having *activated* beliefs firmly entrenched in instinctual egocentric thinking.

The young child does not come to school with an empty head ready to be filled with new ideas and knowledge. The egocentric mind abhors a vacuum. The capacity to suspend judgment pending evidence is a higher order, secondary-nature, skill. The problem of inert knowledge is equivalent to the problem of *activated ignorance*. Children do not *transfer* the knowledge they learn in school to new settings because they already have activated ideas and beliefs to use in those settings.

The child's own emerging egocentric conceptions of children, teachers, parents, fun, work, play, and the physical world are much more activated and real than any alternative conceptions fostered by classroom instruction or textbooks. Only by bringing out the child's own ideas in dialogical and dialectical settings can the child begin to reconstruct and progressively transcend these conceptions. As long as school learning is simply superimposed on top of the child's own activated ignorance, that ignorance will continue to rule in the life-world of the child; scholastic learning will remain largely inert. Perhaps this is partly why so many adults, including those in high positions, often seem to act or talk like egocentric children.

There are, therefore, at least two fundamental justifications for giving children extensive dialogical practice in school: *1)* such practice is essential for all of the intrinsically multi-logical issues that the child must face, and *2)* such practice is essential for the child to come to discover, reconstruct, and ultimately transcend those ideas and beliefs uncritically and unconsciously internalized. A case can be made for the value of dialogical reasoning even with monological issues, as will be shown by the work of Jack Easley on math and science education. But first, let me be more explicit about the nature of dialogical thinking.

✦ Dialogical Thinking in Early School Years

Children begin developing an egocentric identity, point of view, and frame of reference through which they experience, think about, and judge the world. Many of their beliefs come from those around them. Nevertheless, from their earliest days, they come up against opposing points of view, differing interpretations of events, contradictory judgments, and incompatible lines of reasoning. First their parents and peers, later their teachers and other authorities, often disagree with them and thwart their egocentric desires.

But instruction does little to provide children with a way of entering into thoughts and feelings other than their own. Of course, they *hear* what others say, but they do not experience the inner logic of alternative points of view. That children can develop in this direction is demonstrated in their play: "You can be the mommy. I'll be the daddy. And my sister can be the baby." But schools do not, by and large, take advantage of this tendency and use it to construct exercises wherein students present reasons and evidence for alternative conclusions.

Children often use their capacity to think up reasons for and against an idea or decision only when they are already egocentrically for or against it. Of course, they must often bow to the superior power or authority of a parent, teacher, or older peer. But they rarely do so by entering into the point of view of the other and rationally assenting to it. As a result, they do not grasp that they themselves have a point of view. Rather, they tend to make absolute moral judgments about themselves and others. They frequently develop hostile feelings (often repressed) toward themselves or toward those who force them, rightly or wrongly, to accept their point of view. They do not have an opportunity to work out their own thoughts and discover ways of judging *reasons* without judging the *worth of the person* advancing them.

Children need assignments in multilogical issues. They need to discover opposing points of view in non-threatening situations. They need to put their ideas into words, advance conclusions, and justify them. They need to discover their own assumptions and those of others. They need to discover their own inconsistencies and those of others. They do this best when they learn how to role-play the thinking of others, advance conclusions other than their own, and construct reasons supporting them.

Children need to do this for the multilogical issues — the conflicting points of view, interpretations, and conclusions — that they inevitably face in their everyday lives. But perhaps we should go further. All or most of what we learn rationally requires dialogical exchanges and opportunities to judge between conflicting points of view. The work of Jack Easley on math and science education suggests this thesis.

✦ Should Dialogical Instruction Be Used for Monological Issues?

In a series of articles on mathematics and science education, Jack Easley (1983a, b; 1984a) argues that children should learn how to solve virtually all problems — even the most monological and formalistic ones — dialogically or dialectically. He argues that studies indicate that primary school teachers 1) cannot *transmit* knowledge, 2) should therefore leave most discussion of math and science content to pupils, 3) should choose and present appropriately challenging problems and tasks to the pupils, 4) should train group leaders to facilitate dialogical exchanges, and 5) should serve, fundamentally, as moderators of class communication. Most important, children should work in small but heterogeneous groups, trying to convince and understand each other. Through arguing, children discover their own views' strengths and weaknesses and also discover contrasts between their views and the views of others. Here are some of the ways Easely (1984b) formulates these points:

> Primary teachers in the U.S., at least, should leave most discussion of mathematics and physical science content to their pupils. *a)* Cognitive research shows that young children develop and test alternative rational explanations which authoritative exposition can't displace. *b)* The conflicts that arise between presentations by teachers and texts and the pupil's unexamined math-science concepts generate severe anxieties about mathematics and science in most children....
>
> Only by reflection on the alternative schemes in the light of conflicts with standard schemes can revisions be produced....
>
> Those few students who do truly master mathematical or scientific subjects do so through a long process of doubting and challenging authority which few teachers are willing to take the time to do, even in pre-service training....
>
> Teachers of regular primary grade classes should train group leaders on a regular basis to provide appropriate challenges for every member of their group....

Primary children should strive first to develop expression in some form by working in heterogeneous groups, trying to convince each other by clear speaking and writing....

They should also learn to say in advance what kind of contribution to the dialogue they are trying to make: an objection, an alternative view, a supporting point, etc....

I became convinced that teachers should be accepted by school reformers as the persons who are effectively in charge of instruction and who can change only as their perceptions of the classroom context are opened up through dialogues which respect the perceptions they have built from their own experience....

In Kitamaeno School, use of peer group dialogues helped children recognize alternative schemes and deal with them. Organizing children into small working groups around pre-selected appropriately challenging tasks required group leaders with confidence and some training in what to do when things went wrong....

The teachers' role was to present, often very dramatically, the challenging problem they had selected for the lesson, and almost totally abstaining from demonstrating or explaining how to solve it and to serve as master of ceremonies to see that every child had ample opportunity to be heard and took the responsibility to express ideas and to listen critically to those of others....

As children discover they have different solutions, different methods, different frameworks, and they try to convince each other, or at least to understand each other, they revise their understanding in many small but important ways....

As you can see, Easley argues that, irrespective of whether we have a precise and thoroughly defensible monological system for settling certain types of problems, children must work their way to that mono-logic through dia-logic. Since students have alternative beliefs and frames of reference, even regarding scientific and mathematical concepts, they need to confront them or they will remain implicit, unchallenged, and unreconstructed. If we do not provide an environment for children to discover their own *activated* ideas, they may become and remain invincibly ignorant when it comes to putting knowledge into action. Their biases, stereotypes, distortions, illusions, and misconceptions will not dissolve without the purging power of dialogical exchange. They will simply superimpose adult beliefs on top of unreconstructed but still highly activated infantile ones.

Students leave school not only with unreconstructed mathematical and physical ideas but with unreconstructed personal, social, moral, historical, economic, and political views. Students leave school not knowing what they *really* — that is *deeply* — believe. Students leave school with much inert knowledge and even more activated ignorance. Therefore, students do not understand how to write, think, or speak in ways that organize and express what they believe, or read or listen in ways that allow them to understand and assess the thought of another. Students do not know how they respond to the mass media and to what extent it reinforces their subconscious egocentric or sociocentric views. They do not grasp how to read a newspaper or a book critically or how to listen to a lecture critically. They have no *rational* passions. They feel deeply only about egocentric concerns, justifying getting what they want and avoiding what they do not want. If dialogical thinking enables students to reconstruct mathematical and scientific ideas, it is most certainly called for on personal, social, moral, historical, economic, and political ones.

✦ Dialogical Thinking as a Strategy for Breaking Down Egocentric Identifications and Mind Sets

Children must experience dialogical thinking because such thinking is essential for rationally approaching the most significant and pervasive everyday human problems, and without it they will not develop the intellectual tools essential for confronting their own instinctual egocentric thought. Until we discover our own egocentric thinking, we cannot monitor or work through it. Indeed, to hold beliefs egocentrically is to hold them in non-testable ways. As Piaget (1976) puts it:

> Many adults are still egocentric in their ways of thinking. Such people interpose between themselves and reality an imaginary or mystical world, and they reduce everything to this individual point of view. Unadapted to ordinary conditions, they seem to be immersed in an inner life that is all the more intense. Does this make them conscious of themselves? Does egocentrism point the way to a truer introspection? On the contrary, it can easily be seen that there is a way of living in oneself that develops a great wealth of inexpressible feelings, of personal images and schemas, while at the same time it impoverishes analysis and consciousness of self. (p. 209)

Like egocentric children, egocentric adults assimilate everything they hear or experience to their own point of view. They learn how to affect reciprocity — to create the appearance of entering into points of view other than their own. But when there is conflict, they "enter" them only to negate or refute. They never genuinely leave their own mind set.

I am reminded of a distinction drawn by the sociologist, C. Wright Mills (1962), illuminating how people relate to their belief systems. Mills argued that there were three types of believers — vulgar, sophisticated, and "plain" (critical). Vulgar believers can only operate with slogans and stereotypes within a point of view with which they egocentrically identify. Vulgar Marxists use slogans like "Power to the people!" "Smash the state!" "Down with the capitalist pigs!" to badger their would-be opponents. They are not interested in reading books on capitalism or by capitalists, but consider them only as the enemy.

In contrast, sophisticated Marxists do read books on capitalism or by capitalists only to refute them. They stand on their heads if necessary to show that Marxism is in all senses and respects superior to capitalism. They might be intellectually creative, but they use their creativity to further one and only one point of view.

Only critical believers would, in Mills's sense, enter sympathetically into opposing points of view, for only they recognize weaknesses in their own. If they become Marxists, it is because they read Marx as Marx read others — sympathetically and critically. They learn from criticism and are not egocentrically attached to their point of view. They understand they must continually develop and refine it by a fuller and richer consideration of the available evidence and reasoning, through exposure to the best thinking in alternative points of view.

If Mills is right, we also have vulgar, sophisticated, and critical capitalists; vulgar, sophisticated, and critical Christians; vulgar, sophisticated, and critical North Americans, Frenchmen, and Soviets; vulgar, sophisticated, and critical Freudians, and so on. Given their fundamental mode of thinking, their shared capacity to enter into points of view other than their own and to learn from criticism, critical Marxists, capitalists, Christians, Muslims, North Americans, Frenchmen, Soviets, Freudians, and Skinnerians share more in common with each other than they do with their vulgar or sophisticated counterparts.

A fundamental problem of schooling today is that schools in all societies tend to produce vulgar and sophisticated, rather than critical, believers. This problem is mainly due to the lack of dialogical thinking. Most instruction is monological, with various *authoritative* perspectives being nurtured and inculcated. When the inculcated perspective is incompatible with the child's egocentric beliefs, the academically learned perspective is simply superimposed as a facade or veneer. This veneer may itself be egocentrically defended, but the defense is merely *verbal*, because the primary and more primitive system is maintained in behavior. Hence, people can vehemently defend Christianity and yet continually behave in a most un-Christian fashion, apparently and self-righteously oblivious to their contradictions. Or they can defend democracy with passion and abandon, and yet act to undermine all possibility of its being practiced. This is true of any system of beliefs, whether scientific, religious, social, political, or personal. Wherever we find people, we find blatant contradictions between word and deed. Wherever we find people, we find a great deal of ego-defensive self-delusion.

✦ Teaching Critical Thinking in the Strong Sense: School as Purgatory

I would like to use a religious metaphor to characterize the problem of education. For a Catholic, there are three possible divine dispensations as a result of how one lives. In addition to heaven or hell, one may be sent to purgatory, a place in which one must work one's way back to God. The assumption is that one can die with one's thoughts and will still somewhat resistant to God. One then must go through a process of purging one's sinful tendencies. This process involves some pain and struggle, but issues ultimately in a purification of heart and will, a rooting out of one's sinful tendencies, and a reconstruction of one's inner thought.

This concept is apt for understanding what schooling would be if we were to cultivate that very rare breed — the educated, rational person. If we want persons who believe critically, who are neither vulgar nor sophisticated in their beliefs, then we waste our time by trying to make school heaven — all fun and games, all pleasant and satisfying, all positive reinforcement, all sweetness and light, with no confusion, struggle, or dispute. Of course, I take it for granted that we will get nowhere by going to the other extreme and making it hell. The challenge is to foster a process whereby students progressively and over a long period of time rid themselves of their egocentric and sociocentric beliefs and attachments. Presently, it appears that schooling does little more than make people's instinctual egocentrism a bit more sophisticated, at least with respect to those issues, that involve our collective egos.

However, this does not mean that schools that foster dialogical or dialectical thinking would be hotbeds of strident argument, closedminded debate, or personal trauma. Our experience of argument, debate, and controversy occurs now in the context of un-reconstituted egocentric attachment. People now typically argue for egocentric purposes and with egocentric ends in view. They argue now to score points, *defeat* the other person, make their point of view *look* good. They experience "argument" as *battle*, not as a mutual or cooperative search for a fuller understanding.

Yet I know from years of working with students that they *can* learn to reason dialogically in mutually supportive ways, that they can learn to experience dialogical thought as leading to discovery, not victory. To achieve this end we must first ensure that, as soon as possible, they learn to argue for and against each and every important point of view and each basic belief or conclusion that they are to take seriously. We must also raise issues that they care about and which engage their egocentric thoughts and beliefs. We should begin with beliefs that are mildly egocentric and work slowly to those that are deeply embedded in the ego. Then the dialogical thinking we nurture helps develop critical thinking in the strong sense.

Teaching critical thinking in the strong sense means teaching so that students explicate, understand, and critique their own deepest prejudices, biases, and misconceptions, thereby encouraging students to discover and contest their own egocentric and sociocentric tendencies. Only if we experientially contest our inevitable egocentric and sociocentric habits of thought can we hope to genuinely think rationally. Only dialogical thinking about basic issues that matter to the individual provides the kind of practice and skill essential to strong-sense critical thinking. I grant that every student needs to develop the particular skills that Robert Ennis and others have delineated, but I am arguing that *how* these skills are nurtured is crucial.

Students need to develop all critical thinking skills in dialogical settings to develop ethically, rationally, that is, to develop genuine fairmindedness. If simply taught as atomic skills apart from empathically entering into points of view students fear or dislike, critical thinking will in the end simply be used to rationalize prejudices and preconceptions, or convince people that their point of view is *the* correct one. Students will then merely be transformed from vulgar to sophisticated, but not to *critical* thinkers.

✦ Fact, Opinion, and Reasoned Judgment

Unfortunately, many programs designed to enhance critical thinking fail to give students insight into the nature of multilogical issues and the need for dialogical thinking. They often teach as if all questions are reducible either to matters of fact (where science, math, engineering, and technical learning are dominant) or matters of opinion (where personal taste, culture, religion, preference, and faith are dominant). This happens when students are told to divide beliefs or statements into facts and opinions. Neither category allows dialogical thinking. It is presumably unnecessary with facts, because scientific, mathematical, and technological procedures and methods presuppose relatively agreed-upon frames of reference and modes of issue settlement. It is useless with opinions, because presumably one cannot reason in matters of pure taste: *De gustibus non est disputandem.* Schools under the sway of this view take as their first and foremost responsibility teaching students *the facts,* and then secondarily, passing on the shared values and beliefs of the culture.

Unfortunately, a taxonomy that divides all beliefs into either facts or opinions leaves out the most important category: *reasoned judgment.* Most important issues are not simply matters of fact, nor are they essentially matters of faith, taste, or preference. They call for our reasoned judgment. They can be understood from different points of view through different frames of reference. People approach them with different assumptions, concepts, priorities, and ends in view. When analytically applied to these perspectives in dialectical contexts, the tools of critical thinking enable us to grasp genuine weaknesses. The dialectical experience enables us to gain this perspective.

For example, it is exceedingly difficult to judge the case made by a prosecutor in a trial *until* we have heard the arguments for the defense. Only by stepping out of the perspective of the prosecutor and actually organizing the evidence in language designed to make the strongest case for the defense, can we begin to grasp the true strength and weakness of the prosecutor's case. This approach is the only proper way to approach the important issues we face in our lives, and I am amazed that we and our textbooks refuse to recognize it. The most basic issues simply do not reduce to unadulterated fact or arbitrary opinion. True, they often have a factual dimension. But often some of the alleged facts are questionable. And we often must decide which facts are *most* important, which should be made central, and which should be deemed peripheral or even irrelevant. Then, typically, there are alternative arguable interpretations and implications. Make your own list of the ten most important issues and see if this is not true (but beware of the tendency to see your own answers to these issues as self-evident facts!).

✦ The Cultivation of Rational Passions

To grasp the problem of teaching critical thinking skills in a strong sense, we must challenge the reason-versus-emotion stereotype, which fosters the view that a rational person is cold, unfeeling, and generally without passion, whereas an irrational person is passionate but unintellectual. A false dichotomy is set up between reason and passion, and we are forced to choose between the two as incompatible opposites.

But this point of view is profoundly misleading. All action requires the marshaling of energy. All action presupposes a driving force. We must *care* about something to do something about it. Emotions, feelings, and passions of some kind or other underlie all human behavior. What we should want to free ourselves from is not emotion, feeling, or passion *per se*, but irrational emotions, irrational feelings, and irrational passions. A highly developed intellect can be used for good or ill either at the service of rational or irrational passions. Only the development of rational passions can prevent our intelligence from becoming the tool of our egocentric emotions and the point of view embedded in them. A passionate drive for clarity, accuracy, and fairmindedness, a fervor for getting to the bottom of things, to the deepest root issues, for listening sympathetically to opposition points of view, a compelling drive to seek out evidence, an intensive aversion to contradiction, sloppy thinking, inconsistent application of standards, a devotion to truth as against self-interest — these are essential commitments of the rational person. They enable us to assent rationally to a belief even when it is ridiculed by others, to question what is passionately believed and socially sanctioned, to conquer the fear of abandoning a long and deeply held belief. There is nothing passive, bland, or complacent about such a person.

Emotions and beliefs are always inseparably wedded together. When we describe ourselves as driven by irrational emotions, we are also driven by the irrational *beliefs* that structure and support them. When we conquer an irrational emotion through the use of our reason, we do it by using our rational passions. To put this another way and link it more explicitly with the earlier sections of this chapter, our primary egocentric nature is a complex mixture of belief, values, drives, and assumptions. It is an integrated cognitive and affective system. It generates a total frame of reference through which we can come to perceive, think, and judge. When we develop our secondary nature, we develop a countervailing system, equally complex and complete. We may of course experience intense internal struggles between these incompatible modes of being. Both systems can become highly *intellectualized* so that intelligence per se is not what distinguishes them. It is quite possible to find highly intelligent but essentially irrational persons, as well as basically rational ones of limited intelligence. In this way, a highly intelligent but sophisticated (i.e., sophistic) thinker can create the illusion of defending a more rational point of view than that defended by a thinker who is basically rational but not as clever.

Therefore, as educators we should embrace the nurturing of rational passions as an essential dimension in the development of the *thinking* of our students. Teachers must model rational passions. This, of course, presupposes that teachers genuinely have them. It will do no good for a teacher to pretend. This is not a matter of *technique*. This is an important reason why successful critical thinking instruction cannot be achieved as the result of a few weekend in-service workshops.

✦ Critical and Creative Thinking

Just as it is misleading to talk of developing a student's capacity to think critically without facing the problem of cultivating the student's rational passions — the necessary driving force behind the rational use of all critical thinking skills — so too is it misleading to talk of developing a student's ability to think critically as something separate from the student's ability to think creatively. All rational dialogical thinking requires creativity, because dialogical thinking is a series of reciprocal creative acts wherein we move up and back between categorically different imagined roles. We must first of all imagine ourselves in a given frame of reference. Then we must imaginatively construct some reasons to support it. Next we must step outside it and imagine ourselves responding to those reasons from an opposing point of view. Then we must imagine ourselves back in the first point of view to respond to the opposition we just created. Next we must change roles again and create a further response, and so on. The imagination and its creative powers are continually called forth. Each act must fit the unique move preceding it. In dialogical exchange, we cannot predict in advance what another, or indeed what we, will say. Yet what we say, to be rational, must respond to the logic of what the other just said. Furthermore, integrating the strengths of opposing views, and eliminating weak points are also creative and constructive acts. One must creatively develop a new point of view.

Students need not begin by playing both sides of a dialogue simultaneously. But we should continually nurture their ability to frame dialogical exchanges, first brief, then extended ones. Their creative imagination will be continually challenged to develop through this process.

✦ Conclusion

People become educated, as opposed to trained, insofar as they achieve a grasp of critical principles and the ability and passion to choose, organize, and shape their own ideas and living beliefs by means of them. Education is not merely piling up more and more bits and pieces of information. It is a process of autonomously distinguishing true from false. It calls for self-motivated action on our own mental nature and active participation in forming our own character. It requires us to learn to open our mind, correct and refine it, and enable it to learn rationally, thereby empowering it to analyze, digest, master, and rule its own knowledge, gain command over its own faculties, and achieve flexibility, fairmindedness, and critical exactness.

This process cannot be accomplished when learning is viewed monologically. The process of gaining knowledge is at its roots dialogical. Our minds are never empty of beliefs and never without a point of view. They cannot function framelessly. Since our instinctive intellectual drives are initially egocentric, and then typically ethnocentric, we must learn to bring our implicit ideas and reasonings into open dialogical conflict with opposing ones to decide rationally, as best we can, upon their merit as candidates for mindful belief. Our implicit everyday theories of ourselves, our friends and neighbors, our nation and religion, our enemies and antagonists, and our hopes, fears, and premonitions must become overtly known to us that we might learn to continually re-assess them as we enter empathically into more or less alien belief systems.

Children begin by engaging in mere collective monologue, but early on they also begin to respond to the points of view of others. Their play suggests that they enjoy taking on the role of others and acting as though they were someone else. This initial drive must not be allowed to wither

Baby Bear had the smallest bowl.
"Why do I have the smallest bowl?" he said.
"Because you are the smallest bear." said his mother.
"Is that fair?" said Baby Bear.

- *Did Baby Bear **need** as much as the big bears? Why?*
- *Could he eat as much as the big bears? Why?*
- *Did he deserve as much as the big bears? Why?*
- *Do you think it is fair for Baby Bear to have a smaller bowl? Why?*
- *What problems have you seen like the one in this story?*

figure 1

Discussion Plan: Friends

1. Can people talk together a lot and still not be friends?
2. Can people hardly ever talk together and still be friends?
3. Are there some people who always fight with their friends?
4. Are there some people who never fight with their friends?
5. Are there some people who have no friends?
6. Are there people who have friends, even though they have hardly anything else?
7. Do you trust your friends more than anyone else?
8. Are there some people whom you trust more than your friend?
9. Is it possible to be afraid of a friend?
10. What is the difference between friends and family?
11. Are there animals you could be friends with, and other animals you could never be friends with?

figure 2

WHAT DID SARA LEARN?

Making Things Right

The children had damaged the wall. Sara thought they should *make things right*. One way was for them to put a new coat of paint on the wall.

The children's parents might have to pay to have new paint put on the wall. Sara thought that might be another way to *make things right*.

- *What would be fair? Why?*
- *What problems like this have you seen?*
- *What does MAKING THINGS RIGHT have to do with being fair?*

figure 3

For each of the following issues, identify reasons that support each side of the issue.

Issue

Students' grades should be based not only on how much they learn, but also on how hard they try.

Supporting Reasons

1. This policy will encourage students who learn slowly.

2. _____

3. _____

Students' grades should be based only on how much they learn.

Supporting Reasons

1. Teachers don't always know how hard a student is trying.

2. _____

3. _____

Issue

The best way to deal with crime is to give long prison sentences.

Supporting Reasons

1. _____

2. _____

3. _____

Long prison sentences will not reduce crime.

Supporting Reasons

1. _____

2. _____

3. _____

figure 4

"If a man destroy the eye of another, they shall destroy his eye."
                                        Hammurabi, about 1950 B.C.

Convicted of theft, Mustafa was taken into the public square where, before a fascinated crowd, the executioner chopped off his right hand with a sword.

The court ordered Sarah to pay $5,500 for damages to Paul's car and $8,376 in medical bills for injuries to Paul after she crashed into his car while he was stopped for a red light.

Three members of a teen-aged gang beat and robbed a 60-year-old woman standing at a bus stop. The woman was hospitalized for two months and permanently crippled by the beating. The boys were arrested and placed in Juvenile Hall for six months where they were given psychological counseling, released, and placed on probation for one year.

Each of the above situations involves an issue of *corrective justice*. Corrective justice refers to the fairness of responses to wrongs or injuries.

What Do You Think?

1. *What is fair or unfair about each of the above responses to wrongs or injuries?*
2. *What values and interests, other than fairness, might be important to take into account in deciding what might be a proper response to a wrong or injury?*

figure 5

away, but must be cultivated, expanded, and reshaped. Whether we begin with empathy into the thinking and predicaments of characters in children's stories, lead children into reflective philosophical discussions, or provide challenging ethical questions and dilemmas for them to think about, we must lead students to the point that they begin to get comfortable dealing with dialogical issues rationally. Progressively, the issues that students deal with should get more and more complex.

More and more, students should have assignments that challenge their ability to identify and analyze frames of reference and points of view — the frames of reference in their texts, various subject areas, TV programs, news broadcasts and daily papers, the language of their peers and teachers, political speeches and personal discussions, and everyday decisions and ways of living. And they should do this to discover, not that everything is relative and arbitrary, or a matter of opinion, but that all beliefs and points of view are subject to rational analysis and assessment. As they achieve increasing success in this process, their rational passions will develop by degrees and their egocentric defensiveness will concomitantly decrease.

Students will not become progressively more unruly and hard to handle. On the contrary, they will become more and more amenable to reason and the power of evidence. They will, of course, eventually question us and our points of view, but they will do so rationally and hence help us to develop as well. Ideally, the process will pervade the school climate and be reflected in the deepest structures of school life. By this means, schools can perhaps begin to become leading institutions in society, paradigms of rationality, by helping an irrational society become what it itself has said is its own highest goal: a free society of free and autonomous persons.

✦ References

Easley, Jack. (1983a). "A Japanese Approach to Arithmetic," in *For the Learning of Mathematics*, 3 (3).

Easley, Jack. (1983b). "What's there to Talk About in Arithmetic?" in *Problem Solving* (Newsletter, The Franklin Institute Press) 5.

Easley, Jack. (1984a). "Is there Educative Power in Students' Alternative Frameworks?" in *Problem Solving* (Newsletter, The Franklin Institute Press), 6:1–4.

Easley, Jack. (1984b). "A Teacher Educator's Perspective on Students and Teachers' Schemes: Or Teaching by Listening." Unpublished paper, presented at the Conference on Thinking, Harvard Graduate School of Education.

Goffman, Erving. (1959). *The Presentation of Self in Everyday Life*. Garden City, N.J.: Doubleday.

Hayes, J. (1940). *The Complete Problem Solver.* Philadelphia: The Franklin Institute Press.

Mills, C. Wright. (1962). *The Marxists*. New York: Dell.

Piaget, Jean. (1976). *Judgment and Reasoning in the Child.* Totowa, N.J.: Littlefield, Adams.

Toch, H., & Smith, H. C. (Eds.). (1968). *Social Perception.* New York: Van Nostrand.

Whitehead, Alfred. (1929). *The Aims of Education and Other Essays.* New York: Dutton.

* Figures 1, 3, and 5 are from *Justice,* a series produced by *Law in a Free Society,* 5115 Douglas Fir Drive, Calabasas, CA 91302. Figure 2 is from *Pixie: Looking for Meaning,* by Matthew Lipman, in *Philosophy for Children,* Institute for the Advancement of Philosophy for Children, Montclair State College, Montclair, N.J. Figure 4 is from *Thinking Critically,* by John Chaffee, 1985, Houghton Mifflin, Boston.

Chapter 17

Power, Vested Interest, and Prejudice:
On the Need for Critical Thinking in the Ethics of Social and Economic Development

Abstract

In this paper, presented at the International Conference on The Ethics of Development, *held at the University of Costa Rica (1987), Richard Paul argues that mass education is essential to ethically sensitive economic and social development. There are two main reasons Paul advances to support this view: 1) politicians, despite their rhetoric to the contrary, do not typically respond to ethical concerns unless those concerns square with their vested interests, and 2) the mass media in each country — the main source of information regarding development for most people — must be critically analyzed to understand the ethical issues implicit in social and economic development options. As Paul puts it, "neither the leaders of powerful nations and groups nor their 'followers' are likely to analyze or apply the ethical principles relevant to development in a way likely to do justice to those principles. The thinking of the leaders verges toward manipulations, rationalizations, and narrow ways-and-means analysis while the thinking of the followers tends toward naivete, closedmindedness, and intellectual servitude fostered by their restricted sources of information, limited access to education, and traditional egocentric and ethnocentric prejudices."*

✦ We Have Appropriate Ethical Principles

*T*he problem of ethics in economic development is neither verbal nor philosophical, but operational. It isn't that appropriate ethical principles have never been formulated. On the contrary, one could easily identify and set out appropriate ethical principles. The problem is, rather, how to make those principles morally operational, to put them into action when policies and decisions are formulated and implemented by persons and groups in power.

In the next few paragraphs I will provide an incomplete but illustrative list of some moral principles relevant to economic development. For example, the U.S. Catholic bishops, in a pastoral letter on the economy, gave the following "basic and social moral principles" as "guidelines for economic life:"

355

1) Every economic decision and institution should be judged in light of whether it *protects* or *undermines* the *dignity* of the human person. The economy must be at the service of all people, *especially* the poor.

2) Human dignity can be realized and protected only in community. The obligation to "love our neighbor" has an individual dimension, but it also requires a broader commitment to the common good.

3) Everyone has *a right to participate* in the economic life of society. No person or group should be unfairly excluded or unable to contribute to the economy.

4) All members of society have a *special obligation* to the poor and vulnerable. It is our duty to speak for the voiceless, defend the defenseless, and assess lifestyles, policies, and social institutions in terms of their impact on the poor.

5) Human rights are the minimum conditions for life in community. All people have a right to life, food, clothing, shelter, rest, medical care, education, and employment.

6) Society as a whole, acting through private and government institutions, has the moral responsibility to enhance human dignity and protect human rights.

Similar or supplemental principles have been formulated in the U.N. "International Covenant on Civil and Political Rights" (U.N. General Assembly resolution 2200 of 16 December 1966) and the U.N. "International Bill of Human Rights" (U.N. General Assembly resolution 217 of 10 December 1948).

More recently, the U.N. World Commission on Environment and Development issued a report prepared by 21 commissioners who conducted public hearings on five continents, which concluded *1)* that resources must be transferred from the wealthy industrial nations to the poorer developed nations, *2)* that global military expenditures (said to be now $1 trillion a year) use resources that might be employed "more productively to diminish the security threats created by environmental conflict and the resentments that are fueled by widespread poverty," and that "sustainable human progress" can be achieved only through a system of international cooperation that treats economic growth and environmental protection as inseparable.

This report is quite consistent with the ethical principles cited in the American Catholics bishops' letter and the basic U.N. declarations of human rights. The facts upon which they base their ethical judgments are generally accepted by the scholarly community. But the steps being called for sharply contrast with the fundamental mode of operation of powerful nations and groups. Let us now consider why ethical principles are generally moot in the world of economic and political power.

✦ There Are No Practical Incentives for the Powerful to Comply

If actions speak louder than words, then the powerful nations and groups (for example, international corporations) tell us that there is no reason to limit the pursuit of their vested interests, profit, and advantage because of the demands of ethical principles.

The overwhelming majority of nations have condemned the Soviet invasion of Afghanistan, for example, but this condemnation has not persuaded the Soviets to withdraw. The overwhelming majority of nations and the World Court have condemned the U.S.-sponsored invasion of Nicaragua, but the condemnation has not persuaded the U.S. government to desist. Amnesty International and other organizations have documented the extensive use of torture, assassination and terrorism by many nations, but have failed to significantly reduce these ethical violations. Although powerful nations and groups attempt to maintain a positive image in the world press, clearly this image-fostering has little to do with ethical scruples or a willingness to respond to ethical critique. Furthermore, powerful nations spend a great deal of money on covert actions of their intelligence wings enabling them to evade responsibility for much of their own unethical behavior. Hence the fact, for example, that Idi Amin was brought to power by collaborative efforts by the CIA, MOSSAD (Israel), and the MI6 (Britain) is not common knowledge even though scholarly documentation is readily available. Consequently, nations can easily take a strong public stand condemning terrorism while financing it with a lot of money and technical expertise.

The amoral and immoral activities of powerful nations and groups, whether overt or covert, are often at odds with the social, political, and economic development of less powerful nations and groups, so there is a crucial link between the manner in which power is obtained and used and the problems of third world development.

Do not assume I am implying that the leaders of powerful governments and groups are self-consciously or deliberately amoral or immoral in the formulations of their policies and decisions. This I do not intend or believe. Rather my view is that many who rise to political and economic power have highly developed their capacity for rationalizing their vested interests and ignoring viewpoints or lines of reasoning which question what they do. Most discussions over pressing policy decisions focus on ways and means for advancing specific interests; to raise ethical issues in such discussions would seem to the participants "irrelevant", "idealistic", or "hopelessly philosophical". If nothing else, groups vying for power would hesitate to restrict their own use of power, based on ethical considerations, while competing groups, in their view, are not so restricted. Furthermore, since competing groups, in their view, tend to drift toward considering the competing "other" as the "enemy", restricting their activities based on ethical considerations appears to them as "folly".

Jerome Frank has described this tendency with respect to the phenomenon of war in the following way:

> The power of group relationships to determine how the members of groups perceive each other has been neatly shown by the vicissitudes of this image, which always arises when two nations are in conflict and which is always the same no matter who the conflicting parties are. Enemy-images mirror each other — that is, each side attributes the same virtues to itself and the same vices to the enemy. "We" are trustworthy, peace-loving, honorable, and humanitarian; "they" are treacherous, warlike, and cruel. In surveys of Americans conducted in 1942, the first five adjectives chosen to characterize both Germans and Japanese (enemies) included warlike, treacherous, and cruel, none of which appeared among the first five describing the Russians (allies); in 1966 all three had disappeared from American characterizations of the Germans and Japanese (allies), but now the Russians (no longer allies, although more rivals than enemies) were warlike and treacherous. In 1966 the mainland Chinese, predictably, were seen as warlike, treacherous, and sly. After President Nixon's visit to China, these adjectives disappeared from our characterization of the Chinese, whom we now see as hardworking, intelligent, artistic, progressive, and practical.
>
> The image of the enemy creates a self-fulfilling prophecy by causing enemies to acquire the evil characteristics they attribute to each other. In combating what they perceive to be the other's cruelty and treachery, each side becomes more cruel and treacherous itself. The enemy-image nations form of each other thus more or less corresponds to reality.

Of course much of the use of economic resources is motivated today by considerations seen as crucial to the "cold war". Economies and economic and political policies are deeply tied into the role nations and groups appear to play in relation to this struggle between the U.S. and its allies and the Soviet Union and its allies. The superpowers try to prevent anyone from remaining outside of their strategic decisions and policies.

Most citizens find it very difficult to make reasonable ethical judgments about questions of development, when most of their information comes from the public media which are heavily influenced (when not overtly controlled) by a perspective on development of powerful groups.

The picture I am painting is as follows. The leaders of powerful nations and groups are involved in an intense struggle for power, within the context of which ethical principles seem irrelevant or somehow intrinsically embedded in their own vested interests. On the other hand, the majority of citizens in the world are provided with information from sources that are tied, in large part, to these same powerful vested interests. Thus, neither the leaders of powerful nations and groups nor their "followers" are likely to analyze or apply the ethical principles relevant to development in a way likely to do justice to those principles. The thinking of the leaders verges toward practical manipulations, rationalizations, and narrow ways and means analysis while the thinking of the followers tends toward näiveté and closedmindedness fostered by their restricted sources of information, limited access to education, and traditional ethnocentric prejudices. The misinformation and disinformation fostered by the vested interests shape the media representations making the question of development a puzzle to most.

✦ There Is a Need to Foster Critical Thinking in The Education of the Ordinary Citizen

There is little hope that the leaders of powerful nations and groups will of their own volition take ethical considerations seriously in formulating policies and practices that bear on the well-being and development of all. They must be pressured by those not deeply involved in the struggle for political and economic power. But such persons are traditionally ill-prepared to exercise the critical thinking necessary to address the problem of development. Though the relevant ethical principles have been formulated, ordinary people have not been taught those formulations. They have not been encouraged to seek out sources of information not readily accessible in their national public media nor in how to analyze the media critically. They have not developed the conceptual sophistication to see through the bias of their own groups' conceptualizations.

Unless educators in all countries can begin to foster genuine critical thinking in schools accessible to most people, or some other means is developed or generated for helping people free themselves from the self-serving manipulations of their own leaders, it is doubtful that "ethical reasoning" will play its appropriate role in social and economic development. Ethical reasoning, to be effective, cannot be "uncritical" for ethical principles must be applied in the context of human action and interest heavily polluted by distortion and one-sidedness, by vested interests portrayed in the guise of ethical righteousness.

Section IV

Contrasting Viewpoints

Chapter 18

McPeck's Mistakes:
Why Critical Thinking Applies Across Disciplines and Domains

A review of Critical Thinking and Education *by John E. McPeck. Martin Robinson, Oxford, 1981.*

Abstract

In this paper, Richard Paul rejects John McPeck's claim in Critical Thinking and Education *that, since no one can think without thinking about something, critical thinking is nothing more than a conglomeration of subject-specific skills and insights. Paul rejects, in other words, McPeck's view that there are no general critical thinking skills. Paul's argument rests on the fact that most significant and problematic issues require dialectical thought which crosses and goes beyond any one discipline; that many interpretations and uses of discipline-specific information and procedures in exploring real-life issues are inevitably multi-logical.*

$\mathcal{M}$ ost educational commentators and the general public seem to agree on at least one thing: the schools are in *deep* trouble. Many graduates, at all levels, lack the abilities to read, write, and think with a minimal level of clarity, coherence, and critical or analytic exactitude. Most commentators also agree that a significant part of the problem is a pedagogical diet excessively rich in memorization and superficial rote performance, and insufficiently rich in, if not devoid of, autonomous critical thought. This complaint is not entirely new in North American education but the degree of concern and the quiet but growing revolution represented by those attempting to address that concern is worthy of note. (A recent ERIC computer search identified 1,849 articles in the last seven years with *critical thinking* as a major descriptor.[1])

The roots of this multi-faceted movement can be traced back in a number of directions, but one of the deepest and most important goes back as far as Ed Glaser's *An Experiment in the Development of Critical Thinking* (1941) (and his establishing with Watson of the Watson-Glaser Critical Thinking Appraisal) and Max Black's *Critical Thinking* (1946). The manner in which this root of the movement has, after a halting start, progressively built up a head of steam, has been partially chronicled by Johnson and Blair.[2] It is now firmly established at the college and university level affecting there an increasing number of courses that focus on "Critical Thinking" or "Informal Logic", courses designed to provide the kind of shot-in-the-arm for critical thinking that general composition courses are expected to provide for writing.[3] The influence of this current in the movement is being increasingly felt at lower levels of education but in a more variable, if somewhat less effective way.

Enter John McPeck with his book *Critical Thinking and Education* which promises us (on its dust jacket) "a timely critique of the major work in the field", "rigorous ideas on the proper place of critical thinking in the philosophy of education", "a thorough analysis of what the concept is", as well as "a sound basis on which the role of critical thinking in the schools can be evaluated." The book is important not only because it is the first to attempt a characterization of the recent critical thinking movement, but more so because the foundational mistakes it makes are uniquely instructive, mistakes so eminently reflective of "the spirit of the age" they are likely to show up in many more places than this book alone. Unfortunately, because of serious flaws in its theoretical underpinnings, the book doubtless will lead some of McPeck's readers down a variety of blind alleys, create unnecessary obstacles to some important programs being developed, and encourage some — not many, I hope — to dismiss the work of some central figures in the field (Scriven, D'Angelo, and Ennis most obviously). At the root of the problem is McPeck's (unwitting?) commitment to a rarefied form of logical (epistemological) atomism, a commitment which is essential if he is to rule out, as he passionately wants to, *all general skills of thought* and so to give himself *a priori* grounds to oppose all programs that try to develop or enhance such skills.

McPeck's mistakes are, from one vantage point, glaring and fundamental; from another they are seductive, and, as I have suggested above, quite natural. They bear examination from a number of points of view. Certainly most can see the fallacy in inferring that, because one cannot write without writing about something, some specific subject or other, it is therefore unintelligible "muddled nonsense" to maintain general composition courses or to talk about general, as against subject-specific, writing skills. Likewise most would think bizarre someone who argued that, because speech requires something spoken about, it therefore is senseless to set up general courses in speech, and incoherent to talk of *general* speaking skills.

Yet McPeck's keystone inference, logically parallel and equally fallacious in my view, is likely to be seductively attractive to many teachers and administrators in the form in which McPeck articulates it:

> It is a matter of conceptual truth that thinking is always thinking about X, and that X can never be "everything in general" but must always be something in particular. Thus the claim "I teach my students to think" is at worst false and at best misleading.

Thinking, then, is logically connected to an X. Since this fundamental point is reasonably easy to grasp, it is surprising that critical thinking should have become reified into a curriculum subject and the teaching of it an area of expertise of its own ....

In isolation it neither refers to nor denotes any particular skill. It follows from this that it makes no sense to talk about critical thinking as a distinct subject and that it therefore cannot profitably be taught as such. To the extent that critical thinking is not about a specific subject X, it is both conceptually and practically empty. The statement "I teach critical thinking", simpliciter, is vacuous because there is no generalized skill properly called critical thinking. (pp. 4 & 5)

Many would, I suspect, find it equally attractive to conclude with McPeck that "the real problem with uncritical students is not a deficiency in a general skill, such as logical ability, but rather a general lack of education in the traditional sense" and that "... elementary schools are fully occupied with their efforts to impart the three R's, together with the most elementary information about the world around them" and hence have no *time* to teach critical thinking as well. They might not be as comfortable with his notion that "there is nothing in the logic of education that requires that schools should engage in education" and "nothing contradictory in saying 'This is a fine school, and I recommend it to others, even though it does not engage in education.'"

Still, this latter point is mentioned only once, not endlessly repeated in an array of different forms as is his major refrain that "thinking of any kind is always about X". The "X" of this refrain, that to which McPeck believes the logic of all thought is to be relativized, is itself characterized in a litany of synonyms ("the question at issue", "the subject matter", "the parent field", "the field of research", "the specific performance", "the discipline", "the cognitive domain", and so forth) as are the various criteria (the need for "specialized and technical language", "technical information", "field-dependent concepts", "unique logic", "unique skills", "intrafield considerations", "subject-specific information", and so forth) imposed on the critical thinker by the X in question. The hypnotic effect of the continual reiteration of the truism implicit in his major refrain, alongside of a variety of formulations of his major conclusion is such that readers not used to slippery *non-sequiturs* are apt to miss the logical gap from premise to conclusion.

If nothing else, the reader is bound to feel something of the attraction — in this technological, specialists' world of ours — of McPeck's placing critical thought squarely in the center of an atomistic, information-centered model of knowledge. We are already comfortable with the notion that to learn is to amass large quantities of specialized or erudite facts and we know that facts are of different *types*. In other words, we tend to think of knowledge on the model of the computers we are so enamored of: on the one hand, a huge mass of atomic facts (our data bank), and on the other a specific set of categories, McPeck's logical domains, which organize them into higher-order generalizations by formulas and decision-procedures of various kinds. To change one of the formulas or decision-procedures requires technical information about the facts to be manipulated. Critical thought in this context requires understanding of both the data bank and the established procedures.

But it is well to remember that we cannot ask computers multi-categorical questions, especially those kinds that cut across the disciplines in such a way as to require reasoned perspective on the data from a "global" point of view. Such questions, structuring the very warp and woof of everyday life, are typically dialectical, settled, that is, by *general* cannons of argument, by objection (from one point of view) and reply (from another), by case and counter-case, by debate not only about the answer to the question, but also about the question itself. Most social and world problems are of this nature, as are those that presuppose the subject's world view.

For example, consider those social problems that call for judgments on the equity of the distribution of wealth and power, of the causes of poverty, of the justification and limits of welfare, of the nature or existence of the military-industrial complex, of the value or danger of capitalism, of the character of racism and sexism or their history and manifestations, of the nature of communism or socialism, ... The position we take on any one of these issues is likely to reflect the position we take on the others and they are all likely to reflect our conception of human nature (the extent of human equality and what follows from it as so conceived, the nature and causes of human "laziness" and "ambition"), the need for "social change", or "conservatism", even the character of the "cosmos" and "nature".

This point was brought home to me recently when I got into a lengthy disagreement with an acquaintance on the putative justification of the U.S. invasion of Grenada. Before long we were discussing questions of morality, the appropriate interpretation of international law, supposed rights of countries to defend their interests, spheres of influence, the character of U.S. and Soviet foreign policies, the history of the two countries, the nature and history of the C.I.A., the nature of democracy, whether it can exist without elections, who has credibility and how to judge it, the nature of the media and how to assess it, whether it reflects an "American" party line, sociocentrism, our own personalities, consistency, etc. Especially illuminating and instructive was the distinctive pattern that this discussion took. It was eminently clear that we disagreed in our respective world views, our global perspectives. Because we each conceived of the world with something like an integrated point of view, we conceptualized the problem and its elements differently. Specialized information was differently interpreted by us. There were no discipline-specific skills to save the day.

McPeck avoids commenting on such problems except insofar as they presuppose specialized information, which he then focuses on (or dismisses them as belonging to the realm of "common sense"). From a logical atomist's point of view (with everything carefully placed in an appropriate logical category of its own, and there settled by appropriate specialists) dialectical, multi-categorical questions are anomalous, they do not fit in. When they notice them, they tend to try to fabricate specialized categories for them or to break them down into a summary complex of mono-categorical elements. Hence the problem of peace in relation to the military-industrial complex would be broken down by atomists into discrete sets of economic, social, ethical, historical, and psychological problems, or what have you, each to be analyzed and settled separately. This neat and tidy picture of the world of knowledge as a specialist's world is the Procrustean Bed that McPeck has prepared for critical thought. To aspire to critical thought, on this view, is to recognize that it can be achieved only within narrow confines of one's life: "... there are no Renaissance men in this age of specialized knowledge". (p. 7) It is possible only in those dimensions where one can function as a "properly trained physicist, historian, ... [or] art critic," (p. 150), and so learn specialized knowledge and unique skills.

McPeck assumes that for one person to rationally address a multi-categorical problem, he or she would need to be an expert in every pertinent field, an obvious impossibility. Such universal expertise, however, is far from necessary. What *is* necessary is that the individual has a firm grasp of the basic concepts and principles of the pertinent fields, experience thinking within them, and the ability to learn new details and assess relevant details the subjects contribute to understanding the problem. One need not know everything when one takes up a question or problem. One merely needs enough background knowledge and skills to begin to gather and analyze relevant discipline information and insight.

McPeck identifies the bogey man in critical thinking in a variety of ways — "the logic approach", "formalism", "informal logic", "naive logical positivism", "logic simpliciter", and so forth — but the bulk of his book is spent in attacking scholars associated with the informal logic movement (Ennis, Johnson, Blair, D'Angelo, and Scriven). The general charge against them is, predictably, that they have failed to grasp what follows from the logic of the concept of critical thinking — that it is "muddled nonsense" to base it on general skills — and that such misguided attempts necessarily result in "the knee-jerk application of skills" and "superficial opinion masquerading as profound insight", and are thus bound to run aground.

Since McPeck rests so much on his conceptual analysis, it is appropriate to note what he leaves out of it. He does not consider the full range of uses of the word 'critical' as they relate to various everyday senses of the predicate 'thinks critically'. He does not consider the history of critical thought, the various theories of it implicit in the works of Plato, Aristotle,

Kant, Hegel, Marx, Freud, Weber, Sartre, Habermas, and so forth. He does not consider the implications of such classic exemplars as Socrates, Voltaire, Rousseau, Thomas Paine, Henry David Thoreau, or even of an H. L. Mencken, or Ivan Illich, to mention a few that come to mind. He fails to ask whether their critical thinking can or cannot be explained by, or reduced to, specialized knowledge or domain-specific skills. He neglects the rich range of programs that have recently been developed in the field (he has it in mind that in principle there *cannot* be a field of research here). He ignores the possibility that, given the rich variety of programs, reflecting somewhat different emphases, interests, and priorities, it may be premature to attempt to pin down in a few words "the concept of critical thinking". He fails to consider the possibility that the scholars he criticizes may be using the term in an *inductive* sense, hence not presupposing or claiming a definitive analysis of the concept, but restricting their focus rather to some of its necessary, not sufficient, conditions (for example: aiding students in developing greater skill in identifying and formulating questions at issue, distinguishing evidence from conclusion, isolating conceptual problems, identifying problems of credibility, recognizing common fallacies, and coming to a clearer sense of what a claim or an assumption or an inference or an implication is, and so forth).

One result is that his analysis of "the concept of critical thinking" is in all essentials completed in the first thirteen pages of the book with his foundational inference in place by page four. Another is that he gives a most unsympathetic and at times highly misleading representation of most of those he criticizes (Ennis, Glaser, D'Angelo, Johnson, Blair, and Scriven).

In order to have space to develop the broader implications of McPeck's analysis, I will illustrate this latter tendency solely with respect to Robert Ennis, who is at the center of most of his critical remarks in Chapter Three, "The Prevailing View of the Concept of Critical Thinking". McPeck introduces this chapter with three interrelated general charges about the "theoretical foundation" of the prevailing concept: that those who hold it subscribe "to the verifiability criterion of meaning", are "marked by a naive form of logical positivism", and have "an unquestioned faith in the efficacy of science and its methods to settle every significant controversy requiring critical thought". However, nowhere in the chapter does he back up these charges. And I myself do not find anything in the work of Ennis (or of D'Angelo for that matter) that suggest such theoretical commitments.

McPeck focuses his critique on Ennis's article, "A Concept of Critical Thinking", published in 1962, despite Ennis's subsequent published modifications. Furthermore, Ennis makes clear, even in this early article, that he does not take himself to be providing a definitive analysis of the concept; he offers but a "truncated" working definition. He describes his article as providing a "range definition" which has "vague boundaries", based on an examination of "the literature on the goals of the schools and the literature on the criterion of good thinking", and designed merely to "select" "those aspects" which come under the notion of critical thinking as "the correct assessing of statements". He makes it clear that he is leaving out at least one crucial element ("the judging of value statements is deliberately excluded"). He makes clear that his working definition does not settle the question as to how best to teach critical thinking, for example, whether as a separate subject or within subject areas. Finally, it is clear that he is concerned with critical thinking as an open-ended and complicated set of processes that can be set out in analyzed form only for the purpose of theoretical convenience, a list of "aspects" and "dimensions" that can be learned "at various levels".[4]

McPeck's motive for critiquing Ennis's concept is clearly the fact that Ennis does not define critical thinking so as to link it "conceptually with particular activities and special fields of knowledge". (p. 56) And because McPeck sees this conceptual link as necessary, as given *in* the concept, it is, to him, "impossible to conceive of critical thinking as a generalized skill". (p. 56) In other words, Ennis conceives of critical thinking in an "impossible" and therefore incoherent, muddled, and contradictory way. If we are not persuaded of this conceptual link and we read Ennis to be making more modest claims than McPeck attributes to him, most of McPeck's criticisms fall by the wayside.

Let us look more closely, then, at McPeck's model and its implications. It depends upon the plausibility of placing any line of thought into a "category", "domain", "subject area", or "field", which placement provides, implicitly or explicitly, criteria for judging that line of thought. It tacitly assumes that all thinking is in one and only one category, that we can, without appealing to an expert on experts, tell what the appropriate category is, and thus what specialized information or skills are unique to it. Each discrete category requires specialized concepts, experience, skills, etc. Thus, only some limited set of people can develop the necessary wherewithal to think critically within it. Since there are many logical domains and we can be trained only in a few of them, it follows that we must use our critical judgment mainly to suspend judgment and defer to experts when we ourselves lack expertise. It leaves little room for the classical concept of the liberally educated person as having skills of learning that are general and not domain specific. It is worthwhile therefore to set out more particularly, if somewhat abstractly, why it is unacceptable.

First, the world is not given to us sliced up into logical categories, and there is not one, but an indefinite number of ways to "divide" it, that is, experience, perceive, or think about the world, and no "detached" point of view from the supreme perspective of which we can decide on the appropriate taxonomy for the "multiple realities" of our lives. Conceptual schemes create logical domains and it is human thought, not nature, that creates them.

Second, our conceptual schemes themselves can be classified in an indefinite number of ways. To place a line of reasoning into a category and so to identify it by its "type" is heuristic, not ontological — a useful tool, not descriptive of its nature. Even concepts and lines of reasoning *clearly* within one category are also simultaneously within others. Most of what we say and think, to put it another way, is not only open-textured but *multi*-textured as well. For example, in what logical domain does the (technical?) concept of alcoholism solely belong: disease, addiction, crime, moral failing, cultural pattern, lifestyle choice, defect of socialization, self-comforting behavior, psychological escape, personal weakness, ...? How many points of view can be used to illuminate it? Then, is it *in* one or many categories? Or consider the question, "How can society ameliorate the problem of alcoholism?" It cannot be adequately addressed from *one* domain. Nor can the problem be adequately addressed by parsing out its elements and addressing each in isolation from the rest. The light shed by the experts must be synthesized.

Not only conceptualizing "things", but most especially classifying what we have conceptualized, are not matters about which we should give the final word to experts and specialists. To place something said or thought into a category, from the perspective of which we intend to judge it, is to take a potentially contentious position with respect to it. There are no specialists who have the definitive taxonomy or undebatable means for so deciding. The category a thing is in logically depends upon what it is *like*, but all things (including conceptual schemes) are like any number of other things (other conceptual schemes, for example) in any number of ways and so are *in*, any number of logical domains, depending on our purposes.

Consider for example Copernicus' statements about the earth in relation to the sun. These are, you may be tempted to say, astronomical statements and nothing else. But if they become a part of concepts and lines of thought that have radically reoriented philosophical, social, religious, economic, and personal thought, as indeed they have, are they *merely in* that one category? When we begin to think in a cross-categorical way, as the intellectual heirs of Copernicus, Darwin, Freud, and Marx, are there category-specific skills and specialists to interpret that thought and tell us what the correct synthesis of these ingredients is and how it ought to color or guide our interpretation or critical assessment of statements "within" some particular domain or other?

The most important place that knowledge has in any life is, in my view, that of shaping our concept of things overall, our system of values, meanings, and interpretive schemes. This is the domain in which critical thought is most important to us. We spend only a small percentage of our lives making judgments as specialists, and even then we typically give a broader meaning to those acts as persons and citizens.

Hence a business person may place a high value on professional acts as contributing to the social good, may interpret and assess the schools and education on the model of a business, may judge the political process in its relation to the business community and see business opportunities and freedom as conceptually interrelated, and may then unfavorably judge societies not organized so as to favor "free investment of capital" as dangerous threats to human well being. Logical synthesis, cutting across categories, extracting metaphors from one domain and using them to organize others, arguing for or against the global metaphors of others, are intellectual acts ultimately grounded, not in the criteria and skills of specialists, not in some science or any combination thereof, but in the *art* of rational-dialectical-critical thought, in the art of thinking of anything in its relationship to things overall.

Hence, to be rational agents, we must learn to think critically about how we totalize our experience and bring that total picture to bear on particular dimensions of our lives. We cannot, without forfeiting our autonomy, delegate the construction of those crucial acts to specialists or technicians. Students, teachers, and people in general, need to maintain their critical autonomy even in, *especially* in, the face of specialists and even with respect to claims made within specialized areas. If democracy is a viable form of government and way of life, then judgments not only of policy but of world view are the common task of all, not the prerogative of privileged groups of specialists. We need to pay special attention to those *general* skills of critical cross-examination, for they are what enable us to maintain our autonomous judgment in the midst of experts. These pay-off skills of civic literacy and personal autonomy can be articulated best, not in procedures that read like a technical manual, but in *principles* that will often sound platitudinous or have the ring of "general" advice — the principles of clarity, accuracy, consistency, relevance, depth, breadth, precision, completeness, fairness. Platitudes however can become insights and insights definitive of general skills when systematic, case-by-case practice is supported by careful argument for and against. It is a platitude to say, for example, that the press and the media of a nation tend to cover the news so as to foster or presuppose the correctness of the "world view" of that nation or its government. But this bit of "common knowledge" is a far cry from the very important general skill of reading a newspaper so as to note how, where, and when it is insinuating nationalistic biases. Or again, it is one thing to recognize that all "news" is news from a point of view. It is another to be able to read or hear news with the critical sensitivity to see one point of view presupposed and others ruled out. McPeck thinks otherwise:

> ... where there is only common knowledge, there can only be common criticism — which is usually plain enough for one and all to see. This view not only represents a very shallow, or superficial,

understanding of the cognitive ingredients of critical thinking, but it is also forced to underestimate and play down the real complexities that usually underlie even apparently "common" or "everyday" problems. The solutions to "common", "everyday" problems, if they are in fact problems, are seldom common or everyday. In any event, the educational aspirations of our schools are (fortunately) set higher than the treatment of issues that could otherwise be solved by common sense. Where common sense can solve a problem there is hardly a need for special courses in critical thinking. And where common sense cannot solve a problem, one quickly finds the need for subject-specific information; hence, the traditional justification for subject-oriented courses. (pp. 156–157).

The principles may be "common sense" or platitudinous — "consider all and only relevant facts" — but *applying* these principles when their application is not obvious, or when the life-long habit of applying them tendentiously interferes, goes beyond "lowly" common sense. It takes guidance, extended practice, and evaluation of that practice. Far from such work being too lowly for our schools to bother with at any length, it is difficult to imagine a more worthwhile task than developing such judgment to its highest degree in each student. If you believe in democracy you must believe that citizens have the potential to judge. If you believe that one primary function of education is to prepare students for participation in democracy, you must agree that helping students refine their ability to judge social, political, and economic questions (and questions to which these subjects apply) as clearmindedly, fairly, and rationally as possible is among the most important and useful functions of education. Use of "common sense" is not inborn, but developed.

The logics we use, and which we are daily constructing and reconstructing, are far more mutable, less discrete, more general, more open-textured and multi-textured, more social, more dialectical, and even more personal — and hence far less susceptible to domain-specific skills and concepts — than McPeck dares to imagine. We need to base our model of the critical thinker, not on the domain-bound individual with subject-specific skills, but on the disciplined generalist. This means that we ought to encourage the student as soon as possible to recognize that in virtually every area of our lives, cutting across categories every which way, there are multiple conflicting view-points and theories vying for our allegiance, virtually all of whose possible truth call for shifts in our global perspective. Discipline-specific approaches to everyday problems are often partial and one-sided and need to be balanced and "corrected" by other approaches. A critical thinker must not be the captive of the concepts, criteria, or traditions in any one subject or discipline.

The general skills necessary to finding our way about in this dialectical world are more appropriately captured in the work of an Ennis, a D'Angelo, or a Scriven than a McPeck. *General* critical skills and dispositions cannot be learned without content, no doubt, but few would disagree with this point, certainly not Ennis, D'Angelo, or Scriven. The real and pressing question is not whether or not content is necessary to thought (it is), but whether "content" restricts us to thinking *within* as against *across* and *between* and *beyond* categories. If there is such a thing as having a global perspective, and if that perspective not only sets out categories but also implies their taxonomy, and if such a perspective can be assessed only by appeal to general dialectical skills, not domain or subject-specific ones, then McPeck's vision of critical thinking instruction is fundamentally flawed and the move to a greater emphasis on critical thinking in education is more challenging, and to some perhaps more threatening, than has generally been recognized until now.[5]

✦ Footnotes

[1] In addition, there is a growing number of national and international conferences on the subject, for example, the *First* and *Second International Symposium on Informal Logic*, the *First* and *Second National Conference on Critical Thinking, Moral Education, and Rationality*, and the *First International Conference on Critical Thinking, Education, and the Rational Person*.

[2] Blair and Johnson, eds., *Informal Logic, The Proceedings of the First International Conference on Informal Logic*, Pt. Reyes, CA: Edgepress, 1980.

[3] Such a course is now a graduation requirement for all California State College and University system students, as well as for the California Community College system.

[4] Robert Ennis, "A Concept of Critical Thinking." *Harvard Educational Review*, 1962.

[5] Something should be said in passing about McPeck's treatment of Edward de Bono to whose ideas he devotes a full chapter. This is odd, given the book's supposed focus on *critical* thinking, for de Bono has no theory of critical thinking as such, unless his stereotype of critical thinking as uncreative fault-finding qualifies. Indeed, de Bono uses the concept of critical thinking merely as a foil for "lateral" or "creative" thinking, which he of course takes to be essentially different. He holds that we already put too great an emphasis on *critical* thought. Perhaps McPeck includes him because of his celebrity. I find this inclusion inappropriate and the amount of attention devoted to him unjustified, if critical thinking is indeed McPeck's concern. Furthermore, de Bono is *clearly* not in the same league theoretically as an Ennis, D'Angelo, or Scriven, whatever his celebrity, and his kaleidoscopic, helter-skelter development of metaphors, which merely *suggest* rather than theoretically *probe* the character of "lateral" thought, is an easy target for critique.

Chapter 19

Bloom's Taxonomy and Critical Thinking Instruction:
Recall Is Not Knowledge

Abstract

In this brief article, Richard Paul analyses and critiques Bloom's Taxonomy from the perspective of the critical thinking movement. He points out Bloom's achievements in Cognitive Domains and Affective Domains: the analysis of cognitive processes of thought and their interrelationships; the emphasis on the need for these processes (including critical thinking skills and abilities) to be explicitly and mindfully taught and used; the emphasis on critical thinking values, such as openmindedness and faith in reason.

Dr. Paul then argues that Bloom's approach suffers from the following two flaws: 1) the attempt to be "value neutral" is impossible and incompatible with the values presupposed in critical thinking education and 2) Bloom confuses recall with knowledge.

As a result of the way the taxonomy is explained, many teachers identify learning to think critically with merely learning how to ask and answer questions in all of Bloom's categories: knowledge, comprehension, application, analysis, synthesis, and evaluation. Teachers typically take the categories to express objectives which they should teach to in strict order: first give the students "knowledge", then show them how to comprehend it, then how to apply it, etc. Paul, while recognizing that Bloom's distinctions themselves are important, argues that the common understanding of their link to critical thinking is largely misconceived. Teaching critical thinking is not a simple matter of asking questions from each of Bloom's categories; moreover, the categories themselves are not independent but interdependent. Paul shows, for example, how knowledge is not something that can be given to a student before he or she comprehends it. He explains how the critical thinking movement has properly emphasized that getting knowledge is in fact a complex achievement involving thought, and so should be understood as the product of rational thought processes, rather than as recall. This insight needs to be brought into the heart of instruction.

*I*t would be difficult to find a more influential work in education today than *The Taxonomy of Educational Objectives* (Bloom, et al. 1979). Developed by a committee of college and university examiners from 1949 to 1954 and published as two handbooks — *Cognitive Domain* and *Affective Domain* — its objectives were manifold. Handbook I, *Cognitive Domain*, for instance, lists four encompassing objectives.

1. To "provide for classification of the goals of our educational system ... to be of general help to all teachers, administrators, professional specialists, and research workers who deal with curricular and evaluation problems ... to help them discuss these problems with greater precision ...".

2. To "be a source of constructive help ... in building a curriculum ...".

3. To "help one gain a perspective on the emphasis given to certain behaviors ...".

4. To "specify objectives so that it becomes easier to plan learning experience and prepare evaluation devices ...". (pp. 1–2)

The authors also note that the categories of the Taxonomy below can be used "as a framework for viewing the educational process and analyzing its workings" and even for "analyzing teachers' success in classroom teaching." (p. 3)

A generation of teachers have now come of age not only familiar with and acceptant of the general categories of the Taxonomy, but also persuaded that the Taxonomy's identified higher-order skills of analysis, synthesis, and evaluation are essential to education at all levels. For these teachers, critical thinking is essential because higher-order skills are essential. To learn how to think critically, in this view, is to learn how to ask and answer questions of analysis, synthesis, and evaluation. To help teachers incorporate critical thinking in the classroom is to help them ask questions that call for analysis, synthesis, and evaluation. In this view, then, learning to teach critical thinking is quite straightforward. The teacher's thinking does not need to be significantly altered, and no fundamental shifts in educational philosophy are required. The Taxonomy and the ability to generate a full variety of question types are all that an intelligent teacher really needs to teach critical thinking skills.

This view is seriously misleading. According to most advocates of critical thinking, no neat set of recipes can foster critical thinking in students. The single most useful thing a teacher can do is to take at least one well-designed college course in critical thinking, in which the *teacher's own* thinking skills are analyzed and nurtured in numerous ways. In other words, teachers need a solid foundation in critical thinking skills before they can teach them.

What follows is a succinct analysis and critique of Bloom's Taxonomy, from the perspective of the values and epistemological presuppositions of the critical thinking movement. I hope it will contribute to a deeper understanding of the nature and demands of critical thinking instruction.

✦ A One-Way Hierarchy

Though not designed to further critical thinking instruction as such, *Cognitive Domain* contains a wealth of information of use in such instruction. Reading it in its entirety is most rewarding, particularly the sections on analysis, synthesis, and evaluation. These sections disclose that most of the cognitive processes characterized as essential to higher-order questions in fact presuppose use of basic critical thinking concepts: assumption, fact,

---

Bloom's Taxonomy

The Taxonomy of Educational Objectives: Cognitive Domain
1.00 *Knowledge*
    1.10 Knowledge of Specifics
    1.11 Knowledge of Terminology
    1.12 Knowledge of Specific Facts
    1.20 Knowledge of Ways and Means of Dealing with Specifics
    1.21 Knowledge of Conventions
    1.22 Knowledge of Trends and Sequences
    1.23 Knowledge of Classifications and Categories
    1.24 Knowledge of Criteria
    1.25 Knowledge of Methodology
    1.30 Knowledge of the Universals and Abstractions in a Field
    1.31 Knowledge of Principles and Generalizations
    1.32 Knowledge of Theories and Structures

2.00 *Comprehension*
    2.10 Translation
    2.20 Interpretation
    2.30 Extrapolation

3.00 *Application*
The use of abstractions in particular and concrete situations. The abstractions may be in the form of general ideas, rules of procedures, or generalized methods. The abstractions may also be technological principles, ideas, and theories which must be remembered and applied.

4.00 *Analysis*
    4.10 Analysis of Elements
    4.20 Analysis of Relationships
    4.30 Analysis of Organizational Principles

5.00 *Synthesis*
    5.10 Production of a Unique Communication
    5.20 Production of a Plan, or Proposed Set of Operations
    5.30 Derivation of a Set of Abstract Relations

6.00 *Evaluation*
    6.10 Judgments in Terms of Internal Evidence
    6.20 Judgments in Terms of External Criteria

(From the *Taxonomy of Educational Objectives,* Bloom et al. 1974 p. 201)

concept, value, conclusion, premise, evidence, relevant, irrelevant, consistent, inconsistent, implication, fallacy, argument, inference, point of view, bias, prejudice, authority, hypothesis, and so forth. This is clear, for example, in the explanation of analysis:

> Skill in analysis may be found as an objective of any field of study. It is frequently expressed as one of their important objectives by teachers of science, social studies, philosophy, and the arts. They wish, for example, to develop in students the ability to distinguish fact from hypothesis in a communication, to identify conclusions and supporting statements, to distinguish relevant from extraneous material, to note how one idea relates to another, to see what unstated assumptions are involved in what is said, to distinguish dominant from subordinate ideas or themes in poetry or music, to find evidence of the author's techniques and purposes. (*Cognitive Domain*, p. 144)

In other words, if the ability to analyze usually requires students to do such things as distinguish facts from hypotheses, conclusions from evidence, relevant from irrelevant material, note relationships between concepts, and probe and detect unstated assumptions, then it seems essential that students become not only familiar with these words (by teachers introducing them frequently into classroom discussion) but also comfortable with using them as they think their way through analytic problems. This need becomes more evident if we recognize that by analysis, synthesis, and evaluation, the authors of the Taxonomy have in mind only their *explicit* (not subconscious) uses. They rightly emphasize what has become a virtual platitude in cognitive psychology — that students (and experts) who do the best analyses, syntheses, and evaluations tend to do them mindfully with a clear sense of their component elements. So, if the concepts of critical thinking are presupposed in mindful analysis, synthesis, and evaluation, we can best heighten that mindfulness by raising those component concepts to a conscious level.

Although *Affective Domain* implies that it is *value neutral,* many of the examples of higher-order valuing illustrate values intrinsic to education conceived on a critical thinking paradigm, wherein a student:

Deliberately examines a variety of viewpoints on controversial issues with a view to forming opinions about them.

[Develops] faith in the power of reason in methods of experimental discussion.

Weighs alternative social policies and practices against the standards of the public welfare rather than the advantage of specialized and narrow interest groups.

[Achieves] readiness to revise judgments and to change behavior in the light of evidence.

Judges problems and issues in terms of situations, issues, purposes, and consequences involved rather than in terms of fixed, dogmatic precepts or emotionally wishful thinking.

Develops a consistent philosophy of life. (pp. 181–185)

Along with the usefulness of Bloom's Cognitive and Affective Taxonomies, we must bear in mind their limitations for critical thinking curriculum construction. To some extent, the Taxonomies represent an attempt to achieve the impossible: a perfectly neutral classification of cognitive and affective processes that makes no educational value judgments and favors no educational philosophy over any other — one that could be used by any culture, nation, or system whatsoever, independent of its specific values or world view:

> ... to avoid partiality to one view of education as opposed to another, we have attempted to make the taxonomy neutral by avoiding terms which implicitly convey value judgments and by making the taxonomy as conclusive as possible. This means that the kinds of behavioral changes emphasized by *any* institution, educational unit, or educational philosophy can be represented in the classification. Another way of saying this is that any objective which describes an intended behavior should be classifiable in this system. (*Cognitive Domain*, p. 14)

This approach to knowledge, cognition, and education is partly irreconcilable with a commitment to critical thinking skills, abilities, and dispositions:

> To a large extent, knowledge as taught in American schools depends upon some external authority: some expert or group of experts is the arbitrator of knowledge. (*Cognitive Domain*, p. 31)
> ... the scheme does provide levels for the extreme inculcation of a prescribed set of values if this is the philosophy of the culture. (*Affective Domain*, p. 43)
> It is possible to imagine a society or culture which is relatively fixed. Such a society represents a closed system in which it is possible to predict in advance both the kinds of problems individuals will encounter and the solutions which are appropriate to those problems. Where such predictions can be made in advance, it is possible to organize the educational experience so as to give each individual the particular knowledge and specific methods needed for solving the problems he will encounter. (*Cognitive Domain*, p. 39–40)

But precisely because of this attempt at neutrality the category of "knowledge" is analyzed in such a restricted way and the relationship of the categories is assumed to be hierarchical in only one direction. For instance, according to Bloom's Taxonomy, "comprehension" presupposes "knowledge", but "knowledge" does not presuppose "comprehension". The second of these conceptual decisions would be questioned by those who hold that the basic skills and dispositions of critical thinking must be brought into schooling from the start, and that for any learning to occur, they must be intrinsic to every element of it.

✦ Knowledge as Achievement

The critical thinking movement has its roots in the practice and vision of Socrates, who discovered by a probing method of questioning that few people could rationally justify their confident claims to knowledge. Confused meanings, inadequate evidence, or self-contradictory beliefs often lurked beneath smooth but largely empty rhetoric. This led to a basic insight into the problem of human irrationality and to a view of knowledge and learning which holds that to believe or assent without reason, judgment, or understanding is to be prejudiced. This belief is central to the critical thinking movement. This view also holds the corollary principle that critical reflection by each learner is an essential precondition of knowledge. Put another way, those who advocate critical thinking instruction hold that knowledge is not something that can be *given* by one person to another. It cannot simply be memorized out of a book or taken whole cloth from the mind of another. Knowledge, rightly understood, is a distinctive construction by the learner, something that issues out of a *rational* use of mental processes.

To expect students to assent before they have developed the capacity to do so rationally is to indoctrinate rather than to educate them and to foster habits of thought antithetical to the educative process. Peter Kneedler (1985) observed "an unfortunate tendency to teach facts in isolation from the thinking skills" — to *give* students knowledge and some time later expect them to *think* about it. Knowledge, in any defensible sense, is an *achievement* requiring a mind slow rather than quick to believe — which waits for, expects, and weighs evidence before agreeing. The sooner a mind begins to develop rational scruples, in this view, the better.

As Quine and Ullian (1970) put it:

> ... knowledge is in some ways like a good golf score: each is substantially the fruit of something else, and there are no magic shortcuts to either one. To improve your golf score you work at perfecting the various strokes; for knowledge you work at garnering and sifting evidence and sharpening your reasoning skills ... knowledge is no more guaranteed than is a lowered golf score, but there is no better way. (p. 12)

We don't actually know whether students have achieved some knowledge until we have determined whether their beliefs represent something they actually know (have rationally assented to) or merely something they have memorized to repeat on a test. Dewey, as the authors of the Taxonomy recognize, illustrated this point with the following story in which he asked a class:

> "What would you find if you dug a hole in the earth?" Getting no response, he repeated the question: again he obtained nothing but silence. The teacher chided Dr. Dewey, "You're asking the wrong question." Turning to the class, she asked, "What is the state of the center of the earth?" The class replied in unison, "Igneous fusion."

The writers of the Taxonomy attempt to side-step this problem by defining "knowledge" as "what is currently known or accepted by the experts or specialists in a field, whether or not such knowledge, in a philosophical sense, corresponds to 'reality'". (*Cognitive Domain*, p. 32)

The writers of the Taxonomy erroneously assume that the only issue here is the relative *value* of the knowledge, not whether statements merely memorized should be called knowledge at all:

> In these latter conceptions [those which link knowledge to understanding and rational assent] it is implicitly assumed that knowledge is of little value if it cannot be utilized in new situations or in a form very different from that in which it was originally encountered. The denotations of these latter concepts would usually be close to what have been defined as "abilities and skills" in the Taxonomy. (*Cognitive Domain*, p. 29)

This inadvertently begs the question whether blindly memorized true belief can properly be called knowledge at all — and hence whether inculcation and indoctrination into true belief can properly be called education. If knowledge of any kind is to some extent a skilled, rational achievement, then we should not confuse knowledge and education with belief inculcation and indoctrination, just as we should not confuse learning more with acquiring knowledge (we *learn*, are not born with bias, prejudices, and misconceptions, for example). This point, crucial for the critical thinking movement, was well formulated by John Henry Newman (1852):

> ... knowledge is not a mere extrinsic or accidental advantage ... which may be got up from a book, and easily forgotten again, ... which we can borrow for the occasion, and carry about in our hand ... [it is] something intellectual ... which reasons upon what it sees ... the action of a formative power ... making the objects of our knowledge subjectively our own.

The reductio ad absurdum of the view that knowledge can be distinguished from comprehension and rational assent is suggested by William Graham Sumner (1906), one of the founding fathers of anthropology, commenting on the failure of the schools of his day:

The examination papers show the pet ideas of the examiners .... An orthodoxy is produced in regard to all the great doctrines. It consists in the most worn and commonplace opinions .... It is intensely provincial and philistine ... [containing] broad fallacies, half-truths, and glib generalizations ... children [are] taught just that one thing which is "right" in the view and interest of those in control and nothing else.

Clearly, Sumner maintained that provincial, fallacious, or misleading beliefs should not be viewed as knowledge at all, however widely they are treated as such, and that inculcating them is not education, however widely described as such.

✦ Rational Learning

To sum up, the authors of the Taxonomy organized cognitive processes into a one-way hierarchy, leading readers to conclude that knowledge is always a simpler behavior than comprehension, comprehension a simpler behavior than application, application a simpler behavior than analysis, and so forth through synthesis and evaluation. However, this view is misleading in at least one important sense: achieving knowledge *always* presupposes at least minimal comprehension, application, analysis, synthesis, and evaluation. This counter-insight is essential for well-planned and realistic curriculum designed to foster critical thinking skills, abilities, and dispositions, and it cannot be achieved without the development of the teacher's critical thinking.

From the very start, for any learning, we should expect and encourage those rational scruples realistically within the range of student grasp, a strategy that requires critical insight into the evidentiary foundation of everything we teach. We should scrutinize our instructional strategies lest we inadvertently nurture student *irrationality,* as we do when we encourage students to believe what, from the perspective of their own thought, they have no good reason to believe. If we want rational learning (and again, *not all learning is rational*), then the process leading to belief is more important than belief itself. Everything we believe we have in some sense *judged* to be credible. If students believe something just because we or the text assert it, they learn to accept blindly.

Right-answer inculcation is not a preliminary step to critical thought. It nurtures irrational belief and unnecessarily generates a mind-set that must be broken down for rational learning and knowledge acquisition to begin. The structure of our lifelong learning generally arises from our early cognitive habits. If they are irrational, then they are likely to remain so. There are twin obstacles to the development of rational learning: *1)* being told and expecting to be told what to believe (belief inculcation);

and 2) being told and expecting to be told precisely what to do (the over-proceduralization of thought). Together they fatally undermine independence of thought and comprehension.

Bloom's Taxonomy, all of the above notwithstanding, is a remarkable tour de force, a ground-breaking work filled with seminal insights into cognitive processes and their interrelations. Nevertheless, the attempt to remain neutral with respect to all educational values and philosophical issues is a one-sided hierarchical analysis of cognitive processes that limits our insight into the nature of critical thinking. (To minimize misunderstanding, let me express in another way one basic sense in which I consider it misleading to call Bloom's Taxonomy "neutral". By labeling the first category "knowledge" rather than "rote recall", the Taxonomy legitimates calling the product of rote recall "knowledge". Such labeling is educationally tendentious and therefore not neutral.) Successful critical thinking instruction requires that:

- teachers have a full range of insights into cognitive processes and their complex interrelationships.
- Bloom's hierarchy become two-sided.
- teachers see that rational learning is *process*- rather than *product*-oriented — a process that brings comprehension, analysis, synthesis, and evaluation into every act of the mind that involves the acceptance, however provisional, of beliefs or claims to truth, and that thereby fosters *rational* habits of thought and *rational* learning:

> ... the teacher's primary job is that of making clear the bases upon which he weighs the facts, the methods by which he separates facts from fancies, and the way in which he discovers and selects his ultimate norms .... This concept of teaching ... requires that the purported facts be accompanied by the reasons why they are considered the facts. Thereby the teacher exposes his methods of reasoning to test and change. If the facts are in dispute ... then the reasons why others do not consider them to be facts must also be presented, thus bringing alternative ways of thinking and believing into dialogue with each other.
>
> — Emerson Shideler

✦ References

Bloom, Benjamin S., and others. *The Taxonomy of Educational Objectives: Affective and Cognitive Domains.* New York: David McKay Company, Inc., 1974.

Kneedler, Peter. "Critical Thinking in History and Social Science" (pamphlet). Sacramento: California State Department of Education, 1985.

Newman, John Henry. *Idea of a University.* New York: Longmans, Green and Company, 1912.

Sumner, William Graham. *Folkways.* New York: Dover Publications, 1906.

Chapter 20

Critical and Cultural Literacy:
Where E. D. Hirsch Goes Wrong

Abstract

In this paper, originally a talk at the Montclair State College Conference on Critical Thinking: Focus on Social and Cultural Enquiry *(1989), Richard Paul critiques E. D. Hirsch's* Cultural Literacy. *Paul points out several problems with Hirsch's view, primarily that it is based on a didactic theory of education, and so depends on our giving students information to retain, and that what students need most is the ability to think clearly and fairmindedly.*

✦ Hirsch on Cultural Literacy

*T*he term 'cultural literacy' has been popularized by E. D. Hirsch in a book of the same name. It's subtitle is "What Every American Needs to Know". The basic argument of the book is simple. Indeed, it is well characterized in the dust jacket of the hard cover edition as a "manifesto". Hirsch's call to arms is not addressed to the workers of the world but rather to the educators of the world, or, more accurately, *American* educators. Hirsch argues that there is a discrete, relatively small body of specific information possessed by all literate Americans and that this information is the foundation not only of American culture but also the key to literacy and education. Hirsch reasons as follows. Because there is a "descriptive list of the information actually possessed by literate Americans" (xiv), and because "all human communities are founded upon specific shared information" (xv) and because "shared culture requires transmission of specific information to children" (xxvii), it follows that "the basic goal of education in a human community is acculturation". (xvi) Furthermore, because,

> Books and newspapers assume a 'common reader', that is, a person who knows the things known by other literate persons in the culture, ... Any reader who doesn't possess the knowledge assumed in a piece he or she reads will in fact be illiterate with respect to that particular piece of writing. (p. 13)

In his reasoning, Hirsch links the having of a discrete body of information not only with learning to read but also with becoming educated and indeed with achieving success. ("To be culturally literate is to possess the basic information needed to thrive in the modern world.") (xiii) Hirsch plays down the need for critical thinking and emphasizes instead that the information needed for cultural literacy does not have to be deeply understood:

> The superficiality of the knowledge we need for reading and writing may be unwelcome news to those who deplore superficial learning and praise critical thinking over mere information. (p. 15)

The culturally literate, according to Hirsch, often possess common cultural content in a way that is "telegraphic, vague, and limited". (p. 26) Those concerned with critical thinking, on the other hand, Hirsch alleges, are exclusively concerned with "abstract skills" and unconcerned with "cultural content". (p. 27) Yet, he claims, it is precisely this finite quantity of "cultural content" that empowers students to read, write, and achieve success. In Hirsch's mind, therefore, it is a mistake to criticize rote learning:

> Our current distaste for memorization is more pious than realistic. At an early age when their memories are most retentive, children have an almost instinctive urge to learn specific tribal traditions. At that age they seem to be fascinated by catalogues of information and are eager to master the materials that authenticate their membership in adult society. (p. 30)

The result is that Hirsch believes himself to have discovered the "key to all other fundamental improvements in American education", (p. 2) and "the only sure avenue of opportunity for disadvantaged children", (xiii) "traditional literate knowledge", "the information attitudes, and assumptions that literate Americans share" (p. 127) which, if transmitted to students, — even superficially — will make them culturally literate. Once educators recognize these facts, Hirsch confidently believes that "a straight-forward plan" to reform education can be set out. In this plan educators would set aside "abstract formalism" and the ill-conceived focus on critical thinking, "abstract skills", and carry out instead three tasks: *1)* "reach an accord about the contents of the national vocabulary and a good sequence for presenting it", (p. 141) *2)* "shift the reading materials used in kindergarten through eighth grade to a much stronger base in factual information and traditional lores", (p. 140) and *3)* "develop general knowledge tests for three different stages of schooling". (p. 143) These simple steps, Hirsch holds, will ensure that all citizens will become not only culturally literate readers but autonomous persons as well:

> It should energize people to learn that only a few hundred pages of information stand between the literate and the illiterate, between dependence and autonomy. (p. 143)

✦ What's Wrong with Hirsch's View

There are many problems with Hirsch's reasoning. In the first place, it is simplistic. It suffers from the same faults as all panaceas, all attempts to reduce the complex and multi-faceted to the simple and uncomplicated. Reading, culture, and education are more profound than they appear in Hirsch's neat and tidy world. There are many more distinctions to be drawn than Hirsch entertains and many of the concepts which he analyzes superficially need a more refined, a more precise analysis. To understand how to help students become empowered readers and autonomous persons who thrive in the modern world, we must lay our foundations more carefully and deeply than Hirsch suggests. We must draw careful distinctions and come to terms with complexities which he ignores.

1) We must take care to distinguish possessing information from having knowledge. Hirsch uses the terms 'information' and 'knowledge' synonymously throughout his book. Yet "information" may be false, biased, incomplete, or misleading while the word 'knowledge', in contrast, implies solid epistemic grounding. If I *know* something, I do not merely *believe* it. I grasp the evidence or reasons that account for or make intuitive its truth. 'False information' is intelligible. 'False knowledge' is not. As educators, therefore, we cannot be satisfied to merely transmit information. We must be concerned with how students receive and internalize information — if knowledge is an important end of education. As educators we want students to learn how to gain *genuine* knowledge, not simply what is commonly accepted as such. We do not want our students to become informational blotters, open to the manipulation of propagandists. We want them to learn how to question what is presented as the truth. We want them to routinely look for reasons and evidence to support, qualify, or refute what others simply accept uncritically and we want them to *understand* what they learn. This point can be put another way. There are significant differences between the processes of indoctrination, socialization, training, and education. These words should not be used synonymously. Yet apparently Hirsch sees no reason to distinguish them. He recognizes, as far as I can see, no contradiction in the sentence "Jane is very well educated with only one proviso: she cannot think for herself."

2) We must recognize the complexity of society and culture and the extent to which they are necessarily a central point of intellectual and social debate. Since both society and culture, whatever their character, are dynamic, and different groups have an interest in how they evolve and change, these same groups have an interest in how their history is told.

A conservative's account of society and culture differs from a liberal's account. Conservatives play up what liberals play down. Liberals play up what conservatives play down. Often the difference is less a disagreement about what happened, than about whether this or that happening should be included in the account at all. Moreover, after the problem of inclusion is settled, further problems arise regarding how much space to give an event, how it should be characterized, and what we should learn from it. Conservatives often emphasize how past practice is worth preserving; liberals often emphasize how it should be corrected or transformed. These opposing construals have implications for our analysis of social problems and issues.

Much depends on whether one defines culture in terms of articulated ideals (however little they were practiced) or in terms of living practices (however distant from the ideal). So when Hirsch says that "We (Americans) believe in altruism and self-help, in equality, freedom, truth telling, and respect for the national law", (p. 99) his statement is ambiguous. He does not say whether he refers to articulated ideals or living practices. And when he says,

> Besides these vague principles, American culture fosters such myths about itself as its practicality, ingenuity, inventiveness, and independent-mindedness, its connection with the frontier, and its beneficence in the world (even when its leaders do not always follow beneficent policies). (p. 98)

one does not know what status we should give to the term 'myths'. If it is part of our cultural tradition to foster false beliefs about ourselves, then it is odd to consider this dimension of our culture as a manifestation of our belief in "truth telling". Or is belief in our truth telling itself a myth to be transmitted? If so, is it to be transmitted *as a myth?* It is unclear how this dimension of our culture should be "transmitted" to the young. Hirsch tries to side-step this issue by arguing that our national culture is not coherent and therefore,

> What counts in the sphere of public discourse is simply being able to use the language of culture in order to communicate *any* point of view effectively. (p. 103)

What he fails to take into account is that *how we pass on our culture* shapes what *our culture is.* If we pass on our culture so that the young uncritically accept myths as facts, then we cultivate uncritical thinking and uncritical conformity as part of our culture. If, however, we pass on our culture so that students must face the challenge of defining our culture, so that students hear and have to respond to alternative conceptualizations of our culture, then we cultivate critical thinking and independence of thought as part of our culture. These differing approaches to one's understanding of culture and its continuity have implications for our understanding of the process of cultural literacy as manifested in reading.

3) *Reading as a mode of cultural literacy is intrinsically a mode of critically questioning what one reads.* Hirsch repeatedly shows that reading is intrinsically a mode of thinking:

> The reader's mind is constantly inferring meanings that are not directly stated by the words of a text but are nonetheless part of its essential content. The explicit meanings of a piece of writing are the tip of an iceberg of meaning; the larger part lies below the surface of the text and is composed of the reader's own relevant knowledge. (p. 34)

Unfortunately, Hirsch understands this process of inference to be fundamentally an uncritical or robotic process, a process that relies on "telegraphic, vague, and limited" meanings and associations. The issue, as I see it, is not "Does the extraction or construction of meaning depend on inferences based on prior knowledge?" The issue is "How does the *good* reader extract or construct meanings through inference?" Hirsch appears to forget that the information we use to construct meanings are of multiple types, some (when misused in reading) lead us to distort or misconstrue the text. Reading a text is analogous to interpreting a situation. And remember we often construct interpretations as a result of our prejudices, biases, hates, fears, stereotypes, caricatures, self-delusions, and narrowmindedness. Our experience is not then less inferential. The poor reader makes inferences just as much as the good reader. The biased person makes inferences just as much as the relatively unbiased person does. Both reading texts and interpreting situations require insight into the multiple ways we can *mis-read* and *misinterpret*.

Reading is not a good in itself but only as it contributes to our understanding, only as it enriches us, enabling us to see things more truly, more faithfully. By the same token, experience is not a good in itself. Better no experience of a person or culture than a highly distorted experience of that person or culture. If reading and interpretation are to contribute to our education, they must reflect an emerging disciplining of mind and therefore of the mind's inferences. To do this requires a lot more than information that is "telegraphic" or "vague". It requires what might be called, for want of a better term, *critical literacy*.

4) *Critically literate readers must learn to distinguish the sources of the concepts they use to make inferences and most importantly must understand the logic of those concepts*. The critically literate reader routinely distinguishes cultural association from empirical facts, data from interpretations, evidence from conclusions, believing from knowing, having convictions from being stubborn, having judgment from being judgmental, conversation from gossip, mastery from domination.

If in a text the word 'democracy' appears, critically literate readers do not ramble through a panoply of cultural associations, such as images of Democratic and Republican conventions, balloons, ads on T.V., apple pie, motherhood, our government, Abraham Lincoln, ... Instead they probe the conceptual essence of the word 'democracy:' "the people govern". One constructs legitimate paraphrases of the word, such as "a form of government in which political power is in the hands of the people collectively rather than concentrated in the hands of a few". One recognizes that it stands in contrast to oligarchy, monarchy, and plutocracy. One achieves, in other words, command of what the word implies to educated speakers of the English language. One distinguishes educated uses of the word from uneducated or culturally narrowminded uses.

For example, in the U.S. careless speakers often assume a necessary semantic relationship between the word 'democracy' and the word 'capitalism' or 'free enterprise'. They assume that a particular economic system — a market economy — is part of the very meaning of the word 'democratic'. With this culturally biased conceptual assumption they pre-judge a variety of empirical issues.

Critically literate persons continually distinguish undisciplined and often misleading cultural associations from educated use. The word 'love' does not imply to educated speakers of the English language what it implies in Hollywood movies and soap operas. It takes intellectual discipline for speakers of a language to free themselves from the domination of the cultural associations that surround a word or phrase and grasp the trans-cultural meaning inherent in educated use. We tend to forget, for example, that there are educated speakers of English in virtually every country of the world and that the educated use of English, and all other natural languages, is not a simple reflection of the culturally dominant images and associations of any given culture that happens to use it. Learning to speak and write educated English does not presuppose U.S. or British or Australian or New Zealand cultural conditioning.

Hirsch seems oblivious of this essential insight, of this necessary discipline. He never mentions how an uncritical following of a cultural association that flies in the face of educated usage can cause a reader to misconstrue a text.

5) *Background logic, not background knowledge, is the crucial element to reading for understanding.* All writing that purports to convey knowledge or insight is structured by ideas and concepts in some logical relationships to each other. There are four dimensions of background logic that the educated, critical reader can probe: *1)* the source of the ideas or concepts, *2)* the substructure of the ideas or concepts, *3)* the implications or consequences of the ideas or concepts, and *4)* the relationships of the ideas to other ideas, similar and different. Since to read we must use our own thinking to figure out another's thought, critical readers form hypotheses about the author's possible meanings by trying out models from their own thought and experience. What could be meant, what is being implied by this or that sentence? If this is implied how does that square with what appears to be implied in the next and the next sentence? Let's see, could this or that experience of mine be what the author has in mind? If so, then he or she will also imply or assume this. Does he or she? Let me look further in the text.

One begins with the assumption that writers are logical and consistent. One begins with the most charitable interpretation of what they are saying, trying to come up with the strongest most insightful construal consistent with the text. One takes on the author's standpoint imaginatively and empathically. One tries to reason from the author's assumptions. One looks for evidence and experience to support what the author is saying. Only when one cannot find such evidence and support does a critical reader entertain the possibility that the text may be flawed conceptually or empirically.

This mode of critical reading was delineated many years ago by Mortimer Adler in his excellent book, *How to Read a Book*. In it he emphasizes how disciplined critical readers can figure out the basic logic of a text even when they don't have much of the background knowledge that would make it easier to read. This analytic process was used in the circle of people who read the Great Books of the Western World without the technical background in each book's field — psychology, philosophy, economics, physics, ... Armed with good dictionaries and the conceptual resources of their own minds thousands of dedicated readers sloughed their way through culturally diverse texts with minimal background knowledge. What they did is similar to what I did when I spent three days reading technical articles in medical journals at the U.C. Medical School Library to help a family member evaluate the status of research on his medical problem. I had virtually none of the background knowledge of the typical readers (doctors), but I did know how to use a dictionary and the resources of my own mind.

With effort and struggle and some conceptual puzzlement, I was able to identify three distinguishable therapeutic approaches to the medical problem I was researching. I was also able to identify arguments that advocates of each were using in support of their own and in opposition to the other proposed treatments. I was then able to hold my own in subsequent discussions with medical proponents of those approaches. This ability to determine the basic logic of a text in the absence of the standard background knowledge of those it was written for is one of the hallmarks of critically literate readers. It enabled me to read technical articles by cognitive psychologists, anthropologists, economists, and others even though they each presupposed background knowledge within their fields that I lacked.

Having background knowledge presupposed in a text is a matter of *degree*. The less you have, the more you have to figure out. A critically literate reader, like a cryptographer, can reconstruct much of what is not given by reasoning analytically from what is given. It is more important for students to learn that good readers look up unknown references when necessary, go back and reread, and don't simply keep moving on, than for students to be given lots of background. Even the best readers do not immediately understand everything they read. Students need practice learning this kind of reading, as well as practice reading material on which they have background.

Chapter 21

Critical Thinking and
General Semantics:
On the Primacy of Natural Languages

Abstract

Given the frequent sloppiness, vagueness, and obvious irrationality of much human thought, and the rigor, clarity, and usefulness of the physical sciences, many have felt that the answer to irrationality is a more "scientific" approach to language and human problem-solving. As understandable and tempting as this approach may be, it misses some crucial insights into both the nature of human life and understanding, and the nature and value of non-technical, natural, or ordinary language. In this paper, originally presented as the Alfred Korzybski Memorial Lecture *at the Yale Club in New York (1987), Richard Paul critiques the work of the General Semanticist Alfred Korzybski and explores how General Semantics and Critical Thinking can illuminate each other. Both traditions make similar assumptions about human experience: that the meanings we create shape our experience; that irrational habits and patterns of thought are a major cause of irrational behavior; and that people can, by disciplining their thought, become more rational. Korzybski, however, used mathematics and science as models for that improvement. Paul argues for a more "informal", naturalistic model, one in which the flexibility and resources of natural languages (French, German, English, etc.) are valued over artificial or technical languages as tools of thought. Each technical language, by its nature, assumes one perspective or framework; no other can be expressed by it. Natural languages, in contrast, allow for unlimited perspectives to be intelligibly expressed. Technical languages are rigid, natural languages flexible.*

Note to the Reader

Since this paper was read at the Symposium on General Semantics, it presupposed familiarity with the work of Alfred Korzybski. For those unfamiliar with his work, a brief introduction is in order. Korzybski took science to be a model of intellectual power, and began a system designed to free men of "un-sane" and "pathological" habits of using and reacting to language. Such pathology, he thought, could be traced back to Aristotle. His critique of traditional conceptions of language drew upon relativity

393

theory, quantum mechanics, colloidal chemistry, neurology, and mathematical logic. His goal was to show that Aristotelian habits oversimplify reality and thus produce dogmatism, rigidity, and lack of emotional balance. Such habits confuse symbols and what they represent, ignore limitations of abstraction, involve excessive attachment to sharp either-or distinctions, and generate uncontrolled responses — un-sanities requiring semantic therapy. Korzybski's proposed theory includes "indexing" ('man$_1$' to indicate difference in sense from 'man$_2$'), "dating" ('Roosevelt$_{1940}$', 'Roosevelt$_{1930}$'), and adding a symbol to all statements indicating an implicit 'et cetera'.

✦ Introduction

*M*y fundamental objective is to make a case for shifting the emphasis in General Semantics today. For the insights of Alfred Korzybski to have significant influence today and in the future, they must be freed from the limitations of the language he often used to express them. They must also be synthesized with insights which have developed since his major works. I believe that the emphases emerging in the critical thinking field today highlight useful insights that can be incorporated into General Semantics, just as General Semantics highlights useful insights that can be incorporated into the critical thinking movement. I shall proceed as follows. I shall sketch my understandings of the overall thrust of Korzybski's thought, and then analyze what in that thought needs to be emphasized, what de-emphasized, and what added, as it were. In general, I shall argue that Korzybski had too much faith in the possibility of solving human problems by applying scientific methods to them, and too little faith in the power, richness, and flexibility of natural languages like English, French, and German.

One of the insights implicit in critical thinking is that most human problems should be approached through dialogical and dialectical reasoning in natural languages, rather than through tightly disciplined but technically narrow scientific procedures in "artificial" languages. By this I mean that *reasoned judgment,* rather than hypothesis, prediction, and controlled experiment, can solve non-scientific human problems, and ordinary languages are the best medium for discussing them. For example, the disagreement, between Thomas Jefferson and Alexander Hamilton on the interpretation of the U.S. Constitution cannot be settled by facts about the Constitution or even by facts about people and society, but rather by a reasoned assessment in ordinary language. To conduct this reasoned assessment, we must empathically enter into the logic of both of these thinkers' arguments. We must think our way back and forth between their views, consider objections from both sides, consider answers to these objections, and integrate our own insights and experiences into the process. A language like English has excellent conceptual resources for constructing the two opposing sides. We can most readily express our insights and experiences in a natural language such as English.

Moreover, although *I* may settle the issue for myself, at least tentatively, my reasoning does not substitute for the reasoning of anyone else who wants to settle it. Basic human issues must be re-thought by each human. They cannot be settled once and for all in the logic of a scientific language.

Let me put this another way. Korzybski himself raised many important issues that cannot be fundamentally settled by scientific methods expressed in scientific languages. Though he used scientific and mathematical examples throughout his works, the books he wrote did not become part of science. Korzybski did not change any of the hard sciences by his writings, nor did he directly use scientific methods as they are used in the hard sciences themselves (physics, biology, chemistry, etc.). Rather he used scientific and non-scientific insights to construct a frame of reference fundamentally expressed in ordinary language, a philosophy or point of view from which many human failings and follies can be understood. He developed a variety of imaginative and practical devices for heightening our awareness of pitfalls in human thinking. But in his major works he did not write science.

Scientific methods work best only when we focus on ultimately monological rather than multilogical issues. We must distinguish when *one* frame of reference, *one* language, *one* set of laws are the keys to settling an issue from when rationally defensible competing viewpoints must be considered. We have good reason to suppose that the laws of physics, biology, chemistry, geology, and so forth are in harmony with each other and hence capable of being unified into one *logic,* the logic of science. In that sense, all the languages of science in principle can be synthesized. But human creations, our own personalities, the structure of our social groups and cultures, our lives and traditions, our thoughts, feelings, strengths and weaknesses do not display one unified logic, but a complicated network of competing and often contradictory logics. Natural languages have the "openness" to express this contradictory thinking without begging the key questions. Issues requiring an understanding of human behavior often require, therefore, multilogical reasoning in natural languages rather than scientific methods in technical languages for their settlement. And we can often settle them only for ourselves, not for others. Scientific insights may play a role in our thinking but they cannot determine that thinking.

In arguing for greater emphasis on non-scientific, multilogical thinking, I will explain how the quality of such thinking should be assessed. The possibility for assessment, I will suggest, is grounded in universal features or dimensions which can be critically examined in all thinking whose goal is understanding. I will argue also that we need special emphasis on seven traits of mind essential to the rational application of critical thinking principles: intellectual humility, intellectual courage, intellectual empathy, intellectual integrity, intellectual perseverance, faith in reason, and fairmindedness.

People construct the meaning of things from many divergent points of view, within, if you will, the framework of diverse logics. We can insightfully and autonomously participate in that construction only by becoming proficient in multilogical thinking. Korzybski made a significant contribution to our understanding of how this construction of meaning can become more sane and emancipatory. But now we need to add further insights to the process and make contributions of our own. General Semantics of the '80's and '90's should not be General Semantics of the '30's.

✦ General Semantics

General Semantics is a theory of human nature, language, and science whose announced goal is virtually the same as that of the critical thinking movement, namely, the development of rational people in a rational world, of people freed from the entrapments of language, thought, and logic. The foundation for it was laid in Alfred Korzybski's two major works, *Manhood of Humanity: The Science and Art of Human Engineering* (1921) and *Science and Sanity: An Introduction to Non-Aristotelian Systems and General Semantics* (1933). These two seminal insights run throughout the whole of Korzybski's works: that human life is mainly the product of how we construct the meaning of things; and that people can assimilate this insight and reform their minds and behavior in the light of it.

To assimilate this insight, Korzybski argued, people must realize that their day-to-day lives reflect day-to-day evaluations, and that these in turn reflect deep-seated but often unscientific and inappropriate habits of thought. We erroneously and unmindfully assume that we directly observe the world about us and that how we conceptualize and talk about that world reflects reality as it is. In fact, Korzybski argues, we systematically confuse simplistic meanings and rigid absolutistic labels with complex and dynamic realities. We become entrapped in meanings and labels because we have few practical tools for coming to terms with complexity, dynamism, and multi-dimensionality. Furthermore, because our evaluations of life situations are typically one-dimensional, absolutistic, and rigid, we act in ways which are, to a reasonable person, mad, foolish, or infantile. Yet this need not be so. A practical program of education that helps us keep before our minds the complexity, the dynamism, and the multi-dimensionality of the world is possible.

The structure of science and math provides Korzybski with basic models for this program. The languages of science and math, unlike those of natural languages like English, German, Chinese, and so forth, are for Korzybski specially designed to allow for the expression of complexity, dynamism, and multi-dimensionality. Ordinary natural languages, in contrast, encourage us to atomize and dichotomize the world. This is due, Korzybski argues, to Aristotelian assumptions and Aristotelian logic, built into the structure of such language, which blind us to the limitations of abstraction. These assumptions encourage us to use sharp "either-or" distinctions. They undermine our capacity to see the world in a scientific and hence realistic and sane way.

✦ The Need for Shift of Emphasis in General Semantics

Korzybski, at the beginning of the second half of *Science and Sanity* (p. 367), cites the following from Augustus De Morgan:

> Of all men, Aristotle is the one of whom his followers have worshiped his defects as well as his excellencies, which is what he himself never did to any man living or dead; indeed he has been accused of the contrary fault.

I would not go so far as to claim that Korzybski has suffered the same fate as Aristotle, for Aristotle has been slavishly followed for hundreds of years while Korzybski's work is relatively recent. Nevertheless, General Semantics needs to be updated with some insights whose significance has been deeply understood only within the last 30 to 40 years. The most important of these insights are threefold: firstly, the increasing recognition of the richness, flexibility, subtlety, and power of the conceptual resources implicit in the logic of natural languages; secondly, recognition of the insufficiency of mathematical logic as a set of tools for analyzing and critiquing ordinary reasoning; and thirdly, recognition of the important implications of the multi-dimensionality of most vexing human problems. The first set of insights is developed in the later works of Ludwig Wittgenstein and in the writings of such ordinary language philosophers as John Wisdom, J. L. Austin, and Gilbert Ryle. The second set of insights is developed in the writings of informal logicians and critical thinking theorists such as Michael Scriven, Ralph Johnson, J. Anthony Blair, and others. The third set of insights is being highlighted in the critical thinking movement.

Extensive scholarly work has emerged around the first two insights: hundreds of articles and books exploring the logic of concepts embedded in natural language usage and hundreds of articles and books that place practical logic and critical thinking on the foundation of *informal* rather than *formal* logic. These insights call for a modification of Korzybski's emphasis on scientific and mathematical language as paradigms for understanding the relationships among language, thought, logic, and behavior. Indeed, scientific and mathematical languages are much too rigid and technically specialized to serve as our main source of concepts for basic human problems, while natural languages have just the framework neutrality, the subtlety, and the flexibility we need to mediate between competing views and disciplines. Scientific and mathematical languages are tailor-made for what I have called monological problems, those which can be settled by working within one conceptual framework rather than many. Each hard science operates with one evolving but tightly disciplined language. All well-trained physicists around the world share one common set of foundational concepts and foundational understandings, criteria for evaluating the relevance and strength of claims, and established procedures for settling the vast majority of problems that can be generated within the domain of physics. A Soviet and a North American physicist have no problem sharing their thinking and the results of their work.

But hard science has emerged only in the realm of the purely physical and biological domains, not in the human domain, not in the analysis and assessment of human activities and values. This is because many human problems are multilogical rather than monological. By their nature, they can be approached from multiple frames of reference. They cannot be settled within one universally accepted point of view. By their nature they admit to being understood in different ways. The reason for this difference between most problems in the biological and physical worlds and most problems in the human world is in one sense simple.

We humans have no control over the logic of biological and physical nature but we do have significant control over the logic of human nature and society. Human life, unlike chemical behavior, has many logics, not just one logic. The logic and structure of human lives vary in accordance with divergent and often conflicting meanings people bring to the act of living, through their diverse philosophies and ideologies. We of all animals create the logic we live. And we have never collectively agreed what that logic will or should be. This is not a problem created by natural languages or their various structures, for, despite thinking in the same language, there is tremendous variation among speakers regarding basic frames of reference and points of view. Soviet, Chinese, and U.S. economists, historians, and sociologists do not see eye-to-eye, not because of differences in the structure of the natural languages they speak. Economists, historians, and sociologists from the same society speaking the same natural language, approach their subjects with very different conceptual frameworks and points of view. Human multi-dimensionality is often connected with conflicting ways of thinking about and structuring the human world. Sometimes these differences have largely social roots, sometimes largely economic roots, sometimes philosophical or ideological roots, and sometimes personal roots. Most often these various roots are so intertwined and have so grown together that it is impossible to separate them.

My basic point is this: when problems are multilogical rather than monological in nature, we cannot turn to science, by its nature monological, for a model. A science of human life is not possible because human life is not now, nor will it ever be, scientific. It is not now, nor will it ever be, monological. Monological problems can, in the last analysis, be solved within a dominant frame of reference, but human problems require the ability to move back and forth between and among conflicting frames of reference. Human problems require dialogical and dialectical, rather than monological, formal, or procedural, thinking. Korzybski's involvement in science and math, his background in engineering and technical, monological disciplines hampered his ability to fully grasp this important fact. He fails to see that we must look outside the monological disciplines for our paradigms. On the other hand, he is very much aware of the unlimited number of ways the world can be conceptualized and interpreted.

The shift of emphasis I suggest in no way invalidates the various extensional devices Korzybski developed to highlight the uniqueness of every person and event, to remind us of multiple causal influences, of differences in historical and environmental conditions, and of the impossibility of any statement covering all characteristics of a situation. Neither should we forget Korzybski's concern that we keep clearly in mind the inevitable inter-connectedness of events and the ever present danger of reifying our concepts. The heuristic value of such devices to General Semanticists parallels the heuristic value of various fallacy labels developed by critical thinking theorists to heighten our awareness of the pitfalls of various simplistic patterns of thought. Finally, the shift in vision I suggest does not invalidate Korzybski's emphasis on the need to think holistically and multi-dimensionally and to be aware of assumptions hidden in our ways of thinking and talking.

Still this shift would require some basic reorientation within the Korzybskian world view and so I should explain in further detail what that shift, as I envision it, entails.

✦ *Critical Thinking and the Critical Mind*

If human life is by its nature multilogical, then the problem of learning to think critically includes the very difficult task of learning to think clearly, accurately, and insightfully within a variety of conflicting points of view. We must become increasingly more cognizant of how our thought is being shaped by humanly created perspectives, and of their strengths and weaknesses, insights and biases. Taking this task seriously requires us to learn the art of dialogical and dialectical thinking and develop the mental traits which enable us to hold a set of beliefs or use a set of concepts without being dominated by them. These two tasks are interrelated, because dialogical or dialectical reasoning develops the fairminded critical mind only insofar as the thinking reflects certain dispositions or traits of mind.

Let me express this in more detail while I come at it from a somewhat different point of view. As critical thinkers, we begin with the premise that all thinking whose goal is understanding has a logic which, if we develop the appropriate skills, can be explicated, understood and, at least potentially, assessed. Thinking, despite its inevitable particularity, always operates within systems that display universal features. Hence all human thinking:

1) is defined by purposes and ends.

2) affirms or creates meanings and values.

3) embodies some concepts and distinctions and not others.

4) emphasizes some things and not others (puts some things into the foreground of our attention while throwing others into the background).

5) is based on assumptions.

6) advances or uses reasons or evidence.

7) generates implications or consequences.

8) is consistent with or contradictory to other lines of thought.

9) is developed within a point of view or perspective.

10) formulates or highlights some problems or issues and not others.

11) is relatively clear or unclear, elaborated or underdeveloped, deep or superficial, one-dimensional or multi-dimensional, strong or weak, insightful or prejudiced.

A skilled critical thinker is adept at probing into and explicating these dimensions of thought. Skill in Socratic questioning helps the critical thinker bring alternative and conflicting patterns of thought into explicit formulation, while skill in dialogical and dialectical exchange enables the critical thinker to gain insights into the strengths and weaknesses of those patterns.

For example, suppose I was raised in a traditional U.S. "liberal" family and have learned to reason about and interpret events from a liberal perspective. If I learn to think critically, I learn to identify the various elements of the logic of liberal thought, not as facts given in the world, but as guides and foundations in my own thinking. I recognize that others, for example conservatives, have different guides and foundations. I learn to recognize quite explicitly that I begin with some assumptions, rather than others; use some concepts, rather than others; raise some issues, rather than others; look for some kinds of causes of and explanations for social problems; and so forth. I also learn to value entering empathically into the thinking of a wide range of other competing political perspectives. I reason back and forth between them. I role play, in my own mind, various persuasions and perspectives. I learn to critically compare alternative assumptions, alternative objections, alternative implications and consequences. I ransack my experience for events that support these ways of thinking. I begin to integrate insights from other perspectives into my own. My thinking and my perspective evolves. I think of myself less and less as defined by the *substance* of my beliefs and more and more by the critical *processes* that enable me to shape and re-shape them. I realize, more and more, the importance of *how* I think, and of how I relate to that thinking.

My own intellectual traits become more important to me as I see how much the quality and value of my own thinking depends on them. Who I am and *how* I think — rather that *what* I think — become importantly united. I identify myself less and less with particular substantive beliefs. I make common cause, not with those who uncritically reinforce, nor with those who sophistically defend, my substantive beliefs, but with those who critically hold whatever beliefs they hold. I recognize that, as a critical liberal or conservative or radical or socialist or Christian or communist or feminist or atheist or capitalist, I have more in common with those who critically hold their beliefs, even though they may substantively disagree with me, than I have with those who uncritically or closedmindedly defend the substance of what I believe.

So as a critical thinker, I would suggest that Korzybski himself would not identify with the substance of his beliefs at any point in time. He would be willing to abandon, for example, his model of science and mathematics as the fundamental paradigm of knowledge if he came to see the importance of multi-logical "knowledge" and the kind of multi-logical thinking and traits of mind such knowledge requires. Korzybski, as a critical thinker, would be willing to enter empathically into this altered "non-scientific", "non-technical" way of thinking about knowledge that I am now sketching out. Furthermore, Korzybski would be willing to recognize that natural languages have advantages he failed to emphasize and scientific languages disadvantages he failed to highlight. This openness to change of view has characterized most of the great contributors to human knowledge and insight. It is reasonable to postulate then that, if Korzybski had lived to this day, his own views would have undergone significant shifts as a result.

✦ Concluding Remarks

The uncritical or sophistically critical mind is not unmotivated or without traits. The development of a critical mind through critical thinking is not a matter of placing bits and pieces of wisdom into a void. We are each born inclined toward egocentrism. We automatically and painlessly generate fantasies and beliefs that give us pleasure and satisfy our desires. We do not need to be taught how to avoid unpleasant truth nor how to distort, falsify, twist, or misrepresent situations to serve our egocentric interests. We do this quite naturally. Children display great precocity in these "skills" with no training in their backgrounds. The human egocentric mind is tailor-made for self-deception and ready-equipped with what Freud called defense mechanisms. Many of the important meanings we construct for ourselves produce powerful stereotypes, prejudices, delusions, illusions, and narrowmindedness of various kinds. We need a much more developed theory of the cultivation of intellectual traits than we now have in order to realistically combat egocentric thought.

I can reason well in domains in which I am prejudiced — hence, eventually reason my way out of my prejudices — only if I develop a set of mental benchmarks for such reasoning. Of course, one of the insights I will need is the clear recognition that when I am prejudiced, it will seem to me that I am not, and, similarly, that those who are not prejudiced as I am will nevertheless seem to me to be prejudiced. (To a prejudiced person an unprejudiced person will seem prejudiced.) I will come to this insight only to the degree that I have analyzed experiences in which I have first been intensely convinced that I was correct only to find after a series of challenges, reconsiderations, and new reasonings that my previous conviction was in fact prejudiced. I must take this experience apart in my mind, gain a clear sense of its elements and of how these elements fit together (how I became prejudiced; how I inwardly experienced that prejudice; how intensely that prejudice appeared to me to be insight; how I progressively began to break down that prejudice through serious consideration of opposing lines of reasoning; how I slowly came to new assumptions, new information, and ultimately new conceptualizations ...).

Only when one gains analyzed experiences of working one's way, reasoning one's way, out of prejudices can one gain the sort of higher order abilities a fairminded critical thinker requires. To reason one's way out of prejudices in the way suggested above requires that we recognize that our own egocentric drives are the fundamental obstacles to rational living, not forces operating outside of us, not language in itself but language as we are egocentrically inclined to use it. Our capacity to develop a critical mind develops at best alongside of our native egocentric thought. Only through critical analysis directed at our egocentrism can we hope to develop skills in isolating the irrational dimension of our experience. But this skill grows only through time and as a result of very particular educational cultivation.

One implication of the above reasoning is this: if we take seriously the traditional goals of General Semantics, we must go beyond its traditional means. We must reshape and shift our vision somewhat of the roots of the problem. We must give up the view that the structure of natural languages is the fundamental problem. We must learn to use the language we speak with clarity, precision, and accuracy, for it is in natural rather than artificial languages that can we find the linguistic and conceptual resources to develop our critical faculties. We must learn to distinguish monological, technical issues from multi-logical, cross-disciplinary ones. We must develop the art of Socratic questioning and practice dialogical and dialectical exchange. We must empathically enter into and reason within a diversity of points of view. We must develop skill in laying out the logical features of our own thinking and that of others. We must develop our intellectual humility and courage, our intellectual empathy and integrity, our intellectual perseverance, our confidence in reason, and our fairmindedness. And we must do this as part of the very frustrating and difficult task of combatting our ever-lurking egocentric minds.

Most of all we must realize that science cannot tell us how to construct the meaning of things and certainly not how to create a humane world. We must play down the significance of disagreements concerning the substance of thought and look to find others within a diversity of perspectives who critically, rather than simplistically or sophistically, believe what they believe. We must make common cause with critical General Semanticists as well as with critical opponents of General Semantics, if any. We must beware of allegiances based on labels like "American", "Russian", "Communist", "Capitalist", "Christian", "Atheist", "Liberal", "Conservative", "Radical". Only with such a shift of emphasis and vision can the enduring insights of Korzybski be carried forward and honored in the deepest fashion, by being empathically and critically entertained by empathic critical minds.

Chapter 22

The Contribution of Philosophy to Thinking

Abstract

In this paper, originally part of "Philosophy and Cognitive Psychology", Paul argues for the power of philosophy and philosophical thinking for intellectual autonomy. He claims that even children have a need and right to think philosophically and are very much inclined to do so, but are typically discouraged by the didactic absolutistic answers and attitudes of adults. Consequently, the inquiring minds of children soon become jaded by the self-assured absolutistic environment which surrounds them.

The potential of children to philosophize is suggested in a transcript of a 4th grade class-room discussion of a series of abstract questions. Following the transcript, Paul illustrates a variety of ways in which traditional school subjects can be approached philosophically. He closes with a discussion of the values and intellectual traits fostered by philosophical thought, the skills and processes of thought, and the relation of philosophical to critical thought.

*I*n this paper I lay the foundation for a philosophy-based, in contrast to a psychology-based, approach to teaching critical thinking across the curriculum. I lay out the general theory and provide some examples of how it could be used to transform classroom instruction and activities. Nevertheless, I want to underscore the point that I lack the space to cover my subject comprehensively. Interested readers must independently pursue the leads I provide, to see the power and flexibility of philosophy-based approaches to critical thinking instruction. I must content myself with modest goals, with a few basic insights into philosophical thinking, with a few of its advantages for instruction.

There are three overlapping senses of *philosophy* that can play a role in explicating the nature of philosophical thinking: philosophy as a field of study, philosophy as a mode of thinking, and philosophy as a framework for thinking. In what follows, I focus on philosophy as a mode of and framework for thinking and will say least about it as a field of study. Nevertheless, some characterization of the field of philosophy is useful.

Philosophy is steeped in dialogical and dialectical thought. Philosophy is an art rather than a science, a discipline that formulates issues that can be approached from multiple points of view and invites critical dialogue and reasoned discourse between conflicting viewpoints. Critical thought and discussion are its main instruments of learning. More so than any other field, philosophy requires all participants to think their own way to whatever system of beliefs ultimately constitute their thought within the field. This entails that all philosophers develop their own unique philosophies.

In contrast, science students are not expected to construct their own science. Sciences have emerged because of the possibility of specialization and joint work within a highly defined shared frame of reference. Its ground rules exclude what is not subject to quantification and measurement. Sciences are cooperative, collaborative ventures whose practitioners agree to limit strictly the range of issues they consider and how they consider them.

Philosophy, on the other hand, is largely an individualistic venture wherein participants agree, only in the broadest sense on the range and nature of the issues they will consider. Philosophers have traditionally been concerned with big questions, root issues that organize the overall framework of thinking itself, in all domains, not just one. Philosophers do not typically conduct *experiments*. They rarely form *hypotheses* or make *predictions* as scientists do. Philosophical tradition gives us a tapestry rich in the development of individual syntheses of ideas across multiple subject domains: syntheses carefully and precisely articulated and elaborately argued. There is reason for this basic difference between the history of science and that of philosophy.

Some questions, by their nature, admit of collaborative treatment and solution; others do not. For example, we do not need to individually test for the chemical structure of lead or determine the appropriate theory of that structure; we can rely on the conclusions of those who have done so. But we cannot learn the structure of our own lives or the best way to plan for the future by looking up the answer in a technical manual or having an answer determined for us by a collaborative scientific effort. We must each individually analyze these questions to obtain rationally defensible answers. There is a wide range of ways human lives can be understood and a variety of strategies for living them. Rarely, if ever, can answers to philosophical questions be validated by one person for another.

The method of philosophy, or the *mode* of thinking characteristic of philosophy, is that of critical discussion, rational cross examination, and dialectical exchange. Every person who would participate in that discussion must create and elaborate a framework for thinking comprehensively. This discipline in the mode of thinking characteristic of philosophy has roots in the ideal of learning to think with a clear sense of the ultimate foundations of one's thinking, of the essential logic of one's thought, and of significant alternative, competing ways of thinking.

Consider philosophical thinking as a framework for thought. When one engages in philosophical thinking, one thinks within a self-constructed network of assumptions, concepts, defined issues, key inferences, and insights. To think philosophically as a liberal, for example, is to think within a different framework of ideas than conservatives do. What is more, to think philosophically, in this sense, is to *know* that one is thinking within a different framework of ideas than other thinkers. It is to know the foundations of liberalism compared to those of conservativism.

✦ Philosophical and Un-Philosophical Minds: Philosophy as a Mode of Thinking and a Framework for Thinking

Perhaps the best way to show what lies at the heart of the uniqueness and power of philosophy is to consider the contrast in general between un-philosophical and philosophical minds. In doing so, I present the two as idealized abstractions for the purpose of clarifying a paradigm; I realize that no one perfectly illustrates these idealizations.

The un-philosophical mind thinks without a clear sense of the foundations of its own thought, without conscious knowledge of the most basic concepts, aims, assumptions, and values that define and direct it. The un-philosophical mind is unaware that it thinks within a system, within a framework, within, if you will, a *philosophy*. Consequently, the un-philosophical mind is trapped within the system it uses, unable to deeply understand alternative or competing systems. The un-philosophical mind tends toward an intra-system closedmindedness. The un-philosophical mind may learn to think within different systems of thought, if the systems are compartmentalized and apply in different contexts, but it cannot compare and contrast whole systems, because, at any given time, it thinks within a system without a clear sense of what it means to do so. This kind of intra-system thinking can be skilled, but it lacks foundational self-command. It functions well when confronted with questions and issues that fall clearly within its system, but is at its worse when facing issues that cross systems, require revising a system, or presuppose explicit critique of the system used.

Un-philosophical liberals, for example, would be hard pressed to think clearly and accurately within a conservative point of view, and hence would not do well with issues such as "What are some of the most important insights of conservatism?" Un-philosophical psychologists, to take another example, would find it difficult to integrate sociological or economic insights into their thinking. Indeed, thinking un-philosophically in any discipline means thinking reductionistically with respect to insights from other disciplines: one either reduces them to whatever can be absorbed into concepts in one's field or ignores them entirely.

An un-philosophical mind is at its best when routine methods, rules, or procedures function well and there is no need to critically reconceptualize them in the light of a broad understanding of one's framework for thinking. If one lacks philosophical insight into the underlying logic of those routines, rules, or procedures, one lacks the ability to mentally step outside of them and conceive of alternatives. As a result, the un-philosophical mind tends toward conformity to a system without grasping clearly what the system is, how it came to be thus, or how it might have been otherwise.

The philosophical mind, in contrast, routinely probes the foundations of its own thought, realizes its thinking is defined by basic concepts, aims, assumptions, and values. The philosophical mind gives serious consideration to alternative and competing concepts, aims, assumptions, and values, enters empathically into thinking fundamentally different from its own, and does not confuse its thinking with reality. By habitually thinking globally, the philosophical mind gains foundational self-command, and is comfortable when problems cross disciplines, domains, and frameworks. A philosophical mind habitually probes the basic principles and concepts that lie behind standard methods, rules, and procedures. The philosophical mind recognizes the need to refine and improve the systems, concepts, and methods it uses and does not simply conform to them. The philosophical mind deeply values gaining command over its own fundamental modes of thinking.

The discipline of philosophy is the only one at present that routinely fosters the philosophical mind, though there are philosophical minds at work in every discipline. The philosophical mind is most evident in other disciplines in those working on foundational concepts and problems. In everyday life, the philosophical mind is most evident in those who deeply value doing their own thinking about the basic issues and problems they face and giving serious reasoned consideration to the ideas and thinking of others. In everyday life, the philosophical mind is most evident in those not afraid to probe conventional thought, rules, mores, and values, those skeptical of standard answers and standard definitions of questions and problems.

In teaching, the philosophical mind is most evident in those who routinely probe the concepts, aims, assumptions, and values that underlie their teaching;who routinely raise fundamental issues through Socratic questions;who routinely encourage students to probe the foundation and source of their own ideas and those of others; and who routinely encourage students to develop their own philosophy or approach to life or learning based on their own disciplined, rational thought. Need I add that philosophical thinking is not habit for most?

✦ Why Children Need to Think Philosophically

There is a sense in which everyone has a philosophy, since human thought and actions are always embedded in a framework of foundational concepts, values, and assumptions which define a "system" of some sort. Humans are by nature inferential, meaning-creating animals. In this sense, all humans use "philosophies" and even in some sense create them. Even the thinking of very young children presupposes philosophical foundations, as Piaget so ably demonstrated. Of course, if by 'philosophy' we mean explicit and systematic reflection on the concepts, values, aims, and assumptions that structure thinking and underlie behavior, then in that sense most children do *not* philosophize. It all depends on whether one believes that one can have a philosophy without *thinking* one's way to it.

Most children have at least the impulse to philosophize and for a time seem driven by a strong desire to know the most basic *what* and *why* of things. Of course parents or teachers rarely cultivate this tendency. Usually children are given didactic answers in ways that discourage, rather than stimulate, further inquiry. Many parents and teachers seem to think that they or textbooks have appropriate and satisfactory answers to the foundational questions that children raise, and the sooner children accept these answers the better. Such authorities unwittingly encourage children to assent to, without truly understanding, basic beliefs. In effect, we teach answers to philosophical questions as though they were like answers to chemical questions. As a result, children lose the impulse to question, as they learn to mouth the standard answers of parents, peers, and other socializing groups. How many of these mouthed answers become a part of children's lived beliefs is another matter.

Children learn behaviors as well as explanations. They learn to act as well as to speak. Thus they learn to behave in ways inconsistent with much of their conscious talk and thought. Children learn to live, as it were, in different and only partially integrated worlds. They develop unconscious worlds of meaning that do not completely square with what they are told or think they believe. Some of these meanings become a source of pain, frustration, repression, fear, and anxiety. Some become a source of harmless fantasizing and day-dreaming. Some are embedded in action, albeit in camouflaged, or in tacit, unarticulated ways.

In any case, the process of unconsciously taking in or unknowingly constructing a variety of meanings outstrips the child's initial impulse to reflect on or question those meanings. In one sense, then, children become captives of the ideas and meanings whose impact on their own thought and action they do not themselves determine. They have in this sense two philosophies (only partially compatible with each other): one verbal but largely unlived; the other lived but mainly unverbalized. This split continues into adulthood. On the emotional level, it leads to anxiety and stress. On the moral level, it leads to hypocrisy and self-deception. On the intellectual level, it results in a condition in which lived beliefs and spontaneous thought are unintegrated with school learning which in turn is ignored in "real life" situations.

As teachers and parents we seldom consider the plight of children from this perspective. We tend to act as though there were no real need for children to reflect deeply about the meanings they absorb. We fail to see the conflicting meanings they absorb, the double messages that capture their minds. Typically our principal concern is that they absorb the meanings that we think are correct and act in ways that we find acceptable. Reflecting upon their thoughts and actions seems important to us only to get them to think or act correctly, that is, as we want them to think and act. We seldom question whether they deeply agree or even understand. We pay little attention as parents to whether or not conflicting meanings and double messages become an on-going problem for them.

In some sense we act as though we believe, and doubtless many do believe, that children have no significant capacity, need, or right to think for themselves. Many adults do not think that children can participate mindfully in the process which shapes their own minds and behavior. Of course, at the same time we often talk to our children as though they were somehow responsible for, or in control of, the ideas they express or act upon. This contradictory attitude toward children is rarely openly admitted. We need to deal explicitly with it.

I believe that children have the need, the capacity, and the *right* to freedom of thought, and that the proper cultivation of that capacity requires an emphasis on the philosophical dimension of thought and action. Again, by 'the philosophical dimension', I mean precisely the kind of deliberative thought that gives to thinkers the on-going disposition to mindfully create, analyze, and assess their own most basic assumptions, concepts, values, aims, and meanings, in effect to choose the very framework in which they think and on the basis of which they act. I would not go so far as to say, as Socrates was reputed to have said, that the unreflective life is not worth living, but I would say that an unreflective life is not a truly *free* life and is often a basic cause of personal and social problems. I claim at least this much, that philosophical thinking is necessary to freedom of thought and action and that freedom of thought and action are good in themselves and should be given a high priority in schooling. They are certainly essential for a democracy. How can the people rule, as the word *democracy* implies, if they do not think for themselves on issues of civic importance? And if they are not encouraged to think for themselves *in* school, why should they do so once they leave it?

Let me now discuss whether children are in fact capable of this sort of freedom of thought, reflection upon ultimate meanings, values, assumptions, and concepts. The question is both conceptual and empirical. On the conceptual side, the issue is one of *degree*. Only to the degree that children are encouraged in supportive circumstances to reflect philosophically, will they develop proficiency in it. Since few parents and teachers value this sort of reflection or are adept at cultivating it, it is understandable that children soon give up their instinctive philosophical impulses (the basic *why* and *what* questions). It would be foolish to assume that it is the *nature* of children to think and act unreflectively when indeed our experience indicates that they are socialized into unreflectiveness. Since we do not encourage children to philosophize why should they do so?

Furthermore, in many ways we penalize children for philosophizing. Children will sometimes innocently entertain an idea in conflict with the ideas of their parents, teachers, or peers. Such ideas are often ridiculed and the children made to feel ashamed of their thoughts. It is quite common, in other words, for people to penalize unconventional thought and reward conventional thought. When we think only as we are rewarded to think, however, we cease to think freely or deeply. Why should we think for ourselves if doing so may get us into trouble and if teachers, parents, and powerful peers provide authoritative didactic answers for us? Before we decide that children cannot think for themselves about basic ideas and meanings, we ought to give them a real and extended opportunity to do so. No society has yet done this. Unless we are willing to exercise some faith in freedom of thought, we will never be in a position to reap the benefits of it or to discover its true limits, if any.

Let me now explore the conceptual side of the question further by suggesting some kinds of philosophical issues embedded, not only in the lives of children, but also in the lives of adults:

> Who am I? What am I like? What are the people around me like? What are people of different backgrounds, religions, and nations like? How much am I like others? How much am I unlike them? What kind of a world do I live in? When should I trust? When should I distrust? What should I accept? What should I question? How should I understand my past, the pasts of my parents, my ethnic group, my religion, my nation? Who are my friends? Who are my enemies? What is a friend? How am I like and unlike my enemy? What is most important to me? How should I live my life? What responsibilities do I have to others? What responsibilities do they have to me? What responsibilities do I have to my friends? Do I have any responsibilities to people I don't like? To people who don't like me? To my enemies? Do my parents love me? Do I love them? What is love? What is hate? What is indifference? Does it matter if others do not approve of me? When does it matter? When should I ignore what others think? What rights do I have? What rights should I give to others? What should I do if others do not respect my rights? Should I get what I want? Should I question what I want? Should I take what I want if I am strong or smart enough to get away with it? Who comes out ahead in this world, the strong or the good person? Is it worthwhile to be good? Are authorities good or just strong?

I do not assume that children must reflect on all or even most of the questions that professional philosophers consider — although the preceding list contains many concepts that professional philosophers tackle. To cultivate philosophical thinking, one does not force students to think in a sophisticated way before they are ready. Each student can contribute to a philosophical discussion thoughts which help other students to orient themselves within a range of thoughts, some of which support or enrich and some of which conflict with other thoughts. Different students achieve different levels of understanding. There is no reason to try to force any given student to achieve a particular level of understanding. But the point is that we can lead young students into philosophical discussions which help them begin to:

1. see the significance and relevance of basic philosophical questions to understanding themselves and the world about them,
2. understand the problematic character of human thought and the need to probe deeply into it,
3. gain insights into what it takes to make thinking more rational, critical, and fairminded,
4. organize their thinking globally across subject matter divisions,
5. achieve initial command over their own thought processes, and
6. come to believe in the value and power of their own minds.

In the transcript that follows, a normal 4th grade class is led to discuss a variety of basic ideas: how the mind works, the nature of mind, why different people interpret the same events differently, the relationship between emotions and mental interpretations, the nature and origin of personality, nature versus nurture, peer group influence on the mind, cultural differences, free will versus determinism, the basis for ethical and unethical behavior, the basis for reputation, the relation of reputation to goodness, mental illness, social prejudice and sociocentrism, and the importance of thinking for oneself. This transcript represents the first philosophical discussion this particular class had and although it is clear from some of their answers that their present degree of insight into the ideas being discussed is limited, it is also clear that they are capable of pursuing those insights and of articulating important philosophical ideas that could be explored in greater and greater depth over time.

✦ Transcript

The following is a transcript of a 4th grade Socratic discussion. The discussion leader was with these particular students for the first time. The purpose was to determine the status of the children's thinking on some of the abstract questions whose answers tend to define our broadest thinking. The students were eager to respond and often seemed to articulate responses that reflected potential insights into the character of the human mind, its relation to the body, the forces that shape us, the influence of parents and peer groups, the nature of morality and of ethnocentric bias. The insights are disjointed, of course, but the questions that elicited them and the responses that articulated them could be used as the basis of future discussions or simple assignments with these students.

➤ *How does your mind work?*
Where's your mind?

Student: In your head. (Numerous students point to their heads.)

➤ *Does your mind do anything?*

Student: It helps you remember and think.

Student: It helps, like, if you want to move your legs. It sends a message down to them.

Student: This side of your mind controls this side of your body and that side controls this other side.

Student: When you touch a hot oven it tells you whether to cry or say ouch.

➤ *Does it tell you when to be sad and when to be happy?*
How does your mind know when to be happy and when to be sad?

Student: When you're hurt it tells you to be sad.

Student: If something is happening around you is sad.

Student: If there is lightning and you are scared.

Student: If you get something you want.

Student: It makes your body operate. It's like a machine that operates your body.

➤ *Does it ever happen that two people are in the same circumstance but one is happy and the other is sad? Even though they are in exactly the same circumstance?*

Student: You get the same toy. One person might like it. The other gets the same toy and he doesn't like the toy.

➤ *Why do you think that some people come to like some things and some people seem to like different things?*

Student: 'Cause everybody is not the same. Everybody has different minds and is built different, made different.

Student: They have different personalities?

➤ *Where does personality come from?*

Student: When you start doing stuff and you find that you like some stuff best.

➤ *Are you born with a personality or do you develop it as you grow up?*

Student: You develop it as you grow up.

➤ *What makes you develop one rather than another?*

Student: Like, your parents or something.

➤ *How can your parent's personality get into you?*

Student: Because you're always around them and then the way they act, if they think they are good and they want you to act the same way, then they'll sort of teach you and you'll do it.

Student: Like, if you are in a tradition. They want you to carry on something that their parents started.

➤ *Does your mind come to think at all the way the children around you think? Can you think of any examples where the way you think is like the way children around you think? Do you think you behave like other American kids?*

Student: Yes.

➤ *What would make you behave more like the kids around you than like Eskimo kids?*

Student: Because you're around them.

Student: Like, Eskimo kids probably don't even know what the word 'jump-rope' is. American kids know what it is.

➤ *And are there things that the Eskimo kids know that you don't know about?*

Student: Yes.

Student: And also we don't have to dress like them or act like them and they have to know when a storm is coming so they won't get trapped outside.

➤ *O.K., so if I understand you then, parents have some influence on how you behave and the kids around you have some influence on how you behave. ... Do you have some influence on how you behave? Do you choose the kind of person you're going to be at all?*

Student: Yes.

➤ *How do you do that do you think?*

Student: Well if someone says to jump off a five-story building, you won't say O.K. You wouldn't want to do that ....

➤ *Do you ever sit around and say, "Let's see shall I be a smart person or a dumb one?"*

Student: Yes.

➤ *But how do you decide?*

Student: Your grades.

➤ *But I thought your teacher decided your grades. How do you decide?*

Student: If you don't do your homework you get bad grades and become a dumb person but if you study real hard you'll get good grades.

➤ *So you decide that, right?*

Student: And if you like something at school like computers you work hard and you can get a good job when you grow up. But if you don't like anything at school you don't work hard.

Student: You can't just decide you want to be smart, you have to work for it.

Student: You got to work to be smart just like you got to work to get your allowance.

➤ *What about being good and being bad, do you decide whether you're good or you're bad? How many people have decided to be bad? (Three students raise their hands.) (To first student,) Why have you decided to be bad?*

Student: Well, I don't know. Sometimes I think I've been bad too long and I want to go to school and have a better reputation but sometimes I feel like just making trouble and who cares.

➤ *Let's see, is there a difference between who you are and your reputation? What's your reputation? That's a pretty big word. What's your reputation?*

Student: The way you act. If you had a bad reputation people wouldn't like to be around you and if you had a good reputation people would like to be around you and be your friend.

➤ *Well, but I'm not sure of the difference between who you are and who people think you are. Could you be a good person and people think you bad? Is that possible?*

Student: Yeah, because you could try to be good. I mean, a lot of people think this one person's really smart but this other person doesn't have nice clothes but she tries really hard and people don't want to be around her.

➤ *So sometimes people think somebody is real good and they're not and sometimes people think that somebody is real bad and they're not. Like if you were a crook, would you let everyone know you're a crook?*

Students: [Chorus of "NO!"]

➤ *So some people are really good at hiding what they are really like. Some people might have a good reputation and be bad; some people might have a bad reputation and be good.*

Student: Like, everyone might think you were good but you might be going on dope or something.

Student: Does reputation mean that if you have a good reputation you want to keep it just like that? Do you always want to be good for the rest of your life?

➤ *I'm not sure ....*

Student: So if you have a good reputation you try to be good all the time and don't mess up and don't do nothing?

➤ *Suppose somebody is trying to be good just to get a good reputation — why are they trying to be good?*

Student: So they can get something they want and they don't want other people to have?

Student: They might be shy and just want to be left alone.

Student: You can't tell a book by how it's covered.

➤ *Yes, some people are concerned more with their cover than their book. Now let me ask you another question. So if its true that we all have a mind and our mind helps us to figure out the world and we are influenced by our parents and the people around us, and sometimes we choose to do good things and sometimes we choose to do bad things, sometimes people say things about us and so forth and so on.... Let me ask you: Are there some bad people in this world?*

Student: Yeah.

Student: Terrorists and stuff.

Student: Nightstalker.

Student: The TWA hijackers.

Student: Robbers.

Student: Rapers.

Student: Bums.

➤ *Bums, are they bad?*

Student: Well, sometimes.

Student: The Klu Klux Klan.

Student: The Bums ... not really, cause they might not look good but you can't judge them by how they look. They might be really nice and everything.

➤ *O.K., so they might have a bad reputation but be good, after you care to know them. There might be good bums and bad bums.*

Student: Libyan guys and Machine gun Kelly.

➤ *Let me ask you, do the bad people think they're bad?*

Student: A lot of them don't think they're bad but they are. They might be sick in the head.

→ *Yes, some people are sick in their heads.*

Student: A lot of them (bad guys) don't think they're bad.

→ *Why did you say Libyan people?*

Student: Cause they have a lot 'o terrorists and hate us and bomb us ....

→ *If they hate us do they think we are bad or good?*

Student: They think we are bad.

→ *And we think they are bad? And who is right?*

Student: Usually both of them.

Student: None of us are really bad!

Student: Really, I don't know why our people and their people are fighting. Two wrongs don't make a right.

Student: It's like if there was a line between two countries, and they were both against each other, if a person from the first country crosses over the line, they'd be considered the bad guy. And if a person from the second country crossed over the line he'd be considered the bad guy.

→ *So it can depend on which country you're from who you consider right or wrong, is that right?*

Student: Like a robber might steal things to support his family. He's doing good to his family but actually bad to another person.

→ *And in his mind do you think he is doing something good or bad?*

Student: It depends what his mind is like. He might think he is doing good for his family or he might think he is doing bad for the other person.

Student: It's like the underground railroad a long time ago. Some people thought it was bad and some people thought it was good.

→ *But if lots of people think something is right and lots of people think something is wrong, how are you supposed to figure out the difference between right and wrong?*

Student: Go by what you think!

→ *But how do you figure out what to think?*

Student: Lots of people go by other people.

→ *But somebody has to decide for themselves, don't they?*

Student: Use your mind?

➤ *Yes, let's see, suppose I told you: "You are going to have a new classmate. Her name is Sally and she's bad." Now, you could either believe me or what could you do?*

Student: You could try to meet her and decide whether she was bad or good.

➤ *Suppose she came and said to you: "I'm going to give you a toy so you'll like me." And she gave you things so you would like her, but she also beat up on some other people, would you like her because she gave you things?*

Student: No, because she said I'll give you this so you'll like me. She wouldn't be very nice.

➤ *So why should you like people?*

Student: Because they act nice to you.

➤ *Only to you?*

Student: To everybody!

Student: I wouldn't care what they gave me. I'd see what they're like inside.

➤ *But how do you find out what's on the inside of a person?*

Student: You could ask, but I would try to judge myself.

Socratic questioning is flexible. The questions asked at any given point will depend on what the students say, what ideas the teacher wants to pursue, and what questions occur to the teacher. Generally, Socratic questions raise basic issues, probe beneath the surface of things, and pursue problematic areas of thought.

The above discussion could have gone in a number of different directions. For instance, rather than focussing on the mind's relationship to emotions, the teacher could have pursued the concept 'mind' by asking for more examples of its functions, and having students group them. The teacher could have followed up the response of the student who asked, "Does reputation mean that if you have a good reputation you want to keep it just like that?" He might, for instance, have asked the student why he asked that, and asked the other students what they thought of the idea. Such a discussion may have developed into a dialogical exchange about reputation, different degrees of goodness, or reasons for being bad. Or the concept 'bad people' could have been pursued and clarified by asking students why the examples they gave were examples of bad people. Students may then have been able to suggest tentative generalizations which could have been tested and probed through further questioning. Instead of exploring the influence of perspective on evaluation, the teacher might have probed the idea, expressed by one student, that no one is "really bad". The student could have been asked to explain the remark, and other students could have been asked for their responses. In these cases and others, the teacher has a choice between any number of equally thought provoking questions. No one question is the 'right' question.

A general discussion such as this lays the foundation for subsequent discussions by raising and briefly covering a variety of interrelated issues. This can be followed up in small group discussions or made the basis of brief writing assignments or integrated into the discussion of literature, history, or other subject areas. Note the variety of questions that were raised in the preceding discussion:

1. Is the mind like a machine that operates your body?

2. How is it influenced by events?

If something happening around you is sad.

If you get something you want.

3. How is it influenced by its own interpretations and meanings?

You get the same toy. One person might like it. The other gets the same toy and he doesn't like the toy.

When you start doing stuff and you find that you like some stuff best.

4. How is it shaped by significant persons like parents?

Because you're always around them and then the way they act, if they think they are good and they want you to act the same way, then they'll sort of teach you and you'll do it.

5. How is it shaped by cultural forces like peer groups?

Because you're around them.

Like, Eskimo kids probably don't even know what the word 'jump-rope' is. American kids know what it is.

And also we don't have to dress like them or act like them and they have to know when a storm is coming so they won't get trapped outside.

6. Does free will involve more than just inwardly deciding?

You can't just decide you want to be smart, you have to work for it.

You got to work to be smart just like you got to work to get your allowance.

Sometimes I think I've been bad too long and I want to go to school and have a better reputation, but sometimes I feel like just making trouble and who cares.

7. Are minds sometimes deceived by others or self-deceived?

Like, everyone might think you were good but you might be going on dope or something.

You can't tell a book by how it's covered.

The bums, ... not really 'cause they might not look good but you can't judge them by how they look. They might be really nice and everything.

A lot of them don't think they're bad but they are. They might be sick in the head.

A lot of them (bad guys) don't think they're bad.

It depends what his mind is like. He might think he is doing good for his family or he might think he is doing bad for the other person.

Yeah, because you could try to be good. I mean, a lot of people think this one person's really smart but this other person doesn't have nice clothes but she tries really hard and people don't want to be around her.

8. *What are people really like? Should you approach anyone as if they were evil?*

None of us are really bad!

Really, I don't know why our people and their people are fighting. Two wrongs don't make a right.

They might be shy and just want to be left alone.

9. *Should you think as others think or do your own thinking?*

Lots of people go by other people.

You could ask, but I would try to judge myself.

You could try to meet her and decide whether she was bad or good.

When teachers approach their subjects philosophically, they make it much easier for students to begin to integrate their thinking across subject matter divisions. In the preceding discussion, for example, the issues considered involved personal experience, psychology, sociology, ethics, culture, and philosophy. The issues, philosophically put, made these diverse areas relevant to each other. And just as one might inquire into a variety of issues by first asking a basic philosophical question, so one might proceed in the other direction: first asking a question within a subject area and then, by approaching it philosophically, explore its relationships to other subjects. These kinds of transitions are quite natural and unforced in a philosophical discussion, because all dimensions of human study and experience are indeed related to each other. We would see this if we could set aside the blinders that usually come with conventional discipline-specific instruction. By routinely considering root questions and root ideas philosophically, we naturally pursue those connections freed of these blinders.

As teachers teaching philosophically, we are continually interested in what the students themselves think on basic matters and issues. We continually encourage students to explore how what they think about X relates to what they think about Y and Z. This necessarily requires that students' thought moves back and forth between their own basic ideas and those presented in class by other students, between their own ideas and those expressed in a book, between their thinking and their experiences, between ideas within one domain and those in another.

This *dialogical* process (moving back and forth between divergent domains and points of view) will sometimes become *dialectical* (some ideas will clash or be inconsistent with others). The act of *integrating* thinking is deeply tied to the act of *assessing* thinking, because, as we consider a diversity of ideas, we discover that many of them contradict each other. Teachers should introduce the critical, analytic vocabulary of English (to be discussed presently) into classroom talk, so that students increasingly learn standards and tools they can use to make their integrative assessments. Skilled use of such terms as 'assumes', 'implies', and 'contradicts' is essential to rational assessment of thinking.

It would be unrealistic to expect students to suddenly and deeply grasp the roots of their own thinking, or to immediately be able to honestly and fairmindedly assess it — to instantly weed out all beliefs to which they have not consciously assented. In teaching philosophically, one is continually priming the pump, as it were, continually encouraging responsible autonomy of thought, and making progress in degrees across a wide arena of concerns. The key is to continually avoid forcing the student to acquiesce to authoritative answers without understanding them. To the extent that students become submissive in their thinking, they stop thinking for themselves. When they comply tacitly or passively without genuine understanding, they are set back intellectually.

To cultivate students' impulses to think philosophically, we must continually encourage them to believe that they can figure out where they stand on root issues, that they themselves have something worthwhile to say, and that what they have to say should be given serious consideration by the other students and the teacher.

All subjects, in sum, can be taught philosophically or un-philosophically. Let me illustrate by using the subject of history. Since philosophical thinking tends to make our most basic ideas and assumptions explicit, by using it we can better orient ourselves toward the subject as a whole and mindfully integrate the parts into the whole.

Students are introduced to history early in their education, and that subject area is usually required through high school and into college, and with good reason. But the un-philosophical way history is often taught fails to develop students' ability to think historically for themselves. Indeed, history books basically tell students what to believe and what to think about history. Students have little reason in most history classes to relate the material to the framework of their own ideas, assumptions, or values. Students do not know that they have a philosophy and even if they did it is doubtful that without the stimulation of a teacher who approached the subject philosophically they would see the relevance of history to it.

But consider the probable outcome of teachers raising and facilitating discussion questions such as the following:

> What is history? Is everything that happened part of history? Can everything that happened be put into a history book? Why not? If historians have to select some events to include and leave out others, how do they do this? If this requires that historians make value judgments about what is important, is it likely that they will all agree? Is it possible for people observing and recording events to be biased or prejudiced? Could a historian be biased or prejudiced? How would you find out? How do people know what caused an event? How do people know what outcomes an event had? Would everyone agree about causes and outcomes? If events, to be given meaning, have to be interpreted from some point of view, what is the point of view of the person who wrote our text?
>
> Do you have a history? Is there a way in which everyone develops an interpretation of the significant events in his or her own life? If there is more than one point of view that events can be considered from, could you think of someone in your life who interprets your past in a way different from you? Does it make any difference how your past is interpreted? How are people sometimes harmed by the way in which they interpret their past?

These questions would not, of course, be asked at once. But they should be the *kind* of question routinely raised as part of stimulating students to take history seriously, to connect it to their lives, minds, values, and actions. After all, many of the most important questions we face in everyday life do have a significant historical dimension, but that dimension is not given by a bare set of isolated facts. For example, arguments between spouses often involve disagreements on how to interpret events or patterns of past events or behaviors. How we interpret events in our lives depends on our point of view, basic values and interests, prejudices, and so forth.

Few of us are good historians or philosophers in the matter of our own lives. But then, no one has encouraged us to be. No one has helped us grasp these kinds of connections nor relate to our own thought or experience in these ways. We don't see ourselves as shaping our experience within a framework of meanings, because we have not learned how to isolate and identify central issues in our lives. Rather we tend to believe, quite egocentrically, that we directly and immediately grasp life as it is. The world must be the way we see it, because we see nothing standing between us and the world. We seem to see it directly and objectively. We don't really see the need therefore to consider seriously other ways of seeing or interpreting it.

As we identify our point of view (philosophy) explicitly, and deliberately put its ideas to work in interpreting our world, including seriously considering competing ideas, we are freed from the illusion of absolute objectivity. We begin to recognize egocentric subjectivity as a serious problem in human affairs. Our thought begins to grapple with this problem in a variety of ways. We begin to discover how our fears, insecurities, vested interests, frustrations, egocentricity, ethnocentricity, prejudices, and so forth, blind us. We begin to develop intellectual humility. We begin, in short, to think philosophically. Children have this need as much as adults, for children often take in and construct meanings that constrain and frustrate their development and alienate them from themselves and from healthy relationships to others.

✦ *Values and Intellectual Traits*

Philosophical thinking, like all human thinking, is infused with values. But those who think philosophically make it a point to understand and assent to the values that underlie their thought. One thinks philosophically because one *values* coming to terms with the meaning and significance of one's life. If we do so sincerely and well, we recognize problems that challenge us to decide the kind of person we want to make ourselves, including deciding the kind of mind we want to have. We have to make a variety of value judgments about ourselves regarding, among other things, fears, conflicts, and prejudices. This requires us to come to terms with the traits of mind we are developing. For example, to be truly open to knowledge, one must become intellectually humble. But intellectual humility is connected with other traits, such as intellectual courage, intellectual integrity, intellectual perseverance, intellectual empathy, and fairmindedness. The intellectual traits characteristic of our thinking become for the philosophical thinker a matter of personal concern. Philosophical reflection heightens this concern.

Consider this excerpt from a letter from a teacher with a Masters degree in physics and mathematics:

> After I started teaching, I realized that I had learned physics by rote and that I really did not understand all I knew about physics. My thinking students asked me questions for which I always had the standard textbook answers, but for the first time made me start thinking for myself, and I realized that these canned answers were not justified by my own thinking and only confused my students who were showing some ability to think for themselves. To achieve my academic goals I had memorized the thoughts of others, but I had never learned or been encouraged to learn to think for myself.

This is a good example of intellectual humility and, like all intellectual humility, is based on a philosophical insight into the nature of knowing. It is reminiscent of the ancient Greek insight that Socrates himself was the wisest of the Greeks because only he realized how little he really knew. Socrates developed this insight as a result of extensive, deep questioning of the knowledge claims of others. He, like all of us, had to think his way to this insight and did so by raising the same basic *what* and *why* questions that children often ask. We as teachers cannot hand this insight to children on a silver platter. All persons must do for themselves the thinking that leads to it.

Unfortunately, though intellectual virtues cannot be conditioned into people, intellectual failings can. Because of the typically un-philosophical way most instruction is structured, intellectual arrogance rather than humility is typically fostered, especially in those who have retentive minds and can repeat like parrots what they have heard or read. Students are routinely rewarded for giving standard textbook answers and encouraged to believe that they understand what has never been justified by their own thinking. To move toward intellectual humility most students (and teachers) need to think broadly, deeply, and foundationally about most of what they have "learned", as the teacher in the previous example did. Such questioning, in turn, requires intellectual courage, perseverance, and faith in one's ability to think one's way to understanding and insight.

Genuine intellectual development requires people to develop intellectual traits, traits acquired only by thinking one's way to basic philosophical insights. Philosophical thinking leads to insights which in turn shape basic skills of thought. Skills, values, insights, and intellectual traits are mutually and dynamically interrelated. It is the whole person who thinks, not some fragment of the person.

For example, intellectual empathy requires the ability to reconstruct accurately the viewpoints and reasoning of others and to reason from premises, assumptions, and ideas other than one's own. But if one has not developed the philosophical insight that different people often think from divergent premises, assumptions, and ideas, one will never appreciate the need to entertain them. Reasoning from assumptions and ideas other than our own will seem absurd to us precisely to the degree that we are unable to step back philosophically and recognize that differences exist between people in their very frameworks for thinking.

Philosophical differences are common, even in the lives of small children. Children often reason from the assumption that their needs and desires are more important than anyone else's to the conclusion that they ought to get what they want in this or that circumstance. It often seems absurd to children that they are not given what they want. They are trapped in their egocentric viewpoints, see the world from within them, and unconsciously take their viewpoints (their philosophies, if you will) to define reality. To work out of this intellectual entrapment requires time and much reflection.

To develop consciousness of the limits of our understanding we must attain the *courage* to face our prejudices and ignorance. To discover our prejudices and ignorance in turn we often have to *empathize* with and reason within points of view toward which we are hostile. To achieve this end, we must *persevere* over an extended period of time, for it takes time and significant effort to learn how to empathically enter a point of view against which we are biased. That effort will not seem justified unless we have the *faith in reason* to believe we will not be tainted or taken in by whatever is false or misleading in this opposing viewpoint. Furthermore, the belief alone that we can survive serious consideration of alien points of view is not enough to motivate most of us to consider them seriously. We must also be motivated by an *intellectual sense of justice*. We must recognize an intellectual *responsibility* to be fair to views we oppose. We must feel *obliged* to hear them in their strongest form to ensure that we do not condemn them out of ignorance or bias.

If we approach thinking or teaching for thinking atomistically, we are unlikely to help students gain the kind of global perspective and global insight into their minds, thought, and behavior which a philosophical approach to thinking can foster. Cognitive psychology tends to present the mind and dimensions of its thinking in just this atomistic way. Most importantly, it tends to leave out of the picture what should be at its very center: the active, willing, judging agent. The character of our mind is one with our moral character. How we think determines how we behave and how we behave determines who we are and who we become. We have a moral as well as an intellectual responsibility to become fairminded and rational, but we will not become so unless we cultivate these traits through specific modes of thinking. From a philosophical point of view, one does not develop students' thinking skills without in some sense simultaneously developing their autonomy, their rationality, and their character. This is not fundamentally a matter of drilling the student in a battery of skills. Rather it is essentially a matter of orchestrating activities to continually stimulate students to express and to take seriously their own thinking: what it assumes, what it implies, what it includes, excludes, highlights, and foreshadows; and to help the student do this with intellectual humility, intellectual courage, intellectual empathy, intellectual perseverance, and fairmindedness.

✦ The Skills and Processes of Thinking

Philosophers do not tend to approach the micro-skills and macro-processes of thinking from the same perspective as cognitive psychologists. Intellectual skills and processes are approached not from the perspective of the needs of empirical research but from the perspective of achieving personal, rational control. The philosophical is, as I have suggested, a *person-centered* approach to thinking. Thinking is always the thinking of some actual person, with some egocentric and sociocentric tendencies, with some particular traits of mind, engaged in the problems of a particular life. The need to understand one's own mind, thought, and action cannot be satisfied with information from empirical studies about aspects or dimensions of thought. The question foremost in the mind of the philosopher is not "How should I conceive of the various skills and processes of the human mind to be able to conduct empirical research on them?" but "How should I understand the elements of thinking to be able to analyze, assess, and rationally control my own thinking and accurately understand and assess the thinking of others?" Philosophers view thinking from the perspective of the needs of the thinker trying to achieve or move toward an intellectual and moral ideal of rationality and fairmindedness. The tools of intellectual analysis result from philosophy's 2,500 years of thinking and thinking about thinking.

Since thinking for one's self is a fundamental presupposed value for philosophy, the micro-skills philosophers use are intellectual moves that a reasoning person continually makes, independent of the subject matter of thought. Hence, *whenever one is reasoning,* one is reasoning about some issue or problem (hence needs skills for analyzing and clarifying issues and problems). Likewise, *whenever one is reasoning,* one is reasoning from some point of view or within some conceptual framework (hence needs skills for analyzing and clarifying interpretations or interpretive frameworks.) Finally, *whenever one is reasoning,* one is, in virtue of one's inferences, coming to some conclusions from some beliefs or premises which, in turn, are based on some assumptions (hence needs skills for analyzing, clarifying, and evaluating beliefs, judgments, inferences, implications, and assumptions.) For virtually any reasoning, one needs a variety of interrelated processes and skills.

Hence, from the philosophical point of view, the fundamental question is not whether one is solving problems or making decisions or engaging in scientific inquiry or forming concepts or comprehending or composing or arguing, precisely because one usually does most or all of them in *every* case. Problem solving, decision-making, concept formation, comprehending, composing, and arguing are in some sense common to all reasoning. What we as reasoners need to do, from the philosophical point of view, is not to decide which of these things we are doing, but rather to orchestrate any or all of the following macro-processes:

1) *Socratic Questioning: questioning ourselves or others so as to make explicit the salient features of our thinking:*

   a) What precisely is at issue? Is this the fairest way to put the issue?

   b) From what point of view are we reasoning? Are there alternative points of view from which the problem or issue might be approached?

   c) What assumptions are we making? Are they justified? What alternative assumptions could we make instead?

   d) What concepts are we using? Do we grasp them? Their appropriateness? Their implications?

e) What evidence have we found or do we need to find? How dependable is our source of information?

f) What inferences are we making? Are those inferences well supported?

g) What are the implications of our reasoning?

h) How does our reasoning stand up to competing or alternative reasoning?

i) Are there objections to our reasoning we should consider?

2) Conceptual Analysis: Any problematic concepts or uses of terms must be analyzed and their basic logic set out and assessed. Have we done so?

3) Analysis of the Question-at-Issue: Whenever one is reasoning, one is attempting to settle some question at issue. But to settle a question, one must understand the kind of question it is. Different questions require different modes of settlement. Do we grasp the precise demands of the question-at-issue?

4) Reconstructing Alternative Viewpoints in their Strongest Forms: Since whenever one is reasoning, one is reasoning from a point of view or within a conceptual framework, one must identify and reconstruct those views. Have we empathically reconstructed the relevant points of view?

5) Reasoning Dialogically and Dialectically: Since there are almost always alternative lines of reasoning about a given issue or problem, and since a reasonable person sympathetically considers them, one must engage in dialectical reasoning. Have we reasoned from a variety of points of view (when relevant) and rationally identified and considered the strengths and weaknesses of these points of view as a result of this process?

Implicit in the macro-processes, as suggested earlier, are identifiable micro-skills. These constitute moves of the mind while thinking in a philosophical, and hence in a rational, critically-creative way. The moves are marked in the critical-analytic vocabulary of everyday language. Hence in Socratically questioning someone we are engaging in a *process* of thought. Within that process we make a variety of moves. We can make those moves explicit by using analytic terms such as these:

claims, assumes, implies, infers, concludes, is supported by, is consistent with, is relevant to, is irrelevant to, has the following implications, is credible, plausible, clear, in need of analysis, without evidence, in need of verification, is empirical, is conceptual, is a judgment of value, is settled, is at issue, is problematic, is analogous, is biased, is loaded, is well confirmed, is theoretical, hypothetical, a matter of opinion, a matter of fact, a point of view, a frame of reference, a conceptual framework, etc.

To put the point another way, to gain command of our thinking we must be able to take it apart and put it back together in light of its *logic*, the patterns of reasoning that support it, oppose it, and shed light on its rational acceptability. We don't need a formal or technical language to do this, but we do need a command of the critical-analytic terms available in ordinary English. Their careful use helps discipline, organize, and render self-conscious our ordinary inferences and the concepts, values, and assumptions that underlie them.

✦ *Philosophical and Critical Thinking*

Those familiar with some of my other writings will recognize that what I am here calling *philosophical* thinking is very close to what I have generally called *strong sense critical thinking*. The connection is not arbitrary. The ideal of strong sense critical thinking is implicit in the Socratic philosophical ideal of living a reflective life (and thus achieving command over one's mind and behavior). Instead of absorbing their philosophy from others, people can, with suitable encouragement and instruction, develop a critical and reflective attitude toward ideas and behavior. Their outlook and interpretations of themselves and others can be subjected to serious examination. Through this process, our beliefs become more our own than the product of our unconscious absorption of others' beliefs. Basic ideas such as 'history', 'science', 'drama', 'mind', 'imagination', and 'knowledge' become organized by the criss-crossing paths of one's reflection. They cease to be compartmentalized subjects. The philosophical questions one raises about history cut across those raised about the human mind, science, knowledge, and imagination. Only deep philosophical questioning and honest criticism can protect us from the pronounced human tendency to think in a self-serving way. It is common to question only within a fundamentally unquestioned point of view. We naturally use our intellectual skills to defend and buttress those concepts, aims, and assumptions already deeply rooted in our thought.

The roots of thinking determine the nature, direction, and quality of that thinking. If teaching for thinking does not help students understand the roots of their thinking, it will fail to give them real command over their minds. They will simply make the transition from uncritical thought to weak sense critical thought. They will make the transition from being unskilled in thinking to being narrowly, closedmindedly skilled.

David Perkins (1986) has highlighted this problem from a somewhat different point of view. In studying the relationship between people's scores on standard IQ tests and their openmindedness, as measured by their ability to construct arguments against their points of view on a public issue, Perkins found that, intelligence scores correlated substantially with the degree to which subjects developed arguments thoroughly on their own sides of the case. However, there was no correlation between intelligence and elaborateness of arguments on the other side of the case. In other words, the more intelligent participants invested their greater intellectual endowment in bolstering their own positions all the more, not in exploring even-handedly the complexities of the issue.

Herein lies the danger of an approach to thinking that relies fundamentally, as cognitive psychology often does, on the goal of technical competence, without making central the deeper philosophical or normative dimensions of thinking. Student skill in thinking may increase, but whatever narrowness of mind or lack of insight, whatever intellectual closedmindedness, intellectual arrogance, or intellectual cowardice the students suffer, will be supported by that skill. It is crucial therefore that this deeper consideration of the problem of thinking be highlighted and addressed in a significant and global manner. Whether one labels it 'philosophical' thinking or 'strong sense critical thinking' or 'thinking that embodies empathy and openmindedness' is insignificant.

A similar point can be made about the thinking of teachers. If we merely provide teachers with exercises for their students that do no more than promote technical competence in thinking, if inservice is not long-term and designed to develop the critical thinking of teachers, they will probably be ineffective in fostering the thinking of their students.

Teachers need to move progressively from a didactic to a critical model of teaching. In this process, many old assumptions will have to be abandoned and new ones taken to heart as the basis for teaching and learning. This shift can be spelled out systematically as follows.

Theory of Knowledge, Learning, and Literacy

Didactic Theory	*Critical Theory*
1. The fundamental needs of students	
That the fundamental need of students is to be taught more or less *what* to think, not *how* to think (that is, that students will learn how to think if they can only get into their heads what to think). ♦ Students are "given" or told details, definitions, explanations, rules, guidelines, reasons to learn.	That the fundamental need of students is to be taught *how* not *what* to think; that it is important to focus on significant content, but this should be accomplished by raising live issues that stimulate students to gather, analyze, and assess that content.

Theory of Knowledge, Learning, and Literacy

Didactic Theory	Critical Theory

2. The nature of knowledge

That knowledge is independent of the thinking that generates, organizes, and applies it. ♦ Students are said to *know* when they can repeat what has been covered. Students are given the finished products of someone else's thought.

That all knowledge of "content" is generated, organized, applied, analyzed, synthesized, and assessed by thinking; that gaining knowledge is unintelligible without engagement in such thinking. (It is *not* assumed that one can think without some content to think about, nor that all content is equally significant and useful.) ♦ Students are given opportunities to puzzle their way through to knowledge and explore its justification, *as part of* the process of learning.

3. Model of the educated person

That educated, literate people are fundamentally repositories of content analogous to an encyclopedia or a data bank, directly comparing situations in the world with facts that they carry about fully formed as a result of an absorptive process. That an educated, literate person is fundamentally a true believer, that is, a possessor of truth, and therefore claims much knowledge. ♦ Texts, assignments, lectures, discussions, and tests are detail-oriented, and content dense.

That an educated, literate person is fundamentally a repository of strategies, principles, concepts, and insights embedded in processes of thought rather than in atomic facts. Experiences analyzed and organized by critical thought, rather than facts picked up one-by-one, characterize the educated person. Much of what is known is constructed by the thinker *as needed* from context to context, not *prefabricated* in sets of true statements about the world. That an educated, literate person is fundamentally a seeker and questioner rather than a true believer, therefore cautious in claiming knowledge. ♦ Classroom activities consist of questions and problems for students to discuss and discover how to solve. Teachers model insightful consideration of questions and problems, and facilitate fruitful discussions.

Theory of Knowledge, Learning, and Literacy

Didactic Theory	*Critical Theory*

4. The nature of knowledge

That knowledge, truth, and understanding can be transmitted from on person to another by verbal statements in the form of lectures or didactic teaching. ♦ For example, social studies texts present principles of geography and historical explanations. Questions at the end of the chapter are framed in identical language and can be answered by repeating the texts. "The correct answer" is in bold type or otherwise emphasized.

That knowledge and truth can rarely, and insight never, be transmitted from one person to another by the transmitter's verbal statements alone; that one cannot directly give another what one has learned — one can only facilitate the conditions under which people learn for themselves by figuring out or thinking things through. ♦ Students offer their own ideas and explore ideas given in the texts, providing their own examples and reasons. Students come to conclusions by practicing reasoning historically, geographically, scientifically, etc.

5. The nature of listening

That students do not need to be taught skills of listening to learn to pay attention and this is fundamentally a matter of self-discipline achieved through will power. Students should therefore be able to listen on command by the teacher. ♦ Students are told to listen carefully and are tested on their abilities to remember details and to follow directions.

That students need to be taught how to listen critically — an active and skilled process that can be learned by degrees with various levels of proficiency. Learning what others mean by what they say requires questioning, trying on, testing, and, hence, engaging in public or private dialogue with them, and this involves critical thinking. ♦ Teachers continually model active critical listening, asking probing and insightful questions of the speaker.

6. The relationship of basic skills to thinking skills

That the basic skills of reading and writing can be taught without emphasis on higher order critical thinking. ♦ Reading texts provide comprehension questions requiring recall of random details. Occasionally, "main point," "plot," and

That the basic skills of reading and writing are inferential skills that require critical thinking; that students who do not learn to read and write critically are ineffective readers and writers, and that critical reading and writing involve

Theory of Knowledge, Learning, and Literacy	
Didactic Theory	*Critical Theory*
"theme" lessons cover these concepts. Literal comprehension is distinguished from "extras" such as inferring, evaluating, thinking beyond. Only after basic literal comprehension has been established is the deeper meaning probed.	dialogical processes in which probing critical questions are raised and answered. (For example, What is the fundamental issue? What reasons, what evidence, is relevant to this issue? Is this source or authority credible? Are these reasons adequate? Is this evidence accurate and sufficient? Does this contradict that? Does this conclusion follow? Is another point of view relevant to consider?) ♦ Teachers routinely require students to *explain* what they have read, to reconstruct the ideas, and to evaluate written material. Students construct and compare interpretations, reasoning their way to the most plausible interpretations. Discussion moves back and forth between what was said and what it means.

7. The status of questioning

That students who have no questions typically are learning well, while students with a lot of questions are experiencing difficulty in learning; that doubt and questioning weaken belief.	That students who have no questions typically are not learning, while having pointed and specific questions, on the other hand, is a significant sign of learning. Doubt and questioning, by deepening understanding, strengthen belief by putting it on more solid ground. ♦ Teachers evaluate their teaching by asking themselves: Are my students asking better questions — perceptive questions, questions which extend and apply what they have learned? ("Is that why ...?" Does this mean that ...?" "Then what if ...?")

Theory of Knowledge, Learning, and Literacy

Didactic Theory	*Critical Theory*

8. The desirable classroom environment

That quiet classes with little student talk are typically reflective of students learning while classes with a lot of student talk are typically disadvantaged in learning.	That quiet classes with little student talk are typically classes with little learning while classes with much student talk focused on live issues is a sign of learning (provided students learn dialogical and dialectical skills).

9. The view of knowledge (atomistic vs. holistic)

That knowledge and truth can typically be learned best by being broken down into elements, and the elements into sub-elements, each taught sequentially and atomically. Knowledge is additive. ◆ Texts provide basic definitions and masses of details, but have little back-and-forth movement between them. They break knowledge into pieces, each of which is to be mastered one by one: subjects are taught separately. Each aspect is further broken down: each part of speech is covered separately; social studies texts are organized chronologically, geographically, etc.	That knowledge and truth is heavily systemic and holistic and can be learned only by many on-going acts of synthesis, many cycles from wholes to parts, tentative graspings of a whole guiding us in understanding its parts, periodic focusing on the parts (in relation to each other) shedding light upon the whole, and that the wholes that we learn have important relations to other wholes as well as their own parts and hence need to be frequently canvassed in learning any given whole. (This assumption has the implication that we cannot achieve in-depth learning in any given domain of knowledge unless the process of grasping that domain involves active consideration of its relation to other domains of knowledge.) That each learner creates knowledge. ◆ Education is organized around issues, problems, and basic concepts which are pursued and explored through all relevant subjects. Teachers routinely require students to relate knowledge from various fields. Students compare analogous events or situations, propose examples, apply new concepts to other situations.

Theory of Knowledge, Learning, and Literacy	
Didactic Theory	*Critical Theory*

10. The place of values

That people can gain significant knowledge without seeking or valuing it, and hence that education can take place without significant transformation of values for the learner. ◆ For example, texts tend to inform students of the importance of studying the subject or topic covered, rather than proving it by *showing* its immediate usefulness and having students use it.

That people gain only the knowledge they seek and value. All other learning is superficial and transitory. All genuine education transforms the basic values of the person educated, resulting in persons becoming life-long learners and rational persons. ◆ Instruction poses problems meaningful to students, requiring them to use the tools of each academic domain.

11. The importance of being aware of one's own learning process

That understanding the mind and how it functions, its epistemological health and pathology, are not important or necessary for learning. To learn the basic subject matter one need not focus on such matters, except perhaps with certain disadvantaged learners.

That understanding the mind and how it functions, its health and pathology, are important and necessary parts of learning. To learn subject matter in-depth, we must gain some insight into how we as thinkers and learners process that subject matter.

12. The place of misconceptions

That ignorance is a vacuum or simple lack, and that student prejudices, biases, misconceptions, and ignorance are automatically replaced by their being given knowledge. ◆ Little if any attention is given to students' beliefs. Material is presented from the point of view of the authority, the one who knows.

That prejudices, biases, and misconceptions are built up through actively constructed inferences embedded in experience and must be broken down through a similar process; hence, that students must reason their way out of their prejudices, biases, and misconceptions. ◆ Students have many opportunities to express their views in class, however biased or prejudiced, and a non-threatening environment to argue their way out of their internalized misconceptions. Teachers cultivate in themselves genuine curiosity about how students see things, why they think as they do, and the structure of students' thought. The educational process starts where students are, and walks them through to insight.

Theory of Knowledge, Learning, and Literacy

Didactic Theory	*Critical Theory*

13. The level of understanding desired

That students need not understand the rational ground or deeper logic of what they learn to absorb knowledge. Extensive but superficial learning can later be deepened. ♦ For example, historical and scientific explanations are presented to students as givens, not as having been reasoned to. In language arts, skills and distinctions are rarely explicitly linked to such basic ideas as 'good writing' or 'clear expression.'

That rational assent is an essential facet of all genuine learning and that an in-depth understanding of basic concepts and principles is an essential foundation for rational concepts and facts. That in-depth understanding of root concepts and principles should be used as organizers for learning within and across subject matter domains. ♦ Students are encouraged to discover how the details relate to basic concepts. Details are traced back to the foundational purposes, concepts, and insights.

14. Depth versus breadth

That it is more important to cover a great deal of knowledge or information superficially than a small amount in depth. That only after the facts are understood, can students discuss their meaning; that higher order thinking can and should only be practiced by students who have mastered the material. That thought-provoking discussions are for the gifted and advanced, only.

That it is more important to cover a small amount of knowledge or information in depth (deeply probing its foundation) than to cover a great deal of knowledge superficially. That all students can and must probe the significance of and justification for what they learn.

15. Role definition for teacher and student

That the roles of teacher and learner are distinct and should not be blurred.

That we learn best by teaching or explaining to others what we know. ♦ Students have many opportunities to teach what they know, to formulate their understanding in different ways, and to respond to questions from others.

Theory of Knowledge, Learning, and Literacy

Didactic Theory   **Critical Theory**

16. The correction of ignorance

That the teacher should correct the learners' ignorance by telling them what they do not know.

That students need to learn to distinguish for themselves what they know from what they do not know. Students should recognize that they do not genuinely know or comprehend what they have merely memorized. Self-directed recognition of ignorance is necessary to learning. ♦ Teachers respond to mistakes and confusion by probing with questions, allowing students to correct themselves and each other. Teachers routinely allow students the opportunity to supply their own ideas on a subject before reading their texts.

17. The responsibility for learning

That the teacher has the fundamental responsibility for student learning. Teachers and texts provide information, questions, and drill.

That progressively the student should be given increasing responsibility for his or her own learning. Students need to come to see that only they can learn for themselves and that they will not do so unless they actively and willingly engage themselves in the process. ♦ The teacher provides opportunities for students to decide what they need to know and helps them develop strategies for finding or figuring it out.

18. The transfer of learning to everyday situations

That students will automatically transfer the knowledge that they learn in didactically taught courses to relevant real-life situations. ♦ For example, students are told to perform a given skill on a given group of items. The text will *tell* students when, how, and why to use that skill.

That most knowledge that students memorize in didactically taught courses is either forgotten or rendered "inert" by their mode of learning it, and that the most significant transfer is achieved by in-depth learning which focuses on experiences meaningful to the student and aims directly at transfer.

Theory of Knowledge, Learning, and Literacy

Didactic Theory	*Critical Theory*

19. Status of personal experiences

That the personal experience of the student has no essential role to play in education.

That the personal experience of the student is essential to all schooling at all levels and in all subjects; that it is a crucial part of the content to be processed (applied, analyzed, synthesized, and assessed) by the student.

20. The assessment of knowledge acquisition

That a student who can correctly answer questions, provide definitions, and apply formulae while taking tests has proven his or her knowledge or understanding of those details. Since the didactic approach tends to assume, for example, that knowing a word is knowing its definition (and an example), didactic instruction tends to overemphasize definitions. Students practice skills by doing exercises, specifically designed as drill. Successfully finishing the exercise is taken to be equivalent to having learned the skill.

That students can often provide correct answers, repeat definitions, and apply formulae while yet not understanding those questions, definitions, or formulae. That proof of knowledge or understanding is found in the students' ability to explain in their own words, with examples, the meaning and significance of the knowledge, why it is so, and to *spontaneously* recall and use it when relevant.

21. The authority validating knowledge

That learning is essentially a private, monological process in which learners can proceed more or less directly to established truth, under the guidance of an expert in such truth. The authoritative answers that the teacher has are the fundamental standards for assessing students' learning.

That learning is essentially a public, communal, dialogical, and dialectical process in which learners can only proceed indirectly to truth, with much "zigging and zagging" along the way, much back-tracking, misconception, self-contradiction, and frustration in the process. In this process, authoritative answers are replaced by authoritative standards for engagement in the communal, dialogical process of enquiry.

✦ *Bringing a Philosophical Approach Into the Classroom*

Unfortunately a general case for the contribution of philosophy to thinking and to teaching for thinking, such as this one, must lack a good deal of the concrete detail regarding how one would, as a practical matter, translate the generalities discussed here into action in the classroom or in everyday thinking. There are two basic needs. The first is an ample supply of concrete models that bridge the gap between theory and practice. These models should come in a variety of forms: video tapes, curriculum materials, handbooks, etc. Second, most teachers need opportunities to work on their own philosophical thinking skills and insights. These two needs are best met in conjunction with each other. It is important for the reader to review particular philosophy-based strategies in detail.

The most extensive program available is *Philosophy for Children,* developed by Matthew Lipman in association with the *Institute for the Advancement of Philosophy for Children.* It is based on the notion that philosophy ought to be brought into schools as a separate subject, and philosophical reflection and ideas used directly as an occasion for teaching thinking skills. The program introduces philosophy in the form of children's novels. Extensive teachers' handbooks are provided and a thorough inservice required to ensure that teachers develop the necessary skills and insights to encourage classroom discussion of root ideas in such a way that students achieve philosophical insights and reasoning skills. In a year-long experiment conducted by the *Educational Testing Service* significant improvements were recorded in reading, mathematics, and reasoning. *Philosophy for Children* achieves transfer of reasoning skills into the standard curriculum but is not designed to directly infuse philosophical reflection into it.

In contrast, the *Center for Critical Thinking and Moral Critique* at Sonoma State University in California is developing a philosophy-based approach focused on directly infusing philosophical thinking across the curriculum. Handbooks of lesson plans K–12 have been remodeled by the Center staff to demonstrate that, with redesign, philosophically-based critical thinking skills and processes can be integrated into the lessons presently in use, if teachers learn to remodel the lessons they presently use with critical thinking in mind.

We provide a 'before' and 'after', (the lesson plan before remodeling and after remodeling); a critique of the un-remodeled lesson plan to clarify how the remodel was achieved; a list of specific objectives; and the particular strategies used in the remodel. Here is one such example.

Two Ways to Win

(Language Arts — 2nd Grade)

Objectives of the remodeled lesson

The student will:
- use analytic terms such as assume, infer, and imply to analyze and assess story characters' reasoning
- make inferences from story details
- clarify 'good sport' by contrasting it with its opposite, 'bad sport' and exploring its implications

Original Lesson Plan

Abstract

Students read a story about a brother and sister named Cleo and Toby. Cleo and Toby are new in town and worried about making new friends. They ice skate at the park every day after school, believing that winning an upcoming race can help them make new friends (and that they won't make friends if they don't win). Neither of them wins; Cleo, because she falls, Toby, because he forfeits his chance to win by stopping to help a boy who falls. Some children come over after the race to compliment Toby on his good sportsmanship and Cleo on her skating.

Most of the questions about the story probe the factual components. Some require students to infer. Questions ask what 'good sport' means and if Cleo's belief about meeting people is correct.

from *Mustard Seed Magic,*
Theodore L. Harris et al. Economy
Company. © 1972. pp. 42–46

Critique

The original lesson has several good questions which require students to make inferences, for example, "Have Toby and Cleo lived on the block all their lives?" The text also asks students if they know who won the race. Since they do not, this question encourages students to suspend judgment. Although 'good sportsmanship' is a good concept for students to discuss and clarify, the text fails to have students practice techniques for clarifying it in sufficient depth. Instead, students merely list the characteristics of a good sport (a central idea in the story) with no discussion of what it means to be a bad sport or sufficient assessment of specific examples. The use of opposite cases to clarify concepts helps students develop fuller and more accurate concepts. With such practice a student can begin to recognize borderline cases as well — where someone was a good sport in some respects, bad in others, or not clearly either. This puts students in a position to develop criteria for judging behavior.

STRATEGIES USED TO REMODEL

S–10 clarifying the meanings of words or phrases
S–28 supplying evidence for a conclusion
S–23 using critical vocabulary
S–25 examining assumptions

Remodeled Lesson Plan

Where the original lesson asks, "What does 'a good sport' mean?" we suggest an extension. S–10 The teacher should make two lists on the board of the students' responses to the question "How do good sports and bad sports behave?" Students could go back over the story and apply the ideas on the list to the characters in the story, giving reasons to support any claims they make regarding the characters' sportsmanship. S–28 In some cases there might not be enough information to determine whether a particular character is a good or bad sport. Or they might find a character who is borderline, having some characteristics of both good and bad sports. Again, students should cite evidence from the story to support their claims.

The students could also change details of the story to make further points about the nature of good and bad sportsmanship. (If the girl had pushed Cleo down to win the race, that would have been very bad sportsmanship.) To further probe the concept of good sportsmanship, ask questions like the following: How did Toby impress the other children? Why did they think he did a good thing? If you had seen the race, what would you have thought of Toby? Why do we value the kind of behavior we call 'good sportsmanship'? Why don't we like bad sportsmanship? Why are people ever bad sports? S–10

There are a number of places in the lesson where the teacher could introduce, or give students further practice using critical thinking vocabulary. Here are a few examples "What can you *infer* from the story title and picture? What parts of the story *imply* that Toby and Cleo will have some competition in the race? What do Toby and Cleo *assume* about meeting new people and making new friends? Is this a good or a bad *assumption*? Why? Why do you think they made this assumption? Have you ever made similar assumptions? Why? S–25 What can you infer that Cleo felt at the end of the story? How can you tell?" S–23

Only after close examination of specific classroom materials and teaching strategies, can teachers begin to understand how to translate philosophically-based approaches into classroom practice. This requires long-term staff development with ample provision for peer collaboration and demonstration teaching. Only then can one reasonably assess the value and power of a philosophical approach.

✦ Summary and Conclusion

A strong case can be made for a philosophically-based approach to thinking and teaching for thinking. Such an approach differs fundamentally from most cognitive psychology-based approaches. Philosophy-based approaches reflect the historic emphases of philosophy as a field, as a mode of thinking, and as a framework for thinking. The field is historically committed to specific intellectual and moral ideals, and presupposes people's capacity to live reflective lives and achieve an understanding of and command over the most basic ideas that rule their lives. To achieve this command, people must critically examine the ideas on which they act and replace those ideas when, in their own best judgment, they can no longer rationally assent to them. Such an ideal of freedom of thought and action requires that individuals have a range of intellectual standards by which they can assess thought. These standards, implicit in the critical-analytic terms that exist in every natural language, must be applied in a certain spirit — a spirit of intellectual humility, empathy, and fairmindedness. To develop insight into proper intellectual judgment, one must engage in and become comfortable with dialogical and dialectical thinking. Such thinking is naturally stimulated when one asks basic questions, inquires into root ideas, and invites and honestly considers a variety of responses. It is further stimulated when one self-reflects. The reflective mind naturally moves back and forth between a variety of considerations and sources. The reflective mind eventually learns how to inwardly generate alternative points of view and lines of reasoning, even when others are not present to express them.

A teacher who teaches philosophically brings these ideals and practices into the classroom whatever the subject matter, for all subject matter is grounded in ideas which must be understood and related to ideas pre-existing in the students' minds. The philosophically-oriented teacher wants all content to be critically and analytically processed by all students in such a way that they can integrate it into their own thinking, rejecting, accepting, or qualifying it in keeping with their honest assessment. All content provides grist for the philosophical mill, an opportunity for students to think further, to build upon their previous thought. The philosophically oriented teacher is careful not to require the students to take in more than they can intellectually digest. The philosophically oriented teacher is keenly sensitive to the ease with which minds become passive and submissive. The philosophically oriented teacher is more concerned with the global state of students' minds (Are they developing their own thinking, points of view, intellectual standards and traits, etc.) than with the state of the students' minds within a narrowly defined subject competence. Hence it is much more important to such a teacher that students learn how to think historically (how to look at their own lives and experience and the lives and experiences of others from a historical vantage point) than that they learn how to recite information from a history text. History books are read as aids to historical thought, not as ends-in-themselves.

The philosophically oriented teacher continually looks for deeply rooted understanding and encourages the impulse to look more deeply into things. Hence, the philosophically oriented teacher is much more impressed with how little we as humans know than with how much information we have collected. They are much more apt to encourage students to believe that they, as a result of their own thinking, may design better answers to life's problems than have yet been devised, than they are to encourage students to submissively accept established answers.

What stands in the way of successful teaching for thinking in most classrooms is not as much the absence of technical, empirical information about mental skills and processes, as a lack of experience of and commitment to teaching philosophically. As students, most teachers, after all, were not themselves routinely encouraged to think for themselves. They were not exposed to teachers who stimulated them to inquire into the roots of their own ideas or to engage in extended dialogical and dialectical exchange. They have had little experience in Socratic questioning, in taking an idea to its roots, in pursuing its ramifications across domains and subject areas, in relating it critically to their own experience, or in honestly assessing it from other perspectives.

To appreciate the power and usefulness of a philosophy-based approach, one must understand not only the general case that can be made for it but also how it translates into specific classroom practices. One will achieve this understanding only if one learns how to step outside the framework of assumptions of cognitive psychology and consider thinking, thinking about thinking, and teaching for thinking from a different and fresh perspective. If we look at thinking only from the perspective of cognitive psychology, we will likely fall into the trap which Gerald W. Bracey (1987) recently characterized as,

> ... the long and unhappy tendency of American psychology to break learning into discrete pieces and then treat the pieces in isolation. From James Mill's "mental mechanics", through Edward Titchener's structuralism, to behavioral objectives and some "componential analysis" in current psychology, U.S. educators have acted as if the whole were never more than the sum of its parts, as if a house were no more than the nails and lumber and glass that

went into it, as if education were no more than the average number of discrete objectives mastered. We readily see that this is ridiculous in the case of a house, but we seem less able to recognize its absurdity in the case of education. (p. 684)

In thinking, if nowhere else, the whole is greater than the sum of its parts, and cannot be understood merely by examining its psychological leaves, branches, or trunk. We must also dig up its philosophical roots and study its seed ideas as ideas: the "stuff" that determines the very nature of thought itself.

✦ References

Bracey, Gerald W. "Measurement-Driven Instruction: Catchy Phrase, Dangerous Practice." *Phi Delta Kappan.* May, 1987. pp. 683–688.

Paul, Richard W., Binker, A. J. A., & Charbonneau, Marla. *Critical Thinking Handbook: K–3, A Guide for Remodeling Lesson Plans in Language Arts, Social Studies, and Science.* Rohnert Park, California: Center for Critical Thinking and Moral Critique. 1987.

Paul, Richard W., Binker, A. J. A., Jensen, Karen, & Kreklau, Heidi. *Critical Thinking Handbook: 4th–6th Grades, a Guide for Remodeling Lesson Plans in Language Arts, Social Studies, and Science.* Rohnert Park, California: Center for Critical Thinking and Moral Critique. 1987.

Perkins, David. "Reasoning as it Is and Could Be: An Empirical Perspective." Paper given at *American Educational Research Association* Conference, San Francisco. April, 1986.

Chapter 23

Philosophy and Cognitive Psychology:
Contrasting Assumptions

Abstract

This paper was originally written for the Association for Supervision and Curriculum Development (ASCD) meeting, held at Wingspread in 1987 to discuss the ASCD publication, Dimensions of Thinking. *In it, Paul critiques the book for its pedagogical and theoretical bias toward a cognitive-psychological approach to thinking, a bias that largely ignores the contributions of philosophy, as well as those of affective and social psychology. Paul contrasts the very different assumptions that philosophers and cognitive psychologists make when analyzing the nature of thinking.*

O ne of the major objectives of the authors of *Dimensions of Thinking* was to produce a comprehensive, theoretically balanced, and pedagogically useful thinking skills framework. Unfortunately, the value of the present framework is limited by its bias in every important respect toward the approach of cognitive psychology. Virtually all of the research cited, the concepts and terminology used, and the recommendations made for implementation are taken from the writings of scholars working principally in cognitive psychology. The work and perspective of many of the philosophers concerned with thinking is minimally reported. Those whose work is not significantly used include these:

> Michael Scriven, Harvey Siegel, Mortimer Adler, John Passmore, Israel Scheffler, Mark Weinstein, R. S. Peters, Ralph Johnson, J. Anthony Blair, Stephen Norris, John Dewey, Vincent Ruggiero, Edward D'Angelo, Perry Weddle, Sharon Bailin, Lenore Langsdorf, T. Edward Damer, Howard Kahane, Nicholas Rescher, Paulo Freire, Robert Swartz, Max Black, James Freeman, John Hoaglund, Gerald Nosich, Jon Adler, Eugene Garver, (to name some who come readily to mind).

Nor does *Dimensions of Thinking* incorporate significant philosophical contributions to our understanding of thinking from the great philosophers of the last three hundred years. It fails to mention Immanuel Kant's

445

work on the mind's shaping and structuring of human experience, Hegel's work on the dialectical nature of human thought, Marx's work on the economic and ideological foundations of human thought, Nietzsche's illumination of self-delusion in human thought, or Wittgenstein's work on the socio-linguistic foundations of human thought.

Another perspective conspicuously absent from *Dimensions of Thinking* is that of affective and social psychology, especially those studies that shed light on the major obstacles or blocks to rational thinking: prejudice, bias, self-deception, desire, fear, vested interest, delusion, illusion, egocentrism, sociocentrism, and ethnocentrism. The significance of this omission should be clear. The point behind the thinking skills movements (in both cognitive psychology and philosophy) is not simply to get students to think; all humans think spontaneously and continuously. The problem is to get them to think *critically* and *rationally* and this requires insight by students into the nature of uncritical and irrational thought. The massive literature in affective and social psychology bears on this problem; its seminal insights and concepts should be a significant part of any adequate framework for understanding how to reform education to cultivate rational, reflective, autonomous, empathic thought. (Philosophers, I might add, are often as guilty as cognitive psychologists of ignoring the work of affective and social psychologists.) Recently, when I did an ERIC search under the descriptors "prejudice or bias or self-deception or defense mechanism", the search turned up 8,673 articles! This then is a significant omission.

More important than the sheer numerical imbalance in scholarship cited is the imbalance in perspective. There are important differences between those features of thinking highlighted by philosophers in the critical thinking movement and the general approach to thinking fostered by cognitive psychologists and the educators influenced by them. And though there is much that each field is beginning to learn from the other, that learning can fruitfully take place only if some of their differences are clearly set out and due emphasis given to each. After I have spelled out these differences roughly, I will detail what I see as emerging common ground, what I see that gives me hope that these fields may yet work together. But first the down side.

In thinking of the relationship between the traditions of cognitive psychology and philosophy, I am reminded of a couple of remarks by the great 19th Century educator-philosopher John Henry Newman (1912) in his classic *Idea of a University*:

> I am not denying, I am granting, I am assuming, that there is reason and truth in the "leading ideas", as they are called and "large views" of scientific men; I only say that, though they speak truth, they do not speak the whole truth; that they speak a narrow truth, and think it a broad truth; that their deductions must be compared

with other truths, which are acknowledged to be truths, in order to verify, complete, and correct them. (p. 178)

If different studies are useful for aiding, they are still more useful for correcting each other; for as they have their particular merits severally, so they have their defects. (p. 176)

In this case, the "scientific" views of cognitive psychologists need to be corrected by the insights of philosophers, for the whole truth to be apprehended.

Only when we see the differing emphases, assumptions, and concepts, even the differing value priorities of the two disciplines and how the work of those interested in critical thinking reflects them can we begin to appreciate the distinctive contributions of both cognitive psychology and philosophy to instruction for thinking. Few K–12 educators and their education department counterparts recognize the possible contribution of philosophy to instruction for thinking because their own educational background was heavily biased in favor of psychologically and scientistically-oriented courses. Rarely were they expected to articulate a philosophical perspective, to reason and synthesize across disciplinary lines, to formulate their philosophy. Moreover, few feel comfortable with philosophical argumentation and counter-argumentation as a means of establishing probable truth. Well-reasoned philosophical essays do not seem to them to be *research*, properly so called, because they rarely cite empirical studies.

With these thoughts in mind, let us examine 24 contrasting emphases between these two disciplines. I do not assume, of course, that all 24 are always present, but that, on the whole, there is a pattern of differences between the writings of *most* cognitive psychologists and *most* philosophers. In the case of *Dimensions of Thinking*, for example, I am confident that had the co-authors been Lipman, Ennis, Scriven, Scheffler, and Paul, a very different account of thinking would have emerged, one reflective of the contrasts which I now list.

Tendencies of

Cognitive Psychologists	Philosophers
With Respect to:	
1. Approach to thinking	
Approach thinking descriptively.	Approach thinking normatively.
2. Methodology	
Focus on empirical fact-gathering. (This is not to imply that cognitive psychologists do not formulate theories or engage in conceptual analysis.)	Focus on the analysis of cases of "well-justified" thinking in contrast to cases of "poorly justified" thinking.

Tendencies of

Cognitive Psychologists	*Philosophers*

With Respect to:

3. Modes of thinking studied

Focus on expert versus novice thinking, intradisciplinary thinking, and monological thinking.	Focus on rational, reflective thinking, on interdisciplinary thinking, and on multilogical thinking.

4. Value emphasis

Emphasize the value of expertise.	Emphasize the values of rationality, autonomy, self-criticism, openmindedness, truth, and empathy.

5. Authority

Make the authority of the expert central.	Play down the authority of the expert and play up the authority of independent reason.

6. Language used

Generate more technical terminology and make their points in a technical fashion.	Take their terminology and concepts more from the critical, analytic vocabulary of a natural language (e. g., assumes, claims, implies, is consistent with, contradicts, is relevant to).

7. Role of values in thinking

Separate the cognitive from the domain of *a)* value-choices of the thinker and *b)* the overall world view of the thinker (at least when discussing basic mental skills and processes).	Emphasize the role in thinking of values and the overall conceptual framework of the thinker; hence, the significance of identifying and assessing points of view and frames of reference.

8. Place of dialogue

Play down the significance of dialogical and dialectical thinking.	Play up the significance of dialogical and dialectical thinking; view debate and argumentation as central to rational thinking.

Tendencies of

Cognitive Psychologists	**Philosophers**

With Respect to:

9. View of affect

Underemphasize the affective obstacles to rational thinking; fear, desire, prejudice, bias, vested interest, conformity, self-deception, egocentrism, and ethnocentrism.	Emphasize the affective obstacles to rational thinking (this emphasis is correlated with the emphasis on the philosophical ideal of becoming a rational person).

10. Role of teacher

Play down the role of the teacher as autonomous critical thinker (this is perhaps an emerging issue in cognitive psychology).	Make central the role of the teacher as autonomous critical thinker, the need to question her own biases, prejudices, point of view, and so forth.

11. Classroom climate

Play down the need to develop classrooms as communities of inquiry wherein dialogical and dialectical exchange is a matter of course.	Play up the need to develop classrooms as communities of inquiry where students learn the arts of analyzing, synthesizing, advocating, reconstructing, and challenging each other's ideas.

12. Place of intelligent skepticism

Ignore or play down the significance of the student as Socratic questioner, as intelligent skeptic (this too may be an emerging issue).	Make central the significance of questioning; view intellectual advancement more in terms of skill in the art of questioning than in the amassing of an unquestioned knowledge base (the thinker as questioner is connected by philosophers with the disposition to suspend judgment in cases in which the thinker is called upon to accept beliefs not justified by his or her own thinking.)

Tendencies of

   Cognitive Psychologists   *Philosophers*

               With Respect to:

13. Place of empirical research

Cognitive Psychologists	Philosophers
Play up the significance of empirical research in settling educational issues.	Skeptical of empirical research as capable of settling significant educational issues without argumentation between conflicting educational viewpoints or philosophies on those issues.

14. View of the teaching process

Cognitive Psychologists	Philosophers
Give more weight to the significance of teaching as embodying step-by-step procedures (although there is increasing dissent within cognitive psychology on this point).	Play up the significance of dialogical approaches that involve much criss-crossing and unpredictable back-tracking in teaching and thinking; skeptical of step-by-step procedures in teaching and thinking.

15. Identified micro-elements in thinking

Cognitive Psychologists	Philosophers
Emphasize such categories as recalling, encoding and storing, and identifying relationships and patterns — all of which admit to empirical study.	Emphasize identification of issues, assumptions, relevant and irrelevant considerations, unclear concepts and terms, supported and unsupported claims, contradictions, inferences and implications — all of which shed light on thought conceived as the intellectual moves of a reasoning person.

16. Place of micro-skills

Cognitive Psychologists	Philosophers
Separate the analysis of micro-skills from normative considerations.	Link the analysis of micro-skills with normative considerations since, for philosophers, micro-skills are intellectual moves which can be used to clarify, analyze, synthesize, support, elaborate, question, deduce, or induce.

Tendencies of

Cognitive Psychologists	**Philosophers**

With Respect to:

17. View of macro-processes

View macro-processes from the perspective of categories of research in cognitive psychology: problem solving, decision making, concept formation, and so forth.	View macro-processes from the perspective of the overall reasoning needs of a rational person: ability to analyze issues and distinguish questions of different logical types, ability to Socratically question, ability to engage in conceptual analysis, ability to accurately reconstruct the strongest case for opposing points of view, ability to reason dialogically and dialectically (each use of a macro-process is a unique orchestration of some sequence of micro-skills in the context of some issue, problem, or objective).

18. Teaching as a science or art

Present teaching for thinking as a quasi-science, with the assumption that there is a discrete body of information that can be "added up" or "united" and passed on "as is" to the teacher.	Present teaching for thinking as an intellectual art; play down the significance of technical, empirical information as necessary to skill in that art.

19. Place of philosophy of education

Ignore or play down the significance of teachers developing a philosophy of education into which rationality, autonomy, and self-criticism become central values.	Emphasize the importance of each teacher developing an explicit philosophy of education which is openly stated in the classroom; tend to encourage students to do the same, especially in relation to their philosophy of life.

20. Obstacles to rational thinking

Ignore the problem of prejudice and bias in parents and the community as possible obstacles to teaching for rational thinking.	Sensitive to the dangers of community and national bias as possible obstacles to teaching for rational thinking.

Tendencies of

Cognitive Psychologists	*Philosophers*

With Respect to:

21. Place of virtues and passions

Underemphasize the significance of rational passions and intellectual virtues.	Emphasize rational passions (a passion for clarity, accuracy, fairmindedness, a fervor for getting to the bottom of things or deepest root issues, for listening sympathetically to opposing perspectives, a compelling drive to seek out evidence, an intense aversion to contradiction and sloppy thinking, a devotion to truth over self-interest) and intellectual virtues (intellectual humility, intellectual courage, intellectual integrity, intellectual empathy, intellectual perseverance, faith in reason, and intellectual sense of justice).

22. Specialized versus mundane thinking

Orient themselves toward domain-specific thinking, with the "good" thinker often associated with the successful business or professional person, or with a specialist working within a discipline.	Emphasize the link between an emphasis on rational thought and the goals of a traditional liberal education, of the ideal of the liberally educated person and on mundane generalizable skills such as the art of reading the newspaper critically, detecting propaganda and bias in public discourse, advertising, and textbooks, and in rational reorientation of personal values and beliefs.

23. Place of ethics of teaching and the rights of students

Lay insufficient stress upon the relation of teaching for thinking to the ethics of teaching and the rights of students.	Emphasize the link between teaching for critical thinking and developing moral insight, with the rights of students; with the student's "right to exercise his independent judgment and powers of evaluation"; as Siegel (1980) puts it: "To deny the student this right is to deny the student the status of person of equal worth."

Tendencies of	
Cognitive Psychologists	**Philosophers**
With Respect to:	
24. Thinking and one's way of life	
Lay insufficient stress upon the relation of modes of thinking to fundamental ethical and philosophical choices concerning a way of life.	Link emphasis on critical thinking with an attempt to initiate students, as Israel Scheffler (1965) puts it, "into the rational life, a life in which the critical quest for reasons is a dominant and integrating motive."

Those whose thinking about thinking is basically shaped by scholars in one tradition differ from those shaped by the other. They differ in style, direction, and methods for improving thinking. Inevitably problems of misunderstanding and mutual prejudice remain as residues of the historical separation of psychology from philosophy. That psychologists are sometimes skeptical of philosophical approaches to teaching for thinking is poignantly demonstrated by Al Benderson (1984) of the Educational Testing Service. In characterizing "The View From Psychology" (on philosophy's contribution to teaching for thinking) Benderson says:

> Psychologists, who have their roots in research into mental processes, tend to view thinking from a different perspective than do philosophers. ETS Distinguished Research Scientist Irving Seigel, a psychologist, views philosophers who claim to teach thinking skills as encroaching upon a field in which they have little real expertise. "These philosophers are imperialists", he charges. "They don't know the first thing about how kids think." (p. 10)

R. S. Peters and C. A. Mace (1967), two philosophers in turn commenting on the separation of psychology from philosophy for the *Encyclopedia of Philosophy,* say:

> The trouble began when psychologists claimed the status of empirical scientists. At first the philosophers were the more aggressive, deriding the young science as a bogus discipline. The psychologists hit back and made contemptuous remarks about philosophical logic-chopping and armchair psychology. The arguments were charged with emotion and neither side emerged with great credit .... Not all issues between philosophers and psychologists have been resolved, but there has been notable progress toward a policy of coexistence, and here and there some progress toward cooperation has been made. (p. 26)

In the field of teaching for thinking there has been, in my view, much more coexistence than cooperation. The largest and oldest conference tradition in the field (the Sonoma Conferences: two national and six international conferences, the last with a registration of over 1,000 with over 100 presenters and 230 sessions) has had only token participation by cognitive psychologists. The conference on *Thinking* at Harvard, in turn, had only token participation by philosophers. It appears to me that few psychologists or philosophers read widely in the other tradition. The field of education has been dominated by various psychologically-based rather than philosophically-based models of instruction. It is understandable therefore why *Dimensions of Thinking,* written by a team that included no philosophers, fails to successfully represent or integrate the distinctive approach of philosophy toward the thinking skills movement.

Having said this much about the typical failure of cognitive psychologists and philosophers to appropriate the strengths and correct for the weaknesses of their two traditions, I nevertheless want to mention the signs of common themes emerging in the two traditions which may become the basis for integration. Representatives of both traditions are developing a profound critique of what I would call a "didactic" theory of knowledge, learning, and literacy and framing a "critical" alternative. Behind this critique and reconstruction is a growing common sense of how the didactic paradigm impedes the scholastic development of critical thinkers.

✦ Conclusion

Perhaps a growing joint recognition of the need for both cognitive psychologists and philosophers to make common cause against the didactic theory of education will be the impetus for an on-going fruitful exchange of ideas across these rich traditions. It is certainly in the interest of all who consider the ability to think critically to be at the heart of education rightly conceived, for this rapprochement to take place.

✦ References

Newman, John Henry. *The Idea of a University.* London: Langman's, Green, and Co. 1912.

Benderson, Al. "The View from Psychology." *Critical Thinking: Focus 15.* 1984.

Peters, R. S. & Mace, C. A. "Psychology" *Encyclopedia of Philosophy, Vol. 7.* New York: Macmillan Publishing Co., Inc. & The Free Press. 1967.

Paul, Richard W. "Critical Thinking in North America: A New Theory of Knowledge, Learning, and Literacy." *Argumentation: North American Perspectives on Teaching Critical Thinking.* (in press).

Siegel, Harvey. "Critical Thinking as an Educational Ideal" *National Forum.* November, 1980.

Scheffler, Israel. *The Conditions of Knowledge.* Chicago: Scott Foresman. 1965.

Appendix

Appendix A

Glossary:
A Guide to
Critical Thinking Terms and Concepts

with A. J. A. Binker

accurate: Free from errors, mistakes, or distortion. *Correct* connotes little more than absence of error; *accurate* implies a positive exercise of one to obtain conformity with fact or truth; *exact* stresses perfect conformity to fact, truth, or some standard; *precise* suggests minute accuracy of detail. Accuracy is an important goal in critical thinking, though it is almost always a matter of degree. It is also important to recognize that making mistakes is an essential part of learning and that it is far better that students make their own mistakes, than that they parrot the thinking of the text or teacher. It should also be recognized that some distortion usually results whenever we think within a point of view or frame of reference. Students should think with this awareness in mind, with some sense of the limitations of their own, the text's, the teacher's, the subject's perspective. See *perfections of thought.*

ambiguous: A sentence having two or more possible meanings. Sensitivity to ambiguity and vagueness in writing and speech is essential to good thinking. *A continual effort to be clear and precise in language usage is fundamental to education.* Ambiguity is a problem more of sentences than of individual words. Furthermore, not every sentence that can be construed in more than one way is problematic and deserving of analysis. Many sentences are clearly intended one way; any other construal is obviously absurd and not meant. For example, "Make me a sandwich." is never seriously intended to request metamorphic change. It is a poor example for teaching genuine insight into critical thinking. For an example of a problematic ambiguity, consider the statement, "Welfare is corrupt." Among the possible meanings of this sentence are the following: Those who administer welfare programs take bribes to administer welfare policy unfairly; Welfare policies are written in such a way that much of the money goes to people who don't deserve it rather than to those who do; A government that gives money to people who haven't earned it corrupts both the giver and the recipi-

457

ent. If two people are arguing about whether or not welfare is corrupt, but interpret the claim differently, they can make little or no progress; they aren't arguing about the same point. Evidence and considerations relevant to one interpretation may be irrelevant to others.

analyze: To break up a whole into its parts, to examine in detail so as to determine the nature of, to look more deeply into an issue or situation. *All learning presupposes some analysis of what we are learning,* if only by categorizing or labeling things in one way rather than another. Students should continually be asked to analyze their ideas, claims, experiences, interpretations, judgments, and theories and those they hear and read. See *elements of thought.*

argue: There are two meanings of this word that need to be distinguished: *1)* to argue in the sense of *to fight* or to emotionally disagree; and *2)* to give reasons for or against a proposal or proposition. In emphasizing critical thinking, we continually try to get our students to move from the first sense of the word to the second; that is, we try to get them to see the importance of *giving reasons* to support their views without getting their egos involved in what they are saying. This is a fundamental problem in human life. To argue in the critical thinking sense is to use logic and reason, and to bring forth facts to support or refute a point. It is done in a spirit of cooperation and good will.

argument: A reason or reasons offered for or against something, the offering of such reasons. This term refers to a discussion in which there is disagreement and suggests the use of logic and bringing forth of facts to support or refute a point. See *argue.*

to assume: To take for granted or to presuppose. Critical thinkers can and do make their assumptions explicit, assess them, and correct them. Assumptions can vary from the mundane to the problematic: I heard a scratch at the door. I got up to let the cat in. I *assumed* that only the cat makes that noise, and that he makes it only when he wants to be let in. Someone speaks gruffly to me. I feel guilty and hurt. I assume he is angry *at me,* that he is only angry at me when I do something bad, and that if he's angry at me, he dislikes me. *Notice that people often equate making assumptions with making false assumptions.* When people say, "Don't assume", this is what they mean. In fact, we cannot avoid making assumptions and some are justifiable. (For instance, we have assumed that people who buy this book can read English.) Rather than saying "Never assume", we say, "Be aware of and careful about the assumptions you make, and be ready to examine and critique them." See *assumption, elements of thought.*

assumption: A statement accepted or supposed as true without proof or demonstration; an unstated premise or belief. *All human thought and experience is based on assumptions.* Our thought must begin with something we take to be true in a particular context. We are typically unaware of what we assume and therefore rarely question our assumptions. Much of what is wrong with human thought can be found in the uncritical or unexamined assumptions that underlie it. For example, we often experience the world in such a way as to assume that we are observing things just as they are, as though we were seeing the world without the filter of a point of view. People we disagree with, of course, we recognize as *having a point of view*. One of the key dispositions of critical thinking is the on-going sense that as humans we always think within a perspective, that we virtually never experience things totally and absolutistically. There is a connection, therefore, between thinking so as to be *aware of our assumptions* and being *intellectually humble*.

authority: 1) The power or supposed right to give commands, enforce obedience, take action, or make final decisions. 2) A person with much knowledge and expertise in a field, hence reliable. Critical thinkers recognize that ultimate authority rests with reason and evidence, since it is only on the assumption that purported experts have the backing of reason and evidence that they rightfully gain authority. Much instruction discourages critical thinking by encouraging students to believe that whatever the text or teacher says is true. As a result, students do not learn how to assess authority. See *knowledge*.

bias: A mental leaning or inclination. We must clearly distinguish two different senses of the word 'bias'. One is neutral, the other negative. In the neutral sense we are referring simply to the fact that, *because of one's point of view, one notices some things rather than others*, emphasizes some points rather than others, and thinks in one direction rather than others. This is not in itself a criticism because *thinking within a point of view is unavoidable*. In the negative sense, we are implying *blindness or irrational resistance to weaknesses within one's own point of view* or to the strength or insight within a point of view one opposes. Fairminded critical thinkers try to be aware of their bias (in sense one) and try hard to avoid bias (in sense two). Many people confuse these two senses. Many confuse bias with emotion or with evaluation, perceiving any expression of emotion or any use of evaluative words to be biased (sense two). Evaluative words that can be justified by reason and evidence are not biased in the negative sense. See *criteria, evaluation, judgment, opinion*.

clarify: To make easier to understand, to free from confusion or ambiguity, to remove obscurities. *Clarity* is a fundamental perfection of thought and *clarification* a fundamental aim in critical thinking. Students often do not see why it is important to write and speak clearly, why it is important to *say what you mean and mean what you say*. The key to clarification is *concrete, specific* examples. See *accurate, ambiguous, logic of language, vague*.

concept: An idea or thought, especially a generalized idea of a thing or of a class of things. Humans think within concepts or ideas. *We can never achieve command over our thoughts unless we learn how to achieve command over our concepts or ideas.* Thus we must learn how to identify the concepts or ideas we are using, contrast them with alternative concepts or ideas, and clarify what we include and exclude by means of them. For example, most people say they believe strongly in democracy, but few can clarify with examples what that word does and does not imply. *Most people confuse the meaning of words with cultural associations,* with the result that 'democracy' means to people whatever *we* do in running *our* government — any country that is different is undemocratic. We must distinguish the concepts implicit in the English language from the psychological associations surrounding that concept in a given social group or culture. The failure to develop this ability is a major cause of uncritical thought and selfish critical thought. See *logic of language.*

conclude/conclusion: To decide by reasoning, to infer, to deduce; the last step in a reasoning process; a judgment, decision, or belief formed after investigation or reasoning. All beliefs, decisions, or actions are based on human thought, but rarely as the result of conscious reasoning or deliberation. *All that we believe is,* one way or another, *based on conclusions* that we have come to during our lifetime. Yet, we rarely monitor our thought processes, we don't critically assess the conclusions we come to, to determine whether we have sufficient grounds or reasons for accepting them. People seldom recognize when they have come to a conclusion. They confuse their conclusions with evidence, and so cannot assess the reasoning that took them from evidence to conclusion. Recognizing that *human life is inferential,* that we continually come to conclusions about ourselves and the things and persons around us, is essential to thinking critically and reflectively.

consistency: To think, act, or speak in agreement with what has already been thought, done, or expressed; to have intellectual or moral integrity. Human life and thought is filled with inconsistency, hypocrisy, and contradiction. We often say one thing and do another, judge ourselves and our friends by one standard and our antagonists by another, lean over backwards to justify what we want or negate what does not serve our interests. Similarly, we often confuse desires with needs, treating our desires as equivalent to needs, putting what we want above the basic needs of others. *Logical and moral consistency are fundamental values of fairminded critical thinking.* Social conditioning and native egocentrism often obscure social contradictions, inconsistency, and hypocrisy. See *personal contradiction, social contradiction, intellectual integrity, human nature.*

contradict/contradiction: To assert the opposite of; to be contrary to, go against; a statement in opposition to another; a condition in which things tend to be contrary to each other; inconsistency; discrepancy; a person or thing containing or composed of contradictory elements. See *personal contradiction, social contradiction.*

criterion (criteria, pl): A standard, rule, or test by which something can be judged or measured. Human life, thought, and action are based on human values. The standards by which we determine whether those values are achieved in any situation represent criteria. Critical thinking depends upon making explicit the standards or criteria for rational or justifiable thinking and behavior. See *evaluation.*

critical listening: A mode of monitoring how we are listening so as to maximize our accurate understanding of what another person is saying. By understanding the logic of human communication — that *everything spoken expresses point of view,* uses some ideas and not others, has implications, etc. — critical thinkers can listen so as to enter sympathetically and analytically into the perspective of others. See *critical speaking, critical reading, critical writing, elements of thought, intellectual empathy.*

critical person: One who has mastered a range of intellectual skills and abilities. If that person generally uses those skills to advance his or her own selfish interests, that person is a critical thinker only in a weak or qualified sense. If that person generally uses those skills fairmindedly, entering empathically into the points of view of others, he or she is a critical thinker in the strong or fullest sense. See *critical thinking.*

critical reading: Critical reading is an active, intellectually engaged process in which the reader participates in an inner dialogue with the writer. Most people read uncritically and so miss some part of what is expressed while distorting other parts. A critical reader realizes the way in which *reading, by its very nature, means entering into a point of view other than our own,* the point of view of the writer. A critical reader actively looks for assumptions, key concepts and ideas, reasons and justifications, supporting examples, parallel experiences, implications and consequences, and any other structural features of the written text, to interpret and assess it accurately and fairly. See *elements of thought.*

critical society: A society which rewards adherence to the values of critical thinking and hence *does not use indoctrination and inculcation as basic modes of learning* (rewards reflective questioning, intellectual independence, and reasoned dissent). Socrates is not the only thinker to imagine a society in which independent critical thought became embodied in the concrete day-to-day lives of individuals; William Graham Sumner, North America's distinguished anthropologist, explicitly formulated the ideal:

The critical habit of thought, if usual in a society, will pervade all its mores, because it is a way of taking up the problems of life. Men educated in it cannot be stampeded by stump orators and are never deceived by dithyrambic oratory. They are slow to believe. They can hold things as possible or probable in all degrees, without certainty and without pain. They can wait for evidence and weigh evidence, uninfluenced by the emphasis or confidence with which assertions are made on one side or the other. They can resist appeals to their dearest prejudices and all kinds of cajolery. Education in the critical faculty is the only education of which it can be truly said that it makes good citizens. (*Folkways*, 1906)

Until critical habits of thought pervade our society, however, there will be a tendency for schools as social institutions to transmit the prevailing world view more or less uncritically, to transmit it as reality, not as a picture of reality. Education for critical thinking, then, requires that the school or classroom become a microcosm of a critical society. See *didactic instruction, dialogical instruction, intellectual virtues, knowledge.*

critical thinking: 1) Disciplined, self-directed thinking which exemplifies the perfections of thinking appropriate to a particular mode or domain of thinking. 2) Thinking that displays mastery of intellectual skills and abilities. 3) The art of thinking about your thinking while you are thinking in order to make your thinking better: more clear, more accurate, or more defensible. Critical thinking can be distinguished into two forms: "selfish" or "sophistic", on the one hand, and "fairminded", on the other. In thinking critically we use our command of the elements of thinking to adjust our thinking successfully to the logical demands of a type or mode of thinking. See *critical person, critical society, critical reading, critical listening, critical writing, perfections of thought, elements of thought, domains of thought, intellectual virtues.*

critical writing: To express ourselves in language requires that we arrange our ideas in some relationships to each other. When accuracy and truth are at issue, then we must understand what our thesis is, how we can support it, how we can elaborate it to make it intelligible to others, what objections can be raised to it from other points of view, what the limitations are to our point of view, and so forth. *Disciplined writing requires disciplined thinking; disciplined thinking is achieved through disciplined writing.* See *critical listening, critical reading, logic of language.*

critique: An objective judging, analysis, or evaluation of something. The purpose of critique is the same as the purpose of critical thinking: to appreciate strengths as well as weaknesses, virtues as well as failings. *Critical thinkers critique in order to redesign, remodel, and make better.*

cultural association: Undisciplined thinking often reflects associations, personal and cultural, absorbed or uncritically formed. If a person who was cruel to me as a child had a particular tone of voice, I may find myself disliking a person who has the same tone of voice. Media advertising juxtaposes and joins logically unrelated things to influence our buying habits. Raised in a particular country or within a particular group within it, we form any number of mental links which, if they remain unexamined, unduly influence our thinking. See *concept, critical society.*

cultural assumption: Un-assessed (often implicit) belief adopted by virtue of upbringing in a society. Raised in a society, we unconsciously take on its point of view, values, beliefs, and practices. At the root of each of these are many kinds of assumptions. Not knowing that we perceive, conceive, think, and experience within assumptions we have taken in, we take ourselves to be perceiving "things as they are", not "things as they appear from a cultural vantage point". Becoming aware of our cultural assumptions so that we might critically examine them is a crucial dimension of critical thinking. It is, however, a dimension almost totally absent from schooling. Lip service to this ideal is common enough; a realistic emphasis is virtually unheard of. See *ethnocentricity, prejudice, social contradiction.*

data: Facts, figures, or information from which conclusions can be inferred, or upon which interpretations or theories can be based. As critical thinkers we must make certain to distinguish hard data from the inferences or conclusions we draw from them.

dialectical thinking: Dialogical thinking (thinking within more than one perspective) conducted to test the strengths and weaknesses of opposing points of view. (Court trials and debates are, in a sense, dialectical.) When thinking dialectically, reasoners pit two or more opposing points of view in competition with each other, developing each by providing support, raising objections, countering those objections, raising further objections, and so on. Dialectical thinking or discussion can be conducted so as to "win" by defeating the positions one disagrees with — using critical insight to support one's own view and point out flaws in other views (associated with critical thinking in the restricted or weak sense), or fairmindedly, by conceding points that don't stand up to critique, trying to integrate or incorporate strong points found in other views, and using critical insight to develop a fuller and more accurate view (associated with critical thinking in the fuller or strong sense). See *monological problems.*

dialogical instruction: Instruction that fosters dialogical or dialectic thinking. Thus, when considering a question, the class brings all relevant subjects to bear and considers the perspectives of groups whose views are not canvassed in their texts — for example, "What did King George think of the *Declaration of Independence*, the Revolutionary War, the Continental Congress, Jefferson and Washington, etc.?" or, "How would an economist analyze this situation? A historian? A psychologist? A geographer?" See *critical society, didactic instruction, higher order learning, lower order learning, Socratic questioning, knowledge.*

dialogical thinking: Thinking that involves a dialogue or extended exchange between different points of view or frames of reference. Students learn best in dialogical situations, in circumstances in which they continually express their views to others and try to fit other's views into their own. See *Socratic questioning, monological thinking, multilogical thinking, dialectical thinking.*

didactic instruction: Teaching by telling. In didactic instruction, the teacher directly tells the student what to believe and think about a subject. The student's task is to remember what the teacher said and reproduce it on demand. In its most common form, this mode of teaching falsely assumes that one can directly give a person knowledge without that person having to think his or her way to it. It falsely assumes that knowledge can be separated from understanding and justification. It confuses the ability to *state* a principle with *understanding* it, the ability to *supply* a definition with *knowing* a new word, and the act of *saying* that something is important with *recognizing* its importance. See *critical society, knowledge.*

domains of thought: Thinking can be oriented or structured with different issues or purposes in view. *Thinking varies in accordance with purpose and issue.* Critical thinkers learn to discipline their thinking to take into account the nature of the issue or domain. We see this most clearly when we consider the difference between issues and thinking within different academic disciplines or subject areas. Hence, mathematical thinking is quite different from, say, historical thinking. Mathematics and history, we can say then, represent different domains of thought. See the *logic of questions.*

egocentricity: A tendency to view everything in relationship to oneself; to confuse immediate perception (how things *seem*) with reality. One's desires, values, and beliefs (seeming to be self-evidently correct or superior to those of others) are often uncritically used as the norm of all judgment and experience. Egocentricity is one of the fundamental impediments to critical thinking. As one learns to think critically in a strong sense, one learns to become more rational, and less egocentric. See *human nature, strong sense critical thinker, ethnocentrism, sociocentrism, personal contradiction.*

elements of thought: All thought has a universal set of elements, each of which can be monitored for possible problems: Are we clear about our *purpose or goal?* about the *problem or question at issue?* about our *point of view or frame of reference?* about our *assumptions?* about the *claims* we are making? about the *reasons or evidence* upon which we are basing our claims? about our *inferences and line of reasoning?* about the *implications and consequences* that follow from our reasoning? Critical thinkers develop skills of identifying and assessing these elements in their thinking and in the thinking of others.

emotion: A feeling aroused to the point of awareness, often a strong feeling or state of excitement. When our egocentric emotions or feelings get involved, when we are excited by infantile anger, fear, jealousy, etc., our objectivity often decreases. Critical thinkers need to be able to monitor their egocentric feelings and use their rational passions to reason themselves into feelings appropriate to the situation as it really is, rather than to how it seems to their infantile ego. Emotions and feelings themselves are not irrational; however, it is common for people to feel strongly when their ego is stimulated. One way to understand the goal of strong sense critical thinking is as the attempt to develop rational feelings and emotions at the expense of irrational, egocentric ones. See *rational passions, intellectual virtues.*

empirical: Relying or based on experiment, observation, or experience rather than on theory or meaning. *It is important to continually distinguish those considerations based on experiment, observation, or experience from those based on the meaning of a word or concept or the implications of a theory.* One common form of uncritical or selfish critical thinking involves distorting facts or experience in order to preserve a preconceived meaning or theory. For example, a conservative may distort the facts that support a liberal perspective to prevent empirical evidence from counting against a theory of the world that he or she holds rigidly. Indeed, within all perspectives and belief systems many will distort the facts before they will admit to a weakness in their favorite theory or belief. See *data, fact, evidence.*

empirical implication: That which follows from a situation or fact, not due to the logic of language, but from experience or scientific law. The redness of the coil on the stove empirically implies dangerous heat.

ethnocentricity: A tendency to view one's own race or culture as central, based on the deep-seated belief that one's own group is superior to all others. Ethnocentrism is a form of egocentrism extended from the self to the group. Much uncritical or selfish critical thinking is either ego-centric or ethnocentric in nature. ('Ethnocentrism' and 'sociocentrism' are used synonymously, for the most part, though 'sociocentricity' is broader, relating to *any* group, including, for example, sociocentricity regarding one's profession.) The "cure" for ethnocentrism or sociocen-trism is empathic thought within the perspective of opposing groups and cultures. Such empathic thought is rarely cultivated in the societies and schools of today. Instead, many people develop an empty rhetoric of tolerance, saying that others have different beliefs and ways, but without seriously considering those beliefs and ways, what they mean to those others, and their reasons for maintaining them.

evaluation: To judge or determine the worth or quality of. *Evaluation has a logic and should be carefully distinguished from mere subjective prefer-ence.* The elements of its logic may be put in the form of questions which may be asked whenever an evaluation is to be carried out: *1)* Are we clear about *what precisely we are evaluating?; 2)* Are we clear about *our purpose?* Is our purpose legitimate?; *3)* Given our purpose, what are the *relevant criteria or standards* for evaluation?; *4)* Do we have *sufficient information* about that which we are evaluating? Is that *infor-mation relevant to the purpose?;* and *5)* Have we *applied our criteria accu-rately and fairly to the facts* as we know them? Uncritical thinkers often treat evaluation as mere preference or treat their evaluative judgments as direct observations not admitting of error.

evidence: The data on which a judgment or conclusion might be based or by which proof or probability might be established. Critical thinkers distinguish the evidence or raw data upon which they base their inter-pretations or conclusions from the inferences and assumptions that connect data to conclusions. Uncritical thinkers treat their conclu-sions as something given to them in experience, as something they directly observe in the world. As a result, they find it difficult to see why anyone might disagree with their conclusions. After all, the truth of their views is, they believe, right there for everyone to see! Such people find it difficult or even impossible to describe the evidence or experience without coloring that description with their interpretation.

explicit: Clearly stated and leaving nothing implied; *explicit* is applied to that which is so clearly stated or distinctly set forth that there should be no doubt as to the meaning; *exact and precise* in this connection both suggest that which is strictly defined, accurately stated, or made unmistakably clear; *definite* implies precise limitations as to the nature, character, meaning, etc. of something; *specific* implies the pointing up of details or the particularizing of references. Critical thinking often requires the ability to be explicit, exact, definite, and specific. Most students cannot make what is *implicit* in their thinking *explicit*. This deficiency hampers their ability to monitor and assess their thinking.

fact: What actually happened, what is true; verifiable by empirical means; distinguished from interpretation, inference, judgment, or conclusion; the raw data. There are distinct senses of the word 'factual': "True" (as opposed to "claimed to be true"); and "empirical" (as opposed to conceptual or evaluative). You may make many "factual claims" in one sense, that is, claims which can be verified or disproven by observation or empirical study, but I must evaluate those claims to determine if they are true. People often confuse these two senses, even to the point of accepting as true, statements which merely "seem factual", for example, "29.23 % of Americans suffer from depression." Before I accept this as true, I should assess it. I should ask such questions as "How do you know? How *could* this be known? Did you merely ask people if they were depressed and extrapolate those results? How exactly did you arrive at this figure?" Purported facts should be assessed for their accuracy, completeness, and relevance to the issue. Sources of purported facts should be assessed for their qualifications, track records, and impartiality. Education which stresses retention and repetition of factual claims stunts students' desire and ability to assess alleged facts, leaving them open to manipulation. Activities in which students are asked to "distinguish fact from opinion" often confuse these two senses. They encourage students to *accept as true* statements which merely "look like" facts. See *intellectual humility, knowledge.*

fair: Treating both or all sides alike without reference to one's own feelings or interests; *just* implies adherence to a standard of rightness or lawfulness without reference to one's own inclinations; *impartial* and *unbiased* both imply freedom from prejudice for or against any side; *dispassionate* implies the absence of passion or strong emotion, hence, connotes cool, disinterested judgment; *objective* implies a viewing of persons or things without reference to oneself, one's interests, etc.

faith: 1) Unquestioning belief in anything. 2) Confidence, trust, or reliance. A critical thinker does not accept faith in the first sense, for every belief is reached on the basis of some thinking, which may or may not be justified. Even in religion one believes in one religion rather than another, and in doing so implies that there are good reasons for accepting one rather than another. A Christian, for example, believes that there are good reasons for not being an atheist, and Christians often attempt to persuade non-Christians to change their beliefs. In some sense, then, everyone has confidence in the capacity of his or her own mind to judge rightly on the basis of good reasons, and does not believe simply on the basis of blind faith.

fallacy/fallacious: An error in reasoning; flaw or defect in argument; an argument which doesn't conform to rules of good reasoning (especially one that appears to be sound). Containing or based on a fallacy; deceptive in appearance or meaning; misleading; delusive.

higher order learning: Learning through exploring the foundations, justification, implications, and value of a fact, principle, skill, or concept.
Learning so as to deeply understand. One can learn in keeping with the
rational capacities of the human mind or in keeping with its irrational
propensities, cultivating the capacity of the human mind to discipline
and direct its thought through commitment to intellectual standards,
or one can learn through mere association. Education for critical
thought produces higher order learning by helping students actively
think their way to conclusions; discuss their thinking with other students and the teacher; entertain a variety of points of view; analyze
concepts, theories, and explanations in their own terms; actively question the meaning and implications of what they learn; compare what
they learn to what they have experienced; take what they read and
write seriously; solve non-routine problems; examine assumptions;
and gather and assess evidence. Students should learn each subject by
engaging in thought within that subject. They should learn history by
thinking historically, mathematics by thinking mathematically, etc.
See *dialogical instruction, lower order learning, critical society, knowledge,
principle, domains of thought.*

human nature: The common qualities of all human beings. People have
both a primary and a secondary nature. Our primary nature is spontaneous, egocentric, and strongly prone to irrational belief formation. It
is the basis for our instinctual thought. People need no training to
believe what they want to believe: what serves their immediate interests, what preserves their sense of personal comfort and righteousness,
what minimizes their sense of inconsistency, and what presupposes
their own correctness. People need no special training to believe what
those around them believe: what their parents and friends believe,
what is taught to them by religious and school authorities, what is
repeated often by the media, and what is commonly believed in the
nation in which they are raised. People need no training to think that
those who disagree with them are wrong and probably prejudiced.
People need no training to assume that their own most fundamental
beliefs are self-evidently true or easily justified by evidence. People
naturally and spontaneously identify with their own beliefs. They
experience most disagreement as personal attack. The resulting defensiveness interferes with their capacity to empathize with or enter into
other points of view.

On the other hand, *people need extensive and systematic practice to develop their secondary nature, their implicit capacity to function as rational persons.* They need extensive and systematic practice to recognize the tendencies they have to form irrational beliefs. They need extensive
practice to develop a dislike of inconsistency, a love of clarity, a passion to seek reasons and evidence and to be fair to points of view other

than their own. People need extensive practice to recognize that they indeed have a point of view, that they live inferentially, that they do not have a direct pipeline to reality, that it is perfectly possible to have an overwhelming inner sense of the correctness of one's views and still be wrong. See *intellectual virtues.*

idea: Anything existing in the mind as an object of knowledge or thought; *concept* refers to generalized idea of a class of objects, based on knowledge of particular instances of the class; *conception,* often equivalent to concept, specifically refers to something conceived in the mind or imagined; *thought* refers to any idea, whether or not expressed, that occurs to the mind in reasoning or contemplation; *notion* implies vagueness or incomplete intention; *impression* also implies vagueness of an idea provoked by some external stimulus. Critical thinkers are aware of what ideas they are using in their thinking, where those ideas came from, and how to assess them. See *clarify, concept, logic, logic of language.*

imply/implication: A claim or truth which follows from other claims or truths. One of the most important skills of critical thinking is the ability to distinguish between what is actually implied by a statement or situation from what may be carelessly inferred by people. Critical thinkers try to *monitor their inferences to keep them in line with what is actually implied* by what they know. When speaking, critical thinkers *try to use words that imply only what they can legitimately justify.* They recognize that there are established word usages which generate established implications. To say of an act that it is murder, for example, is to imply that it is intentional and unjustified. See *clarify, precision, logic of language, critical listening, critical reading, elements of thought.*

infer/inference: An inference is a step of the mind, an intellectual act by which one concludes that something is so in light of something else's being so, or seeming to be so. If you come at me with a knife in your hand, I would probably infer that you mean to do me harm. Inferences can be strong or weak, justified or unjustified. Inferences are based upon assumptions. See *imply/implication.*

insight: The ability to see and clearly and deeply understand the inner nature of things. Instruction for critical thinking fosters insight rather than mere performance; it cultivates the achievement of deeper knowledge and understanding through insight. *Thinking one's way into and through a subject leads to insights* as one synthesizes what one is learning, relating one subject to other subjects and all subjects to personal experience. Rarely is insight formulated as a goal in present curricula and texts. See *dialogical instruction, higher order learning, lower order learning, didactic instruction, intellectual humility.*

intellectual autonomy: Having rational control of ones beliefs, values, and inferences. The ideal of critical thinking is to learn to think for oneself, to gain command over one's thought processes. Intellectual autonomy does not entail willfulness, stubbornness, or rebellion. It entails a commitment to analyzing and evaluating beliefs on the basis of reason and evidence, to question when it is rational to question, to believe when it is rational to believe, and to conform when it is rational to conform. See *know, knowledge.*

intellectual civility: A commitment to take others seriously as thinkers, to treat them as intellectual equals, to grant respect and full attention to their views — a commitment to persuade rather than browbeat. It is distinguished from intellectual rudeness: verbally attacking others, dismissing them, stereotyping their views. Intellectual civility is not a matter of mere curtesy, but arises from a sense that communication itself requires honoring others' views and their capacity to reason.

(intellectual) confidence or faith in reason: Confidence that in the long run *one's own higher interests and those of humankind at large will best be served by giving the freest play to reason* — by encouraging people to come to their own conclusions through a process of developing their own rational faculties; faith that (with proper encouragement and cultivation) people can learn to think for themselves, form rational viewpoints, draw reasonable conclusions, think coherently and logically, persuade each other by reason, and become reasonable, despite the deep-seated obstacles in the native character of the human mind and in society. Confidence in reason is developed through experiences in which one reasons one's way to insight, solves problems through reason, uses reason to persuade, is persuaded by reason. Confidence in reason is undermined when one is expected to perform tasks without understanding why, to repeat statements without having verified or justified them, to accept beliefs on the sole basis of authority or social pressure.

intellectual courage: The willingness to face and fairly assess ideas, beliefs, or viewpoints to which we have not given a serious hearing, regardless of our strong negative reactions to them. This courage arises from the recognition that *ideas considered dangerous or absurd are sometimes rationally justified* (in whole or in part), and that *conclusions or beliefs espoused by those around us or inculcated in us are sometimes false or misleading.* To determine for ourselves which is which, we must not passively and uncritically "accept" what we have "learned". Intellectual courage comes into play here, because inevitably we will come to see some truth in some ideas considered dangerous and absurd and some distortion or falsity in some ideas strongly held in our social group. It takes courage to be true to our own thinking in such circumstances. Examining cherished beliefs is difficult, and the penalties for non-conformity are often severe.

intellectual curiosity: A strong desire to deeply understand, to figure things out, to propose and assess useful and plausible hypotheses and explanations, to learn, to find out. People do not learn well, do not gain knowledge, unless they *want* knowledge — deep, accurate, complete understanding. When people lack passion for figuring things out (suffer from intellectual apathy), they tend to settle for an incomplete, incoherent, sketchy "sense" of things incompatible with a critically developed, richer, fuller conception. This trait can flourish only when it is allowed and encouraged, when people are allowed to pose and pursue questions of interest to them and when their intellectual curiosity pays off in increasing understanding.

intellectual discipline: The trait of thinking in accordance with intellectual standards, intellectual rigor, carefulness, order, conscious control. The undisciplined thinker neither knows nor cares when he or she comes to unwarranted conclusions, confuses distinct ideas, fails to consider pertinent evidence, and so on. Thus, intellectual discipline is at the very heart of becoming a critical person. It takes discipline of mind to keep oneself focused on the intellectual task at hand, to locate and carefully assess needed evidence, to systematically analyze and address questions and problems, to hold one's thinking to sufficiently high standards of clarity, precision, completeness, consistency, etc. Such discipline is achieved slowly, bit by bit, only in an atmosphere of intellectual rigor and is acquired only to the degree that one develops insight into elements and standards of reasoning.

intellectual empathy: Understanding the need to imaginatively put oneself in the place of others to genuinely understand them. We must recognize our egocentric tendency to identify truth with our immediate perceptions or longstanding beliefs. Intellectual empathy correlates with the ability to accurately reconstruct the viewpoints and reasoning of others and to *reason from premises, assumptions, and ideas other than our own.* This trait also requires that we remember occasions when we were wrong, despite an intense conviction that we were right, and consider that we might be similarly deceived in a case at hand.

intellectual humility: Awareness of the limits of one's knowledge, including sensitivity to circumstances in which one's native egocentrism is likely to function self-deceptively; sensitivity to bias and prejudice in, and limitations of one's viewpoint. Intellectual humility is based on the recognition that *no one should claim more than he or she actually knows.* It does not imply spinelessness or submissiveness. It implies the lack of intellectual pretentiousness, boastfulness, or conceit, combined with insight into the strengths or weaknesses of the logical foundations of one's beliefs.

intellectual integrity: Recognition of the need to be true to one's own thinking, to be consistent in the intellectual standards one applies, to hold oneself to the same rigorous standards of evidence and proof to which one holds one's antagonists, to practice what one advocates for others, and to honestly admit discrepancies and inconsistencies in one's own thought and action. This trait develops best in a supportive atmosphere in which people feel secure and free enough to honestly acknowledge their inconsistencies, and can develop and share realistic ways of ameliorating them. It requires honest acknowledgment of the difficulties of achieving greater consistency.

intellectual perseverance: Willingness and consciousness of the need to pursue intellectual insights and truths despite difficulties, obstacles, and frustrations; firm adherence to rational principles despite irrational opposition of others; a sense of the need to struggle with confusion and unsettled questions over an extended period of time in order to achieve deeper understanding or insight. This trait is undermined when teachers and others continually provide the answers, do students' thinking for them or substitute easy tricks, algorithms, and short cuts for careful, independent thought.

intellectual responsibility: The responsible person keenly feels the obligation to fulfill his or her duties; intellectual responsibility is the application of this trait to intellectual matters. Hence, the intellectually responsible person feels strongly obliged to achieve a high degree of precision and accuracy in his or her reasoning, is deeply committed to gathering complete, relevant, adequate evidence, etc. This sense of obligation arises when people recognize the need for meeting the intellectual standards required by rational, fairminded thought.

intellectual sense of justice: Willingness and consciousness of the need to entertain all viewpoints sympathetically and to assess them with the same intellectual standards, without reference to one's own feelings or vested interests, or the feelings or vested interests of one's friends, community, or nation; implies adherence to intellectual standards without reference to one's own advantage or the advantage of one's group.

intellectual standards: Principles by which reasoning can be judged; requirements of quality reasoning. Intellectual standards are a pervasive part of critical; thinking. Thinking that qualifies as critical thinking is thinking clear, accurate, relevant to the question at issue, fair, precise, specific, plausible, consistent, logical, deep, broad, complete, and significant. Such standards are implicit in all aspects of critical thinking: where standards are not explicitly stated, they are presupposed. (For example, the critical thinker does not merely identify assumptions, but *accurately* identifies *significant* assumptions.)

intellectual virtues: The traits of mind and character necessary for right action and thinking; the traits of mind and character essential for fairminded rationality; the traits that distinguish the narrowminded, self-serving critical thinker from the openminded, truth-seeking critical thinker. These *intellectual traits are interdependent.* Each is best developed while developing the others as well. They cannot be imposed from without; they must be cultivated by encouragement and example. People can come to deeply understand and accept these principles by analyzing their experiences of them: learning from an unfamiliar perspective, discovering you don't know as much as you thought, and so on. They include: intellectual sense of justice, intellectual perseverance, intellectual integrity, intellectual humility, intellectual empathy, intellectual courage, (intellectual) confidence in reason, and intellectual autonomy.

interpret/interpretation: To give one's own conception of, to place in the context of one's own experience, perspective, point of view, or philosophy. Interpretations should be distinguished from the facts, the evidence, the situation. (I may interpret someone's silence as an expression of hostility toward me. Such an interpretation may or may not be correct. I may have projected my patterns of motivation and behavior onto that person, or I may have accurately noticed this pattern in the other.) The best interpretations take the most evidence into account. Critical thinkers recognize their interpretations, distinguish them from evidence, consider alternative interpretations, and reconsider their interpretations in the light of new evidence. *All learning involves personal interpretation, since whatever we learn we must integrate into our own thinking and action.* What we learn must be given a meaning by us, must be meaningful to us, and hence involves interpretive acts on our part. Didactic instruction, in attempting to directly implant knowledge in students' minds, typically ignores the role of personal interpretation in learning.

intuition: The direct knowing or learning of something without the conscious use of reasoning. We sometimes seem to know or learn things without recognizing how we came to that knowledge. When this occurs, we experience an inner sense that what we believe is true. The problem is that sometimes we are correct (and have genuinely experienced an intuition) and sometimes we are incorrect (having fallen victim to one of our prejudices). A critical thinker does not blindly accept that what he or she thinks or believes but cannot account for is necessarily true. A critical thinker realizes how easily we confuse intuitions and prejudices. Critical thinkers may follow their inner sense that something is so, but only with a healthy sense of intellectual humility.

There is a second sense of 'intuition' that is important for critical thinking, and that is the meaning suggested in the following sentence: "To develop your critical thinking abilities, it is important to develop your critical thinking *intuitions.*" This sense of the word is connected to the fact that we can learn concepts at various levels of depth. If we learn nothing more than an abstract definition for a word and do not learn how to apply it effectively in a wide variety of situations, one might say that we end up with no *intuitive* basis for applying it. We lack the insight into how, when, and why it applies. Helping students to develop critical thinking intuitions is helping them gain the practical insights necessary for a ready and swift application of concepts to cases in a large array of circumstances. We want critical thinking to be "intuitive" to our students, ready and available for immediate translation into their everyday thought and experience.

irrational/irrationality: 1) Lacking the power to reason. 2) Contrary to reason or logic. 3) Senseless, absurd. Uncritical thinkers have failed to develop the ability or power to reason well. Their beliefs and practices, then, are often contrary to reason and logic, and are sometimes senseless or absurd. It is important to recognize, however, that in societies with irrational beliefs and practices, it is not clear whether challenging those beliefs and practices — and therefore possibly endangering oneself — is rational or irrational. Furthermore, suppose one's vested interests are best advanced by adopting beliefs and practices that are contrary to reason. Is it then rational to follow reason and negate one's vested interests or follow one's interests and ignore reason? These very real dilemmas of everyday life represent on-going problems for critical thinkers. Selfish critical thinkers, of course, face no dilemma here because of their consistent commitment to advance their narrow vested interests. Fairminded critical thinkers make these decisions self-consciously and honestly assess the results.

irrational learning: All rational learning presupposes rational assent. And, though we sometimes forget it, not all learning is automatically or even commonly rational. *Much that we learn in everyday life is quite distinctively irrational.* It is quite possible — and indeed the bulk of human learning is unfortunately of this character — *to come to believe any number of things without knowing how or why.* It is quite possible, in other words, to believe for irrational reasons: because those around us believe, because we are rewarded for believing, because we are afraid to disbelieve, because our vested interest is served by belief, because we are more comfortable with belief, or because we have ego identified ourselves, our image, or our personal being with belief. In all of these cases, our beliefs are without rational grounding, without good reason and evidence, without the foundation a rational person demands. We become rational, on the other hand, to the extent that our beliefs and actions are grounded in good reasons and evidence; to the extent that we recognize and critique our own irrationality; to the extent that we are not moved by bad reasons and a multiplicity of irrational motives, fears, and desires; to the extent that we have cultivated a passion for clarity, accuracy, and fairmindedness. These global skills, passions, and dispositions, integrated into behavior and thought, characterize the rational, the educated, and the critical person. See *higher and lower order learning, knowledge, didactic instruction.*

judgment: 1) The act of judging or deciding. 2) Understanding and good sense. A person has good judgment when they typically judge and decide on the basis of understanding and good sense. Whenever we form a belief or opinion, make a decision, or act, we do so on the basis of implicit or explicit judgments. All thought presupposes making judgments concerning what is so and what is not so, what is true and what is not. To cultivate people's ability to think critically is to foster their judgment, to help them to develop the habit of judging on the basis of reason, evidence, logic, and good sense. Good judgment is developed, not by merely learning about principles of good judgment, but by frequent practice judging and assessing judgments.

justify/justification: The act of showing a belief, opinion, action, or policy to be in accord with reason and evidence, to be ethically acceptable, or both. Education should foster reasonability in students. This requires that both teachers and students develop the disposition to ask for and give justifications for beliefs, opinions, actions, and policies. Asking for a justification should not, then, be viewed as an insult or attack, but rather as a normal act of a rational person. Didactic modes of teaching that do not encourage students to question the justification for what is asserted fail to develop a thoughtful environment conducive to education.

know: To have a clear perception or understanding of, to be sure of, to have a firm mental grasp of; *information* applies to data that are gathered in any way, as by reading, observation, hearsay, etc. and does not necessarily connote validity; *knowledge* applies to any body of facts gathered by study, observation, etc. and to the ideas inferred from these facts, and connotes an *understanding* of what is known. Critical thinkers need to distinguish knowledge from opinion and belief. See *knowledge.*

knowledge: The act of having a clear and justifiable grasp of what is so or of how to do something. Knowledge is based on understanding or skill, which in turn are based on thought, study, and experience. 'Thoughtless knowledge' is a contradiction. 'Blind knowledge' is a contradiction. 'Unjustifiable knowledge' is a contradiction. Knowledge implies justifiable belief or skilled action. Hence, when students blindly memorize and are tested for recall, they are not being tested for knowledge. *Knowledge is continually confused with recall in present-day schooling.* This confusion is a deep-seated impediment to the integration of critical thinking into schooling. *Genuine knowledge is inseparable from thinking minds.* We often wrongly talk of knowledge as though it could be divorced from thinking, as though it could be gathered up by one person and given to another in the form of a collection of sentences to remember. When we talk in this way, we forget that *knowledge,* by its very nature, *depends on thought.* Knowledge is produced by thought, analyzed by thought, comprehended by thought, organized, evaluated, maintained, and transformed by thought. Knowledge can be *acquired only* through thought. Knowledge exists, properly speaking, only in minds that have comprehended and justified it through thought. Knowledge is not to be confused with belief nor with symbolic representation of belief. Humans easily and frequently believe things that are false or believe things to be true without knowing them to be so. A book contains knowledge only in a derivative sense, only because minds can thoughtfully read it and through that process gain knowledge.

logic: *1)* Correct reasoning or the study of correct reasoning and its foundations. *2)* The relationships between propositions (supports, assumes, implies, contradicts, counts against, is relevant to, ...). *3)* The system of principles, concepts, and assumptions that underlie any discipline, activity, or practice. *4)* The set of rational considerations that bear upon the truth or justification of any belief or set of beliefs. *5)* The set of rational considerations that bear upon the settlement of any question or set of questions. The word 'logic' covers a range of related concerns all bearing upon the question of rational justification and explanation. *All human thought and behavior is to some extent based on logic* rather than instinct. Humans try to figure things out using ideas, meanings, and thought. Such intellectual behavior inevitably involves "logic" or considerations of a logical sort: some sense of what is relevant and irrelevant, of what supports and what counts against a belief, of what we should and should not assume, of what we should and should not claim, of what we do and do not know, of what is and is not implied, of what does and does not contradict, of what we should or should not do or believe. *Concepts have a logic* in that we can investigate the conditions under which they do and do not apply, of what is relevant or irrelevant to them, of what they do or don't imply, etc. *Questions have a logic* in that we can investigate the conditions under which they can be settled. *Disciplines have a logic* in that they have purposes and a set of logical structures that bear upon those purposes: assumptions, concepts, issues, data, theories, claims, implications, consequences, etc. The concept of logic is a seminal notion in critical thinking. Unfortunately, it takes a considerable length of time before most people become comfortable with its multiple uses. In part, this is due to people's failure to monitor their own thinking in keeping with the standards of reason and logic. This is not to deny, of course, that logic is involved in all human thinking. It is rather to say that the logic we use is often implicit, unexpressed, and sometimes contradictory. See *knowledge, higher and lower order learning, the logic of a discipline, the logic of language, the logic of questions.*

the logic of a discipline: The notion that every technical term has logical relationships with other technical terms, that some terms are logically more basic than others, and that every discipline relies on concepts, assumptions, and theories, makes claims, gives reasons and evidence, avoids contradictions and inconsistencies, has implications and consequences, etc. Though all students study disciplines, most are ignorant of the logic of the disciplines they study. This severely limits their ability to grasp the discipline as a whole, to think independently within it, to compare and contrast it with other disciplines, and to apply it outside the context of academic assignments. Typically now, students do not look for seminal terms as they study an area. They do not strive to translate technical terms into analogies and ordinary words they understand or distinguish technical from ordinary uses of terms. They do not look for the basic assumptions of the disciplines they study. Indeed, on the whole, they do not know what assumptions are nor why it is important to examine them. What they have in their heads exists like so many BB's in a bag. Whether one thought supports or follows from another, whether one thought elaborates another, exemplifies, presupposes, or contradicts another, are matters students have not learned to think about. They have not learned to use thought to understand thought, which is another way of saying that they have not learned how to use thought to gain knowledge. *Instruction for critical thinking cultivates the students' ability to make explicit the logic of what they study.* This emphasis gives depth and breath to study and learning. It lies at the heart of the differences between lower order and higher order learning. See *knowledge.*

the logic of language: For a language to exist and be learnable by persons from a variety of cultures, it is necessary that *words have definite uses and defined concepts that transcend particular cultures.* The English language, for example, is learned by many peoples of the world unfamiliar with English or North American cultures. Critical thinkers must learn to use their native language with precision, in keeping with educated usage. Unfortunately, many students do not understand the significant relationship between precision in language usage and precision in thought. Consider, for example, how most students relate to their native language. If one questions them about the meanings of words, their account is typically incoherent. They often say that people have their own meanings for all the words they use, not noticing that, were this true, we could not understand each other. Students

speak and write in vague sentences because they have no rational criteria for choosing words — they simply write whatever words pop into
their heads. They do not realize that every language has a highly
refined logic one must learn in order to express oneself precisely. They
do not realize that even words similar in meaning typically have different implications. Consider, for example, the words explain,
expound, explicate, elucidate, interpret, and construe. *Explain* implies
the process of making clear and intelligible something not understood
or known. *Expound* implies a systematic and thorough explanation,
often by an expert. *Explicate* implies a scholarly analysis developed in
detail. *Elucidate* implies a shedding of light upon by clear and specific
illustration or explanation. *Interpret* implies the bringing out of meanings not immediately apparent. *Construe* implies a particular interpretation of something whose meaning is ambiguous. See *clarify, concept.*

the logic of questions: The range of rational considerations that bear
upon the settlement of a given question or group of questions. A
critical thinker is adept at analyzing questions to determine what, precisely, a question asks and how to go about rationally settling it. A critical thinker recognizes that different kinds of questions often call for
different modes of thinking, different kinds of considerations, and different procedures and techniques. Uncritical thinkers often confuse
distinct questions and use considerations irrelevant to an issue while
ignoring relevant ones.

lower order learning: Learning by rote memorization, association, and
drill. There are a variety of forms of lower order learning in the schools
which we can identify by understanding the relative *lack of logic
informing them.* Paradigmatically, lower order learning is learning by
sheer association or rote. Hence students come to think of history
class, for example, as a place where you hear names, dates, places,
events, and outcomes; where you try to remember them and state
them on tests. Math comes to be thought of as numbers, symbols, and
formulas — mysterious things you mechanically manipulate as the
teacher told you in order to get the right answer. Literature is often
thought of as uninteresting stories to remember along with what the
teacher said is important about them. Consequently, students leave
with a jumble of undigested fragments, scraps left over after they have
forgotten most of what they stored in their short-term memories for
tests. Virtually never do they grasp the logic of what they learn. Rarely
do they relate what they learn to their own experience or critique each
by means of the other. Rarely do they try to test what they learn in
everyday life. Rarely do they ask "Why is this so? How does this relate
to what I already know? How does this relate to what I am learning in
other classes?" To put the point in a nutshell, very few students think

of what they are learning as worthy of being arranged logically in their minds or have the slightest idea of how to do so. See *didactic instruction, monological and multilogical problems and thinking.*

monological (one-dimensional) problems: Problems that can be solved by reasoning exclusively within one point of view or frame of reference. For example, consider the following problems: *1)* Ten full crates of walnuts weigh 410 pounds, whereas an empty crate weighs 10 pounds. How much do the walnuts alone weigh?; and *2)* In how many days of the week does the third letter of the day's name immediately follow the first letter of the day's name in the alphabet? I call these problems and the means by which they are solved "monological". They are settled within one frame of reference with a definite set of logical moves. When the right set of moves is performed, the problem is settled. The answer or solution proposed can be shown by standards implicit in the frame of reference to be the "right" answer or solution. *Most important human problems are multilogical rather than monological,* non-atomic problems inextricably joined to other problems, with some conceptual messiness to them and very often with important values lurking in the background. When the problems have an empirical dimension, that dimension tends to have a controversial scope. In multilogical problems, it is often arguable how some facts should be considered and interpreted, and how their significance should be determined. When they have a conceptual dimension, there tend to be arguably different ways to pin the concepts down. Though life presents us with predominantly multilogical problems, schooling today over-emphasizes monological problems. Worse, and more frequently, present instructional practices treat multilogical problems as though they were monological. The posing of multilogical problems, and their consideration from multiple points of view, play an important role in the cultivation of critical thinking and higher order learning.

monological (one-dimensional) thinking: Thinking that is conducted exclusively within one point of view or frame of reference: figuring our how much this $67.49 pair of shoes with a 25% discount will cost me; learning what signing this contract obliges me to do; finding out when Kennedy was elected President. A person can think monologically whether or not the question is genuinely monological. (For example, if one considers the question, "Who caused the Civil War?" only from a Northerner's perspective, one is thinking monologically about a multilogical question.) The strong sense critical thinker avoids monological thinking when the question is multi-logical. Moreover, higher order learning requires multi-logical thought, even when the problem is monological (for example, learning a concept in chemistry), since students must explore and assess their original beliefs to develop insight into new ideas.

multilogical (multi-dimensional) problems: Problems that can be analyzed and approached from more than one, often from conflicting, points of view or frames of reference. For example, many ecological problems have a variety of dimensions to them: historical, social, economic, biological, chemical, moral, political, etc. A person comfortable thinking about multilogical problems is comfortable thinking within multiple perspectives, in engaging in dialogical and dialectical thinking, in practicing intellectual empathy, in thinking across disciplines and domains. See *monological problems, the logic of questions, the logic of disciplines, intellectual empathy, dialogical instruction.*

multilogical thinking: Thinking that sympathetically enters, considers, and reasons within multiple points of view. See *multilogical problems, dialectical thinking, dialogical instruction.*

national bias: Prejudice in favor of one's country, it's beliefs, traditions, practices, image, and world view; a form of sociocentrism or ethnocentrism. It is natural, if not inevitable, for people to be favorably disposed toward the beliefs, traditions, practices, and world view within which they were raised. Unfortunately, this favorable inclination commonly becomes a form of prejudice: a more or less rigid, irrational ego-identification which significantly distorts one's view of one's own nation and the world at large. It is manifested in a tendency to mindlessly take the side of one's own government, to uncritically accept governmental accounts of the nature of disputes with other nations, to uncritically exaggerate the virtues of one's own nation while playing down the virtues of "enemy" nations. National bias is reflected in the press and media coverage of every nation of the world. Events are included or excluded according to what appears significant within the dominant world view of the nation, and are shaped into stories to validate that view. Though constructed to fit into a particular view of the world, the stories in the news are presented as neutral, objective accounts, and uncritically accepted as such because people tend to uncritically assume that their own view of things is the way things really are. To become responsible critically thinking citizens and fairminded people, students must practice identifying national bias in the news and in their texts, and to broaden their perspective beyond that of uncritical nationalism. See *ethnocentrism, sociocentrism, bias, prejudice, world view, intellectual empathy, critical society, dialogical instruction, knowledge.*

opinion: A belief, typically one open to dispute. Sheer unreasoned opinion should be distinguished from reasoned judgment — beliefs formed on the basis of careful reasoning. See *evaluation, judgment, justify, know, knowledge, reasoned judgment.*

the perfections of thought: Thinking, as an attempt to understand the world as it is, has a natural excellence or fitness to it. This excellence is manifest in its *clarity, precision, specificity, accuracy, relevance, consistency, logicalness, depth, completeness, significance, fairness, and adequacy.* These perfections are general canons for thought; they represent legitimate concerns irrespective of the discipline or domain of thought. To develop one's mind and discipline one's thinking with respect to these standards *requires extensive practice and long-term cultivation.* Of course, achieving these standards is a relative matter and varies somewhat among domains of thought. Being *precise* while doing mathematics is not the same as being precise while writing a poem, describing an experience, or explaining a historical event. Furthermore, one perfection of thought may be periodically incompatible with the others: adequacy to purpose. Time and resources sufficient to thoroughly analyze a question or problem is all too often an unaffordable luxury. Also, since the social world is often irrational and unjust, because people are often manipulated to act against their interests, and because skilled thought often serves vested interest, thought adequate to these manipulative purposes may require *skilled violation of the common standards for good thinking.* Skilled propaganda, skilled political debate, skilled defense of a group's interests, skilled deception of one's enemy may require the violation or selective application of any of the above standards. Perfecting one's thought as an instrument for success in a world based on power and advantage differs from perfecting one's thought for the apprehension and defense of fairminded truth. *To develop one's critical thinking skills merely to the level of adequacy for social success is to develop those skills in a lower or weaker sense.*

personal contradiction: An inconsistency in one's personal life, wherein one says one thing and does another, or uses a double standard, judging oneself and one's friends by an easier standard than that used for people one doesn't like; typically a form of hypocrisy accompanied by self-deception. Most personal contradictions remain unconscious. People too often ignore the difficulty of becoming intellectually and morally consistent, preferring instead to merely admonish others. Personal contradictions are more likely to be discovered, analyzed, and reduced in an atmosphere in which they can be openly admitted and realistically considered without excessive penalty. See *egocentricity, intellectual integrity.*

perspective (point of view): Human thought is relational and selective. It is impossible to understand any person, event, or phenomenon from every vantage point simultaneously. Our purposes often control how we see things. Critical thinking requires that this fact be taken into account when analyzing and assessing thinking. This is not to say that human thought is incapable of truth and objectivity, but only that human truth, objectivity, and insight is virtually always limited and partial, virtually never total and absolute. The hard sciences are themselves a good example of this point, since qualitative realities are systematically ignored in favor of quantifiable realities.

precision: The quality of being accurate, definite, and exact. The standards and modes of precision vary according to subject and context. See *the logic of language, elements of thought.*

prejudice: A judgment, belief, opinion, point of view — favorable or unfavorable — formed before the facts are known, resistant to evidence and reason, or in disregard of facts which contradict it. Self-announced prejudice is rare. Prejudice almost always exists in obscured, rationalized, socially validated, functional forms. It enables people to sleep peacefully at night even while flagrantly abusing the rights of others. It enables people to get more of what they want, or to get it more easily. It is often sanctioned with a superabundance of pomp and self-righteousness. Unless we recognize these powerful tendencies toward selfish thought in our social institutions, even in what appear to be lofty actions and moralistic rhetoric, we will not face squarely the problem of prejudice in human thought and action. Uncritical and selfishly critical thought are often prejudiced. Most instruction in schools today, because students do not think their way to what they accept as true, tends to give students prejudices rather than knowledge. For example, partly as a result of schooling, people often accept as authorities those who liberally sprinkle their statements with numbers and intellectual-sounding language, however irrational or unjust their positions. This prejudice toward pseudo-authority impedes rational assessment. See *insight, knowledge.*

premise: A proposition upon which an argument is based or from which a conclusion is drawn. A starting point of reasoning. For example, one might say, in commenting on someone's reasoning, "You seem to be reasoning from the premise that everyone is selfish in everything they do. *Do* you hold this belief?"

principle: A fundamental truth, law, doctrine, value, or commitment, upon which others are based. Rules, which are more specific, and often superficial and arbitrary, are based on principles. Rules are more algorithmic; they needn't be understood to be followed. Principles must be understood to be appropriately applied or followed. Principles go to the heart of the matter. Critical thinking is dependent on principles, not rules and procedures. Critical thinking is principled, not procedural, thinking. Principles cannot be truly grasped through didactic instruction; they must be practiced and applied to be internalized. See *higher order learning, lower order learning, judgment.*

problem: A question, matter, situation, or person that is perplexing or difficult to figure out, handle, or resolve. Problems, like questions, can be divided into many types. Each has a (particular) logic. See *logic of questions, monological problems, multilogical problems.*

problem-solving: Whenever a problem cannot be solved formulaically or robotically, critical thinking is required: first, to determine the nature and dimensions of the problem, and then, in the light of the first, to determine the considerations, points of view, concepts, theories, data, and reasoning relevant to its solution. Extensive practice in independent problem-solving is essential to developing critical thought. Problem-solving is rarely best approached procedurally or as a series of rigidly followed steps. For example, problem-solving schemas typically begin, "State the problem." Rarely can problems be precisely and fairly stated prior to analysis, gathering of evidence, and dialogical or dialectical thought wherein several provisional descriptions of the problem are proposed, assessed, and revised.

proof (prove): Evidence or reasoning so strong or certain as to demonstrate the truth or acceptability of a conclusion beyond a reasonable doubt. How strong evidence or reasoning have to be to demonstrate what they purport to prove varies from context to context, depending on the significance of the conclusion or the seriousness of the implications following from it. See *domain of thought.*

rational/rationality: That which conforms to principles of good reasoning, is sensible, shows good judgment, is consistent, logical, complete, and relevant. Rationality is a summary term like 'virtue' or 'goodness'. It is manifested in an unlimited number of ways and depends on a host of principles. There is some ambiguity in it, depending on whether one considers only the logicalness and effectiveness by which one pursues one's ends, or whether it includes the assessment of ends themselves. There is also ambiguity in whether one considers selfish ends to be rational, even when they conflict with what is just. Does a rational person have to be just or only skilled in pursuing his or her interests? Is it rational to be rational in an irrational world? See *perfections of thought, irrational/irrationality, logic, intellectual virtues, weak sense critical thinking, strong sense critical thinking.*

rational emotions/passions: R. S. Peters has explained the significance of the affective side of reason and critical thought in his defense of the necessity of "rational passions":

> There is, for instance, the hatred of contradictions and inconsistencies, together with the love of clarity and hatred of confusion without which words could not be held to relatively

constant meanings and testable rules and generalizations stated. A reasonable man cannot, without some special explanation, slap his sides with delight or express indifference if he is
told that what he says is confused, incoherent, and perhaps
riddled with contradictions.

Reason is the antithesis of arbitrariness. In its operation it is
supported by the appropriate passions which are mainly negative in character — the hatred of irrelevance, special pleading,
and arbitrary fiat. The more developed emotion of indignation
is aroused when some excess of arbitrariness is perpetuated in a
situation where people's interests and claims are at stake. The
positive side of this is the passion for fairness and impartial consideration of claims ....

A man who is prepared to reason must feel strongly that he
must follow the arguments and decide things in terms of where
they lead. He must have a sense of the giveness of the impersonality of such considerations. In so far as thoughts about persons enter his head they should be tinged with the respect
which is due to another who, like himself, may have a point of
view which is worth considering, who may have a glimmering
of the truth which has so far eluded himself. A person who proceeds in this way, who is influenced by such passions, is what
we call a reasonable man.

rational self: Our character and nature to the extent that we seek to base
our beliefs and actions on good reasoning and evidence. Who we are,
what our true character is, or our predominant qualities are, is always
somewhat or even greatly different from who we *think* we are. Human
egocentrism and accompanying self-deception often stand in the way
of our gaining more insight into ourselves. We can develop a rational
self, become a person who gains significant insight into what our true
character is, only by reducing our egocentrism and self-deception.
Critical thinking is essential to this process.

rational society: See *critical society.*

reasoned judgment: Any belief or conclusion reached on the basis of
careful thought and reflection, distinguished from mere or unreasoned opinion on the one hand, and from sheer fact on the other. Few
people have a clear sense of which of their beliefs are based on reasoned judgment and which on mere opinion. Moral or ethical questions, for example, are questions requiring reasoned judgment. One
way of conceiving of subject-matter education is as developing students' ability to engage in reasoned judgment in accordance with the
standards of each subject.

reasoning: The mental processes of those who reason; especially the drawing of conclusions or inferences from observations, facts, or hypotheses; the evidence or arguments used in this procedure. A critical thinker tries to develop the capacity to transform thought into reasoning at will, or rather, the ability to make his or her inferences explicit, along with the assumptions or premises upon which those inferences are based. Reasoning is a form of explicit inferring, usually involving multiple steps. When students write a persuasive paper, for example, we want them to be clear about their reasoning.

reciprocity: The act of entering empathically into the point of view or line of reasoning of others; learning to think as others do and by that means sympathetically assessing that thinking. (Reciprocity requires creative imagination as well as intellectual skill and a commitment to fairmindedness.)

relevant: Bearing upon or relating to the matter at hand; *relevant* implies close logical relationship with, and importance to, the matter under consideration; *germane* implies such close natural connection as to be highly appropriate or fit; *pertinent* implies an immediate and direct bearing on the matter at hand (a pertinent suggestion); *apposite* applies to that which is both relevant and happily suitable or appropriate; *applicable* refers to that which can be brought to bear upon a particular matter or problem. Students often have problems sticking to an issue and distinguishing information that bears upon a problem from information that does not. Merely reminding students to limit themselves to relevant considerations fails to solve this problem. The usual way of teaching students the term 'relevant' is to mention only clear-cut cases of relevance and irrelevance. Consequently, students do not learn that not everything that *seems* relevant is, or that some things which *do not seem* relevant are. Sensitivity to (ability to judge) relevance can only be developed with continual practice — practice distinguishing relevant from irrelevant data, evaluating or judging relevance, arguing for and against the relevance of facts and considerations.

self-deception: Deceiving one's self about one's true motivations, character, identity, etc. One possible definition of the human species is "The Self-Deceiving Animal". Self-deception is a fundamental problem in human life and the cause of much human suffering. Overcoming self-deception through self-critical thinking is a fundamental goal of strong sense critical thinking. See *egocentric, rational self, personal contradiction, social contradiction, intellectual virtues.*

social contradiction: An inconsistency between what a society preaches and what it practices. In every society there is some degree of inconsistency between its image of itself and its actual character. Social contradiction typically correlates with human self-deception on the social or cultural level. Critical thinking is essential for the recognition of inconsistencies, and recognition is essential for reform and eventual integrity.

sociocentricity: The assumption that one's own social group is inherently and self-evidently superior to all others. When a group or society sees itself as superior, and so considers its views as correct or as the only reasonable or justifiable views, and all its actions as justified, there is a tendency to presuppose this superiority in all of its thinking and thus, to think closedmindedly. All dissent and doubt are considered disloyal and rejected without consideration. Few people recognize the sociocentric nature of much of their thought.

Socratic questioning: A mode of questioning that deeply probes the meaning, justification, or logical strength of a claim, position, or line of reasoning. Socratic questioning can be carried out in a variety of ways and adapted to many levels of ability and understanding. See *elements of thought, dialogical instruction, knowledge.*

specify/specific: To mention, describe, or define in detail; limiting or limited; specifying or specified; precise; definite. Student thinking, speech, and writing tend to be vague, abstract, and ambiguous rather than specific, concrete, and clear. Learning how to state one's views specifically is essential to learning how to think clearly, precisely, and accurately. See *perfections of thought.*

strong sense critical thinker: One who is predominantly characterized by the following traits: *1)* an ability to question deeply one's own framework of thought; *2)* an ability to reconstruct sympathetically and imaginatively the strongest versions of points of view and frameworks of thought opposed to one's own; and *3)* an ability to reason dialectically (multilogically) in such a way as to determine when one's own point of view is at its weakest and when an opposing point of view is at its strongest. Strong sense critical thinkers are not routinely blinded by their own points of view. They know they have points of view and therefore recognize on what framework of assumptions and ideas their own thinking is based. They realize the necessity of putting their own assumptions and ideas to the test of the strongest objections that can be leveled against them. Teaching for critical thinking in the strong sense is teaching so that students explicate, understand, and critique their own deepest prejudices, biases, and misconceptions, thereby discovering and contesting their own egocentric and sociocentric tendencies. Only if we contest our inevitable egocentric and sociocentric habits of thought, can we hope to think in a genuinely rational fashion. Only dialogical thinking about basic issues that genuinely matter to the individual provides the kind of practice and skill essential to strong sense critical thinking.

Students need to develop all critical thinking skills in dialogical settings to achieve ethically rational development, that is, genuine fairmindedness. If critical thinking is taught simply as atomic skills separate from the empathic practice of entering into points of view that students are fearful of or hostile toward, they will simply find additional means of rationalizing prejudices and preconceptions, or convincing people that their point of view is the correct one. They will be transformed from vulgar to sophisticated (but not to strong sense) critical thinkers.

teach: The basic inclusive word for the imparting of knowledge or skills. It usually connotes some individual attention to the learner; *instruct* implies systematized teaching, usually in some particular subject; *educate* stresses the development of latent faculties and powers by formal, systematic teaching, especially in institutions of higher learning; *train* implies the development of a particular faculty or skill or instruction toward a particular occupation, as by methodical discipline, exercise, etc. See *knowledge.*

theory: A systematic statement of principles involved in a subject; a formulation of apparent relationships or underlying principles of certain observed phenomena which has been verified to some degree. Often without realizing it, we form theories that help us make sense of the people, events, and problems in our lives. Critical thinkers put their theories to the test of experience and give due consideration to the theories of others. Critical thinkers do not take their theories to be facts.

think: The general word meaning to exercise the mental faculties so as to form ideas, arrive at conclusions, etc.; *reason* implies a logical sequence of thought, starting with what is known or assumed and advancing to a definite conclusion through the inferences drawn; *reflect* implies a turning of one's thoughts back on a subject and connotes deep or quiet continued thought; *speculate* implies a reasoning on the basis of incomplete or uncertain evidence and therefore stresses the conjectural character of the opinions formed; *deliberate* implies careful and thorough consideration of a matter in order to arrive at a conclusion. Though everyone thinks, few people think critically. We don't need instruction to think; we think spontaneously. We need instruction to learn how to discipline and direct our thinking on the basis of sound intellectual standards. See *elements of thought, perfections of thought.*

truth: Conformity to knowledge, fact, actuality, or logic: a statement proven to be or accepted as true, not false or erroneous. Most people uncritically assume their views to be correct and true. Most people, in other words, assume themselves to possess the truth. Critical thinking is essential to avoid this, if for no other reason.

uncritical person: One who has not developed intellectual skills (naive, conformist, easily manipulated, dogmatic, easily confused, unclear, closedminded, narrowminded, careless in word choice, inconsistent, unable to distinguish evidence from interpretation). Un-criticalness is a fundamental problem in human life, for when we are uncritical we nevertheless think of ourselves as critical. The first step in becoming a critical thinker consists in recognizing that we are uncritical. Teaching for insight into un-criticalness is an important part of teaching for criticalness.

vague: Not clearly, precisely, or definitely expressed or stated; not sharp, certain, or precise in thought, feeling, or expression. Vagueness of thought and expression is a major obstacle to the development of critical thinking. We cannot begin to test our beliefs until we recognize clearly what they are. We cannot disagree with what someone says until we are clear about what they mean. Students need much practice in transforming vague thoughts into clear ones. See *ambiguous, clarify, concept, logic, logic of questions, logic of language.*

verbal implication: That which follows, according to the logic of the language. If I say, for example, that someone used flattery on me, I *imply* that the compliments were insincere and given only to make me feel positively toward that person, to manipulate me against my reason or interest for some end. *See imply, infer, empirical implication, elements of thought.*

weak sense critical thinkers: 1) Those who do not hold themselves or those with whom they ego-identify to the same intellectual standards to which they hold "opponents". *2)* Those who have not learned how to reason empathically within points of view or frames of reference with which they disagree. *3)* Those who tend to think monologically. *4)* Those who do not genuinely accept, though they may verbally espouse, the values of critical thinking. *5)* Those who use the intellectual skills of critical thinking selectively and self-deceptively to foster and serve their vested interests (at the expense of truth); able to identify flaws in the reasoning of others and refute them; able to shore up their own beliefs with reasons.

world view: All human action takes place within a way of looking at and interpreting the world. As schooling now stands, very little is done to help students to grasp how they are viewing the world and how those views determine the character of their experience, their interpretations, their conclusions about events and persons, etc. In teaching for critical thinking in a strong sense, we make the discovery of one's own world view and the experience of other people's world views a fundamental priority. See *bias, interpret.*

Appendix B

Recommended Readings

The General Case for Critical Thinking

Bailin, Sharon. *Achieving Extraordinary Ends: An Essay of Creativity.* Kluwer-Academic Publishers, Norwell, MA, 1988.

Baron, Joan and Robert Sternberg. *Teaching Thinking Skills: Theory and Practice.* W. H. Freeman Co., New York, NY, 1987.

Blair, J. Anthony and Ralph H. Johnson, eds. *Informal Logic (First International Symposium).* Edgepress, Point Reyes, CA, 1980.

Glaser, Edward M. *An Experiment in the Development of Critical Thinking.* AMS Press, New York, NY, reprint of 1941 edition.

Kennedy, Mary. "Policy Issues in Teacher Education." *Phi Delta Kappan.* May, 1991

Mill, John Stuart. *On Liberty.* AHM Publishing Corp., Arlington Heights, IL, 1947.

Resnick, Lauren. *Education and Learning to Think.* National Academy Press, Washington, D.C., 1987.

Scriven, Michael. *Evaluation Thesaurus.* Point Reyes, CA, Edge Press, 1991

Scheffler, Israel. *Reason and Teaching.* Hackett Publishing, Indianapolis, IN, 1973.

Siegel, Harvey. *Educating Reason: Rationality, Critical Thinking, & Education.* Routledge Chapman & Hall, Inc., New York, NY, 1988.

Sumner, William G. *Folkways.* Ayer Co., Publishing, Salem, NH, 1979.

Toulmin, Stephen E. *The Uses of Argument.* Cambridge University Press, New York, NY, 1958.

Critical Thinking Pedagogy

Brookfield, Stephen D. *Developing Critical Thinkers.* Jossey-Bass, San Francisco, CA, 1987.

Costa, Arthur L. *Developing Minds: A Resource Book for Teaching Thinking.* Revised Edition, Volume 1. Alexandria, VA: ASCD, 1991.

D'Angelo, Edward. *The Teaching of Critical Thinking.* B. R. Grüner, N. V., Amsterdam, 1971.

Lipman, Matthew. *Ethical Inquiry.* Institute for the Advancement of Philosophy for Children, Upper Montclair, N.J., 1977.

Lipman, Matthew. *Harry Stottlemeier's Discovery.* Institute for the Advancement of Philosophy for Children, Upper Montclair, N.J., 1982.

Lipman, Matthew. *Lisa.* Institute for the Advancement of Philosophy for Children, Upper Montclair, N.J., 1976.

Lipman, Matthew. *Mark.* Institute for the Advancement of Philosophy for Children, Upper Monclair, N.J., 1980.

Lipman, Matthew, Ann M. Sharp, and Frederick S. Oscanyan. *Philosophical Inquiry.* University Press of America, Lanham, MD, 1979.

Lipman, Matthew, and Ann M. Sharp. *Philosophy in the Classroom.* 2nd edition, Temple University Press, Philadelphia, PA, 1980.

Lipman, Matthew. *Social Inquiry.* Institute for the Advancement of Philosophy for Children, Upper Montclair, N.J., 1980.

Meyers, Chet. *Teaching Students to Think Critically: A Guide for Faculty in all Disciplines.* Jossey-Bass, San Francisco, CA, 1986.

Norris, Stephen P, and Ennis, Robert H. *Evaluating Critical Thinking.* Pacific Grove, CA: Midwest Publications, 1989.

Paul, Richard and Binker, A. J. A., et al. *Critical Thinking Handbook: K–3rd Grades. A Guide for Remodelling Lesson Plans in Language Arts, Social Studies, & Science.* 2nd edition, Santa Rosa, CA: Foundation for Critical Thinking 1990.

Paul, Richard and Binker, A. J. A., et al. *Critical Thinking Handbook: 4th–6th Grades. A Guide for Remodelling Lesson Plans in Language Arts, Social Studies, & Science.* 2nd edition, Santa Rosa, CA: Foundation for Critical Thinking, 1990.

Paul, Richard and Binker, A. J. A., et al. *Critical Thinking Handbook: 6th–9th Grades. A Guide for Remodelling Lesson Plans in Language Arts, Social Studies, & Science.* Rohnert Park, CA: Center for Critical Thinking and Moral Critique 1989.

Paul, Richard and Binker, A. J. A., et al. *Critical Thinking Handbook: High School A Guide for Redesigning Instruction,* Rohnert Park, CA: Center for Critical Thinking and Moral Critique 1989.

Raths, Louis. *Teaching for Thinking: Theories, Strategies, and Activities for the Classroom.* 2nd edition, Teachers College Press, New York, NY, 1986.

Ruggiero, Vincent. *Thinking Across the Curriculum.* Harper & Row, New York, NY, 1988.

Ruggiero, Vincent. *Art of Thinking.* 2nd edition, Harper & Row, New York, NY, 1988.

Williamson, Janet L. *The Greensboro Plan: Infusing Reasoning and Writing into the K–12 Curriculum.* Santa Rosa, CA, Foundation for Critical Thinking 1990.

College Textbooks (Not Focused on a Specific Discipline)

Barker, Evelyn M. *Everyday Reasoning.* Prentice-Hall, Englewood Cliffs, NJ, 1981.

Barry, Vincent E., and Joel Rudinow. *Invitation to Critical Thinking.* 2nd edition, Holt, Rinehart & Winston, New York, NY, 1990.

Brown, Neil and Stuart Keely. *Asking the Right Questions: A Guide to Critical Thinking.* 2nd edition, Prentice-Hall, Englewood Cliffs, NJ, 1986.

Capaldi, Nicholas. *The Art of Deception.* 2nd edition, Prometheus Books, Buffalo, New York, 1979.

Cederblom, Jerry. *Critical Reasoning.* 2nd edition, Wadsworth Publishing Co., Belmont, CA, 1986.

Chaffee, John. *Thinking Critically.* 2nd edition, Houghton Mifflin, Boston, MA, 1988.

Damer, T. Edward. *Attacking Faulty Reasoning.* 2nd edition, Wadsworth Publishing Co., Belmont, CA, 1987.

Engel, Morris. *Analyzing Informal Fallacies.* Prentice-Hall, Englewood Cliffs, NJ, 1980.

Engel, Morris. *With Good Reason: An Introduction to Informal Fallacies.* 3rd edition, St. Martin's Press, New York, NY, 1986.

Fahnestock, Jeanne and Marie Secor. *Rhetoric of Argument.* McGraw-Hill Book Co., New York, NY, 1982.

Fisher, Alec. *The Logic of Real Arguments.* Cambridge University Press, New York, NY, 1988.

Govier, Trudy. *A Practical Study of Argument.* 2nd edition, Wadsworth Publishing Co., Belmont, CA, 1988.

Hitchcock, David. *Critical Thinking: A Guide to Evaluating Information.* Methuan Publications, Toronto, Canada, 1983.

Hoagland, John. *Critical Thinking.* Vale Press, Newport News, VA, 1984.

Johnson, Ralph H. and J. A. Blair. *Logical Self-Defense.* 2nd edition, McGraw-Hill, New York, NY, 1983.

Kahane, Howard. *Logic and Contemporary Rhetoric.* 5th edition, Wadsworth Publishing Co., Belmont, CA, 1988.

Meiland, Jack W. *College Thinking: How to Get the Best Out of College.* New American Library, New York, NY, 1981.

Michalos, Alex C. *Improving Your Reasoning.* Prentice-Hall, Englewood Cliffs, NJ, 1986.

Miller, Robert K. *Informed Argument.* 2nd edition, Harcourt, Brace, Jovanovich, San Diego, CA, 1989.

Missimer, Connie. *Good Arguments: An Introduction to Critical Thinking.* 2nd edition, Prentice-Hall, Englewood Cliffs, NJ, 1986.

Moore, Brooke N. *Critical Thinking: Evaluating Claims and Arguments in Everyday Life.* 2nd edition, Mayfield Publishing Co., Palo Alto, CA, 1989.

Moore, Edgar. *Creative and Critical Reasoning.* 2nd edition, Houghton Mifflin, Boston, MA, 1984.

Nickerson, Raymond S. *Reflections on Reasoning.* L. Erlbaum, Assoc., Hillsdale, NJ, 1986.

Nosich, Gerald. *Reasons and Arguments.* Belmont, CA Wadsworth 1981.

Ruggiero, Vincent. *Moral Imperative.* Mayfield Publishing, Palo Alto, CA, 1984.

Scriven, Michael. *Reasoning.* McGraw-Hill Book Co., New York, NY, 1976.

Seech, Zachary. *Logic in Everyday Life: Practical Reasoning Skills.* Wadsworth Publishing Co., Belmont, CA, 1988.

Shor, Ira. *Critical Teaching & Everyday Life.* University of Chicago Press, Chicago, IL, 1987.

Toulmin, Stephen E., Richard Rieke, and Alan Janik. *An Introduction to Reasoning.* Macmillan Publishing Co., New York, NY, 1979.

Weddle, Perry. *Argument: A Guide to Critical Thinking.* McGraw-Hill, New York, NY, 1978.

Wilson, John. *Thinking with Concepts.* 4th edition, Cambridge University Press, New York, NY, 1987.

Mathematics and Critical Thinking

Schoenfeld, Alan. *Mathematical Problem Solving: Issues in Research*. Lester, F.K. and Garofalo, J., ed's. Philadelphia, PA: The Franklin Institute Press 1982.

Curriculum and Evaluation Standards for School Mathematics, by the Working Groups of the Commission on Standards for School Mathematics of the National Council of Teachers of Mathematics, Reston, VA 1989.

Professional Standards for Teaching Mathematics, by the Working Groups of the Commission on Standards for School Mathematics of the National Council of Teachers of Mathematics, Reston, VA 1991.

Social Studies and Critical Thinking

Holt, Tom. *Thinking Historically: Narrative, Imagination, and Understanding,* College Entrance Examination Board. New York, 1990

Science and Critical Thinking

Giere, Ronald N. *Understanding Scientific Reasoning.* Holt, Rinehart, and Winston, New York, NY, 1979. (Out of print.)

Radner, Daisie and Radner, Michael. *Science and Unreason.* Wadsworth Publishing Co., Belmont, CA, 1982.

Language Arts and Critical Thinking

Adler, Mortimer. *How to Read a Book.* Simon and Schuster, New York, NY, 1972.

Horton, Susan. *Thinking Through Writing.* Johns Hopkins, Baltimore, MD, 1982.

Kytle, Ray. *Clear Thinking for Composition.* 5th edition, McGraw-Hill Book Co., New York, NY, 1987.

Mayfield, Marlys. *Thinking for Yourself: Developing Critical Thinking Skills Through Writing.* Wadsworth Publishing Co., Belmont, CA, 1987.

Rosenberg, Vivian. *Reading, Writing, and Thinking: Critical Connections.* McGraw-Hill Book Co., New York, NY, 1989.

Scull, Sharon. *Critical Reading and Writing for Advanced ESL Students.* Prentice-Hall, Englewood Cliffs, NJ, 1987.

Zinser, William. *Writing to Learn: How to Write — and Think — Clearly About Any Subject at All,* Harper & Row, Publishers, New York, 1988.

Critical Thinking and the Media

Lazere, Donald. *American Media & Mass Culture.* University of California Press, Berkeley, CA, 1987.

Also of Interest

Baker, Paul J., and Louis Anderson. *Social Problems: A Critical Thinking Approach.* Wadsworth Publishing Co., Belmont, CA, 1987.

Bloom, Benjamin. *Taxonomy of Educational Objectives.* David McKay Co., Inc., New York, 1956.

Dorman, William and Farhang, Mansour. *The U.S. Press and Iran: Foriegn Policy and the Journalism of Deference.* UC Berkeley Press, Berkeley, CA. 1987.

Index